THE NEW CHAUCER SOCIETY

Studies in the Age of Chaucer, the yearbook of The New Chaucer Society, is published annually. Each issue contains a limited number of substantial articles, reviews of books on Chaucer and related topics, and an annotated Chaucer bibliography. Articles explore such concerns as the efficacy of various critical approaches to the art of Chaucer and his contemporaries, their literary relationships and reputations, and the artistic, economic, intellectual, religious, scientific, and social and historical backgrounds to their work.

Manuscripts, in duplicate, accompanied by return postage, should follow the *Chicago Manual of Style,* fourteenth edition. Unsolicited reviews are not accepted. Authors receive free twenty offprints of articles and ten of reviews. All correspondence concerning manuscript submissions for Volume 21 of *Studies in the Age of Chaucer* should be directed to the Editor, Larry Scanlon, Department of English, Rutgers University, New Brunswick, NJ 08903-5054. Subscriptions to The New Chaucer Society and information about the Society's activities should be directed to Susan Crane, Department of English, Rutgers University, New Brunswick, NJ 08903-5054. Back issues of the journal may be ordered from Ohio State University Press, 180 Pressey Hall, 1070 Carmack Rd., Columbus, OH 43210; phone, 614-292-6930, FAX 614-292-2065.

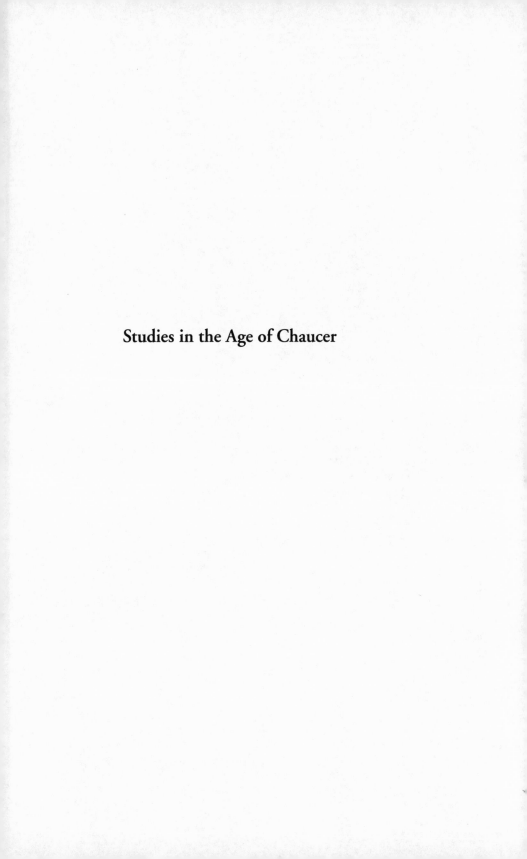

Studies in the Age of Chaucer

Studies in the Age of Chaucer

Volume 20

1998

EDITOR

LISA KISER

PUBLISHED ANNUALLY BY THE NEW CHAUCER SOCIETY

THE OHIO STATE UNIVERSITY, COLUMBUS

The frontispiece design, showing the Pilgrims at the Tabard Inn, is adapted from the woodcut in Caxton's second edition of *The Canterbury Tales.*

ISBN 0-933784-22-8

ISSN 0190-2407

CONTENTS

Studies in the Age of Chaucer

Proving Constant: Torture and *The Man of Law's Tale*

James Landman
University of North Texas

T he third part of Chaucer's *Man of Law's Tale* opens with the torture of King Alla's messenger to extract the vital information that Alla's mother, Donegild, offered the messenger lodging on his way to and from Alla's military camp in Scotland. This information confirms that Donegild had the opportunity to plant the counterfeit letters, delivered by the unfortunate but unwitting messenger, that secure Custance's banishment from Northumberland. The messenger's torture occupies a brief passage (the desired information is quickly obtained), involving a minor character, in the middle of what is considered to be one of Chaucer's "problem" tales. Not surprisingly, the passage has received little critical attention.

The absence of the messenger and his torture in discussions of *The Man of Law's Tale* seemingly befits the messenger's insignificant role in the tale. Perhaps also this absence is a product of an understanding of the Middle Ages that reads an incident such as the messenger's torture as a nonproblematic, albeit unpleasant, attribute of medieval culture. Yet the messenger's torture becomes increasingly troublesome as we inquire into the English analogues of Chaucer's tale, and the legal culture with which its fictional narrator is identified. It is striking that neither Nicholas Trevet's Anglo-Norman *Chroniques écrites pour Marie d'Angleterre* nor John Gower's *Confessio Amantis* (the two English analogues of the tale of Custance) depicts the messenger's torture. It is even more striking that an incident of torture should be inserted into a tale assigned to an English man of law.

1

As a serjeant of law, the Man of Law is near the top of the English legal system, a legal system that in the later Middle Ages was distinguished from its continental European counterparts by the absence of institutionalized judicial torture in its criminal procedure. It is this very distinction that the fifteenth-century English jurist John Fortescue seizes upon in his *De laudibus legum Anglie* to set apart and commend the laws of England as compared with the continental legal system represented in his text by France. Fortescue's condemnation of torture is, however, notably lacking in his fictional predecessor's tale. Indeed, the Man of Law's description of the messenger's torture as part of a process of "wit and sotil enquerynge" (*MLT* 888)[1] suggests approval of a procedure seemingly perceived as a proper method for the retrieval of information from an unreliable source.

This article shall argue that the messenger's torture is not a unique incident within the Man of Law's narrative, nor, despite England's longstanding avoidance of institutionalized torture, is it necessarily an anomaly within a tale told by an English man of law. Instead, the appearance of torture within *The Man of Law's Tale* is a reminder of the fragility of the common-law institutions he represents, and of torture's alluring promise of certainty. This promise shines with particular brightness for the Man of Law—and those like him—whose livelihood and professional reputation depend on the control of narrative, a control that can never be fully achieved within the institutions of the common law. The Man of Law and his colleagues work within a legal system also distinguished by an increasingly insular delegation of the factfinding power to local juries over which men of law exercise little control. In Fortescue's later writing the jury will become the mark of English legal procedure's superiority over the inquisitorial methods assigned to the continent, yet despite the vigor of the *De laudibus*'s defense of English law, both its commitment to the jury and its condemnation of torture prove markedly guarded. And later still, torture eventually, if only temporarily, finds a place in English law.

The treatment of judicial torture in *The Man of Law's Tale*, in other words, places the tale in a complicated and enduring dialogue in English writing on the question of torture's potential to discover the truth. Early in this essay, I will consider how the professional profile of

---

[1] All citations of Chaucer's work are taken from Larry D. Benson, gen. ed., *The Riverside Chaucer*, 3d ed. (Boston: Houghton Mifflin, 1987). Further citations will be made in the text.

Chaucer's Man of Law and the attitudes expressed in his narrative define a legal mentality open to, perhaps even attracted by, torture's promise of securing the "certain" proof of confession—a mentality expressed, to varying degrees, in a broadly defined field of English legal writing that extends well beyond the fourteenth century. I will then consider how the specific issue of judicial torture relates to a more general dialogue on the question of torment and truth within the text of *The Canterbury Tales*, focusing on the juxtaposition in *The Man of Law's Tale* of the tortured messenger and Custance, the tale's tormented heroine, whose relentless proving dominates the Man of Law's narrative. This juxtaposition links the *jurisprudence* of torture enacted in the messenger's torments to a *logic* of torture supporting the application of pain, physical or mental, in the discovery or production of truth.[2] Within *The Man of Law's Tale*, the endless proving of Custance constructs a narrative of endurance that, in its excess, undermines torture's promise of securing a certain truth, particularly when pain produces nothing but silence. There is, however, little to suggest that the tale pursues a narrative strategy meant to expose torture's failings; unlike *The Clerk's Tale*, this tale makes no critique of its heroine's "nedelees" tormenting. And while the Man of Law is a particularly appropriate narrator of this tale of painful provings, the logic of torture informing his narrative is hardly confined to his performance in *The Canterbury Tales*.

I. Trying the messenger

Trevet's *Chroniques écrites pour Marie d'Angleterre*, Gower's *Confessio Amantis*, and Chaucer's *Man of Law's Tale* offer three versions of the story of Custance (or Constance), daughter of the Roman emperor.[3] In an

---

[2] The "jurisprudence of torture" and "logic of torture" are terms taken from, respectively, John Langbein, *Torture and the Law of Proof: Europe and England in the Ancien Régime* (Chicago: University of Chicago Press, 1977), and Page duBois, *Torture and Truth* (New York: Routledge, 1991). The "jurisprudence of torture" refers to laws and procedures constructed around the specific practice of judicial torture; the "logic of torture" refers to a set of assumptions underlying the jurisprudence of torture and other discourses advocating the application of pain in pursuit of truth.

[3] Citations of the *Chroniques* and the *Confessio Amantis* are taken from the following editions: Nicholas Trevet's "Life of Constance," excerpted by Margaret Schlauch from the *Chroniques* in *Sources and Analogues of Chaucer's* Canterbury Tales, ed. W. F. Bryan and Germaine Dempster (New York: Humanities Press, 1958); and *The Complete Works of John Gower: The English Works*, ed. G. C. Macaulay, 2 vols. (Oxford: Clarendon Press, 1901). Further citations will be made in the text.

episode common to all three accounts, Custance, married to her second husband, Alla, the king of Northumberland, gives birth to their son while Alla is on a military campaign in Scotland. A messenger is sent with a letter carrying news of the birth to Alla. Stopping overnight at the residence of Donegild, Alla's mother, the messenger is drugged or made drunk; and while he is unconscious, Donegild replaces the letter he is carrying with a counterfeit letter stating that Custance has been revealed as an elf and has given birth to a monster. Alla sends the messenger home with a reply ordering that Custance and their son be kept to await his homecoming. The messenger, again intercepted and rendered unconscious by Donegild, arrives home with yet another counterfeit letter purportedly from Alla ordering the banishment of Custance and her son. Alla eventually arrives home to discover that his wife and child have been put to sea in the same rudderless boat that carried Custance from Syria to England.

Here the accounts diverge in a subtle way. In both Trevet's and Gower's narratives, the messenger—now a prime suspect—is brought before Alla and interrogated. In Trevet's account, the messenger "finaument dit," or ultimately states, that he is not guilty of treason (p. 176), while Gower's version has the messenger "sodeinliche opposed," or unexpectedly questioned (2.1257). Truly ignorant of the counterfeit letters' contents, the messenger in both versions voluntarily offers information pointing to Donegild's guilt. In neither text is there any indication that the messenger's testimony is coerced.

In *The Man of Law's Tale*, the messenger suffers more than the surprise of unexpected questioning. To quote the tale,

> This messenger tormented was til he
> Moste biknowe and tellen, plat and pleyn,
> Fro nyght to nyght, in what place he had leyn;
> And thus, by wit and sotil enquerynge,
> Ymagined was by whom this harm gan sprynge. (lines 885–89)

This painful escalation of the interrogatory methods used against the messenger is matched by an escalation of the critical rhetoric directed by the Man of Law against the messenger earlier in the tale. Trevet makes the messenger the victim of a drugged drink ("vn maliciouse beyuere" [p. 173]); does not question his intentions in announcing the good news of the birth to Donegild; and limits criticism of the messenger to a relatively innocuous "fol" (p. 174). Gower is somewhat more critical of the messenger. He suggests that the messenger announces the news to

Donegild in hopes of earning a reward (the messenger "thonk deserve wolde" [2.949]), and makes the messenger, on his return journey, drunk with "strong wyn" (2.1008). Neither Trevet nor Gower, however, approaches the Man of Law's censorious description (*MLT* 771–77):

> O messager, fulfild of dronkenesse,
> Strong is thy breeth, thy lymes faltren ay,
> And thou biwreyest alle secreenesse.
> Thy mynde is lorn, thou janglest as a jay,
> Thy face is turned in a newe array.
> Ther dronkenesse regneth in any route,
> Ther is no conseil hyd, withouten doute.

The messenger's susceptibility to drink is part of his general inability to make discriminating judgments, a trait that is emphasized time and again. The messenger first arrives at Donegild's residence chattering about the contents of the sealed letters he carries with the express purpose "to doon his avantage" (line 729); he is unable to restrain himself when offered ale and wine; and when drunk, he talks even more, mindlessly betraying secret information in his possession. He is untrustworthy and corruptible, and these traits are openly despised by the Man of Law.

The Man of Law's critique of the messenger and subjection of him to torture are not coincidentally juxtaposed in the *Tale*. Instead, the particular offenses attributed to the messenger construct the foundation for his subsequent torture, echoing the justifications at the core of the jurisprudence of torture. At the same time, the untrustworthiness attributed to the lowly messenger recalls the untrustworthiness attributed to the lowly poor in the *Prologue* to *The Man of Law's Tale*: the poor whose indigence provokes them to "stele, or begge, or borwe" their sustenance (line 105), and whose envy provokes sinful (and, by implication, groundless) accusations of the rich. The messenger, in other words, displays the traits attributed to the lower classes against whom, in the recurring history of European torture, torture was initially applied, and who also comprise a class suspect to the Man of Law and the legal system he represents.

II. "O prudent folk": Men of law, the jury, and the question of torture

As one commentator on Chaucer's Man of Law has observed, the irony of Chaucer's representation of this pilgrim has, in recent criticism, overwhelmed any other possible meanings of this representation.[4] Yet Sir Edward Coke, drawing on the description of the Man of Law in *The General Prologue*, finds not irony but reason for professional pride in the Man of Law's representation. In the *First Part of the Institutes* (Coke's seventeenth-century glossing of the text of another medieval man of law, Sir Thomas Littleton), Coke writes:

This only is desired, that [Littleton] had written of other parts of the Law, and specially of the rules of good pleading (the heart-string of the Common Law) wherein he excelled, for of him might the saying of our English Poet be verified:
There to he could indite and maken a thing,
There was no Wight could pinch at his writing.
So farre from exception, as none could pinch at it.[5]

The "pinchproof" (unassailable) legal language of Littleton and Chaucer's Man of Law is one of several medieval legal traditions cited with approval in the *Institutes*. In the midst of the *Third Part of the Institutes*'s discussion of torture in England, Coke turns to Littleton's fifteenth-century contemporary, Sir John Fortescue. In the *De laudibus legum Anglie,* Coke argues, Fortescue prefers "the Laws of England . . . for the government of this Country before the Civil Law"; shows "particularly that all tortures and torments of parties accused were directly against the Common Laws of England"; and demonstrates "the inconvenience [of such tortures] by fearfull example." Affirming Fortescue's fifteenth-century description of English jurisprudence, Coke states "there is no Law to warrant tortures in this land, nor can they be justified by any prescription, *being so lately brought in.*"[6]

My emphasis on this final phrase—"being so lately brought in"— underscores an important distinction between the discussions of torture in Coke's *Institutes* and in Fortescue's *De laudibus*. Fortescue maintains a

[4] V. A. Kolve, *Chaucer and the Imagery of Narrative: The First Five Canterbury Tales* (Stanford, Cal.: Stanford University Press, 1984), p. 290.

[5] Sir Edward Coke, *First Part of the Institutes of the Lawes of England, or, A Commentarie upon Littleton* (London: n.p., 1628). Littleton (described on Coke's title page as "not the name of a Lawyer onely, but of the Law itselfe") is the author of the *Tenures*, a fifteenth-century legal treatise. Coke may have found Littleton's language "pinchproof," but he obviously saw room for additional padding. The mise-en-page of the *Institutes*'s commentary on the *Tenures* calls to mind a glossed Scripture, with each passage of the *Tenures* occupying a small portion of a page otherwise filled by Coke's translation of and commentary on Littleton's Law French original.

[6] Sir Edward Coke, *The Third Part of the Institutes of the Laws of England: Concerning High Treason, and other Pleas of the Crown, and Criminal Charges,* 4th ed. (London: n.p., 1669), p. 35; my emphasis.

rigid distinction between England's reliance on the jury for determination of truth and France's use of torture to "extort the truth" in the most serious cases.[7] Despite some shadowy evidence of torture in medieval England, Fortescue's distinction seems basically valid as of the late fifteenth century.[8] Equally valid, however, is Coke's admission that torture has been brought into England, an introduction that Coke alleges was coterminous with Henry VI's reign (and thus with Fortescue's career). Coke's own *Institutes* were written near the end of what John Langbein has labeled England's "century of torture" (1540–1640). In his capacities as Solicitor General and Attorney General, Coke personally had been named as a commissioner to torture in six warrants to torture, and was presumably present in these cases.[9]

Surveying the common law's medieval past to support his articulation of its principles in the seventeenth-century present, Coke makes Littleton and Fortescue emblematic of two common-law fundamentals. Littleton represents "pinchproof" pleading, "the heart-string of the Common Law," while Fortescue represents the common law's prohibition of torture. Coke's own experiences, however, demonstrate that these common-law fundamentals, especially the latter, were not necessarily grounded in an uninterrupted tradition of practice. And the more we move back from the time of Coke to the time of the "English Poet" and his legal contemporaries, the less grounded these fundamentals appear. When we consider the nature of these "fundamentals" in the late fourteenth century, not only do we discover a decidedly formative state of affairs; we also discover that both fundamentals were taking shape against a more (but not much more) fundamental element of the common law—that of trial by jury.

The English legal system described by Coke was, by the fourteenth century, marked by an insularity of which the rules of pleading and the absence of torture were only two components, subordinate and in part attributable to the common law's reliance on trial by jury. But this legal insularity was largely the result of a fairly recent change in European

---

[7] "[T]he civil laws themselves extort the truth by similar tortures in criminal cases where sufficient witnesses are lacking, and many realms do likewise"; Sir John Fortescue, *De laudibus legum Anglie*, ed. and trans. S. B. Chrimes (Cambridge: Cambridge University Press, 1942), p. 49.

[8] Evidence for the practice of torture in England prior to the sixteenth century is examined by James Heath in *Torture and English Law: An Administrative and Legal History from the Plantagenets to the Stuarts* (London: Greenwood Press, 1982).

[9] England's "century of torture" is described in Langbein, *Law of Proof*, pp. 73–139. A table describing the warrants to torture, including those naming Coke as commissioner, is provided on pp. 94–123.

jurisprudence. When the Fourth Lateran Council in 1215 forced western Europe finally to abandon an increasingly discredited use of modes of proof that relied upon theories of divine intervention (the ordeal, for example), England happened to have at hand Henry II's experiments with juries of indictment and the Grand Assize as a solution to the problem of proof made unavoidable by the Fourth Lateran's decree.[10] While continental jurisprudence turned its attention to the confession as the new form of definitive proof, English jurisprudence entrusted determination of fact to its trial juries. Bound to no minimum standard of proof, trial juries simply made the primacy of confession and its attendant use of torture unnecessary in English law; there was, however, no clear prohibition of torture in England, nor was English jurisprudence distinguished by moral or humanitarian objections to torture.[11]

Indeed, within the contours of the two common-law fundamentals described by Coke, we find a certain ambivalence toward the more fundamental institution of the jury: pleading practices are designed to control the jury, and torture, while rejected in English law, is recognized by its most celebrated medieval critic as a possible alternative when trial by jury simply will not work. For if the dominant position of the trial jury as the determiner of fact set the English common law apart from continental legal systems, it did so in a way that was not unconditionally celebrated by men of law. The representation[12] of factual truth by the jury was, and is, imperfect. It is imperfect not only because

[10] For convenient summaries of the Fourth Lateran Council's effect on English legal procedure and on the development of trial by jury, see S. F. C. Milsom, *Historical Foundations of the Common Law*, 2d ed. (Toronto: Butterworths, 1981), pp. 410–13, and J. H. Baker, *An Introduction to English Legal History*, 3d ed. (London: Butterworths, 1990), pp. 578–81. John W. Baldwin analyzes the campaign to discredit theories of divine intervention in the years prior to 1215 in "The Intellectual Preparation for the Canon of 1215 Against Ordeals," *Speculum* 36 (1961): 613–36.

[11] Langbein writes: "Maitland's well known account [of England's avoidance of torture] has never been doubted. The English were not possessed of 'any unusual degree of humanity or enlightenment.' Rather, they were the beneficiaries of legal institutions so crude that torture was unnecessary. . . . To this day, an English jury can convict a defendant on less evidence than was required as a mere precondition for interrogation under torture on the Continent"; Langbein, *Law of Proof*, pp. 77–78.

[12] Juries are often described as the "finders of fact," a term that perpetuates the notion that facts are "merely things found lying about in the world and carried bodily into court." Regardless of the source of the medieval jury's knowledge (self-information, evidence presented in court, community opinion), its verdict is not simply a pouring forth of unmediated fact. It is a rendering, or representation, of the collected knowledge of the individual jurors. For the quoted material and a discussion of the "fundamental phenomenon" of representation, see Clifford Geertz, *Local Knowledge: Further Essays in Interpretive Anthropology* (New York: Basic Books, 1983), p. 173.

the jury might not know all the facts, or might be subject to bribery and intimidation, but also because the jury's representation of fact might not always precisely conform to the dictates of the law it is asked to apply, or might be shaped by considerations or knowledge beyond the purview of the court and its officers. The power to represent the facts determining the outcome of a trial is substantial, and the terms of this power are and long have been of intense interest to the legal profession.

Describing late-twentieth-century American jurisprudence, Clifford Geertz has identified a "long-standing judicial emotion" of "fear of fact," manifested in a professional "distrust of juries."[13] The records of late-medieval English legal practice suggest that this "fear of fact" among men of law is long-standing indeed. But the basis of a fourteenth-century lawyer's fear of fact differs substantially from that of his twentieth-century counterpart. Whereas Geertz associates current professional distrust of the jury with an explosion of fact presumed beyond the comprehension of amateur jurors, a medieval man of law's fear of fact was a fear of the unknown. Medieval jurors were not the passive recipients of facts filtered through rules of evidence: to the extent such rules existed, they were not deemed important enough to record, and even if such rules did exist, their force would have been greatly mitigated by the medieval jury's role as an active producer of fact. The jury's verdict was the terse summation of a collective understanding of fact, and the processes and considerations underlying that understanding were generally inaccessible, hidden behind the final formulation represented by the verdict.[14] The records suggest that lawyers were presenting some evidence to juries in the fourteenth century, but jurors remained free throughout the Middle Ages and beyond to draw on their own personal knowledge in deciding the verdict.[15]

[13] Geertz, *Local Knowledge*, pp. 171–72.

[14] The official records of medieval juries' deliberations are certainly laconic, typically providing only the verdict of "guilty" or "not guilty." Morris Arnold has suggested that at trial, the basis of the verdict might have been subject to closer scrutiny by presiding officials. In at least one area of the law (the property claim of *novel disseisin*), jurors were by statute given the right to articulate the specific factual basis of their verdict and leave determination of guilt or innocence to the court. Juries seemingly embraced this right in novel disseisin actions, but it was not a right generally available to them: special verdicts typically were permissible only at the discretion of the presiding judge. See Morris S. Arnold, "Law and Fact in the Medieval Jury Trial: Out of Sight, Out of Mind," *American Journal of Legal History* 18 (1974): 267–80.

[15] The juror's right to consider personal knowledge in determining the verdict was upheld as late as 1670. See the discussion of *Bushell's Case* in John Marshall Mitnick, "From Neighbor-Witness to Judge of Proofs: The Transformation of the English Civil Juror," *American Journal of Legal History* 32 (1988): 206–7.

It is generally supposed that the jury's central role as determiner of fact was a significant factor in the development of the pleading practices Coke identifies as the "heart-string of the Common Law." It is similarly supposed that these practices were intended to narrow the question of fact submitted to the jury, or even to remove the case from jury consideration by defining the case's issue as a question of law rather than a question of fact.[16] The development of pleading strategies can be traced in the Year Books' transcriptions of pleadings from select cases argued by serjeants at law (and occasionally apprentices) before the justices at Westminster's central courts of Common Pleas and King's Bench. Part of the Year Books' value lies in the fact that they record prospective pleas that are eventually abandoned and, consequently, do not appear in the official plea rolls. And what we see in these more detailed accounts of the pleading process are men of law's often unsuccessful attempts to fashion pleas that might restrict the issue of fact submitted to the jury, or remove the case from jury consideration altogether by defining a new point of law.

The most typical question submitted to the jury was also the least satisfactory for a lawyer interested in defining or circumscribing the factual basis of the jury's verdict. This question was known as the *general issue,* and it followed upon the defendant's flat denial of the plaintiff's allegations. Before retreating to the general issue, however, pleaders could attempt to pursue several strategies. One alternative was to narrow the question of fact submitted to the jury. This strategy, known as either *confession and avoidance* or *justification,* admitted the factual content of the plaintiff's claim, but alleged additional facts that would as a matter of law defeat the plaintiff's claim. If this strategy was successful, the question submitted to the jury would be limited to the veracity of these additional factual allegations. An even more effective strategy for a pleader made anxious by the jury's uncertain verdict was the *demurrer.* This plea again accepted the plaintiff's statement of fact but argued that, as a point of law, the plaintiff had failed to state a cause

---

[16] These suppositions are most clearly argued in Morris Arnold's introduction to *Select Cases of Trespass from the King's Courts, 1307–1399,* ed. Morris S. Arnold, vol. 1 (London: Selden Society, 1985). My summary of pleading practices is heavily indebted to section 2 of Arnold's introduction, titled "The Control of the Jury" (pp. x–xxxi); and to Donald W. Sutherland, "Legal Reasoning in the Fourteenth Century: The Invention of 'Color' in Pleading," in *On the Laws and Customs of England: Essays in Honor of Samuel E. Thorne,* ed. Morris S. Arnold et al. (Chapel Hill: University of North Carolina Press, 1981), pp. 182–94.

of action. If the demurrer was entered as the formal plea, the case would not be submitted to the jury: points of law were determined by justices, not juries, and there would be no facts in dispute. Attempted special pleadings were in practice often abandoned in the face of a panel of justices reluctant to permit exceptions to the general issue. If anything, the justices were too willing to submit to the jury a general issue that could benefit from the clarification of special pleading.[17] And their reluctance to tamper with rules of law pursuant to a demurrer could be taken to the extreme.[18]

If the issue could not be narrowed for or removed from the jury, the pleader could also try to define the jury that would determine the verdict. A case from 1388 illustrates this point. In *Bathe v Jonet and Others*, Bathe brought a trespass action alleging "that on a certain day in a certain year the defendants came to Acton in the same county [of Middlesex] with force and arms, and took and imprisoned and beat him, etc., wrongfully and to his damages to the amount of two thousand pounds." Represented by the lawyer Thomas Pinchbeck, the defendants responded that Bathe was a villein of Sir Matthew Gurney and that they, as Gurney's servants, took Bathe as Gurney's villein and transported

---

[17] The Yearbook for Richard II's second regnal year describes an attempt made by Justice Skipwith to temper his fellow justices' reluctance to permit an exception to the general issue. During the course of pleadings in a property case, a particularly complex issue of bastardy emerges. The perplexed justices of Common Pleas call in Chief Justice Tresilian from King's Bench to help decide the matter. When Tresilian suggests submitting the question of bastardy to the jury as a general issue, Justice Skipwith counters by arguing that "[c]ertainly our law and every law always presumes that one who is born and begotten within the espousals is legitimate and not a bastard; but due to some other special fact he could be a bastard. For instance, if a wife leaves her husband and lives with an adulterer and has a son begotten between them after the espousals, if such facts be found he will be adjudged a bastard. But now if there is some such fact or other which should bastardize [the heir in question] it must be specifically pleaded, on which an issue can be taken specially; and [the demandants] must not take a general issue on the bastardy and thus burden the lay people [i.e., the jury] with deciding the bastardy"; Hil. 2 Richard II, pl. 3; translated in *Year Books of Richard II: 2 Richard II, 1378–79,* ed. and trans. Morris S. Arnold (Cambridge, Mass.: Ames Foundation, 1975), pp. 96–97.

[18] In a famous negligence case, a defendant's lawyer attempts to limit his client's liability by alleging that his servant, not he, started a fire that damaged his neighbors' property. Horneby, representing the defendant, claims "this defendant is destroyed and impoverished forever, if this action should be maintained against him, for some 20 other similar suits will be taken against him in this same matter" [cesty defendant est defait & impoverish pur touts jours, si cest action soit maintenue devers luy, car donques 20 auters tielx suites serront prises devers luy d'autiel matter]. In response, Justice Thirning replies, "What is that to us? It is better that he be completely destroyed, than that the law be changed for him" [Que est ceo a nous. Il est mieulx que il soit tout defait, que la ley soit chaunge pur luy]; Pasch. 2 Henry IV, pl. 5, fol. 18; my translation.

him to the county of Somerset, where Bathe "submitted himself of his own will to the arbitrament of Fulk Fitzwarin and others in respect of the same villeinage and of all other trespasses committed before that time by this same Sir Matthew of his ministers; and the same Sir Matthew did likewise." With the defendants having made an issue of the arbitration, Rickhill, the lawyer pleading for Bathe, had to respond to this new issue, but he did so by insisting that Bathe was taken in Acton in Middlesex and imprisoned *there,* "so that the arbitrament was made under duress of imprisonment *at Acton*" (my emphasis). The Year Book reporter at this point detected an ulterior motive behind Rickhill's strategy: "And Rickhill pleaded in this fashion in order to have a jury of the county of Middlesex."[19]

All of these special pleading practices illustrate the medieval man of law's fear of the power of fact held by the jury, as well as a desire to attain the "pinchproof" professional mastery ascribed to Littleton by Coke, and to the Man of Law by Chaucer. In both Coke's and Chaucer's texts, *pinching* denotes the susceptibility of the legal document or argument to the almost physical probing or testing of one's adversary: it is the search for weaknesses in the body of the text that will open it up to an adversarial interpretation. It is noteworthy, however, that Chaucer describes his Man of Law's pinchproof mastery in terms of his "writyng" (*GP* 326), for even the most tightly constructed oral pleadings remained susceptible to unexpected pinches from an unknown jury. *Bathe v Jonet* demonstrates in a particularly lucid manner the uneasy dynamic between men of law's professional discourse and the jury. The outcome of this case—the "true" story—was seemingly recognized by the pleaders as contingent upon the particular group of jurors summoned to tell it. Notwithstanding the fact that the opposing pleaders were themselves telling contradictory stories, there is something unsettling in the notion that either story might have been certified as true by the appropriate jury. Questions of local intimidation aside, the diverse possible outcomes foreseen and pleaded for in this case point to a problem as potentially disruptive to the integrity of the legal system as Sir Matthew's

[19] As Isobel Thornley suggests, Rickhill's attempt to secure a Middlesex jury was well founded. Sir Matthew Gurney, a soldier of fortune retired to England, apparently presided over a gang of Somerset men who might have influenced a local jury with considerations beyond those of truth and justice. See *Year Books of Richard II: 11 Richard II, 1387–88,* ed. and trans. Isobel D. Thornley (London: Spottiswoode, Ballantyne, 1937), pp. xiii–xvi. I have quoted from Thornley's translation of the case, *Year Books,* pp. 168–70.

gang. Legal outcomes depend on where you go looking for them; there is no precise locus of truth, but multiple loci offering different representations of the truth based on local considerations.

Although a man of law's professional survival requires that the possibility of divergent outcomes be understood and proactively addressed, such a possibility cannot be admitted by the Man of Law. The Man of Law is committed to the notion that a story has only one proper representation, and one correct interpretation. His skills as a legal draftsman are directed toward the task of shutting down the possibility of variant interpretations, erasing any ambiguities in his "writyng" that an adversary could "pynche at" (*GP* 326). He proclaims himself initially at a loss as a teller of tales, since there is "no thrifty tale . . . / That Chaucer . . . / Hath seyd hem in swich Englissh as he kan" (*MLP* 46–49). Chaucer has used up all the tales by telling them once, and the Man of Law sees no reason to revisit a settled story: "What sholde I tellen hem, syn they been tolde?" (line 56). Only a new tale, imported by a merchant, can save the Man of Law from the embarrassment of not satisfying his tale-telling debt to his fellow pilgrims.

The Man of Law, given his profession, is surprisingly skeptical of the value of argumentation. When the Sultan calls upon his advisers to consider ways for him "[t]o han Custance" (*MLT* 208), the Man of Law seems openly dismissive of these advisers' labors. "Diverse men diverse thynges seyden," he narrates. "They argumenten, casten up and doun; / Many a subtil reason forth they leyden" (lines 211–13)—only to arrive at a single solution, marriage. And while the Man of Law upholds a theory of certain truth, he is markedly pessimistic regarding human ability to interpret it. The message of each man's impending death, written in the stars "clerer than is glas" (line 194), is almost always misread: ". . . mennes wittes ben so dulle / That no wight kan wel rede it atte fulle" (lines 202–3). The Emperor of Rome and all his philosophers are unable to read the ominous astrological signs visible when Custance departs for Syria: "Allas, we been to lewed or to slowe!" (line 315).

These opinions against argumentation and interpretation may assume the appearance of professional disavowals, but they are not necessarily inconsistent with the Man of Law's professional self-interest, or the assumptions of his profession. A man of law is very interested in the ambiguities of language, but not because he wants those ambiguities opened up to divergent interpretations. The work of a lawyer is directed toward the closing down of multiple interpretations: in professional "writyng," to anticipate and foreclose challenges to a document's terms, and in professional pleading, to argue for a single proper application of the law in a given case. Although common-law procedure systemically promotes competing accounts of a given case in the initial stages of pleading, the individual man of law is committed to upholding one such account and defeating the other. And ultimately, the system rewards or disappoints this individual effort when the single "truth" represented by the verdict affirms one account over the other. Diverse men might say diverse things, but only one thing can be true.

This assumption helps to explain the Man of Law's reliance on merchants' importation of new narratives, as well as his reluctance to revisit Chaucer's already told tales. Men of law depend on the steady flow of new material because their profession does not permit variant interpretations of a settled narrative. Once the story has been told, and affirmed or negated, that story is over for better or worse. But the Man of Law's insistent refusal to retell Chaucer's tales also betrays an anxiety over the vulnerability of this "legal" hermeneutic of containment, a hermeneutic threatened by a "literary" hermeneutic permitting multiple tellings of a given tale. To reopen a told tale admits the possibility that one's retelling may itself be reopened. It admits, to paraphrase Stanley Fish, interpretive multiplicity instead of interpretive resolution.[20]

Despite the Man of Law's commitment to a theory of a single, certain truth, the dissonance between this theory and the practical maneuverings described in a case such as *Bathe v Jonet* suggests a considerable gap between legal theory and practice. Instead of rousing the truth with the vigor of their advocacy, the men of law in the 1388 case were scrambling to secure a jury more likely to represent the facts favorably. The man of law negotiates for his client the space between the facts of a specific case and the dictates of the law. Yet facts are slippery things, and the justices presiding over the law often prove unwilling to define further the terms of the jury's representation of those facts. The single truth toward which men of law are theoretically driving is not present in fact; instead, representations of these facts are determined by a

---

[20] See Stanley Fish, "Don't Know Much About the Middle Ages: Posner on Law and Literature," in *Doing What Comes Naturally: Change, Rhetoric, and the Practice of Theory in Literary and Legal Studies* (Durham: Duke University Press, 1989), p. 304. Fish writes, "As things stand now in our culture, a person embedded in the legal world reads in a way designed to *resolve* interpretive crises . . . , while someone embedded in the literary world reads in a way designed to *multiply* interpretive crises."

frustrating plenitude of factors, known or unknown, which men of law can only do their best to contain or secure.

From all appearances, medieval juries—civil and criminal—were both aware of and willing to use their power to represent the facts. The discussion thus far has focused on civil juries, for it is in this context that men of law's professional response to the jury can most easily be traced. But the powerful role of the civil trial jury recognized and addressed by the men of law pleading at Westminster was intensified in criminal matters. Because the criminal defendant was denied legal counsel, there was little opportunity for the pleadings that in civil cases tried to isolate discrete issues of fact or remove the case from the jury, and criminal cases were almost invariably tried under the general issue of "not guilty." Moreover, the action of attaint that (in principle) threatened civil juries with severe sanctions for false verdicts was never extended to criminal juries. In sum, at a criminal trial "[t]he jury's power to determine the defendant's fate was virtually absolute."[21] The judges of the assizes before whom most criminal trials were conducted, and in whose number the Man of Law is included (he is a justice "ful often in assise" [*GP* 314]), were more administrators than participants in the trial and its outcome. We must presume that they presided over trials in which the law they were asked to administer was repeatedly subverted by panels of lay jurors following a legal code of their own making.[22] Men of law would thus be in a position to see the law that forms such a strong part of their identity subverted or ignored by lay jurors over whom, as justices of assize, they could exercise little control.

The subversive or subverted jury is a recurring topic of complaint in the late fourteenth century. For example, a parliamentary petition by the Commons in the sixteenth year of Richard II's reign alleges that many "malfesours," indicted of "diverse felonies and trespasses" by the oath of "good and loyal men," have procured favorable jury panels who

---

[21] Thomas A. Green, *Verdict According to Conscience: Perspectives on the English Criminal Trial Jury, 1200–1800* (Chicago: University of Chicago Press, 1985), p. 19.

[22] The phenomenon of trial juries substituting their own legal code for the law they are asked to apply is known as "jury nullification." Green's *Verdict According to Conscience* documents the pervasiveness of this phenomenon among medieval criminal trial juries. And S. F. C. Milsom, criticizing the "miserable history of crime in England," states that "[s]o far as justice was done throughout the centuries, it was done by jurors and in spite of savage laws." Arguing that the early history of crime in England shows "almost a mirror image" of the law's effort to shape the facts, Milsom states that "[j]urors made unacceptable rules produce acceptable results by adjusting the facts"; Milsom, *Historical Foundations*, pp. 403 and 422.

have acquitted them of their offenses. In return, the acquitted malefactors have pursued members of the indicting juries with briefs of conspiracy, alleging misdeeds "committed in other counties where [the malefactors] have alliances and strong friends." As a result, "the loyal and good men do not dare to speak the truth regarding their charges, in very great destruction of the execution of the law of the realm."[23] Regardless of the extent to which such a petition is grounded in fact (and there is ample evidence of jury intimidation or corruption), it also constructs a picture of jury behavior confirming a man of law's worst fears. It establishes an opposition between the "good and loyal men" of the county, who know the truth and are willing to speak it, and the various malefactors and false men, who actively subvert the law by suppressing or purchasing the truth. But this petition and others like it—Langlandian in their emphasis on the corrupting power of wealth and physical force—are used not so much to discredit the institution of the jury as to support arguments for jury reform. Juries can and will produce the truth and uphold the law if they are staffed by "good and loyal men" willing to speak the truth freely. But such men need definition, a need that also presents an opportunity to exclude. The definition that emerges in late medieval statutes and legal writing constructs a limited and uncomfortably fragile theory of human perspicacity and trustworthiness, and it is a definition approved by more than one man of law.

The statutes defining the good and loyal men of the jury share, from Westminster II in 1285 onward, a focus on the material prosperity of prospective jurors. Other requirements such as "next neighbor," "least suspicious," or "of good fame" are combined with either general standards of prosperity ("sufficiently inherited" or "most substantial") or specific income requirements.[24] A statement from a 1436 petition by the Commons seems typical of contemporary opinion: "it is to suppose by reson, that the more sufficient that men be of liflode, of Londes and

---

[23] "[P]lusours Malfesours . . . sont enditez par le serement de bones gentz & loialx . . . de diverses felonies & trespas, & puis par Enquestes procurez & favorables deliverez de mesmes les felonies & trespas; lesqueux Malfesours apres lour deliverance pursuent sovent envers lour Enditours & autres par Briefs de Conspiracie, allegeantz les Conspiracies estre faitz en autres Countees la ou ils ont alliances & amys fortz . . . : Par quoi les loialx & bones gentz n'osent dire la verite de les pointz touchantz lour Charges, en tres grant destruction de l'execution de la Ley du Roialme, & anientissement des ditz Enditours." *Rotuli parliamentorum*, vol. 3 (London: n.p., 1783), p. 306; my translation.

[24] A table of statutes defining juror qualifications, from which these examples are taken, is provided by James C. Oldham in "The Origins of the Special Jury," *University of Chicago Law Review* 50 (1983): 214–221.

Tenements, the more unlikly they are by corruption, brocage, or drede, to be treted or moeved to perjurie."[25] Of course, the term "good and loyal men" excludes without need of further definition women, who were excluded from regular jury service.[26]

As we have seen, *The Man of Law's Tale* displays deep suspicions regarding the ability of any man to see the truth, but there are certain men commended by the Man of Law for their superior prudence and perspicacity. "O riche marchauntz, ful of wele been yee, / O noble, o prudent folk, as in this cas!" (*MLP* 122–23). Worldly in the best sense, well-informed, and free of burdensome cares ("At Christemasse myrie may ye daunce!" [line 126]), the wealthy merchants acquire with their "wynnynges" (line 127) traits that set them apart from the indigent. The poor are wrapped up in their condition, driven to any means to secure their livelihood ("thou most for indigence / Or stele, or begge, or borwe thy despence" [lines 104–5]). They are spiteful, "synfully" accusing their wealthier neighbors for their happier condition, even "bitterly" blaming Christ himself for a misdistribution of wealth that is of their own making (lines 106–9). As the "wise man" says, "'Alle the dayes of povre men been wikke'" (lines 117–18), and such men are not to be trusted. Merchants, on the other hand, have their wits (and wealth) about them: they are "riche, and therto sadde and trewe" (*MLT* 135). They can see opportunities and turn them to their advantage. They are, in other words, men very much like the Man of Law.

Similar opinions are expressed by another man of law, John Fortescue, in his defense of the English jury against the continental jurisprudence of torture. Fortescue's *De laudibus legum Anglie* is often cited for its vivid condemnation of torture. At the same time, Fortescue bases his defense

---

[25] *Rotuli parliamentorum*, vol. 4, p. 501.

[26] The exclusion of women from jury service seems to have been an assumption so deeply embedded as not to merit justification; however, the second part of John Fortescue's *De natura legis naturae* contains an explicit gendering of juridical capacity and functions that not only attempts to deny women any capacity to make judgments, but also establishes clear hierarchies between the juridical role of reason and fact. The realm of fact is, in Fortescue's analysis, gendered as feminine, while reason, a masculine attribute, "corrects" fact, molding it according to the rule of law to produce a truth according to right that supersedes the simple truth according to fact. Knowledge of the truth of fact still produces error if there is ignorance of the law. See Sir John Fortescue, *De natura legis naturae*, trans. Chichester Fortescue, in *The Works of Sir John Fortescue, Knight, Chief Justice of England and Lord Chancellor to King Henry the Sixth*, ed. Thomas (Fortescue) Lord Clermont (London: n.p., 1869; repr., New York: Garland, 1980), pp. 251, 256–58, and 276. This gendering of reason and fact speaks, of course, to the theoretical relationship between men of law and the jury.

of the English jury on grounds that nearly undercut this condemnation, and even implies that torture is at times the only means to get at the truth in the realms where it is used. Fortescue's defense of the jury articulates in greater detail the Man of Law's link between material prosperity and perspicacity, on the one hand, and poverty and myopic corruptibility, on the other. In so doing, it implies that torture is not only imaginable, but at times necessarily (although regrettably) practicable.

Geographical considerations assume an important role in the *De laudibus*, which promotes England's literal insularity as a justification for the realm's legal insularity. Although the *De laudibus*'s Chancellor, in dialogue with the English Prince, demonstrates that torture is inferior to the English jury as a means of determining truth, the Prince asks a bothersome but obvious question: "I wonder very much why this law of England, so worthy and so excellent, is not common to all the world."[27] The Chancellor's response develops his earlier observations on the selection of jurors, who should meet either statutory income requirements or "have lands or rents to a competent value at the discretion of the justices . . . lest through their hunger and poverty they may be easily corrupted or suborned."[28] These requirements are not, unfortunately, easily translated to other realms. England is blessed with a preternatural fertility, being so abundant in its riches that "the men of that land are not very much burdened with the sweat of labour, so that they live with more spirit, as the ancient fathers did, who preferred to tend their flocks rather than to distract their peace of mind with the cares of agriculture." This prosperity makes English men "more apt and disposed to investigate causes which require searching examination than men who, immersed in agricultural work, have contracted a rusticity of mind from familiarity with the soil." And since there are in any given county "various yeoman . . . who can spend more than £100 a year," and

knights, esquires, and others, whose possessions exceed £333 6s. 8d. a year in total, . . . it is unthinkable that such men could be suborned or be willing to perjure themselves, not only because of their fear of God, but also because of their honour, and the scandal which would ensue, and because of the harm they would do their heirs through their infamy.[29]

[27] Fortescue, *De laudibus*, p. 67.
[28] Ibid., p. 59.
[29] Ibid., p. 69.

In contrast, wealth is much more diffuse in other lands, so spread out that it would be impossible to assemble twelve neighbors of sufficient livelihood. Instead, local juries would have to be filled with "paupers who have neither shame of being infamous nor fear of the loss of their goods, since they have none, and are also blinded by rustic ignorance so that they cannot clearly perceive the truth." The conclusion to be drawn from this analysis is well articulated by the Prince:

[T]he [law of France] in the comparison made by you is delivered from all blame, because, though you have preferred the law of England to it, yet it does not deserve odium, since you have not disparaged it or its makers, but have shown only that the land where it rules is the cause of its not eliciting the truth in disputes by so good a procedure as the law of England does. . . . Yet still this superiority of the law of England does not spring from the defects of the other law, but is caused only by the fertility of England.[30]

Torture, as it turns out, is not really condemned: it is an inferior means of discovering the truth, to be sure, but one that seems unavoidable in other realms where determination of the truth cannot be entrusted to a panel of local jurors for want of a sufficient concentration of material wealth.

Fortescue differs from the Man of Law in emphasizing pastoral over mercantile sources of wealth, yet his defense of the English jury is built on assumptions remarkably close to those informing the merchant-praising *Prologue* to *The Man of Law's Tale*. The display of spending power, of material possessions, signifies a discerning mind, one stripped of the blinding rusticity contracted in contact with the soil, when one's daily sustenance must be eked out with burdensome labor. Wealth gives a person something to protect—or lose. Wealth is both liberating and constraining, freeing the mind to search for the truth while guaranteeing, for fear of its loss, that the search will not be diverted by lesser temptations. But this emphasis on wealth—informing Fortescue's, the Man of Law's, and Parliament's various definitions of "prudent folk" and "good and loyal men"—provides unstable support for the jury. If trust-worthiness and perspicacity are defined by wealth, they are as suscepti-ble to loss as is wealth itself. And as the Prince's conclusion makes clear, there are other methods to get at the truth when trust is lacking.

[30] Fortescue, Ibid., pp. 71–73.

19

The fragility of men of law's trust in the jury has been the underlying theme of this section, a fragility manifested in men of law's responses to the jury. We have traced two such responses, both intended to exert some measure of control over this body of laymen. First, we have examined the development of pleading strategies designed to determine the terms of the jury's factual representation, or to determine the very composition of the jury. Second, we have observed efforts to restrict financially the qualifications for jury service, focusing on the linkage in medieval legal theory between trustworthy truthseekers and their material wealth. Combined, these responses outline a theory of the jury shaped by powerful hermeneutical and ideological assumptions. A certain truth is out there, but it is an elusive commodity, subject to the distortions of uncontrollable, obscure, or unknowable factors, discernible only to those men who can patently afford to look for it, and freely offered only by those who cannot afford to hide it. In the absence of such men, more forceful methods of discovering the truth can find a "legitimate" place.

III. The jurisprudence and logic of torture

Given the Man of Law's (and men of law's) assumptions, the appearance of torture in his tale loses its sense of anomaly. The Man of Law, as certain of truth's existence as he is of its ability to elude even the best "mennes wittes" (*MLT* 202), is nonetheless committed to pinning it down. In his tale, the truth often resides with persons who, from his professional perspective, can least be trusted. But in his tale, the Man of Law is not constrained by the unique procedural rules of the common law. He is free to indulge in a narrative experiment with the jurisprudence of torture, demonstrating its brisk efficiency in extorting a confession from the suspect body of the messenger.

There are problems, however, in suggesting that *The Man of Law's Tale* pursues a narrative strategy intended to expose the Man of Law as a potential torturer. I have argued that the Man of Law's profile and the assumptions underlying his narrative conform to a legal mentality that proves notably ambiguous on the question of torture. Yet a mentality willing to consider, even endorse, the efficacy of pain in the production of truth is hardly limited in *The Canterbury Tales* to the Man of Law's narrative. The messenger's torture is only one of several instances of judicial torture described in the *Tales*; and the link in *The Man of Law's*

Tale between the messenger's torments and those of Custance links the jurisprudence of torture to a broader logic of torture that in turn links Custance to the tormented heroines of *The Second Nun's Tale* and *The Clerk's Tale*. I will argue that the juxtaposition of judicial torture and Custance's torments ultimately undermines the claim that torture can secure a certain truth. I am much less willing to argue that this is a narrative strategy intentionally pursued in the tale.

The jurisprudence of torture became part of many distinct European legal systems over the course of the later Middle Ages. Rather than describe these systems individually, this section instead considers the theory behind the particular mode of proof known as *judicial torture*. More specifically, it examines the relationship established between torture and the determination of truth. How is torture justified as a means to the truth? Against whom is it used, and for what reasons? And how does it relate to other discourses, particularly religious discourses, advocating the application of pain in pursuit of the truth—discourses sharing a similar logic of torture?

Judicial torture does not refer to the indiscriminate application of pain: as several recent studies have noted, the expansive semantic sense of torture in modern usage can obscure what is at issue with judicial torture.[31] While there is some dispute over the precise definition of torture, that of the thirteenth-century jurist Azo of Bologna highlights its key elements: it "is the inquiry after truth by means of torment."[32] It developed as a legal practice and set as its goal the recovery of truth in

---

[31] Edward Peters, in the first edition of his study of torture, argues "that judicial torture is the *only* kind of torture, whether administered by an official judiciary or by other instruments of the state. . . . The juxtaposition of familiar terms from one area of meaning to another for dramatic effect is a device of rhetoric, not historical or social analysis. And semantic entropy does not clarify understanding." In the preface to the expanded edition, Peters allows for a "slightly expanded definition" of torture, but still advises avoidance "of the most misleading uses of the term in modern sentimental journalism." See Edward Peters, *Torture* (Oxford: Basil Blackwell, 1985), p. 7; exp. ed. (Philadelphia: University of Pennsylvania Press, 1996), p. vii. Langbein uses the term "judicial torture," but similarly insists that "torture has to be kept separate from various painful modes of punishment used as sanctions against persons already convicted and condemned. No punishment, no matter how gruesome, should be called torture"; Langbein, *Law of Proof*, p. 3. Perhaps the most influential account of torture in recent scholarship—Michel Foucault's *Discipline and Punish*, trans. Alan Sheridan (New York: Vintage–Random House, 1979)—is less specific, focusing on both "judicial" and "punitive" torture (the latter graphically represented in the opening account of the regicide Damien's execution).

[32] Azo's definition is one of several listed by Peters to represent the range (and consistency) of torture's definitions from the third through the twentieth centuries; Peters, *Torture*, pp. 1–2.

an inquisitional context, a recovery purportedly accomplished by the infliction of pain on the body. It was not used indiscriminately: it was to be applied in limited contexts, against certain persons, and subject to certain conditions.

Torture has been a recurring aspect of European jurisprudence since (at least) the time of classical Greek jurisprudence, and it has demonstrated a certain consistency in the course of its translation through the civilizations and legal systems of western Europe. One of its most consistent features has been its initial introduction against certain suspect classes of persons, from which its practice has gradually expanded. The earliest tracts addressing torture in medieval Europe, for example, limit its application to the lowest classes. The *Book of Tübingen* (ca. 1100) condones torture only for known criminals and *vilissimi homines* (the basest of men), excepting "men living honestly who cannot be corrupted by grace, favour and money." Gratian's *Decretum* excludes from a general prohibition on torture accusers of bishops, people in the lowest ranks of society, and slaves.[33] Closer in time and place to Chaucer's England is the example of torture's introduction and expansion in that portion of the Low Countries roughly corresponding to modern Belgium.[34] Torture was introduced in the region first as a police measure in the thirteenth century to give officials the right to use torture in pursuit of criminals. The reaction of citizens to torture's introduction was one of self-interest: torture was permitted, with exceptions carved out for the "propres bourgeois." But as torture's facility for producing confessions made it an invaluable part of legal procedure, the citizens' privileges disappeared and they ultimately became subject to the procedure they had tolerated when used against others. Appearing with what R. C. van Caenegem describes as a "monotonous regularity" from the beginning of the fourteenth century, torture spread across the region as the century progressed.

The association between the lower social classes and torture is, of course, not at odds with the messenger's torture in *The Man of Law's*

---

[33] The *Book of Tübingen* and Gratian's *Decretum* are discussed in Peters, *Torture*, pp. 47–48 and 52–53.

[34] This account is drawn from Raoul C. van Caenegem, "La preuve dans l'ancien droit Belge des origines à la fin du XVIIIᵉ siècle," *La Preuve*, Recueils de la Société Jean Bodin pour l'histoire comparative des institutions, vol. 17 (Brussels: Editions de la Librairie Encyclopédique, 1965), pp. 399–403. The specific areas covered in van Caenegem's analysis are the principalities of Flanders, Artois, Hainaut, Brabant, Namur, and Liège.

Tale, and the Man of Law's representation of the messenger—mindless, eager for favor, susceptible to temptation—is a representation with a distinct historical resonance. Such a class-coded use of torture also has resonance within *The Canterbury Tales.* Instances of judicial torture appear in *The Man of Law's Tale, The Knight's Tale,* and *The Nun's Priest's Tale,* and the similarities and differences among these incidents are telling. One of Chaunticleer's many interpretation-of-dreams exempla in *The Nun's Priest's Tale* describes two travelers forced by a limited number of vacancies to take separate lodgings for a night. One of the travelers appears in the dreams of the other, first warning his sleeping companion of his impending murder, and then appearing after the fact to tell his companion that his body can be discovered in a dung cart. "Mordre wol out," Chaunticleer chides, but it comes out with the assistance of torture (lines 3057–61):

> And right anon, ministres of that toun
> Han hent the carter and so soore hym pyned,
> And eek the hostiler so soore engyned,
> That they biknewe hire wikkednesse anon,
> And were anhanged by the nekke-bon.

As in *The Man of Law's Tale,* the suspect (and lowly) carter and hosteler are put to torments by the presiding officials (here the town ministers), and the application of pain makes them "biknowe" or confess their culpability, just as the tormented messenger "[m]oste biknowe" (*MLT* 886) the details of his travels to and from Alla's camp under the pain of torture.

The threatened use of torture is, in contrast, averted in *The Knight's Tale* when the potential—and noble— subject of torture freely offers his confession. Discovered by Theseus in a grove fighting his cousin Arcite, Palamon "pleynly" confesses "[t]hat I am thilke woful Palamoun / That hath thy prisoun broken wikkedly" (lines 1733–35). Given such a frank and free confession by the young knight, Theseus responds by telling him that because "[y]oure owene mouth, by youre confessioun, / Hath dampned yow, . . . / It nedeth noght to pyne yow with the corde" (lines 1744–46). A "plat and pleyn" (*MLT* 886) confession is extracted from the lowly messenger only under torture, whereas the noble Palamon "pleynly" lays bare his guilt without need of "pyne."

These three descriptions of torture indicate that the legal mentality that defines one's trustworthiness as a speaker of truth on the basis of social rank is not confined in *The Canterbury Tales* to the Man of Law and his tale. They also describe a lexicon of torture in the *Tales: pynen, engynen,* and *tormenten* are all synonyms meaning *to torture.* And these three verbs demonstrate that semantic imprecision on the subject of torture is not only a modern phenomenon. Each of these verbs has related meanings that prove more illuminating than semantically confusing, for they point to gaps between judicial torture's theoretical promise and the realities of its practice, and to links between the judicial practice of torture and other painful productions of "truth."

Engynen, the verb used to describe the process of torturing the Nun's Priest's hosteler, can also mean to contrive or construct something or to trick or deceive someone.[35] Thus, entangled in this verb's semantics are senses of torture, contrivance, and subterfuge. And although this semantic tangle seems potentially contradictory with respect to torture (suggesting that the "true" confession extracted is both constructed and gotten by trickery), it concisely represents the tension between the jurisprudential theory of torture and the realities of its practice.

Modern commentators on the spread of torture in medieval Europe generally agree that the Fourth Lateran Council's ban on clerical participation in ordeals precipitated torture's widespread integration into European jurisprudence. The switch from the certainty of divine judgment to the less reliable standard of human rationality suggested torture, and its promised recovery of the "certain" confession, as a means of negotiating this switch. Torture was deployed within a system of statutory proofs meant to minimize the role of the judge (and unpredictable human reason) in the adjudicatory process. It was used in "blood sanction" cases where death or maiming was the punishment, and was to be applied only upon the establishment of a sufficient foundation of circumstantial evidence known as *indicia.* It addressed a problem arising from the strict law of proof adopted in such cases: the requirement that either the testimony of two eyewitnesses or the confession of the suspect was necessary for conviction. Between sufficient eyewitness testimony and confession lay an intolerable space in which circumstantial evidence (one eyewitness, a discovered weapon, etc.) pointed to, but was not sufficient to convict, a suspect whose confession was not, understandably, forthcoming. As Langbein argues, "No society

---

[35] See the *Middle English Dictionary* [hereafter *MED*] s.v. *enginen.*

will long tolerate a legal system in which there is no prospect of convicting unrepentant persons who commit clandestine crimes. . . . The two-eyewitness rule was hard to compromise or evade, but the confession rule invited 'subterfuge.'"[36] This "subterfuge" of confession was torture: the coercion of the "certain" proof of confession through the application of physical pain.[37]

The distinction between torture, a *means* of extracting proof, and confession, the proof itself, is not irrelevant. Indeed, the jurisprudence of torture insisted that the confession be repeated away from the place of torture, as if to distance the confession from the means by which it was produced. The notion that torture produces the confession recalls the sense of contrivance or constructedness associated with the Middle English *engynen,* and points to a weakness in the justifications of certainty and objectivity underpinning the jurisprudence of torture. Langbein notes that under the jurisprudence of torture, the judge would ideally be rendered an "automaton," administering the law according to objective criteria of proof specified in statutory formulations. Yet the role of the judge described in Jehan Boutillier's *Somme rural* is hardly that of an automaton:

If the person in question be found anyway suspected by strong presumption, [the judge] may and shall put him to torture *according to his physique, for one person can stand more severe torture than another,* . . . and if by dint of torture he will say nothing nor confess the first time, the judge can repeat it the second day, and even the third and fourth *if he sees that the case requires it, and if there be such great presumption and the prisoner be a man of high courage.*[38]

Torture, notwithstanding its promise of delivering the certain proof of the confession, is recognized here as a highly subjective process, to be adapted to the varying constitutions of the persons against whom it is administered.

[36] Langbein, *Law of Proof,* p. 7.

[37] This brief account of torture is drawn from Langbein, *Law of Proof,* pp. 3–17; Peters, *Torture,* pp. 40–73; and Adhémar Esmein, *A History of Continental Criminal Procedure, with Special Reference to France,* trans. John Simpson (Boston: Little Brown, 1913), pp. 78–144.

[38] Quoted in Esmein, *Criminal Procedure,* p. 128; my emphasis. Boutillier held a number of legal positions in and around the southwestern Belgian city of Tournai. His *Somme rural* was written near the end of the fourteenth century. For a description of Boutillier and various features of the *Somme rural,* see Guido van Dievoet, *Les coutumiers, les styles, les formulaires, et les "artes notariae,"* Typologie des sources du moyen âge occidental, fasc. 48 (Turnhout, Belgium: Brepols, 1986), pp. 11–71 passim.

The blend of subjectivity and objectivity in the administration of torture and production of the confession is suggested by the Man of Law's description of the messenger's torture as a process of "wit and sotil enquerynge" applied to extract the "plat and pleyn" confession of the messenger's itinerary. The messenger's torture is "successful" because it gets at its target: a "verbal truth" that can be detached from the victim's body and put to use in the prosecution of the offense in question. This aspect of torture is, as Talal Asad notes, one of the things that distinguishes it from earlier judicial applications of pain, especially in the ordeal. Whereas the ordeal uses physical pain to inscribe judgment on the body of the accused, torture uses physical pain in a hunt for the truth, a hunt in which "violence to the body was a condition for arriving at a judgment and not the form in which judgment was inscribed or read."[39] The utterances brought forth from the tortured body, not the tortured body itself, are the "medium of the truth."[40]

Asad's discussion of judicial torture is of special relevance to *The Man of Law's Tale* because of the connections he makes between judicial torture and the application of pain in pursuit of the truth in other contexts, specifically, that of religious penance. Noting that "the Fourth Lateran Council of 1215, which proscribed ordeals [and precipitated the widespread adoption of judicial torture], also prescribed mandatory annual private confession for all Christians," Asad suggests that "the concern for truth, physical pain, and confession (the very elements that are so central to the practice of judicial torture)" is played out in a "religious history of penance" that roughly corresponds to the historical shift from the jurisprudence of the ordeal to that of torture.[41] In brief, Asad sees a

---

[39] Talal Asad, *Genealogies of Religion: Discipline and Reasons of Power in Christianity and Islam* (Baltimore: Johns Hopkins University Press, 1993), p. 95.

[40] Asad, *Genealogies*, p. 93. Elaine Scarry's analysis of political torture in the twentieth century makes a similar point. "The 'it' in 'Get it out of him,'" Scarry argues, "refers not just to a piece of information but to the capacity for speech itself. The written or tape-recorded confession that can be carried away on a piece of paper or on a tape is only the most concrete exhibition of the torturer's attempt to induce sounds so that they can be broken off from their speaker so that they can then be taken off and made the property of the regime." Scarry's analysis is directed at the use of torture as an instrument of political oppression, but the desire she identifies behind political torture's use—the desire to get at a confession or information that can be detached from the victim and put to use away from the torture chamber—is common to judicial torture. See Elaine Scarry, *The Body in Pain: The Making and Unmaking of the World* (New York: Oxford University Press, 1985), p. 49.

[41] Asad, *Genealogies*, pp. 95 and 97.

transition from the early church's public imposition of painful penances for past deeds to a monastic asceticism that inflicts pain on the body as part of a continual inquiry into and disciplining of the body's potentiality for transgression, to a "new ritual of truth" (expressed in the Fourth Lateran Council's "new regime of penance" that made annual confession to a priest mandatory for all Christians) "in which interrogation plays the central part, in which truth about guilt is no longer inscribed on the body but extracted from it and invested in it—in the form of disciplined words and gestures."[42] While physical pain is, under this new regime, applied only rarely (against the heretic reluctant to confess guilt, for example) other aspects of the new regime of penance bear striking resemblance to the jurisprudence of torture—they display, that is, a similar logic of torture. Suffering (here the mental anguish of acknowledging and articulating one's sins) is used as a means toward the discovery of a truth buried within, and brought forth in the verbal confession. And the discovery of that truth is assigned to official investigators (clerical instead of judicial) trained in a "difficult and dangerous task—how to interrogate, how to listen, and how to identify the guilt that was indicated (or literally created) by the words of the penitent." Again, the discovery of the "objective truth" represented by the confession proves to be a highly subjective process—the interrogating confessor is trained to be sensitive to the specific social status of the penitent and to "types of thought, speech, and action anchored in particular social statuses."[43]

The link made by Asad between judicial torture and religious pain is similar to that made by the Man of Law in his juxtaposition of the messenger's torments and those of his heroine, Custance. The verb *engynen,* already discussed, is probably the most technically specific term in *The Canterbury Tales's* lexicon of torture; *tormenten,* the verb used to describe the messenger's torture, shades into more general connotations of painful suffering, as does *pynen.*[44] *Tormenten* is also associated with three similar heroines in *The Canterbury Tales*—Custance, Griselda of *The Clerk's Tale,* and Cecilia of *The Second Nun's Tale*—and in these three

---

[42] Ibid., p. 117.
[43] Ibid., pp. 119–20.
[44] See *MED,* s.v. *pinen* and *tormenten.* Both verbs often denote the affliction of penitential or spiritual suffering.

cases, we see a consistent use of *tormenten* to describe the application of physical or mental suffering to produce the "truth." We also see, in the move from the old-fashioned hagiography of *The Second Nun's Tale* to the more complicated narratives of *The Clerk's Tale* and *The Man of Law's Tale*, a change in the relationship between truth and bodily pain that mirrors the changes already traced in judicial and penitential practices, and follows the same logic of torture.

Cecilia's torments in *The Second Nun's Tale* represent a ritual of truth production, similar to the judicial ordeal or the early church's public imposition of penance, in which the body itself is the medium of truth; in Cecilia's story, the truth communicated by the martyr's tormented body is the inefficacy of the prefect Almachius's temporal power in the face of divine might. Plunged into "a bath of flambes rede," Cecilia sits "al coold," not sweating a drop and feeling "no wo" (lines 515 and 521). And with her neck carved open by the prefect's "tormentour" (line 527), Cecilia calmly continues "to preche" and arranges the disposition of "hir moebles and hir thyng" (lines 539 and 540). The power of Cecilia's proselytizing utterances is undoubtedly meant to be enforced by her torments, but her torments are not intended to draw forth those utterances—Cecilia has been saying the same things throughout her tale, and her speech is not the product of her pain. Indeed, Cecilia is granted the power to ignore the painful sufferings her tormentor would inflict upon her. She frustrates Almachius's attempt to inscribe his punishing power on her body, although the truth of a superior divine force is still bodily communicated through her miraculous imperviousness to the prefect's torments.

In *The Clerk's Tale*, Griselda herself names what Walter does to her as a "tormentynge" (line 1038), but the terms of her torments are very different from those for Cecilia. Walter torments Griselda with mental anguish—taking their children from her and seemingly murdering them, then stripping her of her "richesse" and sending her back to her father's poor hut—in order to "tempte" and "assaye" her "alwey moore and moore" (lines 458 and 461). Walter, in other words, tests or interrogates Griselda by applying pain (here mental rather than physical) to see if he can produce any proof that Griselda might transgress her vow not to disobey Walter upon pain of death. Walter is searching for something inside Griselda—a confession that she is in truth willing to disobey him, despite all appearances—and his torments are intended to produce an articulation of such a transgressive willingness in her "cheere" or, especially, in her speech. When, for example, Walter's sergeant returns from the first "tormentynge" of Griselda, he tells Walter "of Grisildis wordes and hire cheere / . . . point for point, in short and pleyn" (lines 576–77). Walter is interested in what Griselda said as she experienced the torment of having her child taken from her to be killed, what that torment brought forth from inside her. The sergeant's answer is "short and pleyn" because she said nothing.

Walter's tormenting of Griselda does not, of course, constitute an act of judicial torture, but it certainly follows a logic of torture. It seeks a hidden truth, and it puts Griselda "in angwyssh and in drede" (line 462) to force an articulation of that truth, if it is there, in "Grisildis wordes." Such a truth is not there, or at least it cannot be found by Walter, and this raises a problem in both the logic and jurisprudence of torture, a problem that also appears in the tormenting of Custance. What if the application of pain produces nothing but silence? The certainty of proof promised by torture is gained only when torture has reached a "successful" conclusion, when an "objective" confession has been produced that can be set apart from the subjective uncertainties governing a particular application of pain. An "unsuccessful" application of torture is thus highly problematic: refusal to confess anything should, conversely, prove innocence; but unlike the use of torture that ends in confession, the use of torture that ends in nothing produces nothing that can be taken away from the place of torture and held up as certain proof. The uncertainties implicit in any painful production of the truth are, in other words, foregrounded in the case of the silent victim, and innocence must be determined through inference. The suspect was able to withstand his or her torture, thus the suspect must not be guilty. Or did the interrogator misread this particular suspect? If pain had been administered one more time, would the suspect finally have confessed?[45] Innocence within the logic of torture is a question of accumulation: at what point has a particular suspect withstood so much anguish that innocence has been established? In such instances, the attempt to separate

---

[45] Griselda herself warns Walter that he should "ne prikke with no tormentynge" the "tendre mayden" he has named as his next wife because her more tender "norissynge" would make her less able to endure such pains than the "povre fostred" Griselda (*CIT* 1037–43).

the application of pain as a means of obtaining proof from the proof itself collapses. Innocence is proved by the persuasive force of a narrative of resistance constructed around the articulation of the particular torments endured.

The Clerk's Tale displays a self-awareness that the story of Griselda is precisely such a narrative of resistance, and at first glance its narrator seems to critique the application of pain in pursuit of the truth, emphasizing the excessiveness of Walter's acts. Walter tests Griselda "alwey moore and moore" when there "is no nede" (lines 458 and 461); he catches "yet another lest / To tempte his wyf yet ofter, if he may. / O nedelees was she tempted in assay!" (lines 619–21); he knows "no mesure" (line 622). But, perhaps paradoxically, *The Clerk's Tale* does little to discredit the logic of torture. Walter's torments are excessive only in the context of his need for the certainty he seeks; they become objectionable to the Clerk because Walter has no reason to suspect Griselda of being anything but a good (that is, obedient) wife. And although the Clerk is critical of Walter, by simply retelling the tale of Griselda he too becomes complicit in the logic of torture, especially when, in the tale's notoriously conflicted ending, he tries to impose some meaning on the "nedelees" torments he has described. The force of these torments is so great that there is an almost irresistible need to make sense of how that force could be endured. Yet trying to make sense of such endurance always runs the risk of making sense of torture; an attempted imposition of meaning enables torture to signify something beyond the brutality of its force, even if that brutality is acknowledged and condemned. When that brutality is minimized, or justified as necessary, the logic of torture can run unimpeded, and virtually unquestioned.[46]

---

[46] Kate Millett's account of her childhood experiences with hagiographical and martyrological narratives offers a striking modern example of how the use of torture to signify something else can minimize or obscure the brutal senselessness foregrounded in narratives of endurance. Having been fed a diet of "hundreds of martyrdoms . . . from the nuns in religion classes," Millett describes her response: "Saints and martyrs had a hard time of it but they came through with flying colors, ascended to heaven and a plenteous reward, and then were written up in books where girls like myself wept tears over their sufferings, relished their triumphs. Perhaps we even relished their trials, so much a part of us were, so without danger, so reassuring. They were romances incapable of unhappy endings, without suffering permanent or actual enough to have real meaning as suffering; St. Lawrence on his grill, Catherine breaking her wheel, even Lucy with her breasts sliced off—always magically reattached at the end of the tale."

Such is the case in *The Man of Law's Tale*. The Man of Law is certainly aware of his own heroine's "tormentynge," but there is no sign that he would deem it "nedelees." Presiding, like the Clerk, over a narrative of torments endured, the Man of Law seems even more complicit in the painful provings described in his tale. Describing Custance's "wo" is the Man of Law's exhausting "labour" in his tale (lines 1069–70); his narrative efforts resemble the production of a legal record designed to prove Custance's constancy, and his own exhaustion emphasizes his participation in the process he relates. When the Man of Law juxtaposes this narrative of endurance with the "successful" torture of the messenger, he makes explicit the link between judicial torture and the torments suffered by Custance. And while this juxtaposition may unsettle any claims that torture is a certain means of producing the truth, despite its all too understandable "successes," it also suggests a very different narrative strategy, one designed to heighten the significance of Custance's endurance through contrast with the quick extortion of the messenger's confession.

IV. "So wo is me that I moot be thy tormentour": Proving Custance

Near the end of the second part of *The Man of Law's Tale*, King Alla's constable, acting on the information contained in the counterfeit letter drafted by Donegild and delivered by the unfortunate messenger, puts Custance and her son to sea in the ship that brought Custance to Northumberland. Convinced of Custance's goodness, but obliged to obey Alla's orders on pain of death, the constable exclaims: "O goode Custance, allas, so wo is me / That I moot be thy tormentour, or deye / On shames deeth; ther is noon oother weye" (lines 817–19). Custance—who by now has been forced to leave her home, has witnessed the brutal slaying of her first husband, has endured a lengthy sojourn at sea alone in her boat, and has suffered the murder of her closest friend and been accused of the crime—appeals to another woman

---

These impressions were wiped away by a secularized depiction of Catherine's martyrdom in "Ripley's Believe It or Not." Through this depiction, which "saw the event not only with the eyes of protestant rationalism, but through secularism," one "did not see a martyrdom, one saw an execution." "Ripley," Millett concludes, "had dispensed with fable and illusion." Catherine was "simply a being mercilessly persecuted." See Kate Millett, *The Politics of Cruelty: An Essay on the Literature of Political Imprisonment* (New York: W. W. Norton, 1994), 150–52.

whose torments seem in excess of the limits of imagination and endurance (lines 841–47):

> "Mooder . . . and mayde bright, Marie,
> Sooth is that thurgh wommanes eggement
> Mankynde was lorn, and damned ay to dye,
> For which thy child was on a croys yrent.
> Thy blisful eyen sawe al his torment;
> Thanne is ther no comparison bitwene
> Thy wo and any wo man may sustene."

Clinging to her own child, Custance defiantly walks to her boat, having put what Alla's constable has identified as her most recent torment
in its place (what is it compared to the sufferings of Mary?), while
pointing to the extremities with which real holiness is proved (Mary,
having suffered more woe than any "man may sustene," is now the "glorie of wommanhede"[line 851]).[47]

Having reached the nadir of her fortunes, Custance again proves herself constant: serene, resolute, unshaken in her faith, she gathers what
little remains of her life and takes to her ship. And in case we, as the
Tale's audience, are still uncertain what to make of the numerous and
acute agonies Custance has endured thus far, Alla's constable and
Custance herself make clear that what we are reading is a narrative of
endured torments. Custance is being tormented just as surely as is the
messenger whose torture opens part 3. But what are Custance's torments meant to prove? Why and for whom is such proof needed? The
juxtaposition of Custance's torments with those of the messenger seems
hardly coincidental: how is the messenger's torture meant to inform our
reading of Custance's own torments?

Consideration of these questions might begin by briefly returning to
Custance's apostrophe to Mary, the "glorie of wommanhede" whose torments prove her distance from the "wommanes eggement" through
which "[m]ankynde was lorn." Mary has overcome a presumption of

[47] The association between Custance and her child, and Mary and her son, both draws
attention to what is being tested in this tale (Custance's faith) and draws a line in the
sand. Custance, having endured a series of torments both varied and exhaustingly repetitive, seems to be establishing for her curious tormentor the outer limits of her suffering: "Destroy my child, and you will have gone as far as you can go." It is also at this
point that Custance's torments begin to subside: a few more "just to be sure" tests await,
but Custance seems to have (almost) proved herself.

guilt against her sex traced back to the womanly "eggement" for which she personally has suffered her son's death. Through her suffering, she has proved herself clear of that presumption. Having endured the torment of watching her son be "on a croys ryent," Mary is now the "glorie of wommanhede" yet is set apart from women generally. Although we are all familiar with the woman blamed for the original, mankind-destroying "eggement" in Eden, that woman and her original provocation to sin remain unspecified in Custance's apostrophe. Mary is uniquely possessed of an identity distinct from the generalized "wommanes eggement" that she has painfully transcended. She is a character against type. The tendency toward "eggements"—subversive provocations, instigations, or incitations—remains definitive of woman within *The Man of Law's Tale*.[48] Mary simply proves that this tendency may be resisted. And the association established between Mary and Custance points to the painful task assigned Custance in her tale: like Mary, she must prove herself constant, free of the womanly "eggements" that permeate the tale.

Custance's character is immersed in the turbulent confluence of anxieties, assumptions, and contradictions underlying *The Man of Law's Tale* and impelling its narrator on. Legally bound to tell a tale, the Man of Law finds himself in a crowded field. The competition has already "thriftily" disposed of the supply of narratives, leaving few that the Man of Law can make his own. Taking what he can get, the Man of Law falls upon Custance's tale, itself a "thrifty" tale of Christian virtue freshly delivered by a dependable merchant. But as in his professional life, the Man of Law must take his material as it comes to him, and what he gets in this case is an unstable generic "mixture of hagiography, romance, and chronicle history."[49] Also as in his professional life, the Man of Law

[48] It is with respect to the definition of women in the "Man of Law's Tale" that my reading departs from that of Carolyn Dinshaw. I agree with Dinshaw's observation that there is a blankness (what Dinshaw describes as "an essential blankness") or "no-thing-ness" that defines women in the tale. Dinshaw especially associates this definitive "no-thingness" with Custance, linking it to what she reads as the tale's ideological insistence on woman's passive instrumentality (a trait also defined by Custance). I would argue that feminine blankness plays a more unsettling role in the tale, representing not so much a surface "that will be inscribed by men and thus turned into a tale," but a surface that is essentially unreadable by men, including the Man of Law, and thus suspect because capable of concealment. The Man of Law, in other words, is unsettled by the fear that behind her superficial blankness, Custance might conceal something that could unsettle his tale. See Carolyn Dinshaw, *Chaucer's Sexual Poetics* (Madison: University of Wisconsin Press, 1989), pp. 110–12.

[49] Dinshaw, *Sexual Poetics*, p. 88.

must struggle to maintain control over a narrative that threatens to be subverted by the potential contradictions inherent in its details—details which, by refusing to conform neatly to all the generic frames of the tale, threaten to open the narrative up to unwelcome pinching.

Some of the most elaborate of the Man of Law's efforts to take rhetorical control of his tale occur at points where the details of the narrative push the limits of a particular genre. How, for example, are we to reconcile the carnal realities of Custance and Alla's marriage bed with Custance's holiness? Hagiography and marriage, especially a consummated marriage, are often portrayed as uneasy partners;[50] thus the Man of Law must justify Custance's marital activity as something "skile and right" (line 708). Accordingly, we are told

> For thogh that wyves be ful hooly thynges,
> They moste take in pacience at nyght
> Swiche manere necessaries as been plesynges
> To folk that han ywedded hem with rynges,
> And leye a lite hir hoolynesse aside,
> As for the tyme—it may no bet betide. (lines 709–14)

Holiness, like one's garments, must be thought of as something that can be laid aside from time to time: at the same time, holiness demands that no recognition of pleasure be associated with acts that are "necessaries" to the holy, although "plesynges" to other folk. Pleading on the one hand for a more flexible definition of holiness, while on the other denying the possibility of holiness-threatening pleasure, the Man of Law tries to fashion a pinchproof compromise. Unfortunately, his attempted redefinitions of holiness, necessity, and pleasure only draw more attention to the contradictions he would reconcile.

Similarly, the influence of the divine in the text runs up against the narrative's chronicle-based claim to a grounding in historical fact. The miraculous significance of Custance's three-year solo voyage from Syria to Northumberland is undercut by a host of troubling questions: "Who kepte hire fro the drenchyng in the see?" (line 485), "Who bad the foure spirites of tempest / . . . 'Anoyeth neither see, ne land, ne tree?' " (lines

---

[50] On the relationship between sanctity and virginity, and the focus on the body in female saints' lives, see Elizabeth Robertson, "The Corporeality of Female Sanctity in *The Life of Saint Margaret*," in *Images of Sainthood in Medieval Europe*, ed. Renate Blumenfeld-Kosinski and Timea Szell (Ithaca, N.Y.: Cornell University Press, 1991), pp. 268–87.

491–94), and "Where myghte this womman mete and drynke have / Thre yeer and moore? How lasteth hire vitaille?" (lines 498–99). The answer, of course, is divine intervention. Yet our commitment (or, at least, the Man of Law's commitment) to the notion of divine intervention must be somewhat frail if these questions are arising in the first place.

Belief in divine intervention must be separated from a more general belief in Christian tenets; doubt regarding the former does not necessarily translate into doubt regarding the latter. Indeed, church doctrine had itself invalidated reliance on divine intervention in matters of legal proof. In like manner, there is a distinction between presuming to rely upon divine intervention on human demand (a presumption condemned in the intellectual preparation for the Fourth Lateran Council) and believing in spontaneously produced miracles. Nonetheless, the assumptions underpinning the immanent presence of the divine in *The Man of Law's Tale* do not travel smoothly into the late fourteenth century or the legal world inhabited by the Man of Law, nor do divine acts fit comfortably into a narrative claiming a factual basis. Miracles, especially unobserved miracles, are suspect things; when they have occurred in the past, and are no longer subject to verification, they become more suspect by being even less grounded in the presumed certainty of verifiable fact.[51]

Through the midst of this generic instability sails Custance, the enigmatic emblem of the stability and certainty the Man of Law craves. The notion of enigmatic stability and certainty is, of course, contradictory, but it is a contradiction that drives *The Man of Law's Tale* onward. Custance is at once the emblem of constancy, a signifier of Christianity's unshakable truths, and a flesh-and-blood woman, situated in a specific historical moment and subject to the shifting forces of that moment. The stable truths she represents are constantly beset by religious strife and human passions, forces that always threaten to overwhelm her and, in the process, shake the unshakable truths upon which the credibility of the Man of Law's narrative rests. And equally threatening, Custance is a woman, a suspect category in the *Tale* because of women's perceived

---

[51] Miracles had become suspect to the church itself. Hoping to control popular identification of saints, the church had since the thirteenth century treated canonization "as a judicial inquisitorial procedure. . . . It examined claims [of sanctity] that were assumed to be highly suspicious and it tended not to be generous in its approvals"; Aviad M. Kleinberg, "Proving Sanctity: Selection and Authentication of Saints in the Later Middle Ages," *Viator* 20 (1989): 189–90.

inscrutability and the various women's "eggements" that surround Custance in her tale.

The inscrutable surfaces of women are a recurring motif in the *Tale*, as well as a source of anxiety for the Man of Law. The Sultaness, for example, masterfully constructs artificial surfaces, and the disjunction between her seemingly feminine surface and what lies beneath is repeatedly noted by the *Tale*'s narrator. When the Sultaness conceives her plot against Custance, the Man of Law remarks upon the obfuscating potential of superficial "femynynytee," describing the Sultaness as a "serpent *under* femynynytee" and a "feyned womman" (lines 360 and 362; my emphasis). Upon Custance's arrival in Syria, the Sultaness "[r]eceyveth hire with also glad a cheere / As any mooder myghte hir doghter deere" (lines 396–97). Yet "for al hire flaterynge," the Sultaness "[c]aste *under* this ful mortally to stynge" (lines 405–6; my emphasis). Again, the feminine surface of a motherly appearance and words signifies one thing, but conceals something very different.

Donegild's appearance is similarly deceiving. Thanks to a narrative aside, we know of her aversion to Alla's union with "[s]o strange a creature" as Custance (line 700). This aversion, however, is apparently concealed from everyone else. No one, including Alla, suspects her of counterfeiting the letters that lead to Custance's banishment until the information is tortured out of the messenger. Donegild, even more than the Sultaness, embodies a rupture beneath the surface and the underneath: "Thogh thou heere walke," the Man of Law pronounces, "thy spirit is in helle!" (line 784).

Still more indicative of the *Tale*'s (and its teller's) fear of what is going on beneath feminine surfaces is its treatment of the relationship between Custance and Hermengild. Custance arrives in Northumberland as a complete, and committed, unknown: ". . . what she was she wolde no man seye, / For foul ne fair, thogh that she sholde deye" (lines 524–25). Again, however, there is activity beneath this unreadable feminine surface, even though Custance's role as instigator of this activity is minimized. Custance's exemplary behavior wins over both Hermengild and her husband, the constable (later Custance's self-described tormentor). But Custance's influence on Hermengild, who is secretly converted to Custance's faith before her husband converts, is especially pronounced. Credit for the conversion is given to Jesus, although it is Custance's long stay, prayers, and many tears that win Hermengild over. Like the other Christians scattered about pagan Northumberland, Custance and

Hermengild "in hir privitee / Honoured Crist and hethen folk bigiled" (lines 548–49). Or, at least, that is what we must assume they did: in their privity, Custance and Hermengild's activity is out of our sight, and we cannot really be sure what they are up to. And even if we are willing to accept that the two women are up to honest Christian beguilement, one of those pagans being beguiled is Hermengild's husband, unaware, given all appearances, that Hermengild's love for him has been challenged by her love for Christ.

Accordingly, Custance and Hermengild's privity cannot be tolerated for long: it creates a blind spot in a tale that deplores uncertainty, and it rouses the suspicions of a narrator all too convinced of the mischief that might be enacted behind inscrutable surfaces. Beneath the glare of the bright sun, Custance and Hermengild are exposed before the constable by the blind Christian man who temporarily forgets that "[i]n al that lond no Cristen dorste route" (line 540). Let in on their secret, the constable is also let in on the activities of Custance and Hermengild, enabling him to keep an eye on the no longer privy proceedings of the two women. These proceedings do not remain an issue much longer. Hermengild is soon murdered in the bed on which, in the constable's absence, she and Custance have collapsed together, "forwaked in hire orisouns" (line 596).

The extremity of the response to Custance and Hermengild's alliance is a particularly potent expression of the volatile combination of hermeneutical and ideological assumptions underpinning the Man of Law's narrative. Notions of certain, verifiable, precisely located truths collide with fears of the obfuscating potential of inscrutable, suspect surfaces, surfaces defined as suspect because of their difference from their would-be interpreter. The stability of truth behind these surfaces cannot be trusted, and thus, these surfaces must be gotten through—isolated and penetrated—to get at what is contained beneath. The alliance between Custance and Hermengild, a double threat heightened by Custance's crucial role as the source of the *Tale's* Christian truths, must therefore be broken up, penetrated and overseen by the constable (a man the Man of Law could trust),[52] and eventually, be done away with.

The appearance of judicial torture in *The Man of Law's Tale* is a specifically and, for its narrator, appropriately juridical expression of these

---

[52] Unlike the messenger, Alla's constable "pleynly"—and freely—offers up his account of the circumstances surrounding Custance's banishment (lines 880–84).

underlying hermeneutics and ideologies, but both it and the tormenting of Custance share the same logic of torture. It is a logic that sees physical and mental anguish as a means of getting at the truth, especially when that truth is within a person who belongs to a suspect group—a person who, free of pain, cannot be trusted to speak truthfully. In *The Man of Law's Tale*, the messenger and Custance are linked by the Man of Law's suspicions as surely as their respective torments link the second and third parts of his tale. The lowly messenger, in the Man of Law's contemptuous description, falls easily for the temptation of Donegild's wine, just as the lowly poor are despised in the *Prologue* for falling easily, and wrongfully, for false justifications of their position. Custance, surrounded in her tale by women whose inscrutably feminine appearances and speech obscure (or might obscure) sinister intentions, is similarly subjected to the Man of Law's suspicions.

There is, however, one important distinction between Custance and the messenger. The messenger's tormentor hopes to produce a confession: he suspects that probative information might lurk within the messenger's untrustworthy body, and he applies his tortures to get at it. Custance's ultimate tormentor, the narrator of her tale, hopes that Custance's torments produce nothing, proving that nothing has displaced the truths so precariously represented by Custance. Unwilling to trust Custance's untested appearance or words, the Man of Law relies upon the evidence of torments patiently endured. The evidence of endurance, however, is never conclusive, and can only be strengthened by the collective evidence of repeated tests.

By the end of the tale, it seems as though Custance has almost managed to satisfy her tormentor. The Roman senator who rescues Custance from her second sojourn at sea, describing Custance to Alla, states

> "So vertuous a lyvere in my lyf
> Ne saugh I nevere as she, ne herde of mo,
> Of worldly wommen, mayde, ne of wyf.
> I dar wel seyn hir hadde levere a knyf
> Thurghout hir brest, than ben a womman wikke;
> There is no man koude brynge hire to that prikke." (lines 1024–29)

Custance is almost there, but not quite: even as her virtue is acknowledged, it is qualified (she is the most "vertuous . . . / Of worldly wommen") and defined through the proof of endured pain ("a knyf / Thurghout hir brest," fortunately imagined instead of enacted). No man could bring Custance to the point of wickedness, but not for lack of trying. And indeed, even after the senator's acknowledgment of Custance's virtue, she cannot be left alone. Reunited with Alla, she is not allowed to enjoy her peace for long. Within a year, Alla is dead, and an exhausted Custance, making her way back to Rome, drops to her knees before her father: proved constant, but at a terrible cost.

Whether this is to be considered a "nedelees" cost within the context of *The Man of Law's Tale* or *The Canterbury Tales* generally is a far more difficult question. The Man of Law's profile makes him a particularly appropriate narrator of this tale, but the incidents of torture and endured torment he describes have analogues throughout the *Tales*. *The Clerk's Tale* offers the most overt criticism of painful provings—we may even detect an oblique reference to the Man of Law in the Clerk's description of men who praise such provings "for a subtil wit" (line 459). Nonetheless, the Clerk defines as "nedelees" not so much the general process of "tormentynge" as the particular "tormentynge" of Griselda, an application of painful suffering deemed needless because Walter lacks sufficient grounds to suspect Griselda of disobedience. The critical distance between narrator and tormentor disappears in *The Man of Law's Tale*; the tormenting punishments Custance suffers at the hands of her various adversaries are turned to probative evidence of her constancy in the hands of the *Tale's* distrustful, "pinch-wary" narrator. In the *Epilogue* to the *Tale*, the Host offers the sole commentary on the Man of Law's performance: "a thrifty tale for the nones" (line 1165). The *Epilogue's* relation to *The Man of Law's Tale* as it stands is uncertain, but the Host's words nonetheless serve as a fittingly ambiguous response to the *Tale*, hinting at a pervasive mentality that sees in such a narrative nothing needless, but a "thrifty" compilation of proofs gotten through the "wit and sotil enquerynge" of painful interrogations.[53]

[53] I wish to thank Dan Birkholz, Rita Copeland, Richard Firth Green, Barbara Hanawalt, Colleen Page, Justin Steinberg, David Wallace, and the two *Studies in the Age of Chaucer* readers for their help with this essay at different stages of its preparation. A portion of the essay was presented at the 1994 Modern Language Association conference in San Diego, California.

Criseyde, Cassandre, and the *Thebaid:* Women and the Theban Subtext of Chaucer's *Troilus and Criseyde*

Catherine Sanok
University of California, Los Angeles

Whagen Pandarus first visits Criseyde to inform her of Troilus's love in book 2 of *Troilus and Criseyde*, he interrupts his niece and her companions as they listen to a maiden read "the romaunce of Thebes," a text that turns out to be Statius's *Thebaid*. Throughout *Troilus and Criseyde*, Chaucer borrows widely from the Latin epic, employing Statian invocations and incorporating into his poem elaborate references to the Theban story. In a text replete with allusions to the *Thebaid*, however, the most explicit and extended of them are associated with women. Criseyde reads Statius's poem in book 2, and Cassandre recounts its argument in her interpretation of Troilus's dream of Criseyde's betrayal in book 5. Indeed, the narrative of the love of Troilus and Criseyde is bracketed by the *Thebaid*: Criseyde's reading marks the beginning of the affair, and Cassandre's explanation of Troilus's dream marks its end.

These two extended references and most of the incidental allusions to the *Thebaid* are original to Chaucer's version of the story. In fact, the Theban subtext may well be the most significant addition Chaucer makes to Boccaccio's *Filostrato*.[1] Although the groundwork for an analysis of Chaucer's use of the Latin epic was laid in 1911 with Boyd Ashby Wise's study, *The Influence of Statius upon Chaucer*, subsequent attempts to refine his work were until recently largely confined to tracking down

---

[1] The *Filostrato* is Chaucer's primary source. He also used Benoit de Sainte-Maure's *Roman de Troie* and Guido delle Colonne's *Historia destructionis Troiae*. Chaucer's engagement with Boethius is, of course, also highly important. Winthrop Wetherbee suggests the *Divine Comedy* as another significant source of influence; *Chaucer and the Poets: An Essay on* Troilus and Criseyde (Ithaca, N.Y.: Cornell University Press, 1984).

41

rather than interpreting Chaucer's Statian references.[2] A renewed interest in the Theban material in Chaucer's poem has prompted a reconsideration of Statius's influence, especially in the important work of David Anderson and Winthrop Wetherbee,[3] but has perhaps also served to obscure the marked relationship between the Latin epic and women. Anderson does link Criseyde's reading of the Theban story to Cassandre's summary of it, but he finds the significance of this juxtaposition in a comparison of Pandarus and Cassandre, not Criseyde and Cassandre. Wetherbee is interested in the issue of Theban references in the poem, those derived from Dante and Ovid as well as from Statius, and his broader area of inquiry also obscures the particular conjunction of these two scenes. As the scenes of Criseyde's reading and Cassandre's interpretation suggest, the relationship between women and the Statian epic is highly textual,[4] and a broad interest in allusions to Thebes—or what Lee Patterson calls "Thebanness"—rather than the *Thebaid*, tends to obscure it.

But it is also the strangeness of Chaucer's use of the *Thebaid* that has obscured its striking association with women in *Troilus and Criseyde*. Statius's epic seems at first an extraordinary text to give to female characters, especially to the heroine of a love story, even one as ambiguous as Criseyde. Epic is hardly a genre associated with women in modern critical canons,[5] and Statius's poem, with its vividly gory account of the

[2] Boyd Ashby Wise, *The Influence of Statius upon Chaucer* (New York: Phaeton Press, 1911; rpt. 1967), especially pp. 4–36.

[3] See David Anderson, "Theban History in Chaucer's *Troilus*," *SAC* 4 (1982): 109–33, and Wetherbee, *Chaucer and the Poets*, esp. ch. 4, "Thebes and Troy: Statius and Dante's Statius." See also John Fyler's discussion in "*Auctoritee* and Allusion in *Troilus and Criseyde*," *RPLit* 7 (1984): 73–92. A. C. Spearing questions the assumptions that underwrite the interpretations of Fyler and Wetherbee in "Troilus and Criseyde: The Illusion of Allusion," *Exemplaria* 2 (1990): 263–77. Paul Clogan discusses Criseyde's book and Cassandre's interpretation in relation to the *Thebaid* and the *Roman de Thèbes* in "The Theban Scenes in Chaucer's *Troilus*," *M&H* n.s. 12 (1984): 167–85. Lee Patterson also explores Theban references in *Troilus and Criseyde* extensively, although he seems less interested in the *Thebaid* as a source and intertext than he is in the broad scope of Theban references in Chaucer's poem; *Chaucer and the Subject of History* (Madison: University of Wisconsin Press, 1991), esp. ch. 2, "*Troilus and Criseyde* and the Subject of History," pp. 84–164.

[4] Carolyn Dinshaw's chapter, "Reading Like a Man: The Critics, the Narrator, Troilus, and Pandarus," in *Chaucer's Sexual Poetics* (Madison: University of Wisconsin Press, 1989), pp. 28–64, explores the textuality of the relationship between Troilus and Criseyde through a discussion of how each of the major characters in Chaucer's poem responds to the love story. Her work has informed how I have framed some of the questions I am interested in answering here.

[5] This assumption has influenced arguments about whether Criseyde hears the *Thebaid* or the *Roman de Thèbes*; see below for further discussion of this issue.

siege of Thebes, certainly seems unlikely reading for Criseyde and her female companions. But the *Thebaid* departs from traditional epic in addressing a specifically female perspective, both in Hypsipyle's long narrative of the anger of the Lemnian women at being abandoned for three years by their warring husbands, which occupies most of book 5,[6] and in the final book of the poem, which recounts the grief of the Argive women who have been prevented from burying their dead by the tyrant Creon.[7] Statius brackets the narrative of the Theban war with these two

[6] See especially 5.48–264. The leader of the Lemnian women, Polyxo, calls her companions *viduae . . . Lemniades*, suggesting a parallel between the *rem summam* to which she exhorts them—to avenge their premature "widowhood" by killing the men who have abandoned them in pursuit of war—and the more sympathetic action the Argive widows will undertake in book 12—seeking Theseus's help to secure the right to bury their dead. The women of Lemnos slaughter all of the men on the night they return from their exploits, with the single exception of Hypsipyle's father, who escapes secretly with the help of his daughter. Jason and the Argonauts arrive on Lemnos soon after, and the women, after a futile attempt to defend themselves against the invaders, are forced to accept them as lovers. When rumors of her father's escape finally reach Lemnos, Hypsipyle herself is exiled. She is a servant to the Nemean king Lycurgus when Argive forces encounter her in book 4 of the *Thebaid*. All citations from the *Thebaid* are from A. Klotz, ed., *P. Papini Stati Thebais*, rev. T. C. Klinnert (Leipzig: B. G. Teubner, 1973).

[7] This is the subject of book 12 and is given considerable thematic emphasis by its placement at the close of the poem. That this scene caught Chaucer's imagination is clear from his treatment of it in *The Knight's Tale*, and it may be worth recalling here that the tale is prefaced in several manuscripts by a Latin quotation from the *Thebaid*. Chaucer may well have had this scene in mind in an unremarked Statian allusion in book 4 of *Troilus and Criseyde*, when Criseyde invokes Juno in her promise to return to Troy: "I mene, as helpe me Juno, hevenes quene, / The tenthe day, but if that deth m'assaile, / I wol yow sen withouten any faille" (4.1594–96). Although Criseyde's invocation of Juno recalls the Argive widows' invocation of the bridal Juno for help in securing Theseus's favor so that they might seek the bodies of their loved ones, critics seem to have missed this Statian allusion. This may stem from a pervasive misunderstanding among Chaucer critics of Juno's role in the *Thebaid*, a misunderstanding apparently originating with Wise, who seems to rely on Chaucer's statement in *Anelida and Arcite* that the Theban war stemmed from "[t]he olde wrathe of Juno" (line 51). Wise writes: "In the *Thebaid* Juno is always inimical to Thebes as she is to Troy in the *Aeneid*. Her anger was roused against Thebes because of Jove's relations with Semele and Alcmene." Wise cites 1.12 and 1.256 to support this reading. He goes on to state, "Her wrath was especially baneful on several occasions. She sent Iris to command Somnus to steep the Thebans in forgetfulness, and then incited Tiresias [*sic*: for Thiodamas] to lead a host against them while in their stupor (*Thebaid* 10.81, 126, 162, 282)." He also notes that Juno assisted the Argive widows in gaining Theseus's favor; Wise, *Influence of Statius*, pp. 22–23. With the single exception of 10.282, none of the lines Wise cites fully supports his claims. The reference at 1.12, *quod saevae Iunonis opus*, is part of the catalogue of themes Statius suggests before rejecting them in favor of the tale of the siege of Thebes, a tale instigated in Statius's poem by the anger of Jove, not Juno. In fact, the second citation offered by Wise refers to a passage in which Juno argues *against* the war to Jupiter and in which, moreover, she pardons Jupiter's infidelities: *mentitis ignosco toris*, 1.256. Even Juno's participation in the action of book 10 is considerably more ambiguous than Wise admits: she does send Iris to Somnus (in response to the anguished prayers of the Argive women), but she does so to forestall the Theban plan to harry the Argive camp at night. It is clearly a

extended episodes detailing the emotional cost of military violence for women, who are usually its silent victims. Chaucer inverts this narrative structure in bracketing Criseyde's Trojan romance with the threat of violence represented in his poem by the story of Thebes, read by Criseyde in book 2 and recounted by Cassandre in book 5. This striking association between women and the *Thebaid* opens Chaucer's poem to the theme of women's vulnerability to martial violence that is so powerfully explored by Statius.

If the *Thebaid* has more to say about the female experience of war than does traditional epic, it may well have something to say about Criseyde's experience of war. A widow abandoned by her traitorous father in a besieged city he knows to be doomed, Criseyde knows the vulnerability felt by the women of Lemnos and the women of Argos. Indeed, it is no coincidence that Criseyde herself introduces Statius's epic into Chaucer's poem and that she marks the first interstice of its most pervasive intertextual relationship. As if to understand more fully the implications of her own situation, Criseyde reads the Latin epic that most clearly demonstrates women's vulnerability to martial violence.

When Pandarus arrives at Criseyde's house with news of Troilus's love, he discovers her with two other women who "Herden a mayden reden hem the geste / Of the siege of Thebes, while hem leste" (2.83–84).[8]

---

defensive action, undertaken out of concern for one side of the conflict, not hatred of the other. And although she is responsible for putting the Theban band to sleep, the poem is conspicuously ambiguous in identifying whether Juno or Apollo inspires Thiodamas's frenzy: *sive hanc Saturnia mentem, / sive novum comitem bonus instigabat Apollo* (10.162–63). Juno does carry a torch to illuminate the way for the Argive band in its raid (10.282–84), but this too is done out of her concern for the harassed Argive forces. Juno's anger cannot be called a theme of the poem.

   Wise's misreading of Statius on this point has spread throughout scholarship on *Troilus and Criseyde* and has caused critics not only to ignore Criseyde's invocation to Juno as a possible reference to Statius, but to see one in Troilus's prayer to Cupid in book 5: ". . . so cruel thow ne be / Unto the blood of Troie, I preye the, / As Juno was unto the blood Thebane, / For which the folk of Thebes caughte hire bane" (5.599–602). See, for example, Anderson, "Theban History," p. 131; Barry Windeatt, *Oxford Guides to Chaucer: Troilus and Criseyde* (Oxford: Clarendon Press, 1992), p. 123; and the Riverside edition notes, which refer the reader to a note on the lines in *Anelida and Arcite* that makes the same mistake. Chaucer's narrator does have a strong sense of Juno's enmity, but he does not derive it from Statius; Chaucer has probably borrowed his wrathful Juno from the *Aeneid*. Wetherbee shows that the specific reference to Juno's cruelty toward "the blood Thebane" (5.601) probably derives from canto 30 of the *Inferno*: "Nel tempo che Iunone era crucciata / per Semelè contra'l sangue tebano." Dante relies on Ovid's account in *Metamorphoses* 4.416–542, in which Juno's wrath is amply described; Wetherbee, *Chaucer and the Poets*, pp. 121–22.

   [8] All references to *Troilus and Criseyde* are from Stephen Barney's edition in Larry Benson, gen. ed., *The Riverside Chaucer*, 3d ed. (Boston: Houghton Mifflin, 1987).

Pandarus inquires of the text, "Is it of love?" (2.97), and Criseyde responds (2.100–105):

> This romaunce is of Thebes that we rede;
> And we han herd how that kyng Layus deyde
> Thorugh Edippus his sone, and al that dede;
> And here we stynten at thise lettres rede—
> How the bisshop, as the book kan telle,
> Amphiorax, fil thorugh the ground to helle.

Pandarus acknowledges and dismisses her book in the same breath (2.106–12):

> Quod Pandarus, "Al this knowe I myselve,
> And al th'assege of Thebes and the care;
> For herof ben ther maked bookes twelve.
> But lat be this, and telle me how ye fare.
> Do wey youre barbe, and shew youre face bare;
> Do wey youre book, rys up, and lat us daunce,
> And lat us don to May som observaunce."

The significance of this scene has often been sought in the apparent disjunction between the text Criseyde reads and the one to which Pandarus refers. Most critics of the poem assume that Criseyde reads the vernacular *Roman de Thèbes*, whereas Pandarus describes the Latin *Thebaid* in his reference to twelve books.[9] But the quickness with which critics assume that Criseyde reads a vernacular poem, even "softheaded romantic fiction," instead of Statius's epic reflects both unfortunate

---

[9] Unlike the *Thebaid*, the *Roman de Thèbes* is not divided into twelve books. Ornamented capitals divide the text into verse paragraphs in all manuscripts, but there are no larger structural divisions. Aimé Petit provides a table detailing the placement of the capitals in *Naissances du Roman*, vol. 2 (Geneva: Editions Slatkine, 1985), pp. 1131–61. Both the *Thebaid* and the *Roman de Thèbes* are, of course, anachronistic reading for a Trojan woman, but that does not seem to concern Chaucer here. In fact, Chaucer seems to play with the idea that the literary tradition supersedes chronology in what might be a secular and literary analogue to a Christian understanding of typology. Thus Criseyde, a Trojan woman, can read a Roman poem because it is about Thebes and, more importantly, has a rich, allusive significance, as well as a more literal one, for her life. Similarly, Criseyde knows that her betrayal will be her legacy in the literary tradition before even Troilus has learned of it. As Wetherbee remarks in a different context, "[T]he historical significance of [*Troilus and Criseyde*'s] exemplary narrative derives from an authenticating relation to the classical poetic tradition—from literary history rather than from historicity"; *Chaucer and the Poets*, p. 24. See also Anderson, "Theban History," pp. 123–25.

assumptions about female reading[10] and an anachronistic definition of *romaunce*, which, as Paul Strohm has shown, in Middle English could refer to a Latin text as well as a French one, an "authoritative" work as well as a chivalric narrative. As Strohm cautions, "[O]ne must not seize on the term *romaunce* as a point of critical departure."[11] Strohm's evidence suggests that Criseyde's reference to her "romaunce" cannot be taken as a sure indication of the language of the text, much less its genre. Pandarus's reference to twelve books, a structural feature of classical epics familiar to medieval readers, is a far better indication of genre: it identifies Criseyde's book as a classical epic.[12] It seems to me unlikely that Pandarus should be supposed to mistake which book Criseyde has been reading since she *shows* him the text, pointing out precisely how far they have read: "And here we stynten at thise lettres rede." Several critics, following Alain Renoir, suggest that Pandarus deliberately mistakes the book Criseyde reads in a pedantic display of his knowledge of

[10] For the most egregious example, see John V. Fleming, *Classical Imitation and Interpretation in Chaucer's* Troilus (Lincoln: University of Nebraska Press, 1990), p. 96: "As he comes to frame a story of his own, Pandarus may fairly suspect his niece of the well-attested female weakness for softheaded romantic fiction." Similarly, Paul Clogan suggests that Criseyde and the women of her household "would much prefer the [vernacular poem] with the additional love affairs and chivalric and courtly behavior" even if they could read the Latin epic; Clogan, "Theban Scenes," pp. 178–79. Clogan provides a detailed account of the differences between the *Thebaid* and the *Roman de Thèbes* and the fullest recent argument that Criseyde's book is the *Roman de Thèbes* that I know of; see especially pp. 178–79. The relevant portion of this article has been reprinted, with some revision, as "Criseyde's Book of the Romance of Thebes," *Hebrew University Studies in Literature and the Arts* 13 (1985): 18–28; see esp. pp. 25–26. The argument that Criseyde reads a vernacular text reflects the prevailing critical opinion, endorsed even by feminist critics such as Elaine Tuttle Hansen in *Chaucer and the Fictions of Gender* (Berkeley: University of California Press, 1992), p. 164n. See also Wetherbee, *Chaucer and the Poets*, p. 117, and Barbara Nolan, *Chaucer and the Tradition of the Roman Antique* (Cambridge: Cambridge University Press, 1992), p. 228. Those who take the text to be Statius's include John Norton-Smith, *Geoffrey Chaucer* (London: Routledge and Kegan Paul, 1974), p. 90, and John Fyler, "*Auctoritee* and Allusion," p. 77. The argument for a vernacular text is based on both Criseyde's use of the term *romaunce* and on her description of the text; I address the latter below.

[11] Paul Strohm, "*Storie, Spelle, Geste, Romaunce, Tragedie*: Generic Distinctions in the Middle English Troy Narratives," *Speculum* 46 (1971): 348–59. Strohm points out, "While modern critics have a fairly tidy sense of the mediaeval romance as a narrative poem dealing with the adventures of a chivalric hero, the mediaeval understanding of *romaunce* and of its sources in OF *romanz* and *roman* was considerably less circumscribed . . . ME *romaunce* could mean a work in or translated from French, a work in or from Latin, a narrative poem, any sort of narrative, or an authoritative source" (p. 354).

[12] The twelve-book structure of the *Thebaid* in particular is highlighted in Chaucer's poem by the inclusion of the twelve-line argument of the poem (which serves to specify, in brief, the subject of each book) that interrupts Cassandre's summary in most manuscripts.

the Latin poem,[13] but it seems more likely to me that Pandarus's response is rather a deliberate marker of the Latin epic. Chaucer takes care to identify the text as the *Thebaid* through Pandarus's reaction. Indeed, perhaps the best evidence that Criseyde's text is not the vernacular "romance" is Pandarus's displeasure at her choice of reading material; he is clearly disappointed that she is *not* reading "softheaded romantic fiction," that might make her more susceptible to his plans.[14]

This is not to argue that Chaucer's knowledge of the story of Thebes was not influenced by vernacular treatments of the story of Thebes, either a version of the twelfth-century verse *Roman de Thèbes* or one of its thirteenth- or fourteenth-century prose redactions.[15] As several critics have noted, Criseyde's reference to the death of Laius at the hands of Oedipus clearly reflects such influence. The *Thebaid* recounts only briefly the story of Oedipus, in the voice of Oedipus himself as he prays to Tisiphone to punish his ungrateful and mocking sons,[16] whereas the *Roman de Thèbes* opens with a short summary of Oedipus's life.[17] This summary, as Paul Clogan suggests, is not as fully developed as other

[13] Alain Renoir, "Thebes, Troy, Criseyde, and Pandarus: An Instance of Chaucerian Irony," *Studia Neophilologica* 32 (1960): 14–17. The irony in Renoir's title refers to the possibility that Criseyde could have read her own story in her book, since the *Roman de Troie* follows the *Roman de Thèbes* in most manuscripts.

[14] Gayle Margherita makes the interesting suggestion that "Criseyde's exteriority as reader stands in the way of Pandarus's efforts to textualize her—to inscribe her in the romance he is writing for Troilus"; "Historicity, Femininity, and Chaucer's Troilus," *Exemplaria* 6 (1995): 243–69; quotation from p. 257.

[15] There are several editions of the verse *Roman de Thèbes*: a critical edition by Leopold Constans, *Le Roman de Thèbes*, 2 vols. (Paris: S.A.T.F., 1890), which attempts to reconstruct an originary version of the poem based on all extant complete manuscripts; Guy Raynaud de Lage, ed., *Le Roman de Thèbes*, 2 vols. (Paris: Champion, 1966–1967), which presents an edition of the "short" version of the poem, represented by Bibliothèque Nationale Ms. fr. 784; Francine Mora-Lebrun, ed. and trans., *Le Roman de Thèbes*, (Paris: Le Livre de Poche, 1995), an edition and translation into modern French of British Library, MS Addit. 34114. There is also an English translation of Constans's edition by John Smartt Coley, *Le Roman de Thèbes (The Story of Thebes)* (New York and London: Garland, 1986), Garland Library of Medieval Literature, vol. 44. For the prose redactions, see Constans, ed., 2: cxxiii–cxlv; Guy Raynaud de Lage, "Les 'romans antiques' dans l' *Histoire ancienne jusqu'à César*," *Le Moyen Age* 63 (1957): 267–309, which offers a detailed discussion of the relationship between the most widespread prose version, found in the *Histoire ancienne jusqu'à César*, and the *Roman de Thèbes*, especially the "long" version (found in Geneva, Bibliothèque Bodmer, fol. 186b–269a, and Paris, Bibliothèque Nationale, fr. 375, fol. 36r–67v); Paul Meyer, "Les premières compilations françaises d'histoire ancienne," *Romania* 14 (1885): 1–81; and Brian Woledge, *Bibliographie des romans et nouvelles en prose française antérieurs à 1500*, Supplement (Geneva: Droz, 1975), pp. 120–21.

[16] *Thebaid* 1.60–72.

[17] de Lage, ed., lines 37–536.

additions made by the vernacular poet to Statius's narrative,[18] but it is the most likely source of Criseyde's reference to the death of Laius.

The other evidence used to support the argument that Criseyde's book is the *Roman de Thèbes*—that she refers to Amphiaraus as a *bisshop*—is less conclusive than some scholars suggest. Amphiaraus is introduced in the French poem as *un arcevesque mout cortois*,[19] but I have not found a reference in which he is called an *evesque*.[20] Even if we assume that Chaucer translates the *arcevesque* of the French text as *bisshop*, Criseyde's description of his story complicates the question of Chaucer's source, for the detail that Amphiaraus sinks "to helle" is recorded in only one of the five manuscripts of the *Roman de Thèbes*, London, British Museum, MS Add. 34114. Leopold Constans believed that the description of Amphiaraus's catabasis in this manuscript was an interpolation and relegated it to the appendix of his edition.[21] Although it is of course possible that Chaucer knew this version of the *Roman de Thèbes*, it is certain that he knew the Statian tradition of Amphiaraus's arrival in the underworld, as is witnessed by the Latin argument inserted in Cassandre's summary of the Theban story.

What the contradictory evidence about the identity of Criseyde's book makes most clear is that Chaucer relied on both the Latin and

[18] Clogan, "Theban Scenes," pp. 171–72.

[19] de Lage, ed., line 2056. He is also called an *arcevesque* at lines 2102 and 5029.

[20] Clogan, in a recent reassertion of this argument, says that Amphiaraus is described as an *evesque*, but he does not give line numbers; "Theban Scenes," p. 179. The Riverside notes cite two lines in Constans's edition: line 4791, in which Amphiaraus is called an *arcevesques*, and line 5053, in which the Count of Amicles argues that the Greeks should elect a new *evesque* to replace Amphiaraus, which is not quite the same thing as calling Amphiaraus himself an *evesque*.

[21] Constans, ed., appendix 1, lines 4475–544. Mora-Lebrun restores the lines in her edition; lines 5240–309. In the lines common to all manuscripts, Amphiaraus is swallowed by the earth, but no mention is made of hell:

Car al vespre, soentre none,
La terre crolle et li cieus tone,
Et, si com Deus l'ot destiné
Et cil l'ot dit et deviné,
Terre le sorbi senz enjan,
Com fist Abiron et Datan. (Constans, ed., lines 4833–38; cf. de Lage, ed., lines 5071–76)

[For in the evening, after the ninth hour, / The earth trembles and the heaven thunders; / And, just as God has predestined it / And Amphiareus has foreseen and said, / The earth actually swallows him / As it did Abiram and Dathan (Coley, trans., p. 113)].

See also Petit, who presents several detailed tables analyzing the relationship between the *Thebaid* and the manuscript tradition of the *Roman de Thèbes*, specifying the inclusions of the *Thebaid* and additions to Statius's story found in the different manuscript families of the vernacular poem; *Naissances du Roman*, pp. 1091–1107.

vernacular versions of the Theban story and that he was not too scrupulous about checking his sources for Criseyde's description of her book. Given the conflicting references in Criseyde's account, I think it might be especially important that Chaucer took care to identify Criseyde's text as the Latin epic through Pandarus's reaction. At the very least, I think it worthwhile to consider what kinds of meaning are opened up in Chaucer's poem if we entertain the possibility that Criseyde's book is identified as the *Thebaid*. Spearing's careful distinction between an author's use of a text and allusion to it, formulated in response to the work of Wetherbee and Fyler, is useful here: I'm suggesting that although Chaucer probably also used the *Roman de Thèbes*, he alludes (in what Spearing calls the "strong" sense of the word) to the *Thebaid*, and we should take that allusion seriously.[22]

Criseyde, of course, does not get to hear the end of her book. Few critics seem to take seriously what Criseyde has read as integral to the themes of the poem, but the extent of her reading is marked so specifically that the text seems to me to invite consideration of what Criseyde has and has not been allowed to read. Her reading is, in fact, broken off at exactly the section that holds the most immediate implications for the daughter of Calcas: the story of the Greek seer Amphiaraus. As Criseyde herself reminds us, Amphiaraus's fate was to fall suddenly through the earth, disappearing from the field of battle and arriving, still alive, in the underworld. His fate thus resonates strongly with that of Calcas, who disappears with similar suddenness from Troy, yet later determines the fate of Criseyde's Trojan romance, and ultimately her literary reputation, with his request that she be exchanged for Antenor. Amphiaraus, too, influences the life of the woman he has left behind— his wife, whose greed led her to give away his hiding place where he, like Calcas, sought to escape the doomed future he foresaw for his city. To mollify Pluto, outraged at the threat posed to his sovereignty by the

[22] Lydgate similarly alludes to Statius, although he depended on a vernacular prose version of the story of Thebes for the *Siege of Thebes*, which he imagined as an addition to *The Canterbury Tales*. See Constans's introduction, p. clxi–clxiii, and Axel Erdmann, ed., *Lydgate's Siege of Thebes*, Early English Text Society [hereafter EETS], e.s., vol. 108, (London: EETS, 1911), p. vi. Medieval women seem to have been interested in Lydgate's version of the Theban story: Anne Knevet may have owned Cambridge, Trinity College MS 0.5.2, which contains the *Siege of Thebes*; Anne Paston had another copy; and a manuscript containing the poem, Oxford, Bodleian Lib. Laud MS 416, seems to have been owned by Anne Colvylle, a Syon nun. See Carol Meale, ". . . alle the bokes that I haue of latyn, englisch, and frensch": Laywomen and Their Books in Late Medieval England," in Meale, ed., *Women and Literature in Britain, 1150–1500* (Cambridge: Cambridge University Press, 1993), pp. 141 and 155n.

presence of the still-living Amphiaraus in the underworld, the seer suggests that punishment for the event be reserved for his wife. The Theban narrative, then, itself portends the threat that her still-living father poses to Criseyde. Though not as vengeful as his Theban counterpart, Calcas also works from beyond the boundary he has crossed to affect the life of the woman he has left behind.

But the importance of the sudden violence of Amphiaraus's disappearance for Criseyde's own situation is left unspecified, the pertinent passage left unread by Criseyde and her women. The "lettres rede" describing Amphiaraus's fate at which they stop suggest rubrics either at the heading of a book or a section within a book;[23] that is, they cease reading at the chapter heading that announces Amphiaraus's death, without having read the narrative itself. Criseyde thus knows the fate of the prophet, but has not read the scene of his death nor the battle fury that precedes it. In Statius's epic, Amphiaraus ends his life with a triumphant but horrific burst of violence in which he is metonymically identified with Hades before he arrives there, swallowed suddenly by the earth.[24] The Argive camp tries in vain to interpret Amphiaraus's

[23] Anderson notes that chapter divisions are common in late medieval manuscripts of the *Thebaid*; "Theban History in Chaucer's *Troilus*," p. 120n.

[24] The metonymic identification is accomplished primarily at 7.760–70. I quote from J. H. Mozley's translation in the Loeb edition, *Statius*, vol. 2 (Cambridge, Mass.: Loeb, 1928): "And now the horn-footed steeds snort at the corpses in alarm and probe the ground, and every wheel-track runs o'er bodies and reddens deep with severed limbs. Some the remorseless axle grinds unconscious, but others half-dead from wounds—and powerless to escape—see it as it draws nigh to crush them. Already the reins are wet with gore, the slippery car gives no foothold, blood clogs the wheels and trampled entrails hinder the horses' hooves: then the hero himself madly tears out darts abandoned in the slain and spears projecting from the midst of corpses: ghosts shriek and pursue the chariot."

> [et iam cornipedes trepidi ac moribunda reflantes
> corpora rimantur terras, omnisque per artus
> sulcus et incisis altum rubet orbita membris.
> hos iam ignorantes terit impius axis, at illi
> vulnere semineces—nec devitare facultas—
> venturum super ora vident; iam lubrica tabo
> frena, nec insisti madidus dat temo, rotaeque
> sanguine difficiles, et tardior ungula fossis
> visceribus: tunc ipse furens in morte relicta
> spicula et e mediis extantes ossibus hastas
> avellit, strident animae currumque secuntur.]

Wetherbee's discussion of this episode in the *Thebaid* and of the character of Amphiaraus in general suggests a rather unambiguously positive characterization of the Greek seer, which overlooks lines like these as well as his desire for revenge against his wife; pp. 116–17.

departure as a sign of their future fortunes in war, much as Criseyde and her household seem to read the *Thebaid* as if trying to understand the implications of Calcas's departure. But Criseyde, interrupted by her uncle, is prevented from puzzling out the confusion that attends Amphiaraus's violent movement across boundaries or the threat that departure poses to those who are left behind.

Yet Criseyde may learn the significance of such movement herself much later in the poem. However resonant with Calcas's flight to the Greek camp, the story of Amphiaraus's descent to the underworld is perhaps finally more relevant to Criseyde herself than to her father. Amphiaraus's catabasis traces Criseyde's own vulnerability to the contingencies of war, for his sudden descent to hell not only recalls Calcas's disappearance but also presages Criseyde's sudden departure to the Greek camp. Criseyde and Amphiaraus, juxtaposed in the moment of interrupted reading, share the ability to cross and confuse geographic and narrative borders. These movements upset boundaries that have previously seemed stable or at least firmly maintained: the boundary between life and death and between Troy and the Greek camp. Amphiaraus arrives in the underworld alive, a contradiction that provokes Pluto's fear and anger and, more important for Chaucer's poem, a striking aporia: the Argive camp tries but cannot read this omen. Having trespassed—deconstructed in a very literal way—the boundary between living and dead, Amphiaraus renders interpretation impossible. Those on both sides of the boundary between the world and the underworld, the Argive men and Pluto himself, fail to understand what has happened and what it means. Criseyde's movement across boundaries results in a similar crisis of interpretation. Her relationship to Diomede is famously beyond the powers of the narrator's knowledge or capacity for interpretation. He prefers ignorance or agnosticism on this point: "Men seyn—I not—that she yaf hym hire herte" (5.1050). The narrator's aporia mirrors that of Troilus, who fails to read an abundance of signs—his prophetic dream, Criseyde's failure to return on the assigned date, her increasingly abbreviated responses to his letters. Troilus only understands her continued absence when he sees a sign whose significance he himself had once determined, the brooch he had given Criseyde at her departure "[i]n remembraunce of hym and of his sorwe" (5.1663)—which in its new context, pinned on Diomede's war tunic, can mean only one thing.

Criseyde herself suggests at one point that the story of the Argive seer provides the literary model for her own movement across geographic boundaries. Before departing for the Greek camp, she promises Troilus that if she is ever untrue to him, she will "with body and soule synke in helle!" (4.1554).[25] Her oath resonates strongly with her summary of her reading in book 2; Criseyde virtually promises to imitate Amphiaraus's death. Although her exclamation is clearly rhetorical, it articulates her affinity to Amphiaraus: she too moves suddenly between realms, across borders no one else can transgress. Her reading interrupted at a scene of violent movement across geographical boundaries, Criseyde returns to the Theban story—which is embodied, as we shall see, by Diomede—when she leaves Troy for the Greek camp.

There is perhaps a third, and ironic, allusion to Criseyde's literary kinship with Amphiaraus and his descent to hell, in Troilus's angry rejection of Cassandre's interpretation of his dream. He compares his beloved to Alceste in a reference that further hints that Criseyde, like Amphiaraus, can cross the most impermeable of boundaries. Claiming for Criseyde the virtue and fidelity of Alceste, Troilus mentions the event that entitles her to fame and that Chaucer will explore more fully in the *Prologue* to *The Legend of Good Women*: "For whan hire housbonde was in jupertye / To dye hymself but if she wolde dye, / She ches for hym to dye and gon to helle" (5.1530–32). The reference is strangely appropriate, even knowing as the reader does that Criseyde has already forsaken Troilus: like Alceste, who is, in Troilus's words, substituted for a man "in jupertye," Criseyde is substituted for the captured Antenor. Made to sacrifice her love and her life in Troy to save a man, Criseyde's action is ironically comparable to Alceste's. This allusion echoes and focuses Criseyde's earlier reference to her descent to hell and her relationship to Amphiaraus: like Alceste and Amphiaraus, Criseyde is deprived of her life in Troy because of the self-interest of others.

The extent of Criseyde's reading has additional implications for her affair with Diomede because it marks the limits of her knowledge about his father, Tydeus. Interrupted roughly midway through the text, Criseyde has read of Tydeus's triumphant defeat of the Theban band

---

[25] This stanza opens with another possible borrowing from the *Thebaid*: Criseyde's command to the river Simois to run backward if she prove unfaithful (4.1548–53). Tydeus says that the Inachus and Achelous will run backward before Eteocles would allow Polynices to leave Thebes if he were to visit the city with Jocasta: *Inachus ante retro nosterque Achelous abibit* (7.553); Wise, p. 19, who mistakenly cites book 8 of the *Thebaid*. But see Wetherbee, who suggests that Criseyde's oath echoes the fifth letter of Ovid's *Heroides* (5.25–32), in which Oenone remembers Paris making a similar oath by the Xanthos river; p. 95.

sent to ambush him in book 2,[26] but not of his cannibalism in book 8. In the most disturbing passage of Statius's epic, Tydeus gorges on the brains and "living blood" of Melanippus, the warrior who has fatally wounded him, an act that turns even Pallas, his protector, against him.[27] Anderson notes that although Chaucer does not usually refer to warriors, Greek or Trojan, by their patronymic, Diomede is identified as the son of Tydeus several times in the course of book 5, "as if to make a special point of his genealogy."[28] The repetition of Diomede's patronymic links him insistently with Tydeus and, to someone who has read the *Thebaid*, with Tydeus's horrifying bloodthirstiness. But the significance of his father's name is lost on Criseyde, who has not read this far in Statius's poem. Diomede himself carefully omits reference to the circumstances of his father's death in his effort to convince Criseyde that he is "as gentil man as any wight in Troie" (5.931):

> "For if my fader Tideus," he seyde,
> "Ilyved hadde, ich hadde ben er this
> Of Calydoyne and Arge a kyng, Criseyde!
> And so hope I that I shal yet, iwis.
> But he was slayn—allas, the more harm is!—
> Unhappily at Thebes al to rathe,
> Polymyte and many a man to scathe." (5.932–38)

Diomede interrupts himself at the death of his father, neatly substituting for the story of his inglorious, even monstrous, last moments a rather weak exclamation of sorrow. He covers over, by filling in, the story of his father's death left unread by Criseyde and her household. The precariousness of Criseyde's situation is again figured by her relationship to the *Thebaid*, here by her ignorance of Diomede's ancestry.

---

[26] *Thebaid* 2.527–743.

[27] *Thebaid* 8.735–66. Significantly, the *Roman de Thèbes* omits this scene: Tydeus dies heroically and is deeply mourned by the Greek camp. Throughout the vernacular poem Tydeus is represented as especially noble; as de Lage notes, he is the *héros favori* of the *Roman de Thèbes*; "Les romans antiques et la représentation de l' Antiquité," *Le Moyen Age* 67 (1961): 247–91; quotation on p. 280. The interruption of Criseyde's Theban story is more pointed if we take it to be the *Thebaid*; in that case, Pandarus unwittingly furthers Diomede's love suit as well as Troilus's when he tells Criseyde to "do way" her book.

[28] Diomede is called the "sone of Tideus" at 5.88 and 5.1746, and their relationship is specified at 5.803, 5.932 and 5.1514. For Anderson, the significance of the repetition of Tydeus's patronymic is that Diomede and Criseyde may be cousins; p. 125.

Diomede is identified as the "sone of Tideus" first when he notes the love between Troilus and Criseyde, and it seems to be their love that inspires him to woo her (5.85–98). True to his identity as the son of Tydeus, Diomede sees his pursuit of Criseyde as an act of military aggression: he muses, "[W]hoso myghte wynnen swich a flour / From hym for whom she morneth nyght and day, / He myghte seyn he were a conquerour" (5.792–94). Diomede here seems less interested in securing Criseyde's affection than in winning her from the Trojan she loves: she is merely a pretext for male aggression, the field on which Diomede will name himself victor. Diomede's eagerness to pursue Criseyde in order to become a "conqueror" articulates vividly Criseyde's vulnerability to the situation of war, and does so through a character who is consistently associated with the story of Thebes through his patronymic.

Ironically, then, Pandarus's interruption of Criseyde's reading ultimately serves Diomede's advances just as it had Troilus's. Indeed, the scene of Criseyde's interrupted reading is emblematic of this rupture in the narrative of her Trojan romance: like the Theban story interrupted by her uncle, the story of the love of Troilus and Criseyde is interrupted by her father. Yanked from the narrative Pandarus had constructed to one that Diomede will orchestrate, Criseyde drops not only out of Troilus's life but out of Chaucer's poem as well. Although the poem recounts Diomede's thoughts and early attempts at winning her favor, we know much less about the progress of Criseyde's affection for him in contrast to the extended treatment of her thoughts about Troilus in the early days of their courtship.[29]

As if to signal Criseyde's departure from the Trojan narrative to a Theban one, Cassandre explains Troilus's dream of Criseyde's betrayal by telling the story of Thebes. Indeed, she recounts the argument of the entire *Thebaid*, though it has no clear relationship to Criseyde's affair with Diomede. Her summary is given the authority of the Latin text and intimately identified with it through the twelve-line Latin epitome

---

[29] Compare Criseyde's interior monologue at 2.689–812 to the one at 5.1054–85; she considers her reputation and Troilus's feelings at length, but says of her relationship to Diomede only this: "But syn I se ther is no bettre way, / And that to late is now for me to rewe, / To Diomede algate I wol be trewe" (5.1069–71). Similarly, the narrator professes not to know how long Diomede pressed his suit before Criseyde forsook Troilus (5.1086–92).

of the *Thebaid*, inserted at the midpoint of Cassandre's summary of the Theban war in all but two manuscripts of *Troilus and Crisyde*.[30] The Latin text embedded in Cassandre's speech identifies Statius's poem unequivocally as the source of her knowledge,[31] much as Pandarus's reference to the twelve books of the epic identifies Criseyde's text in book 2. Most editions relegate this passage to the notes as if it were a marginal gloss, peripheral to the poem itself, rather than printing it as part of the text in accordance with the codicological evidence,[32] a decision that undoubtedly reflects the awkwardness of its presence and position in the poem. Cassandre's summary depends closely on precisely the kind of Latin argument that interrupts it; the authoritative gloss seems to have moved from its proper place in the margin into the text of the poem. Cassandre's summary itself has an obscure relation to Troilus's dream and the action of Chaucer's poem, and the Latin argument highlights this obscurity by the strangeness of its placement in the text of the poem. But while Cassandre's interpretation is undeniably enigmatic, her recourse to the story of the *Thebaid* is, I think, central to the kind of interpretation she gives of Troilus's dream. She suggests that in leaving Troy, Criseyde has become part of a different narrative, a narrative that continues the Theban story Criseyde had left off at the commencement of her affair with Troilus.[33]

In his dream, Troilus sees a sleeping boar embrace Criseyde, who kisses the animal affectionately (5.1233–41). In her interpretation of

[30] British Library, Harley MS 2392, and Bodleian, Rawlinson Poet. MS 163. See the textual notes in the Riverside edition, p. 1177.

[31] On this see also Anderson, p. 121. Francis Magoun demonstrates Chaucer's use of both an epitome of the *Thebaid*, of the sort inserted in most manuscripts of *Troilus and Crisyde*, and a broader knowledge of the poem as a whole in Cassandre's summary; "Chaucer's Summary of Statius' *Thebaid* II–XII," *Traditio* 11 (1955): 409–20. Magoun argues that the inserted Latin is authorial, not scribal: "There can scarcely be any question that Chaucer and not a scribe was responsible for the insertion . . . of the Latin argument" (p. 412). This suggests a very literal intertextual relationship; Statius's text is embedded in Chaucer's own. Although, as Spearing has pointed out, identifying a poet's allusions always depends on a subjective, often vague, sense of possibility and likelihood, the inclusion of the argument of the *Thebaid* offers strong evidence that Chaucer intended his reader to understand Cassandre's interpretation in terms of its source.

[32] The exception is Barry Windeatt's edition, *Troilus and Crisyde* (London and New York: Longman, 1984), which prints the Latin verses as part of the text of Chaucer's poem.

[33] Cf. Norton-Smith, pp. 90–91: "When we hear of the epic again [after Criseyde's reading] it is near the end of book V. Cassandra *completes* the whole tragic story, relating the Theban material to Troilus' dream both personally and generally" (emphasis added).

the dream, Cassandre first recounts the Ovidian tale of the Calydonian
boar and identifies Tydeus as a descendant of Meleager.[34] But before she
names Diomede as Tydeus's son, and thus identifies him as the boar of
the dream, Cassandre summarizes the *Thebaid*. I quote the passage in
full, including the Latin verses, to give a sense of the completeness of
her summary, itself an indication of its thematic significance:

> She tolde ek how Tideus, er she stente,
> Unto the stronge citee of Thebes,
> To cleymen kyngdom of the citee, wente,
> For his felawe, daun Polymytes,
> Of which the brother, daun Ethiocles,
> Ful wrongfully of Thebes held the strengthe;
> This tolde she by proces, al by lengthe.
>
> She tolde ek how Hemonydes asterte,
> Whan Tideus slough fifty knyghtes stoute.
> She tolde ek alle the prophecyes by herte,
> And how that seven kynges with hire route
> Bysegeden the citee al aboute;
> And of the holy serpent, and the welle,
> And of the furies, al she gan hym telle;
>
> Associat profugum Tideo primus Polymytem;
> Tidea legatum docet insidiasque secundus;
> Tercius Hemoniden canit et vates latitantes;
> Quartus habet reges ineuntes prelia septem;
> Mox furie Lenne quinto narratur et anguis;
> Archymory bustum sexto ludique leguntur;
> Dat Grayos Thebes et vatem septimus umbris;
> Octavo cecidit Tideus, spes, vita Pelasgis;
> Ypomedon nono moritur cum Parthonopea;
> Fulmine percussus decimo Capaneus superatur;
> Undecimo sese perimunt per vulnera fratres;
> Argiva flentem narrat duodenus et ignem.
>
> Of Archymoris brennynge and the pleyes,
> And how Amphiorax fil thorugh the grounde,

---

[34] Tydeus is traditionally identified as the half brother, not descendant, of Meleager.
Wetherbee notes, however, that Lactantius Placidus's commentary on the *Thebaid* identifies Meleager as the ancestor of Tydeus; Wetherbee, pp. 129–30.

How Tideus was sleyn, lord of Argeyes,
And how Ypomedoun in litel stounde
Was dreynt, and ded Parthonope of wownde;
And also how Capaneus the proude
With thonder-dynt was slayn, that cride loude.

She gan ek telle hym how that eyther brother,
Ethiocles and Polymyte also,
At a scarmuche ech of hem slough other,
And of Argyves wepynge and hire wo;
And how the town was brent, she tolde ek tho;
And so descendeth down from gestes olde
To Diomede. . . . (5.1485–1512)

Given its apparently tangential relationship to Troilus's dream, Cassandre's summary is surprisingly thorough, particularly in comparison with the abrupt conclusion of her interpretation: "This Diomede is inne, and thow art oute" (5.1519). The synopsis of the *Thebaid* given here does more than explain the genealogy of Diomede;[35] in fact, Cassandre's interpretation devotes conspicuously more attention to the story of Thebes than to his ancestry, which is given offhandedly: "And so descendeth down from gestes olde / To Diomede."

Cassandre's use of the *Thebaid* to explain Troilus's dream, perhaps more than the dream itself, signals the depth of Criseyde's betrayal. Through Cassandre's Statian interpretation, Criseyde is closely associated with Diomede's history, a history that begins with his father's participation in the siege of Thebes.[36] Cassandre's reading of Troilus's dream identifies Criseyde's affair with Diomede as part of the Theban story, as a footnote to the *Thebaid*,[37] and thus as a return to Criseyde's earlier reading, set aside by Pandarus in book 2.

[35] Clogan also finds larger significance in Cassandre's apparent digression; he suggests that Cassandre uses the Theban story "to impress upon Troilus the idea of destiny"; "Chaucer's Use of the 'Thebaid,'" *English Miscellany* 18 (1967): 25.

[36] See also Anderson, who argues that Cassandre's interpretation establishes implicit parallels between Troilus's situation and the fall of Troy, especially through Troilus's unbelieving dismissal; "Cassandra's Analogy: *Troilus* V. 1450–1521," *Hebrew University Studies in Literature and the Arts* 13 (1985): 1–17.

[37] But see Wetherbee, p. 129, who rejects Cassandre's explanation as interpretation: "Cassandre's 'historical' reading of Troilus's dream leads to an accurate gloss on the figure of the boar, but it is not therefore a valid *interpretation* of his situation" (the emphasis is Wetherbee's). Patterson similarly argues against Cassandre's summary as interpretation; to him it is "a gloss that replicates its text"; p. 131.

Criseyde, then, crosses a narrative boundary as she crosses a political one and is lost at once to both Troilus and the narrator. Cassandre's implication that Criseyde can be so quickly and so thoroughly associated with the Theban story is striking. Not fixed within a particular story through a political or literary genealogy (unlike Diomede, identified by the Ovidian family attribute, the boar of Meleager, in Troilus's dream), Criseyde can cross political and narrative boundaries more readily than men. Diomede is defined by his genealogy as part of the continuous, even cyclical, story of Thebes. When Cassandre "descendeth down from gestes olde / To Diomede" (5.1511–12), she suggests that Diomede's genealogy is not merely recorded in a literary tradition, but is constituted by it.[38] Her interpretation moves seamlessly from literary "gestes" to the identity of the man for whom Criseyde has betrayed Troilus. Though not a participant in the disastrous siege of Thebes, Diomede is a descendent of the *story* of Thebes—indeed, in Chaucer's poem, of the *Thebaid* itself. Criseyde, in contrast, is not fixed in one story but can move between them precisely because she is a woman, identified not by her ancestry but by whichever man is most intimately connected to her at the moment.[39] She is at different times part of the stories of three men: Calcas, Troilus, and Diomede. Her participation in Calcas's "narrative" illustrates this most simply: Criseyde is introduced as his daughter in the beginning of the poem, before she is even named, but once her relationship with Troilus has begun she is not identified as his daughter again until her father reclaims her in book 4 (4.64–126). Diomede, however, is identified as the "sone of Tideus" consistently, even though his father is not a character in the poem.

As Cassandre's Statian interpretation of the dream suggests, Criseyde's departure from Troy equals departure from her Trojan romance and from the story of Troilus. The movement between military camps corresponds to the movement between narratives, illustrating a convergence of literary and political boundaries that might provide an ontology for the "sliding" position of women within the literary tradition with which Chaucer identifies his poem. Women—or at least

---

[38] This reading of these lines was first suggested to me by Jessica Brantley.

[39] Calcas can also move across political boundaries (an ability clearly related to his special status as a seer) but not with the freedom that Criseyde has. He remains identified primarily as a traitor to Troy, not a participant in the Greek camp.

women like Criseyde, not legally defined by a husband—can cross political boundaries, and the narrative boundaries constructed by them, more readily than men. Criseyde—deemed not essential to the history of Troy by the Trojan council—is traded to the Greeks and becomes part of Theban history.[40]

This kind of interrupted and inserted narrative is something that *Troilus and Criseyde* shares with the *Thebaid*, in which the narrative of Hypsipyle interrupts the narrative progress of the poem's war story.[41] And it is no coincidence that the narrative interruptions in both the *Thebaid* and the *Troilus* are effected through women. Like Criseyde, Hypsipyle is also without a man to protect her once her father departs from Lemnos; indeed, all the Lemnian women are in Criseyde's position. When Jason and the Argonauts arrive, the women recognize that they cannot defend themselves against the invaders and so surrender to them. Having no other recourse, Hypsipyle, like Criseyde, is forced to take her former enemy, Jason, as a lover; but in the absence of a legal relationship, he finally offers no protection and no stability within her Lemnian narrative. Abandoned by Jason, she is ultimately captured by pirates and brought to Nemea in a narrative movement that resembles Criseyde's arrival in the Greek camp. As with Criseyde, Hypsipyle's movement across geographical boundaries is coextensive with a movement across narrative boundaries, since it is in Nemea that she enters and interrupts the Theban story. And like Criseyde, whose affair with Diomede marks a return to the Theban story she reads at the opening of the poem, Hypsipyle enacts a return to an earlier narrative: she is ultimately reunited with the sons she had left behind in Lemnos, who recognize their mother through the story she tells.

Hypsipyle tells her story to the Argive forces on their way to Thebes, inserting her Lemnian narrative into the Theban story and interrupting

[40] Wetherbee also senses that Criseyde is somehow not integral to the "story" of Troy: "Her infidelity to Troilus is important chiefly as a symptom and symbol of the fortunes of Troy, and it is appropriate that she disappear from the story of Troilus and his city once she has abandoned them to their fate"; p. 123.

[41] For Hypsipyle's narrative see *Thebaid* 5.28–498. It falls well before the point in the text at which Criseyde and her maidens are interrupted. Wetherbee calls the Hypsipyle episode the "longest and strangest interruption" in the *Thebaid*. He provides a fascinating argument about the significance of this episode and Hypsipyle's position in Statius's poem for the biography of Statius that Dante invents in the *Purgatorio*; see "Dante and the *Thebaid* of Statius," *Lectura Dantis Newberryana*, eds. Paolo Cherchi and Anthony Mastrobuono (Chicago: Northwestern University Press, 1988), pp. 71–92.

at once the Argive offensive and the martial story of Statius's epic with her own tale of loss. Significantly, Hypsipyle's narrative, which halts the progress of the story of the Theban war for two books of the *Thebaid*, is the most extended exploration of female vulnerability to martial history in Statius's poem,[42] and one in the voice of a woman. Hypsipyle tells the Argive forces the story of the women of Lemnos who try to defend themselves against their vulnerability to the male pursuit of military violence. Angry at being left behind when their husbands, fathers, and brothers go to war, they take revenge by killing them upon their return. But this violence renders them more, not less, vulnerable. When Jason and his men arrive on the island, the women quickly realize that they cannot defend themselves with arms and must instead submit to the invaders. This time their experience of male violence is particularly intimate, as Hypsipyle's own story, familiar to Chaucer's readers from *The Legend of Good Women*, suggests. In the *Thebaid*, her experience stands for the vulnerability of the Lemnian women (5.463–64):

> nec non ipsa tamen thalami monimenta coacti
> enitor geminos, duroque sub hospite mater.
>
> [Made a mother by a fierce guest, I myself bore twins,
> memorial of a forced bridal-couch.]

Criseyde has perhaps learned from her reading of Hypsipyle's narrative the futility of trying to respond actively to military violence. She adopts instead a strategy of submission to the vicissitudes of martial history, abiding by the terms of the prisoner exchange and taking Diomede as her lover just as the Lemnian women had ultimately accepted the Argonauts. Like the Lemnian women, Criseyde is persuaded to accept Diomede's suit because she needs male protection: ". . . she was allone and hadde nede / Of frendes help" (5.1026–27). And, like Hypsipyle, Criseyde can secure male protection only by means of a sexual relationship. The alternative model for women's active intervention in the military affairs of men offered by the *Thebaid*, the story of the

---

[42] Cf. Wetherbee, who calls Hypsipyle's story "a sort of pre-Christian Life of Constance" and suggests that Hypsipyle's life reflects "the violently dislocating course of human history" represented in the *Thebaid*; "Dante and the *Thebaid* of Statius," pp. 80 and 85.

Argive women who convince Theseus to fight for their right to bury their dead, is left unread by Criseyde's household.[43]

The futility of Hypsipyle's attempt to limit her vulnerability to martial violence perhaps explains why Criseyde neglects to mention her story in her brief description of her book. The similarity between Hypsipyle's situation and Criseyde's is likewise left unspecified by Chaucer, though he takes care to mark the extent of Criseyde's reading. Cassandre, too, omits direct reference to Hypsipyle, mentioning only the disastrous consequence of her storytelling: the death of Archemorus, the infant son of King Lycurgus left in her charge, who was killed by a snake sacred to Jupiter while she told her story to the Argive army, and the funeral games in his honor ("the holy serpent, and the welle, / And of the furies, al she gan hym telle; / Of Archymoris brennynge and the pleyes" [5.1497–99]). Neither Criseyde nor Cassandre acknowledges the depth of interest in the human cost of war, represented by the anguish of women, that distinguishes Statius's poem. Cassandre's omissions are particularly striking: following the Latin arguments to the poem, Cassandre omits reference to Jocasta and obscures the role of the Argive women.[44] In fact, she seems to reduce the overwhelming grief of the Argive widows to the single experience of Argia, Polynices's wife: "Argyves wepynge and hire wo" (5.1509).[45] Chaucer's spelling of Argia's name links it closely to the word "Argive," and it would be tempting to see here the blurring of the singular grief of Argia and the collective grief of all the Argive women in a poignant epitome of the personal cost of military violence. But such a reading is not supported by Cassandre's summary: she indicates no interest in the women's

---

[43] The *Roman de Thèbes* differs significantly from the *Thebaid* concerning the action of the Argive widows. Whereas in the *Thebaid* they merely solicit Theseus's intervention, in the vernacular poem Adrastus asks for Theseus's help and then leads "l'ost des femnes" (Constans, ed., line 10070; cf. "l'ost des dames," de Lage, line 10436) to Thebes where they participate in the destruction of the city (which is not recorded by Statius); the women climb the walls to chip away at the mortar with mallets. In stark contrast to Statius's women, the women in the vernacular poem seem to appreciate male military exploits: Ismene and Antigone in particular take great pride in the prowess of their lovers, accepting gifts of war spoils, offering their sleeves to decorate armor, and watching battles from towers or hills. See also de Lage, "Les romans antiques et la représentation de l'Antiquité," p. 273.

[44] On the omissions and confusions in Cassandre's summary, see also Wetherbee, *Chaucer and the Poets*, pp. 130–33.

[45] As in most of her summary, Cassandre here translates from the Latin epitome: *Argiva flentem*.

story presented by the *Thebaid*, and the ambiguity of "Argyves wepyng" seems rather to indicate her carelessness in recounting the events of the twelfth book. She mistakes even the *ignes* that represent the funeral pyres built by the grieving Argive women, for the burning of Thebes itself,[46] an act that focuses on the political significance of Theseus's intervention rather than its very personal significance in the *Thebaid*. As Criseyde mentions the story of Amphiaraus rather than that of Hypsipyle, Cassandre seems to think that the story of military violence has more significance for Troilus's dream than the consequences of that violence for women, even though she is explaining Criseyde's fate. As a seer, Cassandre must realize, even more acutely than Criseyde, the futility of her position, and perhaps her omission of the active role of women in the *Thebaid* reflects her inability to imagine the relevance of Statius's women for her fellow Trojans.[47] By putting the Theban subtext of his poem in the mouths of Criseyde and Cassandre, Chaucer opens the possibility of a Statian reading of his poem, one that would acknowledge human suffering and women's particular vulnerability in times of war, and yet that Statian concern remains unspoken by either of them.

Cassandre does, however, encode in the preface to her Statian story of Thebes a brief reference to a story of a woman's tragic experience of male violence that is strikingly similar to that of Hypsipyle. Recounting the story of the Calydonian boar, Cassandre mentions "a contek and a gret envye" (5.1479) that arose when Meleager presented the boar's head to his beloved Atalanta. As Ovid tells the story, Meleager slew two of his maternal uncles, Plexippus and Toxeus, because they had seized the prize from Atalanta, claiming that the trophy was inappropriate for a girl. Cassandre finishes the narrative hastily in a pointed *occupatio* after naming Tydeus as Meleager's ancestor (5.1482–84):

> But how this Meleagre gan to dye
> Thorugh his moder, wol I you naught telle,
> For al to longe it were for to dwelle.

---

[46] See Wetherbee, *Chaucer and the Poets*, p. 132, n. 20. Wetherbee points out that Chaucer knew the end of Statius's poem well, as is clear from his use of it in *The Knight's Tale*.

[47] I am grateful to one of the *SAC* readers for drawing my attention to the fact that neither Criseyde nor Cassandre says much about women in their references to the Theban story, and for his/her suggestion that this omission may figure the precariousness of their situation.

What Cassandre insists on omitting is the story of Meleager's mother, Althaea, who sees the bodies of her brothers brought to a sacred temple where she is celebrating her son's victory. Ovid explores the tragedy of her position extensively, describing the conflicting loyalties she feels as mother and sister. Althaea literally holds the life of her son in her hands, in the form of a brand she had snatched from the flames at his birth and which represents his life. She is finally overcome with a desire to avenge her brothers and throws the brand into a burning pyre, killing Meleager, before thrusting a knife into her own breast. Like Jocasta and Antigone, Meleager's mother suffers the anguish of a woman who cannot reconcile her loyalties to the men she loves. Male violence here, as in Hypsipyle's narrative of the Lemnian women, leads to women's desperation, which ultimately, and paradoxically, expresses itself by imitating the violence that has caused their suffering. The mention of Meleager's mother and the violence provoked by her conflicting loyalties and deep sorrow introduces to Cassandre's interpretation of Troilus's dream a Statian interest in the consequences of male violence for women. The boar represents the prowess of Diomede's ancestor and the etiology of his family attribute, but it also represents the origin of the "contek" that divided Althaea's loyalties to brother and son.

If Criseyde and Cassandre do not acknowledge the Statian theme of female vulnerability to male violence more overtly, they do recognize the significance of martial violence for their own situation, in marked contrast to the men in Chaucer's poem, Pandarus and Troilus, and even the narrator. Pandarus's abrupt dismissal of Criseyde's reading and Troilus's angry rejection of Cassandre's summary are part of a larger pattern of the male characters' attempts to dismiss martial history, even while they participate in war. The men in Chaucer's poem are also affiliated with the *Thebaid*, though never as explicitly as Criseyde and Cassandre are; but the allusions to the Latin epic associated with the male characters consistently suggest their dismissal of military history. Whereas Criseyde and Cassandre seem to recognize the relevance of the story of the *Thebaid*, the men in *Troilus and Criseyde* sublimate history and martial rhetoric in the service of love and of love-talk.[48]

---

[48] Margherita remarks that the "disavowal [of history] is always associated with the male voice"; "Historicity," p. 253.

The narrator has an explicit and intricate relationship to Statius's poem.[49] The invocations of all five books in *Troilus and Criseyde* recall the *Thebaid*:[50] as Paul Clogan has suggested, such "touches of the *Thebaid* . . . intensify an atmosphere of high antiquity."[51] But recalling the *Thebaid* through such allusion is richly ambivalent. The narrator seems to suggest that the genre or theme of the Latin epic is relevant for his poem, and yet he continually dismisses martial or epic subjects, in the form of the siege of Troy, as anything more than the setting of his tale. He refuses to recount the history of the fall of Troy because it would be a "long digression" (1.143), a dismissal that foreshadows Troilus's rejection of the importance of Cassandre's story of Thebes for his own narrative. As Lee Patterson observes, "[I]n subordinating the historical world of events to the inner world of erotic action the narrator's behavior imitates that of his protagonists."[52] The opening line of *Troilus and Criseyde* suggests this complicity between the narrator and Troilus through a possible Statian allusion that has received much critical attention. The narrator of Chaucer's poem identifies his task as "The double sorwe of Troilus to tellen, / That was the kyng Priamus sone of Troye, / In lovynge, how his aventures fellen / Fro wo to wele, and after out of joie" (1.1–4). Troilus's "double sorwe" may derive from Virgil's reference to the *Thebaid* in Dante's *Purgatorio*: "the savage wars of those twin (*doppia*) sorrows of Jocasta."[53] The narrator seems to claim for his

---

[49] Wetherbee offers an interesting discussion of the thematic similarity between Chaucer's narrator and Dante's Christian Statius; see "'*Per te Poeta Fui, Per Te Cristiano*': Dante, Statius, and the Narrator of Chaucer's *Troilus*," in *Vernacular Poetics in the Middle Ages*, ed. Lois Ebin (Kalamazoo, Mich.: Medieval Institute Publications, 1984), pp. 153–76.

[50] The narrator invokes "Thesiphone" (1.6) at the opening of the poem just as Oedipus calls on Tisiphone in the opening of the *Thebaid*. According to Wetherbee, the *Thebaid* is the only precedent for such an invocation; *Chaucer and the Poets*, p. 32. Book 2 opens with an invocation to Clio, echoing *Thebaid* 1.41. Book 3 calls on Calliope, recalling *Thebaid* 4.34–35. In book 4, the narrator invokes "cruel Mars" (4.25), which recalls *Thebaid* 7.703. The fates, "Parcas, sustren thre" (5.3), invoked in book 5 may derive from *Thebaid* 1.212–13. Chaucer's use of the *Thebaid* in these invocations has long been acknowledged; see especially Wise, *Influence*, pp. 4–20.

[51] Clogan, "Chaucer's Use," p. 29.

[52] Patterson, *Chaucer and the Subject of History*, p. 105.

[53] "Le crude armi / de la doppia trestizia di Giocasta"; *Purgatorio* 22.55–56. The translation and edition are Allen Mandelbaum's, *The Divine Comedy of Dante Alighieri* (New York: Bantam, 1984). But see Spearing, pp. 267–68, who points out that the phrase has an analogue in Chaucer's primary source: *Filostrato* 4.118.2. Given the extensive reference to the *Thebaid* in Troilus and Criseyde, however, it seems entirely possible to me that the phrase is meant to resonate with Virgil's summary of Statius's text in the *Purgatorio*, especially considering the narrator's repeated use of invocations imported from the *Thebaid*. Just as those allusions invoke the epic apparatus of Statius's text, so this allusion invokes its theme.

poem and his protagonist the pathos of Statius's even though the contrast between Troilus's double sorrow and Jocasta's could not be sharper. Jocasta's sorrow is the sorrow of a mother of warring sons, a woman whose loss is inevitable and absolute. Troilus, on the other hand, experiences the double sorrow of his own desire, first unfulfilled and later betrayed.[54]

The distance between the sorrow of Jocasta and Troilus, one the result of military violence and the other of failed love, is collapsed in the allusion, the first example of the displacement of martial rhetoric in the service of romance. A rhetoric of violence is reappropriated from the story of war, here and throughout the poem, for the narrative of romance.[55] Troilus experiences his desire for Criseyde as violence from the beginning when he is first "thorugh-shoten and thorugh-darted" with Criseyde's "look" (1.325). Troilus's repeated insistence that he will die without Criseyde's favor and later her love becomes so familiar that it is easy to ignore the sublimation of the violence of war into the language of love on which it relies.[56] The poem insists on replacing Troilus's concern about the war with his desire for Criseyde and on displacing the threat of violence with the threat of desire (1.463–69):

> Alle other dredes weren from him fledde,
> Both of th'assege and his savacioun;
> N'yn him desir noon other fownes bredde,
> But argumentes to his conclusioun:
> That she of him wolde han compassioun,
> And he to ben hire man while he may dure.
> Lo, here his lif, and from the deth his cure!

Criseyde's "compassioun," not the siege, determines Troilus's life and death; indeed, his preoccupation with Criseyde replaces his "drede" and

[54] Spearing also notes the dissimilarity between Jocasta's sorrow and Troilus's, prompting him to question whether the allusion is merely "an accidental recollection"; p. 268. The allusion is certainly awkward, but it may reflect the narrator's bias or limitations. The possible reference to Jocasta's maternal sorrow here may be echoed in Pandarus's comparison of the lovesick Troilus to weeping Niobe, who mourns her dead children (1.699)—a comparison Troilus rejects as an "olde ensaumple" (1.759–60).

[55] Although this rhetoric of violence, the language of battle appropriated for love, is highly conventional, it is weighted differently in Chaucer's poem by the simultaneous and self-conscious suppression of the story of military violence. In *Troilus and Criseyde*, the martial rhetoric is overdetermined by the military conflict, the historical context that the narrator seeks both to establish and to dismiss.

[56] The instances, of this, sometimes in the voice of Pandarus and sometimes Troilus, are too numerous to catalogue. See especially 1.460–3, 2.323, 2.442.

his concern for the peace of the city. In Troilus's fantasy, Criseyde comes to occupy the emotional space previously taken up by the siege, a space replete with associations of violence and death.[57]

In Pandarus's speech, this displacement of the violence of war exists, of course, in the service of seduction. Pandarus, like the narrator, calls on the Furies and Mars—Statian battle deities—but he does so to authorize speech not about martial violence, but about romantic love. Feigning shock that Criseyde suspects his motives in the love suit he pleads, Pandarus exclaims: "O cruel god, O dispitouse Marte, / O Furies thre of helle, on yow I crye! / So lat me nevere out of this hous departe, / If I mente harm or vilenye!" (2.435–38). The disjunction between the epic convention and the subject matter we saw in the narrator's invocation is echoed here, but this time with a more obvious rhetorical purpose. Pandarus too appropriates Statian martial rhetoric in the service of love, a gesture that seeks to efface the significance of the war that Criseyde herself cannot ignore.

Troilus also invokes Statian gods to assist him in his seduction of Criseyde. One important example is his invocation of the bloodied Mars of *Thebaid* (7.69–71). Praying for the success of Pandarus's machinations to orchestrate a clandestine meeting with Criseyde, Troilus exclaims, "O Mars, thow with thi blody cope, / For love of Cipris, thow me nought ne lette!" (3.724–25).[58] Troilus calls on Mars as the personified war god of the *Thebaid*, and only parenthetically as the lover of

---

[57] The gesture here distancing Troilus's distress from that caused by the war is repeated throughout the poem. Upon discovering the distraught Troilus, for example, Pandarus first assumes he is troubled by the siege (1.552–53) until Troilus responds:

> . . . if thow wene I be thus sik for drede,
> It is naught so, and therfore scorne nought.
> Ther is another thing I take of hede
> Wel more than aught the Grekes han yet wrought,
> Which cause is of my deth, for sorowe and thought. (1.575–79)

Here again, the violence of desire displaces the violence of death: Troilus, who will in fact die in battle at the end of the poem, here attributes the "cause of [his] deth" to Criseyde.

[58] Clogan shows that "blody cope" may derive from glosses of *Thebaid* 7.69–71 in medieval manuscripts of the *Thebaid*; "Chaucer and the *Thebaid* Scholia," *Studies in Philology* 61 (1964): 607–608. Clogan provides a catalogue of glossed manuscripts of the *Thebaid* in "Medieval Glossed Manuscripts of the *Thebaid*," *Manuscripta* 11 (1967): 102–12. On these lines, see also Wetherbee, who identifies Troilus's references as Ovidian; *Chaucer and the Poets*, pp. 102–103.

Venus (Cipris), in a clear illustration of the employment of—even preference for—martial invocations for his romance. By appropriating the deities from martial narrative for a romance, Troilus represents love as war and, more significantly, obscures the significance of public, military history for his personal affairs.

Criseyde is, in contrast, not at all tempted to dismiss the significance of the war for her life. When Pandarus arrives announcing good news, Criseyde immediately assumes it is news of the war: ". . . is than th'assege aweye? / I am of Grekes so fered that I deye" (2.123–24). Criseyde's language implicitly rejects the rhetorical displacement of Troilus's and Pandarus's language: she attributes the threat of death to military violence, not erotic desire. When Pandarus claims that his news is five times better than the end of the siege, Criseyde is incredulous: "What! Bet than swyche fyve? I! Nay, ywys!" (2.128). Her inarticulate confusion at Pandarus's claim reveals a deep sense of the significance of the war to her personal situation.[59] Criseyde's sense of the inseparability of the military and the domestic, of the public and the private, perhaps explains her choice of reading materials. Chaucer assigns to women, to Criseyde and Cassandre, the most pronounced historical consciousness in the poem and the most intimate relationship with the text that represents that knowledge, Statius's *Thebaid.*

In fact, Criseyde only accepts Pandarus's claim that Troilus experiences desire as violence when it is given a literal manifestation in Troilus's experience of actual military violence. Just after Pandarus has informed her of Troilus's love, Criseyde observes Troilus return from battle on a bleeding horse, his own body eloquent testimony to the violence of the war (2.638–42):

> His helm tohewen was in twenty places,
> That by a tyssew heng his bak byhynde;
> His sheeld todasshed was with swerdes and maces,
> In which men myghte many an arwe fynde
> That thirled hadde horn and nerf and rynde. . . .

[59] My own sense of the displacement of history by romance in the poem is much like Lee Patterson's, except on this point. Patterson assigns to all of Trojan society a lack of concern with the martial narrative: "If Books 1 through 3 show us lovers, and a society, determined to avoid their implication within a tragic history, Books 4 and 5 show instead that the local enclave of love can neither withstand nor transcend the pressures of history"; *Chaucer and the Subject of History*, p. 111. But only Troilus is determined to avoid the implications of history; Criseyde is actively concerned with precisely this. See also Margherita, p. 254.

This sight provokes Criseyde's first emotional susceptibility to Troilus. Like Troilus's first experience of desire, Criseyde's response is figured in language that suggests penetration, but it is, significantly, not the violent image of being "thorugh-shoten and thorugh-darted" but the explicitly gentle incorporation of Troilus's image into her heart (2.649–51):

> Criseÿda gan al his chere aspien,
> And leet it so softe in hire herte synke,
> That to hireself she seyde, "Who yaf me drynke?"

The narrator suggests in the subsequent stanza that this susceptibility results directly from precisely the sort of military rhetoric that Criseyde had initially rejected (2.652–58):

> For of hire owen thought she wex al reed,
> Remembryng hire right thus, "Lo, this is he
> Which that myn uncle swerith he moot be deed,
> But I on hym have mercy and pitee."
> And with that thought, for pure ashamed, she
> Gan in hire hed to pulle, and that as faste,
> While he and alle the peple forby paste.

Although she dwells on his excellent birth, person, virtue, and estate, "moost hire favour was, for his distresse / Was al for hire, and thoughte it was a routhe / To sleen swich oon, if that he mente trouthe" (2.663–65). The wounded body of Troilus lends credence to Pandarus's claim that his friend will die without her love; the violence of battle makes Pandarus's martial metaphors for Troilus's desire concrete and threatens Criseyde with the real possibility that Troilus will die. Given the visual realization of a wounded Troilus, Criseyde pulls back from her window in shame, seeming to forget that Troilus has been injured in battle, not in love. It is the sight of Troilus, whose body bears witness to his experience of violence, that renders Pandarus's martial metaphors persuasive.

Despite the narrator's, and the male characters', attempts to suppress the history of Troy in the story of Troilus, the war reasserts itself in book 4. The romance of Troilus and Criseyde is finally subject to the narrative of the siege: the romance ends because Criseyde is traded to the Greeks for the captured Antenor. The female perspective on the war—Criseyde's sense of the significance of public affairs for her private life—is tragically vindicated. Yet even still the male characters continue to fail to see the significance of martial history for romance, as Troilus's rejection of Cassandre's historical interpretation illustrates. Criseyde's choice of reading material, however, reflects her acute sense of history: her own personal and literary history and the historical relationship between Troy and Thebes. Without a legally recognized male protector to anchor her firmly in the Trojan story, she is keenly aware of her particular vulnerability to the fortunes of her city.[60]

Criseyde's reading of the *Thebaid* constitutes the most concrete moment of intertextuality between Chaucer's poem and Statius's; she holds the material text of the Latin epic. This physical association between Criseyde and the *Thebaid* is mirrored in the association established by the genealogy Chaucer invents for Criseyde. In a startling addition to Boccaccio's text, Chaucer's Criseyde identifies her mother as "Argyve," which is also the name Cassandre uses for Argia, the Greek wife of the Theban prince Polynices.[61] Just as remarkable, Chaucer invents for Criseyde a niece named Antigone, a name that refers inescapably to Thebes.

The extraordinary genealogy Chaucer provides for Criseyde has been interpreted literally. Anderson and, following him, Windeatt argue that Criseyde is the daughter of Polynices's widow, and therefore is the cousin of Diomede.[62] To interpret Chaucer's use of the name "Argyve" as straightforward genealogy, however, is to reduce some of its associative power, making the connection between the two women prosaic and

---

[60] A. J. Minnis similarly remarks, "indications of Criseyde's fearfulness abound . . . Criseyde always needs a protector"; *Chaucer and Pagan Antiquity* (Cambridge: D. S. Brewer, 1982), pp. 83–84.

[61] Boccaccio does not name Criseyde's mother at all.

[62] Criseyde and Diomede would be cousins through their mothers, Argia and Deipyle. Noting that the name "Argyve" is also used in Cassandre's summary, Anderson claims that Chaucer "intends the daughter of Adrastus" when he names Criseyde's mother. He also argues that the brooch Criseyde gives to Troilus as a pledge of her love at 3.1370–71 and the one she gives to Diomede at 5.1040–41 are both the "brooch of Thebes" (apparently Chaucer's translation of the *monile Harmoniae* described in *Thebaid* 2.265–305), which Criseyde would have inherited from Argia. Anderson bases this claim on the description of that brooch in the "Complaint of Mars," pp. 127–28. See also Windeatt, *Oxford Guide*, p. 123.

concrete.[63] It seems more useful to consider the thematic significance of Chaucer's effort to link Criseyde to the women, Argia and Antigone, whose mutual suffering and compassion are depicted in the closing book of Statius's epic. Criseyde's relationship to both Argia and Antigone, in fact, makes a genealogical reading of the allusions impossible: there is no way to justify Criseyde as daughter of the Greek woman and cousin of the Theban maiden. Chaucer provides for Criseyde a matrilineal genealogy, one missing from the earlier tradition, and does so with a name that links her to the story of Thebes in a literary, not a literal, way.

Significantly, through this genealogy Criseyde is associated with *both* sides of the Theban war through the two women who represent most vividly the suffering endured by each. Daughter of Argyve and aunt to Antigone, Criseyde mediates between the two women who themselves mediated between the two sides of the Theban war, meeting accidentally on the battlefield when they go separately to bury Polynices, brother to one and husband to the other.[64] As these two women cross boundaries, so too does Criseyde, who like Antigone has a certain allegiance to both sides of the military confrontation. The names of her mother and cousin identify Criseyde with the women's story of Thebes, a story of personal, not political, loss—loss that transcends political boundaries, as Antigone and Argia do when they meet secretly and in defiance of Creon's law to bury the man they both love.

The differences between Criseyde and Statius's Argia, her "mother" in the literary tradition to which Chaucer aspires, are, however, considerable. Unlike Argia, who suffers the death of her husband, Criseyde leaves Troilus before he meets his death; in fact, she seems most moved by Diomede's argument that she should love him because Troy, and therefore Troilus, is doomed. Thinking over Diomede's attempt to persuade her, Criseyde recurs to the "perel of the town" (5.1025) to which

---

[63] Susan Schibanoff offers another possible interpretation of the literary significance of the name of Criseyde's mother in "Argus and Argyve: Etymology and Characterization in Chaucer's *Troilus,*" *Speculum* 51 (1976): 647–58. She shows that the name "Argia," from which Chaucer's "Argyve" seems derived, was etymologized as *providentia* in the pseudo-Fulgentian *Super Thebaidem* and so may have seemed to Chaucer a particularly appropriate name for the wife of Calcas and an ironic one for the mother of "the improvident Criseyde" (p. 647).

[64] On the importance of the meeting between Argia and Antigone for Statius's poem, see Wetherbee, "Dante and the *Thebaid* of Statius," p. 81.

Troilus is exposed as she reconsiders her position. Her "slydynge corage" is her way of avoiding the anguish felt by the Argive women in the *Thebaid*, anguish evoked by Chaucer in the opening of *The Knight's Tale*.[65] Unlike her mother, Argyve, Criseyde exits the story of Troy and Troilus before it becomes a tragedy. Just as she moves across the political boundary separating Troy from the army besieging it, so Criseyde moves, through her genealogy, across the narrative boundary marking off that other city under siege.

Subject to Pandarus's machinations and her own fear, Criseyde is perhaps an awkward avatar of Argia and Antigone. Certainly the redemptive moment of their meeting on the fields of Thebes has no clear analogue in Criseyde's own story. But as the figure most closely associated with the tradition of Statian women through the literary genealogy invented for her by Chaucer, Criseyde introduces into the *Troilus* the possibility of a radically different reading of the events of the poem than that offered by Troilus's laughing *contemptus mundi*, a reading that would acknowledge the poignancy of human suffering in the world that Troilus is privileged to escape and the fragile dignity of those, like Hypsipyle, who acknowledge their vulnerability to the contigencies of history. By giving the women of his poem the most pronounced historical consciousness, and by figuring that consciousness in their association with the *Thebaid*, Chaucer opens his poem to a Statian perspective on martial violence, one that goes far to deny the possibility of victory or real heroism, but not the possibility of compassion born of suffering and loss.[66]

[65] On the necessity of Criseyde's "slydynge," see also Dinshaw, *Chaucer's Sexual Poetics*, pp. 56–64, esp. pp. 57–58.

[66] I would like to thank Claire Banchich, Jessica Brantley, Jennifer Bryan, Christopher Cannon, and V. A. Kolve for reading earlier versions of this essay and for offering many useful suggestions. I am especially grateful to Carole Newlands, whose knowledge of the *Thebaid* was essential to this project from its inception.

Ethics and Interpretation: Reading Wills in Chaucer's *Legend of Good Women*

James Simpson
Girton College, Cambridge

Stanley Fish argues that all interpreters of texts are intentionalists. Readers, he says, "cannot help positing an intention for an utterance if they are in the act of regarding it as meaningful."[1] Once Fish has made this point, however, he goes on to posit that appeal to intention is "methodologically useless." Precisely because every interpretation is intentionalist, appeal to intention cannot constrain interpretation, since intention is indistinguishable from that which it would constrain.[2] And besides, intention gets us no nearer the work, since intention, like everything else about a text, must be construed, and it is construed according to the rules of play of the interpretive "community." A work only "is" as a textual community decides it to be. The momentary prospect of a category (intention) outside and in some ways constraining what the interpretive community decides to be true is immediately withdrawn, since, according to Fish's golden rule, "interpreters are constrained by their tacit awareness of what is possible and not possible to do, what is and is not a reasonable thing to say, and what will and will not be heard as evidence in a given enterprise."[3] Interpreters can be constrained *only* by these considerations, since how they interpret is itself

---

Without implying their agreement, I am grateful to both Christopher Cannon and Jill Mann for their penetrating critiques of this article in earlier forms.

[1] Stanley Fish, "Wrong Again," in his *Doing What Comes Naturally: Change, Rhetoric and the Practice of Theory in Literary and Legal Studies* (Oxford: Clarendon Press, 1989), pp. 103–19 (quotation from pp. 116–17). See also his companion article, "Working on the Chain Gang: Interpretation in Law and Literature," in *Doing What Comes Naturally*, pp. 87–102 (especially pp. 98–99). For a similar argument that understanding intention (in the sense of what an author meant by what s/he wrote) is *equivalent* to "a knowledge of the meaning of what [an author] writes," see Quentin Skinner, "Motives, Intentions, and the Interpretation of Texts," *New Literary History* 3 (1971–72): 393–408.

[2] Fish, "Wrong Again," p. 117.

[3] Fish, "Working on the Chain Gang," p. 98.

determined by the textual community in the first place. To reinterpret a text is, for Fish, and for Richard Rorty, to remake it.[4]

Fish and Rorty's textual communities are cozy and sensible places; the use of the word "community" is itself designed, as it usually is, I think, to suggest their warmth subliminally.[5] History is, however, brimful of textual "communities" that have decided on brutal versions of what is reasonable, and which have remade the records, in exactly the way Fish argues is inevitable, to suit their interpretation. Simply because history offers many examples of brutal textual communities does not of itself, I concede, demonstrate that there is a hermeneutic alternative. In this article I turn to Chaucer's *Legend of Good Women* by way of suggesting that Chaucer does at least propose an alternative. I argue that Chaucer represents himself working within a tyrannical textual "community," and that he asks us faithfully to intuit an unstated and unstatable intention that, by virtue of being unstatable, is necessarily outside the work. The faith we exercise in intuiting that intention offers an alternative both to the tyrannical reading of his patron and to the brutal faithlessness depicted in the legends themselves. Chaucer provokes us to recognize that our interpretive practice has ethical implications, since the issues involved in interpretation are no different from the issues of the "real world" depicted in the narratives themselves. He sharpens this provocation by suggesting resonances between the *Legend* and the last will of a dying author.

I

A variety of late Middle English writing manifests a startling consistency of interest in the will as reader. In a set of key texts we find an

---

[4] Fish, "Wrong Again," p. 107; "Working on the Chain Gang," p. 98. See also Richard Rorty, *Contingency, Irony and Solidarity* (Cambridge: Cambridge University Press, 1989), the main thesis of which is that descriptions of the world gain their force only by their usefulness, and not by their relation to the world they purport to describe; truth is made, not found. See also Richard Rorty, "The Pragmatist's Progress," in Stefan Collini, ed., *Interpretation and Overinterpretation* (Cambridge: Cambridge University Press, 1992), pp. 89–108 (quotation from p. 97).

[5] Relations are not so cozy between textual communities, however, precisely because there can be no appeal to standards of verification or grounds of argument beyond those decided by a single textual community. Richard Rorty is particularly frank about this, in saying that his aim with regard to opponents is not so much to argue against them, as to make them "look bad"; *Contingency*, p. 44. Humiliation by force of elegance or numbers can be the only kind of relation between groups of pragmatists ("textual communities") who make the world in different ways. Rorty's liberalism is only a short distance away from something much less liberal.

acute sensitivity to the psychology of reading, and an equally acute sensitivity to the broadly political implications of the way in which a text is psychologically processed and regulated. In *Piers Plowman*, Will, I have recently argued, is represented as a reader, especially from passus 8 of the B-text onward.[6] The poem earlier represents Conscience as a model reader insofar as he attends to the full text, and to the literal text, no matter how "teneful" it may be; Will's development as a reader, by contrast, displaces the responsible literalism of Conscience by reading according to the pleasure of the text. Will reads as human desire, and the value of his reading is measured not according to his understanding of the text's literal sense and apparent intention, but according to its positive effect on Will himself. In the *Confessio Amantis*, too, I have recently argued that Amans is principally a reader. Once we understand the work as a psychological allegory, in which the will (Amans) interacts with the imagination (Genius), then the action of the poem can be redescribed as a recollection of previously read texts, meditated on in the service of the will's reformation. Genius reproduces texts from the storehouse of the memory in the service of readerly desire, whether concupiscent or rational.[7] Once again, the value of a remembered text is measured not by the understanding of apparent authorial intention; on the contrary, reading is registered as serving the ethical ends of the will's reformation. Like Langland's, Gower's represented hermeneutics can be described as voluntarist: the purpose of reading is that readers regain access to their best desires, not that they gain access to authorial intention, except, of course, if that intention is itself to produce the reader's best desire. And both texts are sensitive to the "political" implications of this recreational reading: for Langland, the reformation of Will as reader requires nothing less than the reformation of the Church, while John Gower's reintegration serves as analogy at least for the reformation of the state.

The reading practices represented in these texts are in theory intentionalist, since the canonical texts being read, especially the Bible, are posited, in an Augustinian tradition, as having the very broad intention

---

[6] See James Simpson, "Desire and the Scriptural Text: Will as Reader in *Piers Plowman*," in Rita Copeland, ed., *Criticism and Dissent in the Middle Ages* (Cambridge: Cambridge University Press, 1996), pp. 215–43.

[7] See James Simpson, *Sciences and the Self in Medieval Poetry: Alan of Lille's "Anticlaudianus" and John Gower's "Confessio amantis,"* Cambridge Studies in Medieval Literature, vol. 25 (Cambridge: Cambridge University Press, 1995), pp. 252–71.

of reforming the will of their readers.[8] If this is the case, then in practice the kind of reading canonical texts ideally provoke looks similar to Fish's account of interpretation, since so much of the hermeneutic initiative lies in the power of readers. For in the case of these canonical texts, readers are free to interpret as they wish (within orthodox limits), as long as they conform to the textual community's demand that reading should revitalize the reader's best desires.[9] But are these *represented* hermeneutic practices the whole story? Even if Chaucer, Langland, and Gower, say, give very high profile to readerly power in the reception of *canonical* texts (the Bible, Ovid), does that mean that they wish the readers of their *own* texts to exercise the same power, even at the expense of authorial "entente"? In this article I want to suggest that Chaucer authenticates *The Legend of Good Women* principally as the expression of a noncanonical, authorial "entente." The "entente" of a canonical text may be taken very broadly indeed, since the reader comes to the text with the preformed conviction that such a text has, at some indeterminate distance from its literal surface, a broadly situated intention to

[8] For Augustine's sense of the intentionalism of Scripture, see, for example, *De doctrina christiana*, 3.27.38. The passage allows, within orthodox limits, various readings of one scriptural text: "For he who examines the divine eloquence, desiring to discover the intention of the author through whom the Holy Spirit created the Scripture, whether he attains this end or finds another meaning in the words not contrary to right faith, is free from blame if he has evidence from some other place in divine books. For the author himself may have seen the same meaning in the words we seek to understand. And certainly the Spirit of God, who worked through that author, undoubtedly foresaw that this meaning would occur to the reader or listener." Translation taken from D. W. Robertson, trans., *Saint Augustine, On Christian Doctrine*, The Library of Liberal Arts (Indianapolis and New York: Bobbs-Merrill, 1958), pp. 101–2.

As for the general intention of Ovidian texts (the canonical texts drawn on, for the most part, by Gower's Genius), any number of *accessus* define Ovid's intention (in the *Heroides*, for example) as being to "commend chaste love . . . or to attack unchaste love." See, for example, A. J. Minnis and A. B. Scott, eds., *Medieval Literary Theory and Criticism, c. 1100–c. 1375* (Oxford: Clarendon Press, 1988), p. 22. See, more broadly, Judson Boyce Allen, *The Ethical Poetic of the Later Middle Ages* (Toronto: University of Toronto Press, 1982), chapter 1.

[9] Fish himself recognizes Augustine's reading directions in book 3 of the *De doctrina christiana* as a model of the way in which a textual community works; see Stanley Fish, "Interpreting the *Variorum*," in his *Is There a Text in This Class?: The Authority of Interpretive Communities* (Cambridge, Mass.: Harvard University Press, 1980), p. 170.

reform its readers.[10] The newly produced text can assume no such confidence on the part of its readers; the presentation of a new text asks that
we attend to authorial agency as existing fairly closely behind and outside the text.[11] This is highlighted in the judicial context of the *Legend*'s
Prologue, since Chaucer's own agency is visibly suppressed there by the
combined sentences of his courtly judges and patrons.

The *Legend of Good Women* offers a spectacular example of a will reading, in the figure of Cupid.[12] The readerly will represented in this work
is a reader of Chaucer's own works, and he is not a political subject,
like the reading wills in *Piers Plowman* and the *Confessio*. He is instead
a potentially tyrannical king, and his cupidinous reading informs his
tyrannical patronage. More recent criticism of the work has rightly argued that the relationship of the *Prologue* to the legends is central to
any coherent interpretation of the poem,[13] and scholars have shown
how Cupid's hopelessly limited conception of virtue constrains and

[10] For a very succinct characterization of the broad hermeneutic tradition to which I
refer here, see E. D. Hirsch, *The Aims of Interpretation* (Chicago: University of Chicago
Press, 1976), pp. 20–22. Hirsch labels the tradition "intuitionism," which "conceives of
the text as an occasion for direct spiritual communion with a god or another person. The
words of the text do not 'contain' the meaning to be communicated; they institute a spiritual process which, beginning with the words, ultimately transcends the linguistic
medium. . . . The authenticity of this communion is determined less by philological investigation than by the vigor of inward conviction, the spiritual certainty of communion." (p. 20).

[11] Tendentiously to use the word "outside" in this context is not to disagree outright
with Derrida's profound point about there being nothing "outside the text" (Jacques
Derrida, *Of Grammatology*, trans. Gayatri Chakravorty Spivak [Baltimore: Johns Hopkins
University Press, 1976] p. 158). I use the word, however, simply by way of inviting deconstruction of Derrida's concept of the "text." Derrida's own practice, that is, would
have it that the very concept of the "text" can only be generated by reference to an "*hors
texte*"; textuality would otherwise become itself a metaphysical entity. For someone who
does not believe in metaphysical entities to say that there is nothing outside the text is
to imply that there is.

[12] Cupid is normally referred to as the "God of Love" in criticism. There can be no
doubt whatsoever that he is properly named "Cupid." See, for example, G.166–72 (the
standard iconography of Cupid); G.313 (the reference to Venus as the God of Love's
mother); and line 1140: "Cupido, that is the god of love."

[13] The point is most powerfully put by Donald W. Rowe, *Through Nature to
Eternity: Chaucer's Legends of Good Women* (Lincoln: University of Nebraska Press, 1988).
pp. 47–51.

flattens the following narratives.[14] With few exceptions, however, critics have not observed that Cupid's posture as patron is determined by his practice as reader.[15] Let us briefly consider the way in which this cupidinous reader exercises his power in the *Legend*. The notion of Cupid as regal patron in poetry of this kind surely derives from Ovid's *Amores*, which begins with the displacement of epic by elegy, as Cupid takes possession of the Ovidian narrator's heart, commanding new and amatory matter (*Amores* 1.1.21–30). For an account of Cupid as potentially tyrannical *reader*, however, I suggest we look instead to Augustine's *De doctrina christiana*. Book 3 of that work is concerned to establish the rules for Christian interpretation of the Old Testament in particular. On the simple principle that Scripture commends nothing but charity, and condemns nothing but cupidity,[16] Augustine develops hermeneutic principles that are themselves informed by charity. Hermeneutic practice is directed by ethical commitments in such a way as to avoid not only the unethical practices described in the Old Testament, but also the carnality of the very letter of the Old Testament itself. The two kinds of reading, charitable and cupidinous, stand in mutually exclusive relationship: "Quanto enim magis regnum cupiditatis destruitur, tanto caritatis augetur."[17] The application of this theory issues in the following account of how figural statements are to be read:

Sic euersa tyrannide cupiditatis caritas regnat iustissimis legibus dilectionis dei propter deum. Seruabitur ergo in locutionibus figuratis regula huiusmodi, ut tam diu uersetur diligenti consideratione quod legitur, donec ad regnum

---

[14] Thus, for example, Elaine Tuttle Hansen, "Irony and the Antifeminist Narrator in Chaucer's *Legend of Good Women*," *JEGP* 82 (1983): 11–31 (see p. 12); Lisa Kiser, *Telling Classical Tales: Chaucer and the Legend of Good Women* (Ithaca, N.Y.: Cornell University Press, 1983), p. 83; Peter L. Allen, "Reading Chaucer's Good Women," *ChauR* 21 (1987): 419–34 (see p. 422); Sheila Delany, *The Naked Text: Chaucer's Legend of Good Women* (Berkeley and Los Angeles: University of California Press, 1994), p. 82.

[15] The exceptions are Kiser, *Telling Classical Tales*, chapter 3, and Allen, "Reading Chaucer's Good Women," p. 422.

[16] *De doctrina christiana*, 3.10.15: "Non autem praecipit scriptura nisi caritatem nec culpat nisi cupiditatem et eo modo informat mores hominum," cited from Joseph Martin, ed., *Sancti Aurelii Augustini de doctrina christiana, libri IV*, Corpus Christianorum Series Latina 32 (Turnholt: Brepols, 1962), p. 87.

[17] *De doctrina christiana*, 3.10.16, p. 88.

caritatis interpretatio perducatur. Si autem hoc iam proprie sonat, nulla pute-
tur figurata locutio.[18]

This fascinating passage underwrites precisely the voluntarist hermeneutics represented in, say, *Piers Plowman*. It places an extraordinary power
in the hands of the reader and removes that power, ostensibly, from the
text itself, or its author, since it directs the reader to keep reading into a
given scriptural text until it should offer up a charitable sense. Whatever
the ostensible *literal* force of the scriptural text, the reader should read
with a charitable "prejudice." That prejudice should be so strong, indeed,
that it becomes the very measure of what is to be taken as figural: if a text
does not lead into the "realm" of charity, then it is, *by definition*, to be understood figuratively. Correlatively, the measure of "literalness" becomes
the charitable sense that the reader perceives: if the text "sounds" charity
"proprie," then it is not to be understood figuratively. This is a radical re-
casting of classical rhetorical norms, since the measure of the figural is located not in the literal meaning of the words themselves, but rather in
their sense as intuited by a charitable will. It is the reader's psychological
disposition that ideally generates the rhetorical status of the text, and
that eventually reads the same meaning ("charity") into every scriptural
text. But if this reading practice is represented in *Piers Plowman* as a liberation for the reader Will, I want now to argue that the very force of that
liberation can be oppressively inverted in the case of the cupidinous
reader. For on the face of it, cupidinous reading looks very similar to charitable reading, since both are generated by the pleasure of the text.

The connections between Augustine's cupidinous reader and *The
Legend of Good Women* are powerful. Cupid is, after all, represented in

---

[18] *De doctrina christiana*, 3.15.23, p. 91. This passage is well known in late-fourteenth-
century England. It is clearly being drawn upon, twice, in the Wycliffite Bible, once in
the Prologue, and once in the Prologue to the Gospel of Matthew: "Such a reule schal be
kept in figuratif spechis, that so longe it be turned in mynde bi diligent considerac[i]oun,
til the expownyng either vndirstonding be brought to the rewme of charite; if eny speche
of scripture sounneth propirly charite, it owith not to be gessid a figuratijf speche . . . if
it seemith to comaunde cruelte, either wickidnesse, either to forbede prophit, either
good doinge, it is a figuratijf speche." Cited from Josiah Forshall and Frederic Madden,
eds., *The Holy Bible . . . made from the Latin Vulgate by John Wycliffe and his Followers*, 4
vols. (Oxford: Oxford University Press, 1850), Prologue, chapter 12, 1:44–45.

the poem as a reader, not only of Chaucer's translation of the *Roman de la Rose*, but also of *Troilus and Criseyde*. In the G version, indeed, he reveals his acquaintance with the "sixty bokes . . . / Of sundry wemen" in Chaucer's possession, including works by Ovid, Livy, Jerome, Claudian, and Vincent of Beauvais (lines 253–316).[19] Cupid is also represented as, potentially at least, a tyrant, since Alceste suggests that his outright judgment of Chaucer resembles the practice of "tyraunts of Lumbardye, / That usen wilfulhed and tyrannye" (G.354–55). Well she might: however much Chaucer is "excused," the "trial" is conducted wholly within the dynamics of Cupid's relationship with Alceste, the narrator's own defense being wholly irrelevant. Alceste argues that a just king should not "dampne a man withoute answere or word" (G.387), and she also says that the meaning of his texts may not have been *his*; he may have translated out of mere habit, "in no malyce" (G.340–45), or else he was bidden by a powerful person to write as he did, "and durste it not withseye" (G.346–47). But when the narrator attempts a defense on the grounds of an authorial "entente," to have done nothing other than promote fidelity in love (G.452–63), he is instantly silenced by Alceste (G.465–68):

> . . . Lat be thyn arguynge,
> For Love ne wol nat counterpletyd be
> In ryght ne wrong; and lerne this at me!
> Thow hast thy grace, and hold the ryght therto.

The processes of this court can work only within the circuit of Cupid's desire, gratified as he is by the intervention of Alceste, and by the exercise of his own grace, unconstrained by the justice of the defendant's case.[20] Such processes could not be further removed from the

---

[19] All citations are taken from Larry D. Benson, gen. ed., *The Riverside Chaucer*, 3d ed. (Oxford: Oxford University Press, 1987). Cupid's reading of the books he cites is characteristically cupidinous, since, on the face of it, some of these works (i.e., "Valerye" and "Jerome agayns Jovynyan") run largely counter to his ideological position (if "Valerye" refers to Valerius of the *Epistola Valerii ad Rufinum*). This point has been made by Alastair J. Minnis, "Repainting the Lion: Chaucer's Profeminist Narratives," in Roy Eriksen, ed., *Contexts of Pre-Novel Narrative: The European Tradition* (Berlin and New York: Mouton de Gruyter, 1994), pp. 153–83 (see p. 157). I cite from the G version by preference, since my argument relates better to the more threatening conditions of that version, although I do not prohibit myself from citing from F when appropriate, since that version (in my view) produces G.

[20] A point made by Rowe, *Through Nature to Eternity*, p. 40.

nuanced hermeneutic and legal practice represented in Machaut's *Jugement dou roy de Navarre*, rightly and often cited as an analogue for the *Legend*.[21] Neither does the process of law here parallel the regenerative world of Nature witnessed by the narrator before he sleeps, where the "tydif, for newfangelnesse" (F.154), beseeches mercy for his infidelity. It is true that the passage superficially resembles the encounter between Cupid and Chaucer, since, in response to the repentance of the tydif, Daunger was

> . . . for a tyme a lord,
> Yet Pitee, thurgh his stronge gentil myght,
> Forgaf, and made Mercy passen Ryght. (F.160–62)

So too does Cupid, at Alceste's prompting, graciously forgive Chaucer. There is an important difference, however: Chaucer never acknowledges his "fault." On the contrary, *after* he has been forgiven, he insists on the wholeness of his "entente" (G.445–63). If Cupid will not be "counterpleted" (a legal term) in right *or* *wrong*, then we can assume that his hermeneutic practice is correlative with his legal practice: both are driven by cupidinous desire, and how could they be driven by anything else? In Cupid's reading the charitable corn is exchanged for the cupidinous "draf," an interpretive metaphor used by both Augustine and Cupid. Cupid sums up his case, and his judgment, against Chaucer by promising a spectacular punishment for Chaucer's heretical inversion of the law of the cupidinous male reader (G.311–16):[22]

[21] Machaut's poem is both more complex and simpler than the *Legend*: more complex because the ethical question raised by Machaut's earlier poem is debated by a wide range of allegorical virtues; simpler because there's no hermeneutic problem—no one doubts what Machaut meant. The only question is the ethical one as to whether or not he was right. The court case, which in Chaucer's poem is over very quickly, occupies most of Machaut's poem. For the text, see R. Barton Palmer, ed. and trans., *Le Jugement dou Roy de Navarre*, Garland Library of Medieval Literature, vol. 45, series A (New York: Garland, 1988).

[22] All but the last line of this passage is an addition to the G version, by which time (presumably post-1394, the death of Queen Anne) its references to heretical textual practices, and their punishment, must have been more pressing in the context of Lollard activity. Two papers at the New Chaucer Society Congress in 1996 argued this (I am grateful to both authors for permission to read these papers): Wendy Scase, "Chaucer and Langland: Censorship and the Clergy," and Helen Phillips, "The Prologue to the *Legend of Good Women*: Registers, Politics, Dates." For Augustine's wheat/chaff metaphors, see, for example, *De doctrina christiana*, 3.7.11, p. 84.

"But yit, I seye, what eyleth the to wryte
The draf of storyes, and forgete the corn?
By Seynt Venus, of whom that I was born,
Although thow reneyed hast my lay,
As othere olde foles many a day,
Thow shalt repente it, so that it shal be sene!"

Chaucer, then, represents himself as operating within a threatening textual "community" whose hermeneutic practices are driven finally by its own power and prejudice. Alceste provisionally recognizes that the "intention" of the text might be either of the original author of a translated text, or of the powerful lord whose command Chaucer dared not disobey. The court in which she pleads does not, however, take time out to consider these possibilities, just as it absolutely refuses to countenance the author's own claim that his intention was only to "forthere trouthe in love" (G.462).

This matches precisely the discursive environment of Richard II's court, as we find it described in the "Record and Process" of Richard's own renunciation of the throne in 1399.[23] Of course this document is a highly charged piece of political propaganda. I refer to it here not by way of suggesting, or denying, that these really were the discursive conditions within which Chaucer worked between 1386 and 1388, when, probably, the *Legend* was first composed, and after 1394, when, probably, the *Prologue* was revised.[24] Whatever the truth of the document, it certainly describes tyranny in terms of willful appropriation of discursive

---

[23] The text is translated in Chris Given-Wilson, ed., *Chronicles of the Revolution, 1397–1400: The Reign of Richard II* (Manchester: Manchester University Press, 1993), pp. 168–89. The Latin text (from which citations are drawn here) is in J. Strachey, ed., *Rotuli Parliamentorum*, 6 vols. (London, 1783), 3: 415–53.

[24] For the dating of the *Legend* and its two prologues, see the *Riverside Chaucer*, p. 1060. The discursive conditions of the middle 1380s (when the struggle between Richard and his most powerful magnates was at its height) were certainly treacherous; see Paul Strohm, "The Textual Environment of Chaucer's 'Lak of Stedfastnesse,'" in his *Hochon's Arrow: The Social Imagination of Fourteenth-Century Texts* (Princeton: Princeton University Press, 1992), pp. 57–74. The discursive conditions of the 1390s were no less fragile and dangerous; see Nigel Saul, "Richard II and the Vocabulary of Kingship," *English Historical Review* 110 (1995): 854–77. Michael Hanrahan, in "Seduction and Betrayal: Treason in the *Prologue* to the *Legend of Good Women*," *ChauR* 30 (1996): 229–40, argues persuasively that the language of treason in the *Prologue* is a response to the struggle for control of "treason" as a concept in the 1380s.

power. Richard is consistently accused of exercising an arbitrary will, "pro sue libito voluntatis," and in each case this exercise of arbitrary will exemplifies specifically discursive infringement. Richard is accused of willfully distorting the process and altering the records of parliament by exploiting, contrary to parliament's intention, a concession to effect some business on officers' powers ("Rex fecit Rotulos Parliamenti pro voto suo mutari et deleri, contra effectum concessionis predicte");[25] he appointed sheriffs whom he knew would in no way resist his will (13); when challenged on the dispensation of arbitrary justice, Richard fiercely replied that the laws were "in his mouth," or "in his breast," and that he did, by his own willful judgment, whatever pleased him ("secundum sue arbitrium voluntatis . . . quicquid desideriis eius occurrerit") (16); he ordered sheriffs to arrest and imprison anyone speaking publicly or privately against him (20); he so terrified his counselors that they dared not speak the truth in giving counsel (23); and he ordered the records of his estate management to be "deleted and erased" (24). The refrain of these charges is reference to the king's arbitrary exercise of "arbitrium voluntatis." The document also records a sermon by Archbishop Arundel, in which the king's childish will is personified: "Cum igitur puer regnat, Voluntas sola regnat, Ratio exul."[26]

The king Cupid acts in just this arbitrary way, and constitutes a textual "community" around him in which the intention of authorial subjects is highlighted precisely as it is suppressed.[27] In this tyrannical and potentially violent environment we are drawn to mark an authorial function in the traces of its suppression. At this point I want to turn from Cupid as readerly will to Chaucer's authorial will, by arguing that there is another sense in which "reading wills" might be applicable to the *Legend*. I want to suggest that the whole text has the resonance of a will, or final testamentary document of a "dying" author.

[25] Paragraph 8 in Given-Wilson, *Chronicles of the Revolution*; all future references will be to this document, and will be referred to by their paragraph number in the text. See also paragraph 19 for willful distortion of parliamentary procedure; Latin text from *Rotuli Parliamentorum*, 3:418.

[26] *Rotuli Parliamentorum*, 3:423.

[27] A connection between the God of Love and Richard was first suggested by J. B. Bilderbeck, *Chaucer's "Legend of Good Women"* (London: Hazell, Watson, and Viney, 1902), pp. 85–87.

The cupidinous reading of the imperious patron prompts us to understand the *Legend* as the expression of an authorial will, or "testament of love."[28]

II

Carolyn Dinshaw and Elaine Tuttle Hansen have proposed two ideas about the God of Love and the narrator. Firstly, they argue persuasively that the God of Love wants only stories of passive women, who suffer in faithful misery.[29] While the narratives of the *Legend* ostensibly promote

---

[28] The phrase "testament of love" is drawn, of course, from the *Confessio Amantis*, 8.2955 (first recension), where Venus commands the aged Gower to greet Chaucer well, since Chaucer has served her well in his youth; now, however,

> . . . in hise daies olde
> Thow schalt him telle this message,
> That he upon his latere age,
> To sette an ende of alle his werk,
> As he which is myn owne clerk,
> Do make his testament of love,
> As thou hast do thi schrifte above,
> So that mi Court it mai recorde. (8.2950–57*)

G. C. Macaulay, ed., *The English Works of John Gower*, 2 vols., Early English Text Society, e.s., vols. 81–82 (London: Oxford University Press, 1900–1901; rpt., 1979). This act of resituating Chaucer's amatory oeuvre in a penitential and legal context, as an "ende" of a given kind of poetry, inclines me to understand this to be a reference to *The Legend of Good Women*. The *Prologue* to *The Man of Law's Tale* also (implicitly) couples the *Legend* and the *Confessio* (lines 45–89). The dates of the two works, which have so much in common, also contribute to the connection; both must have been started about 1385, and both were revised in the 1390s. The phrase "testament of love" cannot help but evoke another text written in this period, Thomas Usk's *Testament of Love* (also probably written in 1385). There are many connections between the *Legend* and Usk's work: like the *Legend*, Usk's text also evokes fidelity in love in a context wherein the author's political fidelity is under question (e.g., 2.3); it is a testamentary work; and it is a "margaret" text. For a possible link between Gower's comment and Usk's work, see David R. Carlson, "Chaucer's Boethius and Thomas Usk's *Testament of Love*: Politics and Love in the Chaucerian Tradition," in Robert A. Taylor et al., eds., *The Centre and Its Compass: Studies in Medieval Literature in Honour of Professor John Leyerle*, Studies in Medieval Culture, vol. 33 (Kalamazoo, Mich.: Western Michigan University, 1993), pp. 29–70 (esp. pp. 29–33). For the *Testament of Cresseid* as another testamentary poem, also (like the *Legend*) written as a way of ending *Troilus and Criseyde*, see Julia Boffey, "Lydgate, Henryson, and the Literary Testament," *MLQ* 53 (1992): 41–56. Here, of course, the testament is composed by Cresseid herself, as a dying author.

[29] Elaine Tuttle Hansen, "Irony and the Antifeminist Narrator," and Carolyn Dinshaw, *Chaucer's Sexual Poetics* (Madison: University of Wisconsin Press, 1989), pp. 65–87.

women, in reality they serve a generally brutalized masculine desire by allowing its repeated satisfaction. Given my understanding of Cupid, I agree with this account of why he wants stories of female fidelity and suffering. From this point, however, Dinshaw, for example, goes on to make a second point. She wants to identify the narrator's interest with that of the God of Love. So far from seeing his authorial intent as suppressed by Cupid, Dinshaw sees it as liberated, given full voice: "Stripped, clipped, and scrubbed, his pagan source texts are like female bodies in the narrator's masculine hands. As he promised, he indeed delivers the 'naked text' of the legends. His *translatio* this time is not the record of his seduction but is, rather, a record of his continual exercise of control over the feminine."[30]

The metaphors of Dinshaw's account implicitly evoke patristic hermeneutic practice in the reception of classical texts. In Deuteronomy 21:10–14, the Israelite soldier is encouraged to take the captive Egyptian woman as his bride on condition that she shall have been properly prepared for her wedding in a new culture—her hair cut, her nails pared, divested of her foreign garments.[31] Jerome defends his use of pagan textual sources by analogy with possession of the beautiful captive woman in this way:

Quid ergo mirum, si et ego sapientiam saecularem propter eloquii venustatem, et membrorum pulchritudinem, de ancilla atque captiva Israelitidem facere

---

[30] Dinshaw, *Chaucer's Sexual Poetics*, p. 86. Hansen argues the same thing in "Irony and the Antifeminist Narrator." Hansen's position in that article is a fuller, and more subtle, interpretation of the *Legend* than Dinshaw's, since Hansen argues that the narrator is being ironized by an authorial Chaucer. Dinshaw leaves unaddressed the question of who (if anyone) presents the narrator, and why. Hansen also allows for another possibility (by and large the one argued for in this article): "A strong case might be made, however, that there is a further irony: the narrator might well be awake to the implications of his treatment, and thus he may be attempting to carry out his imposed sentence while in fact he is poking fun at Cupid by giving him a poem whose effect is exactly the opposite of what the God ordered" (p. 28). Hansen has since changed her mind about the authorial position of Chaucer, arguing that the narrator (and, implicitly, Chaucer) is primarily interested in, and appalled by, the feminization of men in the *Legend*. See her article, "The Feminization of Men in Chaucer's *Legend of Good Women*," in Janet Halley and Sheila Fisher, eds., *Seeking the Woman in Late Medieval and Renaissance Writings* (Knoxville: University of Tennessee Press, 1989), pp. 51–70. The observation that men are feminized in these stories is very revealing; I disagree that it follows from this that Chaucer applauds the brutal means men deploy to escape that feminization.

[31] Dinshaw, *Chaucer's Sexual Poetics*, pp. 22–5.

cupio? Et si quidquid in ea mortuum est, idolatriae, voluptatis, erroris, libid-
inum, vel praecidio, vel rado. . . .[32]

Jerome poses here as the very reverse of the cupidinous reader, ready as
he is to pare away whatever he finds idolatrous or voluptuous in his captured text. But his practice is, of course, a perfect model of cupidinous
reading, given his determination to satisfy his own readerly desire. The
frank comparison with imperialist military practice all but announces
the hermeneutic imperialism that legitimates excision of whatever dis-
pleases in the captured text. Whether or not Chaucer had this text in
mind in his presentation of Cupid as reader, it offers a perfect model of
the kind of excising, invasive cultural transmission implied by Cupid's
imperious and imperialist reading: Cupid, too, demands that Criseyde
be struck out, just as he demands that all women conform to a single
model of Alcestian fidelity, with all else pared away. "[R]eherce of al hir
lyf the grete," he orders the narrator (F.574), thus producing a radically
and revealingly abbreviated, or rather censored, text. If Cupid is identifiable with Augustine's cupidinous reader, the comparison with
Jerome's practice equally reveals that the pose of the charitable reader
can easily mask predatory desire.

I agree with Dinshaw, and many other critics, in her description of
the *Legend*'s rhetorical surface as clipped, stripped, and scrubbed.[33] But
who is generating this sanitation? To suggest, as Dinshaw does, that it
is the narrator strikes me as a serious underreading of the complex relation between author and patronal readership in the *Legend*. As I read
it, the God of Love represents Chaucer's male readership in its most
tyrannical form, outraged by the disappointment of male desire in

---

[32] See Jerome, Epistle 70, in *PL* 22:665: "What is surprising, therefore, if I, too,
should desire to make secular wisdom, on account of its rhetorical elegance and the
beauty of its parts, into an Israelite from its status as handmaiden and captive? If I should
find anything dead in her, either of idolatry, of cupidity, of error, or of libidinous desires,
I will either cut it off, or shave it away." See also Epistle 21, *PL* 22:385. For the history
of the motif, see Henri de Lubac, *Exégèse médiévale*, in *Théologie*, 41–42, 59 (Paris: Aubier,
1959–64), 1:290–304.

[33] R. W. Frank, in *Chaucer and the "Legend of Good Women"* (Cambridge, Mass.: Harvard
University Press, 1972), points in that book's excursus to the consistent use of *occupatio*.
See also Fyler, *Chaucer and Ovid* (New Haven, Conn.: Yale University Press, 1979), p. 99;
A. J. Minnis, *The Shorter Poems: Oxford Guides to Chaucer* (Oxford: Clarendon Press, 1995),
p. 338; Allen, "Reading Chaucer's Good Women," pp. 426–27; and Kiser, *Telling
Classical Tales*, pp. 100–101.

Troilus and Criseyde, and constraining Chaucer's post-*Troilus* work. Just as the God of Love underreads *Troilus and Criseyde*, so too, I'd argue, does Dinshaw underread the *Legend*. Apart from anything else, her position is insensitive to the ways in which authorship is consistently suppressed in the *Prologue*, and in the legends themselves. In the *Prologue*, as Rita Copeland has recently argued, Chaucer replays the structure of events from the *accessus* to Ovid's *Heroides*, where Ovid is under threat from a censorious emperor.[34] I shall return to that, but for the moment I focus on the legends themselves, where there are many instances of dying authors, almost all of them female. This is inevitable, given the *Legend*'s model of the *Heroides*, a text that is nothing if not a reflection on the "death" of authors.

Chaucer has six of his heroines write their letters at the end of their respective legends (i.e., Dido, Hypsipyle, Medea, Ariadne, Philomela, and Phyllis). Each letter provokes a sharp sense of authorial suppression, since not only is each written either by a dying or an abandoned author, aware of the futility of writing, but each is also radically abbreviated, if not wholly excised in the *Legend*. Nowhere is the consciousness of authorial suppression as sharply drawn as in the legend of Philomela. With her tongue cut out, and unable to write, the imprisoned Philomela weaving her narrative powerfully images the silenced female author fighting back by writing back, passing a revolutionary message out of the prison-house of male brutality.[35] I suggest that this image parallels the position of the narrator, on whom the tyrannical God of Love imposes the strictest limits of the sayable in the *Prologue*. Like Philomela, Chaucer transmits messages out of the prison-house of language into which he is put by his powerful male readership. Ostensibly the narrator excises these letters, but it is also plausible to see the excisions as guided by Cupid, "cutting out" the narrator's "tongue" when, from the evidence of the *Rose* and of *Troilus and Criseyde*, he might most want to "speak." Dinshaw's argument that the legends are a record of the "narrator's continued exercise of control over the feminine" does not meet this intense and powerful representation of a woman as writer, and

---

[34] Rita Copeland, *Rhetoric, Hermeneutics and Translation in the Middle Ages: Academic Traditions and Vernacular Texts*, Cambridge Studies in Medieval Literature, vol. 11 (Cambridge: Cambridge University Press, 1991), p. 188.

[35] For a profound reading of the Philomela legend more generally, see Patricia Joplin, "The Voice of the Shuttle Is Ours," in Lynn A. Higgins and Brenda R. Silver, eds., *Rape and Representation* (New York: Columbia University Press, 1991), pp. 35–64. I am grateful to Louise Fradenburg for directing me to this essay.

neither does it account for the *similarity* of position between the imprisoned figures of Philomela and the narrator.[36]

How does the Chaucer-narrator insinuate messages out of the literary prison of readerly will, and so distinguish his agency from that of his tyrannical readership? The *Prologue* and the legends are hyperbolic at every turn, hyperbole being focused with almost surreal insistence on the feminine. In the legends themselves, for example, Dido standing in the temple is so beautiful

> That, if that God, that hevene and erthe made,
> Wolde han a love, for beaute and goodnesse,
> And womanhod, and trouthe, and semelynesse,
> Whom shulde he loven but this lady swete?
> There nys no woman to hym half so mete. (lines 1039–43)

In itself strangely excessive, this panegyric is mere preliminary to the focus of real praise in the poem, Alceste. When she first appears, the narrator declares that even if men sought throughout the world, "Half hire beaute shulde men nat fynde / In creature that formed is by kynde" (G.177–78). Alceste's very perfection places intolerable strains on the capacities of rhetoric, precisely because "no comparisoun" may be made between all the exemplary figures in the ballade (G.203–23) and Alceste: "For as the sonne wole the fyr disteyne, / So passeth al my lady sovereyne" (F.274–75). Alceste puts such pressure on the powers of rhetoric, indeed, that the processes of figuration seem to collapse before her: Chaucer has no "Englyssh" to praise the daisy (F.66), "of alle floures flour / Fulfilled of al vertu and honour" (F.53–54), since "Comparisoun may non ymaked be; / For it surmountede pleynly alle odoures, / And of ryche beaute alle floures" (G.110–12). The daisy, however, is praised only by way of raising the stakes of Alceste's own incomparability, which can be figured by comparing her, in circular fashion, to a daisy. Crowned with daisylike pearls (*margeritae/marguerittes*), her crown "Made hire lyk a dayesye for to sene" (G.156). Visual likeness, verbal pun, and metaphorical identification all point in the one inexpressible direction, to the point where Alceste, with the daisy, can represent

---

[36] Hansen, in "The Feminization of Men" and in *Chaucer and the Fictions of Gender* (Berkeley and Los Angeles: University of California Press, 1992), pp. 9–10, certainly does register the feminization of the narrator. She argues, however, that the narrator wants to escape that, since his "primary concern is . . . to be pleased as a man, and to please other men"; "Feminization," p. 57.

nothing but figuration itself. The moment the nineteen ladies see the daisy, after their ballade eulogizing Alceste's incomparability, they kneel to praise both daisy and Alceste, now conceptually indistinguishable (F.296–98):

> . . . Heel and honour
> To trouthe of womanhede, and to this flour
> That bereth our alder pris in figurynge!

But if Alceste hyperbolically surpasses and represents all the women in the legends, then what of Cupid? What relationship does he have with the men of these narratives? How does he relate, that is, to the male rapists and traitors, as well as to the one or two more noble men, who populate the *Legend*? Alceste seems to be married to Cupid: they arrive together, "The god of Love, and in his hand a quene" (F.213); Cupid describes the daisy, a figure for Alceste, as "myn oune floure" (F.316); and, addressing Cupid, Alceste refers to herself as "youre Alceste" (G.422). Indeed, the mythic personification Cupid figures all men, including Alceste's historical husband, Admetus; for in allowing Alceste's plea for mercy, he declares his ahistorical status as the figure of male desire (G.433–36):

> "Madame," quod he, "it is so longe agon
> That I yow knew so charytable and trewe,
> That nevere yit sith that the world was newe
> To me ne fond I betere non than ye."

If Cupid does personify all men, this establishes an expectation of representational symmetry with Alceste. That expectation is disappointed. Cupid happily promotes the hyperbole of Alceste as the "figure" of all faithful women, since male desire has no complaints about female fidelity and suffering. Within the terms of the Augustinian hermeneutic rule cited earlier, according to which figural expressions should be read until they arrive within the "realm" of charity, Cupid reads the "figure" Alceste in precisely this (a)political way, with the only difference being that the figure must lead directly into the jurisdiction of Cupid. The legends strikingly lack, however, any sustained connection between the male lovers and Cupid. Male desire is certainly represented in all its brutality, but the text offers only suppressed hints of a possible connection between that brutality and Cupid.

The narrator refers, for example, to the "tirannye" of men at the end of the Lucrece sequence (line 1883), recalling Alceste's description of Cupid as a potential tyrant (G.353–55). The Lucrece narrative certainly begins by promising to focus on its political implications, but the promise is withdrawn no sooner than it is made (lines 1680–84):

> Now mot I seyn the exilynge of kynges
> Of Rome, for here horible doinges,
> And of the laste kyng Tarquinius,
> As seyth Ovyde and Titus Lyvius.
> But for that cause telle I nat this storye. . . .

Unlike Gower's treatment of the same story, strategically placed among the explicitly political exempla of book 7 of the *Confessio Amantis*, the Chaucerian narrative marginalizes the exiling of the cupidinous tyrant and focuses instead on the "seynt" Lucrece, who was "yhalwed dere" (line 1871).[37] Any connection between the potentially tyrannical Cupid and the tyrannical king remains muted in the *Legend*. Or, at the beginning of the Philomela sequence, the narrator addresses God as the "ye-vere of the formes," the one who has borne the exemplar of the world in his thought, "Eternaly er thow thy werk began."[38] How, asks the narrator, could such a god have allowed Tereus to be born (lines 2228–34)? This Platonic reference to the predetermination of the world as *opus* provokes us to reflect that the real "giver of forms," or *deus dator formarum*, in the *Legend* is Cupid himself, the personification of male desire who preexists, "sith that the world was newe" (G.435), and predetermines the outcome of each narrative. Put that way, the question becomes "How could you (Cupid) have made anything *different* from Tereus, since you are what motivated him, and since you are what motivates these tales?"

Or again, in the legend of Dido, we read that "Cupido, that is the god of love," took the form of Ascanius, in order to enamor and ensnare Dido (lines 1139–44). This is one of those fascinating moments in Middle English literature when an allegorical project begins to collapse in on

[37] For the political emphases of this narrative in the *Confessio Amantis*, see Simpson, *Sciences and the Self*, pp. 213–15. For the Lucrece story more generally as a "myth of revolution," see Ian Donaldson, *The Rapes of Lucretia: A Myth and Its Transformations* (Oxford: Clarendon Press, 1982), chapter 6.

[38] For a suggestive but inconclusive argument that this Platonic description of God is derived from an *accessus* to the *Metamorphoses*, see Karl Young, "Chaucer's Appeal to the Platonic Deity," *Speculum* 19 (1944): 1–13.

itself.[39] For it is the very figure of Cupid who has ordered these stories, ostensibly to publicize and praise feminine suffering. A moment like this quietly lets the cat out of the bag by revealing that it was Cupid's agency in the first place that *provoked* the feminine suffering. The narrator's attempt to put the cat straight back into the bag only heightens the effect: "but, as of that scripture / Be as be may, I take of it no cure" (lines (1144–45). The suppressed "scripture" here refers to *Aeneid* 1.643–722, where Aeneas orders Ascanius to bear gifts, including the veil once worn by Helen on her way to Troy, to Dido. At the instigation of Venus, Cupid impersonates Ascanius, and carries the gifts himself, with orders to inspire Dido with a secret flame and to beguile her with poison. Dido, "doomed to impending ruin," takes him passionately on her lap, *"inscia Dido, / insidat quantus miserae deus"* (1.719). This Cupid is the narrator's very patron, *"aligeru{s} Amor"* (*Aeneid* 1.663), son of "Seynt Venus, of whom that I was born" (G.313), and capable of impersonating all men. Alceste might stand as a figure for all suffering women, but Cupid's relation to all tyrannical men is eclipsed. For all her surreal inexpressibility, then, Alceste can finally stand only as a reflection, or a "relike," of the sun-king Cupid, rather than as alternative source of illumination. The Man of Law's title for the *Legend*, "the Seintes Legende of Cupide" (*MLH* 61) is from this perspective appropriate, however we understand that "of": the legends are really about, and belong to, their patron.[40] One index of that possession is that Cupid signifies only through faithful women, not brutal men. Whereas the legend of Alceste in the *Confessio Amantis* (7.1783–1984) serves precisely to liberate the king who hears it from tyranny both political and sexual, in the *Legend* Alceste remains a signifier of Cupid.[41]

---

[39] Gower's *Confessio* has a striking and comparable example, where Genius, having listed and condemned each of the classical gods, is asked why he has omitted Venus and Cupid. He replies: "My Sone, I have it left for schame, / Be cause I am here oghne Prest" (5.1382–83). The work would occlude its governing principles, just as, I argue, the *Legend* does.

[40] The Man of Law's appropriation of the *Legend* for Cupid (comparable with the title *The Book of Troilus*) stands in marked contrast to Alceste's title for *Troilus and Criseyde*, to which she refers simply and revealingly as "Crisseyde" (G.344).

[41] For a fuller discussion, see Simpson, *Sciences and the Self*, pp. 282–84. Accounts of Alceste differ sharply, with some critics seeing her as complicit with Cupid (e.g., Rowe, *Through Nature to Eternity*, pp. 40–41; Delany, *The Naked Text*, p. 108; and Lee Patterson, " 'For the Wyves Love of Bathe': Feminine Rhetoric and Poetic Resolution in the *Roman de la Rose* and the *Canterbury Tales*," *Speculum* 58 (1983): 656–95 [see esp. p. 691]). Others understand her as an alternative, if mediatory, figure (Kiser, *Telling Classical Tales*, pp. 42–46; and Jill Mann, *Geoffrey Chaucer* (New York: Harvester Wheatsheaf, 1991), pp. 41–43).

Hyperbole applied to Alceste suits the God of Love: it gratifies male desire, that is, to figure all women as the readiness to suffer. But the hyperbole of Cupid as the figure of male desire clearly does not gratify that desire. For the gratification that Cupid derives from his reading about faithful, suffering women would be fatally flawed were the cause of their suffering traced back to him. Written under Cupid's control, the narrator's pointers to Cupid as the "yevere of the formes," both artistic and emotional, are necessarily covert, but all the more powerful for that. The narrator does not write as one liberated by Cupid, as Dinshaw would have it; on the contrary, he asks us to read his own work as the critique rather than the expression of male desire and male reading. He asks us to read differently from Cupid, not according to the mere pleasure or displeasure of the text, but rather with an eye to authorial intention, an intention that is visible precisely in the traces of its effacement.

Critics have often complained that the legends are repetitive. For this reason, so the argument has often gone, Chaucer got bored with the project.[42] From the perspective of Cupid as reader, however, we might redescribe the features of the *Legend* as the enforced characteristics of the cupidinous reader: like Amans in the *Confessio* or Tarquinius in the *Legend*, Cupid's reading relentlessly replicates the same cupidinous emotional pattern, "Th'ymage of hire recordynge alwey newe" (*LGW* 1760). It is, furthermore, held within very tight and depoliticized discursive limits.[43] Cupid wants one story, that of Alceste, and he wants it explicit: in the F version he charges the narrator with ingratitude for having left Alceste out of the ballade (when in fact the implicit exemplar in that ballade had been Alceste throughout—another example of poor cupidinous reading). In the G version he goes on to command narratives about Alceste, since she hyperbolically contains *all* wifely virtue (G.532–37):

> For of Alceste shulde thy wrytynge be,
> Syn that thow wost that calendier is she

---

[42] See Frank, *Chaucer and the Legend of Good Women*, Excursus, for a history and a persuasive refutation of the idea that Chaucer became bored with the poem. Dinshaw's chapter on the *Legend* in her *Chaucer's Sexual Poetics* is, it might be noted, a more recent addition to the "Chaucer got bored" tradition.

[43] For Amans as obsessive and repetitive reader in the *Confessio Amantis*, see Simpson, *Sciences and the Self*, pp. 254–59.

> Of goodnesse, for she taughte of fyn lovynge,
> And namely of wifhod the lyvynge,
> And alle the boundes that she oughte kepe.

The desire to read Alceste and all women back to the "boundes" that Cupid wants a woman to keep is Cupid's desire, not the narrator's. Like Philomela, the author Chaucer transmits messages out of the prison of readerly power and appropriation. Under the control of a tyrannical readerly "entente," the oppositional text becomes another kind of will, a document, like each of the *Heroides*, written by a "dying" author.

III

If what I have said so far were the whole story, we would have a Chaucer who was indeed "evir . . . all womanis frend."[44] My account of readerly power so far has not, however, mentioned female agency in both the legends and the *Prologue*. Alceste, we should remember, first commissions narratives of faithful and suffering women, because, I can only assume, this suits the interests of women in some ways. Alceste's command capitalizes on the one form of feminine praise that will not antagonize a cupidinous male audience. It is true that she demands stories about "false men" who "betrayen" true women (G.476), but as we have already seen, there is a peculiar Cupidinous logic that allows such stories: Cupid is quite prepared to have stories told of treacherous men as long as their treachery is not related back to Cupid himself. If that condition is observed, then a focus on suffering and faithful women serves a cupidinous desire for women who are only faithful and suffering. Such women become "relics," in both senses, of what Cupid calls "love": by being abandoned, they become numinous. Such stories would erase feminine violence and self-interest, and this erasure suits both Cupid *and* Alceste. The legends, from this perspective, can be seen to be "politically" acceptable, as it were, since they represent the very narrow, anodyne, negotiated space of what is politically allowable, for entirely different reasons, to both men and women, and so avoid the political. If we have seen how Chaucer insinuates messages out of the prison-house of his male readership, let us observe how he also communicates protest against the

[44] The phrase is Gavin Douglas's; see David F. C. Coldwell, ed., *Virgil's "Aeneid,"* *translated into Scottish Verse*, 4 vols., Scottish Text Society, 3d series, vols. 25, 27, 28, 30 (Edinburgh: William Blackwood & Sons, 1957–64), book 1, Prologue, line 449.

constraints of his feminine readership, as long, at any rate, as that readership is part of Cupid's textual "community."

Philomela is described as the author of her legend. She "wrot the storye above," of her own rape (*LGW* 2364). Even before we get to the end of Philomela's story, however, the narrator seeks to close it down: "Now is it tyme I make an ende sone," he says, immediately after he prays that she might be avenged (line 2341). After we have read to the end of Philomela's text, however, the story continues for another twenty-seven lines; it relates the message's transmission, and tries to end with the pathos of the sisters' embrace: "And thus I late hem in here sorowe dwelle" (line 2382). This attempt to end the story does not quite work, either, since this pathetic picture of the sisters suspended in feminine sorrow and solidarity is followed by an *occupatio*. "The remenaunt is no charge for to telle, / For this is al and som . . ." (lines 2383–84), the narrator insists, before warning all women against the labile desire of all men. The *Legend*, as we've seen, refers often to textual suppression. Whenever Chaucer says that it is unnecessary to say something, we should pause, and to pause here is to be reminded of the most terrifying moments in the *Metamorphoses*, where the sisters murder and serve up Tereus's son Itys to him (6.619–74). The terror of the scene is spectacularly suppressed; even the construction used concerning Philomela ("thus was she served") cannot help but evoke the Ovidian scene of serving Itys to Tereus. So far from presenting the "naked text in English" of "many a story," as he defines his "entente" in the opening lines of the *Prologue*, Chaucer instead alludes to the lurid violence suppressed in these texts.[45] To put it another way, if these texts are "naked," they bear the visible and terrible scars of deliberate excisions and even of amputations. The work is anodyne only as long as we read within the terms of its self-interested patrons and readers.

So excisions are made not only by the power of male readers; they also manifest the interests of women readers. The *Legend* is brimful of examples of badly suppressed female agency, ranging from the violence of Medea, Philomela, and Hypermnestra's sisters, all excised; to the rather banal self-interest of Ariadne; to the betrayal of Cleopatra, and,

[45] Fyler, *Chaucer and Ovid*, p. 99, best put the argument for the excisions as meaningful. He has been refuted by Mann, *Geoffrey Chaucer*, pp. 36–38. I fully accept what Mann says about the freedom to manipulate stories in this period without readers necessarily being expected to refer them back to a "source"; in the *Legend*, however, Chaucer draws attention to sources and excisions in a variety of ways; as in the instance discussed here, he is inviting us to notice what is cut out.

especially, to the extraordinary tale of Dido, which is poised between a Virgilian and an Ovidian perspective. In the Virgilian narrative, Dido's magnificent activity and agency are consistently stressed, beside the passivity of Aeneas.[46] All these examples of feminine agency are registered, but finally repressed in each narrative, as the tale returns to rest on an image of female victimization, by way of meeting the joint demand of both Cupid and Alceste. Each of these tales, and indeed the *Legend* as a whole, is a kind of postscript to the finally unfinishable and scandalous text of *Troilus and Criseyde*: each, like *Troilus and Criseyde*, does register feminine agency, but each represses that, since no narrowly consensual literary tradition can contain it.[47] A narrowly consensual tradition is instead locked into the anodyne limits of the politically allowable, that small, depoliticized discursive space acceptable to hostile parties. Any attempt to break the bounds of that space is certain to be dangerous. But the *Legend* is not itself politically anodyne; it is more the *representation* of straitjacketed art, where the strictures of the straitjacket pull violently. The repression of feminine agency involves the correlative repression of authorial agency.

IV

I would, then, apply the model of the *Heroides* to the *Legend* rather more extensively than previous critics: the Ovidian text not only supplies the model of a series of short narratives of betrayed women, but it also offers many models of "dying" authors, authors whose words are only barely audible, barely worth uttering in the face of readerly indifference and power: "*mea pro nullo pondere verba cadunt*," as Ovid's Briseis writes to Achilles (3.98). Like the suicidal Dido writing to the absent Aeneas, the narrator's discursive position borders on futility: "I may wel lese on yow a word or letter, / Al be it that I shall ben nevere the better" (lines 1363–64). As such, the *Legend*'s representation of dying author-heroines evokes not only the content of the *Heroides*, but also the biographical context of that text's production, as given in *accessus* at any rate. Many *accessus* account for the production of Ovidian works within the context of an imagined, and partially true, biography of

[46] Fyler, *Chaucer and Ovid*, pp. 98–115, provides an illuminating conspectus of examples of feminine agency excised from the *Legend*.

[47] Criseyde herself seems to recognize this, in her lament in book 5, lines 1054–77, where she complains not only that "thise bokes wol me shende," but also that "wommen moost wol haten me of alle."

Ovid.[48] The *Heroides* are no exception, presented as they are in some *accessus* as having both a moral and a personal intention. Ovid's ethical intention is to offer models of different kinds of exemplary love; behind this lies a desire to be recalled by Caesar from exile, having offended the Roman matrons with his earlier work, the *Ars amatoria*:

Qui positus in exilio vitam in longo tempore ducens, Romanarum mulierum benivolentiam sibi recuperare cupiens, epistolarum librum coposuit, in quo castas extollendo et incestas deprimendo ponit, ut earum benivolentia recepta, ad statum pristinum reducatur.[49]

This, along with other *accessus*, has it that Ovid writes (like Chaucer) in compensation for past works, and (like Chaucer) that he writes to reintegrate himself with both his feminine readership and his imperial male reader.[50] The content of the *Heroides*, then, suits this imagined biographical context, since the poet himself is also a banished, "dying" author, commanded to write nothing else until he dies but these legends "whil that thou livest, yer by yere" (G.470–71).

In saying, however, that the *Legend* is itself a kind of testament, or will, the last words of a "dying" author condemned to write the same thing until he dies, I seem to be recuperating the humanist Chaucer. I seem to posit an author beyond and sentient of oppressive power structures, to whose last, humane words, and first, originating intentions, we must attend with unquestioning assent.[51] That is not quite my position; there is no way back to a transcendent and originating voice in this text,

---

[48] See especially Fausto Ghisalberti, "Medieval Biographies of Ovid," *Journal of the Warburg and Courtauld Institutes* 9 (1946): 10–59.

[49] "[Ovid], who, living for a long time in exile, wished to recover the good-will of the Roman matrons, composed the book of letters, in which he describes the chaste with praise and the unchaste with criticism, in order that (their good-will recovered) he should return to his prior condition." Ghisalberti, "Medieval Biographies," p. 38, n. 3. The manuscript from which the citation is taken dates from the fourteenth century. See also appendix B, p. 44. The tradition of Ovid writing the *Heroides* in order to placate Augustus is also found in the twelfth-century *accessus* discussed in Ralph J. Hexter, *Ovid and Medieval Schooling: Studies in Medieval School Commentaries on Ovid's "Ars Amatoria," "Epistulae ex Ponto," and "Epistulae Heroidum,"* Münchener Beiträge, vol. 38 (Munich: Arbeo–Gesellschaft, 1986), p. 161.

[50] A point made by Copeland, *Rhetoric, Hermeneutics and Translation*, p. 188; see also Minnis, *Shorter Poems*, p. 393.

[51] I am thinking of (and responding to) Hansen's succinctly put point: "I claim, however, that the attempt to recuperate a feminist Chaucer who does not threaten the humanist Chaucer . . . is misguided"; *Chaucer and the Fictions of Gender*, p. 12.

since the author is already situated within preexisting structures of power, not only of subservience to Cupid, but also of fascinated and obsessive obeisance to Alceste, loving the daisy "ever ylike newe" (F.56). Besides, the example of Philomela serves to remind us that what are apparently final words can simply be the prelude to recriminatory violence. By the same token, the testamentary stance can itself mask a prior violence or treachery, as we can see most clearly in the case of Usk's *Testament of Love.*[52] Chaucer himself may be trying to clear his name from a past violence, his possible rape of Cecilia Chaumpaigne.[53]

I am suggesting, though, that the *Legend's* opening call to give "credence" to books is worth taking seriously: just as no one can talk of heaven and hell with authority, so too no one, the *Legend* implies, can talk safely or authoritatively of the heaven and hell of gender relations. Citing Dante, another exiled poet (G.336), Alceste articulates the rhetorical conditions of Love's court powerfully, if a little too discreetly (G.326–32):

> Al ne is nat gospel that is to yow pleyned;
> The god of Love hereth many a tale yfeyned.
> For in youre court is many a losengeour,
> And many a queynte totelere accusour,
> That tabouren in youre eres many a thyng
> For hate, or for jelous ymagynyng,
> And for to han with you som dalyaunce.

What Alceste characteristically omits, of course, is the subliminal and occasionally explicit directions of Cupid himself, which provoke the "jelous ymagynyng" in the first place. The power of those directions, on the evidence of the *Prologue*, ensures that Cupid hears what he wants to hear, and so precludes the possibility of "gospel" ever being heard in his court, the "*regnum cupiditatis*," as Augustine would put it. The best an unwilling writer of works written at Cupid's command can do is to

---

[52] For the political context of Usk's *Testament* (and particularly Usk's betrayal of his former allies), see Paul Strohm, "Politics and Poetics: Usk and Chaucer in the 1380's," in Lee Patterson, ed., *Literary Practice and Social Change in Britain, 1380–1530* (Berkeley and Los Angeles: University of California Press, 1990), pp. 83–112.

[53] However circumspect its conclusions, the most recent (and the best) contribution to the question of whether or not Chaucer was involved in a rape case (from charges of which he was released in May 1380) would incline me to believe that it *was* a case of rape in the modern sense; see Christopher Cannon, "*Raptus*, in the Chaumpaigne Release and a Newly Discovered Document Concerning the Life of Geoffrey Chaucer," *Speculum* 68 (1993): 74–94.

represent the construction of gender myths *as* a construction, drawing
attention to their terrible excisions. And for readers, too, the discursive
conditions of Cupid's court put real pressure on any sources of information, since they can have been produced only in unpropitious circumstances (G.17–28):

> Thanne mote we to bokes that we fynde,
> Thourgh whiche that olde thynges ben in mynde,
> And to the doctryne of these olde wyse
> Yeven credence, in every skylful wise,
> And trowen on these olde aproved storyes
> Of holynesse, of regnes, of victoryes,
> Of love, of hate, of othere sondry thynges,
> Of which I may nat make rehersynges.
> And if that olde bokes weren aweye,
> Yloren were of remembrance the keye.
> Wel oughte us thanne on olde bokes leve,
> There as there is non other assay by preve.

Chaucer here is asking us to exert pressure on "olde aproved storyes":
by whom were they approved? At the same time, he suggests that we
might invest this new poem with the faithful "credence, in every
skylful wise," that we bring as a prejudice to canonical texts.
Remembrance's key is extremely difficult to find in the relentlessly ahistorical, appropriative conditions of Cupid's court, but texts will, as this
one does, bear the traces of their production and approval. A good readerly "entente" is the premise of understanding a text that speaks the
coded language produced by oppressive conditions, just as Chaucer, listening to the birds, understands a foreign "language" by exercising all
his "entente, / For-why I mette I wiste what they mente" (G.139–40).
And a good authorial "entente" might even rescue old texts, as the narrator suggests in his ignored defense of writing about Criseyde and
translating the *Rose* (G.460–63):

> . . . what so myn auctour mente,
> Algate, God wot, it was myn entente
> To forthere trouthe in love and it cheryce,
> And to be war fro falsnesse and fro vice
> By swich ensaumple; this was my menynge.

In the irredeemably distorted rhetorical conditions of Cupid's court, all
we as readers can do is define the constraints and suppressions that

might efface an authorial "entente" or will. The good faith we exercise in reading toward an authorial "entente," a "*conclusioun*" of someone "fettred in *prysoun*" (the poem's final rhyme; my emphases) at least offers an alternative model of society to the relentlessly tyrannical and faithless practice of the legends themselves. Hermeneutics and ethics are intimately related.

My principal objection to Fish, then, is that insofar as his account of the institution of interpretation is normative, as Rorty's certainly is, it cannot respond to abnormal, "tyrannical" hermeneutic phenomena satisfactorily. He can only say either that such phenomena are not abnormal, but produced by the system, or that they are not hermeneutic interventions, since the interpretive community cannot so judge them. The first of these responses seems to me to offer no ethical defense against brutal textual communities, and the second is gratuitous, since a successfully tyrannical textual "community" does, by definition, have the numbers and power to force acceptance of what it regards as "reasonable." Even if, then, Fish's account of interpretive practice were persuasive as a description, it still seems to me to be ethically vulnerable as a normative model. One way in which I think Fish's account could strengthen its ethical defense, and become a more persuasive normative model, is to offer a fuller welcome to interpretive faith.

As his account stands, Fish certainly recognizes the role of faith in the perception of intentions, since we faithfully posit a meaning not stated by "the words on the page," but he just as quickly neutralizes that by saying that 1) interpretation is necessarily intentionalist, which makes intention methodologically useless; and 2) our faith is, after all, only a fabrication of the interpretive community after all. The first of these points is incorrect. *The Legend of Good Women* reveals faithful perception of intention to be a useful methodological tool, insofar as it can discriminate between competing intentions, let alone discriminating between Chaucer's intended meanings and those he possibly does not and cannot know. The second point seems to me an example of bad faith. An account of the practice of textual communities can only be made on the basis of claiming really to have understood how such communities, whether past or present, really work. If the description itself is founded on such a claim, then it refutes its own argument that textual communities make texts rather than find them. Fish argues, that is, that we are inevitably locked out of understanding of what authors from other textual communities really meant. Such an argument inevitably deploys, however, what are presented as understandings of what writers in other textual communities really meant.

Perhaps Fish, unlike Rorty, has no normative ambitions whatsoever, but merely describes the inevitable characteristics of textual communities. If so, then his description is itself methodologically useless, since it simply describes the way things have to be, and can make no difference to the way we interpret. In that light, his position is also a matter of faith, since it could never conceive of a counterexample. I prefer the faith by which we believe that there really are meanings in texts, to the faith that believes we fabricate such meanings. Reflection on *The Legend of Good Women* reveals that the purely secular faith we exercise in interpreting meanings we believe to be "really there" is only an example of the faith we exercise daily in the various societies we all inhabit. Without such faithful attention to words, and any signs, those "tenues et obscurae notae . . . voluntatis," as Cicero calls them,[54] the very possibility of "community," textual or otherwise, collapses.

---

[54] H. M. Hubbell, ed., *Cicero, De Inventione* (Cambridge, Mass.: Harvard University Press, 1949), 2.48.141, p. 309. In the wider passage from which this is drawn, Cicero is imagining how an intentionalist would argue that the law must be interpreted intentionally, rather than by the letter.

Meanings and Uses of *Raptus* in Chaucer's Time

Henry Ansgar Kelly
University of California, Los Angeles

The question of Geoffrey Chaucer's connection with the *raptus* of Cecily Champain has greatly interested literary historians since the matter first came to light in the 1870s. A recent breakthrough in the discussions came with Christopher Cannon's discovery of a new and different version of a release that Champain made to Chaucer on the same day, May 1, 1380.[1] I wish to review some of Cannon's findings here and to offer further considerations, especially on the various ranges of meanings that were given to the term *raptus* in fourteenth-century England, in the hopes of throwing additional light on the episode and clarifying or expanding its hermeneutic possibilities.

Professor Cannon informs me that many readers of his article have come to the mistaken conclusion that he has proved that Chaucer sexually violated Cecily Champain. His actual conclusion is only that Champain released Chaucer from a charge of sexual violation. I will conclude below that Cannon is probably correct, even though his argument may have to be qualified to some extent, especially with regard to the meaning of *raptus* in legal settings. As we will see, the term was used to mean not only sexual rape but also abduction, short for "ravishing and abducting," sometimes in circumstances where there is no possibility of sexual implications, as when referring to the kidnapping of a male heir.

After reviewing the Champain releases and considering various interpretations of *raptus*, we will discuss ways in which charges of *raptus* were employed, sometimes for different purposes. That is, we will see

[1] Christopher Cannon, "*Raptus* in the Chaumpaigne Release and a Newly Discovered Document Concerning the Life of Geoffrey Chaucer," *Speculum* 68 (1993): 74–94. I am grateful to Professor Cannon (recently my colleague at UCLA) for discussing all aspects of the case with me and for helping me in various ways, including dealing with the Public Record Office at a distance. I am also grateful to Brigette Bedos-Rezak, Paul Brand, and Charles Donahue, Jr., for their very helpful advice on this study.

101

instances in which sexual violation or abduction, with or without forced sex, was alleged without any basis in fact, but simply in order to get other grievances, real ones, into court. On the other side, we will see that when there was a factual basis to the *raptus* charge, a fictitious charge of another kind was sometimes brought against the culprit, notably that of assault, regularly characterized as a savage beating that left the victim barely clinging to life. We will be particularly interested in the options that various kinds of females (underage wards, mature wards, those who owned their own marriage-rights, married women, widows) had in acting against men who wronged them.

My objective is not to come to any definitive solutions, which is not yet possible with the present gaps in our knowledge, but to move the discussion forward and to call for further research in the abundant unstudied archives of the law, following Cannon's admirable example.

I. Cecily With and Without *Raptus meus*

First let us summarize the bare facts of the Champain-Chaucer case and some of their implications. On May 4, 1380, Cecily Champain, identifying herself as "late the daughter of William Champain and his wife Agnes" ("filia quondam[2] Willelmi Chaumpaigne et Agnetis uxoris ejus"), came to Chancery to enroll a document (*scriptum*) stating that on May 1 she released Geoffrey Chaucer from all actions concerning her "rape" (*raptus*) and any other cause. Besides this copy of the release, three other documents seemingly connected with the episode have long been known; they too are enrollment copies, this time from the court of the mayor of London, and, to accept Theodore Plucknett's interpretation, they deal with friends of Chaucer who helped to finance a monetary settlement to Champain. On June 28, 1380, the cutler Richard Goodchild and the armorer John Grove released Chaucer from all actions of law that they had against him, and on the same day Champain similarly released Goodchild and Grove from all actions that she had against them. Four days later, on July 2, Grove acknowledged that he owed Champain ten pounds, payable at Michaelmas.[3] Martin Crow and Clair Olson, the editors of *Chaucer Life-Records*, conclude:

---

[2] For a discussion in 1330 of the meaning of *quondam*, see Donald W. Sutherland, ed., *The Eyre of Northamptonshire*, vol. 2, Selden Society [hereafter SS] vol. 98 (London, 1983), pp. 568–70.

[3] T. F. T. Plucknett, "Chaucer's Escapade," *Law Quarterly Review* 64 (1948): 34. Plucknett is commenting on P. R. Watts, "The Strange Case of Geoffrey Chaucer and Cecilia Chaumpaigne," *Law Quarterly Review* 63 (1947): 491–515.

No more is known as to the nature of this *raptus* than is contained in the records just given, nor have any additional records clarifying the case come to light. Two theories have been advanced to explain the situation: (1) that it was a case of physical rape or seduction; (2) that it concerned the kidnapping or abduction of a young person, possibly in order to make an advantageous marriage. According to either theory Chaucer could have been a principal or an accessory.[4]

As noted above, Christopher Cannon has made a major contribution to our understanding of this episode by discovering another quitclaim that Champain made to Chaucer: on May 7 she came to the Court of King's Bench[5] with a *scriptum* that she asserted was a release made to Chaucer on May 1. This document, however, does not mention her *raptus* but gives only a vague reference to various kinds of charges or actions. Specifically, in place of *omnimodas acciones tam de raptu meo tam de aliqua alia re vel causa* ("all kinds of actions not only concerning my rape but also concerning any other matter or cause"), there are these words: *omnimodas acciones tam de feloniis, transgressionibus, compotis, debitis quam aliis accionibus quibuscumque* ("all kinds of actions not only concerning felonies, trespasses, accounts, and debts, but also all other kinds of actions").[6]

Raptus in the sense of abduction could be charged by indictment of a (grand) jury either as a felony (a capital offense) or as a criminal trespass

---

[4] Martin M. Crow and Clair C. Olson, *Chaucer Life-Records* (Oxford: Clarendon Press, 1966), p. 345; Champain's release is given on p. 343, and the three other documents on pp. 344–45. In my citations of medieval Latin, French, and English I follow modern conventions for *i/j* and *u/v* and use my own capitalization and punctuation.

[5] This was the central court, usually called *Coram rege*, in the fourteenth century. The other central court, later called Common Pleas, dealt only with civil cases and private criminal cases (that is, appeals of felony), while the Crown side of the King's Bench handled criminal cases brought by the king, and the Plea side dealt not only with civil cases but also with felony appeals. See J. H. Baker, *An Introduction to English Legal History*, 3d ed. (London: Butterworths, 1990), pp. 45–46. Baker says that the name "Common Pleas" came into use only in Tudor times, but "Common Bench" can be found well before Chaucer's day. See, for instance, *Year Books of Richard II*, vol. 2, *6 Richard II (1382–1383)*, ed. Samuel E. Thorne et al. (Cambridge, Mass.: The Ames Foundation, 1996), pp. 33–34, where *Bank le Roi* is distinguished from *Comine Bank* (French) or *Communis Bancus* (Latin).

[6] Cannon, *"Raptus,"* p. 89, citing PRO (Public Record Office), KB 27/477 (Easter term, 1380), m. 58d. Champain's release of Goodchild and Grove specifies *omnimodas acciones querelas et demandas tam reales quam personales* ("all kinds of actions, complaints, and demands, whether of property or person"), and Goodchild and Grove's release of Chaucer has *omnimodas acciones querelas et demandas . . . racione alicujus transgressionis convencionis contractus compoti debiti vel alterius rei cujuscumque realis vel personalis* (". . . by reason of any trespass, agreement, contract, account, debt, or any other real or personal matter"). The four formulas also differ in expressing the temporal coverage of the release; see below at n. 75.

(in later terminology, a misdemeanor). *Raptus* as abduction could also be charged as a civil trespass (a "tort," in modern terms) in a suit brought by someone who claims monetary damages (and at the same time seeks a fine for the king, enforceable by imprisonment). When *raptus* refers to a sexual offense, the victim herself could charge the alleged culprit by way of "appeal," as a felony. To my knowledge, no example has yet been found of a woman appealing sexual rape as a criminal trespass, or of suing it as a civil trespass. Though it has been asserted by John Marshall Carter that "if a woman had sexual relations with a man against her wishes, she could theoretically bring an action of trespass against the man," the single example that he gives probably has a different explanation. He describes the case thus: when an appeal of rape was brought by Margery, daughter of Emma de la Hulle, against Nicholas Whatcomb in 1248, the court found that he had carnal knowledge of her but that he did not "forcibly ravish" her; he was declared "in mercy for the trespass," and fined ten marks.[7] But it is likely that Margery originally appealed the crime as felony (with a penalty of death or mutilation), and that when her appeal was "abated" (that is, the charge was found to be deficient), the jury convicted him of a trespass, as happened in other cases of the time.[8] But in this instance, since consensual sex was only an ecclesiastical crime, punishable in the church courts, as is noted at the beginning of Chaucer's *Friar's Tale*,[9] the trespass would have to be something other than *raptus*, say, the forcible breaking of the mother's close "by force and arms" (a standard fictitious charge, as we will see).[10] When charged by way of indictment, sexual rape was usually designated a felony. However, in the quarter-session cases collected by Bertha Putnam,[11]

---

[7] John Marshall Carter, *Rape in Medieval England: An Historical and Sociological Study* (Lanham: University Press of America, 1985), pp. 39–40.

[8] See my "Statutes of Rapes and Alleged Ravishers of Wives: A Context for the Charges Against Thomas Malory, Knight," *Viator* 28 (1997): 361–419, esp. pp. 382–83.

[9] See my *Love and Marriage in the Age of Chaucer* (Ithaca, N.Y.: Cornell University Press, 1975), pp. 169–71. Thomas Aquinas, *Summa theologie* 2–2.69.1 ad 1, gives simple fornication as an example of a crime that is restricted only to the internal forum of confession and not a matter for the external forum; but in England, fornication was indeed prosecuted in the church courts. See my "Right to Remain Silent: Before and After Joan of Arc," *Speculum* 68 (1993): 992–1026, esp. p. 1003, n. 46.

[10] Carter's suggestion that the court reduced the charge when actual coitus could not be proved (p. 40) is belied by the record: coitus was found, but not forced coitus.

[11] Bertha Haven Putnam, *Proceedings Before the Justices of the Peace in the Fourteenth and Fifteenth Centuries* (London, 1938), with "A Commentary on the Indictments" (pp. cxxxiii–clxi) and analytical index (pp. 468–82) by Theodore F. T. Plucknett. Putnam has isolated fifty-three rolls of shire sessions of the peace from 1338 to 1475 and

there are a few examples in which words of felony were omitted—that is, the offense was charged as a trespass.[12]

Charging abduction as a felony or a trespass sometimes seems, from this distance, to be fairly arbitrary, a conclusion that Cannon reached concerning the abduction of wives in studying the court records of 3 Richard II, 1379–80.[13] A slightly later example of such apparent arbitrariness can be seen in the case of abduction that Chaucer investigated as a justice *ad inquirendum* in 1387. He and others were appointed to discover who the malefactors were who ravished and abducted Isabel, daughter and heir of William Hall, being underage and in the custody of Thomas Carshill. The jury indicted three men of the crime and declared their offense a felony: "felonice rapuerunt et abduxerunt,"[14] thus apparently going beyond the original allegation. But unless the jury was sold a complete bill of goods by Carshill, it is difficult to believe that it elevated the offense from a trespass to a felony because sexual rape was involved,[15] since one of the accused, John Lording, was Isabel's husband, and was so recognized by the King's Bench in civil suits that he brought against his accusers and others before and after he pleaded not guilty to the felony charge.[16]

---

printed excerpts from twenty of the rolls; and she also notes (p. lxii) that the sort of cases heard by the Justices of the Peace are identical to those that came before the Crown side of the King's Bench. For some of the formulas used in the cases under discussion, see under "Robbery: Wife and chattels," p. 473, and "Rape," p. 474.

[12] In 1357 (p. 183, no. 17)—cited by Plucknett, "Commentary," pp. clix–clx—a man designated as a common disturber of the peace was charged with abducting a female servant and forcing himself upon her: "cepit et abduxit et concubuit cum ea contra voluntatem suam et contra pacem." In a similar case from the same year and place (Somerset), the alleged victim is a widow, and there is no abduction noted (pp. 184–85, no. 26): "rapuit et cum ea concubuit contra voluntatem suam et contra pacem." In 1363, a rector (parish priest) was accused of the trespass entering a woman's property *vi et armis*, taking her and sleeping with her against the peace ("cepit et cum ea concubuit contra pacem"), with "against her will" doubtless being understood (p. 369, no. 526). Another rector was charged in 1375 (p. 119, no. 157) with the trespass of seizing a wife and forcing her against her will ("rapuit . . . et illam aforciavit contra voluntatem suam"). In 1391 (pp. 219–20, no. 35), a man was charged with the trespass of forcibly entering a house and deflowering a servant against her will ("en countre sa volunte parcocha, pargisa, et defoila") and the next night coming and taking her away to his own service against the statute (concerning the regulation of servants).

[13] Cannon, *"Raptus,"* pp. 87–88.

[14] Crow and Olson, *Chaucer Life-Records*, pp. 375–76.

[15] A principle of this kind was enunciated by one of the justices of the King's Bench in 1409, *Nansegle v Vide*, Yearbook of Henry IV: *Les reports del cases en ley que furent argues en le temps de tres haut et puissant princes, les roys Henry le IV et Henry le V* (London, 1689; rpt., Oxford: Professional Books, 1981), year 11, p. 13; see Kelly, "Statutes of Rapes," pp. 397, 410–12.

[16] Crow and Olson, *Chaucer Life-Records*, pp. 379–81.

In a case earlier in the decade involving Ralph Percy, the brother of Henry Hotspur, commissioners of oyer and terminer were instructed to investigate and judge a ravishing-and-abducting case both as a felony and as a misdemeanor: on February 15, 1384, they were appointed to hear and determine a trespass alleged in a complaint by Percy against John Halsham, namely, ravishing his wife Philippa and abducting her with goods and chattels worth £3,000, and on the next day the same commissioners were appointed to find out what malefactors and breakers of the peace feloniously ravished Philippa, wife of Ralph Percy, knight, and abducted her with Percy's goods and chattels.[17] Like Lording, Halsham was revealed to be the current husband of the allegedly abducted woman.[18]

As noted, ravishing-abducting could be prosecuted not only as a (criminal) felony or a criminal trespass but also as a civil trespass. This is illustrated by Lording's civil suits, and, contrary to what we might conclude from the felony charge delivered by Chaucer's jury, it was also the common procedure in wardship kidnappings.[19] Only one explicit case of ward abduction is to be found in Putnam's criminal rolls: an indictment for ravishing, taking, and abducting an underage male ward; and it is not charged as a felony.[20] But though wardship pleas "sounded in tort rather than crime," as Sue Sheridan Walker puts it in modern terms,[21] there is nevertheless a criminal element in the charge, an allegation that the violence was *contra pacem domini regis*, though not prosecuted as such. This was true also of many other kinds of civil trespass cases, as can be seen in Morris Arnold's collection.[22] However, there was a principle enunciated in 1339 by William Shareshull, a justice of the

[17] PRO, C66/317, m. 20d, recorded in reverse order; briefly summarized in *Calendar of Patent Rolls {CPR}: Richard II*, 2:423–24; for a fuller summary, see *Calendar of the Close Rolls {CCR}*, 2:452: two writs of *Supersedeas* issued on May 28, 1384, suspending the commissions (PRO, C54/224, m. 2d). For published calendars of documents in the PRO, see E. L. C. Mullins, *Texts and Calendars: An Analytical Guide to Serial Publications*, 2 vols. (London: Royal Historical Society, 1978–83), 1:16–36, 2:3–12: Public Record Office Texts and Calendars.

[18] For more on the Percy abduction, see below, and for both Lording and Percy cases, see Kelly, "Statutes of Rapes," pp. 403–7.

[19] See Sue Sheridan Walker, "Wrongdoing and Compensation: The Pleas of Wardship in Thirteenth and Fourteenth Century England," *Journal of Legal History* 9 (1988): 267–307, esp. 286–90.

[20] Putnam, *Proceedings*, pp. 71–72, n.138 (1352).

[21] Walker, "Wrongdoing," p. 268.

[22] Morris S. Arnold, *Select Cases of Trespass from the King's Courts, 1307–1399*, 2 vols., SS, vols. 100, 103 (London, 1985–87).

King's Bench, speaking about a case of an abducted wife, that the Crown had the option of considering a civil trespass conviction to be a felony indictment.[23] It was not always easy to distinguish between criminal and civil actions.[24] We can perhaps be fairly sure that only criminal cases were heard by the justices of the peace (Putnam's cases), and we should be able to presume that only civil trespasses and private crimes (appeals of felony) were heard by the Court of Common Pleas. But in 1382, William Skipwith, one of the justices of Common Pleas, said that since the word *rapuit* ("ravished," "raped") in the writ *De uxore rapta* "sounded in felony," such cases should not be heard by Common Pleas but only by King's Bench.[25] This shows not only that the line between civil and criminal cases of abduction was hard to draw, but also that borderline felony cases were being heard by Common Pleas, and that, since Skipwith's fellow-justices overruled him,[26] the practice continued.

The "accounts" and "debts" mentioned in the May 7 version of the release could refer only to civil and not to criminal charges. Plucknett, in his comment on the May 4 version of the release—which, of course, was the only one he knew—concludes, for reasons to be discussed below, that the *raptus* in question could only be sexual rape, but nevertheless he also concludes that her advisers (who seem to have been skilled) believed that she had a civil remedy for rape, and that her release was a bar to it.[27] But this leaves the question unanswered, he says, of how such a civil release might affect criminal remedies, or whether one could simultaneously bring criminal and civil actions. According to Plucknett, the modern law on the matter goes back only to the seventeenth century, but E. W. Ives cites an interesting abduction case only a century after Chaucer's time, in 1502, which may be relevant in showing what actions a woman well connected with the legal profession could take.

The case is as follows. A twenty-five-year-old widow, Margaret Kebell, was abducted and forced to marry one of her abductors, Roger Vernon, whereupon her relatives secured a commission in London ordering investigations and arrests in Staffordshire, and they also laid

---

[23] *Year Books of the Reign of King Edward III*, Rolls Series, 31b, vol. 3, p. 65. See J. B. Post, "Sir Thomas West and the Statute of Rapes, 1382," *Bulletin of the Institute of Historical Research* 53 (1980): 24–30, esp. p. 25.

[24] See S. F. C. Milsom, "Trespass from Henry III to Edward III," *Law Quarterly Review* 74 (1958): 195–224, 407–36, 561–90, pp. 197 and 584–85.

[25] *Year Books of Richard II*, 2:33.

[26] Ibid., 2:33–34.

[27] Plucknett, "Chaucer's Escapade," p. 35.

information at various quarter sessions (presided over by justices of the peace). After indictments were presented and trials resulted in acquittals, the widow herself appealed her abductors of rape in two counties, and she also pursued several civil actions for trespass in King's Bench and in Common Pleas.[28]

The Staffordshire indictments of March 16, 1502, accused Vernon and his associates of feloniously breaking the close of William Basset with the intention of feloniously ravishing and abducting Margaret, and of actually feloniously ravishing her and taking and abducting her against her will by main force, and feloniously assaulting Basset.[29] An earlier Staffordshire indictment, of February 21, 1502, charged the designated perpetrators with breaking Basset's close, assaulting Margaret to near death, feloniously ravishing her and abducting and carrying her away against her will, and also feloniously taking away £100 of her goods and chattels; the breaking and entering is then counted as a felony, added to which is an assault on Basset, likewise to within an inch of his life.[30] The Derbyshire indictments of March 17, 1502, made accusations of congregating with force and arms at Thorp and causing great terror against the statute on riots and routs, and of

---

[28] E. W. Ives, " 'Agaynst taking awaye of Women': The Inception and Operation of the Abduction Act of 1487," in *Wealth and Power in Tudor England: Essays Presented to S. T. Bindoff*, ed. E. W. Ives et al. (London: Athlone Press, 1978), pp. 21–44, esp. pp. 33–38. By the act of 3 Henry VII (1487), accomplices of the "taking away" of women could be charged as principals. The statute avoids the ambiguous words "ravish" and "ravishment" (see "Statutes of Rapes," pp. 376–77), but the court records continue to use the standard terms, *rapere* and *raptus*.

[29] PRO, KB 9/425 no. 29; KB 27/966 (Hilary term, 1503) Rex (at the end of the roll), m. 6; repeated in KB 27/981 (Michaelmas term, 1506), m. 109.1d (= dorso side of first of four membranes), when Richard Bargh and other defendants cite it (and their acquittal) as part of their defense against Margaret's appeal: according to the indictment, over 200 named and unnamed persons "vi et armis clausum et domos Willielmi Bassett armigeri apud Blore in comitatu Staff. noctanter ac burglariter et felonice fregerunt et intravenerunt ad intencionem felonice rapiendi et abducendi Margaretam Kebell viduam ibidem existentem, et eandem Margaretam adtunc et ibidem inventam felonice rapuerunt et ipsam Margaretam adtunc et ibidem contra voluntatem suam manuforte abinde ceperunt et abduxerunt, et super predictum Willielmum Bassett adtunc et ibidem insultum fecerunt ac ipsum maletractaverunt ita quod de vita ejus disperabatur, contra pacem dicti Domini regis, coronam, et dignitatem suas" ["by force and arms broke the close and homes of William Basset, esquire, at Blore in County Stafford by night and like burglars and feloniously, and entered with the intention of feloniously ravishing and abducting Margaret Kebell, widow, who was staying there, and the same Margaret being found then and there they did ravish, and did take her there and abduct her thence against her will by main force, and upon the said William Basset then and there they did make assault and did maltreat him so that his life was despaired of, against the peace of the lord king and his crown and dignity"].

[30] KB 9/426 no. 11 (Roger Vernon and others); KB 27/966, mm. 6–6d (Richard Bargh and others). The latter record goes on to relate that the king called in the indictments in

assaulting Margaret Kebell such that her life was despaired of, and of feloniously taking and ravishing her against her will and abducting her to *le Peek* in Derbyshire, against the recent statute.[31] A Leicestershire indictment of March 28, 1502, specifies riotous assault upon Margaret and felonious ravishing and abducting of her, against the recent statute, and it charges William Vernon with knowingly receiving the felons at Netherscheyll.[32] Another Leicestershire indictment, of October 3, 1502, accuses Roger Vernon and others of assaulting Margaret at Netherscheyll and feloniously ravishing and abducting her against the recent statute, and William Vernon of receiving them.[33]

On June 17, 1502, Margaret submitted a bill to the king's council: "To prove William Vernon, brother to Sir Henry Vernon, knight, guilty of felous taking and ravishment of Margaret Kebell, widow, and of the felous receiving by the said William Vernon of Roger Vernon and divers other parties privy to the ravishment." In the interrogatories that follow, "taking away" and "ravishment" are used as synonyms both interchangeably and together (by way of "indenture English").[34] Margaret does not refer to sexual interference or forced marriage, either in her bill or in her response to the statement of William Vernon.[35]

On December 9, 1503, Vernon and 109 others were pardoned of "all trespasses, congregations, burglaries and misdeeds for the taking, abduction, or rape" [*capcio, abduccio, vel raptus*] of Margaret Kebell.[36] On March 23, 1504, Vernon was required to give heavy surety to keep the peace toward Margaret, pledging to do no harm to her and specifically promising not to abduct her or cause her to be abducted without her consent ("et preterea quod idem Rogerus absque consensu et assensu ejusdem Margarete ipsam non abducet nec abduci faciet").[37]

January of 1503, and in Michaelmas term the four named defendants (Richard Bargh and three others) were acquitted. In KB 27/969 (Michaelmas 1503) Rex, m. 3 similar indictments of March 16 and February 21 are given against Thomas Folijamb, who is also acquitted.

[31] KB 9/425 no. 34 (a supplementary indictment says that they led her further into Derbyshire and finally out of the county, to unknown parts); KB 27/969 Rex, m. 3d.

[32] KB 9/426 no. 7.

[33] KB 9/437 no. 10.

[34] Printed by I. S. Leadam, *Select Cases Before the King's Council in the Star Chamber*, SS, vol. 16 (London, 1903), pp. 130–37, along with related materials (cf. pp. cx–cxiv) from PRO STAC 1/19/17, 1–3.

[35] PRO, STAC 2/25/68.

[36] *CPR Henry VII*, 2:336–337; the pardon is submitted as a defense in KB 27/990 (Hilary term, 1509) Rex m. 13.1d (see below).

[37] PRO, C 244/153 no. 117 (no. 118 is identical).

Margaret's appeal accuses the culprits of premeditated assault against the king's peace and feloniously taking and abducting her, and she states that immediately after the said felons committed the said felony and rape they fled, and she in timely manner pursued them from vill to vill (in accord with the standard formula).[38] But most records simply specify her appeal as one of rape (*de raptu ipsius Margarete*).[39]

As for the civil suits, one of the King's Bench cases is at an advanced stage and therefore unspecific, referring only to Margaret's plea of trespass against Henry Crichelowe.[40] But another is a standard plea of assault, wounding, and imprisonment, brought against one Ralph Wheledon of Doweall in co. Derby.[41] He is number 48 and Crichelowe is number 105 of the men named in the pardon.[42] In Keilwey's report of the Common Pleas case, which he refers to simply as a trespass plea, he says that when Vernon tried to invoke spousal privilege, Margaret

[38] KB 27/981 (Michaelmas term, 1506), m. 109.1, gives a complete rehearsal of her appeal. The defendants are to answer "de raptu ipsius Margarete et pace domini regis nunc fracte unde eos appellat." She says that when she was in the peace of God and the king on February 1, 1502, at Blore at the sixth hour of the morning, the defendants "felonice ut felones . . . insidiando et insultu premeditato contra pacem ejusdem domini regis . . . predictam Margaretam Kebell . . . contra voluntatem suam vi et armis [the arms are specified] illicite et felonice ceperunt et abduxerunt contra pacem, coronam, et dignitatem dicti domini regis ac contra formam statuti ejusdem domini regis anno regni suo tercio apud Westmonasterium inde editi et provisi; et quam cito iidem felones feloniam et raptum predictos in forma predicta fecissent, fugierunt; eciamque Margareta ipsos recenter insecuta fuit de villa in villam usque quatuor villatas propinquiores et ulterius, quousque, etc." ["feloniously as felons . . . by way of ambush and premeditated assault upon the peace of the same lord king . . . the aforesaid Margaret against her will by force and arms . . . they did unlawfully and feloniously take and abduct against the peace, crown, and dignity of the said lord king and against the form of the statute of the same lord king issued and provided on this matter at Westminster in the third year of his reign; and as soon as the same felons had committed the aforesaid felony and rape, they fled; and likewise Margaret in timely fashion pursued them from town to town through the four nearest townships, whitherever, etc."].

[39] KB 27/979 (Easter 1506), mm. 44, 50–50d; 27/980 (Trinity 1506), mm. 65–65d; 27/983 (Easter 1507), m. 29d; 27/984 (Trinity 1507), m. 26; 27/987 (Easter 1508), m. 27d; 27/988 (Trinity 1508), m. 20.

[40] KB 27/983 (Easter 1507), m. 17.

[41] KB 27/987 (Easter 1508), m. 48: "de placito quare vi et armis in ipsam Margaretam apud Blore insultum prebuit et ipsam verberavit, vulneravit, imprisonavit, et maletractavit, ita quod de vita ejus desperabatur, et alia enormia, etc., ad grave dampnum, etc., et contra pacem domini regis nunc, etc." ["concerning a plea why he made assault upon her at Blore and beat, wounded, imprisoned, and ill-treated her such that her life was despaired of, and other enormities, etc., to the grave harm, etc., and against the peace of the lord king now, etc."]. Ives says there is another case on m. 40, but none appears there or in the vicinity. On m. 45, however, there is an entry referring to the Wheledon case.

[42] Wheledon's town is given in the pardon as Dowell, as in KB 27/979 (Easter 1506), m. 50, where *Roger* Wheledon is no. 50 of the 90 defendants in Margaret's appeal of rape.

responded by saying that the marriage was against her will, and occurred only after threats and harsh imprisonment, and she sought damages.[43] It is clear that she brought up the circumstances of her forced marriage in order to bar Vernon's privilege, but these circumstances may also have been the substance of her complaint. In the event, Vernon's defense was accepted by the justices of the Common Bench: Margaret was to be regarded as Vernon's wife until a Church court said otherwise.[44] Margaret eventually shook off Vernon's marital claims, while continuing her campaign to punish her kidnappers;[45] she obtained a dispensation to marry Ralph Egerton, and became the grandmother of Lord Ellesmere,[46] whose manuscript of Chaucer we all know about.

We see, then, that Margaret used both criminal and civil actions for assault, and she could have added civil suits to the criminal accusation of taking and carrying away goods. Other possible actions of civil trespass which could conceivably be taken in connection with sexual attack and abduction are (to draw on Arnold's categories): threats, besetting, and false imprisonment.

When Plucknett says, "Although compounding a felony was a crime, compounding a trespass was probably not,"[47] we should note that compounding felonies (agreeing with the accused criminal not to prosecute, or to withdraw from prosecution, in return for a consideration of some sort) does not seem to have been criminalized as yet in Chaucer's time,

---

[43] Robert Keilwey, *Reports d'ascuns cases qui ont evenus aux temps du roy Henry le septiême* (London, 1688), fols. 52v–53, rpt. in *The English Reports*, 171 vols. (Edinburgh: W. Green, 1900–1930), 72:210–11.

[44] Ives, "'Agaynst taking awaye,'" pp. 38–39.

[45] Ives did not continue his search for records beyond the death of Henry VII in April of 1509. The last of the documents cited is KB 27/990 (Hilary 1509) Rex, mm. 13.1–13.2: the Staffordshire and Derbyshire indictments of 1502 are put to Richard Forman and others and they plead the pardon of December 9, 1503, for all crimes committed in the *capcio, abduccio, vel raptus* of Margaret Kebell, and also produce a writ dated February 1, 1509, ordering no interference with the pardon. But since the pardon did not cover the charge of taking the £100, they were ordered to stand trial on it a month after Easter.

[46] Ives, "'Agaynst taking awaye,'" pp. 33, 43. Ives says that Egerton was her uncle, that is, her mother's half-brother, but the dispensation was for the third and fourth degrees of consanguinity, making them second cousins once removed. See *Historical Manuscripts Commission, Eleventh Report, Appendix, Part VII* (London, 1888), p. 137: dispensation of June 11, 1509, for Ralph "Eggerton" and Margaret "Rebyll." I should note that the uncle-niece relationship was not prohibited by the levitical degrees and so, at least by this time, would have been easier to dispense than, say, nephew and uncle's wife, but it would still have required special action in Rome. See my "Canonical Implications of Richard III's Plan to Marry His Niece," *Traditio* 23 (1967): 269–311.

[47] Plucknett, "Chaucer's Escapade," p. 35.

but only subject to a fine. At any rate, Cannon's new document seems to show Champain compounding felonies as well as trespasses.

J. B. Post says that in the previous century, before the Westminster statutes of 1275 and 1285, many defendants who were charged with rape (which he defines as forced coitus, sometimes connected with abduction)[48] "concorded with the appellatrixes, either by financial compensation or by marriage."[49] Post sees the situation as changed, at least theoretically, after 1285, when the woman's subsequent consent left the wrongdoer open to Crown prosecution. But the Westminster statutes seem to have been intended to deal primarily with abduction, with or without sexual violation, and they were certainly interpreted in this way in the fourteenth century.[50] It may be, then, that the earlier arrangements concerning appeals of sexual rape continued as before. Withdrawal of appeal would ordinarily entail Crown punishment or fine. For instance, in 1375, a widow named Matilda or Maud Cantilupe withdrew, with a fine, from an appeal of the murder of her husband, leaving the Crown to prosecute the same charge by indictment.[51] Punishment was also forthcoming to the appellant if the appeal was found defective, but the failed appellant nevertheless had the option of prosecuting the felony by grand jury. Furthermore, we see a lot of compromising in the fifteenth century, which Christopher Whittick sees as part of a gradual evolution from the beginning of the fourteenth century.[52]

Another consideration, as we will see, is that a felony could be pardoned by the king as far as the offense against his peace was concerned, with the implication that the aggrieved citizen could similarly pardon the personal offense (even if liable to a fine). If, however, after having promised Chaucer that she would not pursue criminal or civil actions against him, Champain went ahead and did so, Plucknett believes that Chaucer could have used her release only to impede civil cases, since it is "difficult to believe that the release diminished her

[48] J. B. Post, "Ravishment of Women and the Statutes of Westminster," in *Legal Records and the Historian*, ed. J. H. Baker (London: Royal Historical Society, 1978), pp. 150–64, esp. p. 158.

[49] Post, "Sir Thomas West," p. 24.

[50] Kelly, "Statutes of Rapes," pp. 391–95.

[51] G. O. Sayles, *Select Cases in the Court of the King's Bench*, vol. 6, SS, vol. 82 (London, 1965), pp. 174–75. For two other such cases, see ibid., 6:154–56 (1368); 7:215–17 (1413).

[52] Christopher Whittick, "The Role of the Criminal Appeal in the Fifteenth Century," in *Law and Social Change in British History*, ed. J. A. Guy and H. G. Beale (London: Royal Historical Society, 1984), pp. 55–72, esp. pp. 63–64, 71.

criminal remedies."[53] But we are told that releases were sometimes pleaded in response to appeals, and there is record of a widow receiving £20 as compensation for a royal pardon in 1360.[54] We can deduce that this latter was a case in which Milicent, widow of John Waryn of Lockesley, appealed the knight Thomas Shirley of her husband's death; the pardon he received from the king had the standard formula, "Ita tamen quod stet recto," etc. (that is, "So that however he should stand trial in our court if anyone should wish to speak against him concerning the aforesaid death"). The £20 was paid to the widow in two installments, and she executed two receipts, which Shirley kept in his possession, along with the pardon.[55]

Plucknett assumes that the Champain charge dealt with forced coitus because "if only abduction had been involved, then the release would have proceeded from the injured party, viz., the feudal lord, parent, husband or employer of Cecilia."[56] But a case of 1362 shows a woman, Joan, who had been the wife of Nicholas Hotoft, bringing a complaint on her own against Henry Willows and others on a charge of criminal trespass for forcibly entering her close and imprisoning her.[57] That her accusation was one of abduction becomes clear the next year, when another commission of oyer and terminer was set up to investigate her emended complaint. Now she specifies that after she was imprisoned she was taken to unknown places until she swore to marry Henry; and she also alleges that Henry and his accomplices had carried away her goods and assaulted her men and servants. This time she is not identified as having been the wife of Nicholas Hotoft, but simply as Joan Hoto[f]t.[58]

The complaints (*querele*) of Joan Hotoft may have been in the form of "bills." An interesting example of such can be seen in Putnam for 1362,

---

[53] Plucknett, "Chaucer's Escapade," p. 35.

[54] Whittick, "Role of the Criminal Appeal," p. 64. Whittick cites the 1360 case as a meager exception to the fact that the releases are never recited and that there is little evidence of their content. He also mentions a case around 1500 in which a master whose apprentice had beaten a child to death exacted "a release by means of imprisonment on a feigned plea of trespass" (p. 64). He cites another case in 1469 in which widows were forced to agree to make appeals and not to execute releases (p. 68).

[55] The letter of pardon and the two receipts are noted in the *Fifth Report of the Royal Commission on Historical Manuscripts* (London, 1876), p. 369, but Whittick says that the Shirley manuscript collection was later broken up and the three documents recorded in the *Report* have not been traced.

[56] Plucknett, "Chaucer's Escapade," p. 35.

[57] *CPR, Edward III*, 12:288: October 25, 1362; text of original, PRO, C 66/266 m. 20d, below, appendix, no. 1.

[58] *CPR, Edward III*, 12:363: May 2, 1363; text of PRO, C 66/267m. 22d in appendix, no. 2.

in which Alice Lord complained against Geoffrey Wolmonger and John Causton for coming to her by force and arms and demanding that she marry Geoffrey. When she refused, Geoffrey took her by force against her will ("la prist afforce en countre son gre") and threw her on a horse behind John, whereupon she fell to the ground and received such injury that she could not work or walk for two weeks afterwards; then the two men took her ("lamenerunt") to some woods, stopped her cries, and hurt her so much that she was all bloody. The indicting jury found that the things alleged in this bill were true ("in ista billa infrascripta sunt vera") and charged it as a trespass.[59]

In a case of 1379, a woman named Idonia Cophyn, not further identified, simply obtained a writ against Henry Aleyn of Colbrok, who was required by the king to appear before him "to show why with force and arms he took, imprisoned, and maltreated the said Idonia in the parish of St. Clement Without the Bar of the New Temple of London and inflicted other enormities upon her to her grave harm and against our peace."[60]

In a 1364 document we hear of a case of abduction in which the woman is identified only as someone's daughter (like Cecilia Champain), even though it turns out later in the narrative that she was married, or at least had been married at the time. Hugh Bonehomme of Bugthorp is pardoned for a number of offenses, including having abducted, with the help of accomplices, "Agnes, daughter of John Giles of York, and by coercion and threats made her consent to contract an unjust marriage with Simon Porter, and of having carried away goods of Thomas Gilling, then husband of the said Agnes"; the abduction is referred to later in the pardon as a "rape" (*raptus*).[61] A widow or "annulled wife" would presumably have more call to act for herself than a currently married woman, whether or not she owned her own "maritage" (*maritagium*) or marriage-right. (When women's husbands died, their right to remarry reverted to the king or to other feudal lords, but

[59] Putnam, *Proceedings*, p. 344, no. 68; see Plucknett, "Commentary," p. clviii.

[60] PRO, KB 136/5/3/1/2, first of the Middlesex writs for the octave of Martinmas. The writ is addressed to the sheriff, who, if Idonia gives him security for pursuing her claim, is to have Henry produce pledges for his appearance before the king, "ostendendum quare vi et armis ipsam Idoniam apud parochiam sancti Clementis extra barram Novi Templi London. cepit, imprisonavit, et male tractavit et alia enormia ei intulit ad grave dampnum ipsius Idonie et contra pacem nostram." Dated October 22, 1379.

[61] *CPR, Edward III*, 12:515: May 6, 1364; text of PRO, C 66/267 n. 7, in appendix, no. 3.

normally widows were able to marry whomever they wished on pay-
ment of a fine.)[62]

A similar complaint could conceivably be brought by an unmarried
woman—even an heiress who had come of age, if she had purchased her
maritage from her guardian.[63] Such a woman could be in her twenties
or older, as would be the case of Cecily Champneys, daughter of the
baker William Champneys and his wife Agnes, who was left 20s. by her
father in 1360.[64] If the William Champayne whose seal survives from
1354 was Cecily's father, she may have used the same or a similar seal,[65]
just as Thomas Chaucer used his father's seal in 1409.

Cannon says that since the original release of May 1 no longer exists
(or has not been found), we do not know which of the two memoranda
corresponds more closely to it. He leans toward the hypothesis that the
May 4 version is the authentic one, and that Champain was persuaded
to suppress the term *raptus*,[66] but this may not be a plausible solution.
Let us assume that the preparation or at least reading of the original
document of quitclaim was observed by the named witnesses on May 1
and then sealed by Champain with her seal, as stated in both May 4 and
May 7 enrollments. The May 1 original could not have passed into
Chaucer's possession on May 1 if it was to be used on May 4 and again
on May 7 for the enrollments, unless Chaucer gave it back to Champain
temporarily when she went to Chancery and to the King's Bench. Such
maneuverings would not be necessary if the release were an indenture,
with the text copied twice on the same membrane and half given to each
party; but if this were the case, it would undoubtedly say so in the text,
and the text would also say that Chaucer used his seal as well. Chaucer

---

[62] Sue Sheridan Walker, "Free Consent and Marriage of Feudal Wards in Medieval
England," *Journal of Medieval History* 8 (1982): 123–34, esp. p. 126.

[63] See Walker, "Wrongdoing," pp. 292–93, 296. See pp. 289–90, for the case of an
abducted male ward in 1378, whose *maritagium* was assessed by a jury at £10—though
in this case the ward was recovered unmarried—while additional damages were set at
£10. Cf. the £10 that John Grove owed to Cecily Champain.

[64] Crow and Olson, *Chaucer Life-Records*, p. 346.

[65] Roger H. Ellis, *Catalogue of Seals in the Public Record Office: Personal Seals*, vol. 2
(London, 1981), p. 23, entry P 1179. The seal has a shield of arms bearing "three bells
and a lion passant in chief." Two other seals of persons named Champain exist from the
fourteenth century, those of Margery [dame] de Chaumpaigne of county Kent, from
1336, and Ralph Chaumpayn of Cotton Manor, Suffolk, from 1367. See W. de G. Birch,
Catalogue of Seals in the Department of Manuscripts in the British Museum, 2 (London:
Trustees of the British Museum, 1892), pp. 629–30, nos. 8503–5. I am grateful to
Brigette Bedos-Rezak for these references.

[66] Cannon, "*Raptus*," pp. 91–93.

executed an indenture of this kind with Roger Elmham in 1389; Elmham's original "counterpart" still exists in the Exchequer records, and so do the enrollments made by both Elmham and Chaucer.[67] Needless to say, one or other of the enrollments differs in minor ways from the original and the other enrollment (harder to explain are a couple of readings in which both enrollments agree against the original).[68]

Cannon rightly argues that the differences in the Champain enrollments could not be the result of careless copying. We should also reject the notion that Cecily did not have the original release when she went to the two courts but simply described the transaction to the clerk in charge of each office. The purpose of such enrollments was to provide an authentic copy of a document, which could not be done simply on someone's say-so. For the same reason she could hardly have altered the original release after May 4 by having some words erased and bulkier words squeezed in at one point and, at another point, erasing the names of two of the five witnesses and substituting *& aliis*, and expected it to be accepted for enrollment by the King's Bench.[69] It would also have been risky to forge the whole document anew, especially since she had already enrolled the original text in Chancery. It would have destroyed its value for use in court if the three named witnesses were summoned and interrogated separately about "the making, sealing, the time and the place, the manner and time, and the other necessary circumstances surrounding the said deed," including "the substance of the making of the said writing," as specified in a 1318 case in which a release was at issue—and failed to pass muster.[70]

The notion that the five witnesses were regathered some time between May 4 and May 7 and asked to witness a new or emended deed of release that still stated the date of May 1 does not seem very likely. More plausible is the possibility that Cecily Champain created two instruments of release on May 1, perhaps dealing with two different affairs or purposes: one was specifically connected with her *raptus*, which she registered at Chancery, and the other, which did

[67] Crow and Olson, *Chaucer Life-Records*, pp. 406–8.

[68] Ibid., p. 406: both enrollments omit *non depicte* (n. 8); both add *magna* (n. 9). In n. 6, the enrollments have *scomour* ("skimmer") for *soudour* ("solder") among the plumber's implements, but this could be a coincidence; both plumbing items appear further down in the original, under the manor of Eltham (p. 408).

[69] For examples of releases rejected in court because of bad Latin, erasures, and overwriting, see *Le second part de les reports des cases en ley que furent argues en le temps de . . . Roy Edward le tierce* (London, 1679), 24 Edward III (1350), pp. 35, 73–74.

[70] *Reynham v Hatton*, Arnold, no. 4.3 (a case of false imprisonment), p. 40. See below, at n. 164.

not require mention of *raptus*, was registered at the King's Bench.[71]

In any case, it remains probable that Cecily Champain had brought, or threatened to bring, a complaint of *raptus* against Geoffrey Chaucer. According to the summary of the *Life-Records* cited above, Chaucer could have been charged with one of four offenses:

1) Principal perpetrator in a case of forced sexual intercourse.
2) Accessory in such a case.
3) Principal abductor.
4) Accessory to an abduction.

Let us add two more possibilities:

5) Principal in an abduction that involved forced coitus.
6) Accessory in such a case.

Inspiration for these last two categories comes from the further documentation that Cannon provides in the course of his article.

As far as the abduction categories are concerned, we should note that Chaucer could have been a principal abductor of Cecily Champain even though he himself could hardly have intended to marry her, since he is on record in 1381 as still being married to Philippa.[72] We must remember that his own father, John Chaucer, was abducted around 1325 by a woman who wanted him to marry not her but her daughter. The abductor was his aunt, Agnes Westhale, who, along with her accomplice Geoffrey Stace (later her second husband), seized him in an effort to marry him to her daughter Joan. This scheme must have been doomed to failure from the beginning, not only because John was at least two years below the canonical age of valid marriage for boys, namely, fourteen, but also because a papal dispensation to marry his first cousin would have been virtually impossible to obtain for persons of their standing.[73] The culprits were reportedly fined £250 in 1330, but

[71] Paul Brand informs me that it was quite common to make several releases on one occasion, which were not necessarily identical.

[72] Crow and Olson, *Chaucer Life-Records*, p. 77.

[73] Dispensations of this sort (in the second degree of consanguinity) do not seem to have been given even to royalty at this date. Later in the century, Edward III's son Prince Edward was given a dispensation for a slightly lower degree (second degree mixed with third) when he was allowed to marry his first cousin once removed, Joan of Kent. See Karl P. Wentersdorf, "The Clandestine Marriages of the Fair Maid of Kent," *Journal of Medieval History* 5 (1979): 203–31, esp. pp. 217, 223; and see also my "Shades of Incest and Cuckoldry: Pandarus and John of Gaunt," *SAC* 13 (1991): 121–40, esp. pp. 128–29. Of course, the problem would not arise if Joan were only the stepdaughter of Agnes; perhaps Crow and Olson are suggesting this possibility when they identify Joan as "the daughter of Walter de Westhall" (p. 372, n. 1) rather than as "the daughter of Walter

this amount seems too great and may be a mistake, since the tenements of young John were valued at no more than 20*s.* a year.[74]

Both texts of Champain's release(s) of Chaucer, as well as Champain's release of Goodchild and Grove and Goodchild and Grove's release of Chaucer, express the temporal coverage of the respective release in slightly different ways, but all have the equivalent clauses limiting it to all actions in the past, present, and future perfect up to the day of making the document (*quas . . . habere potero . . . usque in diem confeccionis presencium*; "which I shall be able to have up to the day of the confection of the presents"). The future clause is not saying much, since it literally refers only to a small window of opportunity, a matter of hours or days, between the oral agreement and the witnessed sealing of the written version. However, such agreements did not propose to forgo all future actions of whatever sort, but rather to abandon all actions concerning events that may have occurred in the past up to the present. In other words, there were to be no new filings of old quarrels. We will see below an example of a release of ravishment accepted in court as a sufficient response to a civil plea of ravishment.[75]

II. *Raptus* and "Rape" in Law and Literature

Cannon cites documents to support his view that when there is a clear case of abduction only, the words *rapere et abducere* are used together, whereas in cases of forced coitus *raptus* is used alone. To judge from his examples, the active forms of the verb *rapere*, especially the perfect tense, *rapuit*, when used alone, would also seem to be limited to forced coitus. He does acknowledge that the past participle *raptus/rapta* is used to refer to abduction alone, as in the writs *De herede rapto* ("Concerning an abducted heir"—note the masculine form) and *De uxore rapta*, dealing with a charge that someone seized and abducted (*rapuit et abduxit*)

---

and Agnes de Westhall" (p. 3). Derek Pearsall treats the abduction of John Chaucer in *The Life of Geoffrey Chaucer* (Oxford: Blackwell, 1992) as having to do "with the securing of John's inheritance from Robert [John's father], now that his mother had remarried" (pp. 12–14). This would undoubtedly mean that John's mother was an unnamed co-conspirator in the project. By the way, if Pearsall is correct in assuming that the mother's new husband, Richard Chaucer, was Robert's cousin (Crow and Olson, *Chaucer Life-Records*, p. 2, suggest only a possible relationship), a dispensation would have had to be obtained, unless Robert and Richard were related only as fourth cousins or beyond.

[74] Crow and Olson, *Chaucer Life-Records*, p. 3.
[75] See below at n. 160.

another man's wife; but he believes that the noun *raptus*, which "has an independent grammatical existence and a separate history of usage," is not employed in this way.[76]

This may be true in the main, but, as will be seen below, there are enough examples available to show that *raptus* by itself can refer to non-sexual abduction. I do not mean to make it an either/or matter, of course. I support Cannon's caution: "The obsession in Chaucer criticism with making just such a distinction often loses sight of the fact that abduction in practice may easily shade over into something that is hardly to be distinguished from sexual assault."[77] We can add that the opposite is also true: an abduction may have a sexual element that is of secondary importance. An example can be seen in Chaucer's only use of the English noun "rape," when Pandarus tells Troilus, "It is no rape, in my dom, ne no vice,/Hire to withholden that ye love moost" (*TC* 4.596–97).[78] Since Troilus has long been having consensual sex with Criseyde, Pandarus must be speaking primarily about "unlawful detention" rather than sexual violence. It is not a question of abduction, exactly, but of holding back the woman who loves him most. This fits with Pandarus's original advice to Troilus:

> Go ravysshe here! Ne kanstow nat, for shame?
> And other lat here out of towne fare,
> Or hold here stille, and leve thi nyce fare.
>
> Artow in Troie, and hast non hardyment
> To take a womman which that loveth the
> And wolde hireselven ben of thyn assent? (4.530–35)

We see here that "ravish" and "take" are synonyms; the ravishing could consist either of taking her or of keeping her, and it would be done with her assent. In all three cases, the corresponding word in Boccaccio's

[76] Cannon, "*Raptus*," pp. 80 (n. 31), 82. Cf. the similar distinction made by Sue Sheridan Walker, "Punishing Convicted Ravishers: Statutory Strictures and Actual Practice in Thirteenth- and Fourteenth-Century England," *Journal of Medieval History* 13 (1987): 237–50, that the verb form *rapuit* refers to abduction and the noun *raptus* to forcible coitus, but with some blurring in a few cases (p. 237).

[77] Cannon, "*Raptus*," p. 88.

[78] Ed. Stephen Barney, *The Riverside Chaucer*, gen. ed. Larry D. Benson (Boston: Houghton Mifflin, 1987). (Unless otherwise noted, I use the *Riverside Chaucer* for all citations of Chaucer's works.) Needless to say, I exclude the homonym "rape" meaning "haste," which Chaucer also used; other homonyms in use in his time were "rape" meaning "a form of turnip" and "rape" meaning "an administrative district of Sussex."

Filostrato is *rapire*.[79] But Chaucer may have deleted "rape" in line 596 in a later revision and substituted "shame," the reading found in most of the manuscripts. Alternatively, the change may have been scribal, a correction of the mistaken reading "jape" in some of the manuscripts.[80]

Troilus first rejected Pandarus's suggestion because the Trojan war was started on account of this kind of forcible ravishment of women ("For ravysshyng of wommen so by myght" [line 548]). He is doubtless referring to the original ravishment of Hesione by the Greeks, where force was used against her, and to Paris's retaliatory ravishment of the complacent Helen, where any force used was doubtless directed against her husband, Menelaus. Later, when speaking to Criseyde, Troilus tells her that her father may try to talk her into marrying a Greek, either ravishing her with his words or using force: "ravysshen he shal yow with his speche, / Or do yow don by force as he shal teche" (4.1474–75).

Rape as a noun has a long though sparse history of meaning "the act of abducting a woman or sexually assaulting her or both," according to the *Middle English Dictionary*: the first entry is from 1291–92, the second c 1425, and we have seen another example in Chaucer's *Troilus*. The earliest application of the verb *rape* to a woman is by Osbern Bokenham and occurs as late as 1447: he uses it to characterize Pluto's taking of Proserpina. In the next entry, from a paraphrase of the Old Testament, c 1450 (a1425),[81] the word is used of a woman's seduction of a man; the third and last entry is from the anonymous second translation of Higden's *Polychronicon*, ?a1475 (?a1425): Europa was "rapte" (Latin *rapta*) by Jupiter in the form of a bull, that is, carried off by force. We should also note that the participle *raptus/rapta* is used of ecstatics and visionaries; for instance, St. Paul was *raptus* to the third heaven and *raptus* into Paradise (2 Cor. 12:2–4). The noun *raptus* is also used in this sense ("rapture," "ecstasy") in medieval Latin.[82]

In John Trevisa's slightly earlier translation of the *Polychronicon*, in Chaucer's time, he used not "raped" but the French-derived reflex

---

[79] *Filostrato* 4.64, 65, 73; see the stanzas given parallel to Chaucer's in Barry Windeatt's edition of the *Troilus* (London: Longman, 1984), pp. 380–84.

[80] See Barney's textual note to 4.596, p. 1173. Windeatt, p.385, says that the cruder *no rape in my dom* "may reflect Chaucer's translation process here" (assuming, that is, that he later changed it to the less crude *no shame unto yow*).

[81] In the *MED* notation, when a date is followed by another in parentheses, the first refers to the manuscript and the second to time of composition; *c* means *circa* and *a* means *ante*.

[82] The *Revised Medieval Latin Word-List from British and Irish Sources*, ed. R. E. Latham (London: British Academy, 1965), gives instances from c1250 and c1343.

"ravished," which, as we have seen, was also favored by Chaucer. In *The Merchant's Tale*, when describing how Pluto abducted Proserpine, referring to Claudian—meaning his *De raptu Proserpinae*—he makes "ravished" the synonym of "fetched" ("in his grisely carte he hire fette" [line 2233]). Diomede also uses these synonyms: the revenge taken by the Greeks "for fecchynge of Eleyne" will make everyone fear "to ravysshen any queene" (5.890–95). In *Boece*, "ravish" does service not only for *rapere* but also for *raptare, arripere, subripere,* and *rapidus* ("ravishing").[83] Chaucer does use the verb "rape" once, however, in a colloquial expression, to mean "grab": "al that ye may rape and renne."[84]

In this article I will be following the usual practice of the Public Record Office calendars and translate *rapere* as "ravish," the past participle *rapta/raptus* as "ravished," and the noun *raptus* as "rape," letting the context determine when or whether it can be narrowed to abduction or sexual violation or a combination of both, or must be left undecided.[85] To do otherwise, say, to reserve "rape" for cases of sexual violence and "ravishment" for cases of simple abduction, would be to distort the evidence and disambiguate records and events by guesswork.

Giving a broad meaning to "rape" has also been the traditional practice of English letters. When we speak of "the rape of the Sabine women," and, of course, "the rape of Helen" and "the rape of Proserpine," it is mainly seizure and abduction that is meant, even though sexual intercourse may have followed (sometimes *contra voluntatem,* sometimes not).

In one of the examples from *Boece* noted above, we could well speak of "the rape of Philosophy":

Cujus [Socratis] hereditatem cum deinceps Epicureum vulgus ac Stoicum ceterique pro sua quisque parte *raptum ire* molirentur meque reclamantem renitentemque velut in partem praedae traherent, vestem quam meis texueram

---

[83] *Boece* 1 pr. 3.34 (*raptum ire*), 2 pr. 5.69 (*raperis*), 2 m. 7.28 (*rapiet*), 4 pr. 5.23 (*rapiant*), 4 m. 6.37 (*rapiens*), 4 m. 7.34 (*rapuit*); 1 pr. 3.70 (*raptatur*); 5 pr. 6.91 (*arripuit*); 4 pr. 3.111 (*subripuisse*); 1 m. 5.4 (*rapido*), 1 m. 5.56 (*rapidos*), 2 m. 2.5 (*rapidis*), 4 m. 6.9 (*rapidos*). Cf. also 4 pr. 3.105: "ravynour by violence" (*violentus ereptor*).

[84] *CYT* 1422. See Skeat's note for the evolution of the phrase, in *The Complete Works of Geoffrey Chaucer*, 2d ed., 7 vols. (Oxford: Oxford University Press, 1899–1907), 5:431–32. *Rape* here comes from OE *hrepian* (seize), but it was probably influenced by the homonym *rape* (seize), from Latin *rapere*.

[85] One must, however, guard against assuming that every use of "rape" in the calendars corresponds to *raptus* in the original; see the Percy case below (n. 93) for an exception.

manibus disciderunt, *abreptis*que ab ea panniculis, totam me sibi cessisse credentes abiere.

[After him the crowd of Epicureans and Stoics and the rest strove as far as they could to *seize* his [Socrates's] legacy, carrying me off protesting and struggling, as if I were part of the booty, tearing my dress, which I wove with my own hands, and then went off with their *torn-off* shreds, thinking they possessed all of me.][86]

When viewed from this perspective, even *The Rape of the Lock* could be regarded as having an element of sexual violation.

III. *Raptus* as Short for Ravishing-and-Abducting

Cannon mentions two cases of abduction of wife with husband's goods from 3 Richard II (June 22, 1379, to June 21, 1380) using the formula *vi et armis rapuit et eam cum bonis et catallis abduxit* ("he ravished her by force and arms and carried her away with goods and chattels") but also employing the summary formula *de raptu predicto*,[87] "concerning the foresaid rape." We should note first of all that *vi et armis* was often a pure legal fiction from the very beginning of its use in trespass writs and actions.[88] Or, in another analysis, the phrase "was not fictional but rather a low threshold test," alleging some but not necessarily a great deal of force.[89] The cases we are dealing with here correspond to the usage of the title of the relevant writ, *De uxore rapta*,[90] or *De raptu uxoris*,[91] and the

---

[86] Boethius, *Consolation* 1 pr. 3, lines 21–27, trans. S. J. Tester; Loeb *Boethius*, new ed. (Cambridge, Mass.: Harvard University Press, 1973), p. 143. Chaucer's translation is as follows (omitting the glosses): "The heritage of the whiche Socrates whan that the peple of Epycuriens and Stoyciens and many othere enforceden hem *to gon ravyssche* everyche man for his part, they as in partye of hir preye todrowen me, cryinge and debatying therayens, and korven and torente my clothes that I hadde woven with my handes; and with tho cloutes that thei hadden *arased* out of my clothes thei wenten awey wenynge that I hadde gon with hem every del." I italicize the relevant words. *Raptum ire* can be parsed as the future active periphrastic infinitive of *rapere* (*raptum* being the supine of the verb), and *abreptus* is the past participle of *abripere* (from *ab* and *rapere*).

[87] Cannon, "*Raptus*," p. 87.

[88] Milsom, "Trespass," pp. 222–23.

[89] Robert C. Palmer, *English Law in the Age of the Black Death, 1348–1381: A Transformation of Governance and Law* (Chapel Hill: University of North Carolina Press, 1993), p. 159.

[90] Cannon gives the text of the writ on p. 82, from a register of ca. 1320.

[91] In a case from 1314, Sayles, *Select Cases*, vol. 4, SS, vol. 74, p. 60, the writ is referred to as *breve de raptu uxoris*. Similarly, the king's council at the same time refers to it as *breve de transgressione de raptu uxoris alterius et de bonis suis asportatis*, and refers in summary to the charge as "de hujusmodi raptu." See *Rotuli Parliamentorum*, 1:290.

corresponding action, sometimes called *De raptu uxoris cum bonis viri sui.*[92] That is, a wife who is *rapta et abducta,* meaning only "abducted" (literally, "forcibly seized and carried off"), is referred to by shorthand in the more common title only as *rapta,* or, in the alternative title, the alleged offense is referred to as *raptus,* as in the two cited *rapuit et abduxit* cases. The meaning of the term is clear from the context, but when the context is missing, as in the first Champain release, we have no reason, without further information, to conclude that the case refers to sexual rape; it could instead refer only to abduction, or it could be designating a combination of both offenses. A similar example can be seen in the Percy case, mentioned above: John Halsham, having been charged with ravishing and abducting Percy's wife (now actually Halsham's wife), was pardoned by the king (June 7, 1384) for the *raptus* of Philippa of Artheles and for all other felonies and trespasses.[93] We note that Philippa is not identified as anyone's wife and is only referred to by a distorted version of her toponymic (she was the daughter of the earl of Athol).

Cannon also notes a standard plea by defendants in Arnold's collection, in which rape is denied with no mention of abduction: *venit et defendit vim, injuriam, raptum.* He observes that the latest case of this sort comes from 1318, dealing with a father who denies *omnis raptus* of his daughter; that is, he denies categorically that he abducted his daughter.[94] But in a King's Bench case from 1389, *Wyatt v Vicar of Swalcliffe,* the defendant distinguishes between the charges of *raptus* of the woman with the husband's goods, on the one hand, and, on the other hand, the *abductio* of the woman with some of her personal items:

Quo ad raptum predicte Alicie, et [quo ad] bona et catalla predicta, preter pannos lineos et laneos, flammiola, et anulos, dicit quod ipse in nullo est inde cul-

---

[92] This is the usual form in the C version of *Novae Narrationes,* ed. Elsie Shanks and S. F. C. Milsom, SS, vol. 80 (London, 1963), which dates from the early years of Edward II and was frequently copied. See p. 328. One MS of Edward III's time, Rawl. C.49, has *De raptu mulieris cum bonis viri sui,* and another, Dunn 51, has simply *De raptu.*

[93] PRO, C66/317 m. 12. See appendix, no. 12; *CPR Richard II,* 2:399. Another pardon was given to Halsham on 10 July, for all rapes, murders, homicides, common robberies and larcenies and all other felonies of which he stands charged, PRO, C66/318 m. 37, *CPR Richard II,* 2:439. In the *CCR* summary of one of the original commissions (see above, n. 16), the phrase "rape and abduction" is used, whereas in the original record only verbs are used (*rapuerunt, abduxerunt*).

[94] Cannon, "*Raptus,*" pp. 87–88, citing Arnold, *Select Cases of Trespass,* 1:77–80 (8.4–6). The same phrase is used in the 1314 case noted above in Sayles, *Select Cases,* 4:59, and *raptus* is used four other times to sum up the action. In the Year Book for 3 Edward II (1310), a similar case is summarized in the rubric as *De raptu mulieris: Year Books of Edward II,* vol. 4, ed. F. W. Maitland and G. J. Turner, SS, vol. 22 (London, 1907), p. 4.

pabilis. . . . Et quo ad abductionem predicte Alicie et pannorum, lineorum, et laneorum, flammiliorum, et anulorum, dicit. . . .

[As for the rape of the aforesaid Alice, and [as for] the aforesaid goods and chattels, except the linen and woolen cloth, the kerchiefs, and the rings, he says that he is in no wise guilty thereof. . . . And as for the abduction of the aforesaid Alice and the linen and woolen cloth, kerchiefs, and rings, he says. . . .][95]

The defendant is the wife's uncle, a priest, vicar of the church of Swalcliffe in Oxfordshire. He explains here in court that Alice left her husband ("a comitiva dicti Johannis recessit") and lived with him when given permission by the official of the archdeacon of Oxford: she was asking for an annulment on grounds of the husband's impotence, and she feared his violence. The only clothes in question were those she was wearing, and the same was true of the one ring that the husband complained of. The uncle concludes, "This is the way he 'took and abducted' her" ("ipsam in forma predicta 'cepit et abduxit'").[96] In thus denying the *raptus* of his niece, he is only denying any forcible seizure of her and of goods belonging to her husband. It is not likely that there was any nuance in the husband's charge of incestuous sexual violation, or that the vicar was responding to any such connotation.

Another defendant before the King's Bench in 1389 (in the case of *Hamm v Gilbert*) denies "asportation" of the husband's goods and chattels. As for the *raptus* of the wife ("quo ad raptum predicte Margerie"), he says that the husband sent his wife to work for him. The husband persists in maintaining that the defendant "ravished her and still detains her" ("rapuit et eam adhuc detinet"), without any consent or agreement on his own part, contrary to the defendant's allegation. The jury finds that the defendant used no force and arms concerning goods and chattels, but that he did encourage the wife to leave her husband, and that this was why she removed herself ("se elongavit") from his company, without, however, the defendant ravishing her ("absque hoc, quod . . . rapuit"); they assess the defendant's damages to the husband

---

[95] Arnold, *Select Cases of Trespass*, 1:87 (8.15). My translation differs from Arnold's in that where he says "ravishing," I say "the rape" (in keeping with the above-noted PRO practice of translating *raptus* as "rape") and put "the abduction" where he has "abducting." I have also inserted "quo ad" in brackets before *bona et catalla* to underline the fact that, grammatically speaking, the phrase is not governed by *raptus*, since *bona et catalla* is in the accusative rather than the genitive, even though the recorder's intention may have been to refer to "the seizure of the wife and the goods."

[96] Ibid.

(in effect, for alienation of his wife's affections) at 100*s*.[97] The action in this case commenced, according to Arnold's summary, on "a writ and count in common form for abducting the plaintiff's wife along with goods of his."[98] Once again, while it is possible that an element of forcible or unwilling sexual intercourse was included in the husband's charge, if not in the defendant's denial and the jury's negative finding, it seems more likely that the main or only concern was with the defendant's role in the departure of the wife from her husband's home. The husband would hardly have needed to argue that he did not consent to the *raptus* if it denoted forced adulterous sex.[99]

Another similar writ and count resulted in a King's Bench case, *Hampton v Montgomery and Child*, in the following year, 1390, which similarly avoided all use of the terms *abductio* and *abduxit*. The charges were brought by the cordwainer John Hampton against two clerks, Philip Montgomery and William Child. They pleaded "not guilty" concerning the use of force and arms and the goods and chattels ("quo ad venire vi et armis et bona et catalla"), and they gave an explanation concerning the *raptus* of his wife, Katherine ("quo ad raptum dicte Katerine"): her marriage to the plaintiff had been annulled because of her previous marriage to another man, Walter; one defendant, Philip, was Walter's counsel in the annulment proceedings before the archdeacon of the abbot of Westminster, and the other defendant, William, was the wife's counsel. Each defendant admitted that, after the annulment was granted, Katherine left John to seek Walter, but without either clerk ravishing her ("absque hoc, quod ipse dictam Katerinam rapuit"). John, however, continued to insist that Philip and William "ravished the aforesaid Katherine at Southwark, as he supposes by his writ and count" ("predictam Katerinam apud Suthewerk rapuerunt, prout per breve et narrationem sua supponit").[100]

---

[97] Ibid., 1:88–89 (8.16).

[98] Ibid., 1:88.

[99] In this case, the court postponed coming to a judgment after the jury delivered its verdict, but there is no reason to think that its hesitation had anything to do with suspected coitus, forced or unforced, between the defendant and the plaintiff's wife.

[100] Ibid., 1:92–93 (8.19). A 1389 case of "abducting the plaintiff's wife along with goods," *Ware v Halmard*, which also involved annulment proceedings before the archdeacon of Westminster, is given by Arnold, *Select Cases of Trespass*, 1:89–90 (8.17). The husband, Bartholomew Ware, armorer, charges three men with ravishing and abducting his wife Isabel: Thomas, Isabel's son; John, Isabel's son-in-law, married to her daughter; another John, Isabel's cousin. Their story is that when Bartholomew and Isabel found out that they were cousins, Isabel removed herself from Bartholomew, and Bartholomew applied to their ordinary, the archdeacon of the monastery of Westminster (the monk John

The writ for "rape of heir" in a 1337 case, *Bolling v Chestfield*, dealing with the abduction of an heiress, is called *De raptu custodie* and *De raptu de custodia*. Such a writ was allegedly secured by John Chestfield against John Bolling, who, he claimed, had ravished (*rapuerat*) his ward, Joan Lightfoot, out of his custody (*extra custodiam ipsius*).[101] The word *raptus* in such a writ, which was designed for male and female wards, would seem to have no primary reference to sexual violence—though, of course, it was sometimes applied in cases where sexual violence was charged.[102] Rather, it primarily referred to abduction, understood as forcible removal from one's proper custodian. Walker notes that cases of ravished male heirs were more common than those of ravished females; for instance, in 1354, the ratio was 46 to 21.[103]

In a 1391 case, *Lincoln v Simond et al.*, where a man, Thomas Lincoln, claimed the marriage-right of his own daughter, he accused two men and a woman of breaking into his home by force and arms, ravishing and abducting his daughter, Alice, and taking and asporting his goods and chattels—terms normally associated with the writ *De uxore rapta*. One of the defendants, Alan Simond, after protesting that he did not admit that Alice was Thomas's daughter or that Thomas owned her maritage, asserted that he had secretly espoused Alice before Thomas espoused her to another man of his own choice, and that the first spousal had been upheld in the ecclesiastical court (as a valid marriage). Thomas then insisted that this spousal should be adjudged, legally speaking, a *raptus* of his daughter ("et sic dicta affidatio predicte Alicie, sine licencia dicti Thome [patris sui] facta, in lege raptum Alicie adjudicare debet"), because he had thereby lost her maritage, since he could not marry her to anyone.[104] The court postponed coming to a judgment in

---

Stow) for an annulment, which was granted. But during the proceedings, Archdeacon Stow decreed that Isabel was to live in some honest place apart from the company of her husband, and she accordingly spent some time with her son, her son-in-law, and her cousin, the three men whom her husband was now charging with abduction.

[101] Ibid., 1:43–44 (4.6). A jury found that Chestfield had actually not obtained the royal writ *De raptu de custodia*, but had instead pursued his case by means of a bill, which, as we saw above, was a plaintiff's informal petition initiating proceedings in common law.

[102] See Walker, "Punishing Convicted Ravishers," for various circumstances accompanying charged abductions, including the alleged abduction of wives (see below).

[103] Walker, "Free Consent," p. 127 and n. 26.

[104] Arnold, *Select Cases of Trespass*, 1:96–98 (9.2); cf. p. xlv. Arnold translates *affidatio* and *affidatio sponsalium* as "betrothal" and "betrothal of espousals," but he should use a neutral term, since it was surely a question not of betrothals but of marriages. Betrothals (*sponsalia de futuro*) could be broken at will, unless converted into marriage by intercourse;

this case, but the normal solution would have been for the guardian to keep the property of the ward until he was paid the value of the marriage, or else to sue the ward for the amount.[105] A similar situation in 1377 in Yorkshire resulted in a criminal indictment. John Woodhouse (de Wodehous) of Brathwait was indicted for feloniously ravishing Alice, daughter of Richard Jackman, at Woodhouse on August 11, 1377, and feloniously abducting her with goods and chattels of Jackman to the value of 20 marks. When brought before the justices of jail delivery on April 18, 1384, he produced a pardon, dated August 23, 1383, granted at the request of Lady Mohun, upon which he was acquitted. The pardon notes that he was indicted for allegedly having ravished Alice and taken, abducted, (and/or) imprisoned her, and he is pardoned the king's suit for the rape (*raptus*) and other above-mentioned felonies, with the proviso that Alice could speak against him concerning the rape and other aforesaid felonies.[106] It is important to note that, according to this pardon, Alice had the same ability to appeal her abduction as Margaret Kebell would have at the beginning of the sixteenth century. Woodhouse's pardon, like the pardon of Roger Vernon and his accomplices, did not include the taking away of chattels (specified in the Woodhouse indictment as belonging to Alice's father, but in the Vernon indictments as Margaret's own goods). But in Woodhouse's case, he was not held to answer for the chattels. And

---

marriages (*sponsalia de presenti*) could not, and it was only the latter that were at issue in the ecclesiastical cases of "precontract" (which means "previous marriage"). It would make little sense to sue over which of two betrothals came first; Alice could at any time have simply converted either betrothal into marriage on the spot by using the present tense. On precontract, see R. H. Helmholz, *Marriage Litigation in Medieval England* (Cambridge: Cambridge University Press, 1974), pp. 76–77; for the laws on clandestine marriage, see my *Love and Marriage in the Age of Chaucer* (Ithaca: Cornell University Press, 1975), pp. 163–76. See also J. A. Brundage, "Rape and Marriage in the Medieval Canon Law," *Revue de droit canonique* 28 (1978): 62–75: "Abduction of one's own fiancé . . . did not count as rape" in canon law (p. 70, citing *Decretales Gregorii IX* 5.17.6, and also Adhémar Esmein, *Le mariage en droit canonique* [Paris, 1891], 1:392, for the axiom *Non fit raptus propriae sponsae*). When Brundage says that "the abduction of one's wife by someone else was likely to be treated somewhat differently, as 'diversion,' for which both ecclesiastical and secular courts offered separate remedies," his statement needs to be modified for England, where this procedure does not seem to have been common. Brundage cites Helmholz, *Marriage Litigation*, pp. 109–10, but Helmholz here mentions only a single case, in which a man accuses another man in a church court of "subtracting" his wife with her consent, and no reference is made to secular remedies.

[105] *Bracton de legibus et consuetudinibus Angliae*, ed. George E. Woodbine, trans. Samuel E. Thorne, 4 vols. (Cambridge, Mass.: Harvard University Press, 1968), 2:257; Walker, "Free Consent," p. 123; Walker, "Wrongdoing," p. 291.

[106] PRO, JUST 3/80/1 m. 1. See appendix, no. 11.

whereas Margaret really was abducted, it may be that Alice went with Woodhouse willingly. In fact, there may be a reference to them as man and wife later in the same jail-delivery session: William Draper of Wragby, indicted for ravishing Alice wife of John de Wodehousses on June 28, 1379 (the nature of the alleged ravishment is not described), is found not guilty—like all the other defendants, none of whom had pardons to show.[107]

As we can deduce from the examples given above, plaintiffs routinely brought charges of ravishing-abducting against defendants in cases where there was not only no forced sex but also no abduction. In the cases where the plaintiffs claim the supposedly abducted women as their wives, they were following the language of the pertinent writ, *De uxore rapta*.[108] The writ itself purports to be following "the form of the statute," probably that of Westminster II, ch. 34 (1285), with its reference to the goods of the husbands abducted with wives.[109] The next chapter, ch. 35, deals with abducted children, male or female, whose marriage-right belongs to someone: "De pueris sive masculis sive femellis quorum maritagium ad aliquem pertineat raptis et abductis," and provides the necessary writs within the statute itself.[110] We have seen above that both kinds of abductions, of wives and of heirs, were referred to simply as *raptus*, and the same is true of a statute passed in October 1382—that is, two and a half years after Cecily Champain's release of Chaucer. The purpose of the statute was to give the right of appeal to the husband, if the abducted woman was married, or to the next male kin in other cases, when the woman subsequently consented to the "rape" ("post hujusmodi raptum").[111] The text of the Commons' petition in the Rolls of Parliament speaks of ravishment ("apres le ravisement"),[112] but when the Commons unsuccessfully tried to get the statute repealed less than two years later, they also spoke of rape ("apres tiel rape," "apres cel ravissement").[113]

The husbands who used *De uxore rapta* had usually lost their wives not through abduction but through the wives' voluntary separation from

---

[107] Ibid., m. 1d.

[108] See Cannon, "*Raptus*," pp. 82–83, and Kelly, "Statutes of Rapes," p. 393, for the text of the writ, as given in *Early Registers of Writs*, ed. Elsa de Haas and G. D. G. Hall, SS, vol. 87 (London, 1970), p. 181.

[109] *Statutes of the Realm*, vol. 1 (London, 1810), p. 87.

[110] Ibid., p. 88.

[111] 6 Richard II, Stat. 1, c. 6 (1382), *Statutes*, 2:27. See Kelly, "Statutes of Rapes," pp. 371–73, 400–402, as well as Post's two articles (I modify his conclusions somewhat).

[112] *Rotuli Parliamentorum*, 6 vols. (London, 1767–77), 3:139–40.

[113] Ibid., 3:174.

them. As Morris Arnold says, "Probably because the husband-wife relationship is so complex, and the lie in the writ so outrageous, special pleading seems more prevalent in this action than in any other."[114] In other words, it was necessary to allege the violence of *raptus*, both for ward and wife, with or without the possible sexual overtones of the word, in order to get the real complaint into court; once there, the actual circumstances could be explained and appropriate judgment hoped for. Our first instinct, therefore, should be to dismiss the alleged incident as mere boilerplate dictated by the writ. A final example: on March 3, 1379, the tailor John Mare obtained two writs against two East Greenwich men, John Totenham and Thomas Horn, accusing each of ravishing his wife Alice and abducting her and his goods and still detaining them. Since he does not accuse them of acting together, he seems to suggest that his wife could be abducted twice and detained in two places at once.[115]

IV. *Raptus/Rapere*: Seizure, With Coitus Now or Later

Of the documents illustrating appeals by women that Cannon transcribes in their entirety, the first, dealing with Isabel Mohun, taken from the *Coram rege* (King's Bench) rolls, is the most interesting and complicated, and I will analyze it at length below. The second and third are entries from the controlment roll of 3 Richard II (1379–80). Of these two, the second, Agnes Marchal's appeal against Robert Baral, is straightforward: she claims that he came like a felon and lay with her carnally against her will and thus feloniously ravished her (*et sic ipsam felonice rapuit*), and the offense is twice referred to later as "the aforesaid felony of rape" (*felonia predicta de raptu*). The first case, the appeal of Amicia Serle against Roger Snow, is similar in alleging no act of taking the woman away, but only forced intercourse; here, however, it is stated that "he feloniously ravished her of her pure virginity" (*ipsam de pura virginitate sua felonice rapuit*), where the word *rapere* seems to mean "violently deprive," referring to a taking away or destroying of her maidenhood.[116]

---

[114] Arnold, *Select Cases of Trespass*, p. xlv. I analyze all of his cases in "Statutes of Rapes," pp. 398–99, 409. Arnold uses "special pleading" in the nonpejorative seventeenth-century sense of the phrase, meaning the recounting of the peculiar circumstances of a case, as opposed to "general pleading."

[115] PRO, KB 136/5/2/3/1, gathered with the writs of Kent for the quindene of Easter, 1379.

[116] Cannon, "*Raptus*," p. 86, citing KB 29/32, m. 1 (*Marchal v Baral*) and m. 31d (*Serle v Snow*).

Sometimes the virginity is the direct object: he ravished her virginity (from her). The same idiom is found in French: "ravist soun pucellage."[117] In English, the usual verb used is *reve* (it survives today only in *bereave*). Chaucer uses it to describe the two rapes of virgins he portrays, that of Philomela ("he hath reft hire of hire maydenhede, / Maugre hire hed, by strengthe and by his myght" [*LGW* 2325–26]) and that of the maid in *The Wife of Bath's Tale* ("Of which mayde anon, maugree hir heed, / By verray force, he rafte hire maydenhed" [lines 887–88]). He uses the same verb, this time with a double object, for the third sexual rape that he describes, that of Lucretia, but in this case she was bereft not of her virginity, for she was a married woman, but of her life: "And therwithal she rafte hirself hir lyf" (*LGW* 1855). When her rape is recalled by Dorigen in *The Franklin's Tale*, the verb used is "oppresse": "she oppressed was / Of Tarquyn" (lines 1406–7), and the same word is used of virgins: "To been oppressed of hir maydenhede" (line 1385).

In other cases, *rapere* may mean only "seize." This is true of the writ *De uxore rapta*, in which *rapuit, abduxit, et adhuc detinet* means "seized, took away, and still detains." The same may be true in cases of forced sex, even in the formula *eam felonice rapuit et cum ea carnaliter concubuit contra voluntatem ipsius*, which would therefore mean, "he feloniously seized her and immediately lay with her carnally against her will." The latter formula occurs in a case from 1412, where a man was accused of so acting by the command and counsel of his mother.[118] But in such cases it is also possible that the *et* means *sive* or *id est*: so that the *et* joining the words would not mean "and in addition" but would simply add a synonym, in indenture—English style.[119] That is, *rapuit et carnaliter concubuit* could mean no more than *rapuit, id est, carnaliter concubuit*. This may be the meaning of the indictment against Thomas Malory in 1451: *eam felonice rapuit et cum ea carnaliter concubuit*,[120] but the charge also included abduction of wife and goods, and a subsequent appeal, citing the 1382 statute, implied the wife's consent.[121]

---

[117] As in the case of *Alice v John* reported in the 1302 eyre of Cornwall and the 1313–14 eyre of Kent; see Kelly, "Statutes of Rapes," pp. 389–90.

[118] Putnam, *Proceedings*, p. 99, no. 30: "Robertus, filius Thome Howet, . . . ex precepto et consilio Alicie Howet, matris sue, Agnetem, filiam Johannis Clerk, magistri sui, apud Gaddesby, felonice rapuit et cum ea carnaliter concubuit, contra voluntatem ipsius Agnetis."

[119] I owe this suggestion to Christopher Cannon.

[120] Edward Hicks, *Sir Thomas Malory: His Turbulent Career* (Cambridge, Mass.: Harvard University Press, 1928), p. 96.

[121] Kelly, "Statutes of Rapes," pp. 412–15.

A similar interpretation may be called for in the felony case of the countess of Lincoln in 1336, which Cannon analyzes as presenting an ambiguous meaning of *raptus*. According to the indictment, the defendants entered the castle by treachery and took hold of the countess ("comitissam ceperunt") and then took her away (abducted her) from her castle to another castle and there ravished her against her will and against the peace of the king and against the form of the statute thereupon provided, and they did their will concerning her ("et predictam comitissam abduxerunt extra castrum suum predictum usque ad castrum de Somerton et ipsam ibidem rapuerunt, contra voluntatem suam et contra pacem regis et contra formam statuti inde provisi, etc., et voluntatem suam de ea fecerunt"). One of the defendants pleaded not guilty to *capcio, abduccio, raptus, seu felonia predicta sibi imposita*.[122] The statutory reference, if it is to be taken as accurately citing a specific statute, is most likely to be the first part or French section of Westminster II ch. 34 (1285), providing the death penalty for ravishing a woman without her consent.[123] If the ravishment refers to forced sex here, as seems likely, *rapuerunt . . . et voluntatem suam de ea fecerunt* could mean either "seized her and then violated her sexually" or, taking the *et* as explanatory, "seized her, that is, violated her sexually."

However, in other cases the latter interpretation is not possible and *rapuit* appears to mean only "seized," or, at most, "seized with the intention of later violating"; as, for example, in an indictment from 1357 in which a man allegedly *rapuit* a woman, *abduxit* her to a mill, *et cum ea concubuit contra voluntatem suam*.[124] In another case from the same year, a tailor, labeled a common night-stroller and common malefactor and perturber of the peace in the indictment, *rapuit et abduxit* a wife and goods and then *carnaliter cognovit* the wife.[125] Sometimes, of course, one cannot tell whether there was coitus, or full coitus, or not. This is true even in a gruesome indictment from 1413 according to which a man took a ladder one night and broke into (*fregit*) a house and *rapuisset* a woman and *lasaraverit* her clothes (*pannos, lineos, et laneos*), whereupon she raised the hue and cry and the whole village came running, but not

---

Δ [122] G. O. Sayles, *Select Cases in the Court of King's Bench*, vol. 5, SS, vol. 76 (London, 1958), pp. 90–91, discussed by Cannon, *"Raptus,"* pp. 88–89, n. 61. It is noteworthy that the term *felonia* is not used in the narration of the jury's presentment, but it is in the charge that is made against the accused ringleader when he appears in court.

[123] *Statutes of the Realm*, 1:87.

[124] Putnam, *Proceedings*, p. 188, no. 49.

[125] Ibid., p. 190, no. 68.

before he had suffocated and murdered her.[126] The pluperfect subjunctive *rapuisset* and the perfect subjunctive *lasaraverit* may indicate that the woman's cries interrupted his rape attempt before he could complete it.

V. An Appealing Widow and Rapist Husband: *Mohun v Yulecomb*

Let us discuss now the appeal of Isabel Mohun against Henry Yulecomb, the first case of forced coitus that Cannon transcribes.[127] This record, from the *Coram rege* rolls (the Public Record Office KB 27 series of King's Bench plea rolls), like the two controlment-roll entries just discussed, comes from the one year that Cannon thoroughly examined, namely, 3 Richard II (June 22, 1379, to June 21, 1380). The gist of it is as follows. Henry Yulecomb was attached, along with William Yulecomb, his brother, and Lawrence Drew, to respond to Isabel, "who was (*fuit*) the wife of John Mohun," and to her appeal of rape and of breaking of the king's peace (*de raptu et pace . . . fracta*). She claimed that Henry came with the two other men to Bedenek in Cornwall on the evening of November 26, 1376, and feloniously took (*cepit*) her and led (*duxit*) her to Stanerton in the county of Devon and there lay with her carnally against her will on December 1; she was forcibly detained from the aforesaid November 26, 1376, until February 20, 1378, on which day she escaped; and thus he feloniously ravished her (*et sic ipsam felonice rapuit*). William and Lawrence, whom she would also be charging if they were there in court, were present on the aforesaid day and year (i.e., November 26, 1376), aiding and abetting Henry in committing the *felonia predicta* (*de raptu* is not added). And as soon as Henry had committed the *felonia predicta de raptu*, Isabel pursued him from vill to vill (following the standard formula); and if he should deny that he committed the *felonia predicta de raptu*, she is prepared to prove it, as the court wishes.[128]

---

[126] Ibid., p. 102, no. 45.

[127] I give the expanded or regularized forms of the names here; Cannon read the husband's name in the manuscript as "Mann," but he agrees now that it should be transcribed as "Moun."

[128] PRO, KB 27/475 (Michaelmas term, 1379), m. 61, transcribed in Cannon, "*Raptus*," pp. 85–86. The day of the abduction is given as the next Wednesday after the feast of St. Katherine (that is, November 25, a Tuesday), in the fiftieth year of Edward III (that is, 1376); the day of the unwilling coitus is given as the next Monday after the feast of St. Katherine. The day of her escape is given as the twentieth day of February in the first year of Richard II (1378).

We see then that the term *rapuit* is first used after Isabel escaped from her fifteen-month imprisonment, as if the the entire ordeal comprised the felony. Then she seems to limit the felony, in which his accomplices participated, to the initial kidnapping. Finally, she returns speaking of the events of the whole period as a *raptus*. She mentions only one instance of forced coitus, five days after she was seized.

Appeal against a man on a charge of sexual violation was an action traditionally reserved to women, and it may be that this is why Isabel specified the single instance of unwanted sex over a period of a year and a quarter of captivity. There is, however, one early case, *Tolymer v Mounpynzoun* (1315), that may suggest that forced sex was not necessary to the charge. In this case, William Tolymer brings a civil suit against a woman, Christian Mounpynzoun, and a parson, Thomas Holm, saying that they took and abducted (*ceperunt et abduxerunt*) his daughter and heiress Catherine and married her against his (the father's) will to Edmund Mounpynzoun—presumably Christian's son.[129] One of the defendants' lawyers, William Herle, a King's Serjeant,[130] objects that the writ is faulty because the daughter could not be called heiress until her father is dead. Therefore, the writ of ravishment of ward (*ravisement de garde*) is not appropriate, and the father "ought not to have an action; or if there were any action it must be one of rape (*rap*), the suit of which is reserved to the woman."[131] Herle's argument against the writ was not accepted, but there was no challenge to his assumption that a woman could bring an appeal of rape in a case of abduction. But perhaps his assumption was also that she would have to charge, not the mother, but the son to whom she was married, and against whom she would have to allege forcible coitus. However, we have seen in *Jackman v Woodhouse* in 1377 that a daughter could bring an appeal of ravishment and abduction against a man with no explicit allegation of forced sex, and her right to do so was confirmed in the pardon of 1383. But it may be that the situation was different for married women and widows.

In the fifteenth century, in 1436 and 1439, special acts of Parliament were passed to allow abducted and forcibly married women to enter

---

[129] *Year Books of Edward II*, vol. 19 (9 Edward II), ed. G. J. Turner and William Craddock Bolland, SS, vol. 45 (London, 1929), Common Pleas report, p. 31.

[130] John Sainty, *A List of English Law Officers, King's Counsel, and Holders of Patents of Precedence* (London, 1987), p. 5.

[131] Loc. cit.; Herle repeats his objection on p. 32.

appeals of felony against their husbands.[132] After the turn of the next century, Margaret Kebell, discussed above, entered an appeal of "felony and rape" without specifying forced sex but naming the 1487 statute, "Against the Taking Away of Women." Christopher Whittick notes that the statute does not specify the right of appeal, but he points out that when a woman entered such an appeal in 1492, it was received, but only after consultation between the justices of both benches.[133]

We should note, by the way, that when a woman is identified as *que fuit uxor*, having been the wife of someone, we cannot safely conclude, without more evidence, that she is a widow. We know that Maud Cantilupe in the case noted earlier was a widow because her husband had been murdered; but there is a case from 1383–84 of a woman *que fuit uxor Philippi* in which Philip was still very much alive, at least in the summer of 1381, when the offense allegedly took place (June 16, 4 Richard II): a man was indicted for forcibly ravishing her, promising to get her marriage to Philip annulled, and then bigamously marrying her

---

[132] Leadam, *Select Cases Before the Star Chamber*, p. cxii, citing *Rotuli Parl.*, 4:497–98; 5:14–15. In the first case, the widow of a knight, Isabel Butler, says that William Pulle broke into her house with armed misdoers and "felonously and moste horribly ravished" her and led her, naked except for kirtle and smock, to the wilds of Wales, "for which rape" he was indicted before the king's justices of Lancaster, after order was given for his arrest and her rescue. She wants order given that unless he appears in two weeks, he will be attainted of high treason, "considering that the said ravishing is done in more horrible wise and with more heinous violence than any hath been seen or known before this time, and that the said William ravisher is, and of long time hath be, outlawed of felony for man's death foul murdered and slain." In a second petition, she described the event again: William Pulle and other felons lying in wait "felonously there then took and ravished" her and led her into the county of Chester [not to Wales], and there, "to exclude her of her suit and lawful remedy of the said ravishment," imprisoned her for a day (or a week), then forced her to marry him; thereupon he put her in a strong chamber till night, and then "felonously and fleshly knew and ravished" her. She asks that she might "pursue by attorney an effectual appeal . . . of the said ravishment" in spite of the espousals between her and William. In the 1439 case, the petitioner, again the widow of a knight, charges that one Lewis plotted "to ravish the said Margaret and to have her to his wife." He kidnapped her, forced her to undergo a marriage service, and then "against her will ravished her and felonly lay by her." She asks a writ requiring him to answer "the said felony and rape." She refers to his offense interchangeably as "the said ravishment" and "the said rape." Note that in both cases the coitus is said to come only after the forced marriage.

[133] Whittick, "Role of the Criminal Appeal," p. 62. Whittick says that the justices' decision was "presumably by analogy with the admissibility of appeals under the act of 1382." But that act gave suit only to the husband or next of kin in a case in which the woman later consented to the ravishment—the presumption being that the right of appeal by next of kin in cases where the woman did not consent was already granted in the Statute of Westminster II, ch. 34 (1285); *Statutes*, 2:27.

himself.[134] In the case of Isabel Mohun, we know nothing about the status of her former husband, John Mohun, but we will see that another husband, or would-be husband, was in the mix, namely, Henry Yulecomb himself, and that Henry suspected another man, Guy Brian, of masterminding Isabel's prosecution against him.

The record transcribed by Cannon comes from Michaelmas term, 1379, but the events described must be earlier, since Henry has been arrested but has not yet been indicted and has not pleaded. However, less than two months after Isabel's alleged escape, Henry had reportedly been indicted and had received a pardon from the king, or in the king's name (we must remember that Richard II was only eleven years old at this time). The pardon is dated April 9, 1378, and it recounts that Henry Yulecomb stands indicted of having feloniously ravished Isabel Mohun at "Bodennek" on December 22, 1376, but that at the request of the marshall of England, John of Arundel, he is pardoned any breaking of peace connected with the said *raptus*, while still remaining liable to Isabel's charge.[135]

We note that the date of the ravishment of Isabel in Cornwall is given as almost a month later than the one that appears in the document transcribed by Cannon; and we also note that the *raptus*, without any elaboration as to its nature, is said to have allegedly occurred at her residence in Cornwall, not additionally somewhere else later on.

We must not conclude from the terms of the pardon that Henry had admitted to any guilt to the charge of *raptus*, whether it involved only his seizing of Isabel in Cornwall or the full account of events as described in her appeal. Her account is an odd one, and on the face of it suggests something more than she was admitting. If the events of Isabel's appeal are taken to bear a general resemblance to the truth, we may conjecture that Henry's primary motive must have been abduction with a view to marriage, rather than sexual passion leading to forced coitus, and that possibly there had been an betrothal agreement between him and Isabel which she wished to back out of; Henry may have thought that if he could consummate the agreement with copula, it would trigger the canonical provision that betrothals *de futuro* followed by intercourse turned the contract into a marriage *de presenti*. We will

---

[134] Putnam, *Proceedings*, p. 386, no. 8.
[135] PRO, C 66/301; calendared in *CPR Richard II*, 1:182. For text and translation, see appendix, no. 4.

see below that Henry did in fact claim that Isabel was his wife and that she had lived with him, presumably voluntarily, for a year and fifteen weeks.

Four other related King's Bench records from 3 Richard II are noted by Cannon, but not transcribed or summarized. We will see from one of them that Henry was released on mainprise in the autumn of 1379 and ordered to appear again in court in the next Hilary term, that is, in January 1380, but that he failed to appear. Two of the records, which appear together on the same membrane, seem to record what happened at that time. The first concerns the jury hearing Isabel's appeal of *raptus* and *pax fracta*, and it records that the hearing was continued until Easter term.[136] (Easter occurred on March 25 in 1380, meaning that the term would begin three weeks later, on Monday, April 16.) The entry immediately following records Isabel's appearance against William Yulecomb and Lawrence Drew for the aforesaid rape (*de raptu predicta* [*sic*]). On their nonappearance, further order was given for their arrest.[137]

The next record of 3 Richard II unearthed by Cannon is an order to the sheriff of Somerset, apparently requiring him to bring in the three knights who were the mainpernors of Henry Yulecomb, namely, Matthew Gournay, Thomas Trivet, and Thomas Fichet, along with the £200 each had forfeited because of their failure to deliver him to court and to restrain him from trying to prevent Isabel from pursuing her appeal. He not only failed to appear, but he attacked Isabel with a band of miscreants as she was approaching the royal palace in Westminster by the Waterbridge, in order to prevent her from prosecuting her appeal.[138]

We should note that the number of pledges required for appeals of rape was stipulated in the so-called Statute of the Coroner: if the appeal

---

[136] PRO, KB 27/476 9Hilary 1380), m. 30d. See appendix, no. 5.

[137] Ibid. See appendix, no. 6. The Lawrence Drew who was Yulecomb's accused accomplice is identified as the son of Drugo of Wringworth; he may be the Lawrence Drew who was appointed King's Attorney (Attorney General) on September 9, 1381 (with a successor appointed on July 8, 1382); see Sainty, *List of English Law Officers,* p. 43, drawing on *CPR.* Drew is found acting as King's Attorney from 1381 to 1384 in *Calendar of the General and Special Assize and General Gaol Delivery Commissions on the Dorses of the Patent Rolls: Richard II (1377–1399)* (Nendeln, 1977). In 1380, he served as Justice of the Peace in Berkshire (*CPR Richard II* 1:473, 513, 579), and he is seen on commissions in 1382 and 1383 (ibid., 2:25, 290). From 1386 to the end of Richard's reign he served as JP at various times in Berkshire and Wiltshire.

[138] PRO, KB 29/32 m. 52d. See appendix, no. 7.

is recent, and signs of its truth are seen, like bloody clothes, or the hue and cry raised, four or six pledges are to be used, if possible; but if the appeal is without cry and without manifest sign, then two will suffice.[139]

The record of the indictment by the grand jury is the final entry from the King's Bench rolls cited by Cannon. The attempted interception is said to have occurred on Wednesday, April 18, 1380. This date, we may observe, is just three weeks before Cecily Champain came to the King's Bench on May 7 to record her May 1 release of Chaucer from all felony-transgression-account-debt complaints. The indictment against Henry must have been handed down sometime before June 22, 1380, to fall within 3 Richard II. The jury presented that when Isabel came to prosecute her appeal of *raptus*, accompanied by Guy Brian, knight, John Kentcomb, and John Shakel, she was attacked near the Watergate Bridge by Henry Yulecomb, William Yulecomb, Baldwin Yulecomb, John Luke of Bodmin, John Cole (saddler of London), John Fowy, and John Willing of Cornwall. The attackers were arrested by James Lyons, sergeant-at-arms, but the miscreants broke the arrest and escaped.[140]

Thus, in trying to prevent an appeal of rape from being prosecuted, Henry's new accomplices, like William Yulecomb and Lawrence Drew before, were also implicated in a crime of rape.

In faint additions to this entry, one can make out that in the following Michaelmas term, "the Monday after three weeks" (October 22, 1380), the saddler John Cole appeared, and he was mainprised by other saddlers; and outlawry seems to have been declared against the three Yulecombs and the three other indicted accomplices.

Meanwhile, however, Henry Yulecomb had resorted to another measure, namely, obtaining a papal injunction against Isabel's Watergate escort, the knight Guy Brian, whom he blamed for her prosecution of him. There were two knights at this time named Guy Brian, a father and a son, and either one could be the person in question; the father had been especially active in serving as a justice of the peace and performing other official functions in Devon, Dorset, and Somerset.[141] Henry

---

[139] *Statutes* 1:41. This pseudo-statute was based on Bracton; see R. F. Hunnisett, *The Mediaeval Coroner* (Cambridge: Cambridge University Press, 1961). But Bracton does not specify the number of pledges. See Kelly, "Statutes of Rapes," p. 367.

[140] PRO, KB 29/32 m. 43d, Watergate indictment: see appendix, no. 8. This entry is referred to by Crow and Olson, *Chaucer Life-Records*, p. 345, n. 2, citing only "KB 29/32, 3–4 Richard II" without specifying the membrane.

[141] See the *Calendar of Patent Rolls*. The elder Guy seems to have been knighted in 1346

himself managed to be knighted around this time, it seems. His emissary to Rome was probably the chaplain John Dawe, who made proclamation of the papal prohibition on August 5, 1380, in the churchyard of St. Paul's Cathedral in London, immediately after the sermon, in the following terms:

Dominus papa per bullas et processus inhibet domino Guidoni Brian, militi, ne se intromitteret prosequi contra dominum Henricum Yeuelcombe, militem, pro Isabella, uxore ejusdem Henrici, que fuit uxor ejus, et est, et permansit cum eodem Henrico per unum annum et quindecim septimanas, et quod predictus Guido falso et maliciose facit prosecucionem contra eum in curia domini regis ad suspendendum eum. Et qui vult habere inde copiam veniat ad ecclesiam sancti Martini, et habebit.

[The pope by bulls and processes forbids Guy Brian, knight, to intermeddle by proceedings against Henry Yeuelcombe, knight, on behalf of Isabella, the said Henry's wife, who has been, and is, his wife, who lived with the said Henry for one year and fifteen weeks, and the aforesaid Guy falsely and wrongly proceeds against him in the king's court to get him hanged. And anyone who wishes to have a copy hereof, let him come to St. Martin's church, and he shall have it.][142]

On the following November 17, Dawe was charged in the king's court at Northampton for making this proclamation, which he acknowledged; when asked to produce the bulls, he said that they were now in the court of Rome. This unlikely explanation was seemingly accepted, and he was eventually released on condition that he never again go overseas without special license from the king.[143]

We should expect Henry, in addition to the extraordinary resort to papal injunction, to follow the usual course of bringing a writ *de uxore rapta* against Brian, as Roger Vernon was to do against the rescuers of

---

(*CPR Richard II*, 1:248); he was dead by 1391 (ibid. 4:445, 447, 467) and perhaps by June 1386 (3:162). The son is referred to as knight as early as 1377 (*CPR Edward III*, 16:160); he was part of the earl of March's Irish expedition (*CPR Richard II*, 1:409, 449), but it did not arrive in Ireland until May 15, 1380 (Thomas Frederick Tout, "Mortimer, Edmund (II) de," *Dictionary of National Biography*), so that he could still have been available to escort Isabel in April.

[142] Ed. and trans. G. O. Sayles, *Select Cases in the Court of King's Bench*, vol. 7, SS, vol. 88, (London, 1971), pp. 21–22.

[143] Ibid.

Margaret Kebell,[144] and it is likely that such a writ remains to be discovered.

There would also, of course, have been writs from the other side. One such is dated November 29, 1381, addressed to the coroners of Cornwall, ordering the outlawry of William Yulecomb and Lawrence Drew for not appearing in the last Trinity term to respond to Isabel Mohun *de raptu*. The coroner who returned the writ did not receive it until March 28, 1382, but the return was not due until April 21 of that year.[145]

Later in 1382, on October 23, Henry and his brother William received a royal pardon, just as the Parliament that passed the new statute of rapes was winding down. Henry, because of service that he is undertaking for the king in Portugal, is pardoned the king's suit for the *raptus* of Isabel Mohun on which he stands indicted, charged, or appealed, and any decrees of outlawry against him are revoked, but he remains chargeable by others on the foresaid *raptus*. William receives conditional letters of pardon for the same *raptus*.[146] William, by the way, is on record as having been pardoned once before, along with his brother Baldwin, on April 4, 1376, after being indicted or appealed for the death of John Carlyl.[147]

We see then that Henry and William Yulecomb were pardoned for the alleged rape of Isabel, even though Henry had already been pardoned for the earlier incident, and even though, according to Isabel's own accusations, William was involved only in a successful abduction in 1376 and in an attempted abduction in 1380. For a similar case, we can think of Hugh Bonehomme, pardoned for rape in 1364, for having kidnapped Agnes, daughter of John Giles, to persuade her to marry Simon Porter in spite of her being the wife of Thomas Gilling.[148]

---

[144] PRO, KB 27/973 (Michaelmas, 1504) m.1 of warrants (at end of roll): "Staff. Rogerus Vernon ponit loco suo Thomam Skrimsher versus Radulphum Gell nuper de Blore [and seven others] de placito transgressionis contra formam statuti de muliere abducta cum bonis viri inde editi et provisi, etc." See Ives, p. 39, who sums up the yearbook discussions. Ives finds Vernon to be "using the little-known section of Westminster I c. 13, *de uxore abducta cum bonis viri.*" As we have seen, the action was not uncommon a century earlier.

[145] PRO, KB 136/5/5/3/1 (quindene of Easter, 1382), last writ. See appendix, no. 9.

[146] PRO, C66/313, m. 13, reported in *CPR Richard II*, 2:179. See appendix, no. 10.

[147] *CPR Edward III*, 16 vols., (London, 1891–1916), 16:258 (at the request of Thomas Symon, chivaler).

[148] See appendix, no. 3.

Henry and William were pardoned for impending service in Portugal. But just a month after the pardon, order was given to the constable of Dover to arrest the knight Henry Yulecomb and sixteen other men, including William and Baldwin Yulecomb and John Fawy (Fowy), for having rebelled against the king's uncle Edmund, earl of Cambridge, when on a voyage with him. Similar commissions were given to others in England, including Guy Brian, to arrest the same men.[149] Two years later there were more commissions for the same offense,[150] but in the following year all three Yulecombs were pardoned by the king at the supplication of the earl's wife, the countess of Cambridge.[151] In 1388, we find Henry being appointed to a royal commission of inquiry.[152] In the next decade he served as commissioner of array[153] and king's escheator in Cornwall.[154] In January of 1399, Henry finally had successful dealings with another Isabel, but only after she was dead: a royal grant was bestowed on him in virtue of his good service, during the course of which, "by God's visitation," he had gone blind; he was to receive the lands belonging to Isabel Cornewaill, deceased, tenant-in-chief, during the minority of her grandson and heir, Thomas, son of her son David Hendore.[155] Henry's blindness did not prevent him from being included in the duke of Exeter's expedition to Ireland: he received protection for the voyage on May 1 and

---

[149] *CPR Richard II*, 2:256 (November 24, 1382).

[150] Ibid., 2:494 (June 24, 1384, only against Henry and three others, not including his brothers and Fawy; they "behaved rebelliously and frustrated the completion of the expedition" of the earl of Cambridge); 2:348–49 (July 3, 1384, against thirteen men, including the four Watergate fugitives; they "behaved so rebelliously" the earl of Cambridge could not complete the object of his expedition).

[151] Ibid., 2:534 (February 18, 1385).

[152] Ibid., 3:468–69 (May 28, 1388. Henry Ilecome, knight, and others are to inquire if a certain man was an alien and possessed his land illegally).

[153] Ibid., 5:88 (March 1, 1392).

[154] Ibid., 5:653 (December 2, 1395); 6:15 (July 5, 1396), 241 (July 12, 1397). Cf. 5:651 (December 3, 1395): Henry accuses the mayor of Bodmyn, Cornwall, of breaking into his lands, destroying his property, and lying in wait to kill him.

[155] Ibid., 6:479–80, January 25, 1399, for Henry Ivelcombe (i.e., Iuelcombe), knight. There is no record of Isabel's marriage to David Hendore's father. On November 18, 1398 we hear of a vicarage in the diocese of Exeter in the king's gift by reason of the minority of Thomas, son and heir of David Hendor, tenant-in-chief (*CPR Richard II*, 6:447). Isabel was married to Edmund Cornewaille in 1373, and Edmund's mother was also named Isabel (*CPR Edward III*, 15:295–96); an entry in 1389 may indicate that Edmund is dead: Isabel is called both "his wife" and "formerly his wife" (*CPR Richard II*, 4:25).

June 17 of 1399.[156] After Richard II's deposition, his wardship grant was confirmed by the new king.[157]

Meanwhile, new writs continued to be noted on the Watergate indictment, with no notice taken of the pardons of Henry and William from the king's suit in 1382. John Cole eventually turned up again, "made fine," and was released through new mainpernors, and finally, perhaps as late as 1386, was pardoned and dismissed.[158] I have been able to find no further word of Isabel; perhaps we will have to wait until Christopher Cannon's next foray into the Public Record Office.

VI. Releases Undocumented and Documented

We have seen that the king pardoned Henry Yulecomb and his brothers twice for the *raptus* of Isabel, first in 1378 and then in 1382. Isabel herself could have pardoned him as well by withdrawing her appeal at any time. This, of course, would have subjected her to a fine, which she would likely have wished Henry to pay as part of the settlement, along with other considerations. He in turn would undoubtedly have wanted a release from her of the kind that Cecily Champain gave to Chaucer.

A case from the early part of the next century shows the dangers of not having such a release. It concerns still another widow Isabel, *Isabella que fuit uxor*, this time the former wife of Roger Waye. In the county of Devon in 1422, she had a man named Stephen Melya attached, to answer her plea that "with force and arms he broke the close of the said Isabella at Burston and depastured, trod down, and wasted with some beasts her grass, lately growing there, to the value of 40s., and inflicted other outrages upon her, to the serious loss of the said Isabella and against the king's peace." Her attorney, Thomas Foulhill, appearing for her in court and specifying that the incident occurred on July 1, 1420, elaborated on the charges and put the damages at £20. Stephen's attorney, John Burley, denied force and injury and pleaded not guilty. Both parties put themselves on the country. As for the *residuum* of the aforesaid trespass, Stephen's position was that Isabel ought not to have maintained an action against him, because a long time after the trespass was

---

[156] *CPR Richard II*, 6:540, 573.
[157] *CPR Henry IV*, 4 vols., (London, 1903–9), 1:65, November 8, 1399.
[158] Watergate indictment.

supposedly committed, namely, on October 3, 1420, the two parties through the mediation of friends had reached a compromise, promising that they would "stand in high and in low" (*stare in alto et in basso*) by the award of mutually agreed upon arbitrators in Cornwall "both concerning the aforesaid trespass as well as all other trespasses, plaints, and quarrels held, instituted, or to be instituted" ("tam de et super transgressione predicta quam de omnibus aliis transgressionibus, querelis, et debatis . . . habitis, motis, seu movendis"). The arbitrators decided that Stephen should give Isabel one gallon of wine in full satisfaction of everything, and she accepted the gallon of wine in accord with the award. Stephen asserted that he was ready to prove this account of events, but Isabel denied that she had ever made such an agreement, and the case was sent to a jury.[159]

We note that the form of the alleged Isabel–Stephen arbitration, referring first to a specific charge and then to all other actions, corresponds to the May 4 version of the Cecily–Geoffrey quitclaim, rather than to the May 7 version, which first refers generally to various kinds of actions, including felonies, and then even more generally to all possible actions. If Cecily Champain and Geoffrey Chaucer entered upon a similar arbitration with the assistance of friends—for instance, the acquaintances of Chaucer who witnessed the release on May 1—he was fortunate that she not only agreed to the award but also registered it in two courts of law.

An example closer to our interest here can be seen in a 1344 ravishment plea: "When the four defendants showed the court a quitclaim from the plaintiffs, in which they had remitted their action for ravishment, the plaintiffs were amerced for false claim and the ravishers went free."[160] If Cecily Champain had taken Chaucer to court in spite of her release, he would presumably have been on clearer ground if he could have shown the version of the release that mentioned *raptus* explicitly, but the vague language of the May 7 copy would undoubtedly have served just as well.

[159] Sayles, *Select Cases*, 7:257–58: KB 27/643 m. 59.
[160] Walker, "Wrongdoing," p. 287 (Professor Walker informs me that her PRO citation of this case is erroneous, and that she has not yet recovered the correct citation). The plaintiffs in this case accused the defendants of ravishing and abducting a girl, who was a minor in feudal custody, against the will of the plaintiffs, but the defendants showed a *scriptum* remitting and relaxing them.

In another case of ravishment in which a quitclaim figured, this one from 1342, a mother is sued for abducting her son from the custody of his guardian—a fairly typical complaint.[161] Henry of Ravenswath, knight, charges Elizabeth Spring in a writ of trespass with ravishing the heir from his possession ("breve de transgressione per quod ei imponitur ipsam rapuisse predictum heredem extra possessionem ipsius Henrici") on May 5, 1339; Henry claims to own the boy's maritage, the value of which has allegedly deteriorated by the amount of £300. Elizabeth responds by submitting a *scriptum* according to which Henry's father quitclaimed the manor in question to the heir's grandfather, and the terms of the quitclaim indicate that the land is held is socage, not feudal tenure.[162] She asks the court's judgment on whether the quitclaim vitiates Henry's suit. Henry denies that the *scriptum* is his father's doing. Both Elizabeth and Henry call for a trial by jury (*per patriam*) and by the seven witnesses named in the release (*et per . . . testes in predicto scripto nominatos*). Meanwhile the *scriptum* is given to the king's clerk for safekeeping, and he eventually delivers it to one of the justices. Elizabeth's case would have been strengthened, of course, if she could have produced a court enrollment of the release as well as the original. But even as it was, she won the case, at least temporarily—apparently because Henry failed to appear on the appointed day of trial—and was dismissed *sine die.*[163]

If the plaintiff had appeared, along with the witnesses named in the release, the witnesses would have been examined by the jury and possibly by the justices as well, as in a 1318 case of false imprisonment mentioned above, *Reynham v Hatton*: After the jury found the seven defendants guilty, with damages assessed at £100, four of the defendants produced

---

[161] Walker, "Widow and Ward: The Feudal Law of Child Custody in Medieval England," *Women in Medieval Society*, ed. Susan Mosher Stuard (Philadelphia: University of Pennsylvania Press, 1976), pp. 159–72, at 163–65.

[162] As Walker explains (ibid., p. 164), socage was "a free tenure closer to the peasant level in which the land and the heir were placed in the familial custody of a relative who could not inherit in the event of the child's death. . . . Mothers who acted as guardians ('next friends') were especially liable to be involved in litigation if their late husbands held any land by feudal tenure."

[163] PRO, CP 40/324 m. 252. Walker, "Widow and Ward," p. 171, n. 39, recounts a similar case from 1303: "Johanna, widow of Adam de Lorymer, went *sine die* in a plea of ravishing Walter, the son and heir. Johanna disputed the tenurial claims of the plaintiff and the jury supported her. Probably she had taken her son from the plaintiff but he had had no right to the custody, and hence there was no case against her."

a *scriptum* in which the plaintiff allegedly pardoned ("remisit, relaxavit, et omnino imperpetuum pardonavit") all actions and demands that he had against them by reason of trespass, conspiracy, and imprisonment. The plaintiff's attorney denied that the *scriptum* was authentic, and he offered to prove it by the country and by the witnesses. The witnesses were examined separately, their conflicting testimony was recorded in detail and rejected as frivolous, and the *scriptum* was declared false. The four defendants were assessed an extra £50 damages.[164] In a 1390 case, *Colehill v Hankin*, in which the charge was the taking and carrying away of goods and chattels, the defendant pleaded a release of all actions real and personal given him by the executors of the plaintiff's former husband, and he asked immediate judgment of the justices without putting the matter to trial.[165]

VII. Conclusion

Both Isabel Mohun and Cecily Champain seem to have been "women of independent means"; Isabel was the former wife of someone, while Cecily was the "former daughter" of others. Both acted for themselves, Isabel in an appeal of rape, and Cecily in an unknown action or series of actions concerning rape and perhaps other complaints.

We know more about Isabel's situation. She was a widow, or else her marriage to John Mohun had been annulled. Presumably she owned her own "remarriage"; at least, we do not hear of anyone else who did. Henry Yulecomb obviously desired to marry her, and either she resisted and he used force from the beginning, in November of 1376 (her date) or in December of the same year (his date), or else she did agree to marry him and later tried to get out of it, lying about the violence used to take her away and to force intercourse upon her—which, she claimed, occurred only once, even though he detained her for well over a year. It may be that she had to include the reference to unwilling intercourse in order to mount an appeal, or at least she and her lawyers may have believed that such a reference was necessary. Margaret Kebell in a similar situation a century later had an appeal accepted on a simple charge of *raptus*. On the ecclesiastical side, Isabel could have sought an annulment

---

[164] Arnold, *Select Cases of Trespass*, pp. 37–41, *Reynham v. Hatton* (4.3).

[165] Arnold, pp. 173–74 (13.45). This is a case of demurral, that is, denial that the other party has a case (see pp. xxvii, liii). The outcome has not been found.

on the grounds that the marriage was entered into under "force and fear." Back on the secular side, she could have followed the example of the widow Joan Hotoft in 1362, when she charged Henry Willows with criminally breaking and entering and imprisoning her (doc. 1 below), or the same Joan in 1363, when, acting as a nonwidow, she made the same complaints against the same man but added abduction and forced marriage to the charges (doc. 2). Both women could also have brought similar civil suits against the alleged perpetrators. But whatever civil punishments she may have contemplated, Isabel was determined to bring Henry to court as a felon. Perhaps she wished to seek the death penalty for him, as he himself complained about her assistant, Guy Brian. Henry avoided the danger to his neck from the king's side by securing pardons from the king, but the danger from Isabel remained. However, Whittick's study of the appeal process in the fifteenth century leads him to conclude that "the object of an appeal was not vengeance exacted by the defendant's death, but the return of a chattel or a financial settlement after the greatest possible harassment of the other party," a process that he compares to the use of the appeal of rape in the thirteenth century, as reported by Post.[166]

As for Cecily Champain, we are still left with the bare word *raptus* in the first version of her quitclaim, summing up a set of circumstances perfectly well known to the participants but not to us. *Raptus* can certainly mean a sexual violation, short for *raptus et carnalis commixtio contra voluntatem femine*. But *raptus* is also sometimes short for ravishing-and-abducting, and it was used of both male and female wards and also of married women. In the latter case, the terms of the writ *De uxore rapta* required reference to ravishing, abducting, and detaining, even though there was usually no seizure, no sexual violation, no abduction, no robbery from husband, no detention, and even, sometimes, no longer any husband: that is, in some cases the marriage had been annulled in a church court. Thus, even if Isabel Mohun Yulecomb had annulled a marriage to Henry Yulecomb on the grounds suggested above, that she did not give free consent, Henry could have resorted to using the *De uxore rapta* writ, naming Guy Brian as the person who ravished, abducted, and detained her, even though well aware that Brian had done none of these things, but at most, let us say, had only persuaded her to

---

[166] Whittick, "Role of the Criminal Appeal," p. 63, citing Post, "Ravishment of Women," for the thirteenth century.

leave Henry. We have seen Roger Vernon doing this in the case of his forced wife, Margaret Kebell.

Isabel identified herself as having been the wife of John Mohun and made no allusion to the fact that Henry Yulecomb claimed her as his wife. Cecily claimed to be lately the daughter of William and Agnes Champain. She too may have been keeping silent about a claim that some man was making on her as his wife, or she may simply not have mentioned a former or current husband, as in the case of Agnes Giles Gilling (doc. 3 below). By using *quondam* of her parents, she may have been saying nothing more than that they were dead; or, just conceivably, she may have meant to say that she was no longer underage, or that neither they nor anyone else owned her maritage. If her father had owned her maritage (as was the claim in *Lincoln v Simond*, 1391) and she were abducted, he could have referred to her abduction as a *raptus*, and obtained a writ *De raptu de custodia*. But if her father or mother or some other person did not own her maritage and she were abducted by a would-be suitor who enlisted Chaucer's aid, what could she do to obtain satisfaction or damages? On the criminal side, she could have brought an appeal against the perpetrators, whether alleging a real or fictitious element of sexual force, like Isabel Mohun, or not mentioning forced sex, like Alice Jackman, daughter of Richard Jackman, in 1377, where the civil writ *De uxore rapta cum bonis mariti* was altered, in effect, to a criminal appeal *De filia rapta cum bonis patris* (doc. 11 below), or Margaret, widow of Thomas Kebell, later on. She could also, like Joan Hotoft, and like Margaret Kebell's relatives, have laid information at quarter-sessions. Or, like Alice Lord in 1362, in acting against the disappointed suitor who kidnapped her and beat her up, she could have filed a bill of complaint, seeking an indictment for felony or trespass. She could also have brought the sort of civil suits, including assault, that Margaret Kebell did, or obtained a writ charging that she had been taken, imprisoned, and maltreated, like Idonia Cophyn in 1379.

If, on the other hand, Cecily's *raptus* were one of sexual violation, she could clearly have pursued both an appeal and indictment on the criminal side. As for civil remedies, though no examples have yet been found of damages being sought in such cases, one can easily imagine that actions of breaking and entering and assault would be readily available.

Given the inherent ambiguity of the word *raptus*, when abduction and not sexual violation was the main issue, even when both *rapere* and *abducere* were used, there was probably an implicit accusation of sexual violation where the circumstances admitted it: that is, whenever a woman was abducted by a man. If so, that presumptive aspect of the charge would have to be argued or explained away in court. This would clearly be true in criminal prosecutions, but it would also obtain in responses to civil suits of abduction. Such a convention would not have been necessary, of course, in the actions of account and debt mentioned by Cecily in the version of her release discovered by Cannon.

To sum up, given both releases, the one naming *raptus* and the other naming both criminal and civil actions, Cecily's main grievance could have been either abduction or sexual violation or a combination of both. There is more evidence of both criminal and civil remedies being used for abduction than for sexual violation, but it is plausible for the latter as well. If the charge were abduction, say, in the wake of a soured marriage negotiation, an additional charge of unwanted coitus may have been added or even emphasized, in order to make it more convincingly the subject of an appeal of *raptus.*

But whether the charge was meant seriously or fictitiously, whether it involved forced sex—in actuality or only as part of a conventional complaint—or only abduction (with or without an explicit or implicit charge of sexual violation) we must be on guard against concluding that she had proved it or could have proved it, or that it is likely to have been true. Our tours through the legal practices of Chaucer's time should teach us that there are often many complications lying beneath the literal surface of legal records. The grand jury's verdict of "not proven"— or, as they put it in those days, "ignoramus"—is usually the wisest conclusion. Still, it is likely that there was something to the charge, whatever it was, since Chaucer seems to have paid to make it go away. It is pleasant to think that Cecily, acting on her own in a man's world, was able to obtain financial reparations after he had done something actionable against her.

This study has been mainly linguistic and legalistic: I have tried to survey the terms used for the two kinds of rape, sex-rape and abduction-rape, and the realities and fictions that can lie behind them. The second kind of rape gives rise to all sorts of combinations and mixtures of motives and emotions: abduction for the purpose of sex; abduction for the purpose of marriage or arranging a marriage, because of the abductee's wealth or potential wealth; with the abductee willing beforehand or later, or never giving consent to the marriage or the sex that occurs within it. Such distinctions must be kept in mind not only in historical contexts but also in literature.

Let us end by considering Jill Mann's judgment that for Chaucer "rape remains a constant touchstone for determining justice between the sexes; in the *Canterbury Tales* as in the *Legend* [*of Good Women*] it appears as the definitive form of male tyranny, representing a fundamental imbalance between the sexes which human relationships must seek to redress."[167] She is, of course, speaking primarily of the two sexual rapes in the *Legend*, namely, those of Lucretia and Philomela (the latter a case of abduction for purposes of forced sex), and the single sexual rape in the *Canterbury Tales*, at the beginning of *The Wife of Bath's Tale*, where the rape is followed by the hue and cry ("swich clamour / And swich pursute" [lines 889–90]) and the death penalty. Chaucer seems to have the Wife of Bath wonder at the severity of this punishment: "Paraventure swich was the statut tho" (line 893), as if it were not true in her modern England. But, of course, death was the punishment for all felonies, and though it may not have been carried out very often for indictments of rape, in an appeal of rape by the violated woman after a hue and cry, execution should have been inevitable—unless, of course, the traditional compromise of letting the rapist off in exchange for marrying his victim was still feasible in Chaucer's time. That solution does not come into play here (unless we should wish to regard the raped maiden and the Loathly Lady as one and the same person!).

What other rapes is Mann thinking of for her broad statement? She brings up later the foiled rape of Constance in *The Man of Law's Tale* and the plot to make Virginia a sex slave in *The Physician's Tale*, and also, in *The Franklin's Tale*, Aurelius's efforts to secure the affections of Dorigen, which Dorigen thinks of in terms of classical threats of sexual rape. Mann is not concerned with the sex-minded seizers of more or less consenting women in the farcical tales—Nicholas, John and Alleyn, Daun John—but she does include a character in *The Merchant's Tale*, namely, Pluto, for his rape of Proserpine, even though, as we have seen, Chaucer uses the term "fetched" instead of "ravished," for Mann thinks that the grisliness of Pluto's cart makes the event "violent and horrific" and "evokes the terror of the scene." But it seems that any potential terror is

---

[167] Jill Mann, *Geoffrey Chaucer* (Atlantic Highlands: Humanities Press International, 1991), p. 45. She deals with rape on pp. 43–47 (Lucretia and Philomela), 64–66 (Proserpina), 87–89 (*Wife of Bath's Tale*), 97–98 (near-rape in *Pamphilus*), 115 (Dorigen), 137 (Constance), 145 (Virginia), and 167–68 (*Troilus*).

diffused by Chaucer's making Pluto not the god of the underworld but the king of Faery. And even though she says that Pluto's antifeminist remarks are the words of a rapist, she admits that he is "a hen-pecked rapist." We must also acknowledge that Chaucer portrays Proserpine as having long ago consented to her ravished state, like Helen in the *Troilus*, whose rape Mann also discusses.

Since Mann has admitted Pluto and Paris to her list of Chaucerian rapists, I suggest a similar candidate, namely, Theseus. For, not to mention his abduction of the willing Ariadne and Phaedra (and abandonment of Ariadne) in the *Legend of Good Women*, he conquered the Amazons in the land of Feminy by force of arms, and although his subsequent courtship of Hippolyta is omitted—in the *Theseid* he considers her fairer than Helen, whom he had previously abducted (1.130)—we do see the way he deals with his captured ward Emily. He does not give her much room to withhold her consent to marry the winner of the tournament; and, at the end of the story, when she has been a widow for some years, though he does ask her consent to remarry and take Palamon for husband, he does not wait for her reply. We must assume, however, since we are told that she was happy with Palemon, that she was ravished by Theseus's speech (the sort of ravishment that Troilus contrasts with physical force) and gave her full assent. We can, therefore, classify Theseus as a rapist, even a serial rapist; but, since he never refuses any request that women make of him, he approaches the henpecked status of King Pluto in the realm of Faery. We must also remember that Pluto's wife is not the only ravished spouse in *The Merchant's Tale*, for January is "ravished in a trance" every time he looks on May's face, and that in turn brings out the rapist in him: he begins to "menace" her in his heart, threatening to "strain" her in his arms harder than ever Paris did Helen (lines 1750–54). Both January and May, then, are victims of rape, but January is at a disadvantage, since he is the victim of a divine conspiracy: after Venus injured him with her firebrand, he was "so ravished on his lady May" that he was nearly mad and on the point of swooning.

One lesson to take away from all this is that the language of rape has a very wide range in the Middle Ages, and we must not let our hatred for the narrowed meaning of our modern word "rape" mislead us when dealing with past uses of the word, for it will betray us like the most insidious kind of false friend.

Appendix

Documents from the Public Record Office

1. Commission of oyer and terminer, October 25, 1362: Criminal trespass complaint of Joan Hotoft that Henry Willows and others entered her close and imprisoned her. PRO, C (Chancery) 66/266, m. 20d, calendared in *CPR, Edward III*, 12:288.

Audiendo et terminando. Rex dilectis et fidelibus suis Johanni de la Lee, Johanni Knyvet, Waltero de Aldebury, et Thome de Eston, salutem. Ex quadem querela Johanne que fuit uxor Nicholai Hotoft, accepimus quod Henricus atte Wylewes de London, Ricardus de Ardern de London, peltere, Ricardus atte Grene de Hakeneye, Johannes Hereward, Willelmus Hereward, Johannes Sprot, Willielmus Bakere, Willielmus Wyot de Hakeneye, Thomas Hore, peltere, et Ricardus de Tychebourn, et quamplures alii malefactores et pacis nostre perturbatores, clausum ipsius Johanne apud Braghyng vi et armis intraverunt et ipsam Johannem ibidem ceperunt, imprisonaverunt, et male tractaverunt, et alia enormia ei intulerunt, ad grave dampnum ipsius Johanne et contra pacem nostram. Et quia transgressionem predictam, si perpetrata fuerit, relinquere noluimus impunitam, assignavimus vos tres et duos vestrum, quorum vos, prefate Johannes Knyvet, unum esse volumus, justiciarios nostros, ad inquirendum per sacramentum proborum et legitimorum hominum de comitatu Hereford, per quos rei veritas melius sciri poterit de nominibus malefactorum predictorum qui una cum prefatis Henrico, Ricardo, Ricardo, Johanne, Willielmo, Johanne, Willielmo, Willielmo, Thoma, et Ricardo transgressionem illam perpetrarunt, et de transgressione predicta plenius veritatem, et ad eandem transgressionem audiendum et terminandum secundum legem et consuetudinem regni nostri. Et ideo vobis mandamus quod ad certos etc., quos etc., quorum etc., ad hoc provideritis inquisitionem illam facere, et transgressionem predictam audiatis et terminetis in forma predicta. F[. . .] etc. Salvis etc. Mandavimus enim vicecomiti nostro Hereford quod ad certos [etc.,] quos etc., quorum etc., ei sciri facere, venire facere coram vobis ut quorum etc., tot etc., per quos etc., et inquiri. In cujus etc.
Rex, apud Westmonasterium xxv die Octobris.

Hearing and determining. The king to his beloved and faithful John Lee, John Knyvet, Walter Aldebury, and Thomas Eston, greetings. From a

150

complaint of Joan who was the wife of Nicholas Hotoft we have taken it that Henry Willows of London, Richard Ardern of London, pelterer, Richard Green of Hakeney, John Hereward, William Hereward, John Sprot, William Baker, William Wyot of Hakeney, Thomas Hore, pelterer, and Richard Tychebourn, and several other evildoers and disturbers of our peace, entered the close of the said Joan at Braghyng by force and arms, took the said Joan there and imprisoned and maltreated her, and inflicted other enormities upon her, to the grave damage of the said Joan and against our peace. And because we were unwilling to leave unpunished the aforesaid trespass, if it were perpetrated, we assigned you, three and two of you, of whom we wish you, the aforesaid John Knyvet, to be one, as our justices, to make inquest by the oath of good and lawful men from the county of Hereford, by means of whom the truth of the matter can be better known concerning the names of the evildoers who along with the aforesaid Henry, Richard, Richard, John, William, John, William, William, Thomas, and Richard perpetrated that trespass, and the truth of the aforesaid trespass can be more fully known, and to hear and determine the same trespass according to the law and custom of our realm. And therefore we mandate you that to certain men etc., whom etc., whose etc., you shall provide to make the said inquest etc., and hear and determine the aforesaid trespass in the aforesaid form. [?] etc. Saving etc. For we have mandated our sheriff of Hereford that to certain men whom etc., whose etc., to make known to him, to make come before you, so that whose etc., so many etc., by means of whom etc., and have inquest made. In whose etc.

The king at Westminster, the 25th day of October [1362].

2. Commission of oyer and terminer, May 2, 1363: Criminal trespass complaint of Joan Hotoft that Henry Willows and others broke into her close, imprisoned her, took her and her chattels away and kept her captive until she took an oath to marry Henry. PRO, C 66/267, m. 22d, calendared in *CPR, Edward III*, 12:363.

Audiendo et terminando. Rex dilectis et fidelibus suis Johanni de Moubray, Johanni Knyvet, Thome de Ingelby, Johanni Chilterne, et Luce Vynter, salutem. Ex quadam querela Johanne Hoto[f]t accepimus quod Henricus Wylewes de London, draper, Richardus Ardern de London, pelter, Johannes Sprot de London, shereman, Thomas Hore, skynnere, et Richardus Tychebourn, skynnere, ac quidam alii malefactores et pacis nostre perturbatores, clausum et domos ipsius Johanne

apud Braghyng vi et armis noctanter fregerunt et ipsam Johannam ibidem ceperunt, imprisonaverunt, et male tractaverunt, et ipsam sic imprisonatam abinde ad diversa loca ignota duxerunt, et eam sic in prisona, quousque eadam Johanna sacramentum corporale quod se prefato Henrico maritari promittere prestitisset, detinuerunt, et bona et catalla sua ad valenciam quadraginta librarum apud predictam villam de Braghyng inventa ceperunt et asportaverunt, et in homines et servientes suos ibidem insultum fecerunt et ipsos verberaverunt, vulneraverunt, et male tractaverunt, per quod eadem Johanna servicium suum eorundem hominum et servientum per magnum tempus amisit, et alia enormia ei intulerunt, ad grave dampnum ipsius Johanne et contra pacem nostram. Et quia transgressionem predictam, si perpetrata fuerit, relinquere noluimus impunitam, assignavimus vos, quatuor, tres, et duos vestrum, quorum aliquem vestrum vos, prefati Johannes de Moubray, Johannes Knyvet, et Thoma[s], unum esse voluimus, justiciarios nostros, ad inquirendum per sacramentum proborum et legitimorum hominum de comitatu Hereford, per quos rei veritas melius sciri poterit de nominibus malefactorum predictorum qui una cum prefatis Henrico, etc., transgressionem predictam perpetrarunt [continues as above].
Rex apud Westmonasterium, secundo die Maji [1363].

Hearing and determining. The king to his beloved and faithful John Mowbray, John Knyvet, Thomas Ingelby, John Chiltern, and Luke Vynter, greetings. From a complaint of Joan Hotoft we have taken it that Henry Willows of London, draper, Richard Ardern of London, pelterer, John Sprot of London, shearman, Thomas Hore, skinner, and Richard Tychebourn, skinner, and certain other evildoers and disturbers of our peace, by force and arms at night broke the close and houses of the said Joan at Braghyng and took the said Joan there and imprisoned and maltreated her, and, thus imprisoned, took her to divers unknown places and detained her thus in prison until the same Joan had made a corporal oath that she promise to be married to the aforesaid Henry, and they took and carried away goods and chattels to the value of forty pounds found at the aforesaid village of Braghyng, and they made assault upon her men and servants there and beat and wounded and maltreated them, by which the same Joan lost her service of the same men and servants for a long time, and they inflicted other enormities upon her, to the grave damage of the said Joan and against our peace. And

because we were unwilling to leave unpunished the aforesaid trespass, if it were perpetrated, we assigned you, four, three, and two of you, of whom one of you, the aforesaid John Mowbray, John Knyvet, and Thomas, we wish to be one, as our justices, to make inquest by the oath of good and lawful men from the county of Hereford, by means of whom the truth of the matter might be known concerning the names of the aforesaid evildoers who along with the aforesaid Henry, etc., perpetrated the aforesaid trespass [continues as in document 1].
The king at Westminster, the 2nd day of May [1363].

3. Pardon, dated May 6, 1364, of Hugh Bonehomme for various offenses including manslaughter and *raptus*. PRO, C 66/269, m. 7, calendared in *CPR*, *Edward III*, 12:515.

Rex omnibus ballivis et fidelibus suis ad quos etc., salutem. Sciatis quod cum Hugo Bonehumme de Bugthorp indictatus sit, sicut intelleximus, de eo quod ipse die dominica proxima post festum translationis sancti Thome martiris anno regni nostri tricesimo sexto [July 3, 1362] felonice interfecit Gilbertum filium Johannis Grayve de Bugthorp, ac idem Hugo similiter sit indictatus per nomen magistri Hugonis Boni Hominis, aliter vocatus Hugo Bonehomme de Bugthorp, quod ipse simul cum aliis in carnipriveo anno preterito [February 15, 1363] apud Eboracum vi et armis cepit Agnetem filiam Johannis Gyles de Eboraco et ipsam rapuit et secum abduxit et ipsam per cohercionem et minas consentire fecit ad matrimonium injustam contrahendum cum Simone Porter, et bona et catalla Thome Gillyng, tunc mariti dicte Agnetis, ad valenciam viginti marcarum cepit et asportavit, et de eo quod idem Hugo die dominica in quinta septimana quadrigesime anno regni nostri vicesimo tercio [March 29, 1349] bona et catalla Gilberti filii Johannis Grayve ad valenciam duarum marcarum apud Bugthorp cepit et asportavit, et de eo quod prefatus Hugo cum aliis contra prohibicionem nostram sediciose asportavit ad partes transmarinas ducentas marcas sterlingorum in pecunia numerata, videlicet, ad festum sancti Andree anno regni nostri tricesimo primo [November 30, 1357], ac eciam de eo quod ipse ad festum Invencionis sancte crucis anno regni nostri vicesimo tercio [May 3, 1349] venit apud Knyteros juxta Skirpenbek, armatus cum scuto et lancia ad modum guerre, et vadiavit bellum contra Rogerum Clerc, nos de gracia nostra speciali et ad requisicionem tam fratris nostri nuper regis Francie, cujus anime propicietur Deus, quam quorumdam cardinalium qui nobis ex causa specialiter scripserunt, perdonamus eidem Hugoni sectam pacis nostre que ad nos pertinet pro morte et raptu predictis unde sic indictatus, rettatus, vel appellatus existit, ac eciam utlagarias, si que in ipsum hujus occasione fuerint promulgate, et perdonamus similiter eidem Hugoni omnes alias utlagarias in ipsum occasione sedicionis et transgressionum predictarum promulgatas, et firmam pacem nostram ei inde concedimus; ita tamen quod stet recto in curia nostra si quis versus eam loqui voluerit de morte et raptu predictis, et stet etiam recto in eadem curia nostra tam ad sectam nostram quam aliorum de sedicione et transgressionibus antedictis. In cujus etc.

Rex apud Westmonasterium vi die Maji [1364]. [It is noted that on the following July 5 three mainpernors secured Hugh's release on good behavior.]

The king to all his bailiffs and faithful to whom [these letters may come,] greetings. Know that, since Hugh Bonehumme of Bugthorp stands indicted, as we have understood, for that he on the Sunday next after the feast of the translation of St. Thomas Martyr in the thirty-sixth year of our reign [July 3, 1362] feloniously killed Gilbert the son of John Grayve of Bugthorp; and the same Hugh stands similarly indicted, by the name of Master Hugh Goodman, otherwise called Hugh Bonehomme of Bugthorp, for that he along with others on the day of Carnival last year [February 15, 1363] at York by force and arms took Agnes the daughter of John Gyles of York and ravished her and took her away with him and by coercion and threats made her consent to contracting an unjust marriage with Simon Porter, and that he took and carried off the goods and chattels of Thomas Gillyng, at that time the husband of the said Agnes, to the value of twenty marks; and for that the same Hugh on the Sunday of the fifth week of Lent in the twenty-third year of our reign [March 29, 1349] took and carried off goods and chattels of Gilbert the son of John Grayve to the value of two marks, at Bugthorp; and for that the aforesaid Hugh along with others against our prohibition seditiously carried away to places beyond the seas two hundred marks of sterlings in numbered money, viz., on the feast of St. Andrew in the thirty-first year of our reign [November 30, 1357]; and also for that on the feast of the Finding of the Holy Cross in the twenty-third year of our reign [May 3, 1349] he came to Knyteros near Skirpenbek, armed with shield and lance in warlike fashion, and waged a duel against Roger Clerk; we of our special grace and at the request both of our brother recently king of France, on whose soul may God have mercy, and of certain cardinals who have specially for good cause written to us, we pardon the same Hugh the suit of our peace that pertains to us for the aforesaid death and rape whence he stands indicted, charged, or appealed, and also outlawries, if any have been promulgated against him by virtue of this occasion, and we similarly pardon the same Hugh all other outlawries promulgated against him on the occasion of the aforesaid sedition and trespasses, and we grant him our firm peace thereupon. So that however he stand trial in our court if anyone should wish to speak against him concerning the aforesaid death and rape, and that he also stand trial in our same court both regarding our suit and that of others concerning the aforesaid sedition and trespasses. In whose, etc. The king at Westminster, the 6th day of May [1364].

4. Pardon dated April 9, 1378. PRO, C 66 / 301, m. 21; calendared in *CPR Richard II*, 1:182.

Rex omnibus ballivis et fidelibus suis ad quos, etc. Sciatis quod, cum Henricus Yllecombe indictatus existat, ut intelleximus, de eo quod ipse, die Lune proximo ante festum Natalis Domini anno regni carissimi domini et avi nostri Edwardi nuper regis Anglie defuncti quinquagesimo, felonice rapuit apud Bodennek Isabellam que fuit uxor Johannis Moune, nos de gratia nostra speciali et de supplicacione dilecti consanguinei et fidelis nostri Johannis de Arundell, marescalli nostri Anglie, perdonavimus eidem Henrico sectam pacis nostre que ad nos pertinent pro raptu supradicto unde sic indictatus, rettatus, vel appellatus existit, ac eciam utlagariam si qua in ipsum ea occasione fuerit promulgata, et firmam pacem ei inde concedimus. Ita tamen quod stet recto in curia nostra si predicta Isabella versus eum loqui voluerit de felonia supradicta. In cuius, etc.
Rex apud Westmonasterium, ix die Aprilis.

The King to all his bailiffs and faithful subjects to whom, etc. Know that since Henry Yllecombe stands indicted, as we have understood, for having on the Monday before the feast of the birth of Our Lord in the fiftieth year of the reign of our dear lord and grandfather Edward, recently King of England, now deceased [i.e., December 22, 1376], feloniously ravished Isabel, who was the wife of John Moune, at Bodennek, we of our special grace and by supplication of our beloved kinsman and faithful subject, John of Arundell, our marshall of England, have pardoned the same Henry the suit of our peace that pertains to us because of the aforesaid rape whereof he stands indicted, charged, or appealed, and also outlawry, if any for this matter should have been promulgated against him, and we concede to him our firm peace. So that, however, he stand trial in our court if the foresaid Isabel should wish to speak against him concerning the above-mentioned felony. In whose, etc. The king at Westminster, the ninth day of April.

5. Continuation of jury to Easter term, 1380 (April 16). PRO, KB 27/476 (Hilary term, 1380), m. 30d.

Devon. Jurata inter Isabellam, que fuit uxor Johannis Moun, in propria persona sua appellatricem, et Henricum Yeuelcombe, de raptu et pace domini Edwardi nuper regis Anglie, avi domini regis nunc, fracte, unde eum appellat coram domino rege, ponitur in respectum usque a die pasche in tres septimanas, ubicumque, etc., per districtionem juratorum. Quia nullus, etc. Ideo vicecomes habeat corpora omnium juratorum, etc. Idem dies datus est partibus predictis, etc., videlicet predicto Henrico per manucepcionem suam qua prius, etc.

Devon. The jury between Isabel, former wife of John Mohun, appellatrix in her own person, and Henry Yulecomb, concerning rape and the breaking of the peace of the lord Edward, late king of England, grandfather of the present king, whereof she appealed him before the lord king, is placed in respite until three weeks after Easter, wherever, etc., for the distraint of the jurors, because no one, etc. Therefore the sheriff is to have the bodies of all the jurors, etc. The same day is given to the aforesaid parties, etc., viz. to the aforesaid Henry through his mainprise by which earlier, etc.

6. Arrest order. PRO, KB 27/476, m. 30d.

Eadem Isabella in propria persona sua apud se quarto die versus Willielmum fratrem predicti Henrici et Laurencium Drewe filium Drugonis de Wryngworth de raptu predicta [sic], et ipsi non venerunt. Et precatum fuit vicecomiti sicut pluries quod caperet eos. Et vicecomes retornavit quod ipsi non sunt inventi, etc. Ideo sicut pluries preceptum est vicecomiti quod capiat eos si, etc. Et salvo, etc. Ita quod habeat corpora sua coram domino Rege ad prefatum terminum, etc., etc.

The same Isabel appearing in her own person on her own behalf on the fourth day against William, brother of the aforesaid Henry, and Lawrence Drewe, son of Drugo, of Wryngworth, concerning the aforesaid rape, and they did not come. And request was made to the sheriff, as frequently before, that he arrest them, if, etc. And saving, etc. So that he have their bodies before the lord king on the aforesaid date, etc., etc.

7. Order to arrest mainpernors of Henry Yulecomb (after April 13, 1380). PRO, KB 29 / 32 (3 Richard II, 1379–80), m. 52d.

Somerset. Dominus rex mandavit vicecomiti Somerset breve suum clausum in hec verba: Ricardus, rex Anglie et Francie et Dominus Hibernie, vicecomiti Somerset salutem. Cum Matheus Gournay, chevaler, Thomas Tryvet, chevaler, et Thomas Fichet, chevaler, nuper in curia nostra coram nobis manuceperunt pro Henrico Yeuelcombe habendi corpus ejus coram nobis a die sancti Hillarii in xv dies ultimos preteritos ubicumque, etc. [. . .] esserimus in Anglia ad respondendum Isabelle que fuit uxor Johannis Moun de raptu et pace Domini Edwardi nuper regis Anglie, avi nostri, fracta, unde eum appellavit simul cum aliis, et ulterius quousque placitum predictum inter partes predictas terminaretur, et etiam de bono gestu ipsius Henrici erga dictam Isabellam et populum nostrum, et quod eadem Isabella per ipsum Henricum nec per aliquem per eum caperetur nec aliqualiter inclosaretur quin eadem Isabella appellum suum predictum versus eundem Henricum et alios homines appellare vel prosequi posset, quilibet manucaptorum predictorum sub pena ducentarum librarum, sicut per sufficientem redditum (?) et processus inde coram nobis habitos nobis constat, dictusque Henricus in curia nostra predicta ad diem sibi postea prefixum juxta manucapcionem suam predictam coram nobis venire contempsit, et dictam Isabellam quominus appellum suum predictum prosequeretur, aggregata sibi multitudine malefactorum, ipsam Isabellam apud pontem aquaticum palacii nostri Westmonasterii venientem versus curiam nostram in proteccione nostra.

The lord king sends to his sheriffs his writ close in these words: Richard, king of England and France and Lord of Ireland, health to the sheriff of Somerset. Since Matthew Gournay, knight, Thomas Tryvet, knight, and Thomas Fichet, knight, recently mainprised for Henry Yeuelcoumbe of having his body before us, wherever [. . .] we should be in England, on the quindene of Saint Hilary last past, to respond to Isabel, who was the wife of John Moun, concerning rape and breaking the peace of the late king lord Edward, our grandfather, whereof she appealed him along with others, and further, until such time as the aforesaid plea between them should be terminated, and also of the good behavior of the said Henry towards the said Isabel and our people and that the same Isabel not be captured or in any way inhibited by the said Henry or by anyone through him to prevent the said Isabel from appealing or prosecuting her aforesaid appeal against the said Henry and others, each of the aforesaid mainpernors being under pain of 200 pounds, as is clear to us by sufficient return and processes thereon held before us, and since the said Henry contemptuously failed to come before us in our foresaid court on the day later set for him, according to his aforesaid mainprise, and, [to prevent] the said Isabel from prosecuting her aforesaid appeal, with a multitude of malefactors gathered to himself, [he attacked] the same Isabel at the waterbridge of our palace of Westminster as she was coming towards our court, being under our protection.

8. Watergate indictment (before June 22, 1380). PRO, KB 29 / 32, m. 43d.

Midd. Jurata, scilicet [twelve names follow], isto eodem termino coram domino rege apud Westmonasterium presentat quod, cum Isabella, que fuit uxor Johannis Mohoun, prosecuta fuit quoddam breve domini regis de appello de raptu versus Henricum Yeuelcoumbe et alios in curia domini regis coram ipso rege, eademque Isabella habuit diem nunc in tribus septimanis Pasche in appello suo predicto, et quidam Guido de Bryen, chevaler, ipsam Isabellam de London usque Westmonasterio ad appellum predictum in curia regis, ut predicitur, prosequendum, et diem sibi per justiciarios domini regis secundum legem terre datum custodiendum, in quadem batella per aquam duxerit, predictus Henricus Yeuelcoumbe [^. . .] [168] et Willielmus Yeuelcoumbe simul

---

[168] The dim careted note (something like "ij cart. terro –m° a° xiij r.r.p°") seems to be a reference to the thirteenth year of the reign, which would be 1389–90.

cum quampluribus aliis ignotis armatis in loricis et aliis armaturis machinans ipsam Isabellam capere ipsamque ab appello suo predicto totaliter excludere, die Mercurii proximo post tres septimanas Pasche anno regni nunc tercio [April 18, 1380] apud Westmonasterium, videlicet, juxta pontem palacii domini regis Westmonasterii apud Portam aquaticam in presencia justiciarorum domini regis de banco ipsius regis, et manus super ipsam Isabellam miserunt, et ad ipsam capiendam, et in Guidonem de Bryen, chevaler, Johannem Kentcoumbe, et Johannem Shakel venientes cum ipsa Isabella ibidem insultum fecerunt et ipsos verberaverunt, vulneraverunt, et male tractaverunt.

Et dicit quod Jacobus de Lyons, unus servientium domini regis ad arma, immediate ipsos juxta officii sui debitum ipsos arestavit, et ipse Henricus arestum predictum fregit, et quo voluit ivit cum hominibus suis predictis, nullo habito respecto ad arestum predictum.

Item presentat quod Baldewinus Yeuelcombe, Johannes Luk de Bodmyn, Johannes [^. . .] Cole de London. Sadelere, Johannes Fowy, et Johannes Willyng de Cornubia predicto die Mercurii proximo post tres septimanas Pasche anno supradicto omnes transgressiones superius nominatas et declaratas simul cum predictis Henrico Yeuelcombe et Willelmo Yeuelcombe apud predictam portam aquaticam Westmonasterii fecerunt, etc. **Per recorda de anno tercio.**

Per quod preceptum est vicecomitibus quod capiant eos si, etc.

Middlesex. The jury . . . presents that, when Isabel, who was the wife of John Mohoun, prosecuted a writ of the lord king concerning appeal of rape against Henry Yeuelcoumbe and others in the court of the lord king before the said king, and the same Isabel had a day in the present three weeks of Easter for her aforesaid appeal, and a certain Guy de Bryen, knight, would have led the said Isabel from London to Westminster in a boat by water to prosecute the aforesaid appeal and to keep the day granted her according to the law of the land by the justices of the lord king, as is said above, the foresaid Henry Yeuelcoumbe [^. . .] and William Yeuelcoumbe along with several other unknown armed men in breastplates and other armaments, plotting to seize Isabel and completely exclude her from her aforesaid appeal, on the Wednesday next after the three weeks of Easter, the present third year of the reign [April 18, 1380], at Westminster, specifically next to the bridge of the palace of the lord king at Westminster near the Watergate, in the presence of the justices of the lord king of the bench of the said king, and they put hands upon the said Isabel, and, in order to capture her, they also assaulted Guy de Brien, knight, John Kentcoumbe, and John Shakel, who were accompanying the said Isabel to that place, and beat, wounded, and maltreated them.

And the jury says that James de Lyons, one of the sergeants-at-arms of the lord king, immediately arrested them in accord with the duties of his office, and the said Henry broke the aforesaid arrest and departed whither he would with his aforesaid men, having no respect for the aforesaid arrest.

Likewise it presents that Baldwin Yeuelcombe, John Luk de Bodmyn, John Cole of London, saddler, John Fowy, and John Willing of Cornwall on the aforesaid Wednesday following the three weeks of Easter in the above-mentioned year committed all the trespasses named and declared above along with the aforesaid Henry Yeuelcoumbe and William Yeuelcoumbe at the aforesaid Watergate at Westminster, etc. By records of the third year.

By which order is given to the sheriffs to arrest them, if, etc.

9. Writ to the coroners of Cornwall, November 29, 1381. PRO, KB 136/5/5/3/1 (last writ in packet).

Ricardus Dei gracia rex Anglie et Francie et dominus Hibernie coronariis suis in comitatu Cornubie salutem. Cum nuper vicecomitem nostrum comitatus predicti precepimus quod exigi faceret Willielmum fratrem Henrici Yuelcombe et Laurencius Drew filium Drugonis de Wryngworth de comitatu in comitatum [?] quousque secundum legem et consuetudinem regni nostri Anglie utlagarentur si non compararent, et si compararent tunc eos caperet et in prisona salvo custodio faceret, ita quod haberet corpora eorum coram nobis in octobis sancte Trinitatis ultimis preteritis [June 17, 1381], ubicumque tunc essemus in Anglia, ad respondendum Isabelle que fuit uxor Johannis Moun de raptu et pace domini Edwardi nuper regis Anglie avi nostri fracta, unde eos appellat, dictusque vicecomes noster ad diem predictum nichil inde nobis misit; ac jam exigente [?] predicta Isabella accepimus quod predicti Willielmus et Laurencius in comitatu predicto, accione predicta utlagati, existunt, per quod vobis precipimus quod, strictatis rotulis et memorandis vestris, si quam utlagariam in eisdem inveniretis versus predictos Willielmum et Laurencium accione predicta, [eam] mittatis coram nobis a die Pasche in xv dies [April 21, 1382], ubicumque tunc

fuerimus in Anglia, ut ulterius inde fieri faciamus quod de jure et secundum legem et consuetudinem regni nostri Anglie fore viderimus fa-
ciendum, hoc breve emittentes.

Teste R. Tresilian apud Westmonasterium, xxix die Novembris anno
regni nostri quinto [November 29, 1381].

[Dorse] Ego Noelus Padirda, unus coronarius comitatus Cornubie, re-
cepi istud breve apud Lostwcchiel die Veneris proximo ante Dominicam
in Ramis Palmarum [March 28, 1382]. Virtute hujus brevis, strictatis
memorandis rotularum nostrorum [?] de tempore viso inveni quod
Willielmus frater Henrici Yuelcombe utlagatus fuit de felonia die Lune
proximo post festum sancti Mathei apostoli anno regni regis Ricardi
quarto [September 24, 1380].

Et predictum Willielmum ad [. . .] non inveni postea infra comitatum Cornubie. Et quoad Laurencium Drew filium Drogonis de
Wryngworth, de utlagaria sua nullo modo michi constare potest quoad
presens, et ipsum ad capiendum non inveni in comitatu Cornubie. Et
quoad capiendum Henricum nominatum in breve, nihil michi constat
de [. . .] sua.

Noelus Padirda, Robertus Davudel, coronarii regis [?].

Richard by the grace of God king of England and France and lord of
Ireland wishes health to his coroners in the county of Cornwall. Since
we recently ordered our sheriff in the aforesaid county to put in exigents
William brother of Henry Yulecomb and Lawrence Drew son of Drugo
of Wryngworth from county to county, so that according to the law and
custom of our kingdom of England they were to be outlawed if they did
not appear, or if they did appear, that he put them in prison under safe
custody so that he have their bodies before us on the octave of Holy
Trinity just passed [June 17, 1381], wherever we were in England, to
respond to Isabel who was the wife of John Mohun concerning rape and
breaking the peace of Lord Edward late king of England, our grandfather, on which she appeals them, and the said sheriff on the aforesaid
day sent us nothing; and now from the foresaid Isabella we have received
that the aforesaid William and Lawrence, outlawed by the foresaid action, are at present in the foresaid county, in consequence of which we
order you that if, upon examining your rolls and memoranda, you find
any outlawry in them against the aforesaid William and Lawrence on

account of the aforesaid action, you send it before us on the quindene of Easter [April 21, 1382], wherever we then may be in England, so that we may cause further action to be done in accord with what we see is to be done in the matter by law and according to the law and custom of our kingdom of England, upon your sending this writ to us.

Witness Robert Tresilian at Westminster, 29th day of November in the fifth year of our reign.

[Dorse: the Return] I, Noel Padirda, one of the coroners of Cornwall, received this writ at Lostwcchiel on the Friday before Palm Sunday [March 28, 1382]. In virtue of this writ, having examined the memoranda of our rolls in the time specified, I found that William brother of Henry Yulecomb was outlawed for felony on the Monday after the feast of St. Matthew the Apostle in the fourth year of the reign of King Richard [September 24, 1380].

And the foresaid William I have not found for [. . .] afterwards within the county of Cornwall. And as for Lawrence Drew son of Drogo of Wryngworth, nothing can be confirmed to me in any way concerning his outlawry for the present, and I have not found him to arrest him in the county of Cornwall. And as for arresting Henry, named in the writ, nothing appears to me concerning his [. . .].

Noel Padirda, Robert Davudel, coroners of the king.

10. Pardon of Henry and William Yulecomb, October 23, 1382. PRO, C 66/313, m. 13, reported in *CPR Richard II*, 2:179.

Rex omnibus ballivis et fidelibus suis ad quos, etc., salutem. Sciatis quod de gracia nostra speciali et pro bono servicio quod Henricus Ylcombe chevaler alias dictus Henricus Yuelcombe nobis in partibus Portingalie impendit perdonavimus sectam pacis nostre que ad nos pertinet pro raptu Isabelle, que fuit uxor Johannis Moun, unde indictatus, rettatus, vel appellatus existit, ac eciam, utlagarie, si que in ipsum ea occasione fuerint promulgate—et firmam pacem nostram ei inde concedimus. Ita tamen quod stet recto in curia nostra, si quis versus eum loqui voluerit de raptu supradicto. In cuius, etc.

Teste rege apud Westmonasterium, xxiii die Octobris. Per breve de privato sigillo.

Cond. litteras regis de perdonacione habet Willielmus Ylcombe frater Henrici Ylcombe chevaler alias dictus Willielmus Yuelcombe [careted: de raptu predicto]. Teste ut supra. Per idem breve.

The king to all his bailiffs and faithful subjects to whom, etc., good health. Know that of our special grace and for the good service that Henry Ylcombe, knight, otherwise called Henry Yuelcombe, is undertaking for us in the regions of Portugal we have pardoned him the suit of our peace that pertains to us for the rape of Isabel, who was the wife of John Moun, whereof he stands indicted, charged, or appealed, and also any outlawries that may have been promulgated against him on that occasion [have been revoked], and we concede him our firm peace. So that however he stand trial in our court if anyone should wish to speak against him concerning the aforesaid rape. In whose, etc.

Witnessed by the king at Westminster, 23 October. By writ of the privy seal.

William Ylcombe, brother of Henry Ylcombe, knight, otherwise called William Yuelcombe, has conditional letters of pardon of the king—for the above-mentioned rape.

Witnessed as above. By the same writ.

11. Acquittal of John Woodhouse by the justices of jail delivery, April 18, 1384. PRO, JUST 3/80/1, m. 1 (first membrane).

Ebor. Johannes de Wodehous de Brathwayte captus pro eo quod ipse die Martis proximo ante festum sancti Laurencii martyris anno regni regis Ricardi secundi post conquestum Anglie primo [August 11, 1377] apud Wodehous felonice rapuit Aliciam filiam Ricardi Jakman et eam cum bonis et catallis ipsius Ricardi Jakman ad valenciam viginti marcarum ibidem tunc inventis felonice abduxit, unde coram Johanne de Drousfeld et sociis suis custodibus pacis domini regis in Westr. in comitatu Eboraci indictatus est, venit, per custodem gaole ductus, et per justiciarios allocutus qualiter se velit de predictis acquietare, dicit quod dictus rex nunc de gracia sua speciali et ad supplicacionem dilecte sibi domine de Mohun perdonavit eidem Johanni sectam pacis sue que ad [se] pertinuit pro raptu et aliis feloniis supradictis per has ipsius domini regis nunc patentes, quas idem Johannes his profert et que sequuntur in hec verba:

Ricardus Dei gracia rex Anglie et Francie et dominus Hibernie omnibus ballivis et fidelibus suis ad quos presentes littere pervenerint, salutem. Sciatis quod cum Johannes de Wodehous de Braythwait indictatus sit, ut accepimus, de eo quod ipse Aliciam filiam Ricardi Jakman de Wodehous felonice rapuisse debuisset et eandem Aliciam felonice cepisse, abduxisse, imprisonasse contra voluntatem suam, et nos de gracia nostra speciali et ad supplicacionem dilecte nobis domine de Mohun perdonavimus eidem Johanni sectam pacis nostre que ad nos pertinet pro raptu [et] aliis feloniis supradictis unde taliter indictatus, rettatus, vel appellatus existit, ac eciam utlagarias si que in ipsum hiis occasionibus fuerint promulgate, et firmam pacem nostram ei inde concedimus, ita tamen quod stet recto in curia nostra si predicta Alicia versus eum loqui voluerit de raptu et aliis feloniis supradictis. In cujus rei testimonium has litteras nostras nostras [sic] fieri fecimus patentes. Teste me ipso apud Westmonasterium, vicesimo tercio die Augusti, anno regni nostri septimo.

Quarum litterarum pretextu predictus [Johannes] de Wodehous petit se a prisona domini regis deliberari et de raptu et feloniis predictis exonerari. Et inspectis litteris domini regis patentibus predictis consiliatum est quod ipse eat inde quietus, etc.

York. John of Woodhouse of Brathwait, arrested for that he on the Tuesday before the feast of St. Laurence the Martyr in the first year of the reign of King Richard the Second after the Conquest of England [August 11, 1377] at Wodehous feloniously ravished Alice, daughter of Richard Jackman, and feloniously abducted her with goods and chattels of the same Richard Jackman found there to the value of 20 marks, whence he was indicted before John of Drousfeld and his associates, keepers of the peace of the lord king, in Westr. in the county of York, comes, led by the warden of the jail, and, addressed by the justices as to how he wished to acquit himself of the aforesaid, says that the present lord king, of his special grace and at the supplication of the lady of Mohun, dear to him, has pardoned the same John the suit of his peace which pertains to him for the rape and other felonies above-noted, through these letters patent of the said present lord king which the said John here presents, and which follow in these words:

Richard by the grace of God king of England and France and lord of Ireland to all his bailiffs and faithful subjects to which these present letters may come, good health. Know that since John of Woodhouse of Braithwait was indicted, as we have been told, for that he allegedly feloniously ravished Alice, daughter of Richard Jackman of Woodhouse, and took, abducted, imprisoned her against her will, so we of our special grace and at the supplication of our beloved lady of Mohun have pardoned the same John the suit of our peace that pertains to us for the rape and other felonies above-noted whence he is thus indicted, aretted, or appealed, and also outlawries, if any have been promulgated

164

against him on these occasions, and we grant him our firm peace thereof, so that however he stand to right in our court if the aforesaid Alice should wish to speak against him concerning the rape and other felonies above-noted. In testimony of this matter we had these letters patent made. Witness myself at Westminster, the 23rd day of August, the seventh year of our reign.

In virtue of these letters, the aforesaid [John] of Woodhouse asks to be delivered from the prison of the lord king and to be exonerated of the rape and felonies aforesaid. And after the aforesaid letters patent of our lord king are inspected, it is determined that he should go quit thereof, etc.

12. Pardon of John Halsham, June 7, 1384. PRO, C 66/317, m. 12, reported in *CPR Richard II*, 2:399.

Rex omnibus ballivis et fidelibus suis ad quos, etc., salutem. Sciatis quod de gracia nostra speciali et ad supplicacionem carissimi consanguinei nostri comitis Oxon. perdonavimus dilecto ligeo nostro Johanni Halsham sectam pacis nostre que ad nos pertinet, tam pro raptu Philippe de Artheles quam pro omnimodis feloniis et transgressionibus per ipsum quoque modo perpetratis. In cujus, etc.
Rex apud Castrum suum de Corf, vii die Junii. Per litteram ipsius regis de signeto.

The king to all his bailiffs and faithful subjects to whom, etc., good health. Know that of our special grace and at the request of our most dear kinsman the earl of Oxford we have pardoned our beloved liege John Halsham the suit of our peace that pertains to us both for the rape of Philippa of Artheles and for all kinds of felonies and trespasses committed by him in any way. In whose, etc.
The king at his castle of Corfe. By letter of the king himself from the signet.

Unnoticed Extracts from Chaucer and Hoccleve: Huntington MS HM 144, Trinity College, Oxford MS D 29 and *The Canterbury Tales*

Kate Harris
Longleat House

Based on the simple premise that all witnesses (even arrant false witnesses) to the text of Chaucer's *Canterbury Tales* should be available to textual scholars and literary historians alike, the following study seeks also to contribute to the understanding of the reception of Chaucer's work at the close of the Middle Ages. The two manuscripts under consideration here may be viewed against the background of late-medieval monastic book production and particularly monastic history writing of this period: in fact, the unique, bizarre, composite history in one of the volumes concerned could with justice be described as belonging both to the close and the nadir of the latter proud tradition. This article will thus focus not so much on the alterity of the medieval text but on the alterity of one late-medieval monastic reader of Chaucer. It will also show incidentally the effect in these two manuscripts of the infiltration of Chaucer's discourse by that of the reader's preferred genre, the fifth columnist in this case being the preachment or sermon.

Trinity College, Oxford MS D 29 and the much better known San Marino, Huntington Library HM 144 are written in the same idiosyncratic, late fifteenth-century *hybrida* and seem to derive from an Augustinian house in southeast England. As might be expected, they have a number of further features in common: in their layout, size, ruling, irregularity of quiring (irregularity involving the reconciliation of quarto and folio formats), multiplicity of watermarks, and simplicity of programs of decoration, the two manuscripts mirror each other. (The fact that they do not share any of their many watermarks is suggestive of some separation in their dates of production.) As was remarked in the preliminary account of the Trinity manuscript in my essay "John Gower's *Confessio Amantis*: The Virtues of Bad Texts,"[1] the two volumes share two sources, Caxton's edition of the *Polychronicon* and, as it is the purpose of this article to describe, Chaucer's *Canterbury Tales*.[2] (Caxton's edition of Trevisa dates after 2 July 1482 and thus provides a *terminus post quem* for the two collections.[3]) The pair of manuscripts differ widely, however, in that the Huntington volume, which is fascicular in its structure, presents a sequence of distinct short items, while the Trinity volume contains a complex (and rebarbative) prose *cento*, an agglomeration of extracts from many sources assembled to form a prose history beginning with the time of Adam and now ending defectively with that

[1] Derek Pearsall, ed., *Manuscripts and Readers in Fifteenth-Century England: The Literary Implications of Manuscript Studies* (Woodbridge: D. S. Brewer, 1983), pp. 27–40 (see pp. 31–33; the essay was based on a paper read at the first York Manuscript Conference, held in 1981). For further notice of the Trinity manuscript see pp. 67–75 in my D.Phil. thesis, "Ownership and Readership: Studies in the Provenance of Gower's *Confessio Amantis*" (University of York, 1993). I have completed a full description of the Trinity manuscript (including a full breakdown of the sources used) scheduled to appear in Jeremy Griffiths, Kate Harris, and Derek Pearsall, *A Descriptive Catalogue of the Manuscripts of the Works of John Gower*, forthcoming.

[2] For HM 144 see J. M. Manly and Edith Rickert, *The Text of the Canterbury Tales*, 8 vols. (Chicago: University of Chicago Press, 1940), 1:289–94 (a minor correction to this description appears in Daniel W. Mosser, "Manly and Rickert's Collation of Huntington Library Manuscript HM 144 (Hn)," *Papers of the Bibliographical Society of America* 79 (1985): 235–40); see further Joseph Lauritis et al., eds., *A Critical Edition of John Lydgate's "Life of Our Lady"* (Pittsburgh: Duquesne University Press, 1961), pp. 42–43; Ralph Hanna III, *A Handlist of Middle English Prose in the Henry E. Huntington Library*, The Index of Middle English Prose, Handlist I (Cambridge: D. S. Brewer, 1984), pp. 17–20; C. W. Dutschke, *Guide to Medieval and Renaissance Manuscripts in the Huntington Library*, (San Marino, Calif.: The Huntington Library, 1989), 1:197–203, with further bibliography and plate, fig. 148 (f.47ᵛ detail). For the compiler's use of the *Polychronicon* (without notice of his precise source) see also A. S. G. Edwards, "The Influence and Audience of the *Polychronicon*: Some Observations," *Proceedings of the Leeds Philosophical and Literary Society* 17 (1980): 117, n. 2; C. W. Marx, "Beginnings and Endings: Narrative-Linking in Five Manuscripts from the Fourteenth and Fifteenth Centuries and the Problem of Textual 'Integrity,'" in Pearsall, ed., *Manuscripts and Readers*, p. 80, n. 3; C. W. Marx and J. F. Drennan, eds., *The Middle English Prose Complaint of Our Lady and Gospel of Nicodemus*, Middle English Texts (Heidelberg: Carl Winter Universität Verlag, 1988), p. 13.

[3] A. W. Pollard and G. R. Redgrave, *A Short-Title Catalogue of Books Printed in England, Scotland, & Ireland and of English Books Printed Abroad 1475–1640*, 2d ed., rev. and ed. by W. A. Jackson, F. S. Ferguson, and Katharine F. Pantzer (London: The Bibliographical Society, 1986), 13438. For the dating see Paul Needham, *The Printer & the Pardoner: An Unrecorded Indulgence Printed by William Caxton for the Hospital of St. Mary Rounceval, Charing Cross* (Washington, D. C.: Library of Congress, 1986), p. 87, Cx 52.

of Hannibal.[4] This key difference between them accounts for the fact that, although the Huntington volume has long been established among the manuscripts containing extracts from *The Canterbury Tales* (*Melibee* and *The Monk's Tale* appear on ff.81^r–111^v),[5] the presence of material from the same source in Trinity D 29 has passed unnoticed. The aim here is to describe the incidence of extracts from *The Canterbury Tales* in the Trinity history, to present an edition, and to attempt to characterize *The Canterbury Tales* texts in both the Trinity and Huntington manuscripts.

On four occasions the Trinity compiler makes use of Chaucer's *Parson's Tale*; on a fifth and sixth he draws briefly (and repetitively) on the *Melibee*. His first use of *The Parson's Tale*, running from f.2^r line 1 to f.2^v line 31, follows directly upon an account of Adam being placed in Paradise, God's forbidding him to eat of the fruit of the Tree of Knowledge, the creation of Eve, and the devil's envy of Adam and Eve. This passage (for which compare Genesis 2:15–18, 21–25, and 3:1) runs f.1^v line 10–f.2^r line 1 and reads thus:[6]

f.1^v 10   we rede in þe booke of
         Genesis. þat god put Adam in to Paradise. to þat
         yntente ÷ þat he shulde werke therin *and* keep yt. And whan
         he had so doon ÷ he commau*n*dyd Adam. seyng on this wy/
         se ¶ Of all*e* þe treis þat been in Paradise ete thow of.
  15   saue only of þat tre þat standyth in þe myddys of Paradise ÷

---

[4] Besides the sources already named, the Trinity history incorporates material from Gower's *Confessio Amantis, Mandeville's Travels*, Petrus Pictavensis' *Compendium historiae in genealogia christi*, Jacques Legrand's *Livre des bonnes Moeurs* (a copy of the version of the English translation surviving also in British Library, Harley 149) and Wynkyn de Worde's print, *Informacion for pylgrymes vnto the holy londe* (see further Harris 1983 *op.cit.* pp. 32-33). The use of the last text cited may suggest a date for the history after 1500 (the evidence of collation of de Worde's three editions is not, however, completely conclusive). Handlist VIII of *The Index of Middle English Prose*, Sarah Ogilvie Thomson's *Oxford College Libraries* (Cambridge: D. S. Brewer, 1991), refers only to the appearance of the *Polychronicon* in the Trinity manuscript.

[5] The tales, supplied respectively with the running titles "Prou*er*bis" and "The falle Of Princis," are linked by an endnote to *Melibee* on f.99^r, for which see below, p. 188.

[6] Transcription is diplomatic, preserving the lineation, capitalization, and punctuation (largely confined to the use of punctus, lemniscus, and paraph) of the original. Italics indicate expansions, square brackets signify deletions, and half square brackets interlineations; diamond brackets signify loss of text through damage to the manuscript leaves. (When prose is presented continuously, line endings in the original are indicated by vertical slashes.)

þe whiche tre wyl cause þe to knowe good *and* euyl. ete
nat thow of þ*a*t tre. ne touchyt nat. for *and* thou do ÷ thow
shalt dye. ¶ And whan god had co*m*mau*n*dyd hym thus ÷
seyng hym hauyng no felisshyp. nor no helpe lyke vnto
20   hym ÷ than oure lorde sent soche a slombyr in to Adam ÷
þ*a*t he slept. ¶ And than oure lorde toke oute one of his
rybbys *and* conu*er*tyt to a woman. *and* brought hyr to Adam.
to wete what he woolde calle hyr ¶ And whan Adam
sy3 her ÷ he seyde here bonys ar made of my bonys. *and* her
25   flesshe of my flesshe. *and* insomoche þ*a*t she is made of man ÷
she shal be callyd. Virago. ¶ And than oure lorde seyde
to Adam. for soche thyng shal man forsake his fadyr
and his modyr. *and* take hym alonly to his wyfe ¶ And th⌈e⌉y
shalbe two p*er*sonys *and* oon flesshe. ¶ And whan oure
30   lorde had tolde hem thus ÷ he lefte them bothe in Pa/
radise. beyng nakyd *and* wit*h*oute shame. ¶ And whan þe
Deuyl þ*a*t was so sotyl. had aspyed *and* vndirstonde this ÷
that man was made of þe foule slyme of þe erthe ÷
and than put in þ*a*t ioyful place of Paradise ÷ to þ*a*t intent
to kepe yt *and* to werke there in ÷ he had a non in hym selfe
inwardly grete Invye there at. ¶ And than he cam to
f.2ʳ 1   þe woman in lyknesse of a Serpent *and* seyde to her

The extract from *The Parson's Tale* opens (f.2ʳ line 1–f.2ᵛ line 17) with
lines 326–42 from Chaucer's account of the origin of sin in the "secunda
pars penitentie," a passage treating of both the origin of sin in Adam and
Eve and its effect, the presence in all mankind of Original Sin in the form
of concupiscence. It continues (f.2ᵛ lines 17–29) with lines 355–57, part
of Chaucer's account of the progression of sin, deriving from Richard de
Wetheringsett's *Summa de officio sacerdotis*, in which Exodus 15: 9, Moses'
reference to the enemy's threats against the Israelites in his praise of God
after the destruction of the Egyptians in the crossing of the Red Sea, is
glossed as the devil's pursuit and destruction of mankind through sin.
The closing lines of the extract (f.2ᵛ lines 29–31), a grim statement in
which death is seen as the just desert of sinful man, rebelling against
both God and reason, originates in Chaucer's account of how sin turns
all order (God's lordship over reason, reason's lordship over sensuality,
sensuality's lordship over the body) "up-so-doun," part of his disquisition on the "fifthe thyng that oghte moeve a man to contricion" in the
"prima pars penitentie." The lines represent a conflation of *ParsT* 266

("for right as reson is rebel to god / right so is bothe sensuallitee rebel to reson and the body also"), 271 ("and forther ouer / for as muche thanne / as the kaytif body of man / is rebell / bothe to resou*n* and to sensualitee / therfore / is it worthy the deeth"), and perhaps also 268 ("for as muche thanne / as reson is rebel to god / therfore is man worthy to haue sorwe / and to be deed").[7] The whole passage reads as follows:

f.2ʳ 1   ¶ Why com/

mau*n*dyd god yow. þat ye shulde nat ete of eu*er*y tre in Para/
dise ¶ The woman answeryd. Of þe frewte⌈s⌉ quod she of
þe treys in Paradise ÷ we fedyn vs. but of þe frewte of þe

5   tre þ*at* is in þe myddys of Paradise ÷ god forbad vs for to ete
of. noþ*ir* for to touche yt. lest parauenture þ*at* we shulde
dye ¶ Then þe Serpent seyde to þe woman ÷ Nay nay ÷
ye shul nat dyen of dethe forsothe. for god wot þ*at* what day
ye etyn þ*er*of ÷ your eyen shul be opyn. *and* ye shul been as

10   goddys. knowyng good *and* euyl ¶ The Woman sawe þe
frute was good to fedyng. *and* fayre to þe eyen. *and* delectable
to þe syht ÷ she toke of þe frute of þe tre *and* ete þ*er*of. and
than toke yt to her husbonde. *and* he ete yt ¶ And anon
þe eyen of hem openyd. and whan they knewe þ*at* they

15   were nakyd ÷ they toke of ffygge leuys in man*ir* of brechis.
to hyde w*ith* her membrys. ¶ Lo here may we see ÷ þ*at* dedly
synne. hathe first ÷ Suggestiou*n* of þe Deuyl. as shewyth
here be þe Addre. And frowarde delyght of þe flesshe. as
shewyth here be Eve. and aftyr þ*at* ÷ þe consentyng of

20   Resou*n*. as shewyth here be Adam. þ*at* consentyd to þe
etyng of þe ffrute. ʒet stode he in þe state of Innocence.
¶ And of this synne Original toke Adam. and of hem
flessly descendyd be we comen all*e* *and* engendryd of vile
and corupt mateer. ¶ And whan þe soule is put in oure

25   body ÷ ryght a non is contract Original synne. ¶ And
that which was erste. but only peyne of concupiscence
or desyryng ÷ is aftyrward. bothe peyne *and* synne. ¶ And

---

[7] To avoid (or, at least, reduce) the awkward anachronism of presenting a modern, edited text for comparison, the passages in question are quoted from the Hengwrt manuscript (Aberystwyth, National Library of Wales, Peniarth 392; see Paul G. Ruggiers, ed., with introductions by Donald C. Baker and by A. I. Doyle and M. B. Parkes, *The Canterbury Tales, Geoffrey Chaucer, A Facsimile and Transcription of the Hengwrt Manuscript, with Variants from the Ellesmere Manuscript* (Norman: University of Oklahoma Press, 1979).

þerfor been we alle born sonys of wratthe *and* of dampna/
cioun perdurable. yf yt were nat for baptisme. þat we
30 ressayuyn. whiche benemyth vs þe culpe. ¶ But for/
sothe þe peyne dwellyth w*ith* vs. as to temptacion. whi/
che peyne hyte Concupiscence. þat is desyryng. whan
it is wrongfully [desyr] disposyd or ordeynyd in man.
hyt makyth hym coueyte be couetyse of fflesshe ÷ fflessly
35 synne. be syht of his eyen. as to e⌈r⌉thely thyngis. ¶ And
for to speke of Coueytyse. þat is [desyryng] Concupiscens
f.2ᵛ 1 or desyryng. ¶ Aftyr þe lawe of oure membrys. þat were
lawfully made. *and* be ryghtful Iugement of god ÷ I seye for
asmoche as man is nat obeysau*n*t to god ÷ þat is his lorde ÷ þerfor
is þe flesshe to hym obeysau*n*t. throuh co*n*cupiscens or desyryng
5 whiche is clepyd norisshynge of synne. *and* occasyou*n* of synne
¶ Therfor al þe while þat a man hathe w*ith* in hym. þe peyne
of concupiscence or desyryng ÷ it is impossyble but he be
temptyd som tyme. *and* meuyd in his flesshe to synne. ¶ And
this thyng may nat fayle. as longe as he lyuyth. yt
10 may wel wex feble ÷ *and* fayle. be vertu of baptisme. *and* be
þe grace of god. throuh penitence. but fully shal yt neu*ir*
quenche. but þat he shal som tyme be meuyd in hym sylfe.
but ȝif he were al refreynyd be syknesse. or be maledy
or sorcery. or coolde drynkis. ¶ ffor seint Poule Seith.
15 the flesshe coueytyth a geyn þe spiryt. and þe Spirit a/
geyn þe flesshe they be so contrarye *and* so stryuyng ÷ þat a
man may nat done alway as he woolde. ¶ And to thys.
Moyses Seith also. þat þe Deuyl seyth thus. I wole
pursew and chace þe man. be wykkyd suggestiou*n* or inty/
20 syng. ¶ And I wole hente hym ÷ be mevyng *and* steryng of
synne. and I wole departe my poyse *and* my pray ÷ be delybera/
ciou*n*. *and* my lust shalbe a complissid in delyte. I wole drawe
my swerde in consentyng ffor ryght as a swerde departyth
a thyng in two pecys ÷ ryht so consentyng departyth god
25 fro man. and than I wole sle hym w*ith* myn hande in dede
of synne. thus seyth þe feende. ¶ ffor certys than is a man
all*e* dede in soule ¶ And thus is synne acompliscid or fulfillyd
be temptaciou*n* *and* be delyte *and* be concentyng. and than is þe
synne clepyd Actuel or doon in deede ¶ And than þe
30 caytyf body of man. þat is bothe Rebel to god *and* to Resou*n* ÷ is
worthy to dye.

The extract is accompanied by two marginal notes on f.2^r. The first, placed beside *Pars T* 329 (f.2^r line 12) and reading " ¶ Of whens synne | spryngyth *and* how it | entryth in to man.", derives from 321 "And forther ouer / it is necessarie to vnderstonde / whennes þat synnes spryngen / and how they encressen / and whiche they ben." The second, more extensive note, placed at f.2^r line 16 (*Pars T* 331) and now cropped and damaged, details how, in eating the apple, Adam was guilty of all seven of the Deadly Sins: it is unconnected with Chaucer's text and reads as follows:

f.2^r	¶ In þe etyng of þe A
	pyl Adam offendyd
	all*e* þe vij. dedly synny\<s>
	¶ ffirst *in* pr*i*de. whan h\<e>
5	dyd aftyr his owne \<wyl>
	le. *and* not aftyr þe wy\<lle>
	of god. for he dyd co*n*tra
	ry to þat he was comau*n*
	dyd. ¶ In Sacrilege h\<e>
10	synnyd also. whan he \< >
	ageyn þe pr*e*cept of h\< >
	þ*at* was sacrid. *and* fulfi\< >
	his owne talent
	aftyr þe fendy\<s com>
15	mau*n*dme*n*t. ¶ Also \<he syn>
	nyd *in* ma*n*slawtyr w\<han>
	he his owne soule sle\< >
	and alle þ*at* com of hy*m*. fo\< >
	þe feende of helle he \< >
20	toke. ¶ Also he synn\<yd>
	in thefthe. wha*n* he [to\< >]
	stale þ*at* whiche god \< >
	forbad. *and* þ*er*for he wa\< >
	worþy to dye. ¶ A\<lso>
25	he synnyd in forn\<ica>
	cion *etc.* ¶ In Avary\<ce>
	he synnyd. wha*n* he
	covet more þan he
	nede. for he had alle \<para>
30	dise at his wylle ¶ A\<lso>
	in Glotony he synny\<d>

for hy*m* toke more þ<an>
hy*m* nedyd whan h<e>
þe apple þ*at* hym w<as>
35   forbode. ¶ Also in Sl<o>
the he synnyd wor< >
of alle. verte fol< >
f.2ᵛ   < >or whan he was
fallyn in synne. he
had no grace to ryse.
for whan oure lorde
seyde Adam Adam
5   vbi es. than Adam
acusyd þe woman.
and yf he hadde fal/
lyn dou*n* on his kneis
and cryed god me*r*cy ÷ he
10   shulde had me*r*cy.

Closely comparable material occurs in Trinity College, Cambridge MS B.2.18 (262), a variant copy of the *Meditationes vite Christi* in which a partial text of Nicholas Love's translation is preceded by a prefatory narrative of the Fall and the Flood (the material relevant to the present discussion) and an anonymous translation of the *Meditationes* extending down to the "Die Jovis" chapter. At f.2ᵛ lines 17–27 in Trinity B.2.18, after an account of the Expulsion and the sorrows of Adam and Eve in the world and in hell, appears the following:

f.2ᵛ 17   ¶ Adam in etyng of þe appel .' synnyd in al
þe .vij. dedely synnes / ffirst he was proude .' for he
was inobedient in goddes hestys ¶ In wrath he
20   synned / for as Dauid seith. he þ*at* loueþ wykkednes
hateþ his owne soule ¶ In gloteny .' for he ete more
þan him neded ¶ In lechery .' for he brake wedlok
of god in his soule ¶ In slewth .' for he wolde not
do as god badde hym to do ¶ In envy .' for he slow
25   him selfe ¶ In couetyse / for he couetyd more . þan
hym neded / ande so he offended in alle þe .vij. dedly
synnes

After the extract from *The Parson's Tale*, the compiler resumes at f.2ᵛ line 31 with a straightforward narrative of the Expulsion, based on Genesis 3: 8–20, 23, and 21.

The Parson's Tale is next brought into contribution as part of the Trinity historian's rather wayward account of the drunkenness of Noah, in which, contrary to Genesis 9: 25–27 and, be it said, to Chaucer, Noah is said to have cursed Ham and made him thrall to his brothers, Shem and Japheth. The compiler's version received the attentions of a corrector who deleted part of the account and, aping, somewhat stiffly, the style of the Trinity historian's script, entered interlineations and a marginal note describing how Noah's curse fell upon Canaan, Ham's son.[8] The passage in question (f.14ᵛ line 29-f.15ʳ line 1, with the corrector's deletions represented by square brackets and interlineations and marginal additions by half square brackets) reads as follows:

f.14ᵛ29	whan Noe was awakyd ÷ yt was tolde hym how
30	Cam dyd ¶ And than when⌈he⌉ vndirstode yt ÷ he blessyd
	Sem and Iaphet. and [Cam] ⌈Canaan⌉ was cursyd ¶ [And
	than seyde Noe to Sem *and* Iaphet. þat Cam was cursyd. *and* he
	shulde be thralle to them bothe ¶ And Iaphet shulde
	haue his ennerytau*n*ce. *and* shulde be vndyr [obed] obecience
35	to Sem. ¶ And Cam shulde be vndyr obecience *and* thralle
	to them bothe. ¶ And so he was thral *and* vndir subiecciou*n*
f.15ʳ	bothe he *and* all*e* his.]
f.14ᵛ lower	⌈Canaan the sonne of Cam and he was thralle and alle his
margin	progenie to the .vij. degre lyuyd vnder subieccion. ¶ ffor he
	wolde nat curse Cam þ*a*t dyd the trespasse be cause God
	had blessyd hym before. *and* he dyrste nat p*re*sume to curse
	þ*a*t god had blessyd. *and* therfor he cursyd Canaan the sonne of
	Cam.⌉

---

[8] Chaucer's version is confusing in that Canaan is referred to as the son of Noah: see the Trinity corrector's response to 766 below and see Genesis 9:18: "Erant ergo filii Noe, qui egressi sunt de arca, Sem, Cham, et Japheth: porro Cham ipse est pater Chanaan."

175

Again emended by the corrector, a version of *ParsT* 754–56 and 766 then follows:[9]

f.15ʳ 1   ¶ And [754] seint Austyn seith. þat [755] þe con/
       dicioun of Thraldam *and* þe fyrst cause ÷ is for synne. ¶ ffor
       we rede in Genesis. [756] þat gylte deseruyth thraldam.
       but nat nature ÷[766]¶ ffor this name of Thraldam ÷ was
5   neu*ir*. tyl þat Noe seyde to his sonne [Cam] ⌈Canaan⌉ ÷ þat he shulde
       be
       thral [to] ⌈*and*⌉ his [bretheryn] ⌈progenye⌉ for [his] ⌈þe⌉synne ⌈of his
       fadyr⌉.

Forming the third extract, lines 807, 810, and possibly 808 from Chaucer's definition of mercy in the next section of *The Parson's Tale* are brought to bear as a conclusion to the Trinity compiler's prose paraphrase of Gower's story of Constantine and Silvester, derived from the second book of the *Confessio Amantis*.[10] On f.70ᵛ (lines 14–21) he writes:

f.70ᵛ14   ¶ Be this narracioun we may vndirstonde ÷ that
15   [807] Misericorde foluyth Pyte in p*er*formyng
       of cheritabyl wyrkys of mercy. [810]¶ ffor Misericorde
       is for to loue. and for to yeue. and for to relese. and
       for to haue pyte in herte *and* compassioun of þe myschefe
       of thyne evyn cristyn [808[?]]¶ As Crist had of his enemy/
20   es. whan he prayde for them. as he hynge vpon þe
       crosse

---

[9] The text is marked by an uncorrected marginal note, "¶ How thraldom cam vp | first be Cam." The introduction of the error by which Ham is confused with Canaan clearly precedes the compiler's use of Chaucer's text: it seems unlikely, therefore, to stem from the particular copy of *The Canterbury Tales* available to him. Note that the reference in the quotation from St. Augustine (for which see *De Civitate Dei* 19.15) properly includes more precise reference to Genesis 9. *ParsT* 766 reads (the quotation is from Larry D. Benson, gen. ed., *The Riverside Chaucer*, 3d ed., Boston: Houghton Mifflin, 1987; Hengwrt is defective at this point): "This name of thraldom was nevere erst kowth til that Noe seyde that his sone Canaan sholde be thral to his bretheren for his synne." Manly and Rickert, in their edition, record the following variants for "Canaan": "Chaane" in Cambridge, Magdalene College, Pepys 2006, and Philadelphia, Rosenbach 1084 / 1 (*olim* Phillipps 8137); "Chaym" in Cambridge, Trinity College, R.3.3, London, British Library, Egerton 2726 and Tokyo, Takamiya 24 (*olim* Devonshire); "kaym" in London, British Library, Additional 5140, Egerton 2864 and Royal 18 C II, Manchester, Rylands, English 113, Oxford, Bodleian Library, Arch. Selden B 14, Christ Church 152 and Trinity 49.

[10] The extract actually directly follows a short excursus on Constantine's foundation of St. Peter's Church derived from the *Polychronicon* (f.70ᵛ 4–14).

The compiler turns finally to *The Parson's Tale* to provide an analysis of the sin of Amnon, murdered by his brother Absolon for his rape of their sister, Tamar.[11] The passage in question, occurring at f.165ʳ lines 17–30, derives from 865–66 and 868–72 in the section on "luxuria" where Chaucer is writing of fornication, one of the sins making up the species of lechery, "The fifthe fynger of the develes hand" (862). Introduced by a brief bridging passage, "Loo of | this synne comyth many harmys" (f.165ʳ 16–17), the extract reads:

f.165ʳ 17   ¶ ffyrst it is [865] a
         gaynste nature. [866] fo⌈r⌉ alle þat is destruccyoun and enemy
         to nature ÷ is ageynst nature [868] ¶ The secounde is he
20   þat bereuyth A maydyn of hyr maydenhode. for he
         þat so doyth ÷ he chastyth a mayden fro þe hyest degre
         þat is in this present lyfe. [869] and bervyth þat precyus frute.
         þat in latyn hyght Centesimus fructus.
         [870]¶ he þat dothe this. is cause of many damagys and
25   veleneys. [871]¶ ffor certys no more may Maydenhode
         be restoryd. than may an Arme þat is smyttyn fro
         þe body. whiche may neuir returne aȝen for to wex.
         [872]¶ This wot I wel she may haue mercy ÷ yf she
         do penaunce. but neuir shal yt be þat she was corrup/
30   te.

Twice, in almost identical context, the compiler makes use of a single, short, proverbial passage from Chaucer's *Melibee*. Occurring as part of Prudence's advice to Melibee that he has insufficient power to exact vengeance on his enemies, the passage in question (2671–74 in the traditional numbering of Group B²)[12] takes its place at f.32ʳ line 35–f.32ᵛ line 5 in an account of Amazonia, itself part of a more general geography derived largely from the first book of the *Polychronicon*. The passage reads:

f.32ʳ35   [2671]¶ It is a woodnes a man to stryue with a
f.32ᵛ1   more myhty man than he is hym self. [2672]¶ And for to
          stryue with as stronge as hym self. it is perel. [2673]¶ And

---

[11] These events are narrated f. 164ᵛ line 8–f.165ʳ line 16, paraphrased from 2 Regum 13 (1–5, 9, 14–15, 19–20, 28 / 29, 37).

[12] 1481–84 in the numbering of Fragment 7.

for to stryue w*ith* a weker man than hy*m* self. it is
bothe foly *and* shame. [2674] and þ*er*for a ma*n* shulde exchew
5   *and* flee stryuyng asmoche as he myhte.

It is adduced to strengthen the rejoinder made by Thalestris, queen of
the Amazons, to Alexander's demand for tribute as set down in
Polychronicon, book 1, chapter 17 (f.32[r] 28–35):[13]

f.32[r]28   ¶ Of thy wytte is gre/
te wonder. þ*at* thow desyrest to fygthe w*ith* wy*m*men.
30   ¶ ffor yf ffortune fauoure vs. *and* thow be ou*ir*come ÷
[of wy*m*men] it shalbe grete shame *and* vylonye whan
thow arte ou*ir*come of wy*m*men. ¶And yf oure [gd]
goddes be wrothe w*ith* us. *and* suffre þe to haue þe vyc/
tory ÷ yet thou shalt haue [no worship] but lytyl
worship

The identical passage from *Melibee* appears again at f.131[r] lines 11–17,
where—the history having advanced to events taking place during the
rule of Tola, successor to Abimelech—the compiler, recording from the
Polychronicon the conquests of the Scythians, turns again to the foundation, practices, and fortunes of Amazonia. Thalestris' rejoinder to
Alexander appears as on f.32[r] but closes with a short addition (f.131[r]
10–11) not found in the source and probably introduced to make the
transition to the material from the *Melibee* more fluent. Copied with
more facility than on the first occasion, the whole passage reads thus
(f.131[r] 4–17):

f.131[r]4   ¶ Of
5   thy wytte is grete wonder. þ*at* thou desyrest to fyg/
the w*ith* wy*m*men ¶ ffor yf fortune fauoure vs. *and* thow
be ou*ir*come ÷ it shalbe grete shame *and* vylonye whan
thou arte ou*ir*come of wy*m*men. ¶ And yf oure god/
dys be wrothe w*ith* us. *and* suffyr þe to haue þe vycto/
10   ry ou*ir* vs ÷ ȝyt thou shalt haue no worship. for

[13] *Polychronicon Ranulphi Higden monachi Cestrensis; together with the English translations of John Trevisa and of an unknown writer of the fifteenth century*, ed. Churchill Babington [vol-umes 1–2] and Joseph Rawson Lumby [volumes 3–9], Rolls Series (London, 1865–1866), 1:155.

we be wymmen *and* subiectys to men ¶ And þerfor [2671]it
is a woodnes a man to stryue w*it*h a strenger ma*n*
than he is hym self [2672]¶ And for to stryue w*it*h a man
þ*at* is as stronge as he is ÷ it is perel [2673]¶ And for to
15   stryue w*it*h a weker man. it is bothe foly *and* shame.
[2674]and þerfor a ma*n* shulde flee stryuyng asmoche as
he myhte.

In their description of HM 144, Manly and Rickert record plainly
enough that the text in this manuscript is "cut and much edited," but,
in their notice of the origin of the unique variants in the volume's version of *Melibee*, they concede a role to the chances of textual transmission, writing mildly "the interchange of synonyms and minor changes
in the text may have arisen from the inability of the scribe to hold
accurately in his mind a unit of prose text."[14] It will be the main purpose here to show how the texts from *The Canterbury Tales* in both the
Trinity and Huntington manuscripts have been freely subjected to
deliberate extensive editorial intervention and to characterize that
intervention.[15] However, two more minor questions have also to be addressed, first as to the correctness in the case of these two manuscripts
of writing interchangeably of "editor" and "scribe," and secondly as to
the classification of the copy text(s) lying behind their versions of *The
Canterbury Tales*.

In the Trinity history, substantive marginal additions and the presence of deletions and interlineations, all testifying to moments of inde-
cision in the process of composition or, more properly, compilation,
witness to the draft status of the manuscript. The compiler and the
scribe are undoubtedly one and the same. Equally, editing appears to
have been still in progress when the *Melibee* and *The Monk's Tale* were
entered in the Huntington manuscript. The following variants from
these two tales seem to demonstrate that the scribe himself introduced
last-minute changes to the wording of his original by means of deletion
and interlineation:[16]

---

[14] Manly and Rickert, eds., *Canterbury Tales* 1:292; 2:389.
[15] Compare the analysis of HM 144's uniquely "revised" text of the *Gospel of Nicodemus*
given in Marx, "Beginnings and Endings," pp. 77–80, and see also Marx and Drennan,
eds., *Middle English Prose Complaint*.
[16] The text of the *lemma* is from Hengwrt.

Melibee f.83ʳ 2246 wise] wyse ⌈men⌉,[17] f.87ʳ 2379 peruerten] [peruertyn or] ⌈perauentyr⌉ turne, f.88ᵛ 2467 warisshed] [warisshid] ⌈vanyshid or amendyd⌉, f.89ʳ 2476 warisshed] vanisshid ⌈or amendyd⌉,[18] f.92ʳ 2689 moore] [þe more] ⌈be⌉, f.99ʳ 3066 pride and hie[19] presumpcioun] [pryde] high presu*m*pc*i*ou*n* *Monk's Tale* f.100ʳ 3188 trewe] [trewe] ⌈yonge⌉,[20] f.102ᵛ 3367 a certeyn yerys] a⌈fter⌉ certeyn ȝeris, f.104ʳ 3453 dennes] [dennys] ⌈dyuers⌉, f.109ᵛ 3816 this] ⌈þ*at*⌉, f.110ʳ 3830 and another] [and] or any other, f.111ʳ 3906 And as] A⌈s⌉ [nd][21]

Further, on f.85ʳ, occurs the following marginal interpolation, marked for insertion after 2310 in the *Melibee*: "⌈In om*n*i op*er*e m<emen> | to finis. and in | yo*ur* wirkys rem<embir> | the ende.⌉"[22]

Manly and Rickert's collation of the *Melibee* and *The Monk's Tale* in HM 144 (Hn) showed that the manuscript was closely affiliated with London, British Library, Harley 7334 (Ha⁴) and Oxford, Bodleian, Laud 600 (Ld¹), the three copies constituting a subgroup, "a close group," as these editors describe it.[23] Comparison of the *Melibee* extracts in Trinity D 29 and the corresponding passage in HM 144 shows, unsurprisingly, that the latter is somewhat closer to the author's original. The Huntington manuscript reads at f.91ᵛ lines 19–24:

[17] This variant is not unique.
[18] See also below for the doublet introduced at 2480 warisshed] wanisshed or amended.
[19] Hengwrt here reads "by."
[20] This variant is not unique.
[21] The variants at ff.109ᵛ and 111ʳ may represent remedial measures by the scribe. In 3816, British Library, Harley 7334 and Bodleian, Laud 600, with both of which HM 144 is closely affiliated (see below), omit "this." In 3906 Laud omits "as."
[22] See further below, pp. 196–97.
[23] Manly and Rickert, eds., *Canterbury Tales* 2:401. For the classification of the *Melibee* see ibid., 2:371–92, and for *The Monk's Tale*, see 2:397–409. The Harleian manuscript is described at 1:219–30 and the Laud at 1:309–14. *Melibee* is also extracted in Cambridge, Magdalene, Pepys 2006, London, British Library, Arundel 140 and Sloane 1009, and in Stonyhurst College B xxiii (an abridged text). *The Monk's Tale* is extracted in Cambridge, Trinity College, R.3.19 (599) where the text is conflated with the *Fall of Princes* (see further A. S. G. Edwards, "Selections from Lydgate's *Fall of Princes*: A Checklist," *The Library*, 5th ser. 26 (1971): 341–42, and "The Influence of Lydgate's *Fall of Princes c.* 1440–1559: A Survey," *Mediaeval Studies* 39 (1977): 436. Manly and Rickert found HM 144 useful in distinguishing variants introduced for the first time in Harley 7334 from those present in its ancestor (see 1:291). For an interpretation of the relation between HM 144, Laud and Harley, see Charles A. Owen, Jr., *The Manuscripts of the Canterbury Tales* (Cambridge: D. S. Brewer, 1991), p. 118.

f.91ᵛ 19   ffor hit is a woodnes

20   a man to stryue w*ith* a strenger or a mightier ma*n* than hym

self is. And for to stryue of evyn strengthe. þ*at* is as stronge

a ma*n* as hee is. hit is p*er*ile. And for to stryue w*ith* a weker

hit is fooly *and* shame. ¶ And þ*er*for shulde ma*n* flee stryuyng

as moche as he myght.

Still unsurprisingly, collation suggests the close textual connection of
the versions in the two manuscripts. The following variants unique to
HM 144 and Trinity D 29 support this interpretation (the text of the
lemma is succeeded by HM 144, then by the first version at f.32ʳ⁻ᵛ in
Trinity D 29 and finally by the second version at f.131ʳ in the same
manuscript):

2671 Forther moore ye knowen wel that after the comune sawe] ffor] *om.*] And
þerfor, 2672 that is to seyn with] þ*at* is] *om.*] that is, 2673 folye] fooly *and*
shame] bothe foly *and* shame] bothe foly *and* shame

By contrast clear evidence suggests that the extracts from *The Parson's
Tale* in the Trinity manuscript do not derive from a text closely affiliated with Harley 7334 and Laud 600. Only the slightest support can
be summoned for the apparently very obvious notion that the same copy
text lies behind the Trinity compiler's version of *The Parson's Tale* and
the *Melibee* and *Monk's Tale* in HM 144; the following variants might
be cited:[24]

f.2ʳ⁻ᵛ 326 ye] þ*at* ye, 328 þat] ye, 329 þat] *om.*, eet] ete yt, 341 ne] *om.*, ne] *om.*,
842 lo] *om.*, f.15ʳ 755 Genesis nono] ffor we rede in Genesis, 766 that] to, f.70ᵛ
810 as] *om.*, lene] lone, and relesse] and for to relese[25]

The evidence against such a view is very telling. Trinity, for instance,
includes both the substantive omissions in Harley and Laud at 334
("And | that which was erste. but only peyne of concupiscence | . . .
is aftyrward. bothe peyne *and* synne") and 337–38 ("were | lawfully

---

[24] Where Hengwrt is defective, the text of the *lemma* is from the Riverside edition.
[25] The variants are not unique to the Harley and Laud copies. For Manly and Rickert's
classification of the copies of *The Parson's Tale*, see 2: 454–70. The tale is also extracted
in Longleat House MS 29.

made. *and* be ryghtful Iugement of god ÷ I seye for | asmoche as man"). In addition, where Trinity reads "coueyte be couetyse" in 336, Harley turns the verb into an infinitive and for "be," reads "þe," while Laud preserves the infinitive verb only. In 336 also "of flesshe" is correct in Trinity, omitted in Laud, and omitted in part in Harley, this copy reading "of" alone. Again in 338 Trinity has "his lorde" where Harley and Laud both omit "his," "þe flesshe" where Harley and Laud omit the definite article, "whiche" where Harley and Laud have "which that," and "and occasyoun of synne" omitted in Harley. In 340, "thyng" is present in Trinity but omitted in the other two manuscripts. Both Harley and Laud have "parte," not "departe," in 355 and "parties," not "pecys," in 356. Harley 7334 has "deserued" where Trinity has "deseruyth" in 756, "cherldam" where Trinity has "thraldom" in 766,[26] and "harmes" where Trinity has "damagys" in 870—Harley also omits "pyte," present in the Trinity version of 807. If the Trinity compiler did indeed use a single copy text of *The Canterbury Tales* for his work on the Trinity history and the collection in HM 144, it must be assumed that that copy text itself derived at some stage from a divided exemplar having affiliations with more than one textual tradition.

A number (though by no means all) of the unique variants in the Trinity extracts from the *Tales* may be explained straightforwardly enough by the editor's need to extricate them from their immediate context in his source and by his wish to modernize the language of this original or to clarify the articulation of Chaucer's syntax. However, the passages are also slightly abridged. The editor, clearly desiring to transmit only the bare point of his original, stripped his source of inessentials like, for instance, the intensifiers "sothely" and "certes" dropped from *ParsT* 326, 355 and 870, the translator's note in 869, and the simile in 870. In 869, where Chaucer hesitates as to the correct designation in English for the precious fruit of virginity, writing "thilke precious fruyt that the book clepeth the hundred fruyt I ne kan seye it noon ootherweyes in Englissh but in Latyn it highte Centesimus fructus," the Trinity version is reduced to "þat precyus frute. þat in latyn hyght Centesimus fructus." In 870, where Chaucer writes of the man who deflowers a virgin "he that so dooth is cause of manye damages and vileynyes mo than any man kan rekene right as he somtyme is cause of

---

[26] I hesitate to analyze this area of text further for here the Trinity corrector is at work probably without the benefit of any copy text at all.

alle damages that beestes don in the feeld that breketh the hegge or the closure thurgh which he destroyeth that may nat been restoored," the Trinity editor preserves only "he þat dothe this. is cause of many damagys *and* veleneys."[27] The editor also makes lexical intrusions in Chaucer's text, the purpose of all of which is to provide a gloss for his original: the expansion of "folye" to the doublet "foly *and* shame" in all three of his texts of *Melibee* 2673 has already been noted. Unique to the first version of the *Melibee* in the Trinity copy is another such variant: in 2674 "fle" becomes "exchew *and* flee." The text of *The Parson's Tale* in Trinity D 29 includes a sequence of glosses (mostly on the same word); the following variants can be noted:

334 concupiscence] concupiscence or desyryng, 335 concupiscence] Concupiscence. þat is desyryng, 337 concupiscence] Concupiscens or desyryng, 338 concupiscence] concupiscens or desyryng, 339 concupiscence] concupiscence or desyryng, 355 suggestioun] suggestioun or intysyng, 357 acompliced] acompliscid or fulfillyd, actuel] Actuel or doon in deede

There are also a number of more straightforward synonym substitutions:

329 tree] frute, 331 feend] Deuyl [also in the Duke of Northumberland's MS at Alnwick Castle], 341 malefice] maledy, 806 misericorde] mercy [also in Longleat House MS 29].

The two tales in HM 144, in varying degree according to the varying license allowed by their prose and verse forms, provide parallels with the Trinity manuscript in matters of textual detail: as will be seen,

---

[27] The following are also uniqely omitted from the Trinity text: *Parson's Tale* 329 bothe, 332 for truste wel thogh so were þat the feend tempted oon that is to seyn the flessh and the flessh hadde delit in the beautee of the fruyt deffended yet certes til þat reson that is to seyn Adam [this may be a case of eyeskip], 336 And eek coueitise of heynesse by pryde of herte, 337 the firste, 355 in this manere The feend, 756 Thus may ye seen the, 766 erst kowth; *Melibee* f.32ᵉ⁻ᵛ 2671 Further moore ye knowen wel that after the commune sawe, 2672 with a man of euene strengthe that is to seyn, f.131ʳ 2671 or a moore myghty, 2672 a man.

These unique variants may also evidence the editor's attempt to abbreviate his source: *Parson's Tale* 321 And forther ouer it is necessarie to vnderstonde] Of [abridgment, here is for the purpose of turning the text into a marginal note], 754 Augustinus de Civitate libro nono] And seint Austyn seith, 810 The speces of misericorde been] ffor Misericorde is; *Melibee* f.131ʳ 2671 Further moore ye knowen wel that after the comune sawe] And Þerfor, 2672 of euene strengthe that is to seyn with] þat is.

they also reflect a similarity in some of their procedures and more general intention. The *Melibee* and, to a lesser extent, *The Monk's Tale* both provide evidence of an editor set on explaining, glossing his original for his readers. A number of doublets are among the unique variants in the text of *Melibee* in the Huntington manuscript. The following readings may be cited:

2179 vn to the Romayns writeth] writyth vnto þe Romayns. *and* saith, 2187 anoyeþ to the clothes] *and* also in clothes hurteth *and* anoyeth, to the tree] þe tree hurteth *and* apayreth, anoyeth] hurteth and anoyeth, 2303 spoken discretly by ordinance] ordeyned *and* [b] spoken discretly, 2315 wel deme] wel sey nor wel deme, 2316 deme] sey or deme, 2318 viciouse] malycious *and* vicious, 2333 may] may or can, secrely] secretly *and* suerly, 2337 hyde] hyde or kepe, 2364 bountee] bou*n*te *and* good, 2408 doon] done or sey, 2421 wikked] wickyd *and* not good, 2473 desir] wylle *and* desyre, 2480 warisshed] wanisshed or amended, 2487 warnestore] strengthe *and* magnyfy, 2596 depe] grete *and* depe, 2629 shrewes] shrewes *and* wyckyd men, 2673 folye] fooly *and* shame, 2683 for to han pacience] be pacient *and* glad, 2705 moore worth] more worth *and* more profyt, 2706 herte] herte *and* wylle, preyse] co*m*mende *and* preyse, 2767 to desirynge to getyn] to gredy *and* desyrus in getyng, 2797 shapen] borw or shape, goodes] goodes *and* profetis, 2821 richesses] ryches *and* tresure, hapeth] happis. and fortune, 2947 myght] myght *and* pouer, 2980 good herte] good hert *and* wille, 3039 hemself] her body *and* her goodes[28]

A number of synonym substitutions appear uniquely in this same text in HM 144: they are as follows:

2172 warissche] recou*i*r, 2190 hath biraft it me] hit hath taken from me, 2222 algates] yet, 2232 moste haue] ought to take, 2233 for to abregge] to seece, 2238 sooth] trewe, 2258 thar ye nat] þere ye nede nat, 2258 like] wylle, 2260 al displeseth] of alle shal be blamed, 2270 þar hym ne] but he, 2273 soothly] certis, 2274 woot] knowith, 2276 wikked wyues] a chidyng wyfe,[29] 2317 thynges] wordis, 2319 dryue] voyde, 2330 wenen] knowe, 2338 wene sikerly]

---

[28] Ha^4 and Ld^1 read "here body and on hem self." At 2706 the following variant could also be cited: Citees] Cytees *and* tou*n*nes (it is attested elsewhere but not by the manuscripts closely affiliated with HM 144).

[29] Compare the expansion at 2276 and 2277 noted below, p. 187.

trowe verely, 2359 have seyd] spake of, 2365 eek eschue] eschewe also, 2365 soothfastnesse] trouthe, 2375 ne dwelleth] restyth, 2377 ne] yet, neuere] not, 2378 demeth] hopeth, 2379 bountee] good, 2380 beren] doith, 2396 if] wheþir, 2404 wight] wyse man, 2406 weyue] repente, 2421 euery] what, 2456 taught] geuyn, 2473 euery] eche, 2482 noght] neuir, 2488 ful auysely] with good avysement, 2512 it seme] thow suppisist, 2512 siker] suer, certeyne] dyuers, 2639 hope] truste, 2654 ne sustene] nor suffer, 2686 thynken] oughte to know, 2725 putte] to haue, 2732 taketh] is a customyd to pull, 2733 is outher-while] and at last is, 2735 ny] sore, 2758 And the same seith] And to this answeryth, 2760 algates] yet, 2787 Thanne] Lo, richesses] of your goodes, 2793 a manere] wyse, 2814 Afterward] Also, herte] mynde, 2819 his] thi, 2826 Afterward] Aftyr þat, 2829 greet] thy, 2834 loos] name, 2835 loos] name ['or loos' is omitted 2837], 2857 outher while] som tyme, 2883 in thee is] thow mayst, 2903 discouered] shewyd, 2953 right seur] sertayn, 2956 lymyte] licens, 2972 ye nat acorde yow ne haue] not 3e graunte to a corde and, 2975 aboue] be forn, 2995 shopen hem] made hem redy, 3016 agilt] offendid, 3069 giltes] offencis, 3070 do] geue, 3074 tyme] oure, giltes] offencis, to] ayenst[30]

Occasionally rewriting is more intensive; the following might be cited:

2355 by Auctoritee of persones and by Science] and by fayre answeris with resoun shewyd, 2648 thanne haue ye noon oother remedie but for to haue youre recours vn to] Therfor I counsayle yow reserue and yelde vp your mater and quarel vnto, 2658 euery persone to whom men don vileynye take of it vengeance] euery man shulde venge hym þat suffryth wronge, 2663 coman-deth and biddeth hym do synne] he is causer and geuith hym occasion to don another synne, 2704 attempreth hem and stilleth] is ful stille and colde and saith lytel, 2750 the compaignye of poore folk] beggers as thow arte thy self

The demands of the meter preclude the insertion of doublets in *The Monk's Tale*, but a number of synonyms and other simple substitutions

---

[30] The following variants also appear which are not found in the manuscripts closely affiliated with HM 144: 2189 substance] goodis, 2227 holden hem] be, 2269 saue] but, 2301, 2309, 2319, 2372, 2380, 2400 eek] also, 2659 vilenyes] wronges, 3035 renouelle] renewe

(sometimes, admittedly, made in the face of a probably corrupt original)[31] are uniquely inserted in the HM 144 copy of this text:

3204 helle] delue, 3224 hadde] did, so] sore, 3230 wel ny] neere,[32] 3239 vp
plyght] vp lyft,[33] 3246 noon] none ny, 3256 barm] lap, 3269 caytif] Sampson,
3331 hir man] soone, 3352 loute] worship, 3355 assente] consent, 3357
proud] p[ri]nce, 3369 his lyf in feere] he was afeerde, 3390 appetites] Ryott,
3419 heriest] honowrest, 3483 to wyues] but wymmen, 3559 gawreth] gage-
lyth, 2648 tragedie] degre, 3701 of acustumance] a contynuaunce, 3702 In]
Of, 3716 sonnest] sodenly, 3739 bettre] other, 3764 toun] cyte, 3784 greithe]
make redy, 3815 to] nyh, 3833 heir] heythe, 3884 fyn] fal, 3892, 3897
Boydekyns] Allis,[34] 3904 hipes] lymmes, 3926 For] But

The cause of clarification and simplification, with its close ally, modernization, is served in the text of *Melibee* by what might be called an
increase in the level of articulation. A scattering of extra "thens," "fors,"
and "therefores," and a few demonstratives and conjunctions are added
as follows:

2158 vp on] Than vpon, 2160 thre] Than thre, 2192 telleth] Than tellyth
hem, yow gouerne] than gouerne yow, 2240 Whan] Then when, 2244 and] for,
2256 men] þat men, 2271 Youre] Than youre, 2328 whan] Therfor when,
2355 but certes] for, 2368 Salomon] ffor Salomon, 2373 The] ffor þe, 2510
harmes] harmes *and*, 2515 Ouyde] And Ouide, 2518 The] ffor the, 2609 also]
þerfor, 2641 trusteth] Therfor trust, 2706 And] for, 2797 they] than they, 2854
deere sire] þerfor syr, 2887 Whanne] Than whan, 2902 seieth] þerfor saith,
2906 god] That god, 2919 and] Than

The HM 144 *Melibee* and, to a much lesser extent, *The Monk's Tale* both
include a number of further unique minor expansions presumably in-

---

[31] Compare the Ha[4] and Ld[1] readings in 3352 "loue," 3559 "gaulith," 3648 "tegrede,"
and "tegerte," 3390 "arriout." For 3331 see the reading, shared by Ha[4] and Ld[1], in 3330:
whan] whom. There are, further, a few readings attested elsewhere but not in those copies
closely affiliated to HM 144, which may possibly be ascribable to the editor's deliberate
intention to replace the reading of his original with a more readily comprehensible synonym. The following could be cited: 3200 welte] had, 3630 barm] armys, 3738 defame]
defaute, 3796 restrayne] refreyne. Particularly the last, however, looks more like a copying error.

[32] This variant is not recorded by Manly and Rickert.

[33] This involves loss of rhyme.

[34] That is "eile," meaning an awn or beard of grain, a prickle.

troduced mainly to serve the cause of increased clarity and not so far recorded. Thus in *The Monk's Tale* appear the following variant readings:

3239 gates] brasyn gatis, 3246 noon] none ny, 3307 worldes endes] the endes of the worlde, 3318 it maked] she mad hyt, 3326 any] at any, 3370 moore] eny more, 3674 he hire wombe slytte] hyr womb to be slit he, 3820 gerdon] gwerdoun hath, 3902 louede] louyd he[35]

The first of these, introduced into the account of Samson and the gates of Gaza, is of particular note: the editor's urge to introduce complete, "normative" narrative accounts, containing a full complement of customary detail, is attested more strongly in the Trinity history. The more plentiful minor expansions in the *Melibee* are as follows:

2185 maketh] consumeth his bloode *and* makyth, 2189 Iob] man Iop, 2198 hem his cas] his cause vnto them, 2271 my conseil] counsayl of me þat am youre wyf, 2275 wikked] wycked of tounge, (see also the variant noted above: 2276 wikked wyues] a chidyng wyfe), 2277 riotous] ryotus of tounge, 2282 þilke wikked purpos] yow from þat wickyd purpos, 2290 apaised] he appesyd, 2332 lokyng] louyng countenaunce, 2379 Make] Make thou, 2401 and] and knowe, 2404 sholde] shuld neuir, 2512 kepyng of thy persone] keping of thy persone *and* dredyng god, 2517 doute] shulde doute, 2527 And] Also ye shul, 2643 yow] yow vp, 2648 souereyn] hye souereyne, 2649 yow] youre quarel, 2651 Melibe answerde] Now certis quod Melibeus, 2659 iniuries] iniuryes aftyr þe dewe forme of lawe, 2688 semen] shulde seme, 2704 noyses] noyses *and* is ryght loude *and* hote, 2720 ye synnen] ye synne þer by, 2732 taketh] is a customyd to pull, 2733 hound] same hounde, 2797 propre] propir good, another man] oþir men onconciusly, 2817 richesse] worldly ryches, 2832 name] name. *and* dredyth *and* excuyth shame, 2837 name] name with drede *and* excuyng shame, nys but] he is *and* may be callyd, cherl] churle of keende, 2838 Sire] Syre quod dame Prudence, 2840 werres to mayntene] to mayntene your werris, 2890 and they] And oftyme thei, 2897

---

[35] The variants in 3326, 3370, 3674, and 3820 may be the result of attempted adjustments to restore the meter of the verse: with Ha[4] and Ld[1], HM 144 omits "on" in 3326 and "was he" in 3370: in 3674, though HM 144 alone omits "For," both the other copies have a transposed word order. All three read "longeth" rather than "bilongeth" in 3820 ("hath" appears properly at 3818). In 3202 "had" is added after "Adam": this reading is attested elsewhere but not in copies closely affiliated with HM 144.

worth] worthy loue *and* thanke, 2919 shewed] she shewed, 3039 hemself] her body *and* her goodes[36]

The doublets first listed, introduced to serve as instant glosses or to increase emphasis; the synonyms, the scattering of added "thens," "fors," and "therefores" noted just above, as well as the expansions mentioned here, especially insofar as they quite frequently, in the *Melibee* at least, involve reiteration of subjects, objects, and verbs, reducing Chaucer's syntax to smaller discrete units of sense could all be seen as features in keeping with script adjustments in preparation for oral delivery. The additions at 2275–77 in the *Melibee*, insisting on razor-sharp precision in the account of the sin being anatomized, are also, in a different way, particularly typical of this editor.[37]

Whatever their similarities, however, the scribe's strategies for handling his Chaucerian source text in Trinity 29 are only a pale and partial reflection of his more drastic editorial treatment of the *Melibee* in HM 144. (Once again comparison shows that the verse form of *The Monk's Tale* inhibited the scribe, blunting his intention and staying his would-be energetic editorial hand.) Characterization of the more wholesale program of change in the *Melibee* requires a broader brush than has been used so far. This text is both substantially abridged and contains substantive additions, the latter demonstrating that the editor's aim was not primarily, or, at least, not only to change the pace of the tale.[38] Both the running title "Prouerbis" given to *Melibee* in this copy and the endnote which links it to *The Monk's Tale* may supply clues to the editor's interpretation of his source. The endnote on f.99[r] reads:

They that this *present and* forseyde tale | haue or shal Reede ÷ Remembyr the no// | ble prouerbis. that rebukyth Couetise | and Vengeaunse takyng. in truste of | ffortune whiche hathe causyd many | a noble Prince to falle. as we may rede | of them here folluyng.

---

[36] Ha[4] and Ld[1] here read "here body and on hem self." Compare also the following variants in HM 144 attested elsewhere in the manuscripts of *Melibee* but not in those closely affiliated with this copy: 2316 may] he may, 2350 as] as is, 2702 pacience] his pacience, 2965 foryifenesse] for ȝeuenes of synne.

[37] Compare also the "refinements" introduced by the editor at 2512, 2832, and 2837.

[38] The Huntington copy is not the only abridged text of the *Melibee*: Manly and Rickert in their characterization of the copies of this text (2:371–92) single out the version of *Melibee* in Princeton University MS 100 (*olim* Helmingham Hall) and the extracted text in Stonyhurst College B xxiii as having been subjected to drastic cuts. They note many omissions also in Cambridge University Library, Ii 3 26.

Though more apparent in the Trinity history, the editor's twin desires for instant comprehension from his audience and a dominantly
homiletic mode of discourse are perhaps also behind his procedures with
the *Melibee* in HM 144. As will be seen, the regularity with which the
editor adduces chapter and verse is in keeping with his preferred mode:
I would infer from both his editorial performances, but particularly
from that in the Trinity manuscript, that the preachment had a dominant influence on the very character of his thought. It may be that the
actual hierarchy of the scripts he employs in HM 144 affirms this view:
display-script singles out the names of sins, the names of authorities,
and Latin quotations from the same; it also occasionally draws attention
to the articulation of Prudence's argument. In his treatment of the
Melibee, the editor appears to be more interested in the anatomy of sin,
in "sentence," in "morality" than he is in the interchanges between
Melibee and Prudence: on more than one occasion reducing dialogue to
monologue, he makes the undramatic even less dramatic.[39]

Unique minor omissions are multiple in the Huntington version of
the *Melibee*; they are as follows:

2185 soothly, 2255 quod she, 2278 by youre leue þat am nat I for, 2319 sire,
2327 certes, 2350 certes, 2401 and han approued it by manye wise folk and
olde, 2414 Soothly, 2457 for as muche as þat the examinacion is necessarie,
2473 to his owene, 2475 certes, 2486 as ye han herd bifore, 2487 ouer alle
thynges, 2488 seyden also þat in this cas ye oghten for to, 2492 oure lord, 2591
it lettyd nat in as muche as in hem was, 2596 oure lord, 2598 holde and, 2649
after that hym self witnesseth, 2658 ther of, 2666 at the laste maken hem lese
hir, 2671 ye knowen wel that after the comune sawe, 2672 to seyn with, 2762
as the same Salomon seith, 2788 ye shul, by youre wit and by youre trauaile,
2793 haue no matere ne cause to, 2823 so þat ye gete hem, 2850 right in this
wise, 2854 after that Salomon seith, 2868 ye knowen wel þat oon of, gretteste
and, 2888 thynges, 2893 and to preise yow, 2915 hoolly, 2951 ne richesse,
2954 oure lord, 2960 lord, 2974 with outen delay or taryynge, 2975 by ordre
in the presence of Melibe, 3024 and seyde, 3054 and matere, 3055 thyng, 3060
skiles and, 3073 to this[40]

A number of further omissions are not unique to this manuscript and
yet do not occur in the copies with which it is closely associated; thus

---

[39] It is just possible that this change again reflects the kind of reading or "performance" to be accorded to the text in this copy.

[40] Note that earlier in 3073 Harley 7334 has the variant reading shared by HM 144:
"to this effect] this is þeffect."

they may possibly be ascribed to the editor's policy of abridgement. These omissions are as follows:

2201 as ye may heere, 2248 certes, 2265 after that, 2280 soothly, 2296 of heuene, 2325 as ye herde her biforn, 2359 þat they be, 2401 as I haue seyd, 2633 axeth and, 2644 and in hir wit, 2685 as I haue seyd yow her biforn, 2723 with outen, 2780 the same, 2817 Creatour and, 2829 seith Salomon, 2841 and wole algates, 2849 and strenger, 2860 goodly, 2866 in hise epistles, 2878 Certes, 2888 þat ye, 2892 right, 2901 and shewen, 2950 and knowe verraily, 2975 and declared, 2991 that is to seyn the Aduersaries of Melibe, 3005 ye wol, 3008 and gilt, 3022 feyned and, 3030 the sawe of, 3072 outrely

None of the omissions involves actual dislocation of the sense of the original. By halving doublets,[41] and by omitting minor repetitions, intensifiers, and other "redundancies" (he is very consistent in his attack on certain phrases), the editor makes many short cuts in the windings of Chaucer's syntax. If the deliberateness of the process should remain in doubt, a number of minor variants demonstrating that abridgement involved the composition of alternative curtailed versions might be cited:

2186 he seith eek thus þat] And also, 2218 ne sodeynly for to doon] or hasty, 2221 And eek men seyn þat] Therfor, 2251 þat it moste] to, 2254 Whan Dame Prudence ful debonairly and with gret pacience hadde herd al that hir housbonde liked for to seye thanne axed she of hym licence for to speke] Than Prudence spake, 2279 and eek how wel þat I kan hiden and hele thynges þat men oghten secrely to hyde] and yet 3e founde me neuir of þat condicioun, 2280 woot thilke reson stant heere in no stede] forbede, 2493 To this sentence acordeth the prophete Dauid that seith] ffor as the profyt Dauid saith, 2530 of his Citezeins and of his peple] with his pepyll, 2594 by cause þat] for, 2638 ne ye shul nat] nor, after the word of Senek for] ffor Seneca seith, 2639 thynges þat been folily doon and þat been in hope of fortune shullen neuere come] thyngis of foly þat be done in truste of ffortune cometh neuir, 2640 And as the same Senek seith The] ffor þe, 2655 and holden ouer lowe] to wronge, 2665–2666 they sholden by swich suffrance by proces of tyme wexen of swich power and myght þat they sholden putte out the Iuges and the souereyns from hir places and at the laste maken hem lese hir lordshipes] at last in continuaunce þe

---

[41] See 2598, 2615, 2633, 2817, 2841, 2868, 2901, 2950, 2951, 2975, 3008, 3022, 3024, 3054, 3060.

Iugges *and* Sou*i*raynes myght be put doune from her places *and* lordshippis, 2670 is good as now þat ye suffre and be pacient] is bettyr to suffre. than to stryue, 2704 And the same Salomon seith The] ffor þe, 2722 And if ye seye þat] yet,[42] 2726 men haue no cause ne matere to repreuen hym þat defendeth hym] no reprefe be leyde to hym, 2748 right happy that is to seyn If thow be right riche] ryche *and* happy, 2751 seith this Pamphilles] Pamphillus saith

More substantial unique omissions are quite frequent, their deliberateness usually no matter for debate as they involve no loss of basic sense
and quite often some rewriting of the original. If any general tendencies
are to be recognized in the pattern of abridgement they would seem to be
directed towards reducing sequences of examples cited in support of a
single argument (an obvious enough method for curtailing this text), excising some of the matter specific only to Melibee's own case, and, as has
already been noted, promoting monologue as the main strategy of the
text rather than dialogue. From Prudence's speech urging moderation in
weeping, lines 2181–83 are dropped, dealing with the teaching of Seneca
on the proper level of grief to be shown on the death of a friend. Lines
2206–17 are omitted from the debate over the relative benefits of delay
and immediate war on the wronged Melibee's enemies, comprising the
speech of the physicians (notably, given what has just been remarked about
the general tendencies of the editor's policy of abridgement, commencing
"Almoost right in the same wise / the Phisiciens answerden . . .") and part
of the advocate's speech which follows (notably again, the omission including the specific advice that Melibee should set an adequate guard but
not the subsequent more generalized discourse about making war and
wreaking vengeance).[43] From Prudence's discourse on the need to examine counsel and, specifically, to examine the outcome of the action advised,
2411–12 are excised: the excised text includes an element of reca-

---

[42] 2723 "ye seye" is emended to "it is" in consequence.

[43] 2239 was possibly deliberately omitted because it carries neither the action nor the
"sentence" forward (it reads "yet hadde this Melibeus / in his conseil many folk / þat pri-
uely in his ere / conseiled hym certeyn thyng. and conseiled hym the contrarie in general
audience") but the omission might also be a mere copying error due to eyeskip (compare
2240 commencing "Whan Melibeus hadde herd / þat the gretteste party of his conseil
. . ."). From 2263–64, in Prudence's proof of the existence of good women, the following is omitted: "may lightly be preued / for certes sire / oure lord Iesu crist wolde neuere
han descended / to be born of a womman / if alle wommen hadde be wikke." However,
this seems more likely to be a response to a defect in his immediate source rather than a
considered editorial decision: both Harley 7334 and Laud 600 have an omission here
("may . . . of a womman").

pitulation reading "wel seyn they / þat defenden euery wight to assaye / a thyng of which he is in doute / wheither he may parforme it or no ¶ And after / whan ye haue examyned youre conseil / as I haue seyd biforn / and knowen wel þat ye may parforme youre emprise / conferme it thanne sadly."[44] The omission of 2422–53 involves Melibee's request for and Prudence's assessment of his counselors and the counsel offered to him: a rather awkward confounding of the two speakers' words is one of the results—2455 in consequence is edited to begin not "To this sentence / answerde anon dame Prudence / and seyde" but rather "To this sentence | answerde dame Prudence to her [he] husbond Melibeus | and sayde." Lines 2464–65, containing Prudence's advice that the physicians and surgeons should be handsomely rewarded for their wise counsel and their care of Melibee's daughter, are cut. 2495–2504, in which Melibee is told to place reliance on true friends and eschew strangers' counsel, are omitted with the "that" properly opening 2505 being edited to an "And," and the "kepe yow" of 2504 being inserted after "strengthe" in the same line as a consequence. 2504–05, reading in Hengwrt "And after this / thanne shal ye kepe yow in swich manere / that for any presumpcion of your strengthe / þat ye ne despise nat ne attempte nat the myght if youre Aduersarie / so lite / þat ye lete / the kepyng of youre persone for youre presumpcioun," are thus reduced to "And for any presumpcioun of | youre streingthe ÷ kepe yow þat ye despise not þe myght if youre | Aduersarie so lyte þat ye lete þe kepyng for youre persone for | youre presumpcion." The interchange between Melibee and Prudence on what he understands by the advice "to warnestore youre hous" is largely dropped: with the excision of 2521–26, only Prudence's argument that the strongest defense lies in the love of neighbors and dependents remains. Lines 2531–83 are all dropped: they contain Prudence's advice not to proceed precipitately; her critique of the false counselors who promoted immediate war on Melibee's enemies; her unfavorable comparison of Melibee's power and the strength of those adversaries, supported as they are by their close kindred; her casting of doubt on Melibee's authority to exact vengeance; and, finally, her notice of the consequences of such revenge. Line 2584 is edited

---

[44] The omission of 2420, "And eek if so be / þat it be inpossible / or may nat goodly be parformed or kept," may be due to eyeskip on "and," but it has no primary function in the simple argument of the text, merely involving the recital of reasons why counsel might be changed in addition to the reasons already mentioned. The excision may also be ascribed to a desire to simplify: it follows immediately on the tangential statement "for the lawes seyn / that alle bihestes / þat ben deshoneste / ben of no value" which may have been regarded as some sort of clog to easy comprehension.

to accommodate this cut: "Than another poynt is this" is inserted before "thow shalt | vnderstonde þat þe wronge þow hast resceyued. hath cer / | tayne causes. . . ."[45] Lines 2651–53, containing Melibee's urging that failure to avenge his wrongs will encourage another wrong and his authority for this statement, are dropped. The reference to the two authorities cited by Melibee (one of them in fact already cut by the editor) and the narrowing of their application to judges, are lost with the omission of 2660–62. Line 2663 is edited in consequence, commencing not "Also / a wys man seith" but "ffor þe wiseman saith." Prudence's reminder that Melibee's enemies are mightier than he, is excised with the omission of 2667–69: as will be seen below, the passage is actually replaced by a unique addition before 2670. Lines 2681–83, an introductory passage in which Prudence suggests that even if one has the right and license to avenge a wrong yet many arguments can be adduced against actually taking that vengeance. An edited version of 2684 follows the excision (opening not "First and foreward" but simply "For"): a reworked 2683 is introduced before 2686 ("and make yow for to" being replaced by "ye owte mekly to," a reading perhaps also hinting at some corruption in the source of HM 144). In the next passage to be cut (2691–701), beginning tellingly enough "Also / ye owen / to enclyne and bowe youre herte . . . ," Prudence cites the example of Christ's patience from St. Peter's Epistles, the example of the patience of the saints and the fact of the transitoriness of the tribulations of this world when compared with the eternal joy earned by those showing patience, in support of her case for Melibee to display this virtue. The loss of 2708–17, containing Melibee's reply to his wife's disquisition on patience, again sees dialogue reduced to monologue: the editor has to introduce a minor change to 2718 as a consequence of the abridgement—it opens "And" rather than "For." Part of 2726 and all the text down to "is good" in 2729 are omitted: here Prudence analyzes Melibee's own case, driven as he is not by the justifiable need for self-defense but the immoderate desire for revenge. Lines 2730–32 (down to "is lyk") are replaced, as will be seen below, rather than just omitted:[46] in these lines Melibee accepts the wrongful nature of interfering in another man's quarrel—part of 2734 ("right in the same wise is it resoun / þat he haue harm þat by hys inpacience medleth hym / of the noyse / of another

---

[45] The omission of 2627–29 may just be due to eyeskip on "seith."

[46] Notably both Harley 7334 and Laud 600 omit part of 2730 ("of that . . . no wonder"), so intervention may have been forced on the editor by a defective exemplar.

man") is also omitted. Line 2735 is edited to supply an introduction to the speaker of the text lost through the abridgement: "But" is replaced by "Than Melibeus seith." The excision of 2763–64 may have been prompted by the presence here of a recapitulation: the passage reads "By thise resons / þat I haue seyd vn to yow / and by manye othere resons / þat I koude seye / I graunte yow / þat richesses been goode / to hem þat geten hem wel / and to hem / þat wel vsen tho richesses." Line 2765 is edited to open not "And ther fore" but "Therfor saith Prudens." Lines 2798–806 are cut from Prudence's disquisition against avarice. Her recapitulation "now haue I shewed yow / how ye shul do / in getynge richesses / and how ye shullen vsen hem / And" is dropped from 2838–39. The loss of "deere sire / al be it so / þat for youre richesses / ye mowe haue muchel folk. yet bihoueth it nat" from 2844–45 includes the loss of a direct address to Melibee: in 2845 "ne" is replaced with "And þerfor" to accommodate the excision. The element of dialogue is again reduced by the omission of 2862–65, including Melibee's request to Prudence for her advice on what he is to do. The text is quite extensively reordered after 2870: 2882–83 are followed by 2886, 2871–78 and 2880–81, the text then continuing normally from 2887. With 2871 placed after 2886, the new order delays Melibee's intervention on the dishonor of pleading for mercy. Further, 2879 is omitted with the effect of considerably toning down Prudence's assertion that she loves Melibee's "honur and . . . profit / as I do myn owene": 2879 reads "ne ye / ne noon oother / syen neuere the contrarie." Lines 2884–85, containing a very wifely direct complaint to Melibee, are also omitted: the omitted passage reads "yet seye I nat þat ye shul rather pursue to youre Aduersaries for pees / than they shuln to yow ʃ / for .I. knowen wel / þat ye been so hard herted / þat ye wol do / no thyng for me."[47] The final lines of the tale, 3074–78, are also omitted.

There are, further, a small number of omissions which are not unique to HM 144 but are not found in closely affiliated manuscripts: it is possible therefore that they too are the result of the deliberate policy of abridgement by this editor. This may apply to the omission of 2286–87: "Eke some men han seyd / þat the conseilyng of wommen / is outher to deere / or ellis to litel of prys but al be it so / þat ful many a womman is badde / and hir conseil vile and noght worth ʃ yet men founde / ful many a good womman and ful discrete and wys in conseilynge;" the HM

---

[47] The omission of 2993–94, "and answereden . . . ," and 2996–97 may both just be due to eyeskip on "and."

144 text proceeds directly with the examples of good women mentioned in 2285. It may also be the case with 2630–31, which contain an additional reference from St. Paul in a sequence on the judge's duty to punish. The omission of 2978, which is also found elsewhere, may equally be deliberate as its loss does not actually disrupt the basic sense of the passage in which it occurs.

Because they are of the nature of annotation to the text, involving the citation of (Latin) chapter and verse from the Bible in response to the English version in Chaucer's text (though not placed in the margins of the manuscript), the discussion of one or two of the additions to the *Melibee* in HM 144 is slightly problematic, calling for some recourse to the whole corpus of nonauthorial apparatus to the text. It is clearly eminently possible that several different glossators might independently decide to cite the text of a particular passage: equally it is impossible to be entirely certain that some portion of such notes did not exist in the HM 144 editor's immediate source. (As will become apparent, however, neither of the two manuscripts to which this text is closely affiliated, Harley 7334 and Laud 600, include the notes most in question.) In what follows I will endeavor to include as part of the discussion of the additions in this copy mention of the appearance of similar material in the apparatus in other copies.[48] Nine of the additions are ascribed to "þe booke," by which the editor appears to mean, or is under the impression that he means, the Bible. Some of them, however, seem not to be biblical quotations but rather more in keeping with the running titles

---

[48] The marginal apparatus in HM 144 itself is of a different kind: frequently cropped, the notes are fairly often directed towards highlighting the morally educative in the text. (There also seems to be some correlation between the incidence of the marginal notes and the editor's own intrusions in the text.) On f.81^r (2164) appears "¶ Wepe *and* so< >| *with* resou*n*.," on f.82^r (2220) "¶ A prou*er*be" (Bodleian Library, Arch. Selden B 14, for instance, includes similar notes: f.177^r "a comune prou*er*be," f.180^v "prou*er*bium."; see also Lincoln 110 ff.207^r, 209^v, British Library, Egerton 2864 ff.194^v, 195^r), on f.84^r (2274) "¶ Thre thing*es* d<ry>|uyth a ma*n* out< >| his house" (compare Ellesmere "Of .iij. thynges þ*a*t dryuen a | man out of his hous" and Cambridge, Trinity R.3.15 f.225^v (2276) "Of iij thynges | dryueth a ma*n* < >| his hous / / S< >," and British Library, Additional 35286, f.172^r "Of iij thinges that dryuen |a man out of his hous"), on f.85^r (2304) "¶ Whom a M< >| shal chese to b< >| his cou*n*sel.," on f.86^v (2362) "<W>hom a man| < > eschew from | <c>ou*n*sel" (compare Ellesmere "Of conseillo*ur* þ*a*t a man | oghte to eschewe," Additional 35286, f.174^r "Of conseillours that a man | oght to eschue.," and Trinity R.3.15 f.228^r (2363) "howe a ma*n* shalle | eschewe the comp< > | of fooles / Salam < >"), on f.93^v (2777) "ydelnes.," and (2787) "how Man shude | < >is goodis spende. | Auarice."

accorded to the work in this copy, "Prou*er*bis." (Several can be found in the standard reference work of Hans Walther.[49])

At the conclusion to Prudence's advice that grief should be moderated, the Latin version of Job 1:21 is added before the English at 2190 on f.81ᵛ, "D*omin*us dedit d*omin*us abstulit. sicut d*omi*no placuit. ita factu*m* | est. sit nomen d*omi*ni benedictu*m*." Part of this Latin text is also given in Manchester, John Rylands Library MS English 113, f.128ᵛ and in the Cardigan manuscript (University of Texas, Humanities Research Center, HRC Pre-1700 MS 143) f.163ʳ; the whole is given in Bodleian, Hatton Donatus I f.190ᵛ. On f.82ʳ the following is added before 2221 as part of the discourse in favor of ample time being allowed before judgment is given or vengeance exacted (here of course transferred to a different speaker due to the omission of 2206–17): "Om*n*is h*om*o estimat | alt*er*um sicut te ips*u*m. Thou demyst eu*er*y ma*n* as thou arte thi self | ¶ And also þe boke seith. In quo eni*m* iudicas alt*er*um te ips*u*m co*n*|dem*n*as In þ*at* thou Iugest anoþ*ir* ma*n* thi self thou condempnyst."[50] On f.82ᵛ, "¶ Ther / | for þe booke seyth. Meme*n*to finis et in eternu*m* no*n* pec | cabis. Reme*m*byr the ende *and* thow shalt nat don amys" is added before 2231 as part of the speech of the "olde wise" against warmongering and the harsh realities which are the outcome of war. On f.84ʳ, before 2278 is added to Prudence's distinction between the counsel of good women and that of "Iangleresses" immediately before her own protestation of "grete silence . . . grete pacience" and ability to keep a secret, "The boke | seyth. In multi loquio. no*n* effugies peccatu*m*. yn moche | spekynge thow shalt neu*ir* fle synne ¶ And in anoþ*ir* place | hit seith. Sapiens uerbis. in notescit paucis. wyse | wordis nedith not be spokyn softly."[51] The Latin text of Tobias 4:20 is inserted before the English at 2308 on f.85ʳ, "Om*n*i te*m*pore bene / | dic deu*m* *et* pete ab eo ut uias tuas dirigat. *et* | om*n*i te*m*pore consilia tua in ip*s*o p*er*maneant." The marginal interpolation, "In om*n*i op*er*e m< > |to finis. and in | yo*ur* wirkys rem< >| the ende," at 2310, in Prudence's advice on choosing counselors, has already been noted above: the passage is marked for insertion immediately after "Seint Iame also saith. If any of ʒow haue | nede of Sapience ÷ axe hit of god . and afterward then | ʒe shul take cou*n*sel

---

[49] *Lateinische Sprichwörter und Sentenzen des Mittelalters*, Carmina Medii Aevi Posterioris Latina, no. 2, 5 vols. (Göttingen: Vandenhoeck & Ruprecht, 1963–67), and Nova Series, 1982–86.

[50] The second quotation is from St. Paul's Epistle to the Romans 2:1.

[51] For the first quotation see Proverbs 10:19.

in your self. and examyn wel ȝour | thoughtes of swiche thyngis as ȝow thynkith þat is | best for your profyt." On f.88ʳ the same passage is placed before 2398 in Prudence's teaching of "how ye shul examyn your | counseil": it reads here "⌈and⌉ [.]so[..] In omni opere.me / | mento finis. yn all thy werkes remembyr the ende." "Vincit qui patitur. | Suffyr and ouircome." is placed after 2407 ("And yf so be þat thow be | in doute. whether thow maist parfourme a thynge or nat ÷ | chese rather to suffre than to bygynne") on the same page, an addition to Prudence's advice that consideration should be given as to whether advice may be carried through and the likely outcome of any action taken.[52] A passage seeming to contain a number of residual rhymes appears before 2512 on f.89ᵛ, inserted in the much abridged treatment of the men of law's advice that Melibee should safeguard his person: it reads "ffor where as perell is ÷ | grete perell is to abyde ¶ And he saith also. þat euery man in his moste worldly wele. is moste lykly saf only grace ÷ rather | to hurte than to heele." "Michi vindictam et ego retribuam," from Paul's Epistle to the Romans 12: 19, is inserted before the English version of this text at 2650. The Latin forms part of the apparatus in Cambridge University Library, Gg IV 27, f.340ʳ; Magdalene College, Pepys 2006, p. 255; and Trinity College R.3.15, f.234ᵛ, and R.3.3, f.94ʳᵇ, where the text is defective because the leaf is cropped; British Library, Egerton 2864, f.203ᵛ; and Manchester, Rylands 113, f.134ʳ: the opening tag, "Mihi vindictam," alone appears in the McCormick manuscript at the University of Chicago (Regenstein Library MS 564), f.93ʳ, as it does similarly in Bodleian Library, Rawlinson 141, f.104ᵛ. Before 2664 on f.91ᵛ is inserted in Prudence's discussion of the duty of judges to punish "And þerfor þe booke seith | Consencientes et agentes pares pena pu | nientur. þat is to sey ÷ the consenter shal be ponysshyd with | þe doer."[53] The insertion is evidently triggered by 2663, which it immediately follows: "ffor þe wiseman saith. | The Iugge þat correctith not þe synner ÷ he is causer and geuith | hym occasion to don another syne." A little later on the same page appears the addition "And þerfor god hath | ordeyned lawe to ponysshe equalli for euery man and nat euery man to venge his owne quarell." This precedes 2670 (the passage so fixed in the compiler's mind that he used it twice in the Trinity history) and replaces 2667–69, Prudence's unfavorable contrast between Melibee's power and that of his

---

[52] Compare Walther, Nova Series, 442889.
[53] Walther, 3124a.

enemies, which, as has already been noted, is omitted in this copy. It immediately follows the analysis of the outcome of leniency to "shrewes *and* mysdoers" by "Iugges *and* Soueraygnes" as the latter's own overthrow. On f.92ᵛ the omitted 2730–32 are replaced by "¶ ffor he þ*at* is vnpacient. *and* in his yre *and* angyr wyl venge | hym to a cewse a noþ*ir* man. of þ*at* he knowyth ÷ let hym be wel ware | þ*at* he be not culpabil *and* gilty in the same. or in other thyng as | evyl. lest þ*at* hit be openyd *and* disclosyd. þ*at* before was preuy *and* | close. *and* turne to no cou*n*sel. þ*at* before was cou*n*sel." (In 2732 "is lyk to" is replaced by "Soche pepyl may be lykened to.") The replacement for the omitted 2734 which follows just below on the same page is in keeping with the preceding addition, continuing the new focus on impatience, leading to what would now probably be called a "breach of confidentiality": it reads "¶ And so in lyke | wyse. som tyme a ma*n* in angyr constreyneth a nother to speke | *and* discouer. þ*at* he had neu*ir* thought to haue spoke or discou*ir*. And | aftyr þ*at* repent them. whan it is to late. ¶ And so oft tymes is | seen. þ*at* he hathe harme þ*at* medelyth of oþ*ir* me*n*nys deedys." (The text then proceeds, more or less properly, with "where | hit apperteynith no thyng to hym" from 2734.) On f.93ᵛ "¶ ffor þe booke seith. Quod tibi no*n* uis fieri. alij ne | feceris. do thow none otherwise to another. but as thow | woldist be don to thy self." is inserted before 2775, reinforcing Prudence's message that riches are not to be accrued to the detriment of others.[54] A further addition appears just below on the same page: prompted by Prudence's injunction to "flee ydelnes" (2778), it is the first of several changes to the passage treating of that vice. "¶ ffor þe booke seith. Ociositas i*n*imicus e*st* a*n*ime. ydelnes | is enemy to þe soule." is inserted before 2779. After 2779 itself, the text is slightly rearranged: 2783 ("And þ*er*e is a versifyour saith. That þe | ydel man excusith hym in wynter bicause of þe grete colde. And | in somer by enchesou*n* of þe grete hete") succeeds immediately, to be followed by a further insertion: "¶ And þe booke seith. | Qui laboret et manducet. qui no*n* laboreth non | manducet. he þ*at* laboryth shal ete. *and* he þ*at* labor nat shal nat | ete." The text then runs 2780–82, 2785–86, 2784, and 2787 and following, with 2784 edited to read not "For thise causes seith Caton" but "And Catou*n* beddith." On f.97ᵛ (lines 11–15) occurs an insertion of a different

[54] Walther, 26081.

order: a complete rhyme royal stanza is imperfectly absorbed into Chaucer's prose before 2986. It reads:

lest [þat] that thow may say. Alas | to long hathe been the taryeng *and* the delay of my correciou*n*. | A good purpos w*ith* oute begynnyng. good wil w*ith* outen any op*er*a / | ciou*n*. good promys *and* noon execuciou*n*. fourthe dryve. amendys | fro morw to morwe. and neu*ir* doon ÷ causith alle my sorw.

The stanza is traceable to Thomas Hoccleve's *Lerne to dye* (lines 365–71),[55] and is used here to strengthen Prudence's argument that Melibee should not delay in summoning his adversaries to make peace. (In the Trinity history, the scribe's idiosyncratic methods of compounding disparate sources, and the singular processes of association and recollection which lie behind them, are even more apparent and remarkable, because written very much larger.)[56]

The editor's additions to the *Melibee* endorse the view that it is the preachment which is the staple of his literary experience: presumably having undergone a training as concerted as one of Pavlov's dogs, his response to certain keywords (the adducing of related texts) is a deeply engrained reflex action.

---

[55] Frederick J. Furnivall and I. Gollancz, eds., *Hoccleve's Works: The Minor Poems*, rev. and ed. by Jerome Mitchell and A. I. Doyle, EETS, e.s., vols. 61 and 73 (1970): pp. 191–92.

[56] Compare Harris (D. Phil diss., 1993) p. 72.

"Chaucer's Chronicle," John Shirley, and the Canon of Chaucer's Shorter Poems

Julia Boffey
Queen Mary and Westfield College, University of London

A. S. G. Edwards
University of Victoria

T he process of Chaucerian canon formation entered its most distinctive phase during the late fifteenth century and lasted until the end
of the sixteenth. This period saw a series of attempts, in both manuscript and print, to establish the corpus of Chaucer's works and to con-
solidate them in a single entity termed, for the first time in English
literary history, "The Works."[1] The anthologies put together by the
compilers of Oxford, Bodleian Library MS Arch. Selden. B.24, the last
major manuscript collection of Chaucer's works,[2] and for the printed
editions of Pynson (1526), Thynne (1532 and subsequently), Stow
(1561), and Speght (1598 and 1602) are noteworthy for their increasing comprehensiveness and also for the large number of spurious poems
that they included in their formulations of the canon. More than fifty
such poems were added during this period and retained their place until
the end of the nineteenth century.[3]

Modern scholarship has largely pruned these additions from the canon
and established it in what seems a relatively unproblematic form. But

---

[1] A. S. G. Edwards, "Chaucer from Manuscript to Print: The Social Text and the Critical Text," *Mosaic* 28. 4 (1995): 1–12.

[2] See the facsimile (Boydell and Brewer, 1997) with an introduction by Julia Boffey and A. S. G. Edwards; see also A. S. G. Edwards, "Bodleian Library MS Arch. Selden. B. 24: A 'Transitional' Collection," in Stephen G. Nichols and Siegfried Wenzel, eds., *The Whole Book: Cultural Perspectives on the Medieval Miscellany* (Ann Arbor: University of Michigan Press, 1996), pp. 53–67.

[3] R. H. Robbins, "The Chaucerian Apocrypha," in A. E. Hartung, gen. ed., *A Manual of the Writings in Middle English, 1050–1500*, 9 vols. (New Haven, Conn.: Connecticut Academy of Arts and Sciences, 1973), 4:4.

the earlier stages of canon formation—those, that is, before the expansionist phase at the end of the fifteenth century—remain rather unexplored. There has been no systematic attempt to trace the growing patterns of collocation in the manuscript tradition that precede the sixteenth century's more ambitious, and increasingly implausible, attempts to settle the body of Chaucer's works. There remain some indications of an early consciousness of common authorship as a unifying principle, as with the gathering of several of Chaucer's works in Cambridge University Library MS Gg.4.27,[4] but textual collocations were often based, it seems, on generic links in which authorship may have been a reinforcing but not necessarily a primary factor. One sees this in the manuscripts of the so-called "Oxford Group" (Oxford, Bodleian Library MSS Bodley 638, Fairfax 16, Tanner 346, and Digby 181),[5] in which Chaucer's dream-visions and lyrics appear with similar works by Clanvowe, Lydgate, and Hoccleve: *The Cuckoo and the Nightingale, The Complaint of the Black Knight*, and *The Letter of Cupid*, for example. Other patterns of linkage can be discerned at more local levels, as with the groupings of Chaucer's lyrics that can be found in some manuscripts,[6] or even in such curious "mini-anthologies" as London, British Library MS Addit. 10340, in which *Boece* is supplemented with a copy of the lyric "Fortune" and a unique extract from *The General Prologue* depicting the Parson.[7]

But factors other than the literary and thematic seem also to have come into play, and of kinds that resist obvious categorization. These perhaps grew out of a complex of often unrecoverable circumstances linking the earliest attempts to produce Chaucer's works for commercial circulation within the metropolis to individuals with information or texts possibly deriving from Chaucer's own literary circles.[8] While

[4] M. B. Parkes and R. Beadle, intro. to *Geoffrey Chaucer: Poetical Works: A Facsimile of Cambridge, University Library MS Gg.4.27*, 3 vols. (Cambridge: D. S. Brewer, 1979–80).

[5] Eleanor Prescott Hammond, *Chaucer: A Bibliographical Manual* (New York: Macmillan, 1908), pp. 333 ff.; and Aage Brusendorff, *The Chaucer Tradition* (Oxford: Clarendon Press, 1925), pp. 183–200. Some of these are available in facsimile: see John Norton-Smith, intro. to *Bodleian MS Fairfax 16* (London: Scolar, 1979); Pamela Robinson, intro. to *Manuscript Bodley 638* (Norman, Ok.: Pilgrim Books, 1982), and *Manuscript Tanner 346* (Norman, Ok.: Pilgrim Books, 1980). MS Digby 181 is described in R. K. Root, *The Manuscripts of Chaucer's "Troilus,"* Chaucer Society, 1st ser., vol. 98 (London: Oxford University Press, 1914), p. 9.

[6] Julia Boffey, "The Reputation and Circulation of Chaucer's Lyrics in the Fifteenth Century," *ChauR* 28 (1993): 23–40.

[7] See J. M. Manly and E. Rickert, eds., *The Text of The Canterbury Tales*, 8 vols. (Chicago: University of Chicago Press, 1940), 1: 48–51.

[8] Brusendorff, *Chaucer Tradition*, pp. 27–43.

little is known about the roles of figures like Thomas Chaucer[9] or Thomas Hoccleve[10] it seems likely that conjunctions such as that of filial piety and affluence on the one hand, and literary piety and expertise on the other, had important bearings on the early history of both text and canon.

John Shirley has long been recognized as a crucial figure in the early circulation of Chaucer's works, and his multiple fields of professional and familial acquaintance, like his metropolitan connections, may have given him access to a unique mixture of information about Chaucer and his writings. Aspects of Shirley's biography and his scribal activity have yet to be properly studied, although some of the implications of his construction of Chaucer as a figure of poetic and linguistic authority have been reassessed.[11] The enthusiasm of Shirley's efforts on behalf of the authors whose works he transmitted—including both Chaucer and his major fifteenth-century disciple, John Lydgate, as well as lesser figures—is undisputed. The information in the rubrics he supplied to many of his copies contributed in important ways to the conception of the Chaucer canon as it became reflected in the early printed collected editions of Thynne and Stow. Yet the actual quality of the information he transmitted remains largely untested and has not been treated with very much consistency. We wish therefore to explore some texts for which Shirley's claims of Chaucer's authorship have not been readily accepted by posterity, and to relate these untypical rejections of Shirleian authority to certain aspects of the historical construction of the canonicity of Chaucer's works.

I

On folio 38 of Bodleian Library MS Ashmole 59, a manuscript copied by Shirley in the second quarter of the fifteenth century, the following heading appears:

Here nowe folow þe names of þe nyene worshipfullest Ladyes þᵗ / in alle cronycles and storyal bokes haue ben founden of trouþe of / constaunce and vertuous or reproched womanhode by Chaucier.

[9] Jay Ruud, "Against Women Unconstant: The Case for Chaucer's Authorship," *Modern Philology* 80 (1982): 161–64.

[10] On his likely links to the Chaucer circle see E. H. Ingram, "Thomas Hoccleve and Guy de Rouclif," *N & Q* 218 (1973): 42–43.

[11] Seth Lerer, *Chaucer and his Readers: Imagining the Author in Late-Medieval England* (Princeton, N.J.: Princeton University Press, 1993), pp. 117–46.

There follows a poem of nine eight-line stanzas (printed below in the appendix), which ends on folio 39^v. The running title on folio 39^{r-v} is "Þe cronycle made by Chaucier."

The poem recounts the fates of nine worthy women: Cleopatra, Ariadne, Dido, Lucrece, Phyllis, Thisbe, Hypsipyle, Hypermnestra, and Alcyone, a collocation that rather insistently recalls Chaucer's *Legend of Good Women*.[12] But in spite of this and the attribution to Chaucer the text has received virtually no discussion beyond brief entries in such bibliographical works as those of Hammond and Robbins.[13] It is not included in modern editions of Chaucer even though other works dependent upon early attributions of indeterminate authority are canonically enshrined.[14] Nor is there any modern edition.[15]

Yet the reasons that have been advanced for rejecting this poem from the Chaucer canon do not bear very much scrutiny. Skeat, for example, offers a summary dismissal of the poem that is based on important misconceptions. He claims that "the words 'by Chaucier' refer to Chaucer's authorship of the *Legend* only, and not to the authorship of the epitome, which though of some interest, is practically worthless."[16] It is only possible to read the rubric in the way Skeat urges by ignoring Shirley's running title on both sides of fol. 39^{r-v} "Þe cronycle made by Chaucier."

---

[12] This is the order in which they appear in the poem; it differs from that of Chaucer's poem in omitting Philomela and substituting Alcyone, who is misnamed "Alceste." For a text of this poem see below, appendix. All references to Chaucer's text unless otherwise specified are to Larry D. Benson, gen. ed., *The Riverside Chaucer* (Boston: Houghton Mifflin, 1987).

[13] Hammond, *Chaucer: A Bibliographical Manual*, p. 416; Robbins, "The Chaucerian Apocrypha," 4: 1288. It should be noted that the poem presently under discussion is not to be confused with another titled "Nine Ladies Worthy," which appears in Trinity College, Cambridge MS R.3.19 and which was printed in some early Chaucer editions. This poem is no. 2767 in the *Index of Middle English Verse*, ed. Carleton Brown and Rossell Hope Robbins (New York, 1943), henceforward cited parenthetically as "IMEV" by entry number. The poem discussed here is no. 1016 in this work.

[14] For example, *The Riverside Chaucer*, the standard modern edition, includes such poems as "To Rosemounde" (p. 649) and "Womanly Noblesse" (pp. 649–50) on the basis of unique ascriptions in, respectively, Bodleian Library MS Rawlinson Poet. 163, f. 114, and British Library MS Additional 34360, fol. 21^v. Several poems not ascribed to Chaucer also achieve a quasi-canonical status (see pp. 657–60 of *The Riverside Chaucer*).

[15] It was printed in *Odd Texts of Chaucer's Minor Poems*, part 1, ed. F. J. Furnivall, Chaucer Society (London, 1871), pp. vi–viii, and in O. Gaertner, *John Shirley, sein Leben und Werken* (Halle: Ph.D. diss., 1904), p. 66.

[16] Walter W. Skeat, ed., *The Works of Geoffrey Chaucer*, 6 vols. (Oxford: Clarendon Press, 1894), 3: lv. There is no discussion of this poem in Skeat's *The Chaucer Canon* (Oxford: Clarendon Press, 1909).

Brusendorff's objections are more reasoned, but also insubstantial. He gives weight to the fact that the manuscript is copied by John Shirley, but goes on to note that

> it has not proved possible to raise serious objections to Shirley's attributions of poems to Chaucer except in one case, that of the heading in Ashm. 59, f. 38 b. . . . These are, of course, the same nine ladies Chaucer wrote about in his *Legend*, except that Philomene is left out and *Alceste* inserted—though the story told in the last stanza is really not hers, but that of Seys and *Alcyone*. Chaucer would certainly never have commited such an extraordinary mistake: consequently internal evidence goes strongly against Shirley and it is impossible to avoid the conclusion that he wrongly attributed a late anonymous *rifacimento* to the poet.[17]

But there is, of course, nothing to suggest that *Chaucer* wrote "Alceste" (line 75). The only surviving text of the poem was copied some half-century after Chaucer's death and after an undeterminable number of stages of transmission. Moreover, Shirley's texts are generally unreliable, and particularly those in Ashmole 59, a manuscript he copied in his eighties.[18] Given such unreliability it seems entirely probable that, confronted with a form "Alc . . . . e," he simply provided an incorrect homoeograph ("Alcyone" for "Alceste") from memory. The argument that Chaucer would not have made such an error is of no substance in this situation.

Of rather greater significance are some related points that do not seem to have been made. "Alceste" occurs in the poem as a rhyme word, rhyming with "byheste," and so seems a plausible reading. But "Alcyone" would give a syllabically more regular line than "Alceste," and the sense of the rest of the stanza makes clear that it is Alcyone who is being referred to here. This puzzling "Alcyone" stanza is the only one in the poem not based on a figure in *The Legend of Good Women*. But to compound the confusion, the content of line 65, "Whane Seyse þyne husbande fayled þee of byheste," does not correspond to the details of Chaucer's narrative in *The Book of the Duchess*, the only place where he discusses Alcyone, where (unlike the versions of the story in the

---

[17] Brusendorff, *The Chaucer Tradition*, pp. 235–36.
[18] "As [Shirley] died at the great age of ninety, the frequency of careless and garbled texts in the book is easily explained"; E. P. Hammond, "Ashmole 59 and other Shirley Manuscripts," *Anglia* 32 (1907): 321.

Metamorphoses and indeed in Gower's *Confessio Amantis*) no reference is made to Seyx's promise to return. The many peculiarities suggest either that it is an attempt to graft material onto an existing poem from an imperfect exemplar, or that it was subject to more corruption than the rest of the poem. The problems relating to it are of a cumulative and specific kind, and so do not carry much weight in arguments either for or against Chaucer's authorship of the poem.[19]

But if some of the reasons for dismissing the poem from Chaucer's canon lack weight and others seem to raise issues of unresolvable complexity that do not immediately disqualify all of it, is there a sufficient case for including it? Do we assume that the poem is not by Chaucer simply because its content is sometimes at odds with narratives we know Chaucer to have recounted at some point in his poetic career? To do so would be to generate the following syllogism: the facts in this poem are wrong, Chaucer is not wrong, therefore the poem cannot be by Chaucer. Such peculiar logic serves to remind us that we know nothing about the poem's occasion. If it were by Chaucer it could be prentice work or the product of incipient senility. Since we cannot know, we are forced back onto the larger question of Shirley's scribal activity and the reliability of his attributions.

In addition to this manuscript Shirley has left a number of collections, chiefly of Middle English verse and prose, in his own hand: British Library MS Add. 16165 and Harley 78, Trinity College Cambridge R.3.20 and London, Sion College MS Arc.L.402/E.44. Furthermore, a number of other surviving collections seem to be derived from ones compiled by Shirley; the most relevant for the present purposes are British Library MSS Harley 2251 and 7333 and Additional 34360.[20] The scale of his activities establishes him among the more prolific of mid-fifteenth-century scribes.

---

[19] The evidence concerning the poem's relationship to *The Legend of Good Women* is inconsistent. In the Hypsipyle stanza (lines 49–56), for example, the detail that she was "gret with chylde" (54) is not in the *Legend*; and whereas the poem refers to "þy chylde" (56) Chaucer reports "children two" (*LGW* 1568). In addition, whereas the Ashmole poem characterizes Phyllis as "qwene of T[ra]ce" (34) Chaucer does not specify her kingdom (cf. *LGW* 2423). There are, however, some echoes of Chaucer's poem in earlier stanzas; for example: 7–8: cf. *LGW* 696–98; 15–16: cf. *LGW* 2222–24; 21: cf. *LGW* 1238; 24: cf. *LGW* 1351.

[20] For an up-to-date list of manuscripts copied, annotated, or derived from Shirley see Jeremy Griffiths, "A Newly Identified Manuscript Inscribed by John Shirley," *The Library*, 6th ser., no. 14 (1992): 83–93, especially 92–93.

His attributions to Chaucer of various works in these collections provide the sole authority for a number of the shorter poems now in the
canon. For example, he provides the only text and attribution for
"Adam Scriveyn" (in Trinity R.3.20), and the only attribution for "The
Complaint of Mars" (also in Trinity) and "The Complaint of Venus" (in
the same manuscript and in Ashmole 59), for "Fortune" (in the same
two manuscripts), for "Gentilesse" (in the same two manuscripts and
the Shirley-derived Harley 7333), for "The Complaint Unto Pity," in
Harley 78 and the Shirley-derived Additional 34360, and for the
"Complaint to his Lady" (in the same two manuscripts).[21] In addition,
his attributions of *Anelida and Arcite* are of considerable importance,[22]
and still other attributions may be Shirley-derived. Further instances of
the ascription of "Truth" and "Lak of Stedfastnesse" to Chaucer in
Bodleian MS Hatton 73 have been overwritten by other titles, but
sound as if they originated with Shirley.[23] "Truth" is headed "Chauncier
balade vp on his deth bed"[24] and "Stedfastnesse" (according to
MacCracken) 'Geffrey Chauncier sende these Balades to kyng Rychard'
(not unlike the lengthier heading of Harley 7333).[25] The "Chronicle,"
along with others discussed in part II of this article, is one of a very
small number of Shirley's Chaucer attributions that modern scholarship
has rejected.

The case for his reliability must rest on the assumption that Shirley
had some privileged access to information about Chaucer's texts.[26] But
such authority has not usually been extended to the texts themselves.
Shirley's attributions have been given a degree of significance that has
never been accorded to his transcriptions. For the textual authority of
Shirley's manuscripts has generally been seen as notably inferior where

---

[21] For some discussion of Shirley's importance in the Chaucer canon see Brusendorff,
The Chaucer Tradition, pp. 236–86, and Julia Boffey, *Manuscripts of English Courtly Love
Lyrics in the Later Middle Ages* (Woodbridge: D. S. Brewer, 1985), pp. 71–74.

[22] These were recovered in 1908 by H. N. MacCracken by "applying acid"; see his
"Notes Suggested by a Chaucer Codex," *Modern Language Notes* 23 (1908): 212–14.

[23] On these see A. S. G. Edwards, "The Unity and Authenticity of *Anelida and Arcite*:
The Evidence of the Manuscripts," SB 41 (1988): 177–88.

[24] Cf. the heading in Trinity College Cambridge R.3.20, fol. 357: "Balade þat
Chaucier made vp on his deth bedde."

[25] We have examined these erasures under ultraviolet light and have been able to recover less of the text than MacCracken; but the attribution to Chaucer is clearly visible
in both instances.

[26] Brusendorff, for example, suggests that "he must have been in touch with the
Chaucer family"; *The Chaucer Tradition*, p. 235; see also p. 42.

alternative witnesses exist. The assumption seems to be that, however careless his texts, he is a reliable attributor.

There is only limited support for such a view. There are few instances where Shirley or Shirley-derived witnesses provide attributions that can be confirmed by other witnesses, but even in these instances confirmation is not as clear as one might wish. "Truth," ascribed by Shirley in Trinity R.3.20 and in the Shirley-derived Harley 7333, and "Lak of Stedfastnesse" in Harley 7333 are only elsewhere ascribed to Chaucer in the eighteenth-century transcripts that are all that now remains of British Library MS Cotton Otho A.XVIII; the transcripts were made in connection with Urry's 1721 edition of Chaucer, a collection that itself may have been originally Shirley-derived.[27] "Purse" is also ascribed in Cotton and Harley and otherwise only in Magdalene College Cambridge MS Pepys 2006, a very late fifteenth-century collection. Otherwise, only the attribution of the "ABC" in the Pepys and Coventry Corporation manuscripts, which corroborates one of Shirley's in the Sion College manuscript, and those of "The Former Age" (in Cambridge University Library MS Hh. 4.12), and the "Envoy to Scogan" (in Cambridge University Library MS Gg. 4.27) seem to derive from sources unconnected with Shirley.

There are also some grounds for concern about Shirley's reliability as attributor, as Ashmole itself demonstrates. Shirley includes this prefatory rubric to "The Complaint of Venus": "Here begynneþe a balade made þᵗ worþy knight of Savoye in frenshe calde sir Otes Graunsoun translated by Chaucier" (fol. 43ᵛ). There follows the text (omitting lines 33–40) up to line 72, before this rubric appears on fol. 44: "Lenvoye by Thomas Chaucier to all pryncis and princessee [sic] of þis translacoun of þis complaynte and laye." The ten lines that follow are, in fact, lines normally printed as the "Envoy" to "The Complaint of Venus" (lines 73–82). Shirley has already transcribed these lines once before in Ashmole. On fol. 37 begins "a compleynte of þe pleintyff ageinst ageinste [sic] fortune translated oute of ffrenshe into Englisshe by þat famous Rethorissyen Geffrey Chaucier." To the end of this (fol. 38) are appended lines 73–82 of "The Complaint of Venus" again, designated as "Envoy by Chaucyer."[28] This poem immediately precedes "Chaucer's Chronicle."

[27] On this manuscript see George B. Pace, "MS. Cotton Otho A. XVIII," *Speculum* 26 (1951): 306–16.

[28] This collocation also occurs in the Shirley-derived Harley 2251, fol. 45.

Since Shirley's attributions are given such authority by modern Chaucer scholars, what are we saying when we reject his connection of a poem on "the nyene worshipfullest ladies" with Chaucer's name? That we dislike the thought that Chaucer might be muddled, or that he could write such pedestrian verse? Or that we feel Shirley proves himself unreliable here? If we take the latter position, then what are the grounds for accepting his other attributions? That the texts concerned seem to be "better" or more "authentically Chaucerian" pieces? It is not possible to demonstrate in any clear-cut way that "Chaucer's Chronicle" is by Chaucer. But its existence serves to problematize the larger question of the canon of Chaucer's shorter poems. If Shirley is unreliable as an attributor as well as a scribe in this instance, then why should other poems for which he is the sole authority for attribution be accepted as Chaucer's? The question invites a degree of pessimism about our capacity to determine this aspect of the canon with any confidence.

II

Whatever degree of veracity we impute to Shirley's words about specific texts, his expansive conception of Chaucer's oeuvre was undoubtedly influential on the processes of canon formation. His connection with Chaucer of a text which makes reference to *The Legend of Good Women*, in however confused a way, is one very particular instance of what was to become a more general fifteenth- and early sixteenth-century tendency to bundle up Chaucer's shorter poems alongside works that debate issues concerning women. Part of the impetus for this may have come from the early forms in which Chaucer's shorter poems circulated—booklet-derived anthologies, in which the *Legend*, the other dream-visions, and some of the love lyrics were gradually joined by texts such as Hoccleve's *Letter of Cupid* or the English translation of *La Belle Dame sans Merci*.[29]

While the variously pro- or antifeminist Chaucerian stances constructed by this contextualizing seem not to offend modern tastes, modern editors have unanimously ignored the fifteenth-century scribal evidence, originating again with Shirley, which connects Chaucer's

---

[29] Mrs. Priscilla Bawcutt has drawn to our attention a misogynist poem, sometimes thought to be by William Dunbar (SIMEV 3306.8), which in the version in the Lismore MS is attributed to Chaucer.

name with one, or possibly two, poems of an arguably obscene nature. Both are found in British Library MS Additional 16165, the earliest of Shirley's anthologies, which contains what is the first surviving attempt to produce a compilation of shorter poems specifically associated with Chaucer. They are incorporated in a gathering marked by Shirley as "XX," currently fols. 235^r–246^v, which begins with part of the *Supplicacio Amantis* (IMEV 147), continues with Anelida's complaint, extracted from *Anelida and Arcite* (lines 211–350), and concludes with a number of short lyrics and Latin prayers. The first of the poems in question, beginning on fol. 244, where it is headed simply "balade," appears to talk of amatory exploits in terms derived from dicing, fishing, and hunting;[30] its refrain, "thus holde I bett than labour as a reve," has given it the modern title *Balade of a reeve* (IMEV 1635). It is followed on fol. 244^v by a poem ostensibly in praise of ploughing, also headed "balade" (IMEV 2611), which ends rather abruptly on fol. 245^r and is followed by a space before the next item, as if perhaps more material (a further stanza, or an extended colophon) was expected to become available (editions of both are presented here in the appendix). While the running title on fol. 244^r reads "Balade made by halsham" (with reference to the item that precedes the "Balade of a Reeve"), and there is no running title at all on fol. 245^r, that on fol. 244^v reads "Balade by Chau*cer*." Editors have struggled to interpret the sense of this. Furnivall, in a discussion entitled "A Balade or two by Chaucer," eventually thought that both the "Balade of a Reeve" and "The Plowman's Song" might be admitted to the canon.[31] Eleanor Hammond, noting that "it is Shirley's usual custom to make his running title fit the poem which begins on the page below," considered that the Chaucerian designation applied to "The Plowman's Song,"[32] whereas Brusendorff, pointing out that "when one poem stops and another begins on the same page, the running title of this generally refers not to the latter but to

---

[30] Common enough analogies: see the poem known as *Piers of Fulham* (IMEV 71), and Bradford Y. Fletcher and A. Leslie Harris, "The Conceits of 'Piers of Fulham,'" *ELN* 25 (1988): 11–14.

[31] F. J. Furnivall, "A Balade or Two by Chaucer," in *Jyl of Brentford's Testament* (London, 1871).

[32] Eleanor P. Hammond, "Omissions from the Editions of Chaucer," *Modern Language Notes* 19 (1904): 35–38 (p. 37).

[33] Brusendorff, *The Chaucer Tradition*, p. 279.

the former piece," opted for the "Balade of a Reeve."[33] Whatever their differences over Shirley's practice with his running titles (and Brusendorff's hunch seems to be corroborated by the evidence of the "Halsham" running title on fol. 244[r]) these accounts endorse Brusendorff's view that "there cannot be much doubt that we shall have to uphold the canonicity . . . [of these poems] . . . almost solely on the strength of Shirley's MS ascription."[34] But no modern edition contains either text. The possibility that Chaucer enjoyed some fifteenth-century reputation for *double entendre* and obscenity is perhaps strengthened by the appearance of the "Balade of a Reeve" in British Library MS Additional 7578 in close proximity to a comic warning about the physical consequences of lechery (IMEV 551).[35]

The "Chaucerian" claims of these balades are not unlike those of "Chaucer's Chronicle" in Ashmole 59. As that poem, albeit confusedly, refers to *The Legend of Good Women*, so these two could appear in some way to gloss the portraits of the Plowman and Reeve offered in *The Canterbury Tales*, elaborating on the Plowman's dedication to his work ("a trew swynkere and a good was he" [*GP* 531])[36] and the physical manifestations of the Reeve's "coltes tooth" (*RvT* 3889). Understood in these terms, neither need be interpreted as in any way salacious. The "Envoy to Bukton," with its reference to the Wife of Bath, suggests that the composition of short poems with some intertextual connection with the longer works was not an inherently un-Chaucerian practice. The reasons behind the exclusion of these two poems from the canon seem largely to do with the squeamishness—alternatively to be interpreted as the extreme prurience—that reads them as tissues of sexual innuendo inappropriate to Chaucer's oeuvre. Revisionist views of Chaucer's culpability in the Cecily Champaigne affair may find in them some attractive mileage.

---

[34] Brusendorff, *The Chaucer Tradition*, p. 284.

[35] See R. H. Bowers, "A Middle English 'Rake's Progress' Poem," *Modern Language Notes* 70 (1955): 396–98, and R. H. Robbins, "A Warning Against Lechery," *PQ* 35 (1956): 90–95. Neither of these articles takes into account the frame of this poem, which introduces it as a complaint overheard on St. Valentine's eve.

[36] The apocryphal *Plowman's Tale*, which was first incorporated with *The Canterbury Tales* in the 1542 printed edition of Chaucer's works, represents something of the same impulse to extend aspects of the portrait in *The General Prologue*; see the edition by James Dean in *Six Ecclesiastical Satires* (Kalamazoo: Western Michigan University, Medieval Institute Publications, 1991), pp. 51–114.

There remains of course the further possibility that Shirley's invocation of Chaucer in connection with one or both of these poems reflects simply his sense that they "relate" in some way to Chaucer's writing: his general haziness on what was and was not canonical is epitomized in a note in San Marino, Huntington Library MS El. 26.A.13, fols. ii^v-iii, which attributes the "whetstone" stanza from *Troilus* to "Gower."[37] The further contents of MS Additional 16165 anyway testify to a certain take-it-or-leave-it quality in the provision of attributions: while the first part of *Anelida and Arcite*, copied on fols. 256^v–258^v, is headed "Balade of Anelyda qwene of Cartage made by Geffrey Chaucyer," the introduction and conclusion to Anelida's extracted "complaint," on fols. 241^v–243^v, do not mention Chaucer's name. Strangely, too, Shirley seems to have been either unaware or uncaring of the Chaucerian status of what he entitles "Prouerbe" (i.e., the *Proverbs*) at the end of gathering XX of MS Additional 16165, on fol. 246^v. Although the partial copy of the text in British Library MS Additional 10392, copied in 1432 by Shirley's associate John Cok,[38] also omits any note about the authorship of these gnomic verses, in Bodleian MS Fairfax 16 and British Library MS Harley 7578 they are firmly claimed as Chaucer's. Their association, in both of these latter manuscripts, with proverbial lyrics and extracts which Shirley also copied, suggests shared origins, and possibly shared information about authorship which Shirley simply left out, in a casual way, in MS Additional 16165.

The circulation of these stanzas in the context of a small body of proverbial material is also notable. In both Harley 7578 and Fairfax 16 they are copied in sequences that comprise (in different orders) an extract on deceit from Lydgate's *Fall of Princes* (IMEV 674; copied by Shirley in Trinity College Cambridge R.3.20), "Halsham's balade" (IMEV 3504; copied by Shirley in Huntington El. 26.A.13 as well as in the Shirley-derived British Library Additional 34360), and a stanza on "Four things which make a man fall from reason" (IMEV 4230; copied by Shirley in Ashmole 59). Of these, Additional 16165 includes "Halsham's balade" in the same booklet as Chaucer's "Proverbs." This

---

[37] For a description of the manuscript, see C. Dutschke, *Guide to Medieval and Renaissance Manuscripts in the Huntington Library*, 2 vols. (San Marino, Calif.: Huntington Library, 1989), 1:35–39.

[38] On whom see A. I. Doyle, "More Light on John Shirley," *MÆ* 30 (1961): 93–101 (pp. 98–99). The volume is a collection of Latin devotional and ascetical material.

clustering of proverbial material around a short text associated with Chaucer's name may have inspired, or have been in some way connected with the gradual establishment, through the later fifteenth and sixteenth centuries, of Chaucer's reputation for gnomic wisdom. Caxton's 1477 print of *Anelida and Arcite* made use of empty space to associate with this poem a group of proverbial sayings ("When fayth failleth in prestes sawes . . .," "Hit falleth for every gentilman . . .," and "Hit cometh by kynde of gentil blode . . .") the first of which had a wide manuscript circulation (IMEV 3943). The same group of couplets was to appear in every subsequent black-letter edition of Chaucer's works, and eventually—although no early manuscript ascription is recorded— acquired the title "Chaucer's Prophecy."[39] Ironically, versions of the first part of this prophecy, in both English and Latin, are copied by Shirley into MS Ashmole 59, although with no reference to Chaucer.[40] Thynne's incorporation in the introductory pages of his 1532 printed *Workes* of a piece known as "Eight Goodly questions and their answers" (IMEV 3183), in which eight philosophers respond to tricky conundrums ("What is a wise man?" "What is a fool?") may have prompted the appearance of a Scots version of the text in the Bannatyne MS of 1568 (National Library of Scotland MS Adv. 1.1.6) with the colophon "ffinis q Chawseir."[41]

Just as the early printed collections of Chaucer's works extended this construction of Chaucer the sage, so they also associated his name with a growing number of poems which respond in various pro- or antifeminist ways to the questions posed by the *Legend of Good Women*, and recalled in a shorthand way in "Chaucer's Chronicle." In Stow's edition of 1561, that part of the book which purports to present "certaine woorkes of Geffray Chauser, whiche hath not here tofore been printed," includes "The ix Ladies worthie" (IMEV 2767), "A balade, warnyng men to beware of deceiptfull women" (IMEV 1944), and "a balade whiche Chaucer made in ye praise, or rather dispraise, of women for ther

---

[39] See Gertrude H. Campbell, "Chaucer's Prophecy in 1586," *Modern Language Notes* 29 (1914): 195–96.

[40] The Latin distich, titled "Profecia merlini," appears on fol. 72; the English, titled "Prophecia merlini doctoris perfecti" (eight lines in couplets) appears on fol. 78.

[41] See Denton Fox and William A. Ringler, Introduction, *The Bannatyne Manuscript: National Library of Scotland Advocates' MS 1. 1.* (London: Scolar, 1980); the "Proverbs" are also included in these introductory pages.

doublenes" (IMEV 3656, actually Lydgate's "Doubleness"). Thynne's edition of 1532, although not explicitly attributing to Chaucer the spurious pieces concerned, had already underlined the significance to the canon of the topic of women by incorporating texts like *La Belle Dame sans Merci*, Henryson's *Testament of Cresseid*, Hoccleve's *Letter of Cupid*, and shorter poems like *A Praise of Women* (IMEV 228).[42]

These sixteenth-century developments, in extending tendencies evident in Shirley's manuscripts, intensify the complexities that relate to the canon of Chaucer's shorter poems. Shirley established both the mode and the scope of the canon of Chaucer's shorter poems in important ways. His booklet in MS Additional 16165 appears to be the earliest surviving example of what was to become a characteristic form of circulation of shorter poems in the fifteenth century and the first in which poems circulating in this form are ascribed to Chaucer.[43] The motive behind this aspect of the creation of the Chaucer canon was apparently not so much the desire to circulate texts derived from some privileged access to Chaucerian sources as a wish to contextualize these poems in a particular way for Shirley's audience. It seems to have been more the idea of the Chaucerian shorter poem than the authority of particular attributions that concerned Shirley. In linking such poems to Chaucer he gave them status for his audience, which in turn enhanced the status of his own collections. The undertaking became circular and self-fulfilling, and its implications suggest that the grounds for reposing any confidence in Shirley's attributions—which form the basis for this aspect of the canon—may be open to some doubt. The inconsistency with which scholarship has selected from among the various lyrics ascribed to Chaucer is itself a reflection of Shirley's own lack of consistency. We have no clear grounds for rejecting or accepting most of these attributions selectively. In such circumstances the inevitable indeterminacy of the status and authority of these poems might be more clearly appreciated by Chaucer's editors.

---

[42] Also copied into Bannatyne.

[43] On such forms of booklet circulation see Julia Boffey and John J. Thompson, "Anthologies and Miscellanies: Production and Choice of Texts," in *Book Production and Publishing in Britain, 1375–1475*, ed. Jeremy Griffiths and Derek Pearsall (Cambridge: Cambridge University Press, 1989), pp. 279–316.

Appendix

We print below the texts of "Þe Cronycle made by Chaucier" in Bodleian Library MS Ashmole 59, fols. 38^v–39^v and of the "Balade of a Reeve" and "The Plowman's Song" in British Library MS Additional 16165, fols. 244^v–245. Most capitalization and all punctuation are editorial. Contractions have been silently expanded. Occasional virgules and flourishes at the end of lines have been disregarded and not recorded.

f.38^v] Grete rayson <u>Cleopatra</u> is þy kyndnesse   **Cleopatre**
     Be putte in mynde and also þyne hyenesse
     Of Egipte qweene and affter þat was slayne
     Þyne <u>Anthonye</u> by <u>Octovyan</u> þe Romayne
     With gret richchesse þou made his sepulture
     And affter him þee list no lenger dure
     For in a pitte with þee serpentes to take
     Þowe went al naked so þy deþe to make.   8

     <u>Adryane</u> whiche with þy craffty labour   **Adryane**
     Made <u>Theseus</u> to slee þe <u>Minetawre</u>
     And by a threede frome þy faders prysoun
     Made him tescape and þyne housbande bycome
     By helpe of <u>Fedra</u> þy sustre þat with him yeede
     Whilest þou slepte and so he qwytte þy meede
     Whe[r]off þe goddes had of þy pytee rouþe
     And to a <u>sterre</u> transffourmed þee for trouþe. 16

f.39]   Þis noble qweene of <u>Cartage</u> feyre Dydo **Gode dydo qwene**
     Which of pite resceyved <u>Eneas</u> so   **of Cartage**
     Affter frome <u>Troye</u> with tempestes in þe see
     Vnneeþe arryved in to hir cuntree
     Sheo made him lord and sheo his humble wyve
     Wherby ellas sheo loste boþe ioye and lyve
     For whane she wiste þat he was from hir goo
     Vppon his swerde shee roof hir herte atwo.   24

     It is gret right þat youre bountee <u>Lucresse</u> **Lucreste of Rome**
     Be putte in writing and alsoo your goodnesse

Wyff to þe <u>Senatour</u> gode <u>Collatyne</u>
Which thorugh þenvye of Romayne <u>Torqwyn</u>
For yee to him wolde never applye
He ravisshed yowe whereoff it was pyte
With a <u>Tyraunt</u> ful soore ageinst youre wille
He caused yowe for sorowe youre selff to spille.　　32

What noblesse shewed þou <u>Demophon</u> <u>Philles</u>　　**Phillees**
Whome to þine housbande qwene of <u>T[ra]ce</u> þou chas
Comyng frome <u>Troye</u> with tempest al forblowe
As wolde god þou hadest him wele eknowe
Soone he forgate þy fredame and þy trouþe
Whane to his cuntrey he yede: þat was rouþe
Whiche never affter for al his heeste with þee
Efftsones wolde mete, þat made þee soone to dye.　　40

Borne nobully of <u>Babilloygne</u> <u>Thesbe</u>　　**Thesbe of**
Frome þe welle a lyonesse made þee flee　　**Babilloigne**
Where as þou seete Piramus tabyde.
Ellas he foonde þere by þat welle syde
Blody þy wympull and wende þou hadest be sleyne;
For which he karffe þere his hert atweyne.
Which whane þou saughe þou woldest no lenger byde,
But on his swerde þyne hert did thorowe glyde.　　48

f.39ᵛ]　Woo is myne hert for þee, þou <u>Isiphyle,</u>　　**Isiphyle**
<u>Qwene</u> and ladye of <u>Leanoun</u> þe yle,
Wheche wedded was to Iason grekessh man
And gret with chylde lefft þee soone vppon
Fro Medea when he to Colcos yeede
Þat for þe pitee I feele myn hert bleede
To thenke on al þy sorowe and þy woo
Wher thorughe þou dyed and þy chylde alsoo.　　56

<u>Ypermistra</u> þat noble and truwe wyff　　**Ypermistra þe**
Þy faders prysoun made þee to leese þy lyff　　**gode wyff**
Ful pytously, for þat þou wolde not slee
Lyno þine husbande as he comanded þee,
Whiche was þe sone of daun <u>Danao</u>
<u>Egistes</u> broþer, þy fader it fel soo;
And al was but his owen fantasye

Þat he his broþer sone went for to dye.   64

Þe sorowe þou toke þane, O qwene Alceste,   **Þe Qwene**
Whane Seyse þyne husbande fayled þee of byheste, **Alceste**
Whome for to fynde þou sought him ay weoping
Hit happende soo þou saughe him dede fletyng
Vppon þe see and to him leepe anoone
With him to dye, so woo was him begone.
Where þat of yowe þe goodes hade grete pitee
And lyche seemewes transfourmed him and þee.   72

Balade of a Reeve

f.244ʳ]   Hit is no right alle oþer lustes to leese
Þis monþe of <u>May</u> for missyng of on cas;
Þerfore I wol þus my chaunce cheese,
Ageyns <u>love</u> <u>trey</u> ageyns an <u>as,</u>
Hasard a tout and launche an esy pas
In lowe cuntrey þer as hit may not greve:
Þus holde I bett þan labour as a reve.   7

f.244ᵛ]   Sith hit is so þer as hit may not freese
Þat euery wight but I haþe sume solas,
I wol me venge on <u>loue</u> as doþe a <u>breese</u>
On wylde horsse þat rennen in harras;
For maugre <u>love</u> amiddes in his cumpas
I wol conclude my lustes to releeve:
Þus holde I bett þan labour as a <u>Reve.</u>   14

Yit might I seyne 'cryst seeyne,' as whan men fneese,
If I hade leve to hunt in euery chace,
Or fisshen and so myn angle leese
Þat <u>Barbell</u> had swolowed boþe hooke and lace;
Yit launche a steerne and put at suche perchace
To fonde to dompe als deepe as man may dyeve:
Þus holde I bett þan labour as a <u>Reve.</u>   21

[The Plowman's Song]

f.244ᵛ]   Balade
Of alle þe crafftes oute blessed be þe ploughe,
So mury it is to holde to by hinde:
For whanne þe share is shoven inn depe ynoghe,
And þe onlere kerveþe in his kuynde

217

Þe tydee soyle þat doþe þe lande vnbynde,
Ageyns þe hil "Tpruk in, tpruk out" I calle,
For of my ploughe þe best stott is balle.   7

Þe dryver hade a goode at whihche I loughe,
For of þe poynt whan stripped was þe rynde
He dyd dryve in, þeghe þe lande were toughe,
Boþe <u>Rudd</u> and <u>Goore</u> and eke <u>Bayard</u> þe blynde,

f.245ʳ]   Þat beter beestis may þer no man fynde;
Ageyns þe hil "tpruk in, tpruk out" I calle,
For of my ploughe þe best stotte is balle.

REVIEWS

DAVID AERS and LYNN STALEY. *The Powers of the Holy: Religion, Politics, and Gender in Late Medieval English Culture.* University Park: Pennsylvania State University Press, 1996. Pp. 310. $45.00 cloth, $19.95 paper.

The Powers of the Holy is one of those books you keep feeling you've decided about, only to find you haven't. Passionately argued and replete with historical analyses, literary intepretations, theoretical observations, and generally well considered polemics, it is unusual to the degree in which it treats students of Middle English as though we all approach our subject as intellectuals, personally and politically engaged in the fourteenth century as part of our wider engagement in life in the present. While its historicism is broadly consistent with the work of scholars like Paul Strohm, Lee Patterson, and Steven Justice—who, of course, also seek to engage us in the past in a rich variety of ways—its particular drive towards an *ethical* understanding of Ricardian religious and literary culture and how we study it seems reminiscent of feminist scholars with whom the authors are in little sympathy, such as Carolyn Dinshaw and Gayle Margherita. As a consequence of this consciously ethical brand of historicism and the confidence it gives the authors that their subject is relevant to anyone who takes it seriously, this conversational, slightly sprawling book about a quarter century of late-medieval English literary history is likely to be one of those rare studies of Middle English literature that are read by many people who work in quite different areas, and so come to represent our field to a larger world. (For example, the *Bryn Mawr Review* has already published a fine review of the book by a feminist theologian, Jo-Anne McNamara, and I am confident it will be read with care by early modernists.) I have learned a great deal from this book, agree with much that is in it, disagree with much else, and expect to be telling all the students of medieval and early-modern culture and thought I encounter over the next few years that it is one of the books they must read.

The book circles around several themes dealing with gender, politics, literary representation, and the theology of Christ's humanity; three major texts—Langland's *Piers Plowman*, Julian's *Revelation of Love*, and

Chaucer's *Canterbury Tales*; and a handful of late-fourteenth-century historical processes and incidents, especially the Revolt of 1381, the condemnation of Lollardy from the Blackfriars Council of 1382 to the heresy trials of the early fifteenth century, and the troubled relations between Richard II and successive Parliaments through the 1380s. The themes cannot readily be rendered as a single argument or simply related either to the texts discussed or the incidents the book connects with these texts; indeed, the themes are occasionally hard to spot amid the careful readings of particular textual moments of which a good deal of the book consists. But this must be more or less a deliberate policy, as the axiom on which the book is ostensibly built is that the complexity of the interrelationships between cultural discourses makes it necessary to explore these discourses only as they are played out in particular historical contexts. Foucault, Marx, and Quentin Skinner are cited to this effect in the book's joint introduction, and Aers had previously explored this axiom in a published response to a sweeping condemnation of late medieval culture by Kathleen Biddick.[1] While the axiom might seem obvious to some, its implications for Marxist historiography, and its ethical implications, are at once far-reaching and hard to put into practice—as the book's lapses from its own principles indeed show. *The Powers of the Holy* is unified by its fierce concentration on three decades of English history and impassioned desire to find in these decades a key to the processes by which power circulates and the forces of social conformism and protest operate. Ricardian and early Lancastrian England—not twelfth-century France, fourteenth-century Italy, or Tudor England—emerges as an exemplary battleground for conflicting energies which are seen simultaneously as particular to their own time and place and still alive in other forms.

I mean no slight to the collaborative work that has gone into this book by describing its authors' contributions separately; for all the interconnections between the parts of the book, and the conversational tone of both, its voices are confessedly distinct (p. 9). David Aers's three chapters, which constitute part 1, form the most narrowly argued part

[1] Kathleen Biddick, "Becoming Ethnographic: Reading Inquisitorial Authority in *The Hammer of Witches*," chapter 2 of *Figures of Speech: The Body in Medieval Art, History, and Literature*, ed. Allen J. Frantzen and David A. Robertson, Essays in Medieval Studies: Proceedings of the Illinois Medieval Association (1994), vol. 11 (Chicago: Illinois Medieval Association, 1995), pp. 21–37, with a response by David Aers, pp. 38–41. Chapter 1 of the same book, Aers's own "Figuring Forth the Body of Christ: Devotion and Politics" (pp. 1–14), has its own response by Biddick (pp. 15–20). This interesting exchange is clearly drawn on in the book under review but oddly is never cited.

of the book and arouse in this reader the strongest reactions. In these chapters, discussions of *Piers Plowman* and the *Revelation of Love* develop out of a respectful and important critique of Caroline Bynum's *Holy Feast and Holy Fast*. This study is taken partly as a major work of feminist historiography, partly as a representative of a longer scholarly tradition of writing about late-medieval affective spirituality. Arguing that scholars have always paraphrased affective piety, rather than analyzing it, Aers seeks to denaturalize the influential practice of *imitatio Christi* that revolved around passionate identification with Christ in his suffering humanity. Aers notes that "the dominant figurations of Christ's body, *including its alleged 'feminization'*, were *made* dominant, *constituted* as dominant, *maintained* as dominant," in large part by a conservative church and civic hierarchy (p. 34; Aers's italics). It seems to follow that Bynum's hugely influential thesis—that the identification with Christ's humanity through "feast and fast" practiced by late-medieval holy women was a source of empowerment for these women—must be wrong. Far from developing personal or collective autonomy by their self-identification with Christ's suffering humanity, these women (like the modern scholars who have idealized them) reproduced the contours of an official discourse that allowed them the shadow, not the reality, of power. (That is, presumably, they did so in so far as they thought and behaved the way Bynum says they did; Aers's target here is not the holy women themselves but affective piety, and he does not explore the implications of his argument for our understanding of the beguines, Poor Clares, nuns, and religious and lay visionaries who are Bynum's main focus.)

Finally, Aers finds recognition of the true nature of affective piety in Wycliffite and Lollard protests against it (chapter 2)—as expressed in, e.g., *The Testimony of William Thorpe* and the Lollard emphasis on Christ as a preacher—as well as in *Piers Plowman* (chapter 2) and, more unexpectedly, the *Revelation of Love* (chapter 3). In *Piers Plowman*, Christ is active, not passive, his death is a culmination of his life but far from being its sole significant incident, and his humanity unites him with other humans in their multiple passions, rather than being summed up by his own singular one. In Julian's *Revelation*, which feminist scholars such as Elizabeth Robertson have sought to analyze in terms of Bynum's thesis about women's empowerment through their bodiliness, Julian in fact constantly moves away from affective piety and its emphasis on Christ as a suffering body, systematically baffling readerly expectations. Indeed, Aers's analysis of the *Revelation* constructs its progress from the

221

early visions to the later reflections as a progressive rejection of affective piety. In this revisionist account of late-fourteenth-century religious history, Julian joins Langland and the Lollards in a common (if variously nuanced) critique of the "dominant figuration" of Christ's life, in protest against the hierarchization of church and state that this figuration was designed to promote.

This is an important argument that deserves attention as the most cogent critique of *Holy Feast and Holy Fast* yet produced and as a demonstration of the range and international importance of the "reformist" thinking produced by late medieval England. (The argument also generates an extremely helpful close reading of parts of Julian's *Revelation*; the material on *Piers Plowman*, by contrast, I found less deeply engaging than some of Aers's other discussions of the poem.) Yet I have serious disagreements both with what the argument asserts and implies and with the way it is made. Aers's and Staley's introduction had me anticipating a critique of Bynum's "empowerment" thesis that would argue that any detailed study of a specific period of medieval religious history would show her account of holy women, affective piety, and food symbolism to be overgeneralized, and hence simplistic in its assumptions about the nature of "power." But in fact Aers's critique is every bit as grandiose as the thesis it attacks, adopting broad-brush definitions of power and affective piety, and too often amplifying Bynum's always nuanced sense of the tension between center and margin, institutions and reformists, into a fully fledged dichotomy between a powerfully conservative church hierarchy and small bands of plucky dissidents. (The discussion of power on pages 7–9, which objects to Foucault's later rejection of Marxist notions of power, is moving, but to my mind fails to take Foucault's formulations seriously.) Indeed, while I am sure this was not Aers's intention, feminists may take his study as using his Marxist methodology to reinscribe a traditional, pre-Bynum view of medieval holy women (other than Julian) as compliantly marginal. Having pointed the finger at Bynum's tendency to paraphrase, rather than analyze, the structure of affective piety, Aers proceeds to do the very same for Lollard critiques of that piety, passionately identifying with the terms of these critiques in their polemical understanding of Passion meditation and image veneration, and portraying those who produced them in much the same heroizing language Bynum uses of holy women. Despite the invocation of a variety of reformist positions, we come away from this study with the sense that affective piety was simply bad, and that those who engaged in it were reduced to victimhood by their engagement. Only the opiate that Nicholas Love (following St. Paul) calls "spiritual milk," not any more challenging liquor, was ever sucked from Christ's wounds. Moreover, Aers's respect for those who gave their lives to insist on this point in late-fourteenth-century England gives an apocalyptic aura to his presentation of the period, which seems in his account to have had no past and only the most depressing immediate future. The literary history of England before 1380 and after 1410 is a shadowy presence here, and scholars who take a longer chronological view (such as Kathryn Kerby-Fulton or Larry Scanlon) seem to have little impact. Even Margery Kempe, who would have had a lot to say about Aers's argument, and could prove a stumbling block for him, has only a walk-on part as a representative devotional conservative (pages 55–56). Given the developed sense of history in all the writers Aers considers, not to mention his own belief in the importance of historical work, this acceptance of our field's too-pronounced emphasis on "the age of Chaucer" at the expense of the equally important eras from which it came and to which it led seems a pity.

It is still very hard to write dissident analyses of medieval religion, and Aers's adoption of a broadly Protestant critique of the period that belongs in a tradition going back as far as Foxe's *Book of Martyrs* is both understandable and, in this case, highly productive. But to analyze the impact of a complex phenomenon such as affective piety, and the rejection of that piety by some, requires a deeper acknowledgment of the multiplicity of the forms affectivity could take, and of the constantly shifting balances of cultural and social power, than Aers's argument is able to make. If Julian rejects many aspects of the body- and Passion-centered spirituality within which some have understood her, she does not do so simply, but constructs a theology that carefully straddles the very divide between reformism and orthodox devotion that the first two chapters of *The Powers of the Holy* presents as unbridgeable. Julian's sense of her personal and intellectual loyalties, like that of so many of her contemporaries, including Langland and Chaucer, is likely to have been conflicted—it's almost impossible to imagine, for example, how she would have read *The Testimony of William Thorpe*, or *The Lantern of Light*, or Love's strictures against the Lollards in *The Mirror of the Blessed Life of Jesus Christ*. For, as Staley indeed insists in a later chapter, "almost any passage in the *Showings* [i.e., *Revelation of Love*] yields rich evidence of Julian's refusal to oppose systems to one another" (p. 177). Similarly, the fact that Langland's account of the Passion is elliptical and carefully historicized does not mean he would have disapproved of the fervid Passion meditations in *The Prickynge of Love*, nor that much of *Piers Plowman* cannot itself be seen as an expression of a version of "affective piety." Aers has issued a characteristically incisive challenge to scholars of medieval spirituality, and provided a corrective to the idealized picture of late-medieval English devotion in Eamon Duffy's *The Stripping of the Altars*, whose conservative pietism is implicitly the target of many pages of this book. But Aers has not yet, any more than Duffy, presented us with a version of late-medieval English religious history that can be accepted without a good deal of talking back.

Lynn Staley's two main contributions to this book, a second chapter on Julian of Norwich and a long study of "Chaucer and the Postures of Sanctity," make for equally absorbing reading. Less thesis-driven than Aers's three chapters, her approach to her material is more consistent with the one outlined in the joint introduction to the book and reaffirmed in its conclusion. Here, the complexity of the religious scene in late-fourteenth-century England and its importance to our understanding of other aspects of Ricardian culture are at the forefront of the argument. Staley's discussion of Julian's *Revelation* takes the form of a comparative analysis of the earlier and later versions of the text, both of which she sees as products of the 1380s and 1390s, although she explores the generic roots of the Short Text in particular as far back as the English epistles of Richard Rolle, written in the 1340s. (Her discussion of Julian's relation to Rolle and Hilton on pages 131–39 is especially useful for the way it links the strategies employed by the Short Text with specifically English traditions of spiritual writing.) Staley parallels the evolution from an "experience"-based account in the Short Text to a more confidently authoritative (but simultaneously sometimes theologically evasive) voice in the Long Text with the "crisis of authority" she sees as crucial to the period and its literature. Constructing a mosaic picture of this "crisis" as it was perceived by different kinds of people and enacted in the growth of systematic religious persecution during the period, she attempts to find links between these harsh realities and the apparently inward-looking world of Julian's text. I applaud this difficult undertaking. Julian's skill in concealing the "crises" that the *Revelation of Love* cannot help noticing within the labyrinthine windings of her prose makes it all the more important to winkle them out, if we are to learn how to read this astonishing text in relation to its period.

Although I would not make all the connections Staley does—despite the objections to the view raised in this book (e.g., pp. 79–80, n. 4), I still think the Long Text may be partly an early-fifteenth-century work—her linkage of text and historical context is well done, especially in her consideration of the Lord and Servant parable. (It also provides the best model I have encountered for instructors willing to attempt the difficult task of incorporating serious historical analysis into courses on Middle English literature.) The two Julian essays in this volume are the first I know that simply assume her importance as a vital witness to fourteenth-century English religious life. Here, as in Aers's essay, the assumption pays handsome dividends.

Staley's second essay, which reads almost like a sketch for a separate book, again pursues a chronological approach to its subject, analyzing Chaucer's presentation of sanctity in three of *The Canterbury Tales—The Second Nun's Tale, The Tale of Melibee*, and *The Clerk's Tale*—in order to show how these poems engage dialectically with the politico-religious events of the period. All three readings depend on the same association between literary authority and political power developed in the previous chapter, and in this sense should be taken as speculative historical meditations, rather than closely argued historical analyses (this is, indeed, just what makes them so approachable for students). I wish that this eighty-page chapter had been organized in a way that made it easier to read in more than one sitting, and that the parallels Staley is drawing had been made more explicit; as things are, her analysis of the *Tales* tends to disappear under the mass of contextualizing material, especially early in the chapter. But my slight irritation with this problem is entirely because what she has to say is so interesting, making better sense of Chaucer's surprising interest in the first two tales she treats than any other study I know, and going beyond the findings of other recent commentators on *The Clerk's Tale* by not simply explicating but actually attempting to account for the deep gloominess of Chaucer's later thinking. After a period when we have had to choose between "Chaucer the radical" and "Chaucer the time-server," with little to mediate between these two figures, Staley offers a picture of the poet that draws much of its perceptive charity from her analysis of Julian. As the book's epilogue has it, Chaucer and Julian emerge as "two profoundly intelligent minds at once grappling with the need to think independently of dominant codes and the inherent regulations imposed by conventional models *and* avoiding any decisive rupture with the codes themselves"

(p. 263; Staley and Aers's emphasis). The balance of this statement, as well as its refusal to respect the old dichotomies between sacred and secular that still structure our field, should inspire much further thinking along the lines pursued here.

Despite the periodic dogmatism of this book, it deserves our admiration for its acute readings of difficult and important texts, for its desire to raise questions as well to settle them (the epilogue indeed lists several such questions) and, above all, for the sheer energy and joy of its approach to its subject matters. The book will probably make some enemies or, at least, confirm old enmities, perhaps most heatedly as a result of its discussions of gender and power, and of its particular brand of Marxist historicism. It remains, though, a wonderfully creative contribution to Middle English studies: a book that has the knack of leaving its readers at once better informed and at the same time freer to pursue their own inquiries into the field, invigorated by what they have learned. If scholarly collaborations are this much fun, and this productive, let us have more of them.

NICHOLAS WATSON
University of Western Ontario

ANN W. ASTELL. *Chaucer and the Universe of Learning*. Ithaca and London: Cornell University Press, 1996. Pp. xvi, 254. $35.00.

It is difficult to do justice in a brief review to such a plenitude of learning marshalled in support of a catena of fresh, bold, and provocative arguments. Ann Astell's multifaceted thesis elaborated first in her preface asserts that *The Canterbury Tales* is a *summa* whose social estate exposition in *The General Prologue* is succeeded by a philosophical *summa* in exemplary tales; that the contest of tales mirrors the scholastic *quaestiones* and academic competitions of Chaucer's day; and that the Ellesmere redactor orders the tales into a pattern of planetary descent and ascent which makes of pilgrimage and its roadside entertainment on the bumpy road to Canterbury a smooth philosophical soul-journey through the planetary spheres. All of this constitutes, she argues adroitly, an intellectual dialogue with Gower's *Confessio Amantis*, book

7, and a story-telling contest with Dante's *Paradiso*. The Dantean trace is not new, but the details are fresh and stimulating, and more compelling than the Gower nexus.

The elaboration of her polyform argument occupies an introduction, seven chapters, and a brief conclusion. The introduction argues that Chaucer's intellectual milieu and his audience were neither gentry nor nobility, but a new class of nonclerical clerks consisting of a social intelligentsia in the educated upper-middle class. She points to *The House of Fame* with its naïve narrator as a model for the structure of *The Canterbury Tales*, and points to the fragments or story-block divisions of the *Tales* into which the redactor of the Ellesmere text set the tales in imitation of the planetary scheme of a Macrobian soul and body journey (pp. 27–30).

The first chapter, "Chaucer and The Division of Clerks," argues that the Ellesmere scribe would have us read the *Tales* like the clerks to whom the Parson appeals for correction. Chaucer's own Clerk reflects a "clericized" fourth estate (p. 54), in association with the Knight's *bellatores*, the Plowman's *laboratores*, and the Parson's *oratores*. Other pilgrims, including the Wife of Bath, speak for and as clerks whenever they exhibit their knowledge (p. 59). The second chapter, "The Divisions of Knowledge," announces the Ellesmere *Tales* as a *summa* of analogies between divisions of knowledge and divisions of social estates "as part of a conscious dialogue" among Chaucer and Gower and Dante. In this respect, the *Tales* reopens philosophy, submits Dante's *Paradiso*, brought to earth, to interpretation by the pilgrims, and itself constitutes a *Convivio* that matches branches of Philosophy with planetary spheres in exemplary stories and story blocks (p. 85).

Chapter 3, "From Saturn to the Sun: Planetary Pilgrimage in Fragments I and IX," imitates the tour through the chiasmic order of the tales, whose first fragment rehearses a planetary pilgrimage descending from the Knight's Saturn through the Miller's Jupiter and the Reeve's Mars to the Cook's Sun, all in chiasmic relation with the Manciple's solar ascent in Fragment 9 (p. 92). Chapter 4, "Solar Alchemy in Fragments II and VIII," marks Custance and Cecilia as saints of poverty and faith, and their stories as tensions between the language of alchemy and the Word of God. Chapter 5, "Mercurial Marriage in Fragments III–IV–V: Philosophic Misogamy and the Trivium of Woman's Knowledge"—contrasting philosophic misogamy and the trivium of woman's knowledge—links the Wife, Friar, and Summoner to Rhetoric, the Clerk and Merchant to Logic, and the Squire and Franklin to (*un*)Grammar (pp. 175–77). Chapter 7, "Lunar 'Pratique': Law, Medicine, and Theology in Fragments VI and X," whose tales of Physician, Pardoner, and Parson expose the lunar practices of law, medicine, and theology, ends the cosmic tour, noting that the lunar fault of the Pardoner's lapsed memory is countered by the lunar virtue of the Parson's humility. The conclusion reiterates main lines of argument that the "story block," or fragment structure of the *Tales*, "is a purposeful *divisio* and *ordinatio*" comprising "structural breaks necessary for topical location, and thus for meaning" (p. 226), and that Chaucer's choice of a basic ordering principle for the *Tales* is "discoverable and matches that actually in the Ellesmere order" (p. 228).

I cannot but admire Astell's impressive scholarship in this enterprise. Her arguments are bold and backed by a plethora of evidence. Even if I do not *believe* her argument that the Ellesmere redactor saw and ordered the tales into a two-way journey of the soul within a one-way journey of the body, I can only quibble with inconsequential details and a style of argumentation that occasionally detracts attention. For one example, I see an implicit contradiction between an early supposition that the unity of the *Tales* is "an (unfinished) whole" (p. 14) and her well-made point in the conclusion that Fragment 1 figures a bookish Dantean *compilatio* that informs the planetary pilgrimage of the soul (p. 228). Questions of fact also divert attention. The etymology of *book* is not *birch*, and the etymology for *Leonard* is not a critic's, but derives from the martyrologists of the *Legenda Aurea*. The division of Oratores, Bellatores, and Laboratores could not have been "first enunciated" in 1030 (pp. 33–34) if Wulfstan's *Institutes of Polity* listed them earlier. What she means by the "official introduction" to Paris of Aristotle in 1255 escapes me, since Aristotle's Natural Philosophy was proscribed in 1215, and Francis Bacon had lectured there on Aristotelian philosophy in the 1240s. The curricular Trivium can be traced at least as far back as Alcuin in 787.

Some readings of Chaucer seem suspect. Does Palamon marry Emily in the *same grove* of "gardenlike features" where he fought Arcite (p. 102)? If the Knight's comparison of his telling task with plowing a field reflects a Saturnian agrarian deity, can one ignore Absolon's coulter (which in the literature of the day figures the Parson's tongue sowing seeds of truth) in the tale of the Jovean Miller? If the Man of Law's Custance is "a cause of conversion for those to whom she is sent" (p. 142), can we ignore God's voice whose power converts the king and others in her defense (2.683–86)? Can one say that the summoner of the Friar's tale enters into a pact with "the devil himself" (p. 166), when he is but a single *fiend* (3.1448, 1475, 1506)? If the Ellesmere order is a "right" reading of Chaucer's philosophical intent, is it consonant to cite lines not in the Ellesmere (p. 157)? Finally, while I approve the manuscript form *Custance* in preference to *Constance*, I wonder at nonmanuscript *Cecilia* and *Griselda* in preference to *Cecile* and *Grisild(e)*.

Crucial to the intention attributed to the Ellesmere redactor is the chiasmic arrangement of fragment divisions; but, if Chaucer's fragments represent *divisio*, why did he fail to link 3, 4, and 5 into the single philosophical story-block where Astell places them? Putting her entire chiasmic relationship in question is the fact that there are only eight "structural" breaks in the *Tales* and, hence, nine fragments "necessary for topical location, and thus for meaning." The publisher's presentation of the text is agreeable, though there are repetitions of blanket footnotes and unnecessary appeals to "as readers have noted" (e.g., pp. 136–37). I spotted only one obvious typo—*Sorseynt* Leonard (p. 16).

To my taste, this book is filling of fact and rich of speculation, though I miss the Chaucer who indulges in the pleasure of learning and is joyful in the jest it affords him even with the sentence of the theologians. Saturnine and ludic Chaucers are not incompatible (even Hamlet, short of playmates in the dour courts of Denmark, had his moments of merriment); but, my own idiosyncratic taste must not take attention from the splendid achievement of this book, which will stir debate on many a critical terrain. Above all, Astell is everywhere to be taken seriously. She argues with conviction, commitment, and sincerity.

PAUL BEEKMAN TAYLOR
University of Geneva

CATHERINE BATT, ed. *Essays on Thomas Hoccleve.* Westfield Publications in Medieval Studies, vol. 10. Centre for Medieval and Renaissance Studies. Queen Mary and Westfield College, University of London. Turnhout: Brepols, 1996. Pp. ix, 130. Np.

Catherine Batt begins her introduction to this welcome collection with a quote from Hoccleve's *Series* in which the author fears being thought a "double man" for both praising and blaming women in his works. The current interest of literary and cultural critics in Hoccleve has much to do with his "doubleness," the precarious balance in his works between public and private voices, masculine and feminine self-images, sanity and madness. Hoccleve's ambivalent approaches to a range of intertexts, especially his "master" Chaucer's poems, together with his endless questioning of his own poetic practices, make him a compelling subject for postmodern interpretations.

These essays, originally delivered at a conference at the University of London, add to the growing body of new theoretical approaches to Hoccleve. Charles Blyth's "Editing the *Regiment of Princes*" provides a sound argument for a textual methodology that will support these readings by considering Hoccleve in his social and political contexts. Extending the commonsensical approach of David Greetham, his predecessor as general editor of the *Regiment*, Blyth presents the case for using Hoccleve's later holograph poems to reconstruct a "Hocclevean usage" and apply it to the poet's best-known work. As Blyth points out, the survival of Hoccleve's holographs represents a uniquely well documented example of medieval authorship that can be both fruitfully theorized and put to practical editorial use. The prospect of Blyth's new edition, a replacement of Furnivall's error-ridden 1897 EETS volume, should encourage anyone interested in pursuing historicist study of Hoccleve.

In "Chaucer, Christine de Pizan, and Hoccleve: *The Letter of Cupid*," Roger Ellis takes up the thorny question of what exactly Hoccleve *does* to Christine's *Epistre au Dieu d'Amours*. Both Christine and Hoccleve, Ellis suggests, walk a tightrope between antifeminist discourse and its feminist reworkings, especially since their poems are given the voice of a "male and divine" speaker. Ellis abandons earlier critics' attempts to assess Hoccleve's level of sympathy for women by instead reading the *Letter* as the poet's gloss on Christine via Chaucer's *Legend of Good Women*, *Troilus*, *Wife of Bath's Tale*, and finally *Prioress's Tale*. While his reading provides many insights into the *Letter*, Ellis doesn't consider the full implications of these Chaucerian texts for contemporary ideas of gender. For Ellis, Hoccleve makes the *Letter* not more misogynistic than the *Epistre* but rather more ironic, incorporating Chaucer's observations on class and ambiguous sympathy for his male protagonists. But then what are we to make of Hoccleve's final gesture to the

Prioress's Virgin Mary: is it, as Ellis argues, a return to orthodoxy, or is it an even darker irony? While this problem is perhaps just one more reflection of Hoccleve's "doubleness," it seems important to consider just how restrictive Hoccleve's "Chaucerianism" is, and how it shapes his representations of gender.

Fortunately, Batt takes up the relation between Hoccleve's Chaucerian poetics and gender in her wonderful "Hoccleve and . . . Feminism? Negotiating Meaning in the *Regement of Princes*." Batt explores the influence of Chaucer's *Melibee*, in which the feminine represents the very nature of proverbial language and "advice," on Hoccleve's attempts to define himself as a Lancastrian court poet in his "Mirror of Princes" directed to Prince Henry. Hoccleve's engagement with the *Melibee*, as both receiver and giver of political counsel, puts him in both feminine and masculine roles. As Batt puts it, the poet's Chaucerian legacy is a "female impersonation": Prudence's discourse and its various potential interpretations test the very possibility of a politically "responsible" literature. Batt begins her reading of the *Regement* with Hoccleve's vexing "defense" of women based on their bodily roundness at the end of the poem. Wisely avoiding the unanswerable question of how sincere Hoccleve's sentiments are, Batt approaches the work in terms of Hoccleve's dizzying writing of himself and others into traditional and countertraditional gender roles. From his own "feminized" position as abject political subject to his reimagination of Boethius's Lady Philosophy as the Old Man, Hoccleve highlights the politically contingent, ever-changeable nature of "advice." As socially and politically determined contexts of words and texts shift, the court poet's gender itself takes on new meanings.

David Mills's "Voices of Thomas Hoccleve" concludes the volume with an illuminating interpretation of Hoccleve's "doubleness." Mills argues that Hoccleve's extraordinary sensitivity to literary registers and genres is a result of his inability to reconcile his public and private voices or, in other words, to comfortably inhabit the role of a court poet. Mills particularly focuses on the commodification of literary work, its status as a "token of social exchange" ultimately alienated from the poet by a network of political and economic forces. Hoccleve's much discussed "madness" in the *Series* is at once the inevitable symptom of this condition and another topos that the poet must go on to negotiate. Mills's Hoccleve, then, is a radically double man, divided between his

own interests and his readers', yet, to the last, a poet who brilliantly the-
matizes his own alienation.

The readings in Batt's collection add much to our understanding of
an unusually elusive poet and his historical context. The contributions
of all four critics provide us not only with a raft of new ways to read
Hoccleve but with new approaches to the problems posed by post-
Chaucerian, Lancastrian poetry. In regard to issues of textual production, gender and politicized interpretation, these essays point the way
to further work on the difficult relationship of medieval poets to princes
and power.

RUTH NISSÉ
University of Nebraska-Lincoln

MARTHA BAYLESS. *Parody in the Middle Ages: The Latin Tradition.*
Recentiores: Later Latin Texts and Contexts Series. Ann Arbor:
University of Michigan Press, 1996. Pp. xii, 425. $52.50.

Parody is one of the most satisfying forms of literary humor. Its success
depends on a wide knowledge of the target texts, of which the Middle
Ages had an ample supply in the Bible and liturgy, with its verses, responses, hymns, prayers, and a structure known intimately by every
cleric. Almost equally well known were the techniques of biblical
analysis. In its title and preface, Bayless's study explicitly challenges
Paul Lehmann's pioneering *Die Parodie im Mittelalter* (1922, 1963); the
texts she studies and edits largely overlap with Lehmann's, and in some
ways her book could be described as a third (and improved) edition of
Lehmann, though its subtitle might more accurately have been *The
Latin Religious Tradition.*

She restricts herself to self-standing parodies on nonfictional works,
excluding incidental parodies and parodies of genres. For Lehmann's
two broadly based chapters ("Critical, Argumentative, Exultant
Parody," and "Cheerful, Amusing, Entertaining Parody"), Bayless,
after an introduction on methodology, has four very focused chapters,
with the relevant texts (all translated) in appendix 2. Chapter 2 deals
with the mock feast of the *Cena Cypriani*, with its biblical guests and

their antics, and its redactions and derivatives (such as the *Arras Cena*, app. 2.1); she interprets the *Cena* as a parodic allegory. Chapter 3 describes the entertaining pseudosaints Nemo (Nobody, who had seen God) and Invicem (One-Another, who was entertained, abused, and frequently addressed); texts of these rare and barely accessible parodies are in app. 2.2–7, in their various versions. Bayless shows that these immensely funny stories also call into question the literal interpretation of the Bible. Chapter 4 presents the drinker's masses that parody the liturgy (App. 2.10–12), substituting self-indulgence for religion. Chapter 5 describes *centos*, parodies that generally preserve the exact words of their original text (here the Bible) but misplace and reorganize them for satiric effect (the money-gospels, app. 2.8–9) or for pure nonsense (app. 2.13–17). Chapter 6 is a socioliterary analysis, very sensitively done, of the role of parody within medieval Christianity. (App. 1 is a list of parodic texts; app. 2.18 is a digression on mock acrostics).

For seventy-five years Lehmann's studies have held the field, but his sprawling work is hard to use (and not just because it is in German). Bayless's more restricted scope allows her to focus more efficiently, and her refined literary sensitivity produces many insights. This focus comes at a price, however, since she omits a great deal. The omission of incidental parody (such as openings that parody Ovid) is understandable, but it was one of the things that made Lehmann entertaining. More important is the entire neglect of parody for political purposes (Lehmann's *Leidensgeschichte*, anti-Hussite masses, parodic hymns against Piers Gaveston, and other parodies of the hymn "Pange lingua"); these are not even in her list in app. 1, despite its claim to all-inclusiveness, but they are pure parodies or *centos*. The same applies to her omission of parodies based on grammatical texts (erotic, antipeasant, etc.); these *are* listed in app. 1 but are not discussed, even though they would have reinforced her argument that parody was not subversive of its target-text, since presumably no one wanted to abolish Donatus. She touches briefly on "Devil's Letters" (p. 156) but does not put them in her list, which also omits the parodies she discusses on pages 53–56. She lists mock recipes but does not discuss them. All these omissions are forgivable, since there is a corresponding gain in depth of treatment, but I wish her title sounded less comprehensive.

Of the seventeen texts edited in appendix 2, eight have not been edited before in these versions (though most were known in some version or another). Of the rest, most were available in rare or inaccessible journals like *Anzeiger*. Moreover, she provides a full apparatus of variants where previous editions use one manuscript only and (as in 15–16) provides the biblical sources. She has reshuffled and clarified texts edited by Lehmann (particularly the Money Gospels and Drinker's Masses). In several cases (3–5, 11–12) she gives separate texts of what are basically scribal versions (e.g., the Abbreviated Long Nemo, which is not the same as the Short Nemo). This is easier on the reader than printing them as variants in the apparatus (though she has to do this with 2), and also illustrates the way these parodies were subjected to constant revision, expansion, or reduction. This results in some repetitiveness, but in a good cause; what I complain of is the translation of every single version. Surely the non-Latinist would have been content just with the longest of each type? Further, although I would defend the integrity of scribal versions, the scribes should not be followed in absurdities: at page 339, *nutrabis* cannot be from *nutrire*, and can be corrected with minimal ease to *intrabis*.

Some textual matters deserved more attention. For the Long Nemo she prefers to print the fuller Second Recension, while recognizing that the First (represented in OM) has the support of the earliest "witness," Stephen's mock-rebuttal (and "mock" is surely right). It should be noted, however, that the Second Recension must derive from a corrupt archetype. At 49 *dum* (OM) is needed for the sense, and 69 *spretis* (OMH) must be right against *sumptibus*. At 48 *aliud*, although in the Vulgate, is clearly not authentic, since it makes no sense here; it is not in OMALG, and was clearly added by some scribes officiously correcting back to the target-text. Similarly at 74, where the Long and Abbreviated Nemo has simply *Nemo considerat*, some scribes of the Short Nemo add the words *nec percipit corde*, which are liturgically correct but (because of the *nec*) nonsense in context. Possibly 19 *venit* (OMGHP) is to be preferred to *potest venire*, the Vulgate reading, and 101 *misteriis* (OM) to *meritis*. Another example of a scribe "correcting" back to the Vulgate is in the Long Invicem (6/26), which has *superiores*, with the Vulgate, whereas the earlier Short Invicem (7/15) has the correctly modified *superiorem*. Minutiae such as these contribute to the history of the texts (and indeed are the principal reason for providing an apparatus of variants).

No one is without fault, as Cato said, except Nobody (Long Nemo 70–71), and this includes editors. I offer the following corrigenda for a future edition.

p. 54 "for four marks": perhaps "for the three of them at a mark and a penny."

pp. 55–56 *vagam* probably "stray animal"; *verberavissem* apparently = *vapulavissem*.

pp. 65–66 (p. 261): "who do not care to increase their learning for any other reason except to . . ."

p. 68 (p. 273) *per predicta* of later recensions must be correct.

p. 75 "let Nobody light . . ."

pp. 76–78 the Zurich text is clearly very corrupt. We can translate *sapientie illi* as "to that Wisdom" and read *sicut* for *sanctis*, but *quia . . . preventus* and *non etiam . . . eligeretur* must be wrong.

p. 83 The construction is: "We will take care to turn the authorities of the Bible on Nobody's head . . ."

p. 88 "But the brothers of the monastery which he planned to enter . . ."

p. 89 (second quote) for *Quid* (twice) read *Qui*.

p. 90 for "disregard" read "make excuses for."

p. 98 (and pp. 99, 100, 341, 350) *Confitemini* is imperative plural (not "we confess" as she consistently translates); similarly p. 118 *sequamini* "you [not "we"] may follow." In other places she translates *-mini* endings correctly.

p. 100 (last quote) *virgini.*

p. 106 *capitulo* "heading."

p. 106 (and pp. 347, 351) must be "come to Falerna."

p. 107 *decantando* perhaps a pun "decanting."

p. 111 (p. 339) *Sic* for *Sit*, and perhaps *nunc* for *non.*

p. 113 "clearly" (*de claro*), perhaps a pun "from the claret."

p. 114 (p. 352) "it is wicked to condemn wine and must."

p. 115 (p. 353) there is no negative: "lead us into drunkenness" (thus negating Bayless's next remark).

ibid. (and pp. 344, 352) "in the tavern as it is in the die."

p. 117 "paying for carnal things."

p. 118 note that *Lucius* is also the name of a fish.

p. 123 "who descended on behalf of the heretics."

p. 124 "reborn for the devil."

p. 139 delete *ad* before *habenti.*

p. 147 for "perpetually justified" read "instantly made just."

p. 148 *delectabilis* "pleasant."

p. 155 *voluerit* is from *volo* not *volvo.*

pp. 161–62 *autem* should be rendered "but" throughout the passage.

p. 165 (p. 374) *Florenus* perhaps a pun on "florin."

p. 173 "for there are no virgins" would be a better joke.

p. 205 for "are made silly" read "delight."

p. 311/4 perhaps read *eum* for *quem.*

p. 312/53, 55 (and p. 315) *Invicem* is vocative in both cases: "One-Another, do not tell lies."

pp. 339, 343 see above on *nutrabis/intrabis* (cf. p. 354).

p. 340 for *pro quod* read *pro quo* throughout.

ibid. *audemus:* read *audeamus.*

p. 341 *origine.*

ibid. *Ite, mensa . . .* (so translated on p. 345).

ibid. *ut filiorum*: read *et filiorum.*

p. 342 *sternat* "lays low," not "sneezes" (which is *sternuo* or *sternuto*).

p. 344 "rewards": read "fights."

p. 345 for "By Bacchus, the god three times lifted up" read "To the god Bacchus a triple punishment."

p. 350 "thy sense": *sensum* is probably a spelling for *censum* "money."

p. 353 delete "by" before "the cups."

p. 364 *totorum:* read *cocorum* (and translate "cooks" on p. 367); this is the reading of the Septuagint, and is found elsewhere in Latin, as in Gregory and Hildebert, *Epigram* 43.

p. 367 "she (Mary, not Peter) thought she saw a vision."

There are a few typographical slips in the Latin: p. 55 *clamabat, verberaverunt.* p. 68 *castitatem.* p. 113 (second quote) *Domine sancte.* p. 142 *sermonem.* p. 143 *faciem.* p. 265 note to 184–85 *considera.* p. 338 (*Introitus*) *plangunt.* p. 373 *denario.* p. 383 *posuerunt.* p. 401 *lucidos.*

These quibbles notwithstanding, Professor Bayless has produced an excellent study, and I hope she will write more on the subject. She has helped to define parody more closely, by concentrating on the target-texts (Bible and biblical exegesis, gospels and saints' lives, liturgy and hymns) rather than the satirical intent. Although she detects the serious consequences of some of the parodies, she never loses sight of the fact that these clerical *jeux d'esprits* were written primarily for fun.

A. G. RIGG
University of Toronto

JOYCE COLEMAN. *Public Reading and the Reading Public in Late Medieval England and France.* Cambridge Studies in Medieval Literature, vol. 26. Cambridge: Cambridge University Press, 1996. Pp. xiv, 250. $59.95.

Public Reading and the Reading Public pursues two related, but distinct, projects. The first, and more ambitious, is an extended assault upon what its author calls the strong version of orality/literacy theory, that is to say the version espoused, in their different ways, by Jack Goody and Walter Ong (chapters 1–3). The second is a detailed investigation of the practice of public reading (Coleman's term for this practice is "aurality") in the late middle ages in England, France, and Burgundy (chapters 4–7). The relationship between these projects is clear enough: if Goody's position really does imply a "great divide" between literate and oral societies (as Ruth Finnegan has claimed), then public reading can all too easily be dismissed as, at best, a transitional phenomenon and, at worse, a throwback to an earlier age. For this reason, Coleman believes, the way in which poets such as Chaucer represent themselves as writing for oral presentation (a phenomenon first noted by Ruth Crosby) has too often been marginalized as mere "fictive orality" (that is to say, a deliberate or unconscious carryover from a departed age of minstrel performance), a position that derives its force "from the fallacious assumption that 'orality' becomes superfluous upon the appearance of its evolutionary successor 'literacy'" (p. 149).

While the first part of Coleman's case is vigorously and often cogently argued, the book's dust jacket goes too far by claiming that it "offers the first sustained critique of Walter Ong's *Orality and Literacy.*" Critics of the strong theory of orality have not been lacking in the last decade, and it is hard to see how Coleman's theoretical objections really displace those of Ruth Finnegan or Brian Street. Moreover, Coleman shares

Finnegan and Street's penchant for knocking over straw men: Goody, for instance, has always denied that his work on the technology of literacy entails a "single factor determinism," and even Ong might be more charitably interpreted as offering a heuristic rather than empirical account of the great divide. In one important respect, however, Coleman does refocus the debate. Both Street and Finnegan are anthropologists and tend to use the empirical evidence of ethnographic observation to pick holes in Goody's model; neither (despite Finnegan's work on early Ireland) has proved as successful at nullifying the conclusions of cultural and social historians such as Brian Stock or Rosamund McKitterick. Coleman makes much of the fact that a succession of scholars has claimed that each century from the eighth through the fifteenth marks a crucial stage in the transition of Western society from orality to literacy (p. 19), but though her catalogue may force us to take some of these individual claims with a pinch of salt, it hardly invalidates the total enterprise. While Coleman is properly suspicious of the evolutionary or progressive ideology she feels to be implicit in most historical discussions of the development of literacy, she is finally too honest a scholar to blind herself to the obviously transitional status of the Middle Ages as a whole; it may be that the transition took half a millennium (p. 221), but it was no less a transition because of that. The fact that literacy rates were rising throughout the Middle Ages, while everywhere falling far short of those found in the Western world today, cannot but affect our understanding of the differences both among medieval societies and between the Middle Ages and ourselves. Coleman is to be applauded when she argues for a more subtle analysis of mixed or hybrid states, but where she attacks the validity of the overall model she is in danger of weakening her own case.

The second part of Coleman's study (chapters 4–7) shows the value of supplementing historical investigation with techniques drawn from anthropology. The role of the public reader in the late Middle Ages, in court circles at least, might usefully be compared to that of the modern chauffeur; a CEO's preference for being driven to the office no more implies that she herself has never learned to drive than a medieval nobleman's fondness for being read to implies that he was illiterate, and while it is not unreasonable to see such late medieval aurality as a relic of a time when few aristocrats could read (just as chauffeur-driven limousines are clearly survivals from an era when the wealthy maintained coachmen and private carriages), these simple historical associations will never be able to satisfy the anthropologist's demand for thick description—for the move, in Clifford Geertz's words, away "from functionalist accounts of the devices upon which societies rest towards interpretive ones of the kinds of lives societies support." It may well be, for instance, that some medieval aristocrats employed public readers in much the same spirit that some modern business people employ chauffeurs—as a way of displaying their wealth and status (cf. Coleman, p.128), but this is only one of many possible explanations, and it is to Coleman's credit that she constantly reminds us of the potential complexity of an apparently simple cultural phenomenon like aurality. The book is at its best where it attempts what its author calls an "ethnography of reading" in the Middle Ages (for instance, in its analysis of the sociopolitical dimension of aurality on pages 93–96). It is rather a pity, then, that Coleman is not prepared to allow modern criticism the same degree of complexity she finds in medieval aurality. The phenomenon she pillories so energetically under the guise of "fictive orality" masks far more complex issues than she is willing to allow; when all is said and done, critics like Burrow, Mehl, and Pearsall are interested in subtle literary analysis, not in propounding a crude theory of technological determinism.

Joyce Coleman's *Public Reading and the Reading Public* performs a valuable service in reminding us of the limits to private reading in the late Middle Ages. It adds a great deal of new material to Ruth Crosby's two seminal articles and makes a powerful case for regarding aurality as, in her words, the "default option" for literary dissemination in the late Middle Ages. I have only one real quarrel with this aspect of the book. Although Coleman is prepared to accept Chaytor's point that medieval people might read aloud to themselves even in private—for instance, she divides what she calls "dividuality" (that is to say, the solitary reading of written texts) into "voiced private reading" and "silent private reading" (p. 42)—she seems unwilling to accept this as a possible factor in some of the aural situations she discusses. For instance, she admonishes modern scholars (pp. 63–66) for finding "inextricably oxymoronic" the idea of leaf-turning listeners in the *Prologue* of *The Miller's Tale* ("And therefor whoso liste it nat yheere / Turne over the leef and chese another tale"), yet her own account of public readers skipping backward or forward in their texts at the beck and call of peremptory audiences seems to me unnecessarily complicated. Surely the notion of "voiced private reading" resolves this oxymoron considerably more elegantly? There are several other points in the book—for instance, her discussion of the way Gower's Amans reports that he has *heard* something told *above* (p. 187)—where an unwillingness to recognize that private reading might be as much ear-reading as eye-reading weakens her argument. I would not wish to make too much of this criticism, however, for the vast majority of Coleman's examples are unambiguous and taken *en masse* make an overwhelming case for the importance of aurality in the late Middle Ages. This is a book that no one interested in the cultural context of late medieval poetry can afford to ignore.

RICHARD FIRTH GREEN
University of Western Ontario

RITA COPELAND, ed. *Criticism and Dissent in the Middle Ages.* Cambridge: Cambridge University Press, 1996. Pp. xii, 332. $59.95.

Here is a volume of excellence; a reviewer's first response might forgivably be jealousy of those invited to contribute. To an unusual extent these contributors share a common purpose—a desire to provide a multivocal account of medieval culture that breaks down period boundaries and shows the relevance to modern debates of medieval discourses of textuality and interpretation. Far from being monolithic, these discourses are "heterogeneous, conflicted and conflictually invested, even within their own established orders" (p. 1). So writes Rita Copeland in her introduction, calling for a dismantling of "the binarism orthodoxy/dissent" by means of a practice she calls, in quotes, "dissenting reading" (p. 5). Copeland then provides a sustained example of such reading: Prudentius's account of the martyrdom of the grammarian Cassian in relation to William of Malmesbury's report of the death of Eriugena; and the focus of her reading is on the fault lines of cultural dislocation.

Copeland's attention to violence yields place to Jody Enders's opening essay, which argues uncompromisingly that the violence of the medieval classroom stems from that of memory theory itself; torture is the ultimate mnemonic, over which are cast the fictions of beauty and creativity. Our own "hopeful belief" in nonviolence is just that, a necessary social pretense. Enders's discourse serves to connect the classical, medieval, and modern as it ranges from Cicero to Artaud and Stanislavski; though I consider it finally unhistorical in its annihilation of the differences between medieval and modern classrooms and its disregard of educational change even within the last generation, it serves as a vigorous claim for the relevance of medieval practice. There follows a superb essay by Marjorie Curry Woods, "Rape and the Pedagogical Rhetoric of Sexual Violence," which should be set reading for any student of psychoanalysis attempting to understand, say, Freud's gendered reading of a male child's transition from child to adult. Woods explicates the use of three passages describing rape from authoritative works such as school texts in the later Middle Ages. What impresses this reader is her desire to understand, powerfully enacted in historicist close reading. Woods refuses to be reductive, reading *Pamphilus* as, in effect, an early picaresque novel in which—here Woods draws a parallel with Carol Clover's work on horror movies—boys are forced to imagine themselves as victims as well as the possessors of power. There is no elision of historical difference here as Woods insists: "This absolutely patriarchal tradition was neither simplistic nor psychologically crude, and while we may be repelled by its very success, it behooves us to understand what we can of its processes" (p. 74).

After so strong a reading, Martin Irvine's essay on "Heloise and the Gendering of the Literate Subject" seems merely good and informative, especially on the manuscripts and the genre of the Senecan *epistola*. Though it begins by asserting that Heloise had to work with a literate subject that was encoded as masculine, it concludes that the correspondence reveals this subject position to have been negotiable and provisional. The essay might have done more to dramatize its problems with its own terms, but it remains a persuasive account of Heloise as dissenting writer. In the next essay, however, Michael Camille's "The Dissenting Image: A Postcard from Matthew Paris," the dissent is really Camille's—registered against Derrida's use of a postcard showing Matthew Paris's illustration of Socrates and Plato. Camille reads the image historically as the opposite of Derrida's reading (Derrida sees it, perhaps unsurprisingly, as privileging writing over speech), and dissents along the way from other art historians' use and definition of images. Camille's essay is a bravura performance; it may look a little less hyperbolic in the context of his forthcoming study on visual images as pedagogical devices in medieval classrooms. Quieter, but still effective, is Nicolette Zeeman's essay describing the "very fruitful relationship between the medieval schools and vernacular textual culture" (p. 174). Though she does not here prove their influence on actual romance composition, Zeeman gives welcome attention to the commentaries, weighing what they have to say about figuration and implicitly correcting broad-brush generalizations by some other scholars: more criticism than dissent here.

While there is no Chaucer-specific study in the collection, Janet Coleman's brilliant and detailed essay, "The Science of Politics and Late Medieval Academic Debate," should be required reading for all Chaucerians interested in achieving a meaningful formulation of "politics" in relation to Chaucer's work; of particular note is Coleman's identification of Prudence as being at the core of such a definition, "a way of thinking, a consequence of experience rather than a revelation from on high" (p. 189). There follow three essays on English literature. James Simpson's "Desire and the Scriptural Text: Will as Reader in *Piers Plowman*" is beautiful written. It argues that Will moves from being a passive recipient of the Holy Church's broadly scriptural homily to reading Scripture alone in B. 11 and finally to his intellectual deployment of it in B. 13. Will's hope against predestination is a refusal to read literally, one that is authorized by "Langland's voluntarist hermeneutics" (p. 231). Simpson's notion that the shift to a model of lay, private reading in the poem has consequences for "what might be called the politics of culture" (p. 220) sits splendidly beside Ralph Hanna's study of the English translation of Wyclif's Latin exegetical polemic *Vae Octuplex* into what is in effect a Lollard sermon. Hanna argues, first, that Lollard appropriation of "a textual ideology based on specialized training" (p. 246) generally subverts the exclusivity of orthodox textual culture and serves the cause of vernacular translation; and, second, that this particular translation by contrast demonstrates bad faith, both against the scriptural text and against "the single community of the Lollard faithful" (p. 255). The third essay on an English literary theme is Sarah Beckwith's on "Sacramentality and Dissent in York's Theatre of Corpus Christi." Beckwith engages in little close reading either of the York plays or her quotations from Derrida and, especially, Žižek, which badly need further unpacking; but there is more than adequate compensation in the intellectual complexity of Beckwith's argument (and that of the virtual second essay conducted in the footnotes). Rather than adopting a narrowly inquisitorial test of orthodoxy, and desiring to defend the plays both from Lollard attacks and from modern readings of them as anti-Lollard, Beckwith persuasively claims that they stage "an astonishing vernacular encounter" with sacramentality, one which should be read "through the grid of modern hermeneutics" (p. 268). Taking her cue from Ricoeur, Beckwith produces the volume's most challenging model of dissent, in which it is "intrinsic to symbolic formation as such" (p. 265).

Varied as the volume is to this point, all the essays display a commitment to detailed historical reading or to dissenting critical practice or both, and most show an urgent sense that what they have to say engages with modern debate or, as with Woods and Enders, impacts on the nature of modernity itself. By these criteria the final essay, by Steven Justice, is problematic. Its ostensible subject is John of Exeter, Bishop Alnwick's notary in the Norwich heresy hearings of 1429, who deviates from the normal language of record, Latin, in order to record certain responses in English from those under examination. It is crucial to Justice's case that these departures should be unmotivated, a "random event" arising from the fact that "John of Exeter *was bored*" (p. 296). Justice takes this as an occasion to moralize, rebuking fellow scholars for overzealous interrogation of our evidence and finally insisting, in what is best interpreted as a personal statement, that we modern academics have more in common with inquisitors than with their victims. The essay is provocative, then; and it achieved prepublication in *Representations*, a context to which it was far better suited. Here it appears palinodal, not only in relation to Justice's own work on 1381 but also to the rest of the volume. Worse still, its premise is unsustainable: as Susan Crane has shown, the scribe goes into English in order to record wordplay that would be lost in Latin translation ("*Fryday is a fre day*"). If one wanted to moralize, one might say that literary scholars can hardly contribute to the new cultural history without attentive close reading of texts. In any case, the self-dramatizing defensiveness of Justice's piece is at odds with what contributors are doing in most of the rest of this heartening volume, getting on with work they regard as principled and consequential.

DAVID LAWTON
University of East Anglia

GEORGE ECONOMOU, trans. *William Langland's* Piers Plowman: *The C Version: A Verse Translation*. Middle Ages Series. Philadelphia: University of Pennsylvania Press, 1996. Pp. xxxiv, 262. $46.50 cloth, $17.95 paper.

Like Caesar's ancient Gaul, *Piers Plowman* has recently proved unwilling to limit itself to three versions, but those who work with the growing family that goes by that surname will thank George Economou for his attractive verse translation of the C Version. In long lines marked by varied rhythm and strong alliteration, he has given modern voice to the muscular directness of the original. His translation is preceded by a five-page preface; a brief introduction presenting the life and work of William Langland, a summary of the poem, and the principles and practices of this translation; and four pages of selected bibliography of editions, translations, and critical studies from 1960 to the present. The volume concludes with forty pages of explanatory notes and an appendix tabulating the "Major Additions, Omissions, and Transpositions of Material in the C Version." (Unfortunately, a number of typographical and copyediting errors—including the last word of the introduction and a crucial "not" omitted at 22.278a—mar this otherwise handsome volume.)

Arriving on our shelves just in advance of the long-expected third volume of the Athlone edition, this translation offers a modern English rendition of the C Text published in 1978 by Derek Pearsall. Economou acknowledges "improvements" made as a result of readings contributed by George Kane (p.x). Since these are not, unfortunately, identified in the copious endnotes provided for the text, the exact "original" for his translation may be in doubt at times. Along with the recent lively rendition of A by the late Sister Francis Covella, however, we can add this first translation of C to the many verse and prose modernizations of the B Text. General readers and undergraduate students now have trustworthy access to three distinct versions of *Piers Plowman.*

Economou's treatment of the poem's alliterative Middle English for the most part achieves his primary goal of "readabil[i]ty" (p. xxviii). But since, in his brief introduction, he adduces a number of substantial criteria for his translation, it is perhaps fair to employ them in measuring its success. Most of them he meets, but a few (minor) dissatisfactions may cause mixed reactions to the volume, and raise some uncertainty about what exact audience it is intending to address. These reactions are at least in part attributable to the mixed messages the volume itself sends.

To begin with the introduction: its first sentence asserts that William Langland's authorship of the "three successive versions" is "no longer a matter of scholarly controversy" (p. xiii), a handbookish truism that may serve the general or undergraduate reader who does not particularly want to be burdened by scholarly controversies—particularly those that have for so long resisted final solution. But are his

contestable "facts" here—or the extended discussion of the textual relations among the three versions—really *necessary* to the new readers of
Piers Plowman Economou posits as his primary audience? Those first-
time readers may also find the translator's Wittgensteinian ruminations
about the "unique play of the signifier(s)" and the "illusion of semantic
equivalence" (p. xxvii) of less immediate interest (or clear meaning), although they will certainly benefit from his account (pp. xxv–xxvi) of
the poem's punning complexities—even if one of the significant elements in his example ("errant") is not discussed, nor "translated" as the
others are so effectively.

The divided nature of his intended audience(s) is also evidenced by
the useful quotation from Wyclif's *De officio pastorali* (p. xxvi) that he
introduces to cap his discussion of Repentance's "lesson." It is not given
in modern English, even though its language is no easier than that of
the poem he is translating. This is further evidence, I think, of an unsettling mixture of the genuinely introductory and the purely scholarly
competing for primacy in the introduction. Similarly, in the explanatory notes: allusions to *Beowulf*, Chaucer, Shakespeare, and Milton, for
example, will be appreciated perhaps by English majors reading *Piers*
for the first time, but they will find the detailed tables of relations between the B and C Texts in the appendix of little use. On the other
hand, graduate students and others (like Economou himself) interested
in the vagaries of the evolving poem(s) will surely welcome these useful, succinct lists.

His treatment of the Latin lines and phrases that pepper *Piers* also
seems inconsistent. Even after reading his (not altogether clear) explanatory footnote (to Prol. 152–57), I found the irregular treatment
distracting. Some Latin lines are "treated . . . as exceptions . . . because
of their special character and length" (p. 223) and counted in the line
numbers; others are not. But the "special character" of these passages is
not made clear, and others equally long are treated inconsistently
(cf. 16.271a and 17.52a). Latin words contained within an English line
are regularly not translated, while those in separate lines usually are
(though often, as with biblical texts, into *early* modern English). The
flow of the translation is unnecessarily interrupted when readers are
alerted to footnotes that at times do no more than inform them that
Latin *"transgressores"* (1.92) and *"fornicatores"* (2.191) should be translated "transgressors" and "fornicators." Readability would have been

enhanced by translating *all* the Latin (and perhaps even parenthetically referring to uncontroversial sources, such as the many biblical verses).

Finally, his introduction asserts that his goal has not been to "emulate the conventions of alliterative verse" because this might impose "syntactical and linguistic patterns" that would not ring "true to contemporary ears" (p. xxiv). The goal is laudable even if not easily achieved, and the translation at times remains too dependent on modern cognates and the word order of the original (e.g., 1.100, 9.235–39, 11.218–24, and 12.197–202). Some slight departures from his line-by-line translation of the sometimes convoluted syntax of the Middle English might have made these truer to contemporary ears.

Economou has made the final version of *Piers Plowman* accessible in full for the first time in modern English. My qualified praise of his volume derives from what appears to be its uncertainty about how much of the scholarship first-time readers of the poem need to be alerted to if they are to appreciate the passion and learning, and what the translator helpfully terms the "magic realism" (p. xix), of this capacious poem. A teacher willing to complement Economou's introduction and notes will find this an attractive text for survey courses in medieval English literature.

MÍCEÁL F. VAUGHAN
University of Washington

HUW M. EDWARDS. *Dafydd ap Gwilym: Influences and Analogues.* Oxford Modern Languages and Literature Monographs. Oxford: Clarendon Press, 1996. Pp. xiii, 300. $70.00.

Dafydd ap Gwilym, the great poet of medieval Wales, was perhaps twenty years older than Chaucer, whom he never met. His legacy, like Chaucer's, comprises not only a body of poems but also the transformation of the poetry of his nation. Dafydd took up a continuous tradition of bardic poetry that proudly traced itself back to the sixth century, to the bards Aneirin and Taliesin, and with his contemporaries, the "men of the *cywydd*" (*Cywyddwyr*), he changed it utterly. The aristocratic bardic tradition was loosened and enriched by popular and folk traditions; classical and romance influences, the sensibilities of Ovid and the troubadours, became part of Welsh poetry; and the form of poetry itself was changed, with the *cywydd*, a couplet-based form combining popular and bardic versification, becoming dominant. Without forgetting the old forms and old subjects, Welsh poetry found itself singing of new things in new ways. It still sang the praise-poems and elegies and satires of the old bards. But in the work of Dafydd ap Gwilym it sang more often of nature, of the birds and the wind and the changing seasons. And it especially sang of the nature of love, of the winds and seasons of love both high and low.

Dafydd's influence on the poets to follow was immense and permanent: he is still the major poet of the Welsh language. But what influenced him—what specific poems, poets, and medieval topoi were important to him and can be distinguished as formative elements in his poetry? The question of "external" influences—that is, external to Wales—has occupied scholarly study of Dafydd's poetry for most of this century. But here the situation is very different from that of Chaucer, whose sources in Latin, French, and Italian literature, a number of which he swallowed whole, have been fairly clear to see. There is no hard evidence that Dafydd knew either French or Latin (no one has suggested Italian), though his social position and historical situation make it likely that he knew at least something of both. As a lover and a poet he will refer to himself as "Ovid's man" ("dyn Ofydd") or say that he recalls "a psalm from Ovid's book" ("Salm yw 'nghof o lyfr Ofydd"). But do such allusions come directly from his reading of Ovid, from Continental intermediaries such as the *Roman de la Rose*, or from more local traditions, Anglo-Norman or Welsh, of Ovid as a love poet? Forms and motifs from the medieval European lyric tradition echo in Dafydd's verse—the dawn-song, the *sérénade*, the *pastourelle*, along with conventions of *amour courtois* such as the paradoxes of love's sweet pain, the need for secrecy in love, and the mistress's eyes as the agents and weapons of love. Again it would be good to know in specific terms—but we don't—what poems, what passages, from that wider tradition he carried in his memory and whether they came to him directly or through intermediaries of which we know nothing.

The final two chapters of *Dafydd ap Gwilym: Influences and Analogues* survey what is known and what can be surmised of such external influences. But the primary focus is elsewhere, and the rest of the book, about three-fourths of the whole, is concerned mainly with internal influences, in particular with a "submerged tradition" of popular poetry composed and transmitted by wandering minstrels, a class of Welsh jongleurs known collectively as the *Clêr*. When the Edwardian conquest of the last of the independent Welsh princes in 1282 brought to an end princely patronage for the highly trained bards and their highly formal art, they turned for support to the growing class of landed gentry, making circuits from one hall to another. In doing so, they found themselves in the company of other wandering poets and musicians, who lacked formal bardic training and the official sanction of the bardic hierarchy. References to the *Clêr* in bardic poetry, which begin to appear early in the fourteenth century, tend to be disdainful and derogatory. None of their "unofficial" poetry survives from that time. But it has seemed likely that it would have been verse more responsive to an audience desiring entertainment as well as the formalities of praise, that it would have been more open to new forms and fashions in poetry, including those from abroad, and that the work of Dafydd and his contemporaries owes much to interactions with those wandering performers.

In his opening chapters Huw Edwards gathers up in detail evidence pointing to the existence and activities of that elusive class of popular entertainers. He returns often to the point that elements which might seem clearly to have come into Welsh poetic tradition directly from classical or Continental sources could actually derive from "an established blend of native and foreign modes developed in the verse of the *Clêr*." This includes many of the innovations introduced by Dafydd and his contemporaries into the aristocratic tradition. To take just one example, where Edwards has a multitude, the poem "Dan y Bargod" ("Beneath the Eaves") is Dafydd's shivering complaint as he stands in the night before his beloved's locked door drenched by snow and rain. The form, the *sérénade*, has antecedents in Ovid and in Guillaume de Lorris, in Italian and Portuguese literature, and may have been in French popular verse as well. But it also has antecedents, Edwards suggests, in the "begging songs" of Welsh folk tradition—wassailing songs and wren-hunting songs associated with Yuletide. And it is possible that a fusion of all those traditions already existed in the subliterary verse of the *Clêr*, which provided both the basis for Dafydd's poem and the witty and ironic voice he adds to the Continental form.

Edwards points out in conclusion that Dafydd ap Gwilym, by fashioning "a new kind of poetry for a new age," enriched "not only the Welsh literary tradition but that of Western Europe as a whole." The final sentence of the book notes: "Beyond Wales, that contribution has yet to be fully appreciated." That is due in part to much of the scholarly study and critical appreciation of Dafydd's poetry having been conducted in Welsh. Publishing this book in English signals a desire to include a much wider audience in that conversation, and the book will find a place on the shelves of medievalists and others next to other recent studies sharing that aim, notably Rachel Bromwich's *Aspects of the Poetry of Dafydd ap Gwilym* (1986) and Helen Fulton's *Dafydd ap Gwilym and the European Context* (1989). Edwards has not, however, solved all the problems of addressing two audiences, and in a book dense with citation and documentation readers from that wider audience are likely to be presented with frequent minor puzzles. Key technical terms, for example, are in some cases discussed fully (*dyfalu, llatai*) and in others not at all (*awdl, cywyddau rhwystr*); quotations are supplied with translations in the text but not in the extensive notes; the mutation of initial consonants inherent to Celtic languages, which in Welsh changes *Clêr* to *Glêr*, *prydydd* (a principal bard) to *phrydydd*, or *cof* ("memory") to *nghof*, is maintained but never mentioned. Edwards's thoroughness in investigating his material and his accumulative method of argument also make it difficult at times to see the forest for the trees. What he writes of his final chapters applies to the whole: "Some of the analogues identified may appear somewhat trivial when examined in isolation, but seen in the wider context of a considerable body of cumulative evidence even the most minor parallels acquire a more powerful suggestiveness." Suggestive they are indeed, and richly so, though finally the cruel lack of concrete evidence forestalls firm conclusions. Edwards's book is a catalogue of questions rather than answers, a comprehensive gathering of things it would be wonderful to know about this marvelous poet.

ANDREW WELSH
Rutgers University

THOMAS J. FARRELL, ed. *Bakhtin and Medieval Voices.* Gainesville: University Press of Florida, 1995. Pp. xi, 240. $49.95.

Although certain theoretical paradigms prominent in the era of post-structuralism have met with decline or renewed hostility in recent years—deManian deconstruction and psychoanalysis especially—Bakhtin studies surge forward, with no sign of abatement. Thomas

J. Farrell's *Bakhtin and Medieval Voices* furnishes a variety of Bakhtinian readings of medieval texts as well as theoretical overviews on the original Bakhtinian project and its legacy in one of the first collections of its kind. The essays provide not only Bakhtinian readings of Chaucerian poetics (a domain the reader would expect to be well represented), manuscript constitution, folk entertainments, and historiography, but they also provide trenchant insights into the place of theory in contemporary medieval studies.

It was this latter feature of the volume that held especial interest for me as I read, although the theoretical and institutional self-reflection seemed at times variable among the pieces in comparison to Farrell's strident placement, in the volume's introduction, of Bakhtinian theorization in terms of our field's own circumscriptive and hierarchical character. Farrell's introduction opens by providing a clear and sensible review of some of Bakhtin's more notorious terms (*polyphony, heteroglossia, dialogism,* the *carnivalesque*) and considers their continued but often uneven utility for medieval literary studies. The volume thus seeks to shore up what turns out to be a lacuna in Bakhtin's handling of premodern cultural forms: the Middle Ages, which Bakhtin, despite our own "popular" understanding, often only gestured at or caricatured. But following these decisive judgments, the introduction only hints at the political implications of Bakhtin and medieval*ists'* voices. For instance, Farrell writes: "In several recent, relatively open discussions of the general topic of theory and medieval studies . . . calls to reform medieval studies in light of various developments in theory continue to be met with some sense that theory . . . might benefit from more familiarity with medieval studies" (p. 9). The statement, which refers to a general denigration of medieval subjects in postmodern humanistic study and to the volume's mission to help remedy this state of affairs, also describes stratified processes of marginalization *within* the field of medieval studies. That is, theory, which once served as the institutional marker of acquired cachet or cultural capital within literary study in particular and among the university disciplines in general, now can characterize a deficient sort of medievalist—one not trained well enough in the traditional areas of textual criticism, codicology, paleography, and Latin philology. Such a backlash response to the "reforming" of medieval studies itself echoes the official discourse originating from the top of the social hierarchy imagined by Bakhtin to constitute early modern or medieval society. If Bakhtinians are wont to draw parallels between the field of literary or cultural study at large and the structure of the medieval social universe, they must also be willing to see a version of that hierarchical universe among the ranks of medievalists, traditional and theoretical, in which textualists and Latinists occupy the upper echelon, critics the next level, and theorists the lowest levels.

The reformational "spirit" of the volume noted by Farrell, nonetheless, is well fostered in many of the contributions that show strong grounding in traditional interests such as manuscript studies *and* in sociological poetics. The rewarding lead essay in the volume, Andrew Taylor's "Playing on the Margins: Bakhtin and the Smithfield Decretals," rethinks Bakhtin's theories of carnival space in terms of the grotesque and ribald, marginal illuminations in the massive volume of legal formulas found in BL MS Royal 10 E. 4. Taylor reconsiders the functionalist theories of the manuscript's illuminations that have been offered by Mary Carruthers, Michael Camille, Meyer Schapiro, Emile Mâle, and others, before moving to his own appraisal of the text-illumination relationship that merges Bakhtin's dialogical theory with a historically correct review of late-medieval ethical codes concerning human vanity and *curiositas.* Taylor's analysis is fresh, demanding, and theoretically rich, especially in terms of his frequent deferral to the concept of Derridean *différance* in order to explain the modern, institutional tension between historical and dialogical readings of such images: "We should note . . . that what we might call charitable and carnivalesque readings, or Augustinian and Bakhtinian readings, while diametrically opposed, are mutually reinforcing, for each creates in the other the opposing principle that will define its own moral struggle . . ." (p. 30). Yet it's odd how Taylor ends by impugning "popular medievalists" like Victorian medievalist J. J. Jusserand, who sever manuscript images from their adjacent texts in order to "directly" illustrate what "real medieval people" were like. In a word, Jusserand's kind of mutilation represents a modern version of the sin *curiositas*—a conclusion that should strike one as anachronistic, perhaps in the way historically correct medievalists have always inveighed against those who would "apply" modern critical theory (again, psychoanalysis in the main) to premodern texts or sensibilities. The essay's conclusion might itself be taken as a retrograde but *dialogically* active response to the author's brilliant Derridean foundation were we to turn a Bakhtinian eye to Taylor's own pages—a metacritical practice that's in fact invited by his essay's ruling theme of formal "spill-over" that takes place between text and illumination, between document, scriptorium, limner workshop, and the on-going Bartholomew Fair of that actual, ever lively territory in the far eastern reaches of old London that was served by the decretals.

I've spent a good deal of time on Taylor's essay because its *own* dialogic fabric, recoverable through my metacritical inspection, seems to characterize much critical work in contemporary Bakhtin studies in general and among other, very sharp pieces in Farrell's volume in particular. Reading Bakhtinian critics by using Bakhtinian formulas should continue to prove productive (what would Bakhtin make of the polyphonic import in Thomas Farrell's muted yet excessive declaration that the Clerk's Walter is "one of the larger lumps of excrement on the planet"?). Certainly one could argue that a kind of thematic monology, an applicationalist playing-out of one big Bakhtinian theme per project, programs many a Bakhtinian "reading." Nancy Mason Bradbury's "Popular-Festive Forms and Beliefs in Robert Mannyng's *Handlyng Synne*" proffers an astute and on-target rectification of Bakhtin through the work of Aron Gurevich; but it then settles into a largely predictable presentation of laughter and irreverence in Mannyng's popular penitential treatise. Likewise, Lisa R. Perfeti's "Taking Laughter Seriously: The Comic and Didactic Functions of *Helmbrecht*" provides us "with an excellent example" of the Bakhtinian carnivalesque (p. 39); it is a thirteenth-century German tale about a peasant who masquerades as a noble and in the end suffers execution for it. Such thematic attention to social boundaries threatened by transgression also characterizes Jody L. H. McQuillan's historically illuminating essay, "Dangerous Dialogues: The *Sottie* as a Threat to Authority" (although in this case the comparison and contrast between Bakhtinian carnival and the actual French fool-play genre of the sixteenth century could have benefited from attention to some of the more recent critical work conducted directly on Bakhtin and late Middle English theatricality—in particular the research of John Ganim and Martin Stevens). Nonetheless, McQuillan has done well to grill Bakhtin for his narrow definition of "drama" as a strictly "monological" expressive form. Bakhtin, as others have concluded, draws his anachronistic description of drama from the neoclassical theatrical theory of the post-Renaissance period, and indeed I think that McQuillan could have been still harder on Bakhtin along these lines (see p. 64). In all of these essays one finds what is still the governing critical gesture in applied Bakhtin-medieval studies: the thematic idolatrization of the concepts of carnival, transgression, and laughter (see Farrell's point regarding this, discussed below).

Chaucer studies of course find the strongest representation in terms of such applicational theorization out of the Bakhtin orbit. Robert M. Jordan's essay, "Heteroglossia and Chaucer's Man of Law's Tale," makes a good argument for what has hitherto been taken as a stylistically intractable quality. The multiplicity of apostrophic utterances and digressions represent a structure of "interanimational" voices. Nonetheless, Jordan's basic operating assumption—that Geoffrey of Vinsauf's call for "mixed" poetics forms in the *Poetria Nova* and that this poetics presages Bakhtin's own prosaics (pp. 83, 88)—doesn't really take the poetic formalization of such Chaucerian material much beyond the intensive rhetorical modeling made by Robert O. Payne (to whom Jordan dedicates his essay) thirty-five years ago. Jordan, along with H. Marshall Leicester, has been one of the most productive poststructuralists to work on Chaucerian poetics. But this essay seems more a sample or a sketch of what is still needed regarding the intersection of deconstructive and dialogical poetics in contemporary medieval studies.

Steve Guthrie's "Dialogics and Prosody in Chaucer" represents an inspired and intelligent analysis of prosody and actual, or "literal" (as Guthrie asserts, p. 94), linguistic differences in Middle English poetry. Guthrie forwards useful conclusions about the structural relationship between meter (decasyllabic and pentameter) and vocabulary (French vs. English). This leads Guthrie to some bold but clever formulations such as the supposition that "Chaucer's line is ruled by energeia [sic], the animation of linguistic material in tension with a concrete metrical system based in the material itself," while "Gower's line is ruled by ergon, the submission of linguistic material to the authority of an abstract metrical system" (p. 99). Such Chaucerian energeiac (or energetic?) prosody evokes Bakhtinian dialogism, although the interaction of the energeiac and the ergonic names a consequent dialogic process. This broad declaration may sound forced, but I found Guthrie's discussion to have great relevance not only for work in prosody (which, unlike narrative, has gone virtually untouched by Bakhtinian sociological poetics), but also for more fundamental work in stylistics or even History of the English Language pedagogy (Guthrie's generalizations help us to see the semantic and phonic import of French vs. Saxon words for Middle English lexicography).

Of greater importance to me is Guthrie's insistence on the "literal" quality of his polyphonically interrelated "languages," French and English. In one of the collection's most impressive articles, titled "Medieval Authorship and the Polyphonic Text: From Manuscript Commentary to the Modern Novel," Robert J. Sturges cuts to the documentary or indeed *medial* foundation of medieval culture: the manuscript inflected by scribal, compilational, commentational, or authorial interventions. Other essays in the volume treat Bakhtinian thematics or genre (carnival and transgression; exemplary tale and epic narrative), while this essay, not unlike Guthrie's "Dialogics and Prosody in Chaucer," takes off from a literal understanding of Bakhtin's own metaphorical images of dialogue, polyphony, heteroglossia. That is, Sturges shows how "multiple, indeterminate authorship contributes to the polyphony of medieval manuscript texts; they are intertextual . . . and their authors dissolve into a multiplicity of voices in a much more *literal* fashion than is the case with any text produced in a print culture" (p. 123; emphasis added). Fitting Bakhtin's model to the Middle English version of St. Augustine's *Soliloquies* (and using important insights proffered by Gerald Bruns and Robert Hanning), Sturges makes the case quite convincingly.

Nevertheless, one has the feeling that the Bakhtinian model is always somehow heavily tailored to the medieval materials at hand. In one of the two most thoroughgoing theoretical pieces in the collection, Thomas Farrell ("The Chronotopes of Monology in Chaucer's Clerk's Tale") reviews the "applicationalist" bent of most Bakhtinian projects in medieval studies. He rightly scrutinizes the almost dogmatic critical preference to play up the thematics of carnival or dialogue (p. 141) while he champions Bakhtin's more neglected concept of the chronotope (that is, the unique and characteristic "time-space" of a particular genre—such as the wasteland/homeland geography coupled with fifty-year time demarcations in the epic text *Beowulf*). Moreover, Farrell (as in his taxonomically trenchant introduction) charts the distinctions among heteroglossia and dialogue—going so far as to indict even the most important seminal studies on Chaucerian dialogics (namely, by Lars Engle and William McClellan) completed nearly a decade ago. Farrell makes the case for a needed, more sensitized understanding of the monological in narrative poetry; his is a therapeutic response to some of Bakhtin's conceptual shortcomings.

The ongoing project of updating or correcting Bakhtin's conceptual schemes (a theoretical need already glimpsed, as I've noted, in Nancy Bradbury's essay) finds the fullest and most sophisticated expression in Mark A. Sherman's "Problems of Bakhtin's Epic: Capitalism and the Image of History." I found the comparative and overtly politicized carping about the significance of Desert Storm and Bush's New World Order to be somewhat distracting albeit lucid; but Sherman's drive to historicize Bakhtin's misrepresentation of the epic (in favor of its conceptual antinomy, the novel) succeeds well. Bakhtin's vision of epic as the cultural conduit of an "absolute past" cut off from a textual present (p. 184) really stands as the expression of the Russian theorist's own modernist sense of historical discontinuity. Sherman's thesis, one redolent of Richard Berrong's important historicizing of Bakhtin's theoretical production and the Stalinist state of privation, also finds support in his rereading of complicated intertextual moments evident even in the *Odyssey* while it secures its strongest moorings in a good reappraisal of Dante's sense of historical allegory. Clearly allegory enjoys status as a privileged, master mode in Sherman's argument (pp. 190–91, as does allegorical typology for Farrell, pp. 153–54). If Bakhtin idolatrized or fetishized the novel in his relentless description of heteroglossia, some of the more theoretically invested essays in this collection might be seen as attempts to offer other modal or generic candidates for such fetishism: allegory for Farrell and Sherman; translation for Daniel J. Pinti in "Dialogism, Heteroglossia, and Late Medieval Translation." And in all these projects—as in so much that's now produced under the Bakhtinian banner—the figurative powers inherent in how we name or use terms like "dialogue," "polyphony," or "heteroglossia" seem more than ever in need of rhetorical articulation despite the fact that such articulation continues to get skirted. This is why I harped above on the "literal" use of Bakhtin's terms in the opening polemics of the essays by Sturges and Guthrie. Although we see gestures in Farrell and Sherman toward mediating between the legacy of deconstruction (now much in institutional disrepute) and Bakhtinian dialogics (still on the ascent), the need to account for one's literal or figural use of Bakhtin's highly figural, artificial conceptual categories is greater than ever—particularly for the study of medieval texts and culture.

In closing, I assert that this theoretical implication in no way disables or diminishes the effectiveness of what is an outstanding volume;

I merely speak to the future of Bakhtin and medieval studies. I truly enjoyed and was provoked by all of these essays. This volume represents a very rich and powerful combination of theory and credentialed medieval scholarship in an age when both medieval studies and theory are under attack. The proponents of posttheory (neobelletrists, some bodytheorists and queer theorists, neopragmatists and neoappreciationists) and the long-cavilling, antitheory proponents of conservative medieval studies have a volume in *Bakhtin and Medieval Voices* that should challenge, irk, and I hope win them. I sincerely believe that this collection of new essays can have the impact of the now infamous 1990 issue of *Speculum* on the "New Philology." That collection, felicitously cited by Farrell in his smart introduction, provided one of the first workable fusions of theory and traditional, textualism-centered medieval studies. I think that *Bakhtin and Medieval Voices* does the same. Anybody interested in Bakhtin, theory, the literature of the later Middle Ages, and medieval documentary materials should likewise value this volume.

JAMES J. PAXSON
University of Florida

JUDITH FERSTER. *Fictions of Advice: The Literature and Politics of Counsel in Late Medieval England.* Middle Ages Series. Philadelphia: University of Pennsylvania Press, 1996. Pp. xii, 216. $32.95.

The "Mirror for Princes" has often been thought of as an inert genre, in which complaisant scholar-lackeys, whether under solicitation or not, would give princes advice that it was not too painful for them to hear. Be wise and prudent, listen to faithful advisors, keep your promises—these and other similarly bromide exhortations are easy to acquiesce in, it would seem, and impinge little on the actual business of governing. It is the great merit of Judith Ferster's new book that it challenges these easy and self-indulgent assumptions, and makes one think again about some familiar materials. It is not suggested that the writers of these works were brave radicals with original views on the conduct of government policy who were prepared to risk the displeasure of princes, but rather that there was some equilibrium between power and provocation. The prince would do what he would, but he could do it more successfully and for longer if he showed himself receptive to advice; and there might even develop some consensus about what constituted good government in which other interests than the prince's might be given weight.

So Professor Ferster is prepared to find more in these works of advice than has usually been recognized in the past. "The mirrors for princes are not only more topical than they appear to be but also more critical of the powerful than we might expect" (p. 3). Her book examines a series of such works in order to historicize them more fully, to show how their use of familiar materials is often strategically selective, with readjustments of emphasis that would have had important contemporary relevance and impact. She is interested in "the hermeneutics of camouflaged texts" (p. 4), in the possibility of resistance to apparently monolithically powerful regimes, and in arguments against the Foucauldian view that opposition is always co-opted. She is interested in the systems of encoding by which opposition and dissent can be communicated without offending those in power or without provoking repression. Ambiguity is one technique; the use of historical examples, made safe by distance, another. Professor Ferster discusses the kind of political discourse that was possible in late medieval England, when there was no legally enforced censorship (except, it might be noted, of heretical writings), but when authority exercised the usual pressures and constraints upon writers. She emphasizes the growth in the sense that there was a "commonwealth" in which all had a stake and, with the spread of the means of disseminating information, the development of a "political class" that might be interested in its nature and welfare.

Chapters 3–5 introduce the *Secretum Secretorum*, the germinal text for the mirrors for princes, and some of the versions of it that found their way into English, including the translation done by James Yonge in 1422 for the earl of Ormonde. Professor Ferster uncovers some of the self-contradictions within the genre—to govern well, the king must be "well-governed," and to be advised well he must be "well-advised" on whom he takes as his advisors—and recognizes how the stories that are used as exempla may slip and slide (even before they are pushed by modern scholars) and betray their ostensible purpose. But she is prepared always to find a significance in these works, and an interesting mixture of "deference and challenge" in their approach to their admittedly tricky task. She thinks they were influential in history, not so much in the influencing of events as in providing a language in which vulnerable parties could talk about the real business of governing. The issue is one of the greatest importance: how is a prince to select his closest counselors, and what control is to be placed upon his choice? Mirrors for princes were not exactly consulted on these matters, but their language and their "tropes of advice" were a way of talking about policy—or at least a way of not talking about it, of obscuring or encoding in conventional platitudes ("the king's advisors are to blame") what was really happening and being decided.

These first five chapters are a very good beginning. As she showed in her earlier book, *Chaucer on Interpretation* (1985), Professor Ferster is at her best in giving lucid and perceptive summary accounts of broad historical issues and current critical and theoretical practice. She makes generous acknowledgement of the work of previous scholars, but she has her own views to put forward, and offers a nice mixture of "deference and challenge" in her interpretation of the tradition of the mirror for princes.

The last four chapters are on Chaucer's *Melibee*, book 7 of Gower's *Confessio Amantis*, Hoccleve's *Regement of Princes*, and Machiavelli's *The Prince*. These chapters work less well, though there are valuable insights, as for instance in the demonstration of how Rehoboam is picked up from the *Fürstenspiegel* as a way of coding criticism of a king for surrounding himself with immature advisors. The problem is that of the three main approaches Professor Ferster takes to the English works, two work only fitfully and one not at all. She claims that the works, when investigated closely, can be shown to contain topical allusions—but these are rarely clear or specific. They are said to be more outspoken than we thought—but the deference is still deafening, the challenge at most a whisper. The argument that the three works are further interesting in that they "deconstruct the paradigms of advice" seems to me inconsequential. For instance, it is claimed that *Melibee* is ambiguous and self-contradictory in its recommendations about making war and taking advice because the historical circumstances in which it was written were ambiguous on these issues. Thus "deconstruction and historicism can work together" (p. 106). There is something touching here in the desire for rapprochement, but the idea works no better then the sentence.

It will occur to some that the chapters on "fictions of advice" in the English poets are about works of theirs that have customarily been regarded as dull, or at least markedly less interesting than the rest of their output: most readers, for instance, have enjoyed the long, chatty Prologue to the *Regement* much more than the actual advice to princes.

Judith Ferster shows how a good book can now be written on the historical importance of works that had previously been deemed dull, even explaining why they had to be dull in the first place. They do not become any less dull in themselves, but what can be written about them becomes, by substitution, more interesting.

DEREK PEARSALL
Harvard University

PAMELA GRADON and ANNE HUDSON, eds. *English Wycliffite Sermons.* Vols. 4 and 5. Oxford: Clarendon Press, 1996. Pp. 333 and 443. $110.00 and $125.00.

Originally planned as a single volume (see vol. 1: 6–7), these two volumes bring to some kind of conclusion the herculean task of editing the English Wycliffite sermon-cycle. They provide the much-needed commentary on the individual 240 sermons (and two related texts) edited in the first three volumes, part of which is presented as a long, separate section dealing with the polemical issues of Lollard teaching disseminated throughout the cycle. The culmination, though not the end, of an important scholarly project, these volumes constitute an indispensable *vade mecum* to a certain kind of Wycliffite thinking in the vernacular. That there are only just over three pages of *corrigenda* to volumes 1–3 suggests an extremely high level of initial accuracy in transcription and in application of editing policy. The same level of accuracy is carried through in the erudite, judicious, and thoroughly reliable commentary.

Volume 4 opens with a comprehensive discussion of matters of date (before 1400, and probably nearer 1390), authorship, and audience. The editors reconsider the claims of Wyclif and Purvey, the previous candidates, for author, but submit that the writer was anonymous: someone in orders, probably in the university, and with intellectual interests. Displaying little concern for the *pastoralia*, the sermons interestingly draw on the commentary, rather than sermon, tradition. Their brevity also hints at extraliturgical use. The editors conclude that the English cycle belongs to the same production method (collaborative, with horizontal rather than vertical division of labor) as the Wycliffite Bible, *Glossed Gospel* commentaries, and the *Floretum* and *Rosarium* handbooks.

The valuable discussion of polemical issues isolates the sermons' recurrent doctrinal preoccupations with matters such as penance and oral confession, and cites the most favoured locutions in which these discussions are framed. A number of new terms emerge from this present study, providing a useful addition to Hudson's earlier work on Lollard sect vocabulary: for example, *rownyng* (p. 45), pejoratively, "oral confession"; *fable(s)* (pp. 81–82), as opposed to the truth of Scripture; and *prelat* (pp. 103–11). As might be expected, saints are held in low esteem; preaching is essential; the true church is the congregation of *predestinati;* the papacy, church hierarchy (especially cardinals), temporalities, sects, and sins of the clergy are condemned; and the authority of Scripture is absolute (there is useful matter here for those interested in issues of translation, for the discussion touches on the distinction between the material "ink and skin" and the transcendent *sentence*). The sermons reflect Wyclif's later teaching on the Eucharist and show widespread concern for the poor, but contain little discussion of dominion or the status of the ranks in civil society. Comments on war are mainly focused on the Despenser crusade, led by Bishop Henry Despenser of Norwich on behalf of Urban VI, and condemned by Wyclif. There is a dominant concern for persecution.

The notes on the individual sermons, which begin in volume 4 and take up nearly all of volume 5, are scrupulous and yet economical, their two prime purposes being to elucidate obscurities in the text and to point out parallels with Wyclif's Latin sermons and his other writings. Unavoidably, ambiguities remain: for example, the meaning of *schap* in 23 / 55 is not obvious in context. A number of important revisions to *MED* entries are offered in the commentary, but since there is no glossary this information must be retrieved somewhat laboriously from the notes. That the commentary also provides evidence of theological commonplaces and ultimate patristic sources incidentally implies that the radicalism of Wycliffite thinking in the vernacular resides not so much in its complete overturning of the cornerstones of theological belief but rather in its tweaking of the borders of the orthodox.

Volume 5 also contains an "Index to Biblical References in Texts and Commentary"; a key to "Short Texts in Four Collections" (to facilitate identification of material frequently cited by Hudson and Gradon but not commonly available in libraries: from Loserth's edition of Wyclif's *Opera minora*; Buddensieg's of the *Polemical Works*; Arnold's *Select English Works*; and Matthews' *English Works of Wyclif*); *corrigenda* to volumes 1–3; a table of all the sermons (listing number, occasion, and lection); and a rather short bibliography, regretfully containing "only those works which are repeatedly cited, not those only referred to once." The "Index to Biblical References" is invaluable, allowing the reader to identify at a glance the use and frequency of Bible quotations in the English Wycliffite oeuvre, and to compare them with those in non-Wycliffite material. However, the information that "E" stands for the Set 5 Sunday Epistle Sermons (1:7) would bear repeating, both in this index and in the list of abbreviations. These indexes are the counterpart of medieval *florilegia*, insofar as they are devices to aid the retrieval of complex data: the printed book equivalent of the modern computer. Many of the features of these volumes—and of the project as a whole—will be *desiderata* for future editors of medieval sermons and theological works.

With such an ambitious project, it is inevitable that there are a few confusions, especially in the cross-referencing between the volumes: for example, the section in volume 5, "Index to Sermons Mentioned in Chapters 1–2," refers to those chapters in volume 4, to the sermons in volumes 1–3, and to the commentary that is distributed across volumes 4 and 5. Information about the two texts known as *Of Mynystris in þe Chirche* and *Vae Octuplex*, which have justifiable claims to be considered part of the cycle (they are edited in vol. 2), has to be unearthed from volume 1, and might have been worth repeating in the "Plan of the Present Edition" at the beginning of each volume.

In the editors' words, the appearance of these final two volumes "marks a staging post but not a completion," and thus provides an opportunity to cast one's eye back over the project, something both editors would undoubtedly encourage. Given that these compendious, exorbitantly expensive, and scholarly volumes effectively canonize their material, it is useful to remember what the edition excludes, as well as includes. Even though the cycle was produced before the use of English became specifically associated with heresy, it is somewhat curious, given Hudson's earlier assertion that "there is . . . a sense in which it may not be unreasonable to claim lollardy as the heresy of the vernacular, the English heresy,"[1] that these volumes nowhere discuss the role and politics of the vernacular in the last decade of the fourteenth century. It is therefore worth reminding the reader that the sermon-cycle was an elite, academic production, its organization suggesting large-scale financial and intellectual effort, but promulgating after all only one

[1] Anne Hudson, "Lollardy: The English-Heresy?" in *Lollards and Their Books* (London and Ronceverte, W.Va.: Hambledon Press, 1985), pp. 141–63; quotation from p.163.

kind of Lollard vernacular thinking. The so-called "derivatives" of the Wycliffite sermons, such as the series in Lambeth Palace Library 392 and CUL Additional 5338 (see 1: 106–10), may represent not so much derivatives (with all that implies of secondariness and inferiority) as independent vernacular productions, reworking Lollard material in different contexts and for nonacademic audiences. There is in fact a large category of Middle English works, including the set of eighteen sermons in BL Addit. 41321, Bodleian MS Rawlinson C.751 and John Rylands MS English 412, edited by Gloria Cigman,[2] that seem Lollard in attitude though not in every point of doctrine. The appearance of these current volumes signals the time for a reappraisal of the relationship of the vernacular "derivative" productions to the English cycle, and of the nature and trajectory of Lollard thinking in the fifteenth century.

Scholars will gratefully use this extremely reliable edition for the further study of what Nicholas Watson describes as "the tangled history of Lollard thought."[3] The impeccably high standard of scholarship and presentation makes this superb edition a monument of modern philology that will not be surpassed in the foreseeable future.

RUTH EVANS
University of Wales, Cardiff

MICHAELA PAASCHE GRUDIN. *Chaucer and the Politics of Discourse.* Columbia: University of South Carolina Press, 1996. Pp. ix, 200. $29.95.

Michaela Paasche Grudin's engaging and intriguing book appears at a time when Bakhtinian theory is increasingly deployed by feminist, Marxist, and cultural studies critics in the academy. Such work is also becoming more nuanced and sophisticated; where Bakhtin was once cited mostly for the concepts of carnival and folk laughter familiar

---

[2] Gloria Cigman, ed., *Lollard Sermons*, Early English Text Society, vol. 294. (Oxford: Oxford University Press, 1989.)

[3] Nicholas Watson, "Censorship and Cultural Change in Late-Medieval England: Vernacular Theology, the Oxford Translation Debate, and Arundel's Constitutions of 1409," *Speculum* 70 (1995): 822–64.

from the relatively late *Rabelais and His World*, critics now draw on discussions of stylistics, discourse, and genre developed throughout his career. Using a nominally Bakhtinian vocabulary, Grudin's book joins this trend, tracing "Chaucer's concern with discourse," "his perennial interest in talk, talkers, and dialogue" (p. 1), in the *Book of the Duchess*, *Parliament of Fowls*, *House of Fame* (chapter 2), *Troilus and Criseyde* (chapter 3), and several *Canterbury Tales* (chapters 4–9).

Grudin offers several important contexts for Chaucer's interest in the power and possibilities of speech. The first is the "still-oral culture of England," where "talk . . . could be expected to have almost instant practical significance, psychological, social, and political" (p. 2). Second, Chaucer's "almost intuitive yoking of language, character, and experience" (p. 2) parallels humanist debates by Dante, Petrarch, and Boccaccio about speech as a political instrument, an active demonstration of virtue and citizenship. Third, Chaucer possesses a "sense of the critical nature of discourse (and its political character)" that is "radical" and "dramatically timely" (p. 20) when, during Richard II's reign, "severe and arbitrary restrictions on the spoken word both in the city and in the court" (p. 20) were imposed. Its radicalism lies in Chaucer's willingness to give speech untrammeled scope: Grudin asks if "at a time when free speech was severely threatened, Chaucer found a way to sponsor it through the agency of dialogue, thus working with an instrument which is potentially subversive to all authority?" (p. 25).

The author's analysis is shaped by "[t]he dialogic mode—with its questions, disputes, pretensions, and misunderstandings" (p. 19). Grudin uses "dialogic" and "dialogical" throughout "to describe discourse as an interaction, whether actual or implied, between speaker and listener," citing Bakhtin's essay "Discourse in the Novel" (p. 19 and n. 37). Using the dialogic mode, Chaucer "repeatedly explores the ways in which speech refuses to be prescribed and contained" (p. 20). His unique contribution, surpassing the humanists, is his awareness that in the endless play of dialogic exchange, closure is "all but impossible," "only one feature of a whole poetic that is at bottom dialogic and social" (p. 181).

Grudin's methodology and the contexts outlined above all suggest tantalizing possibilities for understanding the place of speech in late medieval English cultures, and how writers like Chaucer might negotiate the political and social through their fictions of discourse. Yet these possibilities remain largely undeveloped; Grudin seems most comfortable with the notion of Chaucer as humanist, recalling the trecento milieu most often. Fascinating observations about, for example, constructions of identity within a largely oral culture (p. 43), or how the Wife of Bath's *Prologue* "embod[ies] the struggles inherent in discourse, particularly . . . between the prevailing ideology and the forces that question it" (p. 100), are raised almost as throwaway comments. Asseverations of the "political reverberations" (p. 55) of texts are alluded to, without exploring what, precisely, these reverberations might be. Grudin seems to get boxed into thematic readings that report how characters in individual tales or poems address and answer each other, explicating "the integrity of speech and action" (p. 15), which sounds much like the familiar question of *entente*.

The real strengths of this study are Grudin's undeniably attentive and sensitively detailed readings, particularly of *The Knight's Tale*, *The Monk's Tale*, and *The Manciple's Tale*. Yet even these would have been enriched by a deeper and more sustained use of Bakhtin, of work outside medieval studies (such as *Feminism, Bakhtin, and the Dialogic*, ed. Dale M. Bauer and Susan Jaret McKinstry [Albany, NY: SUNY Press, 1991]), and by medievalists Lars Engle, William McClellan, and Daniel Pinti. The brief mention of dialogism already noted (p. 19) is the first of only two occasions where Bakhtinian terminology is explored, even briefly. Relying on this single quotation from Bakhtin to define the operative construct of her study, Grudin's arguments about dialogism seem tentative and, I would suggest, narrower than Bakhtin himself intended. Bakhtin developed several terms to describe the ideological uses of language: human language is made up of a wide variety of registers, vocabularies, and discourses (*heteroglossia*); a text may present multiple subjectivities, including the author's (*polyphony*); *dialogism*, an important stylistic and social construct in "Discourse in the Novel," "implies genuine exchange of ideas between different people or different kinds of ideas."[1] Writing about discourse in the novel, Bakhtin also suggested the kind of analysis needed:

. . . in order to understand such dialogue, or even to become aware initially that a dialogue is going on at all, mere knowledge of the linguistic and stylistic profile of the languages involved will be insufficient: what is needed is a profound understanding of each language's socio-ideological meaning and an exact

---

[1] Thomas J. Farrell, "Introduction: Bakhtin, Liminality, and Medieval Literature," in *Bakhtin and Medieval Voices*, ed. Thomas J. Farrell (Gainesville: University Press of Florida, 1995), pp. 1–14; quotation on p. 3. The brief summary of heteroglossia and polyphony draws on Farrell, pp. 2–3.

knowledge of the social distribution and ordering of all the other ideological voices of the era.[2]

There is certainly room in this compact study for such an examination. There are but 182 pages of text, not excluding the lengthy footnotes and copious quotations from Chaucer (in the mediated voice of the Riverside edition). Some chapters are inexplicably short and/or end abruptly: chapters 4 and 7 on the *Knight's Tale* and *Monk's Tale* are barely thirteen and fourteen pages, respectively; a lengthy chapter on *Troilus* stops short while raising the political implications of credulity to refer the reader to an earlier chapter. Chapter 5 on the Wife of Bath's *Prologue* is largely descriptive, despite a provocative opening that analyzes punishments meted out to verbally unruly medieval women (pp. 97–99).

It is a book perhaps overcareful to acknowledge its intellectual debts; Grudin takes great pains to distinguish her ideas from those of previous critics, often employing substantial quotations to demonstrate her points. Primary sources are (nearly always) cited extensively in the original and in translation. Such tactics are laudable in their fairmindedness and scholarly meticulousness, but the voices of Chaucer and the critics become a distracting chorus threatening to drown out the author and her ideas. I would have liked to have heard much more—in her voice.

MARY F. GODFREY
Fordham University

BARBARA A. HANAWALT and DAVID WALLACE, eds. *Bodies and Disciplines: Intersections of Literature and History in Fifteenth-Century England.* Medieval Culture Series, vol. 9. Minneapolis and London: University of Minnesota Press, 1996. Pp. xii, 242. $49.95 cloth, $19.95 paper.

This book is essentially a proceedings volume from a 1993 conference at the University of Minnesota. That occasion brought together five literary scholars and five historians in the hope that the intersections of their shared discourse would lead to greater insight not just into the

---

[2] Mikhail Bakhtin, "Discourse in the Novel," in *The Dialogic Imagination*, ed. Michael Holquist, trans. Caryl Emerson and Michael Holquist (Austin: University of Texas Press, 1981), pp. 259–422; quotation on p. 417.

writings and realities of the later medieval period, but also—and potentially much more importantly—into the ways in which their two
disciplines could best contribute to that end. If that hope thus provided
the subtitle for the present collection, it seems potentially ominous that
Ralph Hanna's first chapter should start things off with the less-than-
optimistic observation that in a modern highway system intersections
are likely to prove the frequent site of "collisions and accidents, often of
the mortal variety (p.1)." Happily, though, conference respondent Paul
Strohm uses the book's "Afterward" to close on a more hopeful note, one
that stresses that in the medieval experience such intersections were
much more often, and surely more congenially, "a *carrefour*: a crossroad
or market square, a place where roads converge and persons with different origins and destinations tarry for purposes of acquaintance and
exchange (p. 223)." Between these two extremes come nine other essays
or chapters, each of which serves to illustrate the metaphorical truth of
either the Hanna or the Strohm thesis—and sometimes both.

If the work manages to cover a wide range of topics, the subjects discussed appear to have been selected with an interdisciplinary focus in
mind. That is, one suspects that students of literature could endlessly
address the uses of metaphor without provoking a historical response
just as historians could explore the niceties of the wool staple without
eliciting much literary reaction. Such purely disciplinary concerns are
avoided here presumably because they would not have encouraged the
kind of mutual exploration that was the original conference's intent, the
kind of dialogue out of which adherents of each discipline would come
better to understand not only what the other had to offer on its own
terms, but also how that discipline could fruitfully be employed to enrich the understandings of their own.

In practice, however, the literary critics speak much more frequently
to that intent than do the historians (and that is a comment made by
one who has long professed both History and Comparative Literature).
The problem, of course, is that whereas contemporary literary studies
place great emphasis on theory, much of it stressing the indeterminacy
of texts, in most instances history does no such thing. Rather, for the
most part its practitioners continue to assume that theirs is a world of
fact, not fictions, and hence that the past has some kind of objective reality. That belief makes their first task one of determining what "the
true facts" are, and, because facts are facts, or so they allege, they tend
violently to reject any objections posed by mere theory. Only in the next
stage, the creation of historical narrative, are they willing to admit the

possibility that the very process of selecting the supposedly important facts—and then of searching out (some would say inventing) the patterns to which they give rise—may be purely interpretive and hence subject to all the uncertainties that modern theory has brought to the study of literature. Thus, even though the historian's factual knowledge is usually derived from texts, scholars of history are likely to respond to theories of textual indeterminacy much as the very literary Dr. Johnson did to Bishop Berkeley's doubts about the universe: not with reasoned logic, but with a swift and vigorous kick. Purely rhetorical though such kicks may be, they are not the stuff out of which fruitful interdisciplinary dialogue is likely to arise.

That observation goes far beyond what any historian claims explicitly here, but the tendency is surely present and goes far toward explaining why *Bodies and Disciplines* is a book in which the literary types have more useful things to say to the historians than those historians have to say in return. For example, in "Brewing Trouble: On Literature and History—and Alewives," Ralph Hanna takes on what he calls "the fine historical work" of Judith Bennett, in particular the way it uses specifics taken from the fictive texts of literature to document what she insists were the misogynistic realities actually experienced by all alewives. Deconstructing these texts as most literary critics would, Hanna soon arrives at rather different conclusions, much more tentative and far less misogynistic.

Whether Hanna is right in his own views about "the tavern as feminized space (p. 1)" matters much less than does his theoretical point, one that should concern all historians, not just Bennett; she is, after all, hardly alone in her willingness to employ literature as a source of historical information. Without such usage, most social history as we now know it would become little more than a pale imitation of its former self. In illustration of the point, all one has to do is to consider what would happen to the work of Barbara Hanawalt, when, in chapter 8, "'The Childe of Bristowe' and the Making of Middle-Class Adolescence," she argues: "The game of exchange between the literary and the historical leads to a fifteenth-century construction of adolescence (p. 155)." Given the claims of earlier historians that adolescence was purely a modern invention, that is potentially an enormously significant conclusion, but it would fade into nothingness were she and every other historian to be denied all use of the literary.

That, obviously, was not Hanna's intent. Rather, his call was more for a historical methodology not blindly insensitive to the nuanced uncertainties inherent in the literary enterprise. That, surely, is not too much to ask. At the same time, though, whether historians respond or not, *Bodies and Disciplines* suggests that as literary studies move more fully to embrace the new historicism, they would do well to ponder the extent to which modern approaches to texts may have undermined the uses to which they put historical findings or, conversely, the extent to which the way they use those findings may implicitly suggest certain caveats about when and where indeterminacy is to be found. That is, as more than a few of the book's chapters demonstrate, new historicists tend to claim that their readings take on added dimensions and depth when the literature with which they are concerned is placed in its proper historical context. Thus, to illustrate, in "Ritual, Theater, and Social Space in the York Corpus Christi Cycle" Sarah Beckwith is at pains to show the extent to which particular scenes take on added resonance when the reader or viewer is made fully aware of just where in York those scenes were meant to be performed: what buildings stood in close proximity, what people either dwelt or worked therein, and what other people one might have expected to encounter outside of them at the time when the plays were written.

As Beckwith's notes demonstrate, these points depend either on her own research into the relevant historical records or on information to be found in works by modern historians. In other words, to make this argument she is proceeding very much as any historian would and, in so doing, she is privileging certain text-based claims as though they were objective facts, the existence of which cannot be brought into doubt through use of the usual deconstructive techniques. Nor is she wrong in so doing, the point being that some facts are more equal than other facts, an Orwellian distinction that both historians and literary critics can all too often overlook, to the detriment of their work. But the shadings here *are* difficult. When a historian states that John was the third of the Plantagenet kings, most people are likely to accept that claim as fact even though they may know that "Plantagenet" was a term introduced only later. On the other hand, while A. A. Milne's proposition— "King John was not a good man / He had his little ways"—may attract the same kind of near-universal acceptance, its existence as a fact is much more problematic because John's character is purely a humanly observed attribute and therefore a subject of at least potential debate. That makes its objective reality much more tenuous than John's numerical position among the Plantagenets, a position that cannot be changed by differing attitudes toward the man. Clearly, too, Beckwith's specifics about fifteenth-century York partake of this same kind of meta-attitudinal facticity.

What these musings suggest is that, maddeningly unreflective though historians can be, their very pragmaticism may have correctives to offer to what one may confidently assume most students of history see as the excesses of modern theoretical assumptions about the nature of texts that, like Bishop Berkeley, can come dangerously close to denying extramental existence in its entirety. This is, however, a Johnsonian subject on which the five historians of *Bodies and Disciplines* are disappointingly silent. Although reviewers are always supposed to review the book before them, not the one that they might have preferred, in the present instance it seems clear that if each chapter from one discipline had been followed by a direct comment from the other, participants and readers alike would have better been able to see the ways in which history and literary studies operating in tandem can produce more lastingly fruitful results than can either of them working in splendid isolation. In short, Hanna's fatality-strewn intersection would have truly become Strohm's life-enhancing *carrefour*.

CHARLES T. WOOD
Dartmouth College

RALPH HANNA III. *Pursuing History: Middle English Manuscripts and Their Texts. Figurae*: Reading Medieval Culture Series. Stanford, Calif.: Stanford University Press, 1996. Pp. x, 362. $39.50.

SETH LERER, ed. *Literary History and the Challenge of Philology: The Legacy of Erich Auerbach. Figurae*: Reading Medieval Culture Series. Stanford: Stanford University Press, 1996. Pp. xii, 301. $45.00.

Pursuing history or challenging history: what's your preference? And is there a difference, for may not any pursuit be also a challenge? Two books, both in the same Stanford series on "reading medieval culture" (with, in the case of Lerer's collection, the added rhetorical convenience that the series uses the same trope of tropes—*figura*—that provoked and animated the career of Erich Auerbach); two books examining the function of history and historiography at a time when it has again become critically fashionable to do so; two books that are both *collectanea* or *florilegia*, bibliographical emulations of the medieval book itself—one organized around the actual writings of one of our most distinguished living textuists and bibliographers, and the other commemorating and evaluating the ongoing presence of a textuist of an earlier generation. Any reviewer, any reader, of these two books together is tempted to ask: did Auerbach make Hanna and his works possible? And/or, more provocatively: is Hanna our current Auerbach? And does the fact that both authors write from an acknowledged *situatedness*—a specific time and place that selfconsciously uses that individual awareness of occupying a particular moment in the cumulative history of textuality—mean that both books can be seen as celebrations of what has elsewhere become known as a "personalist" criticism, so that Auerbach's having written *Mimesis* in Istanbul as a Jewish exile from Nazi Germany is a proper critical precursor to Hanna's opening anecdote of his linguistically tolerant father and of his later having "set up shop as an anti-Chaucerian" (p. 2)?

Consider just some of the autobiographical and polemical contexts provided for Hanna's writings: his determination to "abandon" the "canonical Chaucer [of] the Robinson *Works*" (p. 5); his attacks on the "historical repression" of Chaucerian editors who "denied that [Chaucer's] text had a history of circulation" (p. 4); his acknowledgement that his desire to see medieval books as "fluid, developing entities" has become "almost a fetish" in his work (p. 7); his admission that the six Chaucerian essays are "studies I should have preferred not to have undertaken" (p. 14) but that he had to capitulate to the "inevitability" of Chaucer's "ipsissima verba," just as Shakespeare bestrides the world of later bibliographical work; his acceptance of the Bloomian view of the necessary and "aggressive" killing of the precursor, who in his case is identified as Derek Pearsall, "whose presence I must remove to construct my version of medieval literature" (p. 15). Are not these and many other signs of Hanna's presence in his codicological, textual, and editorial scholarship a recognition that even good old dryasdust philology cannot shelter behind the positivist, objective claims made for it in earlier bibliographical dispensations and evidence that it is as susceptible to autobiographical involvement as any other form of critical discourse? And did not Auerbach pave the way for Hanna's ability to do this?

Of course, I have already shown my own critical sympathies by labeling "philology" as a "discourse" rather than a hard rock of technological security. And I would have to admit that many of the *topics* announced in Hanna's book especially ("The Origins and Production of

Westminster School MS.3," "Two Lollard Codices and Lollard Book Production," "The Hengwrt Manuscript and the Canon of *The Canterbury Tales*," "The Practice of Annotation") might seem to have that rhetorically self-effacing positivism that codicology and bibliography together have traditionally espoused. But while I would not characterize such methods of announcing topics as a critical feint—a device to lead the reader to expect that such techniques as bibliographical description are not amenable to overt critical intervention—I do think the fact that, for example, a) the "Origins" essay contains an attack on dialect maps for not recognizing the effects of migration of scribes (p. 45), b) the "Lollard" essay speculates on the bibliographical effects of "illegal, heretical texts" most likely having been copied in "quasi-clandestine circumstances" (p. 56), c) the "Hengwrt" essay, in its witty distinction between "hard" and "soft" Hengwrtism, addresses the limitations and inevitable anomalies of the descriptive bibliography that supposedly underwrites much of what Hanna appears to be discussing, and d) the "annotation" essay is full of images of "invasion" and authorial "imprisonment" (p. 262), attacks on "ordinary annotation" for being "limp, disconnected, and relatively pointless because of one basic premise it is designed to fulfil: never interpret" (p. 265): all of this and much more is an indication that the modesty? reticence? of Hanna's announced titles does not fully prepare one for the animation, forcefulness, and even polemic of his arguments. And if this is true of the apparently neutrally titled pieces, imagine *a fortiori* how much this animation and speculative edge take over in essays on "Authorial Versions, Rolling Revision, Scribal Error? Or, the Truth about *Truth*," "Producing Manuscripts and Editions," "On the Versions of *Piers Plowman*," or "Presenting Chaucer as Author." Each of these essays contains critical and interpretive riches too numerous even to list here, but the *Piers* essay can be a useful exemplum.

After a brief introduction on the recent history of the *Piers* debate (A, B, C, or a continuously evolving text), Hanna begins with what might at first seem a very dry (indeed "dryasdust") piece on the Ilchester Prologue, full of lists of collations of variants and so on. Ho-hum for those not addicted to tabulations of *lectiones variantes*. A decision *not* to investigate the authoriality of the famous Hophni and Phineas passage in C seems to confirm this refusal to speculate. Even in the next section of the essay, on the R and F manuscripts of B (R includes 180 unique lines not attested elsewhere in the B version), Hanna retains his restrained tone, commenting on the critical issues involved in Skeat's characterization of R as transitional (p. 215) and in Kane and Donaldson's rejection of this thesis (p. 219), largely because they wished to maintain their position that "[i]n no case did Langland craft a version intermediate between B and C" (p. 219). When Hanna then presents the Athlone editors' argument in stemmatic form (p. 223), only to displace this with a two-stage diagram of his own—in which the conventional "tree" form of the stemma is avoided (p. 224)—we may begin to suspect that something is up.

Developing his critique of the necessity for Kane-Donaldson to "protect the integrity of the B manuscript tradition" (p. 226), Hanna then launches into a thirteen-page conclusion of "Thoughts on the Development of Langland's Poem" that not only provides us with his own thesis (that "[t]he poem began, I am reasonably certain, in a tolerably conventional alliterative mode, as a single-vision satire of contemporary conditions" [p. 232], but that its author temporarily lost control over its meaning and dissemination, and therefore sought to "protect his poem against its social consumption by constructing [a] textual overlay as a universal reading experience" [p. 241]) but also raises a range of issues, from John Ball's co-option of Piers in the Peasants' Revolt (p. 240), to the presence of a "London coterie" with a "legal" interest in the topics of the poem (p. 236), to relations of his scenario for *Piers* production to that of Chaucer's *Legend* and the *Troilus*. This last section is a dizzying tour de force of original, highly provocative, and intellectually stirring argument, but an argument that arises directly out of the close (even dense) analysis of codicological features in the first three quarters of the essay. That is, Hanna "pursues" history first by acting as the traditional bibliographer, carefully describing and sifting the documentary evidence; but then he artfully puts this evidence to the test in the attempt to critically "capture" history, if only for our current cultural moment. In so doing he is addressing the challenge he perceives in his introduction, that there is a "serious fault line" between those who are "chiefly interested in books qua books" and who seem "primarily interested in description for its own sake" and those literary scholars who "viewed any bow to the physical volumes as something of a nuisance . . . a formality to be dispensed with" (p. 6). Hanna's scholarly career has been largely devoted to bridging that fault line, to constructing a single "discourse" in which literary "history" is pursued, but it is pursued through an acknowledgement of and even fervor for the bibliographical artifact in which that history is to be found. This book is testimony to his success in building that bridge.

The bridge to be built by the contributors to Lerer's collection might not immediately seem to be across the "fault line" separating literary historians and bibliographers (though Lerer insists on the centrality of textual criticism to Auerbach's general cultural project). But while the bridge directly confronted by this volume is obviously the "legacy" of Auerbach—and specifically the way that *Mimesis* has been both co-opted and misappropriated by the scholarly community—the axis of the book is not simply chronological: this is what Auerbach did in his own moment; this is what we have inherited. For just as Hanna embeds his speculative and interpretive criticism in a philological analysis that is acutely aware of the significance of the concrete artifact as cultural icon, so Lerer takes it as his mission in his volume to emphasize "Auerbach's more subtle and complex adjudications between literary history and philology" and thus to "redress somewhat [the] critical imbalance" whereby Auerbach's main inheritance has been seen within the more conventional terms of the philological duty (and power) to separate truth from falsity and "the authentic from the ersatz" (p. 3). It is not that these tasks of a discipline and a disposition that Jonathan Culler has dismissively labeled "foundationalist" philology ("Antifoundational Philology," *On Philology*, ed. Jan Ziolkowski [University Park: Pennsylvania State University Press, 1990]) should be discarded or disabled, but rather that the sort of commentary dominating Lerer's collection is testimony to a philological and interpretive model that Culler misidentifies as "anti-foundationalist." The basic thesis of Lerer's volume is thus to place in high relief the hermeneutic rather than the "prehermeneutic" nature of Auerbachian philology, and therefore to offer a corrective to such misapprehensions as Paul de Man's claim that in a "return to philology" we encounter a text shorn of that personal, cultural, and interpretive baggage that belletristic criticism is guilty of ("The Return to Philology," *The Resistance to Theory* [Minneapolis: University of Minnesota Press, 1988]).

Now, in the interests of full disclosure, I will admit that neither Culler nor de Man are singled out in Lerer's introduction or in the volume at large as exemplars of the sort of cultural misprision that the book seeks to correct, and that he might not even acknowledge the particular formulation in which I have articulated his thesis. (Jesse M. Gellrich's citing of de Man [p. 276, n. 22; p. 277, n. 32] is on the specific issue of the distinction between *figura* and allegory and does not take on the wider matter of de Man's attitude to Auerbachian philology). For while the essays in the final "Legacies" section of the book inevitably concentrate on the fate of philology and the (mis)appropria-tion of *Mimesis* by the critical establishment, the focus is quite properly on what happened to Auerbach and his work rather than what happened to the philological method that Auerbach promoted. But the lie can im-mediately be given to the misprision that Culler and de Man assume for philology just by noting the rhetoric used by the contributors to Lerer's book in staking out their topics. If the likes of Culler and de Man could have perused just the titles of Hanna's essays they might have been misled into thinking that, yes, philology remains positivist and prehermeneutical and foundationalist; they would have to address the critical maneuvers that Hanna builds on such philological foundations to disabuse themselves, and even then, the typical rhetorical sequence of Hanna's essays (bibliographical analysis > critical and cultural in-terpretation) might just reinforce their prescription for philology. But in Lerer's book we are in a different rhetorical universe. Here the au-thors tend to fly their critical, even ideological, colors bravely at the masthead: witness Suzanne Fleischman's "Medieval Vernaculars and the Myth of Monoglossia," Hayden White's "Auerbach's Literary History: Figural Causation and Modernist Historicism," Kevin Brownlee's "The Ideology of Periodization," Carl Landauer's "Auerbach's Performance and the American Academy, or How New Haven Stole the Idea of *"Mimesis,"* and Geoffrey Green's "Erich Auerbach and the 'Inner Dream' of Transcendence." Even essays with otherwise straightforward topics participate in the current fashion for typographical misprision and de-formation, as for example Claus Uhlig's "Auerbach's 'Hidden' (?) Theory of History." Did Seth Lerer ask the contributors to jazz up their titles a little, or is this rhetorical manner a testimony to the critical ("in-your-face"?) honesty that is not only a characteristic of our cultural cli-mate but is perhaps also the natural culmination of Auerbach's *situat-edness*, of which Hanna's autobiographical exegesis is a significant contemporary exemplum?

I do not imagine that Lerer had to push his contributors into this mode, for such distinguished scholars as Hayden White, Suzanne Fleischman, Kevin Brownlee, Jesse M. Gellrich, and Stephen G. Nichols have already embraced it in their earlier work. The overt acknowledgement of the personal, even idiosyncratic, "take" on a philo-logical topic has become an accepted part of our critical vocabulary and our scholarly self-delineations. Is Auerbach responsible for this? Did he make possible the *situatedness* of White, Fleischman, et al., and (in a more muted form) the situatedness of Hanna?

274

As I did in confronting the riches of Hanna's book, I will have to use the trope of the exemplum to give even the barest response to this question. Take Herbert Lindenberger's "On the Reception of *Mimesis*" (as unprovocative and neutral a title as one may encounter in this book). Lindenberger builds on the fact of *Mimesis* having been written in exile on the very edges of European civilization (Istanbul) and links this geocultural situatedness with the present "central" (!) role of the exilic in much contemporary criticism, citing Edward Said: "Exile, far from being the fate of nearly forgotten unfortunates who are dispossessed and expatriated, becomes something closer to a norm, an experience of crossing boundaries and charting new territories in defiance of the classic canonic enclosures, however much its loss and sadness should be acknowledged and registered" (Said, *Culture and Imperialism* [New York: Knopf, 1993], p. 317, qtd. in Lindenberger, p. 209). The postcolonial, anti-imperialist, politicized criticism of Said looks at first sight an unlikely progeny of *Mimesis*, and Said and Auerbach might appear to be strange critical bedfellows. But consider that Lindenberger, in common with several of the other contributors to this volume, emphasizes the importance to the philological enterprise and to the legacy that Auerbach has bestowed upon us of the famous *confessio* to *Mimesis*: "*Mimesis* ist ganz bewusst ein Buch, das ein bestimmter Mensch, in einer bestimmten Lage, zu Anfang der 1940er Jahre geschrieben hat" ("*Mimesis* is quite consciously a book written by a particular person in a particular place during the early 1940s"); "Epilogomena zu *Mimesis*" (p. 18), qtd. in Lindenberger, p. 291, n. 17.

So, while "on the surface, *Culture and Imperialism* surely does not look like a continuation of Auerbach's project . . . [i]t is most obviously like *Mimesis* in the way it balances insights into specific texts with larger theoretical principles—more precisely, in the way that theory comes directly out of each author's critical practice, indeed the way that theory and practice correct and reshape one another in the course of the argument" (Lindenberger, p. 208).

If Edward Said, an antagonist of the sort of Western and specifically Eurocentric ethic that Auerbach has so often come to represent, can be seen as one of his critical disciples, then the "legacy" of *Mimesis* and its deft calibration and interweaving of the scholarly and the personal is large indeed. And the immense scope of Lerer's collection is testimony to the ubiquitousness of that legacy. White's essay on the modernism of Auerbach's historical method; Carl Landauer's on the "Americanization" of *Mimesis* (to the chagrin of Auerbach's great rival, Ernst Curtius);

Geoffrey Green's on the tensions between the modernism of Auerbach's style of philology and the fractured postmodernism of his "experience of historical multiplicity," linking him with his fellow emigré Vladimir Nabokov (p. 218); Kevin Brownlee's deliberately "revisionist" stake in *Mimesis* as a "great work of interpretative scholarship" that requires such revisionism (p. 156); Lerer's confrontation with, among other things, a style of critical awareness that "blur[s] the line between the philological and the political . . . towards the construction of a scholarly *figura* of their own" (p. 83); these, and so many other "places" in *Literary History and the Challenge of Philology* demonstrate the various ways that that "challenge" can be perceived and met.

Inevitably, there are some "places" where one feels that the statements may be larger and more comprehensive than the occasion warrants. In what is otherwise a highly articulate, both provocative and convincing essay on the [editorial] "myth of monoglossia," Fleischman is led to claim that "current thinking among textual critics reveal[s] the extent to which philology has subtly—and presumably unconsciously—converted our *desire* for regularity and homogeneity in language, for monoglossia, into a moral imperative of rigorous scholarship" (p. 101). While such a prescription *might* still obtain among some editors of Old French, it would be recognizable by most contemporary textual theorists only as a perhaps nostalgic characterization of a now displaced dispensation. The fragmentalism and Pergamanian *anomaly* now endorsed—and practiced—by an array of textuists from Derek Pearsall in medieval studies to Randall McLeod in Renaissance, to Jerome McGann in Romantic and nineteenth century, to Joseph Grigely, Marta Werner, Vicki Mahaffey, and a host of other young scholars in recent literature, art, and music, are sufficient testimony that Fleischman's "monoglossia" has long since vanished as the preferred mode of "current thinking" among textual critics. And even among French theorists and practitioners, the work of Jean-Louis Lebrave, Louis Hay, and of the journal *Genesis*, with an emphasis on the unformed and idiosyncratic *avant-texte* over the idealist critical edition, represent a contemporary consensus very different from that set up as straw man in Fleischman's essay. In fact, even the evidence Fleischman cites for contemporary "standards" within Old French is largely drawn from Albert Foulet and Mary Speer's manual on editing Old French, now two decades old; and a great deal has happened in French textual theory during those twenty years. I hope I do not merely quibble in this corrective to Fleischman's argument, for I would claim that it is this very shift *away* from the idealist monoglossia (Alexandrian *analogy*) she finds in textual theory toward a heteroglossia, a celebration of an idiosyncratic textual *anomaly*, that the "legacy" of Auerbach is to be seen most clearly in contemporary textual studies. The "venerable *bon usage*" (p. 102) has ceded to the partial, the *avant*, and the *brouillions*, in demonstration of the continuance of those postmodernist aspects of Auerbach's philological "character" noted by Geoffrey Green's essay.

Even (perhaps especially) in such moments where one feels the provocation most strongly, the essays in Lerer's book are justly Auerbachian in their setting down of a philological "challenge" which must then be confronted with all the energy, enthusiasm, and vigor that characterizes *Mimesis* itself. So what is the *final* legacy of Auerbach? Much too early to say, of course, but in a sense both Lerer's *Literary History* and Hanna's *Pursuing History* epitomize that legacy in their scholarship, rhetoric, and shape.

DAVID GREETHAM
City University of New York Graduate School

IAIN MACLEOD HIGGINS. *Writing East: The "Travels" of Sir John Mandeville.* Middle Ages Series. Philadelphia: University of Pennsylvania Press, 1997. Pp. ix, 335. $49.95.

Any book that begins its introduction by reference to Adam and Eve announces the scope of its own ambition. Iain Higgins's ambition in *Writing East* is not only admirable but, for the most part, successfully realized. Taking its cue from the peripatetic originary pair, *Writing East* also journeys eastward, moving with Sir John, the narrator and ostensible author of the complex of texts commonly known as "Mandeville's Travels," from the familiar world of western Europe to the East as it was created in the medieval occidental imagination. In his own scholarly excursus, Higgins employs two guiding principles. The first guiding principle is that the East, imagined and reimagined over the course of the fourteenth and fifteenth centuries, is not one but many: the "Travels," that is, encompasses a multiplicity of orients as its narrative moves through Egypt, Palestine, Constantinople, the land of Prester John, India, the Terrestrial Paradise, and back to western Europe again. In its writing of this multiplicity, the "Travels" is one of those essential medieval "artifacts that give expression to the worldly aspirations of medieval Christian culture" (p. 13). Its ideology is thus manifested in its geography.

Higgins's second guiding principle also concerns multiplicity—not, however, in the geography within the text of the "Travels," but in the subsequent textual travels of *The Book of John Mandeville* itself. As Higgins explains (in his book's most original and convincing portions), the "Travels" is not one text but many. Constituted of redactions, versions, translations, and "isotopes" (p. 26), *The Book* is best understood as a "multi-text" (p. viii), "a heterogeneric compilation," "a multinodal network, a kind of rhizome" (p. 18). In its attention to issues of textuality, *Writing East* is a compelling response to recent theoretical controversies about the nature and transmission of medieval texts. Scholars such as Paul Zumthor, Peter Shillingsburg, and Tim William Machan (although only the first is listed in Higgins's extensive bibliography) are among those debating whether it is possible to establish a unified and stable text, whether it is possible to trace the descent of a text from a single, identifiable, and authored (in a modern sense) manuscript source, and, in fact, whether it is desirable to do so. Higgins's implicit answer to each of these questions is "no." Throughout *Writing East*, Higgins demonstrates that *The Book* is not a unified text, nor is it a single text, nor is the earliest extant version authoritative. Reading it as if it were stable or stemmatically determinable is to accept modern premises that falsify the process whereby medieval texts were created. Refuting the dominant schools of modern editing practice that either establish a best text or amalgamate a variety of available texts, Higgins aims for a "palimpsestic or topological reading" that considers the manuscript versions together so as to analyze "the rhetorical strategies and ideological aims" (p. 27) of each.

From the more than 60 French, 44 English, 103 Dutch or German, and 54 Latin manuscripts extant (plus those in Czech, Danish, Irish, Italian, and Spanish), Higgins concentrates on 10: the Continental and Insular Versions (French); the Bodley, Cotton, Defective, Egerton, and Metrical Versions (English); Michel Velser's and Otto von Diemeringen's Versions (German); and the Vulgate Latin Version, discussing others as needed. These ten he chooses according to "the availability of editions and the extent of [his] own interests, training, and linguistic competence" (p. 20), a competence which is impressively illustrated throughout. After an introduction setting out the issues of the book, the middle chapters of *Writing East* follow the *Mandeville*-author's narrative, from the *captatio benevolentiae* of the exordium all the way to the "theological coda." En route, readers encounter "choses estranges" in Constantinople (chapter 3), marvels in Palestine (chapter 4), diversity in "Ynde" (chapter 5), power in Cathay (chapter 6), and piety near Paradise (chapter 7). In every instance, Higgins deploys his palimpsestic method to appraise the significance of the material occurring (or not) in the manuscript versions under scrutiny.

Each chapter follows a similar design that includes, first, an overview of the predominant narrative concerns of the different versions; second, an explanation of the relations of the material to its sources, primarily William of Boldensele's 1336 *Liber de quibusdam ultramarinis partibus* and Odoric of Pordenone's 1330 *Relatio* (though often read through Jean le Long's 1351 modified translation); third, an examination of some of the important redactions, showing how each is ideologically inflected; and, fourth, general conclusions on the narrative strategies and ideological foci of the different manuscripts. It has to be said that faced at times with what seems like overwhelming amounts of detail from unfamiliar texts, one's energies flag. For the most part, however, the rewards of following Higgins's topological readings are well worth the effort. For instance, in the fifth of nine subparts of chapter 8 (subhead: "Papal Approbation, or the Roman Route Home"), Higgins begins with Sir John's meeting with the Pope of Rome (a locational reference that allows Higgins to set this incident within the context of the Great Schism). In the manuscripts in which it occurs, this meeting includes a description of a spherical device (possibly a globe), a *mappamundi*, and a book (known today to be Ranulph Higden's *Polychronicon*) that together serve—the Pope himself informs the traveler—to corroborate what Sir John has written in his own book. To explain the significance of this meeting, Higgins links interpolations occurring in the Cotton, the Defective/Egerton, the Cosin (Latin), and the Velser versions: "Like the world map, the Latin text's world sphere is said to have been made from the papal book, and this raises an intriguing possibility, given the late date of the manuscript [post-1485]. . . . The first extant globe, made at Nuremburg in 1492, cites John Mandeville several times as an authority, and it would be an even greater irony than Velser's scrupulous honesty in the epilogue, if the corroborating sphere named in the Cosin text were the Nuremburg globe or another like it that cited the English Knight. In any case, the Latin text goes the others one better here, since it has Sir John discover the contents of his book on the pope's world sphere" (p. 259). Higgins's commentary here is typical of his study, illustrating not only how carefully he reads his material but also how adroitly he brings together a number of versions to arrive at a nuanced appreciation of the subtle workings of the multitextual *Book*.

Writing East is filled with detailed accounts that are as equally insightful as this discussion of the papal interview. Yet Higgins's method of comparing and contrasting isotopic particulars has its drawbacks as well. First, because he needs to cover so much material as he travels with Sir John to the East and back again, Higgins tends to overload his text with a cornucopia of details. Second, because his methodology requires continual maneuvering among manuscripts in order to read them simultaneously and without prioritizing, Higgins is in danger of losing the reader who is unfamiliar with the redactions except through Higgins's own descriptions. Third, because his concern is "the *discursive* making and remaking of the East" (p. 6; my emphasis), *Writing East* is both wonderfully inclusive and frustratingly circumscriptive in that Higgins does not in the end present a theoretical overview that would tie the local instances together. Like its subject, *Writing East* provides "a textual space within which fundamentally distinct views of the world [can] be articulated" (p. 264). What it does not do is provide an extended theoretical discussion of issues (such as power, otherness, or orientalism) that derive from the multitextual *Book as a whole*.

Despite these drawbacks, *Writing East* is a book that should be read by all scholars interested in "Mandeville's Travels," in the genre of travel literature, in the medieval imagined East, and in the composition and transmission of medieval texts. In his study, Higgins has composed a learned, perceptive, and well-written book (even the preface is a model of its kind). There is, however, one final irony that should not be overlooked: *Writing East*, by proving its case of multitextuality so thoroughly, ends up revealing its own limitations, or rather, the limitations of any work transmitted through the medium of print. By convincing readers of the importance of attending to all manuscripts of *The Book*, Iain Higgins inadvertently frustrates those who are able to attend merely to a few. Perhaps the only medium appropriate to the fully successful realization of Higgins's laudable ambitions is a medium to which manuscript variability itself seems to aspire: hypertext.

Sylvia Tomasch
Hunter College

HENRY ANSGAR KELLY. *Chaucerian Tragedy*. Chaucer Studies, vol. 24. Cambridge: D. S. Brewer, 1997. Pp. xi, 297. $79.00.

For critics familiar with Kelly's work on tragic theory in the Middle Ages, at least since the appearance of his *Viator* article of 1979 ("Aristotle-Averroes-Alamannus on Tragedy: The Influence of the *Poetics* on the Latin Middle Ages"), his new book adds a much appreciated focus on the tragedies themselves. Because the book deals most specifically with Chaucer, about whose works there are as many opinions as there are critics, it is also a thought-provoking book.

Kelly states his methodological approach in the introduction to his book: like Werkmeister, following Marx, Kelly posits "that it is not the business of art historians to make value judgments on what is beautiful and not beautiful . . . [but] their efforts should be directed towards trying to determine the esthetic preoccupations of the artists and their patrons" (p. 9). He adheres to this methodology, rigorously avoiding structural and related forms of analysis throughout the study. Ideology aside, however, the strength of Kelly's book lies, as usual, in the author's balance of exhaustive and well-documented scholarship with a close reading of both primary and secondary sources. His assessments of these sources are bold and authoritative, reflecting generally the good judgment that has become the hallmark of his studies.

Two premises support Kelly's statements on Chaucerian tragedy; one is clearly stated in the book and the other is vigorously implied. First, very little actual medieval theory stands as backdrop to Chaucer's creation in the genre; second, Chaucer cannot be acclaimed an exhaustive scholar.

Chaucer was fortunate in being guided by an unknown glossator [whose original Latin gloss is preserved in Cambridge MS Ii.3.21] to accept a wide-open definition of tragedy, in keeping with the Boethian characterization of the genre. As a result, Chaucer considered all kinds of disasters and all kinds of protagonists eligible for tragedy. (p. 91)

One could also say that Chaucer was fortunate in not pursuing the research that might have led him to the few other, narrower definitions that might otherwise have influenced his working definition of *tragedy*.

In order to provide a full context for Chaucerian tragedy, Kelly begins by discussing Boccaccio's *De casibus* stories, which he proves to have been conceived as moral exempla rather than tragedies. "It was Chaucer who hit upon the idea of calling these narratives tragedies . . ." (p. 11). Kelly then devotes one chapter to Chaucer's early tragic tales, such as the Monk's tragedies, and another chapter to the tragedy of Troilus. There follow two chapters on Lydgate: the first presents Lydgate's various reformulations of Chaucer's definitions of tragedy (as found, for instance, in the *Troy Book*) and the second discusses *The Fall of Princes* in some detail, indicating in passing that it was through Lydgate's work that Chaucer's simplified understanding of tragedy continued in use down to Shakespeare, and beyond. The sixth and final chapter is devoted to Henryson:

Henryson's *Testament of Cresseid* is a tragedy because it is inspired by Chaucer's tragedy, *Troilus and Crideyde*. It also conforms to Chaucer's understanding of tragedy as explained in the *Boece* and *Monk's Tale*. It is a poem about a person of high standing who began in prosperity and ended in misery from which there was no recovery; it bewails this state of affairs, and it draws suitable lessons of mutability and caution. (p. 257)

The organization of chapters in Kelly's book provides, therefore, essential information on the background against which Chaucer worked, the sources that led to Chaucer's unique understanding of tragedy and to the tragedies he produced, and the later medieval English works influenced by Chaucer's understanding.

In his discussion of *Troilus and Criseyde*, Kelly has difficulty treating any notion of *hamartia*, or of an error by Troilus that would precipitate the tragic action, because such an error would have been equated in the Middle Ages with the notion of *sin*. Thus, Kelly dismisses *hamartia*; but he soon alludes briefly to the issue again by mentioning his opinion that Troilus was not in error (sinful) when he fell in love with Criseyde. Dismissal of *hamartia* is important in this study because it allows the author to discuss the Monk's sad stories, which depend upon an "unwar strook" of Fortune for their plot reversal, and the *Troilus*, which structurally is more complex, under the same general definition of tragedy.

Kelly's placing of the *Troilus* under the same definition of tragedy as the one that governs the Monk's tales of woe is necessitated also by his choice of a methodology that avoids aesthetic judgments in favor of seeking more general descriptions and definitions. Kelly signals his fundamental discomfort with this fact by pointing out that Harry

Bailly, who interrupted the Monk's tragedies because they were not well told, would probably have found the *Troilus* "to be well told" (p. 141).

These issues are mentioned here simply to indicate the outer limits of Kelly's study, which is not to be faulted for its avoidance of problems clearly excluded by his introduction. The book gives its readers everything its author promises, and because Kelly, as usual, remains a perfectionist, it represents a very rewarding and satisfying contribution to the scholarship on an important aspect of Chaucer studies. We can be very grateful for the years of thought and research that Kelly has devoted to the study of tragedy and to the production of this volume on Chaucerian tragedy.

NOEL HAROLD KAYLOR, JR.
University of Northern Iowa

BURT KIMMELMAN. *The Poetics of Authorship in the Later Middle Ages: The Emergence of the Modern Literary Persona.* Studies in the Humanities, vol. 21. New York: Peter Lang, 1996. Pp. 288. $49.95.

In this ambitious and often insightful study, Burt Kimmelman has an enormous field to plow. His project is twofold, as indicated in the title; his argument, however, has many strands. His main aim is to show how through autocitations the twelfth-century troubadour Marcabru, Dante, Chaucer, and Langland inscribed themselves, not merely a conventional poetic voice, into their poems. Autocitations, also referred to as "the art of fictional self-inclusion" (p. 2), take various forms, including self-references; explicit naming; conventional, fictionalized versions of the author; and, most important for Kimmelman, discussions by a poem's narrator about the nature of poetry (p. 3). The autocitations shared by the authors above are each poet's attempt to grapple with contemporary theories of language and knowledge and to contribute to the poetic and philosophic tradition to which each is indebted. Identifying the important philosophical and theological ideas and the developments in rhetoric and grammar that shaped how poets conceived of their poetry, Kimmelman discusses each poet in relation to the principal thinkers who influenced him: Marcabru's poetry is discussed in relation to the ideas of Augustine and Anselm, Dante's to those of

Augustine and Thomas Aquinas, and both Chaucer's and Langland's to those of Ockham and other nominalists.

Kimmelman's second aim is to push back to the twelfth century and to detect in the authorship tropes of each of these poets the beginning of modern self-consciousness, and even postmodernism: "Ironically, perhaps, it has taken the urgency and vocabulary of a post-structuralist critique to reveal the very seeds of its epistemological approach in the philosophy of the Middle Ages" (p. 21). Kimmelman frequently insists on the autonomy of language and poetry from language users and the world the poem may only seem to be invoking. He finds Anselm to be the forerunner of postmodernism in Anselm's recognition of "the separateness of language"; that is, the ability of "statements" to "have a 'natural' cogency despite their lack of objective reference" (p. 6). Anselm's ideas about referential and grammatical truth have different functions in Kimmelman's argument, figuring most directly in his discussion of the poems of Marcabru and Guillem IX. But Kimmelman returns to Anselm in each of his chapters, seeing his contributions as "the ground of individual poetic identity" (p. 6).

The first two chapters, "Introduction: Alterity and History" and "Chapter One: Text and Word, History and Fiction," establish the two main critical frameworks that will guide Kimmelman's study: 1) a synthesis of traditional and postmodernist approaches to literature and 2) important developments in medieval language theory, rhetoric, and grammar. While never leaving these discussions behind and also frequently comparing the four different poets, the remaining three chapters focus on poems by Marcabru ("Chapter Two: The Poetics of the 'I'"), Dante ("Chapter Three: The Poet as Text, the Text as Name"), and Chaucer and Langland ("Chapter Four: Poetic Voice, Poetic Text, Thematics and the Individual"). The book also includes an afterword and three brief appendices that examine three different tropes.

Kimmelman is most persuasive and insightful when he is doing close textual analyses of the poems, showing how they engage philosophical debates in surprising and subtle ways. Not all parts of this study, however, are equally successful. Readers may object to his premises, which both establish a too narrowly drawn community in which poets worked and determine the conceptual organization of his book:

My book argues that there were two groups of language users, poets and philosophers, who were writing out of a fecund relationship with one another, during a period of great intellectual tumult lasting for over four hundred years. For us grasping this relationship will mean holding a key to later medieval cosmology and philosophy of language, and to textual autocitation. (p. 2)

This study is largely diachronic rather than synchronic. Kimmelman is not concerned with illuminating the cultural, political, or even literary influences through which philosophical ideas may be refracted in literature. Instead he is interested in how medieval theories of language and epistemology and the poet's poetics intersect:

Speculative grammar, realism and nominalism, often provided the poetic material for poets to be discussed at length: Guillem IX, Marcabru, Dante, Chaucer and Langland. The process in which their poems were created must have been inflected, perhaps directly and certainly indirectly, by the achievements of medieval philosophers whose diction and ideas are so very often present in the poets' verses and whose insights into the nature of language these poets absorbed. (p. 6)

The introduction, in part, reviews mid-twentieth-century to the most recent scholarship on troubadour poetry, critical debates about how to conceive the self or the individual in the Middle Ages, and topics in medieval language theory. This discussion is situated within a larger one on postmodernist issues, particularly those emphasizing the linguistic construction of the self. Kimmelman's task in this chapter is a formidable one, for his own critical approach is largely synthetic. Although not an uncritical reader, he finds persuasive a collection of traditionally historical and postmodernist arguments about the self in medieval literature that are not theoretically compatible. His lack of distinctions, however, tends to make his argument confusing, rather than damaging it, for toward the end of his introduction his synthesis has served to recognize two different conceptions of the "individual," one based on a "psychological critique" and the other on a "textual" one. Kimmelman's study will argue that the "particularized individual emerges" from them both (p. 27). The poets' different kinds of autocitations seem to point to these different selves. Through autocitations authors insert into their poems a fictional self who asserts his place within a poetic tradition. The unique poet beyond the poem, however, emerges from the poet's extended discussion of his poetics.

For each of his poets, except Langland, Kimmelman reviews the philosophical debates which his poets engaged and then shows through close readings how the pertinent philosophical issues become the fabric of the poems. His focus on Marcabru's poems is given a rich context of troubadour verse as a whole and of the language theories of Augustine and Anselm. He shows how Marcabru inscribed a conventional, textual version of himself in his poems by distinguishing himself from other poets whom he dismisses variously, for example, as a "frog" (p. 91), "joglars" (p. 97), and "dogs" (p. 101). Marcabru's elaboration of his poetics is detected in his poems that "wage war on the values of Guillem [IX]" (p. 109). Kimmelman argues that Marcabru's poems debate two uses of language that have their clearest articulation in Anselm's rejection of "Augustine's criterion of intentionality as the most important factor when determining falsehoods" (p. 6). Anselm's qualification that statements can have grammatical truth (*veritas*) apart from their true objective reference (*rectitudo*) (pp. 103–4) allows Marcabru to distinguish his verse, which has rectitude, from Guillem's verse, which merely has *veritas*.

Kimmelman's approach allows him to identify very different poetics for each poet and to make important distinctions among their fictional personae. He examines Dante's autocitation in *The Inferno*, which links Dante and Virgil through the use of pronouns (pp. 27–33), and Dante's elaboration of his poetics, shaped by the *Summa* of Thomas Aquinas, in *Purgatorio* 17 and *Paradiso* 30:

Dante is ultimately able to portray Aquinas' construct, of the material/non-material universe, by bringing the question of making poetry—the question of, finally, an amorphous but decidedly poetic imagination—to bear upon the Thomistic dichotomy. Dante wishes to celebrate a unified world of theology and poetry. (p. 142)

Part of the larger argument in this chapter is that poets increasingly identified themselves with their texts as if the poets "were themselves texts" (p. 123). Although his explanations often involve analogies about what Dante is saying, his textual analyses of Dante's verse focus on how Dante crafts a poetic vision through his many uses of different forms of the verb "to see" and "to imagine" and puns on words for discourse and reason.

The fourth chapter is the least successful, in part because Kimmelman's approach shifts here to a comparison of the "narrative procedures" (p. 166) of Chaucer and Langland, involving frequent descriptive, rather than analytic, comparisons of their projects and narrators. Kimmelman has a very complex understanding of how philosophical issues in Chaucer's works are subordinated to Chaucer's interests in literary realism and his recognition of "a plethora of divergent philosophies ranging throughout the time and place he inhabits" (p. 182). Kimmelman examines how nominalist issues shape Chaucer's emphasis on firsthand experience throughout his works and are given a forum in the *Prologue* to *The Legend of Good Women*. In anticipation of this chapter, Kimmelman has asserted earlier that "after Dante, the authorship trope develops in two directions" represented by Chaucer's persona "Geffrey" and Langland's "Will" (p. 122) and that of the four poets, Marcabru, Dante, and Langland are "pivotal," for their "works exhibit intellectual developments that will include what we may call a 'poetics of the text'" (p. 125). Chaucer's exclusion from the list above seems to result from Kimmelman's privileging of didactic works and his failure to consider *The Canterbury Tales* in which Chaucer's own poetics allows him to examine so many different poetic practices.

Kimmelman builds his argument about Langland's poetics from the recent work of scholars such as John Bowers, George Economou, Laurie Finke, Jill Mann, Anne Middleton, and Lorraine K. Stock. They have already made his points for him, and he reads their scholarship sensitively, citing them at length. In this synthesis, his aim is to further his larger argument of a progression in the development of the authorship trope from Marcabru to Dante to Langland. Each of their personae and poems share salvific aims, with Langland's serving as an epitome in which his persona "Will" is developed as the theme of the poem (*voluntas*).

This book deserved more extensive editing. I found it to repay careful and repeated readings in order to distinguish among Kimmelman's insightful analyses, speculations, and secondary sources that can, at times, overwhelm his argument. There are a few superficial proofreading errors in the form of misspellings and punctuation mistakes. One three-sentence passage on page 9 is repeated on page 28. The book's organization will deter readers interested primarily in any one of his authors, for Kimmelman too frequently discusses them all at once. The chapters are divided into often very brief sections, sometimes of less than three pages. Sections are delineated only by spaces, which often substitute for crucial transitions. Kimmelman, however, has a truly admirable knowledge of scholarship and medieval philosophy, rhetoric, grammar, and literature, and his work shows that literature is the most interdisciplinary form for understanding the world.

AMY W. GOODWIN
Randolph-Macon College

ANNE LASKAYA. *Chaucer's Approach to Gender in the* Canterbury Tales. Chaucer Studies, vol. 23. Cambridge: D. S. Brewer, 1995. Pp. viii, 224. $63.00.

Anne Laskaya's welcome book delivers up a full discussion of gender in Chaucer's *Tales*, masculinity as well as femininity, beginning with an investigation of the ideals of gendered behavior prevalent in late-fourteenth-century England. Previewing her arguments in the introduction, she writes:

Just as [Chaucer's] work can be said to call other ideals into question, so it can be said to call gender ideals into question. It offers up a sophisticated discussion of masculinity . . . while still remaining firmly homosocial and homophobic. Its representations of femininity are also created at a conjunction of inquiry and reinscribed misogyny. (p. 13)

Because so many of Chaucer's narrators are male, the book spends a great deal more time exploring the varieties of male rather than female experience represented in the *Tales*. But this approach results in a study that does not skew our reading of the entire work along an axis that includes only the Wife of Bath, the Second Nun, and the Prioress of the frame, along with several female characters who reside within tales told by male pilgrims. Instead, Laskaya's discussion can close with an acknowledgement of the structural and thematic importance of *The Parson's Tale*:

On the one hand, the game [of storytelling] is a civilizing agent, channelling aggression into play; on the other hand, the *Parson's Tale*, placed in an authoritative final position in the *Tales*, chastises men for their rivalries and expresses a desire for the oneness of man and man, thereby voicing criticisms of a culture which increasingly encouraged competition. (p. 201)

This is no mean feat, as will be evident to all who have followed the influence of feminist criticism on interpretations of Chaucer's texts, and Laskaya is to be thanked for setting her sights on the whole, rather than on a part, of that encyclopedic work.

Her second chapter will perhaps be the most widely cited, as it clearly delineates "four different literary discourses of ideal heterosexual male behavior" that, she readily admits, "were often in tension with one another" (p. 15). She names them: the heroic, or epic, discourse; the discourse of Christian masculinity; the discourse of courtly love; and a "fourth prescription for masculinity [which] promoted the virtue of knowledge above all else" (p. 18). In subsequent chapters, she examines the appearance and critique of these ideals in several tales, including *The Knight's Tale* for heroic discourse, the *Miller's* and *Merchant's Tales* for courtly love, the *Canon's Yeoman's* and *Clerk's Tales* for the intellectual male, and the *Friar's, Summonor's* and *Parson's Tales* for the ideal of Christian masculinity.

Further, Laskaya helpfully articulates gender ideals for both women and men as two series of questions. Since men were expected to rule over others, she says, they were occupied with such questions as: "What are the limits of governance? When does rule become tyranny? What should be the relationship between punishment and mercy? What constitutes just governance for a king, a bishop, a confessor, a husband" (p. 20), or an innkeeper-turned-judge? And since women were expected to submit to the rule of men, they were often *represented* as considering such questions as "Are there any limitations on my obedience to my husband or father? How can I influence the governor? When does influence become rebellion? When does submission become slavery? How do I submit and still maintain self-respect?" (p. 42). Prudence in *The Tale of Melibee* comes out looking quite good in comparison with Custance, Griselde, Virginia, and Dorigen in the chapter entitled "Masculinity, Representations of Ideal Femininity in Men's Narratives, and the Challenge," as Chaucer "depicts in Prudence . . . a strong female intellectual capability" (p. 164).

Also noteworthy is the fact that Laskaya sustains throughout her work the crucial distinction between the lived experience of historical women and the fictionalized experience of Chaucer's invented women. Nevertheless, she argues that Chaucer's three female storytellers tell tales that are filtered through one fewer male consciousness than are the male pilgrims' tales, and it is in these three tales that Laskaya finds a challenge to "male domination and female subordination" (p. 167). She goes on to assert that this challenge is "far greater than any challenge to the culture's assumptions about femininity raised by the male pilgrims' narratives" (p. 167), although they may not impress modern feminists as especially daring.

Aside from wishing Laskaya had included full discussions of Troilus, Pandarus, and Criseyde here, I also wished for a fuller integration of recent scholarship on Chaucer and gender. While the important books of Carolyn Dinshaw[1] and H. Marshall Leicester, Jr.[2] are cited, primarily in footnotes, it seemed that Laskaya could have engaged them both in a more forthright, top-of-the-page manner, especially where the Wife of Bath is concerned. Similarly, Carolyn Walker Bynum's work on female mysticism and the spiritual alliance of women with Christ's suffering body could have figured prominently in her discussion of Christian gender ideals; it might even have led her to modify some of her conclusions about the alienation of historical women from a "male-gendered Godhead" (p. 137).[3] Still, Laskaya's study adds significantly to the growing body of scholarship and criticism on Chaucer's treatment of gender. If she is seen as having her cake and eating it too (that is, asserting that Chaucer's works advance both homosocial *and* protofeminist agendas, for example), then she joins a company of critics who continue to be amazed, and sometimes confounded, by Chaucer's ironies, masks, mimickings, and masquerades—a distinguished group indeed. This book will become the touchstone for all subsequent considerations of the topic well into the foreseeable future.

LAURA L. HOWES
University of Tennessee, Knoxville

---

[1] Carolyn Dinshaw, *Chaucer's Sexual Poetics* (Madison: University of Wisconsin Press, 1989).
[2] H. Marshall Leicester, Jr., *The Disenchanted Self: Representing the Subject in the Canterbury Tales* (Berkeley: University of California Press, 1990).
[3] See Carolyn Walker Bynum, *Holy Feast and Holy Fast: The Religious Significance of Food to Medieval Women* (Berkeley: University of California Press, 1987).

SETH LERER, ed. *Reading from the Margins: Textual Studies, Chaucer, and Medieval Literature.* San Marino, Calif.: Huntington Library Press, 1996. Pp. vii, 160. $12.00 paper.

In their introduction to this book, Seth Lerer and Joseph A. Dane propose as an epigraph R. B. McKerrow's remarks of seventy years ago about the then-new popularity of "bibliographical" methods. *Plus ça change.* . . . But there *have* been changes, of course, as scholars have returned to medieval manuscripts with different assumptions and purposes than those of earlier generations. Illustrating the rewards and occasionally the potential perils of that return, these essays show the range of current textual and codicological approaches to Chaucer and Middle English literature.

In a study of the early reception of the Ellesmere manuscript, A. S. G. Edwards and Ralph Hanna focus on the poem in praise of the De Veres, Earls of Oxford, written on the Ellesmere flyleaves in about the third quarter of the fifteenth century and attributed to "Rotheley." From the definite evidence that the manuscript was owned by the Drurys in the sixteenth century, and the possibility of earlier Paston ownership, Edwards and Hanna infer fifteenth-century ownership by the De Veres, who had connections with both families. They draw together many disparate pieces of evidence to paint a convincing picture of involvement by the De Vere circle in local literary efforts, including connections with Lydgate and with manuscript production at Bury St. Edmunds. The Rotheley poem, itself Lydgatian in vocabulary, gives a (probably) legendary account of how a De Vere ancestor's exploits in the First Crusade led to the family's receipt of its arms. As Edwards and Hanna point out, fidelity to kings, one of the De Vere qualities being celebrated, was a particularly complex thing at the time the poem was apparently written, a period when the De Veres suffered at the hands of Edward IV and Richard III because of their Lancastrian loyalties. The poem looks forward to a restoration of the family's status, which did in fact occur under Henry VII.

Edwards and Hanna contrast this outcome with Chaucer's own permanent loss of status after the triumph of the Appellants in the 1380s; they assert Chaucer wrote *The Canterbury Tales*, which the Ellesmere manuscript "heroicizes," only because he could not "regain the outstanding courtly place he had held before," and thus "exchanged some measure of political power for a much less clearly valuable cultural

standing" (p. 28). The relationship between Chaucer's political and literary careers may have been more complicated than this suggests. He
was, after all, perhaps most productive in the first half of the 1380s,
when he seems to have been quite close to the court; and he may have
chosen not to return to that place and its attendant risks after Richard
II consolidated his power again at the end of the decade. But, perhaps
more important for the study of Chaucer's reception, we cannot know,
as Edwards and Hanna implicitly acknowledge, whether Rotheley and
his patrons were aware of these details of Chaucer's life, including the
fact that a De Vere ancestor, like Chaucer, belonged to Richard's party
and lost out to the Appellants. As is so often the case, we can perceive
a network of relationships between various pieces of evidence—a lavish
manuscript, a copy of Chaucer's *Truth* added to it, the Rotheley poem
added still later—but find it much more difficult to gauge the knowledge and motives of their medieval readers and writers.

Julia Boffey considers the growth of the Chaucer apocrypha and the
existence of divergent "Chaucers" in the fifteenth and sixteenth centuries. Boffey's primary piece of evidence is the attribution to Chaucer,
in two manuscripts, of a one-stanza extract from Walton's translation of
Boethius. One of these manuscripts is Selden B.24, which contains a series of spurious attributions to Chaucer, in addition to much genuine
material, and which contrives to "Scotticize" Chaucer (p. 44). The other
is Cotton Vitellius E.xi, a copy of John of Fordun's *Chronica gentis
Scotorum* and thus another manuscript with Scottish connections. In a
boldly inferential move, Boffey proposes that in Cotton Vitellius, a
"sagacious" English Chaucer is being set parallel to the Scottish historian John of Fordun (p. 44). She argues persuasively that texts of the
kinds contained in these two manuscripts would have been circulating
among Scottish readers such as Archbishop Schevez, who owned Cotton
Vitellius, and the Sinclairs, whose arms appear in Selden B.24. Because
several other copies of the Walton extract appear in manuscripts associated with John Shirley, and Shirley is known to have had an interest in
Scottish history, Boffey goes on to speculate that Shirley "may have
played a role" in transmitting the Walton stanza to Scottish scribes
(p. 45). Finally, she shows why Scottish scribes might well have associated Chaucer with Boethius and thus thought any English verse connected with the *Consolatio* must have been Chaucer's work.

Ardis Butterfield offers a substantial study of the *mise-en-page* of the
Troilus manuscripts in the context of late-medieval French manuscript

culture. She begins with a clear and careful survey of the many features of the *ordinatio* of the *Troilus* manuscripts that mark, for example, beginnings of books and proems, stanzas, and changes in speaker. She goes on to focus on the ways the manuscripts mark two inset genres, the song and the letter, in *Troilus*. Then she compares the ways that shifts in genre or speaker were indicated in manuscripts of other English works, including several of Chaucer's dream-visions, and of French works by such poets as Charles d'Orléans, Machaut, and Froissart. From here she moves to an even larger perspective, as she shows that the sophisticated *ordinatio* of the Machaut and Froissart manuscripts actually represented a culmination of certain longstanding practices in French secular writing. Butterfield aims to outline broader cultural habits of manuscript practice, rather than demonstrate the influence of one particular manuscript on another—although she does believe that "some, at least, of these surviving Machaut manuscripts (or copies derived from them) would have been seen by Chaucer and the influence of their *mise-en-page* felt and experienced by both the poet and his contemporary scribes" (p. 66). Finally, Butterfield argues that authors in Chaucer's period defined themselves partly by appropriating traditionally scribal functions such as the writing of rubrics and the division of a text into parts or books. Thus she sees *Troilus* as "participating in a larger and European cultural enterprise, in which a vernacular author shapes and articulates his identity through the physical form of his writings" (p. 80).

David Lorenzo Boyd argues that the merging of *The Canterbury Tales* with a selection of poems by Lydgate in MS Bodley 686, and the manuscript's unique, expanded form of *The Cook's Tale*, work to contain the subversive energies of Chaucer's fabliaux; the poems of Chaucer and Lydgate are "[a]rranged, contained, and compiled to meet class-specific ethical and social precepts" (p. 88). Unfortunately several major flaws of research and argument limit the essay's power to recover this manuscript's "unique existence" and its "presence in time and space" (p. 96, quoting Walter Benjamin). On paleographical grounds Boyd proposes that the manuscript could have been written as early as 1420; but several of the Lydgate poems it contains are generally believed to date from the mid-1420s, and the manuscript's rubric to Lydgate's *Life of St. Margaret*, which states the poem was written in the eighth year of Henry VI, makes a date before 1430 very unlikely. In addition, apparently following the Manly and Rickert account of the manuscript, Boyd asserts it was "written in several hands" (p. 85) and *The Cook's Tale* was written by "[t]wo contemporary hands" (p. 90, n. 26), but a reexamination in light of current paleographical method reveals the entire manuscript is the work of a single scribe. Boyd favors the theory that "the manuscript might well have been made for a member of the Beauchamp family" (p. 85, n. 10), but this notion seems to reflect Manly and Rickert's habit of using highly conjectural hypotheses to link the *Tales* manuscripts to Chaucer's family and friends. It is hard to imagine that the lines added to *The Cook's Tale*, which stress the practical rewards of imitating one's betters, were intended for an aristocratic audience; and so Ruth Morse's idea, also cited by Boyd, that the manuscript's patrons were members of the merchant class seems much more likely. Perhaps more tellingly, Boyd does not think it is particularly important to distinguish between aristocratic and merchant patrons; he regards both groups as part of what he calls "the hegemony." He uses similarly general terms to explain what might have motivated the patrons to commission such a *de luxe* manuscript: "As the feudal system weakened and incipient capitalism suffered from labor shortages and other disruptions, rising violence and the fear of political and social instability haunted the imagination of empowered groups" (p. 88). The essay's persistent lack of historical specificity means Boyd's call for a "return to the particular and the local" (p. 97) in medieval literary studies remains nothing more than a facile gesture.

D. C. Greetham's "Phylum-Tree-Rhizome" is one of his challenging and entertaining ventures into the newly invigorated field of "textual theory." Greetham begins and ends with the observation that despite numerous challenges to textual stemmatics, the editor of a medieval work probably will still begin by trying to chart a "family tree" for the witnesses to the text he is editing. Greetham himself attempts to rehabilitate stemmatics by exploring alternatives to the family tree model. Drawing parallels between taxonomic methods in textual studies and theoretical developments in biology and linguistics, Greetham proposes the network or rhizome as a new model more suited to the complexities of textual transmission in the Middle Ages and to the electronic technologies that make it possible to represent that complexity in an edition. I am sympathetic to Greetham's reluctance to discard stemmatics entirely, and I suspect that some editors of medieval texts have already arrived at the more flexible understanding of manuscript relationships he outlines. But I have questions about some of Greetham's analogies. He asserts, for example, that what editors used to call "contamination" amounts to the introduction of "female" witnesses that challenge stemmatics' assumption of monogenetic, "nonsexual" descent (pp. 100–101); but both the old metaphor and Greetham's adaptation of it suggest texts (or manuscript copies) reproduce through their own agency, without the intervention of human beings in specific historical circumstances who have many motives for copying, collating, and even altering texts. Despite an occasional nod toward "a socialized view of descent and survival and authority" (p. 103), Greetham's theory often seems remote from the historical concerns that motivate the other essays in this collection.

A postscript prints Anthony G. Cains's copiously illustrated report on his work with "The Bindings of the Ellesmere Chaucer," which was undertaken in conjunction with preparation of the new Ellesmere facsimile. The four bindings discussed by Cains are that of 1911, made by Rivière and Sons, the binding on the Ellesmere when Cains began work in 1994; the previous rebinding of ca. 1802, during which some details were lost from the manuscript through excessive cropping; the original binding of the early fifteenth century; and Cains's own, which he based on the original binding, so far as the evidence for it survives in Ellesmere, and on another fifteenth-century binding still extant in the Huntington's collection. Cains's attention to the damage that has occurred over nearly six centuries, sometimes as the result of earlier attempts at conservation, reminds us of our distance from the fifteenth-century form of even this relatively intact manuscript.

Beyond those reservations already expressed, I have only a few comments about scattered details. In their introduction ("What Is A Text?"), Lerer and Dane imply that the illustrations of the pilgrims in the *Canterbury Tales* manuscripts appear in *The General Prologue*, rather than at the beginnings of the tales (p. 2). Edwards and Hanna provide a new edition of the Rotheley poem; reading it, I wished they had explained more fully their statement that the poem uses "alliterative metre" (p. 20). The poem's use of the "Monk's stanza" for its opening and of rhyme royal for its narrative, not mentioned by them, seems an equally important feature (and possibly further evidence of Rotheley's indebtedness to Lydgate). Butterfield in passing refers to "John Shirley's copy in Trinity R.3.19" of the *Parliament of Fowls* (p. 62); the Trinity manuscript, however, although derived from Shirleian exemplars, was copied about two decades after Shirley's death.

Such minor flaws do not diminish the value of these essays, which at their best combine a wealth of historical and codicological detail with refreshingly imaginative and even adventurous ways of interpreting that evidence.

STEPHEN PARTRIDGE
University of British Columbia

G. A. LESTER. *The Language of Old and Middle English Poetry.* The Language of Literature Series. New York: St. Martin's Press, 1996. Pp. viii, 182. $39.95.

Perhaps the most pertinent observation I might make regarding this book is that it belongs to the "Language of Literature" series, under the general editorship of N. F. Blake. Because this series also includes a volume on *The Language of Chaucer* (by David Burnley [1989]), the sections of Lester's book dealing with Middle English might be more accurately described as "the language of Middle English poetry exclusive of Chaucer." While the avoidance of Chaucer results in a greater number of Middle English examples from writers such as Gower, it also leads Lester to make comments such as the following, regarding the pronunciation of inflectional -*e*: "Much of what is true of Chaucer is also true of his contemporaries" (p. 168, n. 4). Such comments reveal how much of our knowledge of Middle English poetry stems from the study of Chaucer and expose the difficulty of writing usefully on the subject of language in Middle English poetry while avoiding consideration of Chaucer.

With this said, I do want to note that the book manages this difficult task well; one feature obviously in its favor is its sensible and effective organization. Introductory chapters cover "The Social Context" and "The Literary and Linguistic Context." These are followed by paired chapters on "Poetic Diction" and "Structure and Organisation" for both Old and Middle English poetry. Finally, there is one chapter on "Language Varieties," and another in which detailed analyses are carried out on passages from *Beowulf* and *Gawain.* Throughout, Lester stresses continuities between these periods and literatures; his treatment certainly recommends that we appreciate how valuable a knowledge of Old English poetic language can be for an understanding of Middle English works, especially such important poems as Laʒamon's *Brut* and the poems of the Alliterative Revival. And though I occasionally disagree with a gloss or a construal, I think the book as a whole does an admirable job of presenting important information about medieval English poetic language in a clear and accessible manner.

On the other hand, I also found many points in which I felt Lester's book underperformed or misrepresented the state of the field. Much of what Lester has to say about Old English, for example, has a distinctly archaic feel. Specifically, he refers to Old English poems by titles such as "The Arts of Men," "Deor's Lament," and "The Runic Poem," and while all of these titles have been used at one time or another, they are not the most current titles, nor (despite Lester's claim) the titles used in the *ASPR*. Likewise, Lester's comments on the relationship between Old English poetic diction and oral-formulaic theory are based solely on the important early articles by Magoun and Benson, though much more sophisticated treatments of the difficult dynamic of an originally oral tradition recorded only in writing can be found in recent works by John Miles Foley and Katherine O'Brien O'Keeffe. This problem was greatly lessened in the book's Middle English portions, but I did still feel resonances of older perspectives occasionally, especially in the material on Middle English poetic diction, which focused very heavily on the etymological origins of the poetic vocabulary. Except for Lester's discussion of Latinate "aureate" vocabulary in the fourteenth and fifteenth centuries (pp. 97–99), the etymological material may be of more interest to modern philologists than it was to Middle English speakers and poets.

I also had a couple of bibliographic quibbles. At the beginning of chapter 8, Lester writes of "the variety classes distinguished by Randolph Quirk and Sidney Greenbaum in *A Grammar of Contemporary English*" (p. 131). The material cited, however, appears to come from Quirk and Greenbaum's *A Concise Grammar of Contemporary English* (as, indeed, is listed in Lester's bibliography under its British publication title, *A University Grammar of English*), rather than from the title given in the text, which is properly by Quirk, Greenbaum, Leech, and Svartik. It is also important to point out that Lester's bibliography is split into two sections: editions, which are arranged according to the titles of the poems edited; and secondary sources, arranged by authors' names. This occasionally leads to potential confusion when Lester cites editions within his text by editors' names (e.g., p. 162; p. 169, n. 6).

The audience for Lester's book is explicitly defined as "the general reader and beginning student" (p. 3). No knowledge of Old or Middle English is assumed, but Lester writes: "The language was itself the subtlest expression of the whole culture. To understand all its complexities is an impossible task, but to make the attempt immeasurably increases the pleasure and value of a reader's experience" (p. 10). The book is intended to function as neither grammar nor primer, however; instead, it appears to be designed as a supplementary text for those who are learning (or preparing to learn) to read Old or Middle English, serving to increase their appreciation for medieval poets' skilled manipulation of diction and syntax for poetic effect. These ends it serves admirably well, though at nearly forty dollars, it is probably too expensive to assign as a student course-text.

THOMAS A. BREDEHOFT
University of Northern Colorado

JUNE HALL McCASH, ed. *The Cultural Patronage of Medieval Women*. Athens, Ga. and London: University of Georgia Press, 1996. Pp. xix, 402. $60.00 cloth; $25.00 paper.

This meticulously edited collection of twelve essays seeks "to explore the varieties and to test the limits of women's patronage" (p. 3). The appeal made by Rita Lejeune in 1976 for a general work on the patronage of medieval women inspired McCash's labor. With its intention to "hear once again voices that might otherwise have remained silent forever" (p. 1), the volume is largely shaped by the methodological concerns of "herstory" that informed feminist scholarship twenty years ago. It constitutes women as historical agents through painstaking work of recuperation of archival sources, both textual and material (visual and decorative arts and architecture), and the recovery of bibliography. Exemplary in this respect are McCash's overview of cultural patronage of medieval women, essays on patterns of women's literary patronage in England from 1200 to ca. 1475 by Karen K. Jambeck, and a survey of the patronage of Plantagenet Queens by John Carmi Parsons. Specific studies of elite women include essays on Elizabeth de Burgh by Frances A. Underhill, Matilda of Scotland by Lois L. Huneycutt, Isabel of Portugal by Charity Cannon Willard and Leonor of England and her daughters by Miriam Shadis. Essays on the Empress Theodora and on women's role in Latin letters by Anne L. McClanan and Joan M. Ferrante, respectively, offer chronological and geographic perspectives. Madeline H. Caviness's study of women's patronage of the visual arts argues for the blurring of boundaries among patrons, donors, recipients, and users and also emphasizes the strong interest in genealogical projects among elite medieval women. Located as they always were in between their natal and conjugal families, their patronage could refigure genre. Take for instance Matthew Paris's *vita* of St. Edmund, which he translated into a French metrical version for Isabella de Fortibus, countess of Arundel. The Latin hagiography that Matthew renders as romance transforms itself through its dedication to the Countess into a political genealogy commemorating the Marshal rebels to whom Isabel was related through her maternal grandmother.

The intersections between genre, gender, diglossia, and translation at stake in the life of St. Edmund raise important disciplinary questions about the project of this volume. Why the return of herstory (there is no entry for *gender* in the volume's index) in the mid-1990s when the study of gender has made trouble in medieval studies? In his foreward, Stephen G. Nichols emphasizes that "female patronage played a key role in the evolution of the mother tongue from the status of purely informal speech to a stage where, without losing consciousness of its role as discourse, it also functioned as a language, *langue*, in the sense that Latin was a language, *lingua*" (p. xv).

The oxymoronic valence of "female patron" risks going unremarked in this celebration of women's agency. The root of *vernacularity*, as Gabrielle Spiegel reminds us in *Romancing the Past* (Berkeley: University of California Press, 1993), derives etymologically from *verna*, a houseborn slave (p. 66). The root for *patron* comes from a term in Roman law for one who owns slaves. Thus the concatenated terms, *female patron of vernacularity*, captures the powerful contradictions of medieval diglossia—that is, linguistic distinctions between Latin and vernaculars that produced a "different set of values, behavior, and attitudes and was not simply a form of bilingualism" (Spiegel, p. 66). The staging of the female patron in the prologues to both vernacular romances and histories (whether it be Chrétien de Troyes's Marie de Champagne in *Lancelot*, or Nicolas of Senlis's Yolande in his French *Pseudo-Turpin Chronicle*), a figure who is both patron and recipient of the work (slaveowner and slave), uses the "female patron" to put into circulation a troubling exchange, the deadly combat for truth-claims between Latin and the vernacular. The battle over truth-claims between the paternal and maternal tongue are ultimately conservative, since they simply reverse, and do not question, the structures of institutional dominion of Latin literacy. Thus historicized, the question of the "female patron of vernacularity" has paradox to offer.

The contributors, especially Madeline H. Caviness, John Carmi Parsons, and Ralph Hanna III, attempt to grapple with the contradictions of a too easy and unhistoricized assumption of agency for the "female patron," but they stop short of articulating a crucial theoretical question posed by the volume: How does patronage function as a set of textual and material relations long inflected by gender? Readers who wish to follow through with this question will find suggestive parallels in Helen Solterer's study of the "female master" in her book *The Master and Minerva: Disputing Women in French Medieval Culture* (Berkeley: University of California Press, 1995). Christine de Pizan, a "female master" and a "female patron," can instruct us about the risks to contemporary medieval scholars of leaving unaddressed the contradictions of agency embedded in the duality of the "female patron." Christine insisted on calling herself the son (*le fils*) of her father. In so doing she marks the homosociality of genealogy and patronage while at the same time resisting it through disclosure. Such tactics raise questions for the readers of this volume who read it in the "corporate" academy of the late 1990s, in which patronage rules as government and other funding for feminist and queer scholarship and pedagogy becomes increasingly scarce and contested.

KATHLEEN BIDDICK
University of Notre Dame

RUTH MORSE. *The Medieval Medea*. Cambridge: D. S. Brewer, 1996. Pp. xvi, 267. $72.00.

Ruth Morse is a meticulous scholar, and in *The Medieval Medea* she has produced a study worthy of her thoroughness. Hers is a sweeping subject: as she establishes elaborately, the story of Jason and the Argonauts is the earliest secular quest narrative recorded in Western literature. Over it looms the inescapable presence of Medea, constantly (as Morse

300

has it) infusing the tale with a ubiquitous dark vitality even on those few occasions when Jason is center stage alone.

In format the book has an almost old-fashioned feel, scarcely uncomfortable but not much encountered these days when, like as not, ideology is pressed upon us more frequently than scholarship. Morse unfolds her study chronologically, piecing together the beginnings of the Jason legend from what we find remaining in Pindar, Euripides, and Apollonius of Rhodes among the Greeks, and then tracing its development at the hands of Virgil, Ovid, and Seneca. In this process of "handing down," Medea became not only a single character but a topos as well: the eponym for the woman possessed by passion and driven by it to terrifying excesses of every kind. Also along the way a great deal of what passed for history was transferred, and Morse guides us here through Dares and Dictys and Benoît de Sainte-Maure (the Argonauts and their Colchian cargo reach modernity via Troy) to Guido delle Colonne (whose *Historia Destructionis Troiae* "was the direct source of so many medieval interpretations" [p. 92]) to Christine de Pizan in the *Mutacion de Fortune*. What Morse is intent upon showing is how "what we might categorize as mythographical material [becomes] the highest-prestige medieval historiography" (p. 102). Nor is she interested in doing so without commenting sharply here, as in her earlier study *Truth and Convention in the Middle Ages: Rhetoric, Reality and Representation* (1991), on the tendency of contemporary historians to misread the past according to their own conventions. What Morse offers instead (indeed it might be the core concept of the book) is a Heisenbergian caveat about the dangers of believing what you can see to measure, and an appropriate antidote: to follow the bloom back to the root, to focus especially on the context.

Since a great deal of the context Morse must examine is provided by Ovid, she devotes two chapters (out of five) to a careful scrutiny of the Roman poet and his subsequent Christian adaptors. In these we find how, variously, the narratives of Jason and Medea could be allegorized (Morse's primary concern is with the *Ovide Moralisé* and the *Ovidius Moralizatus*) and transformed by Ovid himself into the exotic woman from the East, possessed of occult power and tempestuous passions whose story, altogether horrifying, is nonetheless denied any apprehension as tragedy. Rather, as Morse argues, from Ovid's Medea comes a cautionary icon for the Middle Ages and beyond. This figure, *mutatis mutandis*, stalks further through the writings of Chrétien de Troyes, Raoul Lefevre, and, more briefly in the final chapter, entitled "Some

Medieval Medeas," of Dante, Petrarch, and Boccaccio, Chaucer, Gower, and Lydgate, and ultimately Christine de Pizan.

That the final chapter of Morse's book should thus provide the primary locus for the greatest number of exclusively medieval authors, as well as the title of the work itself, is both telling and puzzling. For if one were to have to say what *The Medieval Medea* is about, lacking the title as a clue, it seems doubtful many would call it a book about the Middle Ages. Indeed, in the seven-page conclusion entitled "Silence, Exile and Cunning Intelligence," which serves as a coda to the rest, Morse herself remarks, "This book takes its place in a succession of studies of these legends which have been the purview of classicists and anthropologists, for none of whom have the Middle Ages been of prime interest" (p. 240). And indeed, Morse has it right. Much of the old-fashioned texture of *The Medieval Medea* comes suddenly clear when, following this directive, Morse's study is placed in line with ethnoliterary works of the last century. Here, as there, we find great reach and sweep, but little time to squander on any single medieval author save Lefevre, on whom Morse writes with wisdom and authority. The result of Morse's choice of models will be, predictably, that puzzlement about the title, and a vague sense among medievalists when the final page is turned of disappointment rather difficult to pin down. But it is a sentiment to be resisted, as a second reading, or a third, rewardingly establishes. True to her claim that to apprehend something truly we must place it fully in context, Morse delivers a Medea feminists should encounter fresh, and strive again to know.

R. F. YEAGER
University of North Carolina, Asheville

JACQUELINE MURRAY and KONRAD EISENBICHLER, eds. *Desire and Discipline: Sex and Sexuality in the Premodern West.* Toronto, Buffalo, and London: University of Toronto Press, 1996. Pp. xxviii, 311. $21.95 paper.

In a properly run Republic of Letters, special orders of merit would be reserved for conference organizers. They must serve first as some combination of budget travel agent, social worker, dietician, and huntmaster. They must then edit a volume of conference papers in which written unity appears by magic out of performed multiplicity. The conference papers—products of the hundred accidents of scholarly obsession, competence, ambition, delay—must be presented as so many "flowering branches" rising from one "verdant field of research" (p. vii). Or other metaphors to that effect. Of course, the same Republic of Letters would also offer medals for reviewers of conference volumes, who often confront not so much a flowering tree as a public plot planted by diverse hands to contrary tastes.

The fifteen essays gathered in this volume had their first germination in a conference on "premodern" sex and sexuality. The editors prefer "premodern" to alternate labels because it "highlights the similarities and continuities" in Europe from the twelfth through the seventeenth centuries. "Premodern" may also be more marketable, as Nancy Partner suggests in her vivid rebuke to standard medieval scholarship. The rhetoric of labeling aside, the papers in this volume do not seem to highlight similarities or continuities. They share few interests and fewer methodological assumptions or procedures. Where the papers cluster chronologically (six of them are at work in the sixteenth and early seventeenth centuries), the material discontinuities are still enormous. Ivana Elbl collects instances of sexual irregularities in Portuguese colonial records from the 1490s through the 1550s. Carol Kazmierczak Manzione finds cases of sexual misconduct adjudicated by the governors of a London charity hospital between 1560 and 1580. Guy Poirier summarizes fantasies about Middle Eastern and North African sexual mores from sixteenth-century French travel writing. Rona Goffen's elegant analysis of the three Paduan frescoes completed by Titian in 1511 discovers unexpected lessons about the burdens of marital chastity. So the four papers trace out material from adjacent decades, but they do so without intersecting. Even where essays in the volume seem to be treating identical or closely related material, they do not engage. Robert Shephard recovers sexual innuendo in gossip about Elizabeth I and James I, while Joseph Cady sorts through a richer trove for attacks on Henri III and his *mignons*. But the papers make contradictory theoretical assumptions about the reconstruction of historical homoerotic identities. Such a contradiction might have been the occasion for an exciting exchange; it provokes in fact only dismissive cross-references in two footnotes (p. 122, n. 49, and p. 153, n. 80, to which compare Poirier's casual judgment on the French evidence at p. 160).

It must also be remembered that the plantings in this plot were arranged for the fall of 1991. They appear in print more than five years later. That is quite a span in the racing development of the history of sexuality. It is, indeed, almost a quarter of the whole history of the (verdant?) field if we go by the editors' own chronology, which starts in 1976 with Foucault's *History of Sexuality*, vol. 1 (p. ix). Most of the authors seem to have revised the annotation of their papers after presentation, but the added works are most often their own. In consequence, some of the volume's arguments sound belated. They address views in terms that have since been revised or entirely redone. Cady, for example, engages in a heavy-handed polemic against what he terms the "new inventionism" of gay history. This seems to be the position usually called "social constructionism," which Cady caricatures as holding that "homosexuality is a relatively new historical 'invention'" (p. 123). (It would be somewhat more accurate to move the quotation marks: " 'homosexuality' is a relatively new historical invention.") Cady says that the view was "popularized first by the works of Jeffrey Weeks, Michel Foucault, and Alan Bray" (p. 123), but when discussing it he cites only the (very faulty) English translation of Foucault (1978) and David Halperin's *One Hundred Years of Homosexuality* (1990). He does not cite any of the dozen volumes that have changed the terms of debate since 1990. To cite some obvious examples: the introduction to Sedgwick's *Epistemology of the Closet* (1990) or "How to Bring Your Kids Up Gay" in her *Tendencies* (1993), half a dozen of the essays in the *Inside / Out* anthology edited by Diana Fuss (1991), Judith Butler's *Bodies that Matter* (1993), Halperin's own *Saint Foucault* (1995), or Leo Bersani's *Homos* (1995).

What I perceive as belatedness may be instead a more deliberate rejection. Cady's essay is not the only one in this volume that seems curiously innocent of gender theory, and the number of remarks against Foucault in the introduction by Jacqueline Murray seem to position the anthology as a sober, scholarly alternative to the excesses of theory. To which one wants to say: Of course there have been silly misuses of Foucault, as there have been needless mystifications in high theory. But Foucault and high theory have at least one advantage. They typically make clear the larger stakes and the deeper unities in any particular investigation.

If the volume seems as a whole both motley and belated, not to say reactionary, it does offer fine individual papers. Beyond those by Partner and Goffen already mentioned, I would single out at least three others. Dyan Elliott shows how Bernardino of Siena's remarks on the marriage debt might open a little more room for female agency. Garrett Epp makes some sense out of the wearying profusion of sexual images in Matthew of Vendôme's *Ars versificatoria*. Barrie Ruth Straus searches cunningly in Chaucer's *Parliament* and *Knight's Tale* and in Margery Kempe for the suppressed voice of women's desires. These branches do indeed flower.

MARK D. JORDAN
Medieval Institute, University of Notre Dame

JOHN CARMI PARSONS and BONNIE WHEELER, eds. *Medieval Mothering*. Garland Reference Library of the Humanities. The New Middle Ages Series, vol. 3. New York and London: Garland Publishing, 1996. Pp. xvii, 384. $60.00.

The title of this volume has been very carefully chosen, for it is not just about mothers in the literal sense, as the editors stress in their introduction, but also about "nurturant behavior" (p. xv). The book begins with a challenge from the editors to the stereotypical images of motherhood in the Middle Ages—a serene Madonna holding her baby close, or "a careless aristocrat who callously rejects her children, sending them into fosterage, monastic life, and warfare" (p. ix). They note that mothering can take many forms, and can be practiced by men as well as women (though in this volume only two male examples are discussed).

This collection will be of interest to medievalists in various disciplines, though the majority of the essays deal with religious texts and historical women. "Fiction" is rather thinly represented: Patricia Ann Quattrin sees Herzeloydë in Wolfram's *Parzival* as a spiritual symbol comparable to Augustine's mother; John Carmi Parsons compares the intercession of the pregnant queen in the Middle English romance *Athelston* with that of the historical Queen Eleanor at Calais as reported by Froissart; Allyson Newton argues for the displacement of the feminine and maternal in *The Clerk's Tale* in favor of the masculine and paternal; and there are overlapping studies of mothers in Norse sagas by Jenny Jochens and Stephan Grundy. Rhetorical use of maternal images and vocabulary in religious contexts is analyzed by Susanna Greer Fein in her study of Aelred of Rievaulx's letter to his sister, and by Maud Burnett McInerney and Andrew Sprung in their discussions of Julian of Norwich.

The two examples of male nurturing are both special cases. In "The Maternal Behavior of God," Pamela Sheingorn argues that Joseph was pushed into the background for much of the Middle Ages because God plays the roles of father and also of elderly husband to the young Virgin. Rosemary Drage Hale demonstrates how Joseph became a more admired and influential figure in the late Middle Ages, perhaps because of the waning of the Marian cult; in this period he is often depicted holding the baby Jesus, or walking hand in hand with Him. It is a pity that there is no discussion of any other fathers or father-figures; the Knight of La Tour Landry and the Ménagier of Paris are two obvious candidates.

The most interesting essays in this collection focus on the scope and potential (or limitations) of women's maternal roles. One of the most striking is Felice Lifshitz's "Is Mother Superior?: Towards a History of Feminine *Amtscharisma*," in which she discusses various monastic rules and uses the convent of Niedermünster in the tenth and eleventh centuries as a case study. She shows that monastic rules for women were defined in male terms; the abbess was rarely called *mater*, and was in fact a "female father." The investiture ceremony for abbesses differed significantly from that for abbots: the new abbess was not given a *baculum* or staff, but merely a copy of the monastic rule (p. 131):

... by virtue of the stipulations of the rule itself she is a female father who stands in the stead of Christ; by virtue of her ordination ceremony she is a castrated father, or at least a deformed one, for she bears no staff; finally, also by virtue of her ordination ceremony, she occupies a maternal throne.

Lipschitz concludes that "Mother Superior is a singularly incomplete and misleading translation of the title *abbatissa*" (p. 131).

In discussing the secular world, a number of contributors work hard to show how caring and devoted medieval mothers could be, with mixed success. Barbara Hanawalt challenges the criticism of a fifteenth-century Italian merchant, much quoted by modern historians, that the English were not loving parents because they fostered their children very young. She makes a convincing case for the maternal devotion of Lady Lisle (hardly a medieval mother), who sent her daughters off to live with French families but kept closely in touch with them by letter, and worked hard to find them suitable positions at court and suitable husbands. The Paston grandmothers discussed by Joel Rosenthal fit the medieval time frame, but are much less rewarding subjects; he seems to be applying modern expectations of the role of grandmother, but is forced to admit that there is little relevant evidence available. There is more information to be had about the queens who are the subject of the next group of essays: Marjorie Chibnall on the Empress Matilda, Lois Huneycutt on Margaret of Scotland and her female descendants, Kimberly LoPrete on Adela of Blois, and Miriam Shadis on Berenguela of Castile. It is hard to be sure how to assess the relative importance of their maternal emotions and their sense of *Realpolitik*; Shadis, like Parsons, stresses that for aristocratic medieval women motherhood offset the weakness implicit in their gender, and concludes that there are "differences between motherhood and womanhood as routes to power, evidently with motherhood dependent upon womanhood but also surpassing it" (p. 351). Of course political ambitions do not preclude the possibility of genuine maternal affection: as Nancy Partner remarks in the elegant essay that ends the collection, "sincerity and strategy sometimes coincide nicely, and clever people recognize their opportunities" (p. 373). Her subject is not an ambitious queen, but the virtuous mother of Guibert of Nogent, who abandoned her young son without warning in order to live a semimonastic life. Partner analyzes his famous autobiography in psychoanalytical terms, arguing that Guibert's presentation of his relationship with his parents can be seen as Oedipal. His mother, apparently repelled by sex, was "an uneasy, reluctant player in the inflexible script of aristocratic family life" (p. 371). Clearly her defection caused Guibert lasting distress, even though he was proud of her piety.

Medieval Mothering begins with an essay that suggests considerable ambivalence about maternity in the Middle Ages: William MacLehose shows that the blood and milk necessary to nourish a child were believed to be potentially toxic and dangerous. The final essay by Partner is a vivid account of a woman who resisted her "natural" reproductive and nurturing role. We are not told much in this volume about general social attitudes to good and bad mothering. How much advice or comment was available in medical manuals or courtesy books, for instance? The editors pose the question, "Can we reasonably read back into the Middle Ages our modern cultural expectations that mothering equals warm nurturing?" (p. xv). No definite answer emerges from these essays, nor are we offered a response to another editorial question, "[W]hat and where are the gaps between maternal and paternal roles?" Fathers and male nurturers other than God and Joseph are hardly mentioned. It would be interesting to know more about the theory and practice of monastic "mothering," and about the roles of male and female teachers, and of foster parents (the latter are mentioned here mostly in connection with the sagas, but occur in many other forms of literature too). The editors point out that most of the information available about mothering comes, inevitably, from male writers, but there are some female sources who are not tapped here, such as Christine de Pizan. We might also ask what and where are the gaps between aristocratic and nonaristocratic mothering; very little is said here about life outside courts and noble households. These essays vary considerably in quality, but the topic is a rich one; it is to be hoped that the appearance of this volume will prompt further studies of medieval mothering, both literary and historical.

ELIZABETH ARCHIBALD
University of Victoria

O. S. PICKERING, ed. *Individuality and Achievement in Middle English Poetry*. Cambridge: D. S. Brewer, 1997. Pp. xi, 227. $71.00.

In his preface, O. S. Pickering remarks that "the influence of a 1960s English department dies hard," and this collection of critical essays certainly does reflect many of the formalist approaches that dominated medieval criticism during the 1960s and 70s. Indeed, one of the explicit purposes of this collection is to counterbalance "the recent growth of theoretical, socio-historical and bibliographical approaches to the study of Middle English literature [that] has led to a decline in the amount of literary appreciation, and to the neglect . . . of poets who are not at the centre of the present-day taught canon." The volume contains twelve essays, five on ME lyric poetry (broadly defined), three on ME drama, and four dealing with longer narrative works. They are arranged roughly in chronological order, with each essay focusing on a distinctive aspect of a particular work or a small cluster of works.

In the first of the several essays on lyric poetry, Karl Reichl proposes that the apparent simplicity of many early Middle English secular lyrics—a simplicity suggestive of popular songs—actually belies the writers' conscious and sophisticated imitation of such works. Reichl believes, however, that some of the lyrics in MS Rawlinson D.913 come close to being true reflections of folk poetry, and he cites "Maiden in the mor lay" as an example. On the whole Reichl's argument is persuasive, though the connection he attempts to establish between "Maiden in the mor lay" and certain Portuguese and Spanish ballads seems more tenuous.

In his own contribution to the collection, Oliver Pickering comments on the distinctive stylistic features shared by a small group of fourteenth-century religious poems, and suggests the possibility of their common authorship. The most essential feature of this group, he finds, is the use of concentrated visual images not unlike those that occur in seventeenth-century "metaphysical poetry." Pickering refers to four of these poems—the "Dispute between Mary and the Cross" being the best known—as the *Dispute* group, and he associates them with other somewhat similar poems—e.g., *The Devils' Parliament* and Richard Maidstone's translation of the seven penitential psalms. This larger group of poems, Pickering believes, reflects a tradition of religious poetry "distinguished by compressed argument and daring image." In another article on Middle English religious lyrics, Julia Boffey discusses the lyric strategies that underlie many late-medieval religious lyrics such as those found in Balliol College MS 354 (Richard Hill's MS). Boffey shows how these poems manage to encapsulate subject matter that "is amenable to much more capacious exposition, and to find ways of making it arresting and memorable." Her essay also deals with *titulus*-verses—poems written to accompany wall paintings or other visual images—and on the relationship between *pictura* and *litteratura*. Her discussion of Lydgate's *Testament* and the series of carved wooden plaques in Holy Trinity Church at Long Melford is particularly compelling.

In his discussion of *The Simonie*, Derek Pearsall considers the ways in which this powerful poem of complaint against the times is like and unlike other works belonging to this genre of satiric poetry. Pearsall believes that *The Simonie* is not a poem in which the depiction of social corruption is for the purpose of initiating reform; rather, it is the expression of a vision of the world in which the flourishing of evil stems from God's plan for the punishment of sinners. As a result, Pearsall argues, the poem has a timelessness that makes attempts to historicize it largely irrelevant.

Thorlac Turville-Petre's essay examines "Ne mai no lewed lued," one of the poems in MS Harley 2253 that concerns a very specific contemporary situation. (This is one of the several poems on social, political, or historical topics in the Harley MS, as Turville-Petre points out, that is *not* to be found in G. L. Brook's *The Harley Lyrics*, the standard edition of the English poems.) The speaker in the poem has been summoned to the ecclesiastical court because he has gotten a young woman pregnant and she is insisting that he wed her—something he is not eager to do. The situation is further complicated by a second woman who also claims he has contracted to marry *her*. Turville-Petre shows how any initial sympathy we might have for the young man "is dissipated little by little, and when it comes to the sentence imposed upon him, to be whipped like a dog at the church . . . and then to be married off by a priest, it seems little more than he deserves."

The longer works discussed in the collection include the *Owl and the Nightingale*, *St. Erkenwald*, and *The Siege of Jerusalem*. David Lawton's discussion of hunting and hawking in the *Siege of Jerusalem* analyzes the specific use of this topos in the *Siege* and also relates it to other alliterative poems in which hunting and hawking figure prominently. Lawton's interesting discussion makes one look forward to the forthcoming edition of *The Siege of Jerusalem*, a work that—due to its stark portrayal of violence against the Jews—"even its editors cannot love." Alexandra Barratt focuses on "Avian Self-Fashioning and Self-Doubt" in the *Owl and the Nightingale*, demonstrating the ways in which this pair of avian debaters are "seething masses of neurotic insecurity." Although I can't agree with her that the poem's humor has been largely ignored by recent commentators, Barratt couldn't be more right in her basic contention that the *Owl and the Nightingale* "is a very funny poem which deserves to be more widely read." John Burrow, in his brief essay on *St. Erkenwald*, considers the effect of the poet's intentional employment of redundancy at strategic moments in the poem: "[T]he *Erkenwald* poet can, at his best, achieve a texture in which traditional redundancies of alliterative verse—alliteration itself, 'formulae', 'variation'—play a full part in what is at the same time densely expressive poetic writing."

The final three essays in the collection concern Middle English drama. Myra Stokes discusses the Wakefield Master's masterful "studies in human nastiness," proving him to be "an expert pathologist of anger and ill-will." She explores this aspect of his dramatic art in all six of the plays attributed to him, beginning with the *Mactatio Abel*, the one play not written in his trademark stanza. In his discussion of the N-Town *Mary Play*, Peter Meredith offers an interesting variety of observations and speculations about an actor's use of "connyng," "personne" and "voice," and about the social contexts in which the play might have been performed. Avril Henry, finally, calls attention to the dramatist's use of unusual rhymes at important moments in *The Castle of Perseverance*, and concludes that it "is not certain whether rhyme-variation in the play reflects extreme sensitivity or ear in the medieval audience, or a craftsman's private delight, or devotional decoration for the glory of God, or simply flamboyant contemporary taste."

All in all, this is a very appealing collection of essays, partly because it is so refreshingly old-fashioned, but even more so because it calls to our attention a wonderful array of lesser-known works that are very deserving of attention. A pair of the essays have as their principal concern two such works—*The Simonie* and "Ne mai no lewed lued"—and in most of the other discussions our attention is drawn to many intriguing but relatively obscure poems, such as "The Festivals of the Church" (*Index* 3415), which contains among other things a stanza on Christ's circumcision; or the lyric poem that warns worldly girls of their mortality, found in MS Harley 116 (*Index* 2136); or Lydgate's *Testament* (*Index* 2464), a poem written late in his life in which he laments his misspent youth. What this group of essays does, finally, is to remind us of the many notable Middle English poems that we rarely have a chance to consider and that we even more rarely have a chance to incorporate into our teaching.

JOHN W. CONLEE
College of William and Mary

SANDRA PIERSON PRIOR. *The Fayre Formez of the Pearl Poet*. Medieval Texts and Studies, vol. 18. East Lansing: Michigan State University Press, 1996. Pp. xiv, 222. $37.95.

This is a fine book of formalist New Criticism of the four well-known Middle English poems—*Pearl*, *Cleanness*, *Patience*, and *Sir Gawain and the Green Knight*—assigned to the anonymous *Pearl*-poet of the fourteenth century. The major strength of the book is not only in what it says about these poems especially in the context of ecclesiastical iconography, illustrating the adage *ut pictura poesis*, but also in what it does by pointing the way for future scholars to pursue. The book provides insights into the formal structures or "fair forms," both visual and verbal, of these poems. Most importantly, the book dwells on the apocalyptic content of the poems, which is its significant contribution to scholarship. Prior sees the apocalyptic ideas of doom, death, punishment, and reward in various forms and shapes repeated and cleverly manipulated by the poet in these four works.

Prior shows that there is a providential plan in the process of sacred history in the Bible. The increasing intensity of sin invites God's intervention, which is characteristically a call to conversion. Punishment brings sinners to their senses and helps them reform their lives. Once sinners are converted, the historical process leading to damnation is reversed and postponed. On the other hand, good deeds and a virtuous life on earth are rewarded not only with the eternal enjoyment of the beatific vision of God but also with the anticipation of glory on earth in the grace of the sacraments, like the Eucharist. Existentially speaking, grace is the beginning and foreshadowing of heavenly joy and glory on earth. Thus, Prior correctly points out two important facets of Biblical and English apocalyptic thought. First, the process of history is reversible in the sense that human history is not naively linear, with an absolute beginning and inevitable end in entropic fashion. Salvation history is, rather, circular in movement, with creation, destruction, and reconstruction or with creation, sin, punishment, and conversion; punishment is constantly thwarted by conversion. Second and consequently, the fact of conversion can and does almost interminably postpone the inevitable doom.

Prior demonstrates how the poet develops this providential pattern of salvation history in an orderly fashion from the first poem to the last. *Pearl* is characterized by the apocalyptic vision of the end borrowed almost verbatim from John's Apocalypse. *Cleanness* is a return to the beginning of sacred history with the early stories of Adam, Noah, and Abraham followed by the later story of Daniel. *Patience* retells the story of Jonah with very obvious apocalyptic overtones. Finally, *Gawain* is a fictional account of a modern Christian and his society. *Gawain* also represents a return to the world and time and literary context of *Pearl*, stressing the pattern of circularity. However, this sweep of history leaves a lacuna—of the period between the time of Daniel and Gawain. Why not incorporate *St. Erkenwald* into this tectonic structure as the fourth book, with *Patience* as the central work, giving us the following chiasmic pattern: *Pearl* (A), *Cleanness* (B), *Patience* (C), *St. Erkenwald* (B'), *Gawain* (A')?

Prior's basic premise, that apocalypticism plays a major role in the works of the *Pearl*-poet, is to be taken seriously. It is worth pointing out that *Pearl* is more apocalyptic than made out in the present book, provided we view it against the literary genre of the apocalypse, which often involves an otherworldly journey and the encounter of the visionary with his alter ego—as in the book's Asian analogues. In Zoroastrian tradition, at death the departing soul meets its *daena*, or the allegory of good deeds, in the person of a beautiful young maiden (compare the *Pearl* maiden) who leads the deceased's soul across a river. It seems that the English poet adroitly exploits apocalyptic motifs such as death, judgment, and reward in *Pearl*, albeit ambiguously. Future *Pearl* students could test and see whether the chiasmic pattern used by the Book of Apocalypse is also employed by the Middle English poet in versification.

Prior is at her best in exploiting the apocalyptic ideas and motifs, especially doom and conversion, found in *Cleanness* and *Patience*. She develops thoroughly the providential pattern of salvation history with special reference to the sacramental typologies of baptism and the Eucharist in these poems.

Gawain seems to pose problems for Prior in the discussion of apocalyptic ideas and motifs. It is the fair form of chivalric romance that seems to disguise the apocalyptic aspect of the poem. Beneath the veneer of romance apparently based on Celtic and Arthurian sources, there lie classical and Islamic subtexts in the poem. A careful comparison of the figure of the Green Knight with Virgil's Charon, his classical antecedent, shows that the Knight is green, old, and netherworldly, as the ferryman Charon is. This perspective would place *Gawain* squarely within the literary genre of the apocalypse with an otherworldly messenger and a vision of hell—the green chapel surrounded by a moat / river over which Bertilak leaps by using his ax handle as Charon could do from hell across the river Styx. Also, there is in the English poem the association of the Green Knight with the Islamic otherworldly green Khadir, who spares the life of a merchant on New Year's Day in the *Arabian Nights*, which also provides the motif of the severed speaking head.

This discussion leaves *St. Erkenwald* in limbo. Arguably, Prior discounts this work as a work of the *Pearl*-poet on the grounds that it is not in the same manuscript (Cotton Nero A. 10) and that it is not in the same dialect, in spite of the many similarities found between it and *Gawain*. Though there does not exist a scholarly consensus on the unity of authorship of these five poems, a case can be made for their common authorship on the same grounds used for the four poems discussed above—their apocalypticism.

In traditional Catholic teaching, the four eschata or "last things" are Death, Final Judgment, Heaven, and Hell. Church teaching also has emphasized particular judgments (the Augustinian "little judgments" referred to by Prior) which each soul must be subject to immediately after death—with a possible dispatch to Limbo, as in the case of the souls of unbaptized infants, to Heaven, to Hell, or to temporary Purgatory, as in the case of those dying with unforgiven and unexpiated venial sins but with forgiven and not fully expiated mortal sins. The good pagan of *St. Erkenwald* seems to have been lodged in Purgatory, like Dante's Virgil, since the poem refers to fire and suffering, which are inconceivable in Limbo; further, the place is temporary, as Purgatory is, for the noble pagan is released from suffering after he receives baptism from St. Erkenwald. Therefore, Prior's treatise on apocalyptic motifs in the works of the *Pearl*-poet raises the possibility of arguing for the common authorship of these five poems.

Though one may cavil at Prior's limiting of the meaning of *forma* and at the exclusion of Aristotelian-Platonic-Scholastic treatises on *forma substantialis,* her rhetorical application of "fair forms" illuminates the formal structuring of the four poems. I encountered only one typo in the book with regard to English words; however, I cannot say the same with regard to Latin. We may dismiss this shortcoming by saying that our computers do not come equipped with Latin spell-checkers! It is regrettable, however, that the bibliography, published in 1996, does not include many works published in the nineties, suggesting that Prior did not consult much recent scholarship.

Sandra Pierson Prior's book is a significant contribution to scholarship on the apocalyptic dimensions of the medieval works it covers, opening the door to opportunities for future scholars.

ZACHARIAS P. THUNDY
Northern Michigan University

SUZANNE REYNOLDS. *Medieval Reading: Grammar, Rhetoric and the Classical Text.* Cambridge Studies in Medieval Literature, vol. 27. Cambridge: Cambridge University Press, 1996. Pp. xvi, 235. $54.95.

Narrowly construed, the subject of this book is the glossing of Horace's *Satires* by grammar teachers in England and northern France during the second half of the twelfth century; but in the manner of the grammarians' glosses, its title discloses a wider authorial intention. In terms of Reynolds's larger purpose, the glosses on Horace's poems illustrate how the pagan classics were read in the Middle Ages, since the ancient Roman poets were studied principally as a means toward learning Latin as a foreign language. "If classical *auctores* are an instrumental part of learning Latin," Reynolds asks, "what precisely does it mean that students 'read' them? How does this affect our notion of what medieval reading was? And how far was that reading shaped by the discipline— *grammatica*—of which it appears to be an integral part?" (p. 11). Her answer is that the reading of such texts was mediated by an "expert reader," whose glossing belongs to a "culturally enshrined practice of using literary texts to teach Latin" (p. 31) that is both shaped by and in turn helps to shape the discipline of *grammatica*.

Horace's *Satires* provide an excellent way into this mediation not only because they were so widely used by twelfth-century Latin teachers (more than eighty twelfth-century copies survive; p. 14), but also because their complexity and difficulty elicit the full range of the glossators' activity. Not the least of Reynolds's achievements is to introduce order into the apparent chaos of heavily glossed pages such as the one that she reproduces and edits as a "case study" (pp. 32–43). By paying close attention to the functions of individual glosses within a coherent teaching program, she is able to group them into distinct categories. At the most elementary level are "lexical glosses in the vernacular" or "translation glosses," which converted the Latin text into a source of new vocabulary. More sophisticated but still focused on single words are glosses that convey information about inflection ("morphological glosses") and glosses that provide lexical information—often including etymologies—in Latin ("synonym glosses"). An important but largely neglected category of glosses are the assorted slashes, dots, letters, and numbers used to identify words that belong to the same syntactic unit or to rearrange such units into "normal" word order ("syntax glosses"). Finally, and most sophisticated of all, are the glosses of tropes, which require "the expositor to recreate and mimic the originating thought of the author" (p. 130). While all these varieties of gloss may appear together on the same page, the relative frequency of each kind depends in large part on the level of student addressed. Following the medieval teachers, Reynolds divides the student-readers of classical texts into two major categories: elementary students of Latin (*pueri*) and more advanced students (*provecti*). Drawing primarily—but by no means exclusively—on two sets of glosses, one directed to elementary and the other to advanced students, she contrasts the more "pragmatic" elementary glosses, which convey data to be memorized, with the advanced glosses, which engage more overtly with theoretical issues.

The relationship between pedagogy and theory, whether covert or overt, is a major focus of the book, and Reynolds discovers some fascinating connections between the glosses of the grammar teachers and the language theories of such figures as Adelard of Bath, William of Conches, and Peter Helias. She displays her learning to best effect in the central chapters (4–8), where she relates the ways in which single words were glossed to twelfth-century theoreticians' preoccupation with the doubleness of the word, with its "first imposition" of naming things and its metalinguistic "second imposition" of naming the names themselves. Less persuasive is her claim that the use of syntactic glosses to convert the artificial word order of the poetic text into the "natural" word order of nonliterary prose and vernacular speech reveals "a tension between accepted notions of reading (the glosses) and writing (the text)" (p. 110) that amounts to a disciplinary conflict between grammar as exposition and rhetoric as composition. Here the theoretical position is at odds with pedagogical practice: the same persons generally taught both grammar and rhetoric during the Middle Ages and the evidence suggests that such teachers saw the two disciplines as complementary rather than adversarial. If there is a "tension" in these syntactic glosses, it is not so much between grammar and rhetoric or even between vernacular and Latin word order as it is between prose and verse: the radical disruption of "normal" word order that such glosses "correct" results above all from Horace's writing in meter. Moreover, in medieval as in ancient times, both the comprehension and the production of metrical discourse were taught under the aegis of grammar.

Reynolds's emphasis on disciplinary boundaries is curious in any case, since she goes on to show how the distinction between grammar and rhetoric dissolves when the glossators expound the intention behind figurative language and so appropriate the function of the author (chapter 10). In seeking the authorial intention behind figurative passages in Horace's text, the glossators were committed to a literal reading, a fact that calls into question the modern assumption that allegory dominated medieval exegesis of pagan texts. As Reynolds shows, medieval exegetes were sensitive to satire's literal purpose—to reprehend vice—and therefore located its ethical value in the "naked text" rather than in a truth hidden beneath the integument of fable. In other words, the glosses served to clarify the surface of Horace's text, not to strip it away. The "new kind of literal reading" that Reynolds describes provides not so much a general model for medieval reception of classical texts as a valuable lesson in the need to contextualize all models of medieval reading not only in terms of time, place, audience, and institutional function, but also in terms of genre.

By looking so carefully at the margins and between the lines of the *Satires*, Reynolds is able to discover some central truths about the ways in which these classical Latin poems were read by, or perhaps better, for medieval students. The categories of mediation that she identifies were applied to other classical texts and even to medieval school texts, such as the fifteenth-century glossed copies of the *Poetria nova* and the *Architrenius* that I happened to examine after reading her book. Yet, as Reynolds demonstrates in some detail, these various techniques of mediation were not mere mechanisms for homogenizing the pagan past but rather flexible tools that enabled medieval teachers to respond not only to the needs of different levels of students but also to the particularities of unique and complex texts. Reynolds effectively shows how medieval teachers at one particular time and place made one such text accessible to beginning and more advanced students of Latin; but the question many readers will find themselves asking is why medieval teachers persisted for so many centuries "in the tacit conviction that difficult Latin literature in verse might serve as the basis for learning the Latin language" (p. 154). Reynolds waits until the very last page of her book to raise that larger question directly, and then only to acknowledge the paradox.

MARTIN CAMARGO
University of Missouri

PETER ROBINSON, ed. Chaucer: *The Wife of Bath's Prologue on CD-ROM*. The *Canterbury Tales* Project. Cambridge: Cambridge University Press, 1996. 1 computer disk; 80 pp. booklet. $240.00.

This is the first installment of the *Canterbury Tales* Project, an undertaking that proposes to make available all data fundamental to reconstructing the textual history of Chaucer's poem. It is an impressive first installment, certain to make evident the value of the larger Project and likely to become a benchmark for similar products in other literary and historical specialties. It demands that its users develop skills with mouse and computer screen well beyond what I suspect most Chaucerians have, and it demands care, even caution, in deriving its extraordinary data. It rewards these skills and this caution with a view of the future and with complete textual data for *The Wife of Bath's Prologue*, data available in no other single source, including Manly and Rickert's *The Text of the* Canterbury Tales.

The CD-ROM contains facsimile-quality digital images of all fifty-eight fifteenth-century witnesses to the Wife's *Prologue* (some 1,200 pages of fifty-four manuscripts and four printed editions), transcriptions of these witnesses in both regularized and unregularized spelling, word-by-word collations of the transcriptions, and, as described in the booklet that accompanies the disk, "spelling databases grouping every occurrence of every spelling of every word in every witness by lemma and grammatical category" (p. 13). The disk also includes Daniel W. Mosser's codicological descriptions of each of the fifty-eight witnesses (a preliminary version of the materials for Mosser's anticipated *Descriptive Catalogue of the Manuscripts and Pre-1500 Printed Editions of the* Canterbury Tales) and Stephen Partridge's transcriptions and collations of all glosses to the Wife's *Prologue*. Mosser and Partridge each provides an essay that introduces the principles underlying his contribution. Further, the disk contains two essays reprinted from *The Canterbury Tales Project Occasional Papers Volume I* (see *SAC* 17 [1995]: 301, no. 23): one by Robinson and Elizabeth Solopova on the theory and principles of transcription of the witnesses, and one by Norman Blake on editing *The Canterbury Tales*.

The manuscript images on the disk can be magnified or printed. Collations and spelling databases are available at the click of a mouse, as are lists that enable comparison of a given line in the witnesses that contain it. Split-screen technology makes it possible to compare manuscript with manuscript, transcript with manuscript, or multiple combinations of manuscript, transcript, and apparatus. The base text for the collations is "a very lightly edited" version of the Hengwrt manuscript, but the collations can be read against any of the fifty-eight witnesses. The disk is fully searchable in both normal language and SGML code. The data can be cut-and-pasted into word processors, and users can add their own hypertext links, bookmarks, and annotations to the disk. Robinson estimates that the disk contains somewhere around 10 million items of information about individual words, their parts of speech, variant spellings, and relations with other occurrences, etc. These data are tied together in a web of some two million hypertext links. God's plenty indeed.

Such a summary description of the materials on the disk and the ways they can be used disguises the work's enormous potential and its possibilities for confusing or frustrating its users. Computer adepts will capitalize on the gold mine of information without having to pause long in confusion. Computer preliterates will probably never get past the confusion. Most of us, however, have much to learn much from the disk, not only about the manuscripts of *The Wife of Bath's Prologue* but also about computer technology. In a month or two of working recurrently with the disk, I have learned how to make my own links and annotations, how to develop sophisticated searches, how to toggle between the CD-ROM and various word processors, etc. In short, I have learned how to manipulate the technology to move toward using the vast quantities of information here, although I do not imagine that I have exhausted the potential for complex searches. The instructional booklet that accompanies the disk is helpful, but not thorough in explaining processes or abbreviations; the "help" screens on the disk itself are extensive.

Facing this first installment of the Project is something like facing Manly and Rickert's *Text of the* Canterbury Tales for the first time, despite the important differences between the two. Perhaps the most important difference is that Robinson's CD is only a beginning. Manly-Rickert includes various surmises and conclusions about the textual history of *The Canterbury Tales* as well as textual data for the entire work. Robinson's CD includes data from the *Wife's Prologue* only—the kind of data from which Robinson and Blake promise to generate their own surmises and conclusions, but raw data nevertheless. I imagine that the codes and charts and bland typeface of Manly-Rickert were as intimidating in 1940 as the electronic wizardry of the CD-ROM is today, and though the Manly-Rickert blizzard of sigils and abbreviations has become more familiar with time, Robinson's *Wife's Prologue* benefits from more normal language in the collations. Nevertheless, the multiple-screen technology produces some baffling codes of its own. Terms like "regapp," "unregapp," "linapp," and "revwtxt" are used to label individual screens, meaning (I think) "regularized apparatus," "unregularized apparatus," "line apparatus," and "review witnesses to the text of a given line" respectively. "Fulltext" labels a number of different kinds of screens, creating possibilities for confusion when multiple screens are open simultaneously, and none of these screen-labels identifies which witness is being viewed, making possible much greater confusion. When comparing transcripts of individual manuscripts, for example, I often find it necessary to scroll to the top or bottom of a given screen to recall which manuscript I am viewing.

Moreover, scrolling itself causes some problems, especially when one manipulates the manuscript images and certain parts of the apparatus. Magnification or reduction of a given image brings one back to the top of the image, requiring recurrent back-scrolling to reach the point of interest when attempting to examine closely a particular word or flourish. However, because one can here closely examine magnifications of individual words, flourishes, even marks of punctuation, the irritation of scrolling is minor compared with the rewards.

Scrolling any collation screen produces a curious glitch. The top of the screen conveniently includes the base-text version of the line under consideration, yet once scrolled off-screen, the base-text line reappears in a scrambled version when one scrolls back to it. Such glitches and the issues of labeling above make it necessary that users be very cautious about the information they carry away from the disk.

An extended example will help clarify the kinds of information available and the caution necessary in deriving it. The CD enables users to examine any given word or line of the *Wife's Prologue* in a number of ways. Clicking on the line number to, say, line 1, produces a "revblk" screen (a bit of code I have not broken). The screen usefully informs us that in forty-seven witnesses, line 1 appears after a rubric; in seven, it appears first without a rubric; and in four the line is "out," or does not appear at all. Clicking on the icon next to forty-seven produces a "revwtxt" screen that reads "Single-click on any line to move to that line in the transcription. Number of witnesses with this reading in line 1: 47." The screen then lists each witness in which line one appears after a rubric, even though the text in the list is not fully formatted. That is, the text of the lines listed on this screen is normalized in ways that it is not elsewhere on the disk, making it necessary that users are careful not to use this text instead of the more precise version of the base-text.

A similar search route produces another, almost identical, "revwtxt" screen. Clicking on the word "Experience" in the base-text results in a "regapp" screen that identifies all variants of the opening word of the *Wife's Prologue*, forty-two of which agree with the lemma, seven reading "Experiment," and four out. Clicking on the number "42" brings another "revwtxt" screen very easily confused with the one above. It reads "Single-click on any line to move to that line in the transcription. Number of witnesses with this reading in line 1:42," and it lists each witness to line 1 that has the word "Experience" in initial position, a list very similar to the one above. The information on the two "revwtxt" screens is accurate, precise, and useful, but one screen is too easily confused with another, especially when one or both is held open for future reference. There is simply no way to distinguish them except by remembering which is which or by repeating the searches. With multiple screens and frequent rearrangement of screens, memory is not sufficient. Redoing the search for certainty is easy enough, and that is the point I wish to make: users must confirm the information they derive because the system of labeling on the disk is insufficient to the point of potential confusion.

Similar caution is necessary in using the spelling databases where the complicated taxonomy of grammatical categories can lead users to make incorrect assumptions about the data they are viewing. Calling up the verb "be" in the All-witness Spelling Database produces the impressive datum that the verb occurs 12,828 times in 172 spellings. This is further broken down to tell us that the verb occurs 1,040 times as an infinitive in 12 spellings, with 902 occurrences spelled "be"; 19, "bee"; 73, "ben," etc. The five occurrences of "ben" with a terminal flourish and the three occurrences where it has a macron over the "n" are distinguished from unadorned "ben," as are other variations. It takes a bit of scrolling, however, to discover that the "be" spelling also occurs as an infinitive in initial position 59 times, in addition to the 902 listed previously, with capped (56) and uncapped (3) occurrences listed separately. Another bit of scrolling finds that the "be" spelling of the infinitive also occurs 366 more times in rhyme position, but it takes a good ten or so more screens to find listed the one occurrence of "be" as an indicative present singular, the 183 occurrences of indicative present plural, and the 159 occurrences of the subjunctive present singular. Continued scrolling (or paging) discovers the remaining instances of subjunctive, impersonal, and participial instances of the verb in its "be" spelling. This is impressive data indeed, and with a 200 MHz Pentium computer, it took me just over a minute to do this scrolling, although on a 100 MHz model with a slower CD-ROM drive it took well over five. The minimum equipment required to run the CD is a 386 or faster PC with at least a double-speed CD-ROM drive, Windows 3.1+, and 8 MB of RAM (or Macintosh System 7 or later, double-speed CD-ROM drive, and 4 MB RAM), but I am sure that the disk would be very frustrating to use on minimal equipment. I suggest that users work on very fast machines, that they double-check their search paths, and that they make certain they derive complete information. On the other hand, for the purposes of this review, I easily cut-and-pasted above quotations from the "revwtxt" screens, and I printed the data about "be" just as easily, enabling me to check the data without having to scroll more than once on a slow machine.

Like Manly-Rickert, the CD-ROM is intended primarily for those interested in textual and editorial issues, a basic reference tool for libraries. But the disk shows the potential for the overall Project to go well beyond Manly-Rickert in some important ways. Partridge's information about the glosses is much more extensive than that in Manly-Rickert. Mosser's descriptions of the witnesses are more detailed than Manly and Rickert's, and they benefit from the many recent advances in codicology. The spelling databases of the *Canterbury Tales* Project in particular will be a resource for historical linguists unavailable in Manly-Rickert, indeed unavailable anywhere else at present with the possible exception of the archives of the *Middle English Dictionary*.

Furthermore, the CD supersedes Manly-Rickert in at least one fundamental way: the graphic capabilities of electronic publication make for very refined transcriptions and the transcripts are all here for the checking. I cannot pretend to have checked transcriptions on the CD at all exhaustively, but I can say that what I have checked has been 100 percent accurate. According to Robinson, each transcription was checked at least three times, and wherever possible, checked and double-checked against the manuscript itself as well as a reproduction. To transcribe the witnesses of the *Wife's Prologue*, Robinson and Solopova developed a unique transcription policy, detailed in their essay included on the disk. While they acknowledge that no transcription can duplicate a manuscript, Robinson and Solopova provide a system of "graphemic" transcription that distinguishes a number of abbreviations, superscripts, marks of punctuation, and special or terminal characters that are beyond the alphabet or ASCII code. This makes for, as they put it, very "rich" transcription that is more open to error than a less complicated system. Awareness of this potential for error has apparently encouraged the transcribers to be highly cautious, and if the entire Project achieves what seems to be the standard of this disk, it will be very high indeed. When they wrote their essay describing the transcription method, Robinson and Solopova hoped that their final check of the transcripts would "find less than one correction for every four thousand characters," and presumably the final check took care of those. They hope that scholars who check their transcripts will find them "perfectly reliable." I did not check four thousand characters in each or any of the fifty-eight witnesses, but I did spot-check various collations against the manuscript images, against Manly-Rickert, and against John Fisher's unpublished Variorum collations of the *Wife's Prologue.* I did not discover any errors on the CD, and I was recurrently astonished at how much information it includes.

There can probably never be a simple, single, or final test of Robinson and Solopova's method, of the *Wife of Bath's Prologue* on *CD-ROM*, or of the *Canterbury Tales* Project more generally. Their success will depend upon how much they are used, imitated, and relied upon. So, I am at something of a loss to pronounce judgment on any of them now, so early in what will be their scholarly legacy. Nevertheless, the labor involved in producing this one disk is enormous, exacting, and justified. Peter Robinson's vision in embarking on the task is to be commended. He developed the electronic collation program that underlies the enterprise and was instrumental in developing the *Canterbury Tales* Project to make possible this first installment. The disk testifies that Robinson's vision is both practical and exciting. The Web page of the *Canterbury Tales* Project (http:www.shef.ac.uk/uni/projects/ctp/Main/occ.html) promises that a CD-ROM of *The General Prologue* will be available late in 1997, *The Nun's Priest's Tale* in 1998, and that significant progress is under way for the transcription of all of fragments 1 and 7. May they all be as careful as Robinson's first CD, and may they become less daunting with familiarity.

MARK ALLEN
The University of Texas at San Antonio

ROSENTHAL, JOEL T. *Old Age in Late Medieval England.* Middle Ages
Series. Philadelphia: University of Pennsylvania Press, 1996. Pp. xv,
260. $39.95.

Late medieval poets often portray old men as foolish, incompetent, be-
sotted in love, or impotent—witness January of *The Merchant's Tale*, the
pilgrim Miller and Reeve, "John Gower" of *Confessio Amantis*, or
Langland's narrator, ravaged by Elde (B passus 20; C passus 22).
Medieval iconographic depictions of old age (*senectus*) display a feeble,
poverty-stricken, bent figure supported by a crutch. These literary and
artistic views do not necessarily reflect everyday attitudes toward senior
citizens in late medieval England, as Joel T. Rosenthal demonstrates in
his fine recent study of *Old Age in Late Medieval England.* It would be
more factual to proclaim, with Chaucer's Knight, "Elde hath greet
avantage," or again, "In elde is both wysdom and usage." The evidence
suggests that Englishmen of the later Middle Ages respected old people, hoar upon their heads, and that more people than might be thought
enjoyed productive careers into what today we conceive of as old age.
This does not mean, however, that late medieval English society quali-
fies as a "gerontocracy," as Rosenthal hastens to point out.

Rosenthal, a social historian who has written often and well about
medieval gender and family issues, evaluates aging from cultural and
historical perspectives. He examines "Some Data and Data Sets," including Inquisitions Post Mortem, Proofs of Age, and the Scrope and
Grosvenor Depositions (part 1); various material drawn from "Three-
Generation Families," including Last Wills and Testaments (part 2);
and "Full Lives and Careers," case studies including Genealogies,
Bishops' Records (drawn from Emden), and literary documents that disclose perceptions and *mentalitées* toward old age (part 3). Of special interest to Chaucerians are "The Scrope and Grosvenor Depositions"
(chapter 3) and "Men and Women of Letters" (chapter 10), both of
which contain reflections on Chaucer's life and career.

Rosenthal treats his prosopographical data with considerable caution.
He is keenly aware that his sources may not be fully trustworthy from
a modern statistical viewpoint, since they were assembled in codified,
formulaic ways. Those giving testimony frequently relied on folk memory or invoked parables, hearsay, or round numbers ("forty years and
somewhat more"). Nonetheless, the Inquisitions Post Mortem and
Proofs of Age are, says Rosenthal, "a mine of information far beyond any

other body of extant material"—"if," he adds, "used with care" (p. 15). He can and does read this material as "social discourse" (p. 42). Rosenthal has recourse to Durkheim's concept of "social facts" and the more recent notion of "social memory" (p. 13) to approach his data sets as repositories of information concerning old age.

Rosenthal argues backward from the heir's attested age to locate the probable age (within a range) of the predecessor. For example: "A son of 40 years and more must have meant a father in his early to mid-60s, and if the data are accurate the chances are that the father might have been in his late 60s or beyond" (p. 31). In his case study of the English bishops from 1399 to 1485, he compiles a fascinating table (9-4) that shows the date of first benefice (when known), date of nomination to the episcopacy, and year of death. The final column shows the length of total service in the church ("Pre- + as bishop"). Some men spent most of their career in lesser benefices while others were quickly nominated to the bishopric. Simon Sydenham's pre-episcopal career lasted 40 years; he was bishop for 7 years. Thomas Bourgchier (born 1410), by contrast, was bishop for 53 years but his pre-episcopal service lasted only 7 years. Of the ninety bishops in table 9-4, one (William Waynflete) served for 70 years, four for 60 or more, six for 50 or more, twenty-three for 40 or more, fourteen for 30 or more, and seventeen for 20 or more. Rosenthal remarks that longevity itself was an important factor in an episcopal career: "No matter how talented and well-connected one might be at the beginning of a career, if one did not survive a certain number of years one did not live to become a bishop" (p. 135).

For the Scrope-Grosvenor Hearings—the famous trial in the Court of Chivalry in which Chaucer gave testimony on behalf of Sir Richard Scrope, the eventual winner in this case—fully 29 percent of Scrope's deponents were age sixty or more, whereas only 7 percent of Sir Robert Grosvenor's deponents were that old. Nearly 80 percent of Scrope's deponents testified that they were aged forty or more—"a distinctly gray-bearded group," comments Rosenthal (p. 47)—whereas 54 percent of Grosvenor's witnesses were that age. Chaucer in his testimony claimed that he was "xl ans et plus armeez par xxvii ans." From this statement Chaucerians have determined that Chaucer was born about 1340 and that he lived to "fifty years and more," an age attained by about one in six landholding men in late medieval England. In the Scrope-Grosvenor trial, age, stability, and nobility mattered, since the issue was which family had the right to bear the device "azure a bend or." "In this unique proceeding," says Rosenthal, "much more than in the run of Proof of Age determinations, age was likely to be equated with gravity and credibility" (p. 46).

Rosenthal considers retirements in late medieval England. For most people in this time retirement was not an option; but for those who enjoyed significant careers, especially in the church, retirement was sometimes possible. The issues Rosenthal tackles are: when did people choose to retire and under what circumstances? He concludes that there were no pressures to continue working and no concept of "golden years": "We have moralizing about the final stages of the life line, but no one spoke about the potential pleasures and opportunities of golden years, now upon them, except for homilies about spiritual freedom from sensuality" (p. 113). Nor did senior men step aside to make room for younger generations: "If he was to stay in line, and if he chose to stay in line, tough luck for those behind him" (p. 114). Kings did not retire from the throne; prelates did not as a rule abdicate. There were distinct advantages to remaining on the job as long as possible. Age had its privileges.

Chaucerians will discover few surprises in Rosenthal's chapter on "Men and Women of Letters." He provides well-known autobiographical material from the writings of Chaucer, Gower, Hoccleve, Lydgate, Trevisa, and others—material about which he is properly skeptical. Yet these familiar statements have a somewhat new look in context of the demographic data presented in Rosenthal's previous chapters. He concludes that patrons were not interested in supporting "boy geniuses" but rather "stable and trustworthy figures who could be relied on to trumpet their own political virtues and values" (p. 166).

As Rosenthal observes in his preface, old age has become a "hot topic" in medieval and modern studies. Within the last dozen years (and within three years of each other), three studies of the ages of man—by Elizabeth Sears, Mary Dove, and J. A. Burrow—appeared. In 1992 Alfred David gave a memorable Presidential Address on "*Old, New*, and *Yong* in Chaucer" at the New Chaucer Society Conference (published in volume 15 of *SAC*). More recently, Shulamith Shahar contributed *Growing Old in the Middle Ages* (1995; English translation 1997). Rosenthal's study is not the last word on this important topic; but with his creative scrutiny of published material, Rosenthal shows how it might be done.

JAMES M. DEAN
University of Delaware

PIOTR SADOWSKI. *The Knight on His Quest: Symbolic Patterns of Transition in* Sir Gawain and the Green Knight. Newark: University of Delaware Press, 1996. Pp. 289. $37.50.

With its poetic richness and interpretive multivalence, *Sir Gawain and the Green Knight* has happily accommodated modern discussions based on a wide variety of critical approaches. In the first chapter of his book, Piotr Sadowski reviews a number of those discussions, grouping them into five major categories, which he labels the ethnological-genetic, the literary critical, the theological, the psychological, and the literary historical (p. 27). Missing from the list, it will be noticed, are any of the poststructuralist approaches that have been so important in the critical work of the recent past. Sadowski's own analysis, while it does not completely ignore newer contributions, is generally informed by older, more traditional conversations about the poem. Although the choice to position himself away from the most *au courant* criticism does limit what Sadowski can contribute to the study of the poem, it is less troublesome than the ahistoricized context Sadowski produces for the *Gawain*-poet. Among the categories he has identified, Sadowski characterizes his own approach as "closest to historical criticism with elements of literary criticism and source study" (p. 44). Yet rather than localizing the poem within its likely provenance, a provenance that has been fruitfully explored (despite the *Gawain*-poet's anonymity) both by historians and by literary scholars, Sadowski instead sets it within the old monolithic Middle Ages, in which texts from different centuries and different locations across Europe are presumed to "represent an essentially homogenous and unified picture of the world, of the kind spoken of some time ago by C. S. Lewis" (p. 15).

Such presuppositions may put off some prospective readers. Nonetheless, the book is not without interest. Along with its anatomy of traditional approaches to *Sir Gawain and the Green Knight*, Sadowski's first chapter also includes a delineation of his own critical framework, that of systems theory. He is perhaps too sanguine about the exactness and objectivity of his approach, about its capacity to offer a "holistic view of literary reality" (p. 49). Yet he is at the same time surely accurate in praising the systemic approach for its versatility and complexity. The approach allows Sadowski to come at the poem from a variety of angles, examining the relations among text, author, and audience as he considers the mythic patterns manifested in the elements of Gawain's quest. In this view, Gawain becomes a kind of Everyman, presented

327

with a set of tests and transitions that force him to confront the in-
evitable limitations of the human condition. Following the introduc-
tory discussion are chapters entitled "The Temporal Structure of *Sir
Gawain*," "The Greenness of the Green Knight," "Sir Gawain's
Pentangle," "Gawain's Threefold Temptation," and "The Head and the
Loss Thereof."

The systemic approach, with its use of charts and diagrams to quan-
tify observations, serves Sadowski best in the book's fourth chapter, "Sir
Gawain's Pentangle: The *Imago Hominis* and the Virtue of Temperance."
Drawing on the poem's description of the pentangle as "a syngne þat
Salamon set sumquyle / In bytoknyng of trawþe" (lines 625–26),
Sadowski makes connections with salient biblical passages before moving on to consider the numerological symbolism associated with the
number five and the geometrical properties of a pentangle (most notably, the properties of the golden section ratio inherent in its construction), with the ultimate goal of illuminating Gawain's virtues as
they are reflected in the sign. Sadowski's observations are evocative
rather than definitive, and readers unfamiliar (or uncomfortable) with
geometry may not find enough documentation and explanation to follow the argument fully. Moreover, even in this chapter Sadowski shies
away from particularity as he considers the intellectual context that
might have produced the poem's elaborately explicated sign of the pentangle: "It is not unlikely that the *Gawain*-poet was himself familiar
with some Hermetic and Neoplatonic texts," Sadowski writes, "because
the intellectual sophistication of the pentangle passage clearly calls for
some definite source of this kind as an inspiration" (p. 127). The statement makes an important point, yet surely a more specific and localized
examination of its implications would have added to its value. Where
might a fourteenth-century poet from the Northwest Midlands have
come into contact with such texts? Which "definite source" would be a
possible candidate for his reading? Here and throughout his book,
Sadowski leaves such questions unconsidered. Yet at the same time, his
attention to the geometrical proportions and the symbolism of the pentangle reiterates the *Gawain*-poet's vital investment in this aspect of
medieval learning, rightly emphasizing the significance of number in
the meaning of the poem.

The chapter on the pentangle, then, provides worthwhile observations, even if they are vitiated by the same limitations that characterize
the book from its outset. Another crucial limitation to Sadowski's interpretations of the poem as a whole, though, is the lack of attention to

women, and most importantly, to the role of Morgan. Twice, Sadowski alludes to her centrality to the workings of the plot (pp. 154, 214–15), yet both these mentions are very brief. Sadowski seems aware of the lack, for in an endnote he acknowledges that he has only "cursorily dealt" with "the enigmatic role played by Morgan le Fay" (p. 262, n. 102.) But beyond the neglect of Morgan, Sadowski also fails to mention Gawain's antifeminist outburst (lines 2414–28). Even without emphasizing feminist approaches, any reading of the poem in its entirety (which Sadowski purports to be giving) will fall short if it fails to account for such prominent and perplexing elements. Here, Sadowski's commitment to older and more traditional approaches to the poem seems to hamper his ability even to see aspects of the poem that newer discussions have brought into focus.

Sadowski writes that his aim in the book is "not the purity of methodological approach or a validation of a theory, but rather the exciting intellectual adventure of engaging in a mental interaction with the *Gawain*-poet through his text" (p. 49). The particular adventure Sadowski sets for himself is constrained by his omission of some of the poem's important elements and of its specific historical context. Yet even with its limitations, the book does evoke some of the complex traditions that *Sir Gawain and the Green Knight* embodies.

DONNA CRAWFORD
Virginia State University

M. C. SEYMOUR, gen. ed. *Authors of the Middle Ages: English Writers of the Late Middle Ages: Vol. 3, Nos. 7-11.* Aldershot, Hants.: Variorum; and Brookfield, Vt.: Ashgate Publishing, 1996. Pp. vi, 256. $67.95.

The present hardback volume comprises five studies of individual named authors that have also been made available by the publishers as separate paperback titles. Accordingly, a double system of pagination is provided; references in the contents pages are to the individual paginations (though references below are to the running pagination). As I have noted in an earlier review of Ralph Hanna's *William Langland* in this series, the slim format of the individual pamphlet-style versions of these studies makes them ideal for slipping into a pocket or briefcase when one is engaged in library work.

In the present volume, the medieval authors and their modern commentators are as follows: William Caxton, by N. F. Blake; Reginald Pecock, by Wendy Scase; Robert Henryson, by Douglas Gray; William Dunbar, again by Douglas Gray; and John Capgrave, by M. C. Seymour, who also serves as the general editor of the subseries. (A second subseries on Historical and Religious Writers of the Latin West is edited by Patrick Geary.)

The separate studies have been written according to a flexible set of common guidelines, aiming to give the biographical facts for each author, including a review of scholarship; a detailed list of works and manuscripts; a printing or listing of documentary and other sources for the author's life; and a selective secondary bibliography. The precise arrangement for including these elements varies slightly from study to study according to immediate requirements, but all are present.

Thus, appendices to the individual studies contain a calendar of biographical references for Caxton and documents for Pecock's life printed in full or in excerpts, while those for Henryson (almost nonexistent) and Dunbar appear in footnotes; the considerably more numerous records of Capgrave's life are used passim in the narrative text or appear in the footnotes, and are supplemented by a short table of dates. In the cases of Pecock and Capgrave respectively, Scase and Seymour are able to include previously unknown biographical and contextual information that marks a useful advance in scholarly knowledge of these writers. (Two potentially misleading typos occur on page 52 of the Caxton appendix, where the dates in documents I.T. 2 and 3 should read "1493–96" in both instances.)

One of the most useful features of these studies is the full listing of manuscripts and early prints of works written by the individual authors (or, in the case of Caxton, works issued from his press, though a list of manuscript copies from Caxton prints would also have been welcome). These lists are up-to-date, reliable, and extremely handy for quick reference.

The lengths of the studies naturally vary according to the amount of surviving information: Caxton occupies 68 pages, Pecock 72, Henryson 18, Dunbar 16, and Capgrave 56. All, however, contain solid factual information in a concise manner. In the main, the modern commentators have tried to treat their authors objectively and later scholarship judiciously. Purely literary criticism rarely intrudes—Blake comments briefly on Caxton's style as translator and critic (pp. 36, 37–38), Gray makes some favorable aesthetic judgments on Dunbar (pp. 185–86), while Seymour castigates regularly Capgrave's writing and scholarly abilities (for example, pp. 218, 221, 225, 233–34, 235).

To borrow a term from Derek Pearsall, whose similarly constructed monograph on John Lydgate appeared in 1997, the present studies are "bio-bibliographies," whose primary purpose is to provide a solid foundation for further study. Essentially, then, these studies concentrate on basic factual material, similar to what one might expect in a well-crafted introduction to a modern EETS edition. Therein lies their utility and value: they collect, synthesize, and print otherwise disparate materials and provide fair and expert guidance to the evaluation of the original sources and later scholarship.

LISTER M. MATHESON
Michigan State University

GALE SIGAL. *Erotic Dawn Songs of the Middle Ages: Voicing the Lyric Lady.* Gainesville: University Press of Florida, 1996. Pp. xii, 241. $49.95.

This careful and sensitive reading of the *alba* in Occitan, Old French, Middle High German, and Middle English is discreetly and convincingly revisionist in both its methods and conclusions. That it succeeds so well is testimony not only to Gale Sigal's scholarship but also, depressingly, to the manner in which received opinion can be perpetuated for so long in the face of contrary evidence. The inability of students of the lyric to offer a proper assessment of the female voice in the *alba* is mainly due, Sigal argues, to their failure to distinguish the genre from the larger body of *canso*, of which it is usually considered a part. It is also refreshing to read a book that celebrates, like the *alba*, the vitality and eloquence of the female voice, rather than condemn the nature and causes of its repression.

The introduction (pp. 1–20) provides a critical review of scholarship (in particular by Hatto, Savile, and Dronke) and briefly raises issues that will be treated in more detail in later chapters. In particular, Sigal notes the paradox of the female voice being articulated by what one must suppose to be male authors; the empathy of male poets with the female subject transcends medieval misogyny and humanizes the courtly *domna.*

331

In chapter 1, "The Alba Lady: Literary Perspectives" (pp. 23–50), Sigal takes to task earlier scholars such as Savile and Fries for fitting the lady of the *alba* into existing, but inappropriate, categories, usually derived from other genres of the courtly lyric. A brief review of the presentation of women in some narrative genres provides material for comparison, although the courtly romance (where the similarities are surely greater) is given only passing mention. This chapter, like most of the others, also contains some sensitive detailed commentary on individual lyrics. The general humanization of the *alba* lady also implies unabashed intimacy and frank sexuality, resulting in a radically different presentation of women.

Chapter 2, "The *alba* Lady: Sex Roles and Social Roles" (pp. 51–93), opens with the observation that in the *alba*, the lady often initiates the love affair, a fact once more overlooked by earlier scholars. The male-dominated world is excluded from the *alba*, as the love relationships in these poems are defined by mutuality and reciprocity; the lovers, however, are seen as powerless to change the problematic situations in which they find themselves. Despite the frequent presence of the *gelos*, love in the *alba* is not always adulterous; the Middle High German *tageliet* and Chaucer's reworking of the genre in *Troilus and Criseyde* are cases in point.

The relative social positions of the lovers form the subject of chapter 3, "Eros in the Socius" (pp. 94–130). Again, the *alba* forms a clear contrast with other lyric genres, since the relationship between the lovers is presented as horizontal rather than hierarchical. Despite the lover usually being technically the lady's social inferior, the significant social relationship in the *alba* is that between the pair of lovers and the husband, the latter clearly socially superior. Yet as regards the lovers alone, the *alba* is subversive, since it disdains class as well as marriage; if the lovers are alienated from society by the pervasive presence of the *lauzengiers*, they enjoy the approval of God.

Sigal examines the symbolism of night and dawning in chapter 4, "Eros and Dawning Identity" (pp. 133–68). The lovers are alive while the rest of the world sleeps; night obscures the perception of time and stresses the immediacy of the present. Despite, or perhaps because of, Sigal's attempts to demonstrate the development of the *alba* tradition beyond the Middle Ages, there are some rather dizzying chronological leaps in this chapter, particularly as she moves from Donne ("The Sunne Rising") backward through Chaucer, Heinrich von Morungen, and

Giraut de Bornelh. This chapter is nevertheless notable, in my opinion, for an excellent reading of Giraut's "Reis glorios" and its shift in voice from the lady to the lover's male companion, here the *gaita*. The reciprocity of *alba* love also leads through the inseparability of the lovers to an almost androgynous symbiosis.

In chapter 5, "First Light: Mask and Masquerade" (pp. 169–94), Sigal argues that the protagonists of the *alba* reflect a new sense of the self in the second half of the twelfth century, love being the agent of that transformation. This is a much more problematic issue than Sigal seems to admit, content as she is to cite the usual studies on the subject (mainly Morris and Hanning). I am not sure there is an easy way to deal with this subject: it is complex, far from monolithic in nature, and intimately bound up with contemporary developments in philosophy and theology. Nevertheless, the received view that romance heroes are individuals as opposed to the collective and representative heroes of the *chanson de geste* stands in need of revision and refinement. In the last part of the chapter, Sigal shows how dawn is a loaded symbol, the *alba* freezing an untenable situation at the height of its emotional intensity. It symbolizes both union and separation and the transition between them.

In her conclusion, "The Fractured Self" (pp. 195–203), Sigal shows that, despite the symbiosis of the lovers, the *alba* paradoxically separates body from heart, contrasting presence and absence, union and separation. There are notes on pages 205–14, a bibliography on pages 215–29, and an index on pages 321–41.

Since the complete corpus of *albas* is not large, Sigal is able to consider examples from a number of languages and, as I have pointed out, the postmedieval life of the genre. While this comparative approach works well for the most part, there is a sense in which the individual poems by Giraut de Bornelh, Cadenet, Gace Brulé, Heinrich von Morungen, Wolfram von Eschenbach, and others demand to be situated in more depth in their own linguistic and cultural traditions. On the other hand, this would have doubled the length of the book and perhaps detracted from the presentation of the corpus as a coherent tradition. In sum, however, this book provides an excellent reassessment of the *alba* and its originality and is an important contribution to our understanding of the medieval lyric.

KEITH BUSBY
The University of Oklahoma

PAUL BEEKMAN TAYLOR. *Chaucer's Chain of Love*. Madison and Teaneck: Fairleigh Dickinson University Press, 1996. Pp. 215. $35.00.

Taylor begins his thorough study by discussing the background of Theseus's famous First Mover speech as Chaucer's "encyclopedic reference book for his poetic enterprise" (p. 19). In that speech, as in its background, the European intellectual tradition of the *catena aurea* from Homer through Dante (admirably surveyed on astonishingly few pages), the cosmos and its triune structure are seen as held in place by the chain of love, the central binding principle in Chaucer's medieval world as well as the central dramatic principle in his textual universe.

After this introductory chapter, the critic's perspective zooms in on the horizontal chain of love, the earthly, linear temporality (connected to God's eternity) of human life described by Theseus as "progressiouns" and "successiouns." In this part, which represents the second substantial treatment of literary and extraliterary time in Chaucer's poetry since Paul Strohm's splendid chapter 5 in his *Social Chaucer* (Cambridge, Mass.: Harvard University Press, 1989), Taylor (who is unaware of Strohm's study) intends to demonstrate how the storytelling (i.e., art-making) pilgrims, who kill and transcend time on the way to Canterbury, emulate God's own timelessness in that their stories are in time but do not move with it: "Retelling story, like the hag's riddling choice, retrieves the past, so that pilgrimage recollected is grace retrieved, sin and time redeemed" (p. 55). He also makes some suggestive observations about female protagonists' conceptual and male protagonists' perceptual dealings with time, but overlooks how many of the supposedly female perceptions are framed by the male narrator's wishful gaze.

Taylor then investigates *The Legend of Good Women* as a text that exposes the women's (and perhaps the poet's?) vain attempt to link the sight and linguistic signs of love with an insight into and true expression of its deeper form, and reads *Troilus and Criseyde* and *The Knight's Tale*—two plots that repeat the threefold process of amatory possession (visual, verbal, physical) typical of the stories in *LGW*—as texts that reveal how man's *ratio* and words may either direct affections toward unworthy or worthwhile objects, "but do best when they hold him to those activities proper to time and place in his life" (p. 75). Next, the Clerk's Grisilde, unlike the Franklin's impatient Dorigen, is held to exemplify how the womb of a woman mediates God's providence by serving both the measurable process of natural time and the progress of redemptive time. She is the vehicle through which "an idle life sets itself on a track toward a future good higher on the chain of love" (p. 106). Taylor similarly shows the extension and varying levels of love's chain by pitching the knight's serious concern for the glory days of secure monarchical order against the uproarious fourteenth-century disarray in the responses of the Miller, Reeve, and Cook.

Several other tales (e.g., WBT, PardT) also undergo Taylor's allegorizing readings as more or less successful quests for physical or spiritual love, a universalizing strategy that sometimes brings the critic dangerously close to forcing his theoretical choice too schematically onto the literary texts and which reminds readers of Robertsonian techniques or other trends that would favor a moral and Christian Chaucer. Thus, the incomplete Tale of Sir Thopas is supposed to figure the incompleteness of the pilgrimage and its binding book while the completeness of the Tale of Melibee becomes an "emblem of the completeness of God's design which one is liable to read as confusion" (p. 132). The specter of nominalism, which might well have served as a philosophical correspondence to explain what Taylor terms open-endedness or indeterminacy,[1] is invoked several times (pp. 57, 89, 143, 156) only to disappear into oblivion. However, this is scarcely surprising with a critic who is convinced that the late medieval writer "prefers the Boethian model to various opposing Scholastic and Nominalist speculations" and was "too cautious to take the confident stance of the zealot and proselitizer" (p. 156).

This latter statement may characterize Taylor at least as much as Chaucer, especially when one remembers the study's puzzling prologue. Perhaps to safeguard against the current antiphilological rhetoric in the academy, he tries too hard to please both sides of the debate. He joins— rather zeugmatically—the Hirschean idea that "[a] reading of Chaucer suggests its own theory" with the truism that "[t]here are many rooms in the mansion of Chaucerian criticism," and further claims that he has "no stake in any particular critical stance" because the poet's texts are "ideologically open-ended" (p. 16). However, the very reasonable methodological (hence theoretical) resolve to read—in the wake of

---

[1] For such a reading see Hugo Keiper, "'I wot myself best how y stonde': Literary Nominalism, Open Textual Form and the Enfranchizement of Individual Perspective in Chaucer's Dream Visions," in Literary Nominalism and the Theory of Rereading Late Medieval Texts: A New Research Paradigm, ed. Richard J. Utz (Lewiston: Edwin Mellen Press, 1995), pp. 205–34.

Arthur Lovejoy and Emil Wolff—the *catena aurea* as the dominating dramatic principle in Chaucer's spiritual and textual world on the basis of highly nuanced semantic and solid philological observations, to concentrate on an "exposition of Chaucer's play with ideas" (p. 16) and not on a history of ideas or mentalité, is only weakened by this curiously apologetic *captatio*. Although the volume could have gained through a final round of editorial fine-tuning (see, e.g., the book's back flap, which inverts the content of chapters 5 and 6, and a number of unfortunate typos) as well as through the inclusion of Katherine Tachau's *Vision and Certitude in the Age of Ockham* (Leiden: Brill, 1988) and Linda Holley's *Chaucer's Measuring Eye* (Houston: Rice University Press, 1990) on the topic of "sight," Taylor's investigation, in its learnedness and accuracy, is a welcome contribution to the ideologized realm of Chaucer studies in the nineties. Once one has accepted its basic (moral?) premise, the book's impressive array of detailed philosophic and linguistic analysis and its depth of interpretive insight (esp. on the connectedness or mediation of sight and word, time and narrative form, memory and design) rival Jerome Mandel's recent *Geoffrey Chaucer: Building the Fragments of the* Canterbury Tales (1992), which attracted, not surprisingly, the same publisher.

RICHARD J. UTZ
University of Tübingen / University of Northern Iowa

N. S. THOMPSON. *Chaucer, Boccaccio, and the Debate of Love: A Comparative Study of* The Decameron *and* The Canterbury Tales. Oxford: Clarendon Press, 1996. Pp. x, 364. $72.00.

The author of this engaging and learned work insists that he is out to prove only that it takes more than the search for verbal parallels to investigate the possible connections between *The Decameron* and *The Canterbury Tales.* He also acknowledges that the kind of evidence for influence that he explores is not likely to change the minds of those who will admit nothing less than positive evidence in such matters. Yet he is himself convinced that his comparative readings of the two works yield results that show, at least, stronger connections between them than have been hitherto shown, if not conclusive reasons for believing

Chaucer knew and used Boccaccio's *Decameron* when he wrote *The Canterbury Tales*. And this is exactly as it should be if one is to revive this old question from the affirmative point of view.

Some readers, however, may find Thompson's approach as old-fashioned as the question it addresses, for his account of what happens when we look beyond what the textual eye sees is based on critical resources that are largely traditional in their interpretive orientation. The book's carefully argued thesis depends almost exclusively upon close and complex readings of the framing structures of *The Decameron* and *The Canterbury Tales* and of specific parallel narratives within those structures. The cultural context of the study has been defined predominantly by the conventions of literary and intellectual history. Recent theoretical paradigms and systems are scantly present in Thompson's method, though he does use the term *reader-response* (without reference to Kenneth Burke) to name one of the intended effects of Boccaccio's and Chaucer's narrative strategies upon their audiences. Though this will please some members of our common Chaucerian enterprise more than it will others, it should not prevent anyone interested in the book's subject from giving it an open-minded reading.

Thompson's organization of his argument follows a similar pattern throughout most of the book. First, a concept such as diversity (in chapter 1) is introduced with some commentary on its medieval cultural particularities. This is followed by subsections in which the concept as it functions in Boccaccio and Chaucer is analyzed. These are, in turn, followed by a comparative summary and conclusion. The topical concepts with which Thompson titles the remaining six chapters—Reading the Signs, The Literary Debate, The Autonomy of Fiction, The Comic Tales: Fabliaux or Novelle?, The Romances: Noble and Ignoble Love, and The Three Griseldas—give some idea of the shape of the work. In every chapter, Thompson writes with extraordinary attention to the details in the texts he has selected as the bases for his argument that *The Canterbury Tales* resembles *The Decameron* both in the ways their authors represent their understanding of the nature and aims of writing as well as in the ways they handled analogous story materials. One of the most important of the correspondences investigated in the first half of the book is that between the *brigata*'s concerns with "utile" and "diletto" in *The Decameron* and the pilgrims' oppositions of "sentence" and "solas" and "earnest" and "game" in Chaucer. These lead to the creation in each work of a moral laboratory in which the reader is provoked into making discriminations between virtue and vice and finds himself working his way through a labyrinth of appearances and reality that ultimately acts as an instrument of self-knowledge. This and other narrative aspects of the two fictions that are discussed early in the book then inform the treatment of their analogue tales in the second half of the study. These are divided into a "comic" group—*The Miller's Tale* and *Decameron* 3.4; *The Reeve's Tale* and 9.6; *The Shipman's Tale* and 8.1—and a "serious" group—*The Merchant's Tale* and 7.9; *The Franklin's Tale* and 10.5; and *The Clerk's Tale* and 10.10. The heart of Thompson's work, the analyses of these groups emphasize their common concern with the subject of marriage, generating a debate that examines the sources of order and stability for society and individual.

Just as it is impossible for a review to convey fully an argument like the one Thompson makes, it is also difficult to indicate disappointments with much thoroughness. Still, a responsible accounting must at least state the major issues that elicited some degree of reservation. Since the book's argument depends upon the notion that Chaucer took some very important cues from Boccaccio in his conception and execution of *The Canterbury Tales* as a whole, it is surprising to find that Thompson does not devote more time to the tales of pilgrims who have not been traditionally associated with *The Decameron*. For example, his comparisons—teasingly brief themselves—of Dioneo as paradoxical and teasing narrator to the Pardoner and Wife of Bath may have been missed opportunities to strengthen his case, especially since the discussions of Dioneo's role in *The Decameron* are so interesting. So, too, the decision not to extend the context of his inquiry to include an ample consideration of other Chaucerian appropriations of works by Boccaccio limits Thompson's claims to have explored the relationship between the two writers thoroughly. *Troilus and Crisyede* is mentioned several times without any sustained discussion of its Boccaccian provenance, and even the four pages given to *The Knight's Tale* barely acknowledge, much less address, the extent and manner of Chaucer's adaptation of the *Teseida*. It is difficult, for me at least, to think about what Chaucer might have done with *The Decameron* without qualifying that proposition with what he actually did with the *Filostrato* and the *Teseida*, including somewhere in the consideration the recognition that prose and verse sources may constitute a meaningful difference in the ways in which one writer may draw on the works of another.

Three other details of a minor nature are, perhaps, worth pointing out. First, Thompson's extensive bibliography omits the singular study by Stavros Deligiorgis, *Narrative Intellection in the* Decameron (Iowa City: University of Iowa Press, 1975) in which Boccaccio's work is subjected to intense thematic scrutiny and analysis. Second, I must disagree with the statement on page 72 that Chaucer's characterization of the pilgrims "anticipates Cubism by some five hundred years. . . . As with Cubist works, it is left to the observer to disambiguate the lines which both depict and obfuscate meaning." I seriously doubt that anybody who knows how to look at modern art would regard Cubist works in this way. Like the attempts to explain the allegorical space of *Piers Plowman* as "surrealistic," this analogy does intellectual justice to neither of its terms. Last, and on a lighter note, on page 211, the Miller's daughter Malyne in *The Reeve's Tale* is further "disparaged" by being renamed Malkyn, whose maidenhead, according to Holy Church, no man wants (*Piers Plowman*, C 1.180).

Finally, it must be said that *Chaucer, Boccaccio, and the Debate of Love* first entered this world as an Oxford doctoral thesis. The thesis, according to the author's acknowledgement note, became this book. Yet to one who turned to it after a term of reading theses and dissertations in eager anticipation of a change in reading program karma, it seems to have retained too much of its former incarnation for comfort. This excellent and intelligent study could have been an elegant book had it been revised to omit the relentless repetitions, recapitulations, summaries, the "as we have just seen" and "I shall now argue," and other rhetorical signposts of the thesis level of existence. This personal complaint notwithstanding, N. S. Thompson has made an impressive and valuable debut with this work.

GEORGE D. ECONOMOU
The University of Oklahoma

THERESA TINKLE. *Medieval Venuses and Cupids: Sexuality, Hermeneutics, and English Poetry.* Figurae: Reading Medieval Culture Series. Stanford: Stanford University Press, 1996. Pp. xiii, 294. $39.50.

This is an excellent book: clear and intelligent, innovative and well-balanced. Basing her analysis on formidable and penetrating research into mythographic writings, Theresa Tinkle destroys the all too long entrenched belief that medieval writing on Venus and Cupid, as love deities, planetary powers, and personifications of passion, can be adequately interpreted in terms of authoritative reifications like the "two loves" or "courtly love." No such simple and hegemonic duality as the two loves emerges from the material, whether iconographical, poetic, or philosophical, usually cited to sanction such interpretations. Classical and medieval iconology was multiple, flexible, inconsistent, and historically subject to change and development. Tinkle's account of Alberic brings out clearly not only the "chaotic polysemy" (p. 61) created by his encyclopedism, analogous to the multiplicity and multivalence discernible in other twelfth-century discourses, but also the sense of "the sequentiality of the creation of meanings" (p. 61), and of the discrete realms of different kinds of meaning, discernible in his writing. The discovery of multiple readings emerges from this book as not merely a twentieth-century taste; it seems for many of the great medieval mythographers a consequence of their efforts to codify ancient poetry and myth-making. They are, in Tinkle's title for chapter 2, "semiotic nomads." It proves impossible to make a distinction, as she says on page 32, "between problematic 'literary' and pellucid 'source' texts."

Chapter 2 offers an overview of the tradition of mythographic writing as "one of the very few discourses on sexuality that span the entire Middle Ages" (p. 43), and then outlines the classical sources for the medieval tradition. There follow succinct analyses of several key mythographers, including Augustine, Fulgentius, and Isidore, considered as writers responding from the perspectives of different Christian eras to the challenge of interpreting and evaluating pagan mythology and fiction for Christian culture. Some mythographers, including Bernardus Silvestris, Boccaccio, and Christine de Pizan (that trio of names alone surely amply indicates the absence of a monolithic inherited tradition) are poets. Conversely both the authors of medieval poetry and also on occasion their scribes, commentators, or imitators may follow mythographic systems of interpretation slavishly. Some poets in their handling of these personifications of human love limit and determine their readers' interpretations; others—notably but not exclusively Chaucer—transfer the task or authority of interpretation to their readers.

Venus, as the supposed focus of an age-old dilemma at the very heart of human desire, conceived as masculine desire, has dominated scholarly writing; gender difference and the evolution of Cupid/Amor has engaged less academic attention. Tinkle clearsightedly corrects the distortion introduced into much mainstream iconography, literary history, and criticism not only by the overexclusive modern embrace of the "two loves" concept, which obscures the importance of other dichotomies like the contest between Ganymede and Helen (and she writes well on Alain de Lille), but also by the bias among modern scholars toward locating conflict in opposed images of the female (the two Venuses as Eve and Mary) and ignoring the history and problematic potentialities of the figure of Cupido, "desire."

Tinkle writes perceptively (pp. 67–70) of the mixture of careful analysis and confusion in Boccaccio's encyclopedic efforts to catalogue classical mythology in the *Genealogia,* and she lays welcome emphasis on the central significance of his Promethean self-image as poet—and as modern, vernacular poet in a Christian era—in the proems to that work. Tinkle discusses Christine de Pizan's *Epistre d'Othéa* as a programmatically contemporary didactic essay that uses parallels between ancient and modern chivalry as commentary on her own society and nation. Christine, Tinkle argues, is innovative both in the precision with which she turns mythography to social commentary (conservative in implication) and also in simultaneously translating what Tinkle calls "clerkly mythography" (p. 73) into the vernacular and attributing it to a female divinity as authority figure. While this is true, it passes over Christine's audacious and drastic transformation of the rich poetic multiplicity of Ovid's *Metamorphoses* into a far more rigid and scholarly genre: retrospectively turning it into something like the mythographies and moralizations derived from it. Given Tinkle's developing agenda of tracing the birth of a poetics focused on sensual pleasure, a poetics of desire, it is a loss that she could not give more attention to this particular metamorphosis.

Tinkle's critical analysis weaves together issues of gender, hermeneutics, politics, and poetics with an assured hand, and the analysis of medieval literature is enlivened and illuminated by references forward to later writers as diverse as Mark Twain, Keats, and Adrienne Rich. At the center of her book is an exploration of Chaucer's poetry and its power to suggest to the reader affinities between apparently disparate ideals of sexuality, class ideology, and poetry. Chapter 6 includes a persuasive argument of the centrality of the astrological references to the challenge to chauvinist exegesis in *The Wife of Bath's Prologue*. Tinkle shows Chaucer in *The House of Fame* and *The Knight's Tale* inheriting a nexus of images and implications and creating a new nexus of dynamic and dialectic recombination. His juxtaposition of mythographic and romance conventions challenges the assumptions of both and raises questions about human sensuality and chivalric myth that offer implicit social critique rather than a simple verdict against class-based carnality or "courtly love." Tinkle's study provides new perspectives on issues that have been authoritatively raised during the last fifteen years by critics such as Patterson and Nolan. Late medieval poets' transformations of Latin mythographic *auctoritas* into vernacular freedom and accessibility parallels, as she points out, tensions associated with Wycliffite translation (she might have taken more account of *The Legend of Good Women* in this context), Lydgate, and the author of the *Assembly of Gods* precisely because, compared with Chaucer's more subtle play with multiple traditions, they often deploy the authoritative systems begotten by mythography, reveal points of stress where Latin hermeneutics meet vernacular poetry, and foreground questions of interpretation in typically fifteenth-century fashion.

In her last chapter Tinkle sees Chaucer's *Troilus* celebrating Venus, with her potential to symbolize both sensuality and affinities with cosmic order, as the muse for a new kind of English poetry, reaching back beyond French models to Ovid as originary *auctor* for a poetics of sensuality dignified with classicizing and intellectual *gravitas*. She also proposes Chaucer as the originator of the fifteenth-century transformation of Cupid into a figure for antimisogynist discussion of masculine sexual aggression. It might be profitable to investigate the presence of similar trends in French fourteenth-century literature, but the precise lines of influence in this particular development of courtly writing are hard at present to trace.

Tinkle writes pleasantly, authoritatively, succinctly, and with wit. It is hard to give more than a summary impression of this complex book and its union of scholarship and critical argument. It is an impressive and exhilarating achievement. The title is refreshingly apt. Titular pluralizations are a fashionable precaution for the ideologically circum-spect author; here Theresa Tinkle convincingly displays the multiple, discordant, and creatively chaotic nature of her subjects and the deep historical roots of their conflicted meanings, while in no way dissolving, but on the contrary strengthening, her readers' awareness of the pro-fundity of medieval poets' engagement with the figures of Venus and Cupid and the philosophical importance of the poetic structures cen-tered upon them.

HELEN PHILLIPS
University of Nottingham

DAVID WILLIAMS. *Deformed Discourse: The Function of the Monster in Mediaeval Thought and Literature.* Montreal and Kingston; London and Buffalo: McGill-Queen's University Press, 1996. Pp. xiv, 392. $55.00.

David Williams's challenging study of the monster in medieval thought and literature goes well beyond the catalog-style discussion that seems to be a typical feature of books and articles in this subject area. Williams offers a framework of understanding for monstrosity, contending that in medieval cosmology, and specifically in Pseudo-Dionysian thought, the idea of the monster has a centrality to the scheme of things that postmedievals have to recover. The monster is not *contra naturam*, but rather *extra naturam*. Williams quotes Isidore's *Etymologiae* 11.3.1–2: "Varro says that portents are things which seem to have been born contrary to nature, but in truth, they are not born contrary to nature, because they exist by the divine will, since the Creator's will is the nature of everything created. . . ." The monstrous can be seen to have a major function within the scheme of things be-cause of a series of moves Pseudo-Dionysius offers in his cognitive sys-tem that effectively constitute a deformed discourse, or the proper in-terpretation of sacred symbols. Pseudo-Dionysius, readers of *The Cloud of Unknowing* and related treatises will remember, offers the negative path to God: what God is not is easier to consider than what He is. Operationally this negation yields to paradoxical utterances and the failure to make any positive predication about God; this failure, however, liberates the knower from the "logical" limits of predication and points to a transcendent possibility. As Cusa has it, God is the coincidence of opposites. The monster is similarly a sign of negation, pointing to the paradox of "what is" and "what is not" or the transcendent. Amplifying John Scotus Eriugena and his *Periphyseon*, Williams can argue that in Eriugena's worldview "God the Creator is also seen as monster." Eriugena is a key figure for Williams because he sees the ninth-century thinker as creating a teratological symbolism based on a liberal interpretation of Pseudo-Dionysius.

Having established the philosophical basis for his book in negative theology, Williams goes on to the second part of his grand argument, which part gives the necessary links between the general theory of monsters and the specific representations of them in select texts. Part 2, "Taxonomy," is, in one sense, the catalog of monsters so often seen in scholarship, but here it comes forward not as a descriptive inventory of things that go bump in the night but in the context of a considered theory of forms, based on the history of ideas. Williams does not lose sight of the foundation he established earlier, repeating the central ideas of negative theology and paradoxical utterances from time to time in his taxonomy with good rhetorical effect. Admittedly such a taxonomy is "a system of categories of nothing," a contradictory "structuring of disorder," and yet the "requirement of an affirmative discourse that attempts to understand the negative." Foucault's famous comment on the Chinese encyclopedia and its taxonomy of animals is a proper motto to this theme that the "exotic charm of another system of thought" makes us understand "the limitation of our own, the stark impossibility of thinking that." Williams's first taxonomic divide is "The Body Monstrous," wherein size (i.e., pygmies, giants), locus and position (antipodes, shape-shifters), the head (multi-, bi-, tri-, a-cephalic, as well as the human-headed animal), the mouth, the eyes, ears, and lips, and the genitals (disembodied, *vagina dentata*, and the hermaphrodite) are ordering categories. Since the body as *mikrokosmos* in Neoplatonic thought contains the world in miniature, Williams, like Isidore before him, chooses an apt model for his system. Polyphemus and Ulysses, for example, reenact the Pseudo-Dionysian monstrous moment when the former asks "Who are You?" and the latter responds "I am/I am not"; the female saints who disguise themselves as monks and enter monasteries are encoded examples of the Divine as androgyne. The second divide is "Nature Monstrous": animal (man and animal combined, one animal with another of a different species), various denizens of earth, air, fire, water, vegetal combinations, and mineral combinations. As with monsters of the human body, Williams offers Pseudo-Dionysian profiles of centaurs, satyrs, dragons, sirens, the vegetable lamb, the wak-wak tree, etc. The final divide of "Monstrous Concepts," an interesting but comparatively undeveloped taxonomy suggesting that the Anthropomorphic Alphabet and Prodigious Numbers, where monsters reside in zoomorphic initials or where Boethius discusses numbers likened to monsters, respectively, belong as part of the monstrous world.

All these preliminaries prepare for the analysis of texts on three heroes (Alexander, Orpheus, and Gawain in *Sir Gawain and the Green Knight* [*SGGK*]) and three saints (Christopher, Denis of Paris, and Wilgefortis). Though much of the monster theory comes from late antique and early medieval periods, the focus on mainly later medieval texts is a little surprising. Williams does not, for example, capitalize on his earlier study of *Cain and Beowulf* here, and his choice of texts suggests a Mediterranean view of the Middle Ages (rather than a Northern one) where, of course, Neoplatonic thinking might be seen to be more at home. Clearly the analysis of Gawain in *SGGK* is the text comparatively more isolated from the others in this selection of six, given its sources. Williams offers a reading of *SGGK* that emphasizes many good, strong formalist features, however, rather than Pseudo-Dionysian elements. In the bustling *SGGK* industry there will be readers who will dispute points of detail in Williams's discussion (for example, the reading of the old hag), but the spirit of play and game in *SGGK* is perhaps the most notably absent major theme.

Deformed Discourse is an important "thesis book." Williams makes it clear that he is not attempting a full-scale history of ideas; that there were other, competing perspectives on cosmology, such as the Thomistic; and that the Pseudo-Dionysian view did not prevail as culture became early modern. Properly, he sets out to prove what he sets out to prove, and this clarity should mollify those who fear the "totalizing" tendencies of the thesis-book genre or who might wonder why sometimes the exposition of the Pseudo-Dionysian seems to be only more broadly Neoplatonic, or why, finally, Pseudo-Dionysian elements help us to understand the phenomenon of Wilgefortis better than other approaches. After all, finding transcendental meaning hidden under the surface of things is a basic medieval move animating even the Robertsonian reading of medieval culture, and the existence of monsters, furthermore, may be a function of human psychology of whatever stripe, Freudian, Jungian, or Lacanian. The Danes would take no comfort from the Pseudo-Dionysian view of things as Grendel approached the door, nor does the terror in *Grettissaga* seem cosmological. Still the perspective Williams presents will find its necessary place in any thoughtful approach to medieval monsters and their place in the medieval scheme of things, for he brings our time closer to the medieval worldview than any mere descriptive study.

Minor points: there are some 90 black-and-white illustrations, some murky and lacking sharpness. There are a bibliography and an index, but footnotes tend to be understated. There are also occasional odd lapses, e.g., the identification of the ox with Matthew (p. 12), proofing errors, etc.

PAUL E. SZARMACH
Western Michigan University

BOOKS RECEIVED

Allaire, Gloria. *Andrea da Barberino and the Language of Chivalry*. Gainesville: University Press of Florida, 1997. Pp. xi, 183. $49.95.

Allen, Valerie, and Ares Axiotis, eds. *Chaucer: Contemporary Critical Essays*. New Casebooks Series. New York: St. Martin's Press, 1996. Pp. xi, 268. $39.95.

Bestul, Thomas H. *Texts of the Passion: Latin Devotional Literature and Medieval Society*. Middle Ages Series. Philadelphia: University of Pennsylvania Press, 1996. Pp. viii, 264. $39.95.

Biller, Peter, and A. J. Minnis, eds. *Medieval Theology and the Natural Body*. York Studies in Medieval Theology, vol. 1. York: York Medieval Press, 1997. Pp. x, 244. $81.00.

Blamires, Alcuin. *The Case for Women in Medieval Culture*. Oxford: Clarendon Press, 1997. Pp. viii, 279. $75.00.

Boitani, Piero, and Anna Torti, eds. *Medievalitas: Reading the Middle Ages*. The J. A. W. Bennett Memorial Lectures, 9th Ser., Perugia, 1995. Cambridge: D. S. Brewer, 1996. Pp. x, 183. $71.00.

Brewer, Charlotte. *Editing* Piers Plowman: *The Evolution of the Text*. Cambridge Studies in Medieval Literature, vol. 28. Cambridge: Cambridge University Press, 1996. Pp. xv, 459. $64.95.

Brewer, Derek and Jonathan Gibson, eds. *A Companion to the* Gawain-Poet. Arthurian Studies, vol. 38. Cambridge: D. S. Brewer, 1997. Pp. xi, 442. $89.00.

Burton, T. L. and Rosemary Greentree, eds. *Chaucer's* Miller's, Reeve's, *and* Cook's Tales: *An Annotated Bibliography 1900 to 1992*. The Chaucer Bibliographies, vol. 5. Toronto, Buffalo, and London: University of Toronto Press, 1997. Pp. xix, 287. $75.00.

Carruthers, Leo. *L'Anglais Médiéval*. L'Atelier du Médiéviste Series, vol. 4. Turnhout: Brepols, 1996. Pp. 256. 1100 BF.

Consoli, Joseph P., ed. and trans. The Novellino *or* One Hundred Ancient Tales: *An Edition and Translation Based on the 1525 Gualteruzzi, editio princeps*. Garland Library of Medieval Literature, vol. 105A. New York and London: Garland Publishing, 1997. Pp. xxviii, 188. $49.00.

Cooper, Helen, and Sally Mapstone, eds. *The Long Fifteenth Century: Essays for Douglas Gray*. Oxford: Clarendon Press, 1997. Pp. xi, 362. $85.00.

Cox, Catherine S. *Gender and Language in Chaucer*. Gainesville: University Press of Florida, 1997. Pp. x, 196. $49.95.

Craun, Edwin D. *Lies, Slander, and Obscenity in Medieval English Literature: Pastoral Rhetoric and the Deviant Speaker*. Cambridge Studies in Medieval Literature, vol. 31. Cambridge: Cambridge University Press, 1997. Pp. xiii, 255. $59.95.

Dean, James M. *The World Grown Old in Later Medieval Literature*. Medieval Academy Books, no. 101. Cambridge: The Medieval Academy of America, 1997. Pp. xi, 379. $50.00.

Durling, Nancy Vine, ed. *Jean Renart and the Art of Romance: Essays on Guillaume de Dole*. Gainesville: University Press of Florida, 1997. Pp. vii, 240. $49.95.

Eckhardt, Caroline D., ed. *Castleford's Chronicle or The Boke of Brut*. 2 vols. Early English Text Society, vols. 305–6. Oxford: Oxford University Press, 1996. Pp. xvi, 1065. $125.00.

Eldredge, L. M., ed. *The Wonderful Art of the Eye*. A Critical Edition of the Middle English Translation of *De Probatissima Arte Oculorum* by Benvenutus Grassus. Medieval Texts and Studies, vol. 19. East Lansing: Michigan State University Press, 1996. Pp. xiii, 120. $24.95.

Ferrante, Joan M. *To the Glory of Her Sex: Women's Roles in the Composition of Medieval Texts*. Women of Letters Series. Bloomington and Indianapolis: Indiana University Press, 1997. Pp. xii, 295. $19.95 paper.

Foster, Edward E., ed. Amis and Amiloun, Robert of Cisyle, *and* Sir Amadace. Middle English Texts Series. Kalamazoo, Mich.: Medieval Institute Publications, 1997. Pp. vi, 153. N.p.

Fowler, David C., Charles F. Briggs, and Paul G. Remley, eds. *The Governance of Kings and Princes: John Trevisa's Middle English Translation of the* De Regimine Principum *of Aegidius Romanus*. Garland Medieval Texts, vol. 19. New York and London: Garland Publishing, 1977. Pp. xxix, 439. N.p.

Fradenburg, Louise, and Carla Freccero, eds. *Premodern Sexualities*. New York and London: Routledge, 1996. Pp. xxiv, 276. $19.95 paper.

Geary, Patrick J., gen. ed. *Authors of the Middle Ages: Historical and Religious Writers of the Latin West*. Vol. 4, nos. 12–13. Gregory the Great and Fredegar. Brookfield, Vt.: Ashgate Publishing, 1996. Pp. vi, 138. $55.95.

Gillespie, James L., ed. *The Age of Richard II*. New York: St. Martin's Press, 1997. Pp. viii, 256. $55.00.

Gold, Barbara, Paul Allen Miller, and Charles Platter, eds. *Sex and Gender in Medieval and Renaissance Texts: The Latin Tradition*. SUNY Series in Medieval Studies. Albany: State University of New York Press, 1997. Pp. viii, 330. $22.95 paper.

Gregg, Joan Young. *Devils, Women, and Jews: Reflections of the Other in Medieval Sermon Stories*. SUNY Series in Medieval Studies. Albany: State University of New York Press, 1997. Pp. x, 275. $20.95 paper.

Hahn, Thomas, and Alan Lupack, eds. *Retelling Tales: Essays in Honor of Russell Peck*. Cambridge: D. S. Brewer, 1997. Pp. vi, 359. $81.00.

Haug, Walter. *Vernacular Literary Theory in the Middle Ages: The German Tradition, 800–1300, in its European Context*. Cambridge Studies in Medieval Literature, vol. 29. Cambridge: Cambridge University Press, 1997. Pp. xiv, 426. $74.95.

Howes, Laura L. *Chaucer's Gardens and the Language of Convention*. Gainesville: University Press of Florida, 1997. Pp. xi, 142. $39.95.

Justice, Steven, and Kathryn Kerby-Fulton, eds. *Written Work: Langland, Labor, and Authorship*. Middle Ages Series. Philadelphia: University of Pennsylvania Press, 1997. Pp. ix, 347. $45.00.

Karnein, Alfred. *Amor est passio: Untersuchungen zum nicht-höfischen Liebesdiskurs des Mittelalters*. Hesperides: Studies in Western Literature and Civilization, vol. 4. Trieste: Edizioni Parnaso, 1997. Pp. 188. $28.00 paper.

Klassen, Norman. *Chaucer on Love, Knowledge and Sight*. Chaucer Studies, vol. 21. Cambridge: D. S. Brewer, 1995. Pp. xi, 225. $53.00.

Knight, Stephen, and Thomas Ohlgren, eds. *Robin Hood and Other Outlaw Tales*. Middle English Texts Series. Kalamazoo, Mich.: Medieval Institute Publications, 1997. Pp. xv, 723. $35.00.

Labarge, Margaret Wade. *A Medieval Miscellany*. With introduction by N. E. S. Griffiths. Ottawa: Carleton University Press, 1997. Pp. xi, 292. N.p.

Lerer, Seth. *Courtly Letters in the Age of Henry VIII: Literary Culture and the Arts of Deceit*. Cambridge Studies in Renaissance Literature and Culture, vol. 18. Cambridge: Cambridge University Press, 1997. Pp. xiv, 252. $59.95.

Lindley, Arthur. *Hyperion and the Hobbyhorse: Studies in Carnivalesque Subversion*. Newark: University of Delaware Press, 1996. Pp. 197. $33.50.

Looze, Laurence de. *Pseudo-Autobiography in the Fourteenth Century: Juan Ruiz, Guillaume de Machaut, Jean Froissart, and Geoffrey Chaucer.* Gainesville: University Press of Florida, 1997. Pp. xi, 211. $49.95.

Lynch, Andrew. *Malory's Book of Arms: The Narrative of Combat in* Le Morte Darthur. Arthurian Studies, vol. 39. Cambridge: D. S. Brewer, 1997. Pp. xx, 169. $53.00.

Magennis, Hugh. *Images of Community in Old English Poetry.* Cambridge Studies in Anglo-Saxon England, vol. 18. Cambridge: Cambridge University Press, 1996. Pp. ix, 212. $54.95.

McCarl, Mary Rhinelander, ed. The Plowman's Tale: *The C. 1532 and 1606 Editions of a Spurious Canterbury Tale.* The Renaissance Imagination Series. New York and London: Garland Publishing, 1997. Pp. 318. $72.00.

Millett, Bella. *Annotated Bibliographies of Old and Middle English Literature, Vol. 2:* Ancrene Wisse, *the Katherine Group, and the Wooing Group.* Annotated Bibliographies of Old and Middle English Literature Series. Cambridge: D. S. Brewer, 1996. Pp. x, 260. $71.00.

Mullally, Evelyn, and John Thompson, eds. *The Court and Cultural Diversity.* Papers from the Eighth Triennial Congress of the International Courtly Literature Society. Cambridge: D. S. Brewer, 1997. Pp. x, 426. $90.00.

Nichols, Stephen G., and Siegfried Wenzel, eds. *The Whole Book: Cultural Perspectives on the Medieval Miscellany.* Ann Arbor: University of Michigan Press, 1996. Pp. viii, 188. $37.50.

Noomen, Willem, ed. *Nouveau Recueil Complet des Fabliaux (NRCF),* vol. 9. Assen: Van Gorcum, 1997. Pp. xxv, 366. $80.00.

Pask, Kevin. *The Emergence of the English Author: Scripting the Life of the Poet in Early Modern England.* Cambridge Studies in Renaissance

Literature and Culture, vol. 12. Cambridge: Cambridge University Press, 1996. Pp. x, 218. $49.95.

Pearsall, Derek. *John Lydgate (1371–1449): A Bio-bibliography*. *English Literary Studies*. Monograph Series, no. 71. Victoria: University of Victoria, 1997. Pp. 95. $9.50 paper.

Pfeffer, Wendy. *Proverbs in Medieval Occitan Literature*. Gainesville: University Press of Florida, 1997. Pp. x, 155. $49.95.

Potkay, Monica Brzezinski, and Regula Meyer Evitt. *Minding the Body: Women and Literature in the Middle Ages, 800–1500*. Twayne's Women and Literature Series. New York: Twayne Publishers, 1997. Pp. xi, 238. N.p.

Rigby, S. H. *Chaucer in Context: Society, Allegory and Gender*. Manchester Medieval Studies. Manchester and New York: Manchester University Press, 1996. Pp. xii, 205. $59.95.

Robinson, P. R., and Rivkah Zim, eds. *Of the Making of Books: Medieval Manuscripts, Their Scribes and Readers. Essays Presented to M. B. Parkes*. London: Scolar Press, 1997. Pp. xiii, 324. $68.95.

Rosenberg, Samuel N., Margaret Switten, and Gérard Le Vor, eds. *Songs of the Troubadours and Trouvères: An Anthology of Poems and Melodies*. Garland Reference Library of the Humanities, vol. 1740. New York and London: Garland Publishing, 1998. Pp. xi, 378. $85.00.

Russell, George, and George Kane, eds. Piers Plowman: *The C Version*. London and Berkeley: Athlone Press and University of California Press, 1997. Pp. xi, 700. $145.00.

Salda, Michael N., and Jean Jost, eds. *Chaucer Yearbook: A Journal of Late Medieval Studies*. Vol. 3. Cambridge: D. S. Brewer, 1996. Pp. 234. $59.00.

———. *Chaucer Yearbook: A Journal of Late Medieval Studies*. Vol. 4. Cambridge: D. S. Brewer, 1997. Pp. 217. $63.00.

Saul, Nigel. *Richard II*. Yale English Monarch Series. New Haven and London: Yale University Press, 1997. Pp. xiv, 514. $35.00.

Scattergood, John, and Julia Boffey, eds. *Texts and Contexts: Papers from the Early Book Society*. Dublin: Four Courts Press, 1997. Pp. 252. $55.00.

Spiegel, Gabrielle M. *The Past as Text: The Theory and Practice of Medieval Historiography*. Parallax: Revisions of Culture and Society Series. Baltimore and London: Johns Hopkins University Press, 1997. Pp. xxii, 297. $39.95.

Sponsler, Claire. *Drama and Resistance: Bodies, Goods, and Theatricality in Late Medieval England*. Medieval Cultures Series, vol. 10. Minneapolis and London: University of Minnesota Press, 1997. Pp. xvii, 209. $21.95 paper.

Taylor, Jane H.M., and Lesley Smith, eds. *Women and the Book: Assessing the Visual Evidence*. The British Library Studies in Medieval Culture. Toronto and Buffalo: University of Toronto Press, 1997. Pp. 287. $75.00.

Townsend, David, trans. *The* Alexandreis *of Walter of Châtillon: A Twelfth-Century Epic*. Middle Ages Series. Philadelphia: University of Pennsylvania Press, 1997. Pp. xxix, 214. $37.50.

Vauchez, André. *Sainthood in the Later Middle Ages*. Trans. Jean Birell. Cambridge: Cambridge University Press, 1997. Pp. xxvii, 645. $95.00.

Voaden, Rosalynn, ed. *Prophets Abroad: The Reception of Continental Holy Women in Late-Medieval England*. Cambridge: D. S. Brewer, 1996. Pp. xiii, 197. $63.00.

Wallace, David. *Chaucerian Polity: Absolutist Lineages and Associational Forms in England and Italy*. Figurae: Reading Medieval Culture Series. Stanford, Cal.: Stanford University Press, 1997. Pp. xix, 555. $55.00.

Watt, Diane, ed. *Medieval Women in Their Communities*. Toronto and Buffalo: University of Toronto Press, 1997. Pp. xii, 250. $50.00.

353

Wilcox, Helen, ed. *Women and Literature in Britain, 1500–1700*. Cambridge: Cambridge University Press, 1996. Pp. xiv, 306. $54.95 cloth, $18.95 paper.

Williams, Jeni. *Interpreting Nightingales: Gender, Class and Histories*. Sheffield: Sheffield Academic Press, 1997. Pp. 299. $49.50.

An Annotated Chaucer Bibliography
1996

Compiled and edited by Mark Allen and Bege K. Bowers

Regular contributors:

Bruce W. Hozeski, *Ball State University* (Indiana)
George Nicholas, *Benedictine College* (Kansas)
Martha S. Waller, *Butler University* (Indiana)
Marilyn Sutton, *California State University at Dominguez Hills*
Larry L. Bronson, *Central Michigan University*
Glending Olson, *Cleveland State University* (Ohio)
Jesús Luis Serrano Reyes (*Córdoba*)
Winthrop Wetherbee, *Cornell University* (New York)
Elizabeth Dobbs, *Grinnell College* (Iowa)
Masatoshi Kawasaki, *Komazawa University* (Tokyo, Japan)
William Schipper, *Memorial University* (Newfoundland, Canada)
Daniel J. Pinti, *New Mexico State University*
Erik Kooper, *Rijksuniversiteit te Utrecht*
Amy Goodwin, *Randolph-Macon College* (Virginia)
Cindy L. Vitto, *Rowan College of New Jersey*
Richard H. Osberg, *Santa Clara University* (California)
Margaret Connolly, *University College, Cork* (Ireland)
Juliette Dor, *Université de Liège* (Belgium)
Mary Flowers Braswell and Elaine Whitaker, *University of Alabama at Birmingham*
Denise Stodola, *University of Missouri-Columbia*
Cynthia Gravlee, *University of Montevallo* (Alabama)
Gregory M. Sadlek, *University of Nebraska at Omaha*
Cynthia Ho, *University of North Carolina, Asheville*
Richard J. Utz, *Universität Tübingen* (Tübingen, Germany)
Thomas Hahn, *University of Rochester* (New York)
Rebecca Beal, *University of Scranton* (Pennsylvania)

Valerie Allen, *University of South Florida*
Stanley R. Hauer, *University of Southern Mississippi*
Mark Allen, Gail Jones, and Connie Sabo-Risley, *University of Texas at San Antonio*
Andrew Lynch, *University of Western Australia*
Brian A. Shaw, *University of Western Ontario*
Joyce T. Lionarons, *Ursinus College* (Pennsylvania)
John M. Crafton, *West Georgia College*
Robert Correale, *Wright State University* (Ohio)
Bege K. Bowers, *Youngstown State University* (Ohio)

Ad hoc contributions were made by the following: Steve Ellis (*University of Birmingham*); Thomas Garbáty (*University of Michigan*); Cynthia Klekar and Eileen Krueger (*University of Texas at San Antonio*); Shannon Lewis (*Memorial University*); Cecelia Mecca (*University of Scranton*); Pamela K. Mott (*University of Alabama at Birmingham*); and Dana Symons (*University of Rochester*).

The bibliographers acknowledge with gratitude the MLA typesimulation provided by Terence Ford, Director, Center for Bibliographical Services of the Modern Language Association; postage from the University of Texas at San Antonio Division of English, Classics, and Philosophy; and assistance from the library staff, especially Susan McCray, at the University of Texas at San Antonio.

This bibliography continues the bibliographies published since 1975 in previous volumes of *Studies in the Age of Chaucer.* Bibliographic information up to 1975 can be found in Eleanor P. Hammond, *Chaucer: A Bibliographic Manual* (1908; reprint, New York: Peter Smith, 1933); D. D. Griffith, *Bibliography of Chaucer, 1908–53* (Seattle: University of Washington Press, 1955); William R. Crawford, *Bibliography of Chaucer, 1954–63* (Seattle: University of Washington Press, 1967); and Lorrayne Y. Baird, *Bibliography of Chaucer, 1964–73* (Boston: G. K. Hall, 1977). See also Lorrayne Y. Baird-Lange and Hildegard Schnuttgen, *Bibliography of Chaucer, 1974–1985* (Hamden, Conn.: Shoe String Press, 1988).

Additions and corrections to this bibliography should be sent to Mark Allen, Bibliographic Division, New Chaucer Society, Division of English, Classics, Philosophy, and Communication, University of Texas at San Antonio 78249-0643 (FAX: 210-458-5366; E-MAIL:

MALLEN@LONESTAR.JPL.UTSA.EDU). An electronic version of this bibliography (1975–97) is available via the New Chaucer Society Web page (via http://ncs.rutgers.edu) or via TELNET connection (UTSAIBM.UTSA.EDU; type "library" at the applications prompt, "cho chau" at the request for a database, and "stop" to exit the database). Authors are urged to send annotations for articles, reviews, and books that have been or might be overlooked.

Classifications

Abbreviations of Chaucer's Works

ABC	*An ABC*
Adam	*Adam Scriveyn*
Anel	*Anelida and Arcite*
Astr	*A Treatise on the Astrolabe*
Bal Compl	*A Balade of Complaint*
BD	*The Book of the Duchess*
Bo	*Boece*
Buk	*The Envoy to Bukton*
CkT, CkP, Rv–CkL	*The Cook's Tale, The Cook's Prologue, Reeve–Cook Link*
ClT, ClP, Cl–MerL	*The Clerk's Tale, The Clerk's Prologue, Clerk–Merchant Link*
Compl d'Am	*Complaynt d'Amours*
CT	*The Canterbury Tales*
CYT, CYP	*The Canon's Yeoman's Tale, The Canon's Yeoman's Prologue*
Equat	*The Equatorie of the Planetis*
For	*Fortune*
Form Age	*The Former Age*
FranT, FranP	*The Franklin's Tale, The Franklin's Prologue*
FrT, FrP, Fr–SumL	*The Friar's Tale, The Friar's Prologue, Friar–Summoner Link*
Gent	*Gentilesse*
GP	*The General Prologue*
HF	*The House of Fame*
KnT, Kn–MilL	*The Knight's Tale, Knight–Miller Link*
Lady	*A Complaint to His Lady*
LGW, LGWP	*The Legend of Good Women, The Legend of Good Women Prologue*
ManT, ManP	*The Manciple's Tale, The Manciple's Prologue*
Mars	*The Complaint of Mars*
Mel, Mel–MkL	*The Tale of Melibee, Melibee–Monk Link*
MercB	*Merciles Beaute*

MerT, MerE–SqH	*The Merchant's Tale, Merchant Endlink– Squire Headlink*
MilT, MilP, Mil–RvL	*The Miller's Tale, The Miller's Prologue, Miller–Reeve Link*
MkT, MkP, Mk–NPL	*The Monk's Tale, The Monk's Prologue, Monk–Nun's Priest Link*
MLT, MLH, MLP, MLE	*The Man of Law's Tale, Man of Law Headlink, The Man of Law's Prologue, Man of Law Endlink*
NPT, NPP, NPE	*The Nun's Priest's Tale, The Nun's Priest's Prologue, Nun's Priest's Endlink*
PardT, PardP	*The Pardoner's Tale, The Pardoner's Prologue*
ParsT, ParsP	*The Parson's Tale, The Parson's Prologue*
PF	*The Parliament of Fowls*
PhyT, Phy–PardL	*The Physician's Tale, Physician– Pardoner Link*
Pity	*The Complaint unto Pity*
Prov	*Proverbs*
PrT, PrP, Pr–ThL	*The Prioress's Tale, The Prioress's Prologue, Prioress–Thopas Link*
Purse	*The Complaint of Chaucer to His Purse*
Ret	*Chaucer's Retraction {Retractation}*
Rom	*The Romaunt of the Rose*
Ros	*To Rosemounde*
RvT, RvP	*The Reeve's Tale, The Reeve's Prologue*
Scog	*The Envoy to Scogan*
ShT, Sh–PrL	*The Shipman's Tale, Shipman–Prioress Link*
SNT, SNP, SN–CYL	*The Second Nun's Tale, The Second Nun's Prologue, Second Nun–Canon's Yeoman Link*
SqT, SqH, Sq–FranL	*The Squire's Tale, Squire Headlink, Squire–Franklin Link*
Sted	*Lak of Stedfastnesse*
SumT, SumP	*The Summoner's Tale, The Summoner's Prologue*

TC	*Troilus and Criseyde*
Th, Th–MelL	*The Tale of Sir Thopas, Sir Thopas–Melibee Link*
Truth	*Truth*
Ven	*The Complaint of Venus*
WBT, WBP, WB–FrL	*The Wife of Bath's Tale, The Wife of Bath's Prologue, Wife of Bath–Friar Link*
Wom Nob	*Womanly Noblesse*
Wom Unc	*Against Women Unconstant*

Periodical Abbreviations

AHR	*Afro-Hispanic Review*
Allegorica	*Allegorica: A Journal of Medieval and Renaissance Literature*
Anglia	*Anglia: Zeitschrift für Englische Philologie*
Anglistik	*Anglistik: Mitteilungen des Verbandes deutscher Anglisten*
ArAA	*Arbeiten aus Anglistik und Amerikanistik*
Archiv	*Archiv für das Studium der Neueren Sprachen und Literaturen*
BAM	*Bulletin des Anglicistes Médiévistes*
BJRL	*Bulletin of the John Rylands University Library of Manchester*
ChauR	*Chaucer Review*
Cithara	*Cithara: Essays in the Judaeo-Christian Tradition*
CL	*Comparative Literature* (Eugene, Ore.)
CLS	*Comparative Literature Studies*
ContempR	*Contemporary Review* (London, England)
CrSurv	*Critical Survey*
DAI	*Dissertation Abstracts International*
ÉA	*Études Anglaises: Grand-Bretagne, États-Unis*
Edebiyât	*Edebiyât: The Journal of Middle Eastern Literatures*
EJ	*English Journal* (Urbana, Ill.)
ELH	*ELH*
ELN	*English Language Notes*
ELWIU	*Essays in Literature* (Macomb, Ill.)
EMS	*English Manuscript Studies, 1100–1700*
Encomia	*Encomia: Bibliographical Bulletin of the International Courtly Literature Society*
ES	*English Studies*
Exemplaria	*Exemplaria: A Journal of Theory in Medieval and Renaissance Studies*
Florilegium	*Florilegium: Carleton University Papers on Late Antiquity and the Middle Ages*
HLQ	*Huntington Library Quarterly: A Journal for the History and Interpretation of English and American Civilization*
InG	*In Geardagum: Essays on Old and Middle English Language and Literature*

JBAL	*Journal of British and American Literature* (Komazawa University)
JEGP	*Journal of English and Germanic Philology*
JELL	*Journal of English Language and Literature*
LittPrag	*Litteraria Pragensia: Studies in Literature and Culture*
Lore&L	*Lore and Language*
MA	*Le Moyen Age: Revue d'Histoire et de Philologie*
MÆ	*Medium Ævum*
M&H	*Medievalia et Humanistica: Studies in Medieval and Renaissance Culture*
Mediaevalia	*Mediaevalia: A Journal of Mediaeval Studies*
MedPers	*Medieval Perspectives*
MFN	*Medieval Feminist Newsletter*
MFra	*Le Moyen Français*
MLR	*The Modern Language Review*
Mosaic	*Mosaic: A Journal for the Interdisciplinary Study of Literature*
MP	*Modern Philology: A Journal Devoted to Research in Medieval and Modern Literature*
MS	*Mediaeval Studies* (Toronto, Canada)
N&Q	*Notes and Queries*
NLH	*New Literary History: A Journal of Theory and Interpretation*
Parergon	*Parergon: Bulletin of the Australian and New Zealand Association for Medieval and Renaissance Studies*
PLL	*Papers on Language and Literature: A Journal for Scholars and Critics of Language and Literature*
REALB	*REAL: The Yearbook of Research in English and American Literature* (Tübingen, Germany)
RenQ	*Renaissance Quarterly*
RES	*Review of English Studies*
Review	*Review: Latin American Literature and Arts* (New York, N.Y.)
RmR	*Rocky Mountain Review of Language and Literature*
SAC	*Studies in the Age of Chaucer*
Scriptorium	*Scriptorium: Revue Internationale des Études Relatives aux Manuscrits/International Review of Manuscript Studies*
SeijoB	*Seijo Bungei* (Tokyo, Japan)
SEL	*Studies in English Literature, 1500–1900*
SiM	*Studies in Medievalism*

SMELL	*Studies in Medieval English Language and Literature*
SN	*Studia Neophilologica: A Journal of Germanic and Romance Languages and Literature* (Uppsala, Sweden)
SoAR	*South Atlantic Review*
SoRA	*Southern Review: Literary and Interdisciplinary Essays* (Gippsland, Australia)
SP	*Studies in Philology*
Speculum	*Speculum: A Journal of Medieval Studies*
Style	*Style* (DeKalb, Ill.)
Text	*Text: Transactions of the Society for Textual Scholarship*
TLS	*Times Literary Supplement* (London, England)
Traditio	*Traditio: Studies in Ancient and Medieval History, Thought, and Religion*
UMSE	*University of Mississippi Studies in English*
Viator	*Viator: Medieval and Renaissance Studies*
W&I	*Word and Image: A Journal of Verbal/Visual Enquiry*
YWES	*Year's Work in English Studies*

Bibliographical Citations and Annotations

Bibliographies, Reports, and Reference

1. Allen, Mark, and Bege K. Bowers. "An Annotated Chaucer Bibliography, 1994." *SAC* 18 (1996): 317–96. Continuation of *SAC* annual annotated bibliography (since 1975); based on *MLA Bibliography* listings, contributions from an international team, and independent research. A total of 352 items, including reviews.
2. Allen, Valerie, and Margaret Connolly. "Middle English: Chaucer." *YWES* 75 (1994): 167–200. A discursive bibliography of Chaucerian scholarship and research in 1994; divided into four categories: general, *CT*, *TC*, and other works.

See also nos. 5, 11, 59, 68, 113, 118.

Chaucer's Life

3. Meale, Carol M. "Reading Women's Culture in Fifteenth-Century England: The Case of Alice Chaucer." In Piero Boitani and Anna Torti, eds. *Mediaevalitas: Reading the Middle Ages* (*SAC* 20 [1998], no. 64), pp. 81–101. Examines the life, tomb, and library of Alice Chaucer—granddaughter of the poet—to suggest how we might reconstruct a women's literary culture of the fifteenth century. Alice's literary taste was influenced by her father, Thomas Chaucer; by the French connections of her two husbands; and by her role as mother, and possibly educator, of her politically important son.
4. Pask, Kevin. "'England's Olde Ennius': Geoffrey Chaucer." In Kevin Pask. *The Emergence of the Author: Scripting the Life of the Poet in Early Modern England.* Cambridge Studies in Renaissance Literature and Culture, no. 12. Cambridge: Cambridge University Press, 1996, pp. 9–52. Traces the process by which Chaucer's biography developed through Bale, Leland, Spenser, Speght, Thynne, Dryden, Urry, and Johnson. Topics include laureation, Chaucer in print, nationalistic and humanistic impulses, and Chaucer as a symbol of cultural exchange.

Facsimiles, Editions, and Translations

5. Alexander, Michael, ed. *The Canterbury Tales: The First Fragment: The General Prologue, The Knight's Tale, The Miller's Tale, The Reeve's Tale, The Cook's Tale: A Glossed Text.* London; New York; Ringwood, Victoria; Toronto; Auckland: Penguin, 1996. xvi, 293 pp. Reproduces *The Riverside Chaucer* texts of *GP*, *KnT*, *MilT*, *RvT*, and *CkT*, with original glosses on left-hand pages facing the text on the right-hand pages. Includes a brief descriptive introduction, a select bibliography, and thirty pages of informational notes.

6. Coghill, Nevill, trans. Foreword by Melvyn Bragg. Introd. by John Wain. *The Canterbury Tales.* New York: Barnes and Noble, 1994. 288 pp; 282 illus. A reprint of the 1952 Coghill translation (*Mel* and *ParsT* in synopsis only), with extensive color and black-and-white illustrations from a variety of medieval sources: all of the Ellesmere illuminations; woodcuts from Caxton's second edition of *CT* and from Wynkyn de Worde; and a variety of medieval maps, tapestries, windows, panels, and manuscripts. Illustrations depict details of the narratives and their backgrounds.

7. Costomiris, Robert Douglas. "Editorial Authority: William Thynne and the Construction of the Chaucer Canon in the Henrician Age." *DAI* 56 (1996): 4783A. William Thynne, the first true editor of Chaucer's œuvre, performed fewer duties for the royal household than has been believed; thus, he had more time for editing. Familiar with the three previous printings and with many manuscripts, he built on Caxton's edition and apparently relied most heavily on one manuscript, Tanner 346.

8. Machan, Tim William. "Speght's *Works* and the Invention of Chaucer." *Text* 8 (1996): 145–70. Examines how the form and ideology of Thomas Speght's Renaissance editions of Chaucer contribute to the monumentalization of the man and his works. Speght's critical apparatus, his expansion of Chaucer's corpus, and even the size and title pages of his editions contribute to Chaucer's preeminent mythical status.

9. Nakamura, Tetsuko. "Theory and Practice of Chaucerian Modernisations in Eighteenth Century Britain with Particular Reference to George Ogle's *Clerk's Tale.*" In Roger Ellis and René Tixier, eds. *The Medieval Translator/Traduire au Moyen Age*, 5 (*SAC* 20 [1998], no. 74), pp. 322–33. Surveys eighteenth-century translations of portions of Chaucer's *CT*, examining Ogle's translation of *ClT* as an

example in which the translator adapted the original to contemporary taste. Ogle's Walter and Griselda are a couple with human feelings and sentiments.

10.   Remley, Paul G. "Questions of Subjectivity and Ideology in the Production of an Electronic Text of the *Canterbury Tales.*" *Exemplaria* 8 (1996): 479–84. An electronic text of *CT* can give explicit attention to important philological issues—e.g., metrics, Middle English dialects, pronunciation, etymologies—so that class time can be devoted to the literary, historical, social, and theoretical issues raised by Chaucer's text.

11.   Robinson, Peter M. W., ed., with contributions from N. F. Blake, Daniel W. Mosser, Stephen Partridge, and Elizabeth Solopova. *The Wife of Bath's Prologue on CD-ROM.* Cambridge: Cambridge University Press, 1996. CD-ROM with printed instructional booklet and editor's introduction, 80 pp. Contains original-spelling transcripts of all fifty-four manuscripts and four pre–1500 printed editions of *WBP*, with digitized images of every page of text contained in these sources (1,200 images in all). The transcripts are linked with two collations, one unregularized and one regularized, so that any reading of any word or line can be compared with the corresponding word or line in all other texts. The CD-ROM also contains transcripts of all glosses, new descriptions of each witness, spelling databases for all the witnesses, introductions to each transcript, and articles by the contributors. See also no. 339.

See also nos. 74, 114, 165, 192, 276, 281.

Manuscripts and Textual Studies

12.   Boffey, Julia. "Annotation in Some Manuscripts of *Troilus and Criseyde.*" *EMS* 5 (1995): 1–17. Examines the layout and annotation of some of the sixteen surviving manuscripts of *TC*, focusing on Bodleian MSS Rawlinson Poet 163 and Selden B. 24. Repetition of headings and glosses may indicate that some parts of *TC* existed as discrete fragments with headings to clarify their arrangement.

13.   ———. "Short Texts in Manuscript Anthologies: The Minor Poems of John Lydgate in Two Fifteenth-Century Collections." In Stephen G. Nichols and Siegfried Wenzel, eds. *The Whole Book: Cultural Perspectives on the Medieval Miscellany* (*SAC* 20 [1998], no. 100), pp. 69–82. Discusses whether British Library MS Harley 116 and Cambridge

University Library MS Hh 4.12 were meant to be anthologies or whether the quire signatures indicate discrete works that came together by accident. Includes remarks on *PF*, *Form Age*, and *ClT.*

14. Bourgne, Florence. "Corpus Chaucérien et corporéite des vertus. Le MS Cambridge Gg 4.27 (1)." In Marie-Claire Rouyer, ed. *Le corps dans tous ses états*. Bordeaux: Université Michel de Montaigne, 1995, pp. 69–79. The surviving illustrations accompanying *ParsT* in Cambridge University Library MS Gg 4.27 reflect the personification of penance as a tree and a growing tendency toward concretization and didacticism in the late Middle Ages. As aspects of the *ordinatio* and *compilatio* of the manuscript, the illustrations are a manifestation of increased corporeality.

15. Butterfield, Ardis. "*Mise-en-page* in the *Troilus* Manuscripts: Chaucer and French Manuscript Culture." *HLQ* 58 (1996): 49–80. In addition to large formal sections, the *ordinatio* of fifteenth-century *TC* manuscripts marks categories of text and genre shifts (songs, letters, lyrics). Such practice, resembling that in manuscripts of Machaut and Froissart, suggests that *TC* participates in a cultural process in which scribal prerogatives of dividing the text and subordinating certain features to a larger conceptual hierarchy are closely aligned with new ideas of authorship. Also printed in no. 97.

16. Cains, Anthony G. "Notes and Documents: The Bindings of the Ellesmere Chaucer." *HLQ* 58 (1996): 127–57. Discusses the disbinding, preservation, and rebinding of Huntington Library MS EL 26C9. Provides new information regarding earlier bindings, inks, pigments, the relationship of text and decoration, repairs, etc. Also printed in no. 97.

17. Cavin, John A., III. "The Aesthetics of Textual Criticism Revisited." *DAI* 57 (1996): 198A. Considers the opposing theories of James Thorpe and G. Thomas Tanselle and emphasizes the need for full understanding of the aesthetic of meter, as with Chaucer's "heroic" line.

18. Dixon, Lori Jill. "The 'Canterbury Tales' Miscellanies: A Contextual Study of Manuscripts Anthologizing Individual 'Canterbury Tales.'" *DAI* 57 (1996): 674A. Sixteen fifteenth-century *CT* manuscripts—anthologized on the basis of theme, subject, or interest—survive. They reveal middle-class taste through their moral and devotional content and indicate the popularity and availability of Chaucer exemplars.

19.   Edwards, A. S. G. "Bodleian Library MS Arch. Selden B. 24: A 'Transitional' Collection." In Stephen G. Nichols and Siegfried Wenzel, eds. *The Whole Book: Cultural Perspectives on the Medieval Miscellany* (*SAC* 20 [1998], no. 100), pp. 53–67. Examines various aspects of late-medieval manuscript compilation in light of Selden B. 24, a "transitional collection" that extends the Chaucerian canon and connects with the emerging print culture.

20.   ———, and Ralph Hanna III. "Rotheley, the De Vere Circle, and the Ellesmere Chaucer." *HLQ* 58 (1996): 11–35. Although Ellesmere ownership in the fifteenth century cannot be proved, a preponderance of evidence indicates association with Bury St. Edmunds and a family circle that included the Pastons, Drurys, and De Veres, suggesting a context within which the manuscript was used. Particularly important is the largest entry on the flyleaves, Rotheley's poem honoring the De Veres (*Index* 1087), a transcription of which follows in an appendix. Also printed in no. 97.

21.   Hanna, Ralph, III. "Miscellaneity and Vernacularity: Conditions of Literary Production in Late Medieval England." In Stephen G. Nichols and Siegfried Wenzel, eds. *The Whole Book: Cultural Perspectives on the Medieval Miscellany* (*SAC* 20 [1998], no. 100), pp. 37–51. Using Winchester College MS 33 as a touchstone for examining the difficulties of apprehending medieval texts, Hanna attributes the miscellaneous nature of collections of vernacular works in manuscripts to the difficulties of textual supply rather than to randomness.

22.   ———. *Pursuing History: Middle English Manuscripts and Their Texts.* Stanford, Calif.: Stanford University Press, 1996. xii, 362 pp. Revised versions of fourteen essays by Hanna, plus an introduction and two new essays: "On Stemmatics" and "On the Versions of *Piers Plowman.*" All eight Chaucerian essays have been revised for consistency. The introduction describes how the canonization and reputation of Chaucer's works have dehistoricized much reading of Middle English works. According to Hanna, traditional presentation of Chaucer's works (and of other Middle English works) accords poorly with their presentation in manuscripts, amounting to a misrepresentation of the medieval experience of encountering the works.

23.   Mooney, Linne R. "More Manuscripts Written by a Chaucer Scribe." *ChauR* 30 (1996): 401–7. Two recently identified Trinity College manuscripts written by the "Hammond" scribe (who worked in

London ca. 1460–85), a prolific copier of Chaucer, contain medical, scientific, and legal materials, indicating that this scribe included among his patrons members of the knightly and merchant classes.

24. Pearsall, Derek. "Theory and Practice in Middle English Editing." *Text* 7 (1994): 107–27. Surveys recent discussions of the editing of medieval texts, calling for a consistent and sensitive concern for authorial intention, however evasive. Shows how manuscripts of *CT* and *TC* reflect Chaucer's likely revision of his works and how such revision is—and is not—reflected in editions and commentary.

25. Portnoy, Phyllis. "The Best-Text/Best-Book of Canterbury: The Dialogic of the Fragments." *Florilegium* 13 (1994): 161–72. Recent debates over the editing of *CT* reflect "best-text" (Hengwrt) versus "best-book" (Ellesmere) views, but both sides continue to make editorial assumptions about unity and closure. A better approach would be to recognize a genuinely dialogic relationship among all the parts, in which no single voice or order provides an authenticating perspective.

26. Robinson, Peter M. W. "Collation, Textual Criticism, Publication, and the Computer." *Text* 7 (1994): 77–95. Explores the advantages of computerized collation programs such as *CASE*, *TUSTEP*, and *Collate*, commenting on how they can expedite traditional editing. Cites many applications to *CT.*

27. Seymour, M. C. "The Manuscripts of Chaucer's *Legend of Good Women.*" *Scriptorium* 47 (1993): 73–90. Surveys issues in the textual history of *LGW*, e.g., its production in booklets and evidence of readership. Also describes codicological details of the ten surviving manuscripts that include the poem. Does not address the two versions of *LGWP.*

28. ———. "The Manuscripts of Chaucer's *Parlement of Fowls.*" *Scriptorium* 47 (1993): 192–204. Surveys issues in the textual history of *PF*, e.g., the role of Cambridge University Library MS Gg 4.27; the status of the roundel; and the influence of the poem. Also describes codicological details of the fourteen surviving manuscripts that include the poem, except those that include *LGW.* Manuscripts that include both poems are described in no. 27.

29. Wolfe, Matthew Clarke. "Constructing the Chaucer Corpus: A Study of Cambridge University Library, MS. Gg. 4.27." *DAI* 57 (1996): 2499A. Argues that Gg is the earliest surviving effort to create a corpus of Chaucer's poetry and that codicological analysis of the

manuscript reveals much about the reception of Chaucer in the fifteenth century.

See also nos. 11, 170, 172.

Sources, Analogues, and Literary Relations

30. Bianciotto, Gabriel. *Le Roman de Troyle.* Publications de l'Université de Rouen, no. 75. Rouen: Université de Rouen, 1994. 2 vols. 859 pp. Challenges Robert Pratt's view that *TC* was based on Beauvau's French *Troyle*, comparing the similarities among Boccaccio's *Filostrato*, *TC*, and the *Roman de Troyle.* Includes a detailed historical analysis of the Beauvau family in the fifteenth century and asserts the literary importance of Louis de Beauvau.

31. Galloway, Andrew. "A Fifteenth-Century Confession Sermon on 'Unkyndeness' (CUL MS Gg 6.26) and Its Literary Parallels and Parodies." *Traditio* 49 (1994): 259–69. Observes parallels between a confessional sermon and the following: the Wit section of *Piers Plowman*, the "Somme le Roi," *Mankind*, and both *SumT* and *PardT.* Includes a text of the Middle English sermon.

32. Hagedorn, Suzanne Christine. "Abandoned Women: Studies of an Ovidian Theme in the Works of Dante, Boccaccio, and Chaucer." *DAI* 56 (1996): 2671A–72A. Ovid undercuts epic male heroism, treating the emotional cost to the women deserted by Achilles, Theseus, Ulysses, and Aeneas and casting a shadow on these heroes in the works of Dante, Boccaccio, and Chaucer (*KnT*, *LGW*, and *TC*). Bakhtin's views illuminate the conflict between Virgilian and Ovidian treatments of Dido in Chaucer's work.

33. Kendrick, Laura. "Beyond the Question of Who Influenced Whom: The Shaping of the Individualist Consciousness in Eustace Deschamps's *Miroir de mariage* and Chaucer's *Canterbury Tales*." *BAM* 49 (1996): 7–37. Challenges assumptions underlying traditional studies of sources and relative chronology, suggesting that similarities between Deschamps's work and Chaucer's are evidence of late-fourteenth-century literary style and common *mentalités.* Compares ways Chaucer and Deschamps manipulate their readers.

34. Scudder, Patricia Heumann. "Chaucer's Vergil, Troy and the Medieval Commentary Tradition." *DAI* 57 (1996): 1130A. Chaucer

puts the allegorized Latin epic to various uses in five works: *HF, TC, KnT, MilT* (as comic and unsuccessful rebellion against the hierarchies of *KnT*), and *LGW.*

35. Spearing, A. C. "Chaucerian Authority and Inheritance." In Piero Boitani and Anna Torti, eds. *Literature in Fourteenth-Century England* (*SAC* 7 [1985], no. 71), pp. 185–202. Explores literary inheritance and father-child relations in Chaucer's works. Chaucer's "unfavourable attitude toward the power of the father" is reflected in his plots and in his attitudes toward his literary ancestry. Of Chaucer's descendants, Skelton, Henryson, and Douglas inherited "skeptical independence" from Chaucer.

36. Wallace, David. "Dante in English." In Rachel Jacoff, ed. *The Cambridge Companion to Dante.* Cambridge: Cambridge University Press, 1993, pp. 237–58. Surveys engagement with Dante by writers in English, from Chaucer to Seamus Heaney. Discusses Dantean influence on the Hugelyn section of *MkT* and on other portions of *CT, HF, Lady*, and *TC.*

See also nos. 103, 112, 116, 117, 126–28, 148, 152, 159, 164, 167, 179, 185, 190, 192, 198, 202, 206, 215, 216, 224, 228, 229, 233, 234, 253, 257, 260, 263, 266, 268, 271, 273–75.

Chaucer's Influence and Later Allusion

37. Batt, Catherine. "Hoccleve and . . . Feminism? Negotiating Meaning in *The Regiment of Princes.*" In Catherine Batt, ed. *Essays on Thomas Hoccleve* (*SAC* 20 [1998], no. 59), pp. 55–84. Examines the "defense-of-women" section near the end of Hoccleve's *Regement* (5090–194) as a meditation on literary influence and the need for the poet to comment on political issues. The defense alludes both to the Wife of Bath and to Prudence of *Mel*, emulating Chaucer's attitudes toward proverbial wisdom and toward the need for poets to be conscious of audience reception when giving practical advice.

38. Boffey, Julia. "Charles of Orleans Reading Chaucer's Dream Visions." In Piero Boitani and Anna Torti, eds. *Mediaevalitas: Reading the Middle Ages* (*SAC* 20 [1998], no. 64), pp. 43–62. Explores possible influences of Chaucer's dream poems on the works of Charles of Orleans, especially on the dream episodes in the English poems of British

Museum MS Harley 682 attributed to Charles. Similarities in pattern and verbal detail may have been mediated by other texts or derive from common sources.

39. ———. "Proverbial Chaucer and the Chaucer Canon." *HLQ* 58 (1996): 37–47. Unique Scottish attribution of "Walton's Prosperity" (a copy of *Index* 2820) to Chaucer in British Library MS Cotton Vitellius E. 11 suggests fifteenth-century reception of Chaucer as "fount of proverbial wisdom." Also printed in no. 97.

40. D'Agata d'Ottavi, Stefania. "Blake's Chaucer: Scholasticism *post litteram.*" In Piero Boitani and Anna Torti, eds. *Mediaevalitas: Reading the Middle Ages (SAC* 20 [1998], no. 64), pp. 115–28. William Blake's painting *The Canterbury Pilgrims* and his commentary on it in a *Descriptive Catalog* (1809) are a "complex allegory of life, where the classicist belief in the imitation of nature is thoroughly discarded." Blake returns to a "scholastic" approach to art and life and rejects Chaucer's naturalism, sacrificing ambiguity to allegory.

41. Ellis, Roger. "Chaucer, Christine de Pizan, and Hoccleve: *The Letter of Cupid.*" In Catherine Batt, ed. *Essays on Thomas Hoccleve (SAC* 20 [1998], no. 59), pp. 29–54. Questions how well Thomas Hoccleve's translation of Christine de Pizan's *Epistre au Dieu d'Amours* captures the "wit of the original," arguing that the translation was influenced by *LGW* and by other Chaucerian works and suggesting that Christine's original may also reflect the influence of *LGW.*

42. Ellis, Steve. "Chaucer, Yeats, and the Living Voice." *Yeats Annual* 11 (1995): 45–60. W. B. Yeats's early interest in Chaucer as a populist poet gave way to a "more occasional interest in the aristocratic and esoteric elements of Chaucer's works." For only a brief time, after receiving a copy of the Kelmscott Chaucer in 1907, Yeats idealized Chaucer for what he perceived to be a fusion of art and life. Later, Yeats became sensitive to Chaucer's complexities.

43. Hodder, Karen. "Elizabeth Barrett and the Middle Ages' Woeful Queens." *SiM* 7 (1996): 105–30. Explores the influence of medieval models of women on Barrett's poetry, arguing that, among others, Chaucer's works deserve greater attention in this respect. Considers Barrett's modifications of *Anel* in *Chaucer Modernized* and assesses aspects of *ClT, KnT,* and *TC.*

44. Kyriakakis-Maloney, Stella. "The Resuscitation of Romance: William Morris's 'The Earthly Paradise.'" *DAI* 56 (1996): 2694A.

Morris's effort to alter romance to the art of the community evokes the image of Chaucer as a forerunner. The envoy sends the book forth to meet its public and its master, Chaucer.

45. Pace, Claire. "Blake and Chaucer: 'Infinite Variety of Character.'" *Art History* 3 (1980): 388–409. Examines William Blake's painting of the Canterbury pilgrims for its artistic value and its place in the history of taste. Blake's *Descriptive Catalog*, which accompanied the first exhibition of the painting, and his *Prospectus* for a subsequent engraving of the pilgrims reflect his views on characterization and his admiration of Chaucer. Pace surveys pictorial depictions of Chaucerian materials before Blake and comments on the rise of Chaucer's popularity in the eighteenth century.

46. Page, Stephen. "John Metham's *Amoryus and Cleopes*: Intertextuality and Innovation in a Chaucerian Poem." *ChauR* 31 (1996): 201–8. The influence of Lydgate's *Troy Book* on Metham's work is often cited by critics. However, in terms of scene and tone, Metham is more indebted to Chaucer's *TC* and *Legend of Thisbe* than to Lydgate.

47. Pinti, Daniel J. "Teaching Chaucer Through the Fifteenth Century." *Exemplaria* 8 (1996): 507–11. Because a Chaucer class is often a student's only medieval course, we should incorporate fifteenth-century Chaucerian writing into our classes to expose students to the active reception of literary works, the social and/or literary uses to which Chaucer's texts may be put, and the historical construction of a "major author."

48. Schlacks, Deborah Davis. *American Dream Visions: Chaucer's Surprising Influence on F. Scott Fitzgerald.* Studies on Themes and Motifs in Literature, no. 5. New York: Peter Lang, 1994. x, 234 pp. Argues from internal and external evidence that Fitzgerald's works were strongly influenced by Chaucer's dream poems. In particular, Chaucerian themes, characterizations of females, and dream structures occur in Fitzgerald's early works, especially *The Great Gatsby*, as do parallel concerns with creativity and the role of the artist. The influence is less pervasive in later works by Fitzgerald, but his concern with the artist-protagonist continues.

49. Tomko, Andrew Stephan. "William Dunbar's Poetics: A Reconsideration of the Chaucerian in a Scottish Maker." *DAI* 56 (1996): 3950A. Though recent studies of Dunbar emphasize the traditional, the Scottish, and the Renaissance elements of his poetry, his aureate verse derives from familiarity with the rhetoric of Dante and Boccaccio, and

his prosody from Chaucer. He is closer to Chaucer than to poets of the early sixteenth century.

50. Underwood, Verne Michael. "John Lane's 'Tritons Trumpet.'" *DAI* 57 (1996): 1155A. Lane's previously unedited and unprinted pastoral poem of 1621, modeled on Spenser's *Shepheardes Calender*, follows Chaucer in using verse narratives of varying genres (e.g., fabliau and romance) to illustrate its themes (the vices of the age; superiority of the pastoral to the court life).

51. Winstead, Karen A. "John Capgrave and the Chaucer Tradition." *ChauR* 30 (1996): 389–400. Though Capgrave's *Life of St. Katherine* does not mention Chaucer or his characters and does not quote from Chaucer's texts, it bears a marked similarity to the technique of *TC*. Capgrave seems interested in issues raised by Chaucer but not, like Hoccleve and Lydgate, in "becoming" a Chaucerian.

See also nos. 35, 188, 190, 236, 255.

Style and Versification

52. Hanks, D. Thomas, Jr., Arminda Kamphausen, and James Wheeler. "Circling Back in Chaucer's *Canterbury Tales*: On Punctuation, Misreading, and Reader Response." *Chaucer Yearbook* 3 (1996): 35–53. Shows how modern punctuation obscures subtleties of Chaucer's poetry, drawing examples from *CT*. Unpunctuated, Chaucer's verse has a rich poetic syntax, especially in the ways it compels readers to posit one meaning, adjust that meaning to a second meaning, and come away with a double sense.

See also nos. 17, 49, 223, 275.

Language and Word Studies

53. Cannon, Christopher. "The Myth of Origin and the Making of Chaucer's English." *Speculum* 71 (1996): 646–75. Linguistic claims that Chaucer's English is the origin of English literary language are self-fulfilling, based on the "myth," in the sense of Levi-Strauss, that Chaucer originated English poetic tradition. The *OED* credits Chaucer with the first citation of 1,180 words (many of them introductions from French

and Latin) because the compilers worked under the influence of the myth, as the compilers of the *MED* continue to do.

54. Dane, Joseph A. "*Queynte*: Some Rime and Some Reason on a Chaucer[ian] Pun." *JEGP* 95 (1996): 497–514. Larry Benson's understanding of "queynte" as an adjective (*SAC* 9 [1987], no. 54) is untenable since it depends on a rhyme pattern inadmissible in Chaucer. The true meaning is the traditional one of "pudendum."

55. Fisher, John H. *The Emergence of Standard English.* Lexington: University Press of Kentucky, 1996. ix, 208 pp. Prints eight previously published essays with a new introduction, all pertaining to the influence of bureaucratic and literary language on the standardization of English. Chronicling the development of Fisher's idea that standard written English arose out of bureaucratic scribal practice, the introduction explores relations between the Chancery Standard and Tudor English. For the reprinted essays that relate directly to Chaucer, see *SAC* 12 (1990), bibliography entry no. 18; *SAC* 16 (1994), no. 54; and *SAC* 18 (1996), no. 64.

56. Kanno, Masahiko. *Chaucer's Words: A Contextual and Semantic Approach.* Tokyo: Eihosha, 1996. Discusses Chaucer's epithetic adjectives, stock phrases, and asseverations. Also considers his transformations of traditional similes and metaphors into fresh ones for poetic effects.

57. Park, Sae-gon. "The Transition from the Impersonal to the Personal Construction in English—with Reference to Data Analysis of the Sentences that Contain Infinitives." *JELL* 41 (1995): 827–45 (in Korean, with English abstract). Draws examples from *Beowulf* and *CT* to demonstrate transitions in impersonal constructions in the Middle English period, especially evident in uses of the expletive "it" with an infinitive ("it happed hym to ride").

See also nos. 170, 197, 267.

Background and General Criticism

58. Arthur, Karen Maria. "Speculum Mortis: Reflections of Chivalry and Courtly Society in the Age of Chaucer." *DAI* 56 (1996): 2671A. Warfare and plague made English people of the later fourteenth century unprecedentedly aware of death. The Black Prince and John of Gaunt's first father-in-law, despite their heroic image in chronicles, died

of unromantic diseases. Like *Sir Gawain and the Green Knight*, *KnT* and *TC* combine seemingly meaningless death with the courtly and chivalric, revealing Chaucer's philosophic probing.

59. Batt, Catherine, ed. *Essays on Thomas Hoccleve.* Westfield Publications in Medieval Studies, no. 10. [Turnhout, Belgium]: Brepols, 1996, in association with the Centre for Medieval and Renaissance Studies, Queen Mary and Westfield College, University of London. 130 pp. Four essays by various authors focus on editing Hoccleve's works, his variety of styles, and the relation of his works to those of Chaucer and Christine de Pizan. Includes a bibliography, an index, and an introduction that surveys critical approaches to Hoccleve. For essays that pertain to Chaucer, see nos. 37 and 41.

60. Bauer, Kate A. "The Portrayal of Parents and Children in the Works of Chaucer, Gower, and the Pearl-Poet." *DAI* 56 (1996): 3949A. Cross-disciplinary evidence (since the publication of Aries's *Centuries of Childhood*) indicates that strong love between parents and children existed in medieval culture. Chaucer, Gower, and the *Pearl*-poet represent children and family ties with some realism and considerable idealization.

61. Beidler, Peter G. "Teaching Chaucer as Drama: The Garden Scene in the *Shipman's Tale.*" *Exemplaria* 8 (1996): 485–93. Introducing small readers' theatre productions of scenes from Chaucer into the classroom reinforces the sounds of Middle English for students, allows them to get personally involved in the class, focuses their attention more closely on Chaucer's text, and emphasizes the large dramatic element of *CT*.

62. Besserman, Lawrence. "Augustine, Chaucer, and the Translation of Biblical Poetics." In Sanford Budick and Wolfgang Iser, eds. *The Translatability of Cultures: Figurations of the Space Between.* Stanford, Calif.: Stanford University Press, 1996, pp. 68–84. Augustine's emphasis on charity and cupidity in *De doctrina Christiana* and his discussion of the relations among gospel narratives in *De consensu evangelistarum* suggest that he equates secular and biblical poetics. Similarly, Chaucer justifies his poetry by connecting it with the Bible in *GP*, *Th–MelL*, and *Ret*, thereby linking himself to a learned tradition of Augustinian interpretation.

63. ———, ed. *The Challenge of Periodization: Old Paradigms and New Perspectives.* New York: Garland, 1996. xxiv, 245 pp. Thirteen

essays originally presented as lectures at the Center for Literary Studies at the Hebrew University of Jerusalem between September 1991 and January 1993. Each essay reexamines the relation of a major author, genre, or theme to traditional understanding of literary periods, challenging such labels as "medieval," "Renaissance," and "modern." The collection includes a reprint (pp. 29–49) of Larry D. Benson, "The Beginning of Chaucer's English Style" (*SAC* 19 [1997], no. 60).

64. Boitani, Piero, and Anna Torti, eds. *Mediaevalitas: Reading the Middle Ages.* J. A. W. Bennett Memorial Lectures, 9th ser., Perugia, 1995. Cambridge: D. S. Brewer, 1996. x, 183 pp. Ten essays by various authors on topics that include depictions of nature, Chaucer and his reception, Spenser, and medievalism. For individual essays that pertain to Chaucer, see nos. 3, 38, 40, 190, 255, and 260.

65. Bragg, Lois. "Chaucer's Monogram and the 'Hoccleve Portrait' Tradition." *W&I* 12:1 (1996): 127–42. Read in accord with the medieval one-handed alphabet, the hand positions in Chaucer's Hoccleve portrait form the monogram GC. These positions appear to be a constant in the tradition of Chaucer portraiture, including the Ellesmere miniature. Such devices were used in medieval portraiture to particularize otherwise typical and timeless images.

66. Brewer, Derek. "Arithmetic and the Mentality of Chaucer." In Piero Boitani and Anna Torti, eds. *Literature in Fourteenth-Century England* (*SAC* 7 [1985], no. 71), pp. 155–64. Examines arithmetical aspects of Chaucer's poetry in an effort to understand the mind of the man. The arithmetical devices of such works as *RvT*, *ShT*, and *SumT* indicate the strong vein of "modernistic rationalism" in Chaucer, a distinctive feature of his mentality.

67. Bruhn, Mark Joseph. "Episodes in English Verse Romance." *DAI* 57 (1996): 690A. Study based on theories of Fowler (genre) and Jakobson (metaphor and metonymy) reveals that English verse romance from the thirteenth to the twentieth centuries is typically episodic, with variations attuned to changing intent.

68. Burrow, J. A., and Thorlac Turville-Petre. *A Book of Middle English.* 2d ed. Oxford: Basil Blackwell, 1996. xii, 373 pp. A revision of the 1992 edition (*SAC* 16 [1994], no. 52), the second edition includes—in addition to the fourteen original non-Chaucerian works— three Chaucerian texts: *PF*, *RvT*, and *PrT*. The texts include notes, glossary, and brief bibliographies and introductions.

69. Carruthers, Mary. "The Poet as Master Builder: Compositional and Locational Memory in the Middle Ages." *NLH* 24 (1993): 881–904. Dante and Chaucer use "buildings of the imagination" to organize lists of names, lists less informational than "inventional"—sets of associated plots or ideas that may reverberate in the work in which they appear. Examples from *HF* and *BD*, as well as from Dante's *Inferno*, help clarify the technique, which Carruthers explores further as a monastic procedure for composing prayers and for studying Scripture.

70. Charnley, Susan Christina De Long. "'I Wol Nat Serve . . .': Authority and Submission in Late Medieval English Literature." *DAI* 57 (1996): 2030A. Examines right relations of individuals in the medieval Christian hierarchy as shown in the writings of Chaucer, Gower, Langland, the *Pearl*-poet, Julian of Norwich, and Guillaume de Deguileville.

71. Coleman, Joyce. "An 'Ethnography of Reading' in Chaucer." In Joyce Coleman. *Public Reading and the Reading Public in Late Medieval England and France* (*SAC* 20 [1998], no. 72), pp. 148–78. Internal evidence in Chaucer's works indicates that he expected his works to be read aloud—both by himself to an immediate, first audience and by prelectors to later audiences. Chaucer's references to the reception of his work, his references to the reception of others' works, and his depictions of reception indicate the community of hearers assumed in his literature.

72. ———. *Public Reading and the Reading Public in Late Medieval England and France.* Cambridge: Cambridge University Press, 1996. xiv, 250 pp. Argues that public reading was popular because people enjoyed listening to books in company. Aural audiences included literate upper-middle-class and upper-class readers well into the Renaissance, when aural reading changed. Elite audiences preferred the social experience of literature long after the rise of print and expanding literacy. For the chapter that pertains to Chaucer, see no. 71.

73. Dauby, Hélène, with an introduction by André Crépin. "Catalogue de l'Exposition: Chaucer et les cultures d'expression française." *BAM* 39 (1991): 615–24. Briefly describes the books and materials exhibited at the January 11, 1991, Sorbonne conference on Chaucer-French relations.

74. Ellis, Roger, and René Tixier, eds. *The Medieval Translator/Traduire au Moyen Age, 5.* [Turnhout, Belgium]: Brepols, 1996. xvi, 488 pp.; illus. Twenty-five essays from the Fourth Cardiff

Conference on the Theory and Practice of Translation in the Middle Ages, 26–29 July 1993. The essays address topics of translation in the Middle Ages and translation of medieval authors. For the essays that pertain to Chaucer, see nos. 9, 94, and 159.

75. Epstein, Robert William. "'At the Stremes Hed of Grace': Representations of Prince and Poet in Late Medieval English Court Poetry." *DAI* 57 (1996): 1631A. Before Richard II's deposition, Chaucer affected an apolitical stance, while Gower became pro-Lancastrian. Poetic self-representation later gave way to politicized views in the works of Hoccleve, Scogan, and Lydgate. The dissertation also treats Margery Kempe, James I of Scotland, and George Ashby.

76. Erzgräber, Willi. "Die antiken Episoden in Chaucers frühen erzählerischen Werken." In Bernd Engler and Kurt Müller, eds. *Exempla: Studien zur Bedeutung und Funktion exemplarischen Erzählens.* Schriften zur Literaturwissenschaft, no. 10. Berlin: Duncker & Humblot, 1995, pp. 55–77. Examines the structural and thematic roles of the Ceys and Alcyone episode in *BD*, the Dido episode in *HF*, and the Dream of Scipio in *PF.*

77. Ferster, Judith. *Fictions of Advice: The Literature and Politics of Counsel in Late Medieval England.* Philadelphia: University of Pennsylvania Press, 1996. xii, 216 pp. Outlines the mixture of authorial deference and criticism within a mostly English mirror-for-princes tradition, from the *Secretum secretorum* to Machiavelli. Historicizes the works of James Yonge, John Gower, and Thomas Hoccleve within particular political contexts, assessing the ruler/counselor agency established in each case. For a chapter that pertains to Chaucer, see no. 225.

78. Flores, Nona C., ed. *Animals in the Middle Ages: A Book of Essays.* New York: Garland, 1996. xvi, 206 pp. Discusses animals as symbols in medieval culture and includes four essays that consider works by Chaucer. See nos. 79, 210, 243, and 269.

79. ———. "*Effigies Amicitiae . . . Veritas Inimicitiae*: Antifeminism in the Iconography of the Women-Headed Serpent in Medieval and Renaissance Art and Literature." In Nona C. Flores, ed. *Animals in the Middle Ages: A Book of Essays* (SAC 20 [1998], no. 78), pp. 167–95. Oblique mention of Chaucer's comparison of Fortune to the "fraudulent serpent" in *MerT* and of his reference to the "smiler with the knife" in *KnT.*

80. Folks, Cathalin B. "Of Sondry Folk: The Canterbury Pilgrimage as Metaphor for Teaching Chaucer at the Community College."

Exemplaria 8 (1996): 473–77. Like Chaucer's pilgrimage, community colleges accept all comers and promise a miraculous transformation of a clientele representing a cross-section of society. The students-pilgrims prefer the spoken to the written word, requiring frequent reading aloud and dramatization, with leadership by a professor-host who exhibits a Chaucerian mixture of humor and patience.

81. Garbáty, Thomas J. "A Description of the Confession Miniatures for Gower's *Confessio Amantis* with Special Reference to the Illustrator's Role as Reader and Critic." *Mediaevalia* 19 (1996, for 1993): 319–43. Examines illuminations in manuscripts of Gower's *Confessio Amantis*, arguing that they reflect contemporary difficulties in distinguishing between the author and the fictional persona. Includes depictions of Chaucer in miniatures and comparisons with Chaucer's self-depictions in poetry.

82. Glejzer, Richard Robert. "Invention, Instrumentality, and Sexuation in Chaucer and Lacan." *DAI* 57 (1996): 675A. Examines the relationship of Jacques Lacan's theories to Chaucer's sense of sexuality in *NPT*, *ClT*, and *WBPT*.

83. Goodman, Thomas A. "On Literacy." *Exemplaria* 8 (1996): 459–72. Chaucerians must encourage or revive linguistic and cultural literacy of the Middle Ages among students and colleagues, both because the Middle Ages are of significant interest in popular culture and because they offer access to "familiar difference," fostering critical awareness in interpretation and communication.

84. Grudin, Michaela Paasche. *Chaucer and the Politics of Discourse.* Columbia: University of South Carolina Press, 1996. ix, 200 pp. A recurrent concern in Chaucer's works is the relation between society and discourse, a concern Chaucer shares with Italian humanists. In *BD*, Chaucer demonstrates the reciprocity of speaker and listener; the playfulness and lack of closure in *HF* indicate the "instability of discourse." In *PF*, the Ciceronian ideal of a discursively ordered society is challenged by the birds' cacophony. *TC* examines how speech itself is a way of understanding human behavior and human interactions. The authoritative discourse of *KnT* is challenged by *MilT* and *RvT* and contrasted by Walter's hidden intentions in *ClT*. *WBP* demonstrates that discourse cannot be restrained. In *SqT* and *FranT*, speech misused and speech misunderstood are counterpointed. The responses of the Knight and the Host to *MkT*—itself a rhetorical tour de force—indicate a "ten-

sion between discourse and its receivers." *ManT* indicates the necessity for poetic artfulness and perhaps for guile. Throughout his career, Chaucer emphasized the uncertain nature of social discourse by imitating orality and resisting closure.

85. Hagen, Susan K. "Interdisciplinary Chaucer." *Exemplaria* 8 (1996): 449–53. An undergraduate Chaucer course exploring the late fourteenth century as a time of political, economic, religious, technological, and epistemological change can both enrich students' experiences of the texts and help them realize that twentieth-century American culture is also a construction.

86. Hass, Robin Ranea. "Naked Truth, Feminized Language, and Poetics: Paradigms of Femininity from the Rhetoricians to Chaucer." *DAI* 56 (1996): 3949A–50A. In the light of medieval *artes poetriae*, rhetoric is perceived as feminine. Chaucer's hagiography, courtly romance, and fabliaux demonstrate rhetoric in various modes: as chaste, "pedestal," and wanton, especially as voiced by the Clerk and the Wife of Bath.

87. Jennings, Margaret. "The 'Sermons' of English Romance." *Florilegium* 13 (1994): 121–40. Thematic sermon structure, as delineated in English *artes praedicandi*, influenced romances as well as other genres. This influence can be seen in *Sir Amadace*, *Sir Gawain and the Green Knight*, *KnT* (Theseus's speech on order), *WBT* (the loathly lady's lecture), *TC* (Criseyde's discourse on jealousy in *TC* 3.987–1054), and Robert Henryson's *Testament of Cresseid.*

88. Jost, Jean E. "Chaucer, Geoffrey." In Steven H. Gale, ed. *Encyclopedia of British Humorists: Geoffrey Chaucer to John Cleese.* 2 vols. New York and London: Garland, 1996, vol. 1, pp. 228–43. Surveys the humor and structural comedy of Chaucer's works, especially *CT*, examining individual tales and commenting on *BD*, *HF*, and *PF*. Chaucer achieves comic effects through narrative resolution and by manipulating time, place, and circumstances. The article includes a bibliography of critical commentary on Chaucer's comedy.

89. Kelly, Kathleen Coyne. "If a Trope Looks like a Trope: The Ape Metaphor in Middle English Texts." *Allegorica* 16 (1995): 3–16. Explores how Chaucer capitalized on extrinsic and intrinsic connotations in his ape metaphors. Kelly provides backgrounds to the metaphors from other medieval texts and, following Michael Riffaterre, theorizes about how such metaphors can operate in nonallusive ways.

90. Kiessling, Nicolas. *The Incubus in English Literature: Provenance and Progeny.* [Pullman]: Washington State University, 1977. [iv], 104 pp. Includes passim references to Chaucer's works and reprints as "Monks and Incubi in Chaucer" (pp. 51–55), a slightly revised version of "The Wife of Bath's Tale, D 878–81," *ChauR* 7 (1972): 113–17.

91. Kimmelman, Burt. *The Poetics of Authorship in the Later Middle Ages: The Emergence of the Modern Literary Persona.* Studies in the Humanities–Politics–Society, no. 21. New York: Peter Lang, 1996. 288 pp. Explores the emergence of the modern, first-person persona as manifested in autocitation. Assessing the influence of Augustine, Anselm, Ockham, and others, Kimmelman traces the development of autocitation in the works of Guillem IX, Marcabru, and Dante, focusing primarily on Langland and Chaucer. Kimmelman studies Chaucer's persona most closely in *LGWP* but also comments on *PF, TC, ClT, Ret,* and *CT.*

92. Kinney, Clare R. "Theory and Pedagogy." *Exemplaria* 8 (1996): 455–57. Recent critical theory emphasizes reading from the margins to interrogate problematic "master narratives." When one teaches Chaucer to undergraduates, however, such interrogation may become "naturalized" as a new master narrative for students unaware of critical or historical tradition.

93. Kitson, Annabella. "Astrology and English Literature." *ContempR* 269 (1996): 200–207. Illustrates a variety of ways astrology has been used in literature, drawing examples from Chaucer, Shakespeare, John Webster, and Samuel Beckett. Cites examples from *Mars, MilT,* and *FranT,* as well as Hypermnestra in *LGW.*

94. Koff, Leonard Michael. "'Awak!': Chaucer Translates Bird Songs." In Roger Ellis and René Tixier, eds. *The Medieval Translator/Traduire au Moyen Age,* 5 (*SAC* 20 [1998], no. 74), pp. 390–418. Briefly sketches a medieval philosophy of animal language in relation to medieval notions of translation as a communal ideal. In *ClT,* Chaucer presents translation as a form of revelation; in *SumT,* it is transgressive; in *KnT,* a kind of disguise. In *ManT,* translation is replaced by silence to indicate that incomprehensibility is a moral rather than a linguistic phenomenon.

95. Landman, James Henry. "Langland, Chaucer, Fortescue: Force of Law and Popular Voice, 1377–1471." *DAI* 57 (1996): 2492A. The complicated matrix of late-medieval law, with its efforts to seek truth

(even by torture), sheds light on the historical dynamics of various works.

96.   Lázaro Lafuente, Luis A., José Simón, and Ricardo J. Sola Buil, eds. *Proceedings of the IIIrd International Conference of the Spanish Society for Medieval Language and Literature.* Madrid: Universidad de Alcalá de Henares, 1996. 288 pp. Includes seven essays that pertain to Chaucer; texts in English and Spanish variously. See nos. 102, 129, 164, 192, 212, 261, and 270.

97.   Lerer, Seth, ed. *Reading from the Margins: Textual Studies, Chaucer, and Medieval Literature.* San Marino, Calif.: Huntington Library, 1996. vii, 160 pp. Simultaneously publishes the essays that appear in *HLQ* 58:1 (1996). See nos. 15, 16, 20, 39, and 155.

98.   Machan, Tim William. "Thomas Berthelette and Gower's *Confessio.*" *SAC* 18 (1996): 143–66. Contrasts the printing history of Gower's *Confessio Amantis* with that of *CT*, describing how Berthelette's 1532 printing of the *Confessio*—the only edition between Caxton and the nineteenth century—contributed to the critical privileging of Chaucer over Gower. Berthelette's prefatory discussion, his printing format, his penchant for ethical and religious works, and his failure to revise and update the presentation of the *Confessio* encourage a view of Gower as a conservative, moral poet.

99.   Mead, Jenna. ". . . The Anti-Imperial Approaches to Chaucer (Are There Those?): An Essay in Identifying Strategies." *SoRA* 27 (1994): 403–17. A postcolonial meditation on "what is Chaucer in the changing reality that is the context of Australia," which focuses on portions of four texts: a conversation between Meaghan Morris and Stephen Muecke, Ralph Elliott's 1968 comments on the development of the Australia and New Zealand Association for Medieval and Renaissance Studies, a Frank Moorhouse short story that mentions Chaucerian Stephen Knight, and Gayatri Spivak's view that Chaucer is a component in an imperialist project.

100.   Nichols, Stephen G., and Siegfried Wenzel, eds. *The Whole Book: Cultural Perspectives on the Medieval Miscellany. Recentiores*: Later Latin Texts and Contexts. Ann Arbor: University of Michigan Press, 1996. viii, 188 pp. Nine essays by various authors and a closing commentary address organization, inclusion, and definition of medieval miscellanies—Latin, French, and English. The essays were first presented at a colloquium at the University of Pennsylvania in 1993. For the essays that pertain to Chaucer, see nos. 13, 19, and 21.

386

101. Patterson, Lee. "The Disenchanted Classroom." *Exemplaria* 8 (1996): 513–45. Max Weber's distinction between an "ethics of commitment" and an "ethics of responsibility" can help make the connection between theoretical assumptions and pedagogical practices explicit. An "ethics of commitment" leads to the idea of the teacher as prophet; an "ethics of responsibility" encourages specialization and leads to a historicist approach.

102. Pérez Lorido, Rodrigo. "English Secular and Ecclesiastical Music in the Fourteenth Century: Some Literary References." In Luis A. Lázaro Lafuente, José Simón, and Ricardo J. Sola Buil, eds. *Proceedings of the IIIrd International Conference of the Spanish Society for Medieval Language and Literature* (SAC 20 [1998], no. 96), pp. 247–59. Though not a practicing musician, Chaucer had a better-than-average knowledge of late-fourteenth-century French monodic and English polyphonic music. This knowledge is evident in his specific and accurate use of musical terminology.

103. Petrina, Alessandra. "Incubi and Nightmares in Middle English Literature." *Atti Dell'Istituto Veneto di Scienze, Lettere ed Arti* 152 (1993–94): 391–422. Surveys the connections in classical and Christian literature between incubi and nightmares. Documents the intersections of these traditions in Middle English literature, where such night visitations are more frequent than in Continental literature. Comments on dreams and visitations in *WBT* and *TC* and assesses an analogue, from a thirteenth-century exemplum collection, of the incubus/friar scene in *WBT*.

104. Richmond, Velma Bourgeois. "Teaching Chaucer in a Small Catholic Liberal Arts College." *Exemplaria* 8 (1996): 495–506. Theoretical studies of Chaucer often discourage student interest because of their difficulty and narrow focus. Teaching Chaucer to a diverse population in a small liberal arts college requires materials and activities such as videos, slides, dramatic productions, examples of the use of Chaucer as children's literature, and discussion of moral issues.

105. Rose, Christine. "'Diverse Folk Diversely They Seyde': Teaching Chaucer in the Nineties." *Exemplaria* 8 (1996): 443–48. Despite the increasing difficulty of retaining the Chaucer "canon" in university curricula of the 1990s, Chaucer-teaching is alive and flourishing, as evidenced in the colloquium on teaching at the 1994 New Chaucer Society meeting and the papers printed in the *Exemplaria* 8:2 (1996) special issue on teaching.

106. ————. "Postscript: An Internet Pilgrimage." *Exemplaria* 8 (1996): 547–51. The electronic "preprints" of "Teaching Chaucer in the Nineties" revealed both the extent to which professors and students have become electronically literate and large disparities in the availability of electronic resources. Ironically, no papers suggested the internet or WWW as teaching tools; most papers did not stimulate on-line discussion.

107. Ross, Valerie Ann. "The Tradition of Subversion in Medieval Vernacular Literature: A Feminist Analysis of Selected Works by Marie de France and Geoffrey Chaucer." *DAI* 56 (1996): 3950A. Chaucer and Marie de France simultaneously contribute to the development of vernacular literature and subvert its conventions through parody, pastiche, and resistance to existing gender models.

108. Scattergood, John. *Reading the Past: Essays on Medieval and Renaissance Literature*. Portland, Ore.; and Dublin: Four Courts Press, 1996. 310 pp. A collection of nineteen essays previously published by the author, ten on Chaucer.

109. Summit, Jennifer. "The Goose's Quill: The Production of Female Authorship in Late Medieval and Early Modern England." *DAI* 57 (1996): 240A. After the anonymity of earlier times, fourteenth-century writing reveals increasing individuation and attention to the gender of an author. Chaucer's fictional women writers indicate an anxious sense on his part of declining *auctoritas*, whereas Margery Kempe and Christine de Pizan exploit the dislocation to extend genres and break with tradition.

110. Taylor, Mark Norman. "Chaucer and the Dialectic of Love: Transformations in the Literary Love Tradition since Marcabru." *DAI* 57 (1996): 207A. The outworn paradigm of courtly love has been discarded but not superseded by a model flexible enough to contain the many variations developed by "moralists and gameplayers." Treats troubadour verse, French and English romances and lyrics, and Chaucer.

111. Tinkle, Theresa. *Medieval Venuses and Cupids: Sexuality, Hermeneutics, and English Poetry*. Stanford, Calif.: Stanford University Press, 1996. xv, 294 pp. Mythographic tradition provided Chaucer and his contemporaries a wide variety of significations for the figures of Cupid and Venus. Tinkle surveys this variety from antiquity forward, showing that vernacular representations of Cupid and Venus derived complex meanings from such mythographic traditions as moralization,

medicine, philosophy, astrology, and iconography. Depictions of Cupid and Venus by Chaucer, Gower, Lydgate, James I, Boccaccio, and Christine de Pizan (among others) reflect medieval constructions of sexuality. Chaucer "shuns Cupid's deceits in favor of Venus's patronage," abandoning French models and constructing a less class-based, more "natural" order that set the English standard. Discussed at length are *KnT*, *WBT*, *ParsT*, *HF*, *PF*, and *LGWP*. Some attention is given to *SqT* and *TC*.

See also nos. 258, 264.

The Canterbury Tales—General

112. Astell, Ann W. *Chaucer and the Universe of Learning*. Ithaca, N. Y.; and London: Cornell University Press, 1996. xvi, 254 pp. In the Ellesmere arrangement, *CT* forms a unified whole, modeled on the seven planets and on the traditional divisions of philosophy and offering a "planetary pilgrimage" and a philosophical "journey of the soul." Like Gower's *Confessio Amantis*, *CT* is an "ordered collection of exemplary stories," structurally tripartite. The two works are also similar in that each "involves its reader as an active participant in the construction of its meaning." A planetary scheme connects *CT* and Dante's *Paradiso*, even though their audiences differ and Chaucer has "[n]o unequivocally authoritative guide for his pilgrims." Not a court poet, Chaucer belongs among the literate and bookish crowd of England, and his work is best viewed in the genre familiar to his audience.

113. Cooper, Helen. *The Canterbury Tales*. 2d ed. Oxford Guides to Chaucer. Oxford: Oxford University Press, 1996. xiii, 439 pp. A revision of the 1989 edition (*SAC* 13 [1991], no. 97), with updated discussions of critical issues—especially social and historical matters—and more extensive bibliographies.

114. Feinstein, Sandy. "Hypertextuality and Chaucer, or Reordering *The Canterbury Tales* and Other Reader Prerogatives." *Readerly/Writerly Texts* 2 (1996): 135–48. The selectivity of oral performance and scribal practice parallels the selectivity of hypertext presentation, raising questions about the order of the tales in *CT*. In *MilP*, the narrator enjoins readers to arrange the tales as they wish, adumbrating options potentially available in hypertext editions.

115. Fellows, Jennifer, Rosalind Field, Gillian Rogers, and Judith Weiss, eds. *Romance Reading on the Book: Essays on Medieval Literature Presented to Maldwyn Mills.* Cardiff: University of Wales Press, 1996. x, 307 pp. Collection of essays on medieval romance that contains recurrent references to *FranT*, *KnT*, *MLT*, *MilT*, *PhyT*, and *Th*. For an essay that pertains to Chaucer, see no. 179.

116. Guerra Bosch, Teresa. "The Religious Satire in *The Decameron* and *The Canterbury Tales.*" *Philologica Canariensia* (1994): 181–91. Comments on examples of ecclesiastical satire in *CT* and *The Decameron*, arguing that Chaucer viewed contemporary abuses as comic, though Boccaccio's ironies are "slyer."

117. Kawasaki, Masatoshi. "Chaucer's Narrative Game." *JBAL* 31 (1996): 1–18 (in Japanese). Considers the backgrounds and narrative structures of Chaucer's comic tales. Chaucer's fabliaux are less serious than are their sources and analogues, although some of the resemblances are disturbing.

118. Lambdin, Laura C., and Robert T. Lambdin, eds. *Chaucer's Pilgrims: An Historical Guide to the Pilgrims in* The Canterbury Tales. Westport, Conn.; and London: Greenwood, 1996. xiv, 398 pp. Thirty-two essays by various authors who define and describe the professions, vocations, and avocations of Chaucer's pilgrims. Individual essays pertain to each of the pilgrims mentioned in *GP*—including the five guildsmen, the Host (innkeeper), and the narrator (writer and pilgrim)—and to the pilgrims who approach the pilgrimage late—the Canon (canon and alchemist) and the Canon's Yeoman. The guide includes an index and a selected bibliography in addition to the selected bibliographies that accompany each essay. See nos. 131, 133–37, 139–41, 144, 150, 153, 156, 161, 180, 183, 187, 189, 193, 197, 207, 208, 213, 218, 219, 227, 231, 237–39, 241, and 245.

119. Larson, Wendy Rene. "Exile, Confession, Vision: Discourses of Subjectivity in Anglo-Saxon and Middle English Literature." *DAI* 57 (1996): 206A. Analysis based on Foucault and Butler shows that, in a wide variety of medieval texts including *CT*, the speakers' situations affect their social position and their ability to refashion genres.

120. McIlhaney, Anne E. "Sentence and Judgment: The Role of the Fiend in Chaucer's *Canterbury Tales.*" *ChauR* 31 (1996): 173–83. In *CT*, generally, and in *MLT*, *FrT*, *PhyT*, *PardT*, and *PrT*, specifically, devils act as agents of God to tempt evildoers. Although they fail, evildoers in

CT are armed with the God-given ability to avoid such temptation through their reason, discretion, and wit.

121. McLaughlin, Becky Renee. "Pilgrimage Gone Awry: The Theatrics of the Chaucerian Unconscious." *DAI* 57 (1996): 2493A. *CT* develops "horror and abjection" through struggles for mastery of many kinds, leaving its characters suspended between the Tabard and Canterbury amid images of mutilation and death. Chaucer critics may also be seen as pilgrims struggling among themselves for mastery.

122. Mann, Jill. "Parents and Children in the 'Canterbury Tales.'" In Piero Boitani and Anna Torti, eds. *Literature in Fourteenth-Century England (SAC* 7 [1985], no. 71), pp. 165–83. The parent-child relationship is one of the central motifs of *CT*. Mann focuses on *MkT*, *MLT*, *PrT*, *PhyT*, and *ClT* to argue that Chaucer explores not only the power relations between parent and child but also parallel relations and the relations of the human with the supernatural.

123. Olsen, Alexandra H. "The Rise of the Middle Class in Middle English Literature." *InG* 17 (1996): 51–56. Discusses references to the middle class in Arthurian literature and relates *SqT*, *Th*, and *ShT* to the medieval "commercial revolution." Arcite, in *KnT*, is a type of Horatio Alger, beginning as a page, gaining status, and marrying into nobility.

124. Rigby, S. H. *Chaucer in Context: Society, Allegory, and Gender.* Manchester Medieval Studies. Manchester and New York: Manchester University Press, 1996. xii, 205 pp. Surveys the polarities in critical assessments of *CT*, focusing on four oppositions: realism vs. stereotypicality, monologic vs. dialogic approaches, allegorical vs. humanist (ironic) approaches, and misogyny vs. feminism. Assesses opposed critical views in light of the social, political, and literary conventions of Chaucer's day, using a "contextual approach" to conclude that Chaucer's works do not reflect modern views or modern literary goals. Instead, Chaucer's works remind us that his society confronted social and aesthetic issues differently than ours does and that current views—like those of Chaucer's day—are a product of history. Rigby emphasizes *GP*, *KnT*, *NPT*, *WBPT*, *Mel*, and *ParsT*.

125. Scoppettone, Stefanie Anne. "The 'Canterbury Tales': The Aesthetics of Humor." *DAI* 57 (1996): 2496A. Though Chaucer has been scorned for creating humor, the bulk of *CT* is serious, and seriousness and humor should no longer be perceived as mutually

antagonistic. Chaucer's humor develops as a structuring "glue" arising through literary methods that subvert genre and style.

126. Serrano Reyes, Jesús L. *Didactismo y moralismo en Geoffrey Chaucer y Don Juan Manuel: Un estudio comparativo textual.* Córdoba: Servicio de Publicaciones, Universidad de Córdoba, 1996. 385 pp. Argues that Don Juan Manuel's *El Conde Lucanor* and Chaucer's *CT* have many parallels and that *CT* may have been influenced by Manuel's work. Explores the presence of both authors in Spain and compares their didactic methods and their many *sententiae.* Explores in greatest detail the relations between Exemplum 50 of *El Conde Lucanor* and *FranT*, and Exemplum 20 and *CYT*.

127. ———, Antonio León Sendra, and Mercedes Robles Escobedo. *Séneca y Chaucer, I: Influencia Senequista en* The Canterbury Tales. Córdoba: Publicaciones de la Universidad de Córdoba, 1996. 108 pp. Demonstrates the influence of Seneca's moral philosophy on *CT* by assessing Chaucer's quotations of Seneca. Translates Latin and Middle English quotations into both Spanish and modern English.

128. Thompson, N. S. *Chaucer, Boccaccio, and the Debate of Love: A Comparative Study of* The Decameron *and* The Canterbury Tales. Oxford: Clarendon, 1996. x, 354 pp. *The Decameron* should be seen as a source of *CT* despite the lack of verbal parallels. Each work forms "an itinerary for the reader, if a highly indirect one, towards the good." *The Decameron* leads to Griselda, while *CT* leads to the Parson's penitential treatise, but both works depict labyrinthine, disrupted worlds and obliquely indicate that the only true way is the way of virtue. Thompson considers literary self-consciousness, genre, and the relations of art and morality. Includes an extended discussion of *ClT* and the version of the Griselda tale in Boccaccio and Petrarch.

129. Vila de la Cruz, Mª Purificación. "El mundo de Chaucer en *The Canterbury Tales.*" In Luis A. Lázaro Lafuente, José Simón, and Ricardo J. Sola Buil, eds. *Proceedings of the IIIrd International Conference of the Spanish Society for Medieval Language and Literature* (*SAC* 20 [1998], no. 96), pp. 267–74. The structure of *CT* reflects aspects of Chaucer's world, in particular the structure of gothic cathedrals.

130. Willocks, Stephanie. "Our Classrooms and Chaucer's *Canterbury Tales.*" *EJ* 85:7 (1996): 122–24. Advocates imitative role-playing as a way to teach Chaucer. Students select pictures from

newspapers and magazines, create characters from the pictures, and develop stories for the characters to tell. Stories are told during an imaginary journey, actually a partial tour of campus.

131. Wilson, Katharine. "'What Man Artow?': The Narrator as Writer and Pilgrim." In Laura C. Lambdin and Robert T. Lambdin, eds. *Chaucer's Pilgrims: An Historical Guide to the Pilgrims in* The Canterbury Tales (*SAC* 20 [1998], no. 118), pp. 369–84. Considers Chaucer's narrative persona in *CT* in two manifestations: as writer and as pilgrim. Writers were necessarily reciters in Chaucer's day, with opportunities in government, in religion, and as itinerant performers. Pilgrims encountered discomfort and danger, although Chaucer's pilgrims seemed prepared for both. Wilson provides details of social history for both "avocations" of Chaucer's pilgrim persona.

See also nos. 2, 6, 18, 24–26, 33, 36, 45, 52, 80, 84, 88, 209, 242, 243.

CT—The General Prologue

132. Bainbridge, Virginia. "From Medieval to Modern: Local Communities and National Government Intervention." *CrSurv* 8 (1996): 84–92. Traces the development of English "central government control over local institutions," discussing the emergence of local groups and mentioning the *GP* guildsmen.

133. Conlee, John W. "A Yeman Had He." In Laura C. Lambdin and Robert T. Lambdin, eds. *Chaucer's Pilgrims: An Historical Guide to the Pilgrims in* The Canterbury Tales (*SAC* 20 [1998], no. 118), pp. 27–37. With the Knight and the Squire, Chaucer's Yeoman composes the "basic English fighting unit—a unit sometimes referred to as a 'lance.'" Details of the Yeoman's *GP* sketch capitalize on the various connotations of "yeoman" and depict the Yeoman as a skilled warrior and forester.

134. Lambdin, Laura C., and Robert T. Lambdin. "An Haberdasher. . . ." In Laura C. Lambdin and Robert T. Lambdin, eds. *Chaucer's Pilgrims: An Historical Guide to the Pilgrims in* The Canterbury Tales (*SAC* 20 [1998], no. 118), pp. 145–53. Surveys the development of various fashions in late-medieval England in an attempt to explain the rising importance of haberdashers and why Chaucer may

have included one among his *GP* guildsmen. Also comments on the history and status of the haberdashers' guild.

135. Morgan, Gwendolyn. ". . . A Webbe. . . ." In Laura C. Lambdin and Robert T. Lambdin, eds. *Chaucer's Pilgrims: An Historical Guide to the Pilgrims in* The Canterbury Tales *(SAC* 20 [1998], no. 118), pp. 170–79. The inclusion of the weaver among the guildsmen of *GP* "is an anomaly" insofar as the typical weaver of the age was "an exploited, usually propertyless laborer." Morgan surveys the history of weavers and their role in the English wool trade.

136. Pigg, Daniel F. "With Hym Ther Was a Plowman, Was His Brother." In Laura C. Lambdin and Robert T. Lambdin, eds. *Chaucer's Pilgrims: An Historical Guide to the Pilgrims in* The Canterbury Tales *(SAC* 20 [1998], no. 118), pp. 263–70. The *GP* sketch of the plowman reflects the ambiguities of late-medieval attitudes toward labor. It depicts ideals of working-class spirituality and the social realities of agriculture.

137. Richardson, Thomas C. "Harry Bailly: Chaucer's Innkeeper." In Laura C. Lambdin and Robert T. Lambdin, eds. *Chaucer's Pilgrims: An Historical Guide to the Pilgrims in* The Canterbury Tales *(SAC* 20 [1998], no. 118), pp. 324–39. Characterizes the Host by examining the social history of his profession as an innkeeper and its possible associations with prostitution. In his interactions with other pilgrims, the Host reveals a "desire to be entertained with merry stories" and an obsession with male sexuality.

138. Standop, Ewald. "Wann es Frühling wird: Wann brachen Chaucers Pilger nach Canterbury auf?" *Anglistik* 7 (1996): 91–98. Chaucer's depiction of time in the opening of *GP* is modeled on either Guido delle Colonne's *Historia Destructionis Troiae* or Boccaccio's *Ameto*, although Chaucer mistakenly inverted the mention of April and the cliché about March.

139. Stephens, Rebecca. ". . . And a Tapycer." In Laura C. Lambdin and Robert T. Lambdin, eds. *Chaucer's Pilgrims: An Historical Guide to the Pilgrims in* The Canterbury Tales *(SAC* 20 [1998], no. 118), pp. 192–98. Briefly surveys the medieval history of tapestry- or rug-making as background to the portrait of the tapicer in *GP*.

140. Uhlman, Diana R. ". . . A Dyere. . . ." In Laura C. Lambdin and Robert T. Lambdin, eds. *Chaucer's Pilgrims: An Historical Guide to the Pilgrims in* The Canterbury Tales *(SAC* 20 [1998], no. 118), pp. 180–91. Surveys the process and business of dyeing in the Middle

Ages, commenting on the economic status of the dyers' guild and individual dyers in late-medieval England. Briefly assesses Chaucer's depiction of the dyer as one of the guildsmen in *GP*.

141. Wasserman, Julian N., and Marc Guidry. "... And a Carpenter. . . ." In Laura C. Lambdin and Robert T. Lambdin, eds. *Chaucer's Pilgrims: An Historical Guide to the Pilgrims in* The Canterbury Tales (*SAC* 20 [1998], no. 118), pp. 154–69. As background to the *GP* carpenter—one of the guildsmen—this essay surveys the prospects and activities of medieval carpenters: their organization into guilds and the guild hierarchy, their relations with masons and iron mongers, their techniques and tools of lumbering and building, regulation of their wages and workdays, etc.

142. Wimsatt, James I. "John Duns Scotus, Charles Sanders Peirce, and Chaucer's Portrayal of the Canterbury Pilgrims." *Speculum* 71 (1996): 633–45. Relates the *GP* portraits to the philosophy of realism expressed by Scotus and Peirce. Chaucer's realism is especially like Peirce's in its emphasis on behavior, historical coordinates, and the use of lively action or dynamic process to define the "real general" conveyed by the characters' activities.

See also nos. 5, 62, 118, 124, 131, 144, 150, 151, 153, 156, 161, 165, 180, 187, 189, 193, 197, 207, 208, 218, 219, 227, 231, 238, 239, 241, 245.

CT—The Knight and His Tale

143. Amtower, Laurel. "Mimetic Desire and the Misappropriation of the Ideal in *The Knight's Tale*." *Exemplaria* 8 (1996): 125–44. In *KnT*, Chaucer presents three conceptions of knighthood, each arising from individual desires that displace social responsibility. Arcite and Palamon's rivalry is based in mimetic desire for ontological being. Theseus arbitrates their rivalry by ritualizing the violence such desire engenders. He thus defines Arcite's death as a necessary sacrifice that restores communal order.

144. Calabrese, Michael A. "A Knyght Ther Was." In Laura C. Lambdin and Robert T. Lambdin, eds. *Chaucer's Pilgrims: An Historical Guide to the Pilgrims in* The Canterbury Tales (*SAC* 20 [1998], no. 118), pp. 1–13. Summarizes the medieval history of knighthood and its status in late-fourteenth-century England, exploring implications of de-

tails in the *GP* sketch of the Knight, especially those that relate to the "Crusading spirit" in its positive and negative connotations.

145. Jones, Terry. *Chaucer's Knight: The Portrait of a Medieval Mercenary*. London: Methuen, 1994. xxiv, 322 pp. First published in 1980 (see *SAC* 5 [1983], no. 137), Jones's study appeared in a revised edition in 1985. The 1994 version reprints the 1985 edition, with a new introduction. The argument is much the same as in the original— reading the Knight as a professional mercenary and as Chaucer's means to critique contemporary military politics. The introduction responds to Maurice Keen's critique (see *SAC* 7 [1985], no. 139) and records Jones's thoughts while writing the book and revising it.

146. Luttrell, Anthony. "Chaucer's Knight and the Mediterranean." *Library of Mediterranean History* 1 (1994): 127–60. The discrepancies in the Knight's military curriculum reflect Chaucer's attempt to represent a desire for peace at home and for the transfer of destructive military activity to distant frontiers in Prussia and the Mediterranean. Luttrell explores the history of English knights (their various missions, their modes of fighting, and their motivation) to explain ambiguities of the Knight and Chaucer's attitude toward the Mediterranean.

147. Schulz, Andrea K. "Theriomorphic Shape-Shifting: An Experimental Reading of Identity and Metamorphosis in Selected British Medieval Texts." *DAI* 56 (1996): 4765A. The universal theme of metamorphosis, compelled or voluntary, relates to both the natural mutability of human life and the boundaries and hierarchies set by society, as shown in four texts ranging from *KnT* (Actaeon) through Gower's Ovidian passages, Welsh myth, and Shakespeare's *A Midsummer Night's Dream*.

See also nos. 5, 32, 34, 43, 58, 79, 87, 94, 111, 115, 123, 124, 149.

CT—The Miller and His Tale

148. Beidler, Peter G., Jennifer McNamara Bailey, Christine G. Berg, Sister Elaine Marie Glanz, Anne M. Dickson, Tracey A. Cummings, and Elizabeth M. Biebel. "Dramatic Intertextuality in the *Miller's Tale*: Chaucer's Use of Characters from Medieval Drama as Foils for John, Alisoun, Nicholas and Absolon." *Chaucer Yearbook* 3 (1996): 1–20. Six

brief essays from a graduate seminar explore how select medieval plays of the Flood, Nativity, Annunciation, and Slaughter of the Innocents and Jean Bodel's *Le jeu de Saint Nicolas* illuminate Chaucer's characters in *MilT*.

149. Briggs, Frederick M., and Laura L. Howes. "Theophany in the *Miller's Tale*." *MÆ* 65 (1996): 269–79. *MilT* develops the theme of "pryvetee," which in Chaucer refers to both human genitalia and divine secrets. Echoes of Exodus and its tradition of commentary reinforce the theme and enable Chaucer to suggest an orientation of the *Tale* as a theological response to *KnT*.

150. Lambdin, Laura C., and Robert T. Lambdin. "The Millere Was a Stout Carl for the Nones." In Laura C. Lambdin and Robert T. Lambdin, eds. *Chaucer's Pilgrims: An Historical Guide to the Pilgrims in* The Canterbury Tales (*SAC* 20 [1998], no. 118), pp. 271–80. Consistent with contemporary social and economic conditions, the Miller of *GP* aspires to the gentry although he "is still rooted in the peasantry." Bridging the courtly *KnT* and the low-class *RvT*, Chaucer's *MilT*—like the Miller's profession—reflects "changes that were occurring in England."

See also nos. 5, 34, 93, 114, 115.

CT—The Reeve and His Tale

151. Everest, Carol A. "Sex and Old Age in Chaucer's *Reeve's Prologue*." *ChauR* 31 (1996): 99–114. Chaucer is versed in medieval medical theories, which underlie the physical and emotional descriptions of the Reeve in both *GP* and *RvP*.

152. Haug, Walter. "Die Lust am Widersinn: Chaos und Komik in der mittelalterlichen Kurzerzählung." In Dorothee Lindemann, Berndt Volkmann, and Klaus-Peter Wegera, eds. *"Bickelwort" und "wildiu mære": Festschrift für Eberhard Nellmann zum 65. Geburtstag*. Göppingen: Kümmerle, 1995, pp. 354–65. Compares *RvT* with its analogue in Boccaccio's *Decameron* and with the Middle High German *Studentenabenteuer*, exploring their concerns with disorder and its effects.

153. McDonald, Richard B. "The Reve Was a Sclendre Colerik Man." In Laura C. Lambdin and Robert T. Lambdin, eds. *Chaucer's Pilgrims: An Historical Guide to the Pilgrims in* The Canterbury Tales (*SAC* 20 [1998], no. 118), pp. 288–99. Describes what it meant to be a reeve in terms of social status, day-to-day life, and relations with

people of other professions, especially clerks. The viciousness of the Reeve of *GP* and *RvT* is consistent with what medieval people expected of reeves.

154. Watson, Jessica Lewis. *Bastardy as a Gifted Status in Chaucer and Malory.* Studies in Mediaeval Literature, no. 14. Lewiston, N. Y.; Queenston, Ontario; and Lampeter, Wales: Edwin Mellen, 1996. x, 90 pp. In Chaucer's *RvT* and Malory's *Morte D'Arthur*, illegitimacy is not a negative notion. The Reeve is unorthodox in his negative view of the illegitimacy of Symkyn's wife and of the sexual liberation of Symkyn's daughter. Chaucer, however, discloses a less critical view, enabling his readers to consider bastardy and sexual play in a positive light.

See also nos. 5, 66, 68.

CT—The Cook and His Tale

155. Boyd, David Lorenzo. "Social Texts: Bodley 686 and the Politics of the Cook's Tale." *HLQ* 58 (1996): 81–97. The unique ending of *CkT* in MS Bodley 686 (ca. 1420–1440) reaffirms the preservation of traditional social systems and the obedience that they entail in the face of rising violence and the fear of political and social instability. Also printed in no. 97.

156. Hieatt, Constance B. "A Cook They Had With Hem for the Nones." In Laura C. Lambdin and Robert T. Lambdin, eds. *Chaucer's Pilgrims: An Historical Guide to the Pilgrims in* The Canterbury Tales (*SAC* 20 [1998], no. 118), pp. 199–209. Comments on each of the three appearances of the Cook in *CT*—the *GP* sketch, *CkP*, and *ManP*—providing historical and cultural background for Chaucer's "proprietor of a cookshop," including several recipes.

157. Pinti, Daniel J. "Governing the *Cook's Tale* in Bodley 686." *ChauR* 30 (1996): 379–88. By adding forty-five lines in "quasi-Langlandian" alliterative personification allegory to *CkT*, the Bodley scribe creates a second distinctive narrative voice that competes with Chaucer's own. The deliberate moral ending "governs" both Perkyn and Chaucer, who left "some badly-spun text threatening to unravel."

158. Woods, William F. "Society and Nature in the *Cook's Tale.*" *PLL* 32 (1996): 189–205. Explores ways *CkPT* respond to themes raised earlier in fragment I and focuses on how *CkT* provides a "powerfully

suggestive" urban setting in which the regulated life of Perkyn's master is contrasted by the mercurial, primal, savage world of thievery and prostitution.

See also no. 5.

CT—The Man of Law and His Tale

159. Dor, Juliette. "L'énigme du *Prologue du Conte de l'Homme de Loi*: Chaucer et l'auto-plagiat." In Roger Ellis and René Tixier, eds. *The Medieval Translator/Traduire au Moyen Age*, 5 (*SAC* 20 [1998], no. 74), pp. 376–89. Examines the differences between Chaucer's poverty prologue to *MLT* and its source, Innocent III's *De miseria condicionis humane*, attributing these differences to the influence of Renaud de Louens's *Livre de Mellibee et Prudence*, which Chaucer translated closely as his *Mel*. *MLP* combines elements of Innocent's treatise and Chaucer's own *Mel*.

160. Forste-Grupp, Sheryl L. "Signifying Acts: Writing in the Middle English Romances." *DAI* 57 (1996): 674A–75A. Analysis of legal documents and letters (especially treacherous or forged) in Middle English romances reveals that these fictions (including *MLT*) reflect popular attitudes of the 1300s and 1400s. Though speech had been preferred earlier, written documents came to be accepted as society became literate.

161. Hornsby, Joseph. "A Sergeant of the Lawe, War and Wyse." In Laura C. Lambdin and Robert T. Lambdin, eds. *Chaucer's Pilgrims: An Historical Guide to the Pilgrims in* The Canterbury Tales (*SAC* 20 [1998], no. 118), pp. 116–34. Surveys the development of the legal profession in medieval England as background to understanding how the *GP* sketch of the Man of Law is a "thumbnail sketch of a common lawyer," focusing on his status as a "sergeant." *MLT* capitalizes on the myth that English common law had ancient roots, perhaps even grounded in divine law.

162. Schibanoff, Susan. "Worlds Apart: Orientalism, Antifeminism, and Heresy in Chaucer's *Man of Law's Tale*." *Exemplaria* 8 (1996): 59–96. The Man of Law uses the discourses of orientalism and antifeminism to suggest the proximity of Islam to Christianity and of women to men, as well as the necessity of reinscribing Muslims and women as clearly delimited Others. *MLT* attempts to forge a sense of fraternity among the quarrelsome male pilgrims.

163. Winstead, Karen A. "Saints, Wives, and Other 'Hooly Thynges': Pious Laywomen in Middle English Romance." *Chaucer Yearbook* 2 (1995): 137–54. Addresses medieval writers' uses of saints' lives in Middle English romances of persecuted laywomen. *Le Bone Florence of Rome*, *The King of Tars*, *Emare*, and *MLT* exemplify the influence of, and variations from, early pious romances. The conclusions, however, endorse a new kind of legend: one that affirms the value of family, marriage, and social order and praises the saint who sacrifices to protect her family and obey her husband. The vindication of patriarchal authority found in these romances resulted from insecurities about gender issues in the late Middle Ages.

See also nos. 115, 120, 122.

CT—The Wife of Bath and Her Tale

164. Aguirre, Manuel. "A Link Between the *Wife of Bath's Tale* and Its (Disputed) Irish Source." In Luis A. Lázaro Lafuente, José Simón, and Ricardo J. Sola Buil, eds. *Proceedings of the IIIrd International Conference of the Spanish Society for Medieval Language and Literature* (*SAC* 20 [1998], no. 96), pp. 9–14. Reexamines the meaning of "sovereignty," proposes that *The Wedding of Sir Gawen and Dame Ragnell* is a link between *WBT* and its ultimate Irish source, and reformulates the question of sources.

165. Beidler, Peter G., ed. *Geoffrey Chaucer: The Wife of Bath: Complete, Authoritative Text with Biographical and Historical Contexts, Critical History, and Essays from Five Contemporary Critical Perspectives.* Case Studies in Contemporary Criticism. Boston and New York: Bedford–St. Martin's, 1996. xiii, 306 pp. Based on the Hengwrt manuscript, this edition of *WBPT* and the Wife's sketch from *GP* is designed for classroom use. It includes notes and glossary, a biographical sketch of Chaucer, a guide to pronunciation and verse, and a summary of historical contexts. Beidler surveys the history of responses to the Wife of Bath, and accompanying essays and bibliographies introduce five critical approaches—new historicist, Marxist, psychoanalytic, deconstructionist, and feminist—and apply them to the Wife. The introductions to the critical approaches are by Ross C. Murfin; for the applications, see 168, 169, 171, 173, and 177.

166.   Brown, Carole Koepke. "Episodic Patterns and the Perpetrator: The Structure and Meaning of Chaucer's *Wife of Bath's Tale.*" *ChauR* 31 (1996): 18–35. Episodes in the first part of *WBT* parallel events in the second. This "step parallelism structure" reveals a "pattern of attenuation" that emphasizes the development of the knight, who becomes less impulsive and more reflective through the course of the *Tale.*

167.   Dauby, Hélène. "Chaucer et Gower: Esquisse comparative de leurs attitudes morales et politiques." In Danielle Buschinger and Wolfgang Spiewok, eds. *Économie, politique, et culture au Moyen Age: Acte du Colloque, Paris, 19 et 20 mai 1990.* WODAN ser., no. 5. [Amiens]: Université de Picardie, 1991, pp. 55–63. Compares Chaucer's *WBT* and Gower's *Tale of Florent* as indices to the authors' social and moral outlooks. Whereas Gower consistently emphasizes maintaining a hierarchical status quo, Chaucer's concern for the individual and his recurrent ambiguities indicate a more complex philosophy.

168.   Finke, Laurie. "'All Is for to Selle': Breeding Capital in the Wife of Bath's Prologue and Tale." In Peter G. Beidler, ed. *Geoffrey Chaucer*: The Wife of Bath (*SAC* 20 [1988], no. 165), pp. 171–88. A Marxist reading of *WBPT* that regards the "link between sexuality and monetary gain" as the "key to the sexual economy of the Wife's performance." *WBP* reflects the violence potential in "primitive accumulation," an early stage of capitalism defined by Karl Marx. Through the pillow lecture on gentility in *WBT*, the violence is transformed into a "political idyll" of socioeconomic leveling and marital bliss.

169.   Fradenburg, Louise O. "'Fulfild of Fairye': The Social Meaning of Fantasy in the Wife of Bath's Prologue and Tale." In Peter G. Beidler, ed. *Geoffrey Chaucer*: The Wife of Bath (*SAC* 20 [1998], no. 165), pp. 205–20. Psychoanalytic analysis of *WBP* reveals the development of the narrator's identity through the history of her losses and pleasure, suggesting the failure of society to structure her desires. Through fantasy, *WBT* idealizes a version of the past and suggests the potential for achieving a new ideal.

170.   Green, Robert F. "The *Canterbury Tales*, D117: *Wrighte* or *Wight?*" *N&Q* 241 (1996): 259–61. Challenges E. Talbot Donaldson's emendation of the Hengwrt reading *wight* (*WBP* 117); *wight* corresponds to good Middle English syntax and makes perfect sense.

171.   Hansen, Elaine Tuttle. "'Of His Love Daungerous to Me': Liberation, Subversion, and Domestic Violence in the Wife of Bath's Prologue and Tale." In Peter G. Beidler, ed. *Geoffrey Chaucer*: The Wife

of Bath (*SAC* 20 [1998], no. 165), pp. 273–89. The Wife of Bath's reference to being beaten by Jankyn and the rape in *WBT* indicate the violent nature of sex, yet the text glosses over this violence, making it seem normal. Although Chaucer's position as poet may have inclined him to identify with women, he did not escape male perspective or achieve a truly feminist perspective.

172. Kennedy, Beverly. "Cambridge MS. Dd.4.24: A Misogynous Scribal Revision of the *Wife of Bath's Prologue?*" *ChauR* 30 (1996): 343–58. Cambridge MS Dd. 4.24 contains a unique version of *WBP*: it adds five antifeminist passages and renumbers the Wife's husbands, making that section more organized and coherent. It is not possible to determine whether these changes were the work of Chaucer or that of later scribes.

173. Leicester, H. Marshall, Jr. "'My Bed Was Ful of Verray Blood': Subject, Dream, and Rape in the Wife of Bath's Prologue and Tale." In Peter G. Beidler, ed. *Geoffrey Chaucer*: The Wife of Bath (*SAC* 20 [1998], no. 165), pp. 234–54. Treats the Wife of Bath as a subject in the process of self-definition who simultaneously seeks to deconstruct the society that constitutes that process. Leicester focuses on the dream of blood in *WBP* (577–82) to show the difficulty of determining any single meaning. He deconstructs "Paradventure" in *WBT* (893) to explore the indeterminable relations between rape and lawful marriage and, more generally, the indeterminacy of any text.

174. McKinley, Kathryn L. "The Silenced Knight: Questions on Power and Reciprocity in the *Wife of Bath's Tale*." *ChauR* 30 (1996): 359–78. The old hag's curtain lecture, which changes the knight from selfish to selfless, is made possible through the romance genre. The silence of the knight signifies "radical freedom," not the end of an "authentic personality."

175. Minnis, Alastair. "Anthropologizing Alisoun: The Case of Chaucer's Wife of Bath." *REALB* 12 (1996): 203–21. Assesses differing opinions of female preaching and teaching in medieval orthodoxy and in the Lollard movement, arguing that Chaucer's depiction of the Wife of Bath and the loathly lady in *WBT* confronts these opinions. Just as *PardT* confronts whether an immoral man can tell a moral tale, *WBPT* explores the validity of female preaching.

176. Morrison, Susan Signe. "Don't Ask; Don't Tell: The Wife of Bath and Vernacular Translations." *Exemplaria* 8 (1996): 97–123. *WBPT* address the relationship between vernacular texts and female audiences. Vernacular translations of authoritative texts allow women to

enter the discourse of power, creating a new discourse that validates not only the existence of a different truth for women but also Chaucer's authority as a vernacular author.

177. Patterson, Lee. "'Experience Woot Well It Is Noght So': Marriage and the Pursuit of Happiness in the Wife of Bath's Prologue and Tale." In Peter G. Beidler, ed. *Geoffrey Chaucer: The Wife of Bath* (*SAC* 20 [1998], no. 165), pp. 133–54. A new-historicist reading that focuses on the conditions of marriage depicted in *WBPT* to show how the Wife uses the late-medieval marital system for her own private, emotional advantage. She capitalizes on the social and economic opportunities of wifedom and widowhood rather than seeking to challenge them.

178. Pelen, Marc M. "Chaucer's Wife of Midas Reconsidered: Oppositions and Poetic Judgment in the *Wife of Bath's Tale.*" *Florilegium* 13 (1994): 141–60. The interpolated story of Midas's wife evokes Ovidian concern with poetic judgment and suggests Chaucer's perspective on the differing attitudes of the hag and the knight toward love and marriage. Complex Ovidian echoes imply the failure of Midas's wife to understand the significance of his preference for Pan's music over Apollo's, and, by extension, the Wife's failure to acknowledge a more cosmic view of love and poetry than the purely experiential one she espouses.

179. Shepherd, Stephen H. A. "No Poet Has His Travesty Alone: 'The Weddynge of Sir Gawen and Dame Ragnell.'" In Jennifer Fellows, Rosalind Field, Gillian Rogers, and Judith Weiss, eds. *Romance Reading on the Book: Essays on Medieval Literature Presented to Maldwyn Mills* (*SAC* 20 [1998], no. 115), pp. 112–28. "The Weddynge" recalls *WBP* and *WBT* "in a spirit of creative adaptation and emulation," as part of a conscious travesty of this and other sources.

180. Slover, Judith. "A Good Wive Was Ther of Biside Bath." In Laura C. Lambdin and Robert T. Lambdin, eds. *Chaucer's Pilgrims: An Historical Guide to the Pilgrims in* The Canterbury Tales (*SAC* 20 [1998], no. 118), pp. 243–55. Surveys medieval attitudes of and about women as background to the *GP* sketch of the Wife of Bath, *WBP*, and *WBT*. Reads the Wife as a conscious manipulator of antifeminist texts, her husbands, and the convention of romance—all aspects of her protoliberation.

181. Stapley, Ian Bernard. "Marriage as Exchange, from Chaucer to Defoe." *DAI* 57 (1996): 1154A. Aware that their husbands (as chosen by their families or communities) will determine the nature of their lives, women have sought to choose their own husbands, a daring

assumption of sovereignty in a patriarchal society. The Wife of Bath, Shakespeare's *Shrew*, and *Moll Flanders* are among the many women characters treated.

182. Wynne-Davies, Marion. "'The Elf-queen, with Hir Joly Compaignye': Chaucer's *Wife of Bath's Tale*." In Marion Wynne-Davies. *Women and Arthurian Literature: Seizing the Sword*. New York: St. Martin's, 1996, pp. 14–35. While the Wife of Bath's character is protofeminist, the rape of the maiden and the submission of the woman at the end of *WBT* point to a dominant patriarchal attitude. By embedding Arthurian myth into the *Tale* and presenting the Wife as a fictional character, Chaucer scrutinizes gender relations without threatening the patriarchal system.

See also nos. 11, 37, 82, 86, 87, 90, 103, 111, 124, 206.

CT—The Friar and His Tale

183. Hagen, Karl T. "A Frere Ther Was, a Wantowne and a Meryee." In Laura C. Lambdin and Robert T. Lambdin, eds. *Chaucer's Pilgrims: An Historical Guide to the Pilgrims in* The Canterbury Tales (*SAC* 20 [1998], no. 118), pp. 80–92. Summarizes the history and organization of the four fraternal orders, focusing on the Franciscans and Dominicans. Chaucer's Friar and the friar of *SumT* are fictional renderings of the antifraternal outlooks of William of St. Amour and Richard Fitz-Ralph.

184. Kendrick, Laura. "Friar Hubert's Lisp." *BAM* 50 (1996): 37–57. Friar Hubert practices false-seeming by faking a Francophone lisp, replacing dentals with sibilants, in order to increase his social prestige and his seductiveness. Kendrick also explores why Parisian French was considered "sweet."

See also nos. 120, 187.

CT—The Summoner and His Tale

185. Fletcher, Alan J. "The Summoner and the Abominable Anatomy of Antichrist." *SAC* 18 (1996): 91–117. Attests two early-fifteenth-century analogues of *SumP* and describes several echoes of Wycliffite antifraternal sentiment in *SumT*: concern with letters of

fraternity and trentals (i.e., commissioned masses for the dead), venal preaching, fraternal claims to be the salt of the earth, and challenges to the Church by peasant and aristocratic classes combined. Chaucer articulates Lollard views in the Summoner's materials, but he does not affirm them.

186. Hasenfratz, Robert. "The Science of Flatulence: Possible Sources for the *Summoner's Tale*." *ChauR* 30 (1996): 241–61. The source for *SumT* 2253–79 can be found in the medieval notion of the "wheel of the twelve winds," where each wind (depicted in manuscript art as a "spoke") ends in the mouth of a human face. Such a motif was associated not only with atmospheric conditions in scientific texts but also with the scholastic-scientific traditions parodied by Chaucer's *Tale*.

187. Keller, James. "A Sumonour Was Ther with Us in That Place." In Laura C. Lambdin and Robert T. Lambdin, eds. *Chaucer's Pilgrims: An Historical Guide to the Pilgrims in* The Canterbury Tales (*SAC* 20 [1998], no. 118), pp. 300–313. Examines the structure of the medieval ecclesiastical court system and the role of the summoner, or apparitor, within that system. The Summoner and the summoner of *FrT*, as portraits of "two damned souls," reflect Chaucer's knowledge of the "duties and corruptions of the apparitor."

See also nos. 31, 66, 94, 183.

CT—The Clerk and His Tale

188. Bliss, Lee. "The Renaissance Griselda: A Woman for All Seasons." *Viator* 23 (1992): 301–43. Focuses on Elizabethan versions of the Griselda story but includes discussion of how the context of *CT* dislocates both allegorical and literal readings of *ClT*. Efforts to resolve this dislocation prompt Elizabethan and later versions.

189. Dillon, Bert. "A Clerk Ther Was of Oxenford Also." In Laura C. Lambdin and Robert T. Lambdin, eds. *Chaucer's Pilgrims: An Historical Guide to the Pilgrims in* The Canterbury Tales (*SAC* 20 [1998], no. 118), pp. 108–15. Reads the Clerk's sketch in *GP* as an idealized depiction of academic life in fourteenth-century Oxford, summarizing typical activities and outlooks.

190. Edwards, Robert R. "'The Sclaundre of Walter': The *Clerk's Tale* and the Problem of Hermeneutics." In Piero Boitani and Anna Torti, eds. *Mediaevalitas: Reading the Middle Ages* (*SAC* 20 [1998], no. 64),

pp. 15–41. *ClT* maintains a tension between the interpretive multiplicity of Boccaccio's version of the tale and the hermeneutic closure of Petrarch's translation. The integration of Griselda and her heirs into hereditary hierarchy may help explain the fifteenth-century popularity of *ClT*.

191. Weber, Diane Looms. "A Look at Socialized Violence in Chaucer's 'Clerk's Tale.'" *DAI* 56 (1996): 3599A. Since the fourteenth century can be seen as a distant mirror of postmodern culture, "Walter's abuse and Griselda's passive resignation" merit study in the light of twentieth-century psychological insights.

See also nos. 9, 13, 43, 82, 86, 94, 122, 128.

CT—The Merchant and His Tale

192. Castillo, Francisco J. "La divulgación de la obra de Chaucer en España: Algunas observaciones sobre una versión indirecta de *The Merchant's Tale*." In Luis A. Lázaro Lafuente, José Simón, and Ricardo J. Sola Buil, eds. *Proceedings of the IIIrd International Conference of the Spanish Society for Medieval Language and Literature* (*SAC* 20 [1998], no. 96), pp. 75–88. A previously unknown Spanish translation of *MerT* derives not from Chaucer's original but from the English translation by Alexander Pope. Castillo provides biography of Canary Islander Graciliano Alfonso Naranjo, who may have been the author of the Spanish version.

193. Reale, Nancy M. "A Marchant Was Ther with a Forked Berd." In Laura C. Lambdin and Robert T. Lambdin, eds. *Chaucer's Pilgrims: An Historical Guide to the Pilgrims in* The Canterbury Tales (*SAC* 20 [1998], no. 118), pp. 93–107. Reads the Merchant's sketch in *GP* as a depiction of a duplicitous man and assesses January in *MerT* as a reflection of the Merchant's commercial outlook, which, in turn, reflects Chaucer's experience with the mercantile world of London.

194. Rudat, Wolfgang E. H. "Chaucer's Merchant and his Shrewish Wife: The Justinus Crux and Augustinian Theology." *Cithara* 35:1 (1995): 24–38. A "palimpsestic" reading of *MerT* reveals the irony with which the Merchant treats January and with which Chaucer treats the Merchant, enriching and complicating the *Tale*'s identification between the Merchant and January.

See also no. 79.

CT—The Squire and His Tale

195. DiMarco, Vincent. "The Dialogue of Science and Magic in Chaucer's *Squire's Tale.*" In Thomas Kühn and Ursula Schaefer, eds. *Dialogische Strukturen/Dialogic Structures: Festschrift für Willi Erzgräber zum 70. Geburtstag.* Tübingen: Gunter Narr, 1996, pp. 50–68. The apparent "magic" of *SqT* is explicable via medieval understanding of the rational explanation of marvels. Surveying medieval attitudes toward science and technology, DiMarco argues that the gifts of *SqT* are presented as scientific objects that operate in accord with principles such as the "multiplication of species," the assumption that objects influence one another by emitting corporeal likenesses of themselves.

196. ———. "The Historical Basis of Chaucer's *Squire's Tale.*" *Edebiyât,* n.s., 1:2 (1989): 1–22. The setting and select characters of *SqT* have historical basis in the reigns of Özbeg Khan of the Golden Horde at Sarai (ruled 1313–41) and Mamluk sultan el-Melik en-Nasir at Cairo (ruled variously 1291–1340). Their failed alliance influenced the politics of the fourteenth-century Crusades, and Mongol custom may underlie several details of *SqT*.

197. Huey, Peggy. "A Yong Squier." In Laura C. Lambdin and Robert T. Lambdin, eds. *Chaucer's Pilgrims: An Historical Guide to the Pilgrims in* The Canterbury Tales (*SAC* 20 [1998], no. 118), pp. 14–26. Explores the lexical and cultural meaning of "squire" as background to the *GP* sketch of the Squire. Chaucer's portrait is an idealized one, counterpointed by the lack of rhetorical skill in *SqT*.

See also no. 123.

CT—The Franklin and His Tale

198. Edwards, Robert R. "Source, Context, and Cultural Translation in the *Franklin's Tale.*" *MP* 94 (1996): 141–62. Although the influence of Boccaccio's *Filocolo* on *TC* is uncertain, examination of various manuscripts of *Filocolo* suggests that Chaucer uses the love questions of *Filocolo* 4 as a source of *FranT*. Moreover, translating the culture of book 4 into *FranT* enables Chaucer to interrogate the world of *FranT*.

199. Flake, Timothy H. "Love, *Trouthe*, and the Happy Ending of the *Franklin's Tale.*" *ES* 77 (1996): 209–26. Challenges the discussion of Angela M. Lucas and Peter J. Lucas (*SAC* 15 [1993], no. 215), arguing

407

that the marriage of Dorigen and Arveragus "is a poetic expression of freedom and love brought to life by the power of *trouthe*," a force so much greater than illusion that it converts the squire and the magician to *gentilesse*. The source of the happy ending is in the way these virtues are presented by the Franklin.

200. Friedman, John B. "Dorigen's 'Grisly Rokkes Blake' Again." *ChauR* 31 (1996): 133–44. Dorigen's home is in "lower" Brittany around Carnac and the Locmariaquer peninsula, an area replete with menhirs and dolmens. These megalithic pagan structures are the "grisly rokkes blake," and Dorigen's fear of them is both physical and spiritual.

201. Kearney, John. "Chaucer's 'Franklin's Tale': 'Trouthe,' 'Routhe,' and the 'Rokkes Blakke.'" *South African Journal of Medieval and Renaissance Studies* 4 (1994): 95–107. In *FranT*, the seriatim pity of the characters makes it possible for others to move through the worldly truth that it is necessary to suffer in time, toward the greater truth of unchanging stability. The rocks represent the need for worldly suffering.

202. Larson, Leah Jean. "Love, Troth, and Magnanimity: The 'Weltanschauung' of the Breton Lay for Marie de France to Chaucer." *DAI* 57 (1996): 1610A. The world view of the Breton lay, as conceived by Marie de France, changed little before 1400. In *FranT*, Chaucer expands the genre with increased emphasis on passionate and "egalitarian" love in marriage, troth, and magnanimity, as solution to the marriage debate.

203. McEntire, Sandra J. "Illusions and Interpretations in the *Franklin's Tale*." *ChauR* 31 (1996): 145–63. Aurelius usurps and reinterprets Dorigen's speech. Through such devices, Chaucer subtly makes listeners and readers aware that what may appear to be real, whether concrete or ideological, may be illusion. The Franklin's intent is to assert his social equality with other travelers rather than to address issues of chastity, honor, and virtue.

204. Parry, Joseph D. "Dorigen, Narration, and Coming Home in the *Franklin's Tale*." *ChauR* 30 (1996): 262–93. The word "hoom," appearing numerous times in *FranT*, changes according to the character with whom it is associated. This is especially true of Dorigen, whose "hoom" reflects her most moral self.

205. Pulham, Carol A. "Promises, Promises: Dorigen's Dilemma Revisited." *ChauR* 31 (1996): 76–86. Argues that oral promises were binding in the largely oral, late-medieval culture and considers the

contemporary "seriousness" of both Dorigen's marriage vow to Arveragus in *FranT* and her contradictory promise to Aurelius.

206.   Salisbury, Eve. "The Middle English Breton Lays: Four Texts and Their Contexts." *DAI* 56 (1996): 3950A. Despite the apparent variability of the genre in English, six Breton lays demonstrate distinctive characteristics, developed in part by the turbulent fourteenth- and fifteenth-century England that produced them. Though they deal with difficult issues of community life, these English lays emphasize "family values" and conclude happily. Salisbury assesses *FranT*, *WBT*, and four anonymous lays.

207.   Sembler, Elizabeth Mauer. "A Frankeleyn Was in His Compaignye." In Laura C. Lambdin and Robert T. Lambdin, eds. *Chaucer's Pilgrims: An Historical Guide to the Pilgrims in* The Canterbury Tales (*SAC* 20 [1998], no. 118), pp. 135–44. The ambiguous social and legal status of franklins in fourteenth-century England makes it difficult to know whether Chaucer's Franklin was a member of the gentry or an aspirant to the gentle class. Sembler surveys critical opinions about the Franklin's gentility.

See also nos. 93, 115, 126.

CT—The Physician and His Tale

208.   Eleazar, Edwin. "With Us Ther Was a Doctour of Phisik." In Laura C. Lambdin and Robert T. Lambdin, eds. *Chaucer's Pilgrims: An Historical Guide to the Pilgrims in* The Canterbury Tales (*SAC* 20 [1998], no. 118), pp. 220–42. Describes medieval medical education and explains the theory and practice of medieval physicians and surgeons as background to the *GP* sketch of the Physician. Some details of the sketch accord well with typical medieval medical activities, while others suggest possibilities of malpractice or unethical behavior. Chaucer's portrait is equivocal.

209.   Hirsh, John C. "Chaucer's Roman Tales." *ChauR* 31 (1996) 45–57. Considers Chaucer's two tales set in ancient Rome—*PhyT* and *SNT*—maintaining that each is "particularly concerned with political corruption"; "the depravity of those who wield the state's power has quite undermined it." Hirsh notes a possible "progression" in certain late tales, which "give evidence of a growing authorial disinclination to

privilege the ideal and ordered, but rather to engage the incongruous, the eccentric, and the palpably false or unjust."

210. Sprunger, David A. "Parodic Animal Physicians from the Margins of Medieval Manuscripts." In Nona C. Flores, ed. *Animals in the Middle Ages: A Book of Essays* (*SAC* 20 [1998], no. 78), pp. 67–81. Discusses manuscript drolleries that represent physicians, commenting on the conventional clothing of Chaucer's Physician and the flask or jordan the Physician holds in the Ellesmere illumination.

See also nos. 115, 120, 122.

CT—The Pardoner and His Tale

211. Aspinall, Dana E. "'I Wol Thee Telle Al Plat': Poetic Influence and Chaucer's Pardoner." *UMSE* 11–12 (1993–95): 230–42. A psychoanalytic reading of the Pardoner that views him as one who struggles to escape the influence of his father-figure (God) and simultaneously to escape literary models posed in the Bible. Freud and Harold Bloom enable us to see the struggle between id and ego in the Pardoner and a parallel struggle in the Pardoner's efforts both to supersede and to reject his literary precursors.

212. Lázaro Lafuente, Luis A. "Irony and Humour in *The Pardoner's Tale.*" In Luis A. Lázaro Lafuente, José Simón, and Ricardo J. Sola Buil, eds. *Proceedings of the IIIrd International Conference of the Spanish Society for Medieval Language and Literature* (*SAC* 20 [1998], no. 96), pp. 207–15. Surveys the kinds of irony and humor in *PardPT* for the ways they characterize the Pardoner.

213. Smith, Elton E. "With Hym Ther Rood a Gentil Pardoner." In Laura C. Lambdin and Robert T. Lambdin, eds. *Chaucer's Pilgrims: An Historical Guide to the Pilgrims in* The Canterbury Tales (*SAC* 20 [1998], no. 118), pp. 314–23. Briefly describes the history of confession and the granting of indulgences in church tradition. Also explicates details of *PardPT*.

214. Snell, William. "Chaucer's *Pardoner's Tale* and Pestilence in Late-Medieval Literature." *SMELL* 10 (1995): 1–16. Assesses *PardT* in light of contemporary literature about pestilence, arguing that Chaucer both distances the *Tale* from his audience and critiques Flemings.

215. Wenzel, Siegfried. "Another Analogue to *The Pardoner's Tale.*" *N&Q* 241 (1996): 134–36. An exemplum in Oxford Bodleian Library

MS Bodley 859, from *Distincciones*, no. 118—attributed to John Bromyard (ca. 1350)—is the earliest analogue to *PardT*.

See also nos. 31, 120, 175, 230.

CT—The Shipman and His Tale

216. Beidler, Peter G. "The Price of Sex in Chaucer's *Shipman's Tale*." *ChauR* 31 (1996): 5–17. It is impossible to determine an exact modern value of the 100 francs in *ShT*, but internal, economic, and comparative literary evidence indicates that $5,000 is "a specific lower limit to the value of that amount in 1990s U.S. dollars." Although Chaucer makes the amount more conservative than in Boccaccio's analogous tale, the merchant is generous to his wife, who has an inflated self-valuation.

217. Ganim, John M. "Double Entry in Chaucer's *Shipman's Tale*: Chaucer and Bookkeeping Before Pacioli." *ChauR* 30 (1996): 294–305. Double-entry bookkeeping, which Chaucer could have learned in Italy, contains "a system of rhetoric as well as a technique." The plot of *ShT* can be seen as a series of parallel accounts, with the ending as the "closing of the books" on the final transaction.

218. King, Sigrid. "A Shipman Ther Was, Wonynge Fer by Weste." In Laura C. Lambdin and Robert T. Lambdin, eds. *Chaucer's Pilgrims: An Historical Guide to the Pilgrims in* The Canterbury Tales (*SAC* 20 [1998], no. 118), pp. 210–19. The *GP* description of the Shipman depicts him as a typical privateer, one modeled, perhaps, on the historical John Hawley and Piers Risselden. *ShT* reflects a cynical attitude, aimed especially at the merchant of the *Tale*.

See also nos. 61, 66, 123, 227.

CT—The Prioress and Her Tale

219. Hourigan, Maureen. "Ther Was Also a Nonne, a Prioresse." In Laura C. Lambdin and Robert T. Lambdin, eds. *Chaucer's Pilgrims: An Historical Guide to the Pilgrims in* The Canterbury Tales (*SAC* 20 [1998], no. 118), pp. 38–46. Briefly surveys the history of medieval nunneries, the typical responsibilities of a prioress, and critical attitudes toward the Prioress and *PrT*.

220. Kellogg, A. L. "The Possible Unity of Chaucer's Prioress." *Chaucer Yearbook* 3 (1996): 55–71. Examines details of the *GP* sketch of the Prioress and the sensibility of *PrT* for the ways they clash, exploring their details in light of medieval convent learning and practice. The Prioress may have learned her courtliness as a devotee of Queen Anne and her attitudes toward Jews and children from such reading as Robert de Boron's *Roman de l'Estoure dou Graal* or the *Meditationes vitae Christi*.

221. Kelly, Henry Ansgar. "A Neo-Revisionist Look at Chaucer's Nuns." *ChauR* 31 (1996): 115–32. Based on medieval religious rules and regulations, particularly those related to orders of nuns, the medieval norm of nuns is revealed in Chaucer's depiction of the Prioress, a depiction that is not negative.

222. Marvin, Corey J. "'I Will Thee Not Forsake': The Kristevan Maternal Space in Chaucer's *Prioress's Tale* and John of Garland's Stella Maris." *Exemplaria* 8 (1996): 35–58. A reading of *PrT* in the mode of Julia Kristeva reveals it to be the narrative of the "litel clergeon's" entry into selfhood and subjectivity by a traumatic passage from the maternal "chora," represented by the singing of *Alma redemptio mater*, through abjection, into the symbolic order of language and the Father.

223. Osberg, Richard H. "A Voice for the Prioress: The Context of English Devotional Prose." *SAC* 18 (1996): 25–54. The naive, heavily repetitive, oratorical style of *PrT* appears to be influenced by late-medieval devotional prose written by men for women. Broader patterns of recurrence signal oppositions in the *Tale* that subvert its feminine voice and its claims to authenticity. The rhetoric of apostrophe fails to replace the absence of the subverted voice, leaving the Prioress less a character than a style. The article includes a chart of repetitive rhetorical devices.

224. Utz, Richard J. "Hugh von Lincoln und der Mythos vom jüdischen Ritualmord." In Werner Wunderlich and Ulrich Müller, eds. *Herrscher, Helden, Heilige. Mittelalter-Mythen*, no. 1. Konstanz: Universitätsverlag, 1996, pp. 710–22. Surveys the medieval mythographic accounts about Little Hugh (e.g., Matthew Paris, Chaucer's *PrT*); transformation into popular ballads, nursery rhymes, and Romantic verse (Child, Arnim, Brentano, Heine); and modern appropriations in A. Zweig's *Ritualmord in Ungarn* and Bernard Malamud's *The Fixer*. Explains the anti-Semitism in *PrT* as originating in unsolved conflicts within medieval Christianity.

See also nos. 68, 120, 122.

CT—The Tale of Sir Thopas

See nos. 62, 115, 123.

CT—The Tale of Melibee

225. Ferster, Judith. "Chaucer's 'Tale of Melibee': Advice to the King and Advice to the King's Advisers." In Judith Ferster. *Fictions of Advice: The Literature and Politics of Counsel in Late Medieval England* (*SAC* 20 [1998], no. 77), pp. 89–107. Blends a "historicist" approach that sees *Mel* as topical to the later 1380s with "formalist" emphasis on its discontinuities and contradictions. Concludes that "in the context of the Appellants' struggles with Richard II, . . . the deconstruction of the ideology of advice was a challenge not to the king, but to the ruling elite who had challenged him."

See also nos. 37, 62, 124, 159, 258.

CT—The Monk and His Tale

226. Boenig, Robert. "Is the *Monk's Tale* a Fragment?" *N&Q* 241 (1996): 261–64. *MkT* is not fragmentary, although the Knight misunderstands its common fourteenth-century technique of closure. Boenig provides parallel examples from Chaucer and Machaut.

227. Hermann, John P. "A Monk Ther Was, a Fair for the Maistrie." In Laura C. Lambdin and Robert T. Lambdin, eds. *Chaucer's Pilgrims: An Historical Guide to the Pilgrims in* The Canterbury Tales (*SAC* 20 [1998], no. 118), pp. 69–79. Summarizes the history, ideals, and practice of medieval monks as background to understanding the *GP* sketch of the Monk and the monk of *ShT*. The Monk is preoccupied with the diversions of monastic administration, while the Shipman's Daun John is more sinister.

228. Spillenger, Paul. "'Oure Flessh Thou Yaf Us': *Langour* and Chaucer's Consumption of Dante in the *Hugelyn*." *Chaucer Yearbook* 3 (1996): 103–28. Explicates the Ugolino episode of *MkT* as an instance of Chaucer's self-consciousness about borrowing from sources, especially Dante. Explores the courtly, Boethian, Boccaccian, and Dantean nuances of *langour* and argues that, as Ugolino passively suffers his role as a cannibal in hell, so Chaucer presents the poet who borrows from others.

229.   Taylor, Paul B. "L'Histoire de Néron par le 'Grant Translateur, Noble Geoffrey Chaucier.'" In Jean R. Scheidegger, ed. *Le Moyen Âge dans la modernité: Mélanges offerts à Roger Dragonetti, Professeur honoraire à l'Université de Genève.* Paris: Champion, 1996, pp. 427–42. Explores Chaucer's adaptation-translation of Jean de Meun's account of the fall of Nero. In *MkT*, Chaucer capitalizes on Boethian references to Nero and presents Nero as responsible for his fall in fortune.

See also nos. 36, 122.

CT—The Nun's Priest and His Tale

230.   Camargo, Martin. "Rhetorical Ethos and the 'Nun's Priest's Tale.'" *CLS* 33 (1996): 173–86. The ethos of the Canterbury preachers reveals Chaucer's distinctive self-consciousness about medieval rhetorical issues. The Pardoner's emphasis on pathos contrasts the Parson's emphasis on logos. *NPT* is an act of self-display in which the narrator preaches against flattery to ingratiate himself. The Host responds astutely to each, and, with the others, reveals Chaucer's anxiety about his own role.

231.   Cox, Catherine. "And Preestes Thre." In Laura C. Lambdin and Robert T. Lambdin, eds. *Chaucer's Pilgrims: An Historical Guide to the Pilgrims in* The Canterbury Tales (*SAC* 20 [1998], no. 118), pp. 55–68. Describes the medieval ecclesiastical hierarchy and places Chaucer's Nun's Priest in the hierarchy, identifying the training and responsibilities of medieval priests and the particular activities of priests who ministered to cloistered nuns and accompanied them while they traveled.

232.   Galván Reula, J. F. "Chaucer, narrador moderno y ejemplo de clasicismo." *Epos: Revista de Filología* 1 (1984): 19–34. Focuses on *NPT* as an example of Chaucer's combination of linguistic ambiguity and limited or unreliable narration, his "modern" features. Chaucer's works are classics because his techniques accord well with the narrative theories of modern critics such as Wayne Booth and Tzvetan Todorov.

233.   Rowland, Beryl. "The Wisdom of the Cock." In Jan Goosens and Timothy Sodmann, eds. *Third International Beast Epic, Fable and Fabliau Colloquium, Münster 1979: Proceedings.* Köln and Wien: Böhlau, 1981, pp. 340–55. Surveys several classical, oriental, and exegetical traditions of the symbolic or exemplary value of the cock, variously an

emblem of wisdom, pugnacity, or stupidity. Chaunticleer of *NPT* is un-usual in combining many qualities, for later literary roosters embody single values. Rowland concludes with comments on Herman Melville's story "Cock-a-doodle-doo!"

234. Wheatley, Edward. "Commentary Displacing Text: *The Nun's Priest's Tale* and the Scholastic Fable Tradition." *SAC* 18 (1996): 119–41. Compares the structure and interpretive techniques of *NPT* with those of scholastic fable commentaries widely used in medieval class-rooms, arguing that Chaucer capitalized on these similarities to encour-age readers to recognize the inseparability of text and commentary, ex-perience and education. Various details of *NPT* recall the medieval classroom and its texts, and the fable commentaries are reflected in the seriatim arrangement of Chaunticleer's summary of his dream, the vari-ous interpretations of Chaunticleer and Pertelote, the fox-and-rooster plot, and the interpretive conclusion.

See also nos. 82, 124.

CT—The Second Nun and Her Tale

235. Blamires, Alcuin. "Women and Preaching in Medieval Orthodoxy, Heresy, and Saints' Lives." *Viator* 26 (1995): 135–52. Includes among its examples a discussion of *SNT.*

236. Jankowski, Eileen S. "Reception of Chaucer's *Second Nun's Tale*: Osbern Bokenham's *Lyf of S. Cycyle*." *ChauR* 30 (1996): 306–18. Lexical similarities and broad organizational strategies in Bokenham's legend suggest that his sources were *SNT*, the *Legenda*, and the *Passio*. Bokenham reveals an early-fifteenth-century appreciation of Chaucer's skill as author and translator.

237. Stephens, Rebecca. "Another Nonne with Hire Hadde She." In Laura C. Lambdin and Robert T. Lambdin, eds. *Chaucer's Pilgrims: An Historical Guide to the Pilgrims in* The Canterbury Tales (*SAC* 20 [1998], no. 118), pp. 47–54. Summarizes the conventions of medieval monas-tic life and comments on the hagiography of *SNT*. In all except the fact that she speaks, Chaucer's Second Nun embodies the ideal of the me-dieval nun.

See also no. 209.

CT—The Canon's Yeoman and His Tale

238. Chism, Christine N. "I Demed Hym Som Chanoun for to Be." In Laura C. Lambdin and Robert T. Lambdin, eds. *Chaucer's Pilgrims: An Historical Guide to the Pilgrims in* The Canterbury Tales (*SAC* 20 [1998], no. 118), pp. 340–56. Describes the office of canon and the science of alchemy as background to the Canon, who chooses not to join the Canterbury pilgrimage. The history of corruption and reform among canons is a "touchstone" for understanding the character Chaucer creates, and the development of alchemy helps clarify Chaucer's association of the science and religion. Chism also raises questions about similarities between alchemy and poetry.

239. Lambdin, Robert T., and Laura C. Lambdin. "His Yeman Eek Was Ful of Curteisye." In Laura C. Lambdin and Robert T. Lambdin, eds. *Chaucer's Pilgrims: An Historical Guide to the Pilgrims in* The Canterbury Tales (*SAC* 20 [1998], no. 118), pp. 357–68. Characterizes the Canon's Yeoman as a "personal servant of a religious officer," although details of *CYP* indicate that he might more accurately be described as an alchemist's fire-tender or "puffer." The essay examines the importance of fire and temperature control in alchemical practice and reads details of *CYPT* as evidence that the Canon's Yeoman is in the process of reformation.

See also no. 126.

CT—The Manciple and His Tale

240. Cox, Catherine S. "The Jangler's 'Bourse': Gender, Renunciation, and Chaucer's Manciple." *SoAR* 61 (1996): 1–21. As a character "capable of saying one thing but meaning quite another," the Manciple ridicules the "wisdom of the mother" at the end of *ManT*. The crow suffers for the "feminine behavior" of talking too much, and the Manciple talks "as if a woman" to "warn against such speech." Like *ManT*, Chaucer's *Ret* uses a rhetoric of renunciation to speak out against silence.

241. Fisher, John H. "A Gentil Maunciple Was Ther of a Temple." In Laura C. Lambdin and Robert T. Lambdin, eds. *Chaucer's Pilgrims: An Historical Guide to the Pilgrims in* The Canterbury Tales (*SAC* 20 [1998], no. 118), pp. 281–87. The *GP* sketch of the Manciple is interesting insofar as it reflects Chaucer's possible associations with the Inns of Court.

416

The profession was a rare one in Chaucer's day, although there are similarities between reeves and manciples. The antagonism between the Manciple and the Cook in *ManP* is justified historically.

242. Ginsberg, Warren. "Chaucer's Canterbury Poetics: Irony, Allegory, and the *Prologue* to *The Manciple's Tale*." *SAC* 18 (1996): 55–89. Irony and allegory displace meaning in opposite directions, and in *ManP* they conspire to simultaneous affirmation and negation. Like Christ's parable of the wicked servant (Luke 16:1–9), the Manciple's verbal assault on the Cook indicates the way to salvation in a condemnatory gesture. Like *Ret* in canceling and affirming poetry, *ManP* encourages silence and restates the beginning of the pilgrimage, articulating a poetics of analogy that runs throughout *CT*.

243. Kordecki, Lesley. "Making Animals Mean: Speciest Hermeneutics in the *Physiologus* of Theobaldus." In Nona C. Flores, ed. *Animals in the Middle Ages: A Book of Essays* (*SAC* 20 [1998], no. 78), pp. 85–101. The overt hermeneutic directives of many animal books are evident in *HF, WBP*, and, especially, the silencing of the crow in *ManT*. The latter combines with the Parson's "antiliterary prologue" to undercut the whole of *CT*.

244. Raybin, David. "The Death of a Silent Woman: Voice and Power in Chaucer's Manciple's Tale." *JEGP* 95 (1996): 19–37. Reads *ManT* as a "story both of a wife who cuckolds her jealous husband and of a sexually aware trickster [the crow] who uses his knowledge, voice, and wit to gain freedom from his gilded cage." Both the wife and the crow seek freedom, but unlike the silenced wife, the crow effectively uses reasoned speech to liberate itself.

See also nos. 94, 156.

CT—The Parson and His Tale

245. Smith, Esther M. G. "And Was a Poure Persoun of a Toun." In Laura C. Lambdin and Robert T. Lambdin, eds. *Chaucer's Pilgrims: An Historical Guide to the Pilgrims in* The Canterbury Tales (*SAC* 20 [1998], no. 118), pp. 256–62. Comments on ecclesiastical reform of the late Middle Ages as background to the Parson's sketch in *GP* and presents *ParsT* as a confessional manual.

246. Tamaki, Atsuko, and Tadahiro Ikegami. "Meaning of Chaucer's Parson as a Narrator." *SeijoB* 155 (1996): 1–22 (in

Japanese). Explores why the Parson is neither a rector nor a parish priest, examining historical contexts and speculating about Chaucer's intentions, especially as they relate to backgrounds to the *Summa de poenitentia*.

See also nos. 14, 111, 124, 128, 230, 247.

CT—Chaucer's Retraction

247.   Shynne, Gwanghyun. "The Allegory of the *Retraction* and the Retraction of Allegory." *JELL* 42 (1996): 3–21 (in Korean, with English abstract). The allegory of *ParsPT* assumes that literature can somehow represent truth, while the theology of *ParsPT* emphasizes the impossibility of humanity's comprehending such truth. *Ret* espouses a mediating negative allegory that indicates divine ineffability and thereby equates secular and sacred poetries as limited—and equivalent—means to truth.

See also nos. 62, 240, 242.

Anelida and Arcite

See no. 43.

The Book of the Duchess

248.   Hamaguchi, Keiko. "The *Book of the Duchess* as Consolatio." *Tosa Women's Junior College Journal* 3 (1996): 19–35. Argues that *BD* satisfies the principal features of the consolatio, while recognizing the poem's dream-vision characteristics. Examines dialogue, the frame, the role of narrator-dreamer as narrator-therapist who leads the Black Knight to Blanche—a true superior guide who, in turn, consoles the Knight and her mourners, including John of Gaunt and Chaucer.

249.   Hendershot, Cyndy. "Male Subjectivity, *Fin Amor*, and Melancholia in *The Book of the Duchess*." *Mediaevalia* 21 (1996): 1–26. The discourse of *fin amor* places the male subject in a feminine position; in *BD*, the absence of White problematizes this feminization of the male, producing melancholia that endangers the Black Knight's psychic stability and the dominant fiction of masculine stability. The

narrator's attempt to console the Black Knight defends the fiction of masculine wholeness.

250. Shippey, T. A. "Chaucer's Arithmetical Mentality and *The Book of the Duchess*." *ChauR* 31 (1996): 173–83. Chaucer's knowledge of medieval mathematical imagery is evidenced in several ways, beginning with his reference to "Argus, the noble countour," who is Algus, the great Arab mathematician Al-Khwarizmi. By refiguring the beginnings and endings of selected passages as set forth in *The Riverside Chaucer* and other editions, additional mathematical references emerge.

251. Vickery, Gwen M. "*The Book of the Duchess*: The Date of Composition Related to the Theme of Impracticality." *ELWIU* 22 (1995): 161–69. Argues that *BD* was composed after John of Gaunt made plans to remarry—or even after his second marriage—and that the poem constitutes both an elegy on the death of Blanche and a "carefully argued justification of Gaunt's second marriage." Further, this justification is covertly undercut, indicating Chaucer's disapproval of the marriage to Constance.

See also nos. 69, 76, 84, 88.

The House of Fame

252. Boitani, Piero. "Introduction: An Idea of Fourteenth-Century Literature." In Piero Boitani and Anna Torti, eds. *Literature in Fourteenth-Century England* (*SAC* 7 [1985], no. 71), pp. 11–31. Reads *HF* as an index to English literary culture of the late fourteenth century—as "Chaucer's idea of fourteenth-century literature." The variety of genres of the work, its complex relations with literary traditions, its concerns with science and mysticism, its mythography, and its sheer expansiveness indicate the mentality of Chaucer and his literary culture.

253. Grady, Frank. "Chaucer Reading Langland: *The House of Fame*." *SAC* 18 (1996): 3–23. *HF* recalls *Piers Plowman* in its vocabulary, its apocalyptic pursuit of truth and authority, its dream-vision genre, its signature passages, and its unfinished state. Both poems manipulate conventions and challenge readers' presuppositions in ways that make it likely that Chaucer knew a version of Langland's work.

254. Kennedy, Thomas C. "Rhetoric and Meaning in *The House of Fame*." *SN* 68 (1996): 9–24. Considers three rhetorical features of *HF*

(introductory features, *occupatio* and the inexpressibility *topos*, and repeated rhyme) to refute John Matthews Manly's view (1926) that Chaucer's early writing lacked originality and that his use of rhetoric was extrinsic to the meaning of his poems.

See also nos. 34, 36, 69, 76, 84, 88, 111.

The Legend of Good Women

255. Delany, Sheila. "The Friar as Critic: Bokenham Reads Chaucer." In Piero Boitani and Anna Torti, eds. *Mediaevalitas: Reading the Middle Ages* (*SAC* 20 [1998], no. 64), pp. 63–79. In his *Legend of Holy Women*, Osbern Bokenham "offers something formally similar but ideologically opposite" to *LGW*. Bokenham parodies Chaucer's work, thus reasserting the hagiographical genre that Chaucer undercut, and indirectly critiques Chaucer's and Gower's uses of rhetoric for secular purposes.

256. Hanrahan, Michael. "Seduction and Betrayal: Treason in the *Prologue* to the *Legend of Good Women*." *ChauR* 30 (1996): 229–40. When an angry God of Love accuses the narrator of a breach of faith, Alceste rebukes the god for believing false counselors. This action reflects the political situation of Chaucer's time. The Lords Appellant had attacked Richard II's corrupt counselors for giving him evil advice—a violation of trust and therefore *treason* in the medieval sense of the word.

257. Morse, Ruth. *The Medieval Medea*. Cambridge: D. S. Brewer, 1996. xvi, 267 pp. Surveys the depictions of Medea in medieval literature and its backgrounds, focusing on how, in the Middle Ages, the character reflects issues of dynastic rivalry, legitimacy, and presumptions about the passions of females. Comments on how Chaucer's depiction of Medea in *LGW* involves a double reversal, whereby Jason is feminized and Medea is suppressed.

258. Wallace, David. "Anne of Bohemia, Queen of England, and Chaucer's Emperice." *LittPrag* 5 (1995): 1–16. Describes the rich Bohemian culture that Anne brought with her to England in 1381 and suggests various ways Chaucer may have been influenced by the connection with Bohemia. In the original version of *LGWP*, references to Anne indicate the extent to which she embodied for Chaucer the ideal of a wife as mediatrix, also a motif in *Mel*.

See also nos. 27, 32, 34, 41, 91, 93, 111.

The Parliament of Fowls

259.   Bertelot, Craig E. "'My Wit Is Sharp: I Love No Taryinge': Urban Poetry in the *Parlement of Foules*." *SP* 93 (1996): 365–89. Argues that "the character paradigm that Chaucer creates . . . specifically for the lower birds in *PF* originates from his understanding of the rising social importance of urban culture in England, even though these birds themselves do not come from cities." Addresses the themes of love and governance and suggests that Chaucer provides not one but a collection of answers to the burning question that the dreamer faces.

260.   Kiser, Lisa J. "Alain de Lille, Jean de Meun, and Chaucer: Ecofeminism and Some Medieval Lady Natures." In Piero Boitani and Anna Torti, eds. *Mediaevalitas: Reading the Middle Ages* (*SAC* 20 [1998], no. 64), pp. 1–14. Assesses the depiction of female-gendered Nature in Brunetto Latini's *Il Tesoretto*, Alain de Lille's *De planctu naturae*, Jean de Meun's *Roman de la Rose*, and Chaucer's *PF*. A modern ecofeminist approach to these depictions helps disclose the binary thinking that underlies them and reveals a surprising variety in the way they reflect power relations between classes and genders.

261.   Sola Buil, Ricardo J. "Dreaming and Speaking in *The Parliament of Fowls*." In Luis A. Lázaro Lafuente, José Simón, and Ricardo J. Sola Buil, eds. *Proceedings of the IIIrd International Conference of the Spanish Society for Medieval Language and Literature* (*SAC* 20 [1998], no. 96), pp. 261–65. Questions whether Chaucer's deviations from traditional literary standards disguise or disclose personal messages.

See also nos. 13, 28, 68, 76, 84, 88, 111.

Troilus and Criseyde

262.   Børch, Marianne. "Poet & Persona: Writing the Reader in *Troilus*." *ChauR* 30 (1996): 215–28. In *TC*, Chaucer creates a persona who embodies two conflicting modes of response, thus leaving it up to the reader to find a reconciliation.

263.   Bradley, Ann. "Sarpedon's Feast: A Homeric Key to Chaucer's 'Troilus and Criseyde.'" *DAI* 56 (1996): 4763A. Chaucer's *Troilus*

derives from three reflections of the *Iliad*: the classical, the Christian-allegorical, and the romance. Sarpedon's feast is central to *TC*, with classical, Scholastic, and finally Dantesque treatment of free will, fate, and transcendence.

264. Brewer, Derek. "Some Aspects of the Post-War Reception of Chaucer: A Key Passage, *Troilus* II 666–679." In Stefan Horlacher and Marion Islinger, eds. *Expedition nach der Wahrheit: Poems, Essays, and Papers in Honour of Theo Stemmler, Festschrift zum 60. Geburtstag von Theo Stemmler.* Heidelberg: C. Winter, 1996, pp. 513–24. Critiques approaches to *TC* that separate the narrator of the poem from Chaucer, briefly tracing modern ideas of character and irony from Kittredge to Donaldson and Muscatine and on to deconstruction and feminism. New Critics and their descendants are wrong to impose a "hermeneutics of suspicion" on Chaucer.

265. Chamberlain, Stephanie Ericson. "'How Came That Widow In': The Dynamics of Social Conformity in Sidney, Marlowe, Shakespeare and Hooker." *DAI* 56 (1996): 2691A. In the flux that overturned feudal patriarchal society, the position of the widow was destabilized; the social station of Chaucer's Criseyde contrasts with that of Shakespeare's Cressida, as well as that of widows in other Renaissance works.

266. Clogan, Paul M. "Visions of Thebes in Medieval Literature." In Gerald Gillespie, Margaret R. Higonnet, and Sumie Jones, eds. *Visions of History, Visions of the Other.* Vol. 2 of Earl Miner, gen. ed. *ICLA '91 Tokyo: The Force of Vision.* 6 vols. Proceedings of the 14th Congress of the International Comparative Literature Association. Tokyo: University of Tokyo Press, 1995, pp. 144–51. Depictions of Thebes indicate various medieval views of history. *Roman de Thèbes* blurs contrasts between pagan and Christian, classical and historical. Boccaccio's *Teseida* resists the modernization and secularization of romance tradition. *TC* suggests that romance decorum has eroded the historical and moral vision of the classical epic.

267. Gray, Douglas. "Chaucer and the Art of Digression." *SMELL* 11 (1996): 21–47. The English word "digression" is first recorded in *TC* 1.143, where the narrator comments on the fall of Troy. This digression anticipates ideas and images that occur later in the poem and reflects the narrator's difficulty in coming to a conclusion.

268. Heinrichs, Katherine. "Troilus' 'Predestination Soliloquy' and Machaut's *Jugement du Roy de Behaigne.*" *MFra* 35–36 (1994–95): 7–15. Explores similarities between the lovelorn knight of Machaut's

Jugement and Troilus, including their mutual concern with Fortune and their misunderstanding of Providence, their failure to comprehend human freedom, and the ways their speeches combine seriocomic befuddlement with earnest philosophical inquiry.

269. Hinton, Norman. "The Werewolf as *Eiron*: Freedom and Comedy in *William of Palerne*." In Nona C. Flores, ed. *Animals in the Middle Ages: A Book of Essays* (*SAC* 20 [1998], no. 78), pp. 133–46. Comparison of the protagonist of *William of Palerne* with Chaucer's Troilus makes William seem "a paragon of decision," while Alisaundrine is like Pandarus in bringing lovers together.

270. León Sendra, Antonio R. "Friendship in Chaucer Through a Textual Analysis." In Luis A. Lázaro Lafuente, José Simón, and Ricardo J. Sola Buil, eds. *Proceedings of the IIIrd International Conference of the Spanish Society for Medieval Language and Literature* (*SAC* 20 [1998], no. 96), pp. 217–46. Examines an exchange between Troilus and Pandarus to explore the theme of public versus private life in *TC*. Explores the relation between friendship and the public-private dialectic.

271. Milliken, Roberta Lee. "Neither 'Clere Laude' nor 'Sklaundre': Chaucer's Translation of Criseyde, and Sensual and Holy Locks: A Study of Hair in Women's Hagiography." *DAI* 56 (1996): 2672A. Comparison of Criseyde with Boccaccio's Criseida shows that Chaucer sets forth her characterization in Books 1–3: she is fearful, alone, aware of her position, and easily manipulated. These traits, which foreshadow her future, are less evident in Boccaccio's treatment.

272. Oka, Saburo. "Religious Sentiments in Chaucer's *Troilus*." *SMELL* 11 (1996): 1–20. The love triangle of *TC* (Troilus, Criseyde, and Diomede) is mirrored in a narrative triangle, in turn reflecting a Trinitarian religious outlook. Chaucer's narrative anxiety parallels his anxiety that his religious message may not be fully understood.

273. Sadlek, Gregory M. "Bakhtin, the Novel, and Chaucer's *Troilus and Criseyde*." *Chaucer Yearbook* 3 (1996): 87–101. Defines *TC* as a novel because it partakes heavily of the linguistic qualities that Bakhtin associates with novelization, including contemporaneity, fusion of genres, and open-endedness. Most important, *TC* is dialogic in its adaptations of Boccaccio's *Filostrato*, courtly conventions, Boethian thought, and Christian outlook.

274. Utz, Richard J. "'For All That Comth, Comth by Necessitee': Chaucer's Critique of Fourteenth-Century Boethianism in *Troilus and Criseyde* IV, 957–58." *ArAA* 21 (1996): 29–32. In *TC*, Chaucer adapts

Boethian thought to expose the dangers of the radical determinism of John Wyclif. Such determinism fails to remedy Troilus's loss of Criseyde, posing dangers to society as well as to the individual.

275. Watts, William. "Translations of Boethius and the Making of Chaucer's Second 'Canticus Troili.'" *Chaucer Yearbook* 3 (1996): 129–41. Examines details of verse and style in *TC* 3.1744–71 for the ways they reflect the sources of the passage: Boethius's *Consolation of Philosophy*, Jean de Meun's *Li livres de Confort*, and *Bo.* The examination seeks to understand Chaucer's attempt to forge an English poetic language.

See also nos. 2, 12, 15, 24, 30, 32, 34, 36, 43, 46, 51, 58, 84, 87, 103.

Lyrics and Short Poems

276. Duncan, Thomas G., ed. *Medieval English Lyrics, 1200–1400.* London: Penguin, 1995. xlviii, 266 pp. Having normalized the language "in accordance with the grammar and spelling of late fourteenth-century London English," Duncan divides this "comprehensive selection" of lyrics into four thematic groups, three of which include lyrics attributed to Chaucer. Part 1 (Love Lyrics) includes "Now Welcome, Somer," *Ros, Wom Nob, Wom Unc,* the "Canticus Troili," *Compl d'Am, MercB,* and *Bal Compl.* Part 2 (Penitential and Moral Lyrics) includes *For, Truth,* and *Gent.* Part 4 (Miscellaneous Lyrics) includes *Purse.* An extensive commentary provides textual, contextual, and linguistic information, and appendices treat music, meter, and a "Syllabic Analysis of Middle English Verse."

277. Gray, Douglas. "Songs and Lyrics." In Piero Boitani and Anna Torti, eds. *Literature in Fourteenth-Century England* (*SAC* 7 [1985], no. 71), pp. 83–98. Characterizes the nature and conventions of Middle English lyrics, looking briefly at representative examples. Includes discussion of Chaucer as both a representative lyricist and one who breaks boundaries in his short poems.

The Former Age

278. Galloway, Andrew. "Chaucer's *Former Age* and the Fourteenth-Century Anthropology of Craft: The Social Logic of a Premodernist Lyric." *ELH* 63 (1996): 535–53. *Form Age* emphasizes not so much

former innocence as prelapsarian lack of technical knowledge. Though the speaker takes his stance between the first age and the present, he employs ironic diction, aligning himself with the latter. Besides recognized sources, Chaucer draws on Scholastic praise of technology, as well as reactions (especially Lollard) against it. The anti-Wycliffite Roger Dymmok turned anti-Royalist by 1398, Norton-Smith's date for the poem.

See also no. 13.

The Complaint of Mars

279. Van Dyke, Carolynn. "The Lyric Planet: Chaucer's Construction of Subjectivity in the *Complaint of Mars.*" *ChauR* 31 (1996): 164–72. The multiple voices in *Mars* mask the identity of the real lyric subject. An examination of these voices reveals that the real lyric subject is the reader, who discovers that he or she is not, like Mars, an autonomous self.

280. Williams, Sean D. "Chaucer's Complaint of Mars." *Expl* 54 (1996): 132–34. The affair between Mars and Venus enfigures three analyses of love: the least negative, "courtly" definition; the classical, "lascivious" definition; and the deterministic vision implied by the statues of the gods as planets.

See also no. 93.

A Complaint to His Lady

See also no. 36.

Chaucerian Apocrypha

281. Dane, Joseph A. "Bibliographical History Versus Bibliographical Evidence: The Plowman's Tale and Early Chaucer Editions." *BJRL* 78 (1996): 47–61. Assesses Francis Thynne's references to *The Plowman's Tale* and *The Pilgrim's Tale* in his *Animadversions* on Speght's edition of Chaucer, concluding that no sixteenth-century printer tried to pass off the latter as Chaucer's. Although *The Plowman's Tale* was consistently in the hands of Chaucer's printers, his association with *The Pilgrim's Tale* is a "bibliographical fantasy."

282. Delasanta, Rodney K., and Constance M. Rousseau. "Chaucer's *Orygenes upon the Maudeleyne*: A Translation." *ChauR* 30 (1996): 319–42. Chaucer's translation of this work, alluded to by Alceste in *LGW* (G. 404–18), has since been lost. Authors use MS Corpus Christi 137 as a basis for their work.

283. Forni, Kathleen Rose. "Studies in the Chaucerian Apocrypha." *DAI* 57 (1996): 206A. The body of Chaucerian apocrypha, "largely ignored" since 1900, deserves reconsideration for its relation to the canon and to Chaucer's reputation. The latter was affected less by the apocrypha than by linguistic factors and changing tastes. Medieval literary practices valued individual authorship so little as to make almost all writing to some degree communal.

Book Reviews

284. Amodio, Mark C., ed. *Oral Poetics in Middle English Poetry* (*SAC* 18 [1996], no. 71). Rev. Carl Lindahl, *SAC* 18 (1996): 167–70.

285. Arn, Mary-Jo, ed. *"Fortunes stabilnes": Charles of Orleans's English Book of Love* (*SAC* 19 [1997], no. 76). Rev. Julia Boffey, *MÆ* 65 (1996): 319–20.

286. Barney, Stephen A., ed. *Studies in* Troilus: *Chaucer's Text, Meter, and Diction* (*SAC* 17 [1995], no. 21). Rev. C. David Benson, *MLR* 91:1 (1996): 186–88; Robert F. Yeager, *MÆ* 65 (1996): 134–35.

287. Baswell, Christopher. *Virgil in Medieval England: Figuring the* Aeneid *from the Twelfth Century to Chaucer* (*SAC* 19 [1997], no. 292). Rev. Charles Burnett, *MÆ* 65 (1996): 299–300; Valerie Edden, *N&Q* 241 (1996): 310.

288. Benson, Larry D. *A Glossarial Concordance to the* Riverside Chaucer (*SAC* 17 [1995], no.2). Rev. Paul Schaffner, *Chaucer Yearbook* 3 (1996): 151–56.

289. Blake, N. F. *William Caxton and English Literary Culture* (*SAC* 17 [1995], no.12). Rev. Mark Addison Amos, *Chaucer Yearbook* 3 (1996): 157–61.

290. Bronfman, Judith. *Chaucer's* Clerk's Tale: *The Griselda Story Received, Rewritten, Illustrated* (*SAC* 18 [1996], no. 199). Rev. Amy W. Goodwin, *SAC* 18 (1996): 178–81; Charlotte C. Morse, *N&Q* 241 (1996): 79–80; Edward Wheatley, *MFN* 21 (1996): 46–47.

291. Brown, Peter. *Chaucer at Work: The Making of the* Canterbury Tales (*SAC* 18 [1996], no. 136). Rev. Lillian M. Bisson, *SAC* 18 (1996): 181–83.

292. Buffoni, Franco. *I racconti de Canterbury: Un'opera unitaria* (*SAC* 18 [1996], no. 137). Rev. Traugott Lawler, *Speculum* 71 (1996): 395–97.

293. Burrow, J. A., and Thorlac Turville-Petre. *A Book of Middle English* (*SAC* 16 [1994], no. 52). Rev. J. Hunter, *Lore&L* 13 (1995): 86–87.

294. Calabrese, Michael A. *Chaucer's Ovidian Arts of Love* (*SAC* 18 [1996], no. 34). Rev. Peter Brown, *MÆ* 65 (1996): 133–34; Marilynn Desmond, *SAC* 18 (1996): 183–86; Robert R. Edwards, *Speculum* 71 (1996): 931–33; Kathryn L. McKinley, *M&H* 23 (1996): 126–30; Theresa Tinkle, *JEGP* 95 (1996): 227–29.

295. Calin, William. *The French Tradition and the Literature of Medieval England* (*SAC* 18 [1996], no. 35). Rev. R. Barton Palmer, *SAC* 18 (1996): 186–90.

296. Chamberlain, David, ed. *New Readings of Late Medieval Love Poems* (*SAC* 17 [1995], no. 274). Rev. Barrie Ruth Straus, *SAC* 18 (1996): 190–95.

297. Chance, Jane. *The Mythographic Chaucer: The Fabulation of Sexual Politics* (*SAC* 19 [1997], no. 85). Rev. Mark Allen, *SAC* 18 (1996): 195–98.

298. Cowen, Janet, and George Kane, eds. *Geoffrey Chaucer: The Legend of Good Women* (*SAC* 19 [1997], no. 18). Rev. Leo Carruthers, *ÉA* 49 (1996): 223–24; Joseph A. Dane, *SAC* 18 (1996): 200–205.

299. Crane, Susan. *Gender and Romance in Chaucer's* Canterbury Tales (*SAC* 18 [1996], no. 139). Rev. Thomas L. Burton, *ES* 77 (1996): 504–5; Phillipa Hardman, *RES,* n.s., 47 (1996): 564–65; Charlotte C. Morse, *Speculum* 71 (1996): 709–11; Marcelle Thiébaux, *JEGP* 95 (1996): 225–27.

300. Delany, Sheila. *The Naked Text: Chaucer's* Legend of Good Women (*SAC* 18 [1996], no. 265). Rev. Dieter Mehl, *Anglia* 114 (1996): 269–71.

301. Desmond, Marilynn. *Reading Dido: Gender, Textuality, and the Medieval* Aeneid (*SAC* 18 [1996], no. 82). Rev. Leslie Cahoon, *SAC* 18 (1996): 205–9; Nicola F. McDonald, *MÆ* 65 (1996): 121–22; Wendy Chapman Peek, *MFN* 22 (1996): 39–43.

302. Ecker, Ronald L., and Eugene J. Cook, trans. The Canterbury Tales *by Geoffrey Chaucer* (*SAC* 17 [1995], no. 13). Rev. John Micheal Crafton, *SAC* 18 (1996): 198–200.

427

303. Edwards, Robert R., ed. *Art and Context in Late Medieval English Narrative: Essays in Honor of Robert Worth Frank, Jr.* (*SAC* 18 [1996], no. 85). Rev. Rodney Delasanta, *SAC* 18 (1996): 209–13; H. L. Spencer, *N&Q* 241 (1996): 76.

304. ———, and Vickie Ziegler, eds. *Matrons and Marginal Women in Medieval Society* (*SAC* 19 [1997], no. 224). Rev. Corinne J. Saunders, *N&Q* 241 (1996): 471–72.

305. Fleming, John V. *Classical Imitation and Interpretation in Chaucer's* Troilus (*SAC* 14 [1992], no. 259). Rev. Marilynn Desmond, *CL* 48 (1996): 377–81.

306. Frese, Dolores Warwick. *An* Ars Legendi *for Chaucer's* Canterbury Tales: *A Reconstructive Reading* (*SAC* 15 [1993], no. 150). Rev. Marilynn Desmond, *CL* 48 (1996): 377–81.

307. Ganim, John M. *Chaucerian Theatricality* (*SAC* 14 [1992], no. 138). Rev. Marilynn Desmond, *CL* 48 (1996): 377–81.

308. Gellrich, Jesse M. *Discourse and Dominion in the Fourteenth Century: Oral Contexts of Writing in Philosophy, Politics, and Poetry* (*SAC* 19 [1997], no. 168). Rev. Andrew Galloway, *SAC* 18 (1996): 213–22.

309. Hanawalt, Barbara A., ed. *Chaucer's England: Literature in Historical Context* (*SAC* 16 [1994], no. 89). Rev. David G. Allen, *Chaucer Yearbook* 3 (1996): 192–94.

310. Hansen, Elaine Tuttle. *Chaucer and the Fictions of Gender* (*SAC* 16 [1994], no. 90). Rev. Joy Wallace, *Parergon* 10:2 (1992): 210–11.

311. Havely, Nicholas R., ed. *Chaucer*: The House of Fame (*SAC* 19 [1997], no. 22). Rev. J. D. Burnley, *RES*, n.s., 47 (1996): 562–63; A. S. G. Edwards, *JEGP* 95 (1996): 229–31.

312. Heffernan, Carol Falvo. *The Melancholy Muse: Chaucer, Shakespeare, and Early Medicine* (*SAC* 19 [1997], no. 284). Rev. Susan Baker, *RMR* 50 (1996): 189–90.

313. Hill, John M. *Chaucerian Belief: The Poetics of Reverence and Delight* (*SAC* 15 [1993], no. 108). Rev. Marilynn Desmond, *CL* 48 (1996): 377–81.

314. Jost, Jean E., ed. *Chaucer's Humor: Critical Essays* (*SAC* 18 [1996], no. 94). Rev. Roy J. Pearcy, *SAC* 18 (1996): 227–31.

315. ———, and Michael N. Salda, eds. *Chaucer Yearbook: A Journal of Medieval Studies* 2 (1995). Rev. Julia Boffey, *Encomia* 17 (1995): 28–29.

316. Justice, Steven. *Writing and Rebellion: England in 1381* (*SAC* 18 [1996], no. 95). Rev. David Fowler, *Review* 18 (1996): 1–30.

317. Kay, Sarah, and Miri Rubin, eds. *Framing Medieval Bodies* (*SAC* 19 [1997], no. 239). Rev. Alexandra Barratt, *N&Q* 241 (1996): 205; Karma Lochrie, *AHR* 101 (1996): 461.

318. Kiser, Lisa J. *Truth and Textuality in Chaucer's Poetry* (*SAC* 15 [1993], no. 113). Rev. Marilynn Desmond, *CL* 48 (1996): 377–81.

319. Klitgård, Ebbe. *Chaucer's Narrative Voice in* The Knight's Tale (*SAC* 19 [1997], no. 172). Rev. Lois Roney, *SAC* 18 (1996): 232–34.

320. Kooper, Erik, ed. *Medieval Dutch Literature in Its European Context* (*SAC* 18 [1996], no. 38). Rev. David Wallace, *SAC* 18 (1996): 234–38.

321. Lerer, Seth. *Chaucer and His Readers: Imagining the Author in Late-Medieval England* (*SAC* 17 [1995], no. 50). Rev. Donald C. Baker, *ELN* 34:1 (1996): 94–96; C. David Benson, *RES,* n.s., 47 (1996): 232–33; Mary Carruthers, *MP* 93 (1996): 375–77; Andrew Welsh, *RenQ* 49 (1996): 154–55.

322. Lomperis, Linda, and Sarah Stanbury, eds. *Feminist Approaches to the Body in Medieval Literature* (*SAC* 17 [1995], no. 103). Rev. Juliette Dor, *Archiv* 233 (1996): 133–36.

323. McAlpine, Monica. *Chaucer's Knight's Tale: An Annotated Bibliography, 1900–1985* (*SAC* 15 [1993], no. 5). Rev. Stephanie Hollis, *Parergon* 10:2 (1992): 228–29.

324. Machan, Tim William. *Textual Criticism and Middle English Texts* (*SAC* 18 [1996], no. 29). Rev. Julia Boffey, *N&Q* 241 (1996): 72–73; A. S. G. Edwards, *MÆ* 65 (1996): 313–14; John H. Fisher, *JEGP* 95 (1996): 109–11; Bella Millett, *SAC* 18 (1996): 243–47.

325. Mandel, Jerome. *Geoffrey Chaucer: Building the Fragments of the Canterbury Tales* (*SAC* 16 [1994], no. 147). Rev. Charles A. Owen, Jr., *Chaucer Yearbook* 3 (1996): 208–10.

326. Margherita, Gayle. *The Romance of Origins: Language and Sexual Difference in Middle English Literature* (*SAC* 18 [1996], no. 108). Rev. Anne Clark Bartlett, *MFN* 22 (1996): 49–52; Paul Theiner, *SAC* 18 (1996): 247–51.

327. Meale, Carol M., ed. *Readings in Medieval English Romance* (*SAC* 18 [1996], no. 109). Rev. Susan Crane, *SAC* 18 (1996): 251–54.

328. Minnis, A. J., ed. *Chaucer's* Boece *and the Medieval Tradition of Boethius* (*SAC* 17 [1995], no. 220). Rev. Richard J. Utz, *Anglia* 114 (1996): 112–14.

329. ———, with V. J. Scattergood and J. J. Smith. *The Shorter Poems* (Oxford Guides to Chaucer) (*SAC* 19 [1997], no. 112). Rev. Peter

Mack, *TLS*, Apr. 5, 1996, pp. 23–24; Charlotte C. Morse, *N&Q* 241 (1996): 323–24.

330. Myles, Robert. *Chaucerian Realism* (*SAC* 18 [1996], no. 111). Rev. N. F. Blake, *ES* 77 (1996): 110–11; Peter Brown, *MÆ* 65 (1996): 133–34; Russell A. Peck, *Speculum* 71 (1996): 469–71; Daniel Ransom, *JEGP* 95 (1996): 540–42; William Watts, *SAC* 18 (1996): 257–60.

331. Nolan, Barbara. *Chaucer and the Tradition of the Roman Antique* (*SAC* 16 [1994], no. 30). Rev. Peter Mack, *TLS*, Apr. 5, 1996, pp. 23–24.

332. Owen, Charles A., Jr. *The Manuscripts of* The Canterbury Tales (*SAC* 15 [1993], no. 28). Rev. Klaus Bitterling, *Anglia* 114 (1996): 109–12.

333. Patterson, Lee. *Chaucer and the Subject of History* (*SAC* 15 [1993], no. 124). Rev. Gabrielle Mueller-Oberhauser, *Anglia* 114 (1996): 556–60.

334. Paxson, James J. *The Poetics of Personification* (*SAC* 18 [1996], no. 116). Rev. Mark Allen, *MÆ* 65 (1996): 110–11; Clare R. Kinney, *SAC* 18 (1996): 266–68; R. A. Shoaf, *Style* 29 (1995): 158–61.

335. Pearsall, Derek. *The Life of Geoffrey Chaucer: A Critical Biography* (*SAC* 16 [1994], no. 5). Rev. Erik Kooper, *Madoc* 7 (1995): 155–59.

336. Plummer, John F., III. *The Summoner's Tale* (*SAC* 19 [1996], no. 23). Rev. E. G. Stanley, *N&Q* 241 (1996): 469–70.

337. Quinn, William A. *Chaucer's "Rehersynges": The Performability of* The Legend of Good Women (*SAC* 18 [1996], no. 267). Rev. Betsy Bowden, *M&H* 23 (1996): 171–72; J. D. Burnley, *RES*, n.s., 47 (1996): 562–63; Donald W. Rowe, *SAC* 18 (1996): 272–75.

338. Rand Schmidt, Kari Anne. *The Authorship of the* Equatorie of the Planetis (*SAC* 17 [1995], no. 233). Rev. N. F. Blake, *RES*, n.s., 47 (1996): 233–34; Ebbe Klitgård, *ES* 77 (1993): 503–4; Linne R. Mooney, *Speculum* 71 (1996): 197–98; Linda Ehrsam Voights, *Isis* 86 (1996): 642.

339. Robinson, Peter, ed., with contributions from N. F. Blake, Daniel W. Mosser, Stephen Partridge, and Elizabeth Solopova. *The Wife of Bath's Prologue on CD-ROM* (*SAC* 20 [1998], no. 11). Rev. Michael Fraser, *Computers & Texts* 12 (1996): 21–25; John Naughton, *Magazine of the Cambridge Society*, Feb. 1997, pp. 65–67.

340. Rooney, Anne. *Hunting in Middle English Literature* (*SAC* 17 [1995], no. 111). Rev. Sandra Pierson Prior, *SAC* 18 (1996): 278–80.

341. Saunders, Corinne J. *The Forest of Medieval Romance: Avernus, Broceliande, Arden* (*SAC* 17 [1995], no. 114). Rev. J. R. Goodman, *SAC* 18 (1996): 285–88.

342. Scanlon, Larry. *Narrative, Authority, and Power: The Medieval Exemplum and the Chaucerian Tradition* (*SAC* 18 [1996], no. 120). Rev. Nicola McDonald, *RES*, n.s., 47 (1996): 560–62; Sally Mapstone, *N&Q* 241 (1996): 467–68; Elizabeth Scala, *M&H* 23 (1996): 174–78; A. C. Spearing, *SAC* 18 (1996): 289–94.

343. Spearing, A. C. *The Medieval Poet as Voyeur: Looking and Listening in Medieval Love-Narratives* (*SAC* 17 [1995], no. 117). Rev. Carolynn Van Dyke, *Chaucer Yearbook* 3 (1996): 219–24.

344. Stevens, Martin, and Daniel Woodward, eds. *The Ellesmere Chaucer: Essays in Interpretation* (*SAC* 19 [1997], no. 26). Rev. Peter Mack, *TLS*, Apr. 5, 1996, pp. 23–24.

345. Sturges, Robert S. *Medieval Interpretation: Models of Reading in Literary Narrative, 1100–1500* (*SAC* 15 [1993], no. 131). Rev. Jeanette Beer, *Chaucer Yearbook* 3 (1996): 231–34.

346. Whitaker, Muriel, ed. *Sovereign Lady: Essays on Women in Middle English Literature* (*SAC* 19 [1997], no. 133). Rev. Faye Walker, *SAC* 18 (1996): 304–8.

347. Wilkins, Nigel. *Music in the Age of Chaucer, with Chaucer Songs* (*SAC* 19 [1997], no. 134). Rev. Leo Carruthers, *ÉA* 49 (1996): 225–26.

348. Wilson, Katharina M., and Elizabeth Makowski. *Wykked Wyves and the Woes of Marriage: Misogamous Literature from Juvenal to Chaucer* (*SAC* 14 [1992], no. 189). Rev. Arlyn Diamond, *M&H* 19 (1992): 147–58.

349. Wimsatt, James. *Chaucer and His French Contemporaries: Natural Music in the Fourteenth Century* (*SAC* 15 [1993], no. 45). Rev. Peter Mack, *TLS*, Apr. 5, 1996, pp. 23–24; Margaret Rogerson, *Parergon* 11:2 (1993): 165–66.

350. Woodward, Daniel, and Martin Stevens, eds. *The* Canterbury Tales *by Geoffrey Chaucer: The New Ellesmere Chaucer Facsimile* (*SAC* 19 [1997], no. 30). Rev. Peter Beadle, *TLS*, Apr. 19, 1996, p. 33.

431

Author Index—Bibliography

Index